Gross Pathology of Avian Diseases

Text and Atlas

Tahseen Abdul-Aziz
Veterinary Pathologist (Avian)
Rollins Animal Disease Diagnostic Laboratory
North Carolina Department of Agriculture
and Consumer Services
Raleigh, North Carolina
USA

H. John Barnes
Professor
Department of Population Health and Pathobiology
College of Veterinary Medicine
North Carolina State University
Raleigh, North Carolina
USA

The American Association of Avian Pathologists

Copyright © 2018 by
American Association of Avian Pathologists, Inc.

All Rights Reserved

Printed by Omnipress
Madison, WI 53704

Library of Congress Catalog Number 2018930598
International Standard Book Number 978-0-9789163-9-8

Copies available from
American Association of Avian Pathologists

AAAP, Inc
12627 San Jose Blvd., Suite 202
Jacksonville, Florida 32223-8638
AAAP@aaap.info

Contents

Introduction v
Unhealed Navels, Omphalitis, Yolk Sac Infection 1
Neonatal Septicemia 6
Salmonella Enteritidis Infection in Broiler Chickens 11
Colibacillosis with Tracheitis Caused by Infectious Bronchitis Virus in Broiler Chickens 13
Swollen-Head Syndrome in Broiler Chickens 15
Inflammatory Process (Cellulitis) in Broiler Chickens 16
Pasteurella multocida Infection (Fowl Cholera) 18
Erysipelas in Turkeys and Pheasants 24
Riemerella anatipestifer Infection in Ducks 28
Ornithobacterium rhinotracheale (ORT) Infection in Turkeys 30
Bordetellosis in Turkeys 31
Infectious Coryza 32
Bacterial Peritonitis, Salpingitis, and Salpingoperitonitis 35
Orchitis 38
Staphylococcal Tenosynovitis of the Gastrocnemius Tendon 40
Bacterial Tenosynovitis of Foot Tendons in Broiler Breeders 42
Bacterial Osteomyelitis and Femoral Head Necrosis 43
Spondylitis (Vertebral Osteoarthritis) 46
Gangrenous Dermatitis (Clostridial Cellulitis, Blue Wing Disease) 48
Necrotic Enteritis 50
Ulcerative Enteritis in Quail 53
Focal Duodenal Necrosis in Table-Egg Layers 55
Avian Mycobacteriosis 56
Mycoplasma gallisepticum Infection in Turkeys (Infectious Sinusitis) 59
Mycoplasma gallisepticum Infection in Hobby Chickens 60
Mycoplasma synoviae Infection 61
Mycoplasma iowae Infection 64
Avian Chlamydiosis 68
Newcastle Disease in Chickens 71
Infectious Laryngotracheitis (ILT) 74
Avian Influenza 78
Infectious Bursal Disease (IBD) 83
Inclusion Body Hepatitis and Hepatitis-Hydropericardium Syndrome in Chickens 87
Hemorrhagic Enteritis in Turkeys 89
Chicken Infectious Anemia 90
White Chick Syndrome 92
Avian Hepatitis E Virus Infection in Chickens 95
Viral Tenosynovitis in Chickens 98
Avian Pox 100
Turkey Viral Hepatitis 102
Duck Viral Enteritis 103
Duck Viral Hepatitis Type A 105
Paramyxovirus Infection in Pigeons (Pigeon Paramyxovirus) 107
Herpesvirus Infection in Pigeons 110
Pacheco's Disease 112
Proventricular Dilatation Disease 113
Polyomavirus Infection in Budgerigars and Other Psittacine Birds 115
Psittacine Beak and Feather Disease 117

Cutaneous and Mucosal Papillomas 120
Marek's Disease 122
Lymphoid Leukosis. 134
Myelocytic Leukosis (Myelocytomatosis) 139
Nephroblastoma in Chickens. 142
Third-eyelid Aspergillosis 143
Mycotic Keratitis Caused by *Aspergillus*. 144
Respiratory Aspergillosis. 146
Crop Candidiasis (Crop Mycosis, Thrush) 152
Comb Candidiasis 153
Intestinal Coccidiosis in Chickens 154
Renal Coccidiosis in Geese. 159
Histomoniasis (Blackhead). 160
Trichomoniasis 165
Spironucleosis (Hexamitiasis) 167
Sarcocystis rileyi Infection in Ducks 169
Sarcocystis falcatula Infection 169
Crop Capillariasis. 170
Cheilospirura hamulosa Infection of Ventriculus 172
Tetrameres spp. Infection of Proventriculus 173
Hadjelia truncata Infection in Pigeons. 175
Eustrongylidosis (Verminous Peritonitis) 176
Ascaridiasis. 178
Heterakis isolonche Infection in Pheasants 181
Syngamus trachea Infection 182
Cestodiasis in Chickens 184
Collyriclosis (Cutaneous Trematodiasis). 188
Lice, Mites, and Ticks 191
Scaly Leg Mites 196
Subcutaneous Mite 197
Respiratory Mites. 198
Nutritional Encephalomalacia 199
Rickets 201
Broiler Chicken Breast Myopathy ("Wooden Breast"). 204
Deep Pectoral Myopathy (Green Muscle Disease). 205
Sternal Bursitis. 207
Ruptured Gastrocnemius Tendon. 210
Spondylolisthesis ("Kinky Back") 213
Spinal Cord Contusions in Turkeys 214
Tibial Dyschondroplasia 215
Osteoporosis in Caged Layers 218
Angular Limb Deformities (Valgus and Varus Deformities). 220
Rotation of Tibiotarsus 222
Atherosclerosis in Birds 223
Pulmonary Hypertension Syndrome (Ascites) in Broiler chickens 225
Round-Heart Disease (Dilated Cardiomyopathy) in Turkeys 228
Acute Pancreatic Necrosis in Psittacines. 231
Fatty Liver Hemorrhagic Syndrome 232
Hepatic Lipidosis Syndrome in Turkeys 234
Aflatoxicosis in Ducks 237
Hemosiderosis and Iron-Storage Disease 238
Necrohemorrhagic Hepatopathy in Chickens Following *Salmonella* Enteritidis Bacterin Injection 240

Oral, Pharyngeal, Esophageal, and Laryngeal Squamous Cell Carcinoma (SCC) in Hobby Chickens 243
Traumatic Ventriculitis 244
Intussusception in Poultry 245
Cloacitis in Broiler Breeder Hens 247
Dehydration in Baby Chicks (Baby Chick Nephropathy) 249
Urolithiasis (Ureteral Calculi) 251
ZZW Triploid Chicken 253
Persistent Cystic Right Oviduct 254
Regression (Involution, Atresia) of Ovarian Follicles 256
Female Reproductive Tract Adenocarcinomas 258
Ovarian Granulosa Cell Tumor 263
Oviductal Leiomyomas 265
Amyloidosis 268
Cerebellar Hypoplasia in Chicks 270
Footpad Dermatitis (Pododermatitis) 272
Avian Keratoacanthoma (Dermal Squamous-Cell Carcinoma) in Broiler Chickens 274
Cutaneous Xanthoma 275
Cataract 276
Ammonia-Induced Corneal Erosion 277
Miscellaneous 279
Index 298

INTRODUCTION

Birds are amazing animals. They can do everything that mammals can do, except they are more efficient. Additionally, almost all birds have the ability to fly, handling all of the complexity that flight entails. Fossil evidence indicates even flightless birds evolved from birds that previously could fly. Flight is essential to the preservation of a species; the majority of recently extinct birds have been flightless. Weight, weight distribution, and energy production are important factors in birds' ability to fly. Birds have minimized mass and maximized function. As a result, changes in organ structure and distribution compared to mammals have occurred. It is essential to recognize normal tissues before one can recognize abnormal tissues.

Gross (anatomic) pathology refers to the macroscopic changes in tissues and organs that result from a disease. Avian pathology is a sub-specialty that has its roots in the broad field of gross pathology. Initial diagnostics for an individual animal that is ill, including birds, typically includes a complete blood count and metabolic (chemistry) panel. However, when a population of birds, i.e. poultry flock, is affected, the flock becomes the patient and the approach is to "biopsy" the flock. Initial diagnostics for an avian population is to select a sampling of birds that represent the spectrum of the disease including recently dead, clinically affected, and one or two birds showing early or no signs of disease. Birds are euthanized and necropsied. Gross lesions that are recognized, described, and interpreted provide an immediate clinical diagnosis and permit appropriate interventions to be made to protect the remainder of the flock. Speed in making a clinical diagnosis and instituting interventions is essential as diseases can rapidly affect the entire flock. Gross lesions are often characteristic, but can be pathognomonic in some cases. Findings at necropsy also provide direction on what samples to collect for additional diagnostics to confirm the clinical diagnosis. Necropsy of dead or dying individual birds is also indicated to confirm the clinical diagnosis, collect further samples for diagnosis, make sure other birds or animals are not at risk, and correlate clinical findings with necropsy findings. Sections in the *Gross Pathology of Avian Diseases: Text and Atlas* are organized by diseases, which are grouped by etiology. Each section consists of text and pictures of gross lesions. The majority of pictures have been taken *in situ* to show exactly how the lesions appear at necropsy. Although gross lesions are emphasized, etiology and, if applicable, pathogenesis of the disease process and transmission of infectious agent are included. Over 1200 figures show the gross pathology of over 120 avian diseases. The overwhelming majority of pictures come from diagnostic cases that we have seen during our careers as avian pathologists. We wanted to publish this book so that those involved in the diagnosis of avian diseases and necropsy of birds could benefit from our extensive collections of gross lesions in birds. Several figures are included for some diseases to show gross lesions in organs and tissues that vary in distribution, extent, and severity depending on factors related to the host and etiology. Additionally, lesions evolve over time.

The book by no means covers all diseases of birds, but we hope that this edition will be the foundation for future editions in which additional diseases are included. Special thanks go to those who contributed pictures from their collections to use in the book; their contributions are acknowledged in the legends of their photos. We invite avian pathologists to contribute their cases to future editions of *Gross Pathology of Avian Diseases: Text and Atlas*. In addition, we welcome comments from colleagues about the book. We thank the American Association of Avian Pathologists (AAAP) for publishing the book. This book is a companion to *Avian Histopathology*, also published by the American Association of Avian Pathologists. We hope that the *Gross Pathology of Avian Diseases: Text and Atlas* will be on the bookshelves of anyone involved in the diagnosis of avian diseases.

Tahseen Abdul-Aziz
H. John Barnes

Gross Pathology of Avian Diseases
Text and Atlas

Tahseen Abdul-Aziz
H. John Barnes

Unhealed Navels, Omphalitis, Yolk Sac Infection

Omphalitis and yolk sac infections are common findings in poultry that die during the first week post-hatching. Yolk sac infection can result from non-specific environmental bacteria or be a manifestation of a specific disease, e.g., salmonellosis.

Unhealed navels and omphalitis. Omphalitis is inflammation of the navel (umbilicus). The navel in birds is the opening through which the yolk sac is retracted into the body cavity shortly before hatching. In chickens, this occurs at about day 19 of incubation. After hatching, the navel area must remain clean and dry to ensure proper healing and prevent infection. It is common for tissue to be trapped in the healing navel, which results in a persistent 'string' or 'button'. Trapped tissue acts as a wick for bacteria to enter the body cavity. With the yolk sac just inside and usually adhering to the internal navel, it is most frequently infected along with the umbilicus. Unhealed navels also serve as portals of entry for bacteria. Infrequently, bacteria bypass the yolk sac and cause peritonitis in the absence of yolksacculitis.

Proper incubation is essential for normal closure of the umbilicus. Factors contributing to delayed healing and/or infection of the navel include (1) excessive fogging at transfer from the incubator to hatcher, (2) high humidity in the hatcher, (3) overheating in the late incubation or hatching process, (4) exploding contaminated eggs (5) dirty hatching trays, (6) removing birds from the hatcher before the majority of them are dry, (7) transferring newly hatched chicks to wet trays, (8) placing chicks on damp belts, (9) excess wetting in vaccination cabinet, (10) and placing chicks in dirty transportation boxes.

With omphalitis, the area around the unhealed navel becomes swollen, reddened, and edematous. Although the infection may extend from the navel to the yolk sac, baby chicks or poults with omphalitis may or may not have yolk sac infection, i.e. infection may be confined to the navel. Conversely, it is also possible for yolk sac infection to occur in the absence of omphalitis. In these cases, the organism enters the yolk sac from the intestinal tract. However, in most cases both the umbilicus and yolk sac are inflamed.

Mild 'physiological inflammation' of the navel is normal and often present during the first day or two following hatching. It should not be confused with bacterial infections, which are more severe, present for several days, and usually associated with yolksacculitis. Urates in the unhealed umbilicus are seen when the urachus is patent.

Yolk sac infection (Yolksacculitis). Heavy contamination of the eggshell is the most important factor involved in yolksacculitis. Immediately after laying, eggs are hot, moist, and porous. As egg contents cool, they shrink and produce an internal negative pressure, which results in bacteria on the surface of the egg being drawn through pores in the shell into the egg. The cuticle is moist when the egg is laid, but soon dries, blocking the pores, and preventing microbial penetration. However, because the cuticle does not fully protect against bacterial penetration immediately after laying, large numbers of bacteria may penetrate the eggshell if the surface of the egg is heavily contaminated or moist. Motile bacteria can directly penetrate shell pores if there is sufficient moisture. Sweating of eggs removed from the egg cooler in a humid environment is a common way in which moisture contributes to egg contamination. Embryos with infected yolk sacs may die before hatching. Eggs infected with gas-producing bacteria, especially *Pseudomonas*, may explode in the incubators (these are called "exploders", "rots", or "bangers"). Other chicks may hatch with infected yolk sacs. After hatching, bacteria continue to multiply in the yolk sac, causing yolksacculitis. The infection may spread from the yolk sac causing septicemia and death of the bird. Bacteria commonly isolated from infected yolk sacs include *E. coli*, *Pseudomonas aeruginosa*, *Enterococcus*, and *Proteus*.

To minimize the numbers of birds with yolk sac infections, nest boxes must be well littered, accessible, and sufficient in numbers. Nest material needs to be dry. Eggs should be gathered frequently. Good management of nest boxes will minimize floor eggs, which become heavily contaminated with bacteria. Floor eggs should be handled separately.

Under normal conditions, yolk sacs are gradually absorbed during the first week post-hatching. Normal yolk sacs are flaccid and contain thick, viscous, homogenous, yellow, yellow-green, or green yolk. Infected yolk sacs vary in size and appearance; some of them may be small while others are large and turgid, filling the abdominal cavity and distending the abdomen. Large, infected yolk sacs are fragile and easily ruptured during necropsy. The wall of the yolk sac may have prominent blood vessels or appear hemorrhagic. The consistency of the yolk is an important criterion in diagnosing yolksacculitis. Yolk becomes watery, lumpy, thick and curdled, or inspissated. Color can range from bright yellow to dark brown. Often there is an offensive odor. Infection may extend through the yolk sac wall into the body cavity, causing peritonitis.

Young birds surviving acute yolksacculitis are usually undersized. Variably sized yolk sacs with thickened, inflamed walls persist for weeks, often adhering to the duodenum or other parts of the intestinal tract and body wall.

Contents of chronically infected yolk sacs range from thick inspissated exudate to curd-like masses that typically adhere as a layer on the inner surface of the yolk sac. Causative bacteria are readily isolated from chronic yolksacculitis. Rarely the chronically infected yolk sac and elongated yolk sac stalk wrap around an intestinal loop causing strangulation.

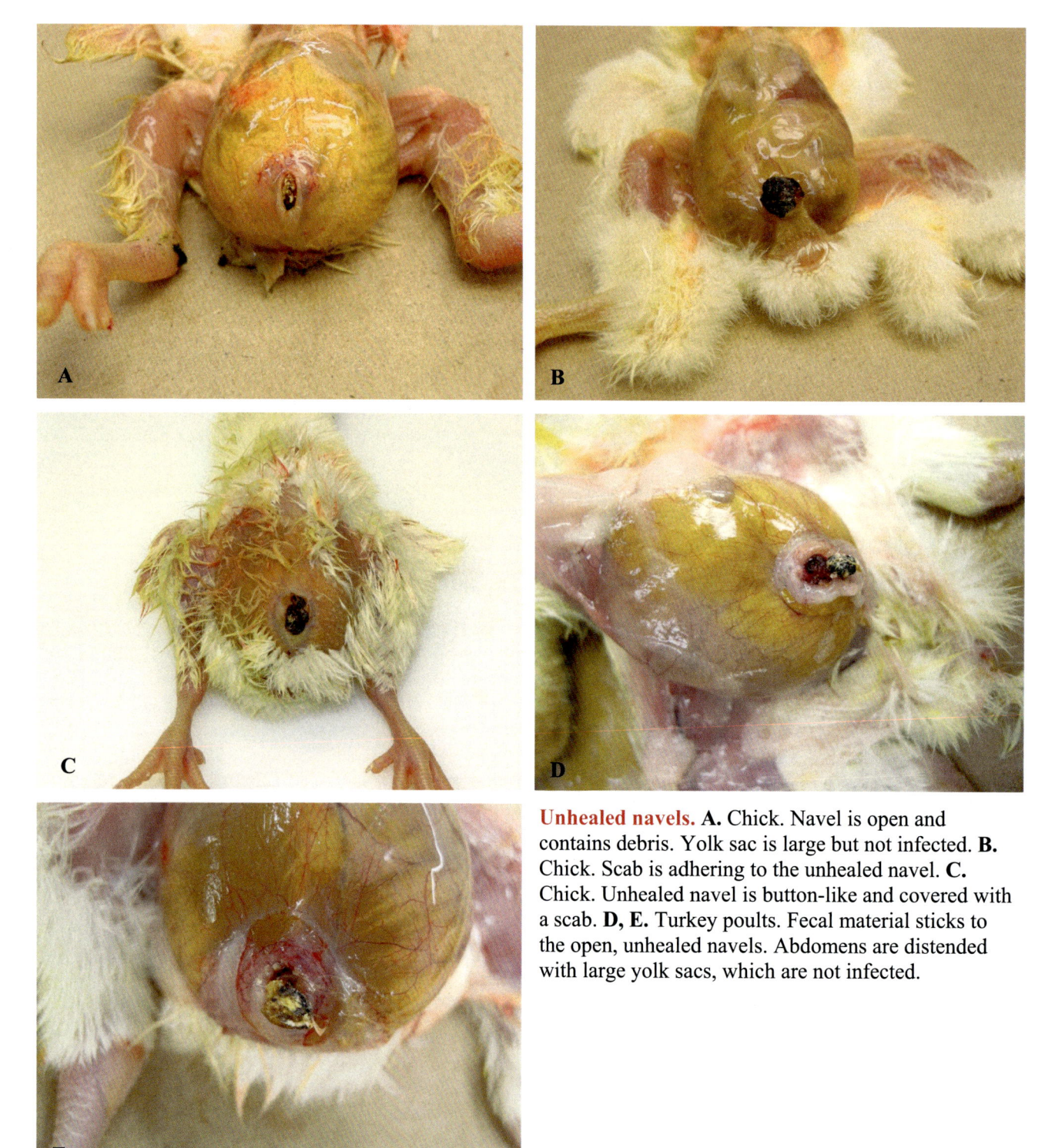

Unhealed navels. A. Chick. Navel is open and contains debris. Yolk sac is large but not infected. **B.** Chick. Scab is adhering to the unhealed navel. **C.** Chick. Unhealed navel is button-like and covered with a scab. **D, E.** Turkey poults. Fecal material sticks to the open, unhealed navels. Abdomens are distended with large yolk sacs, which are not infected.

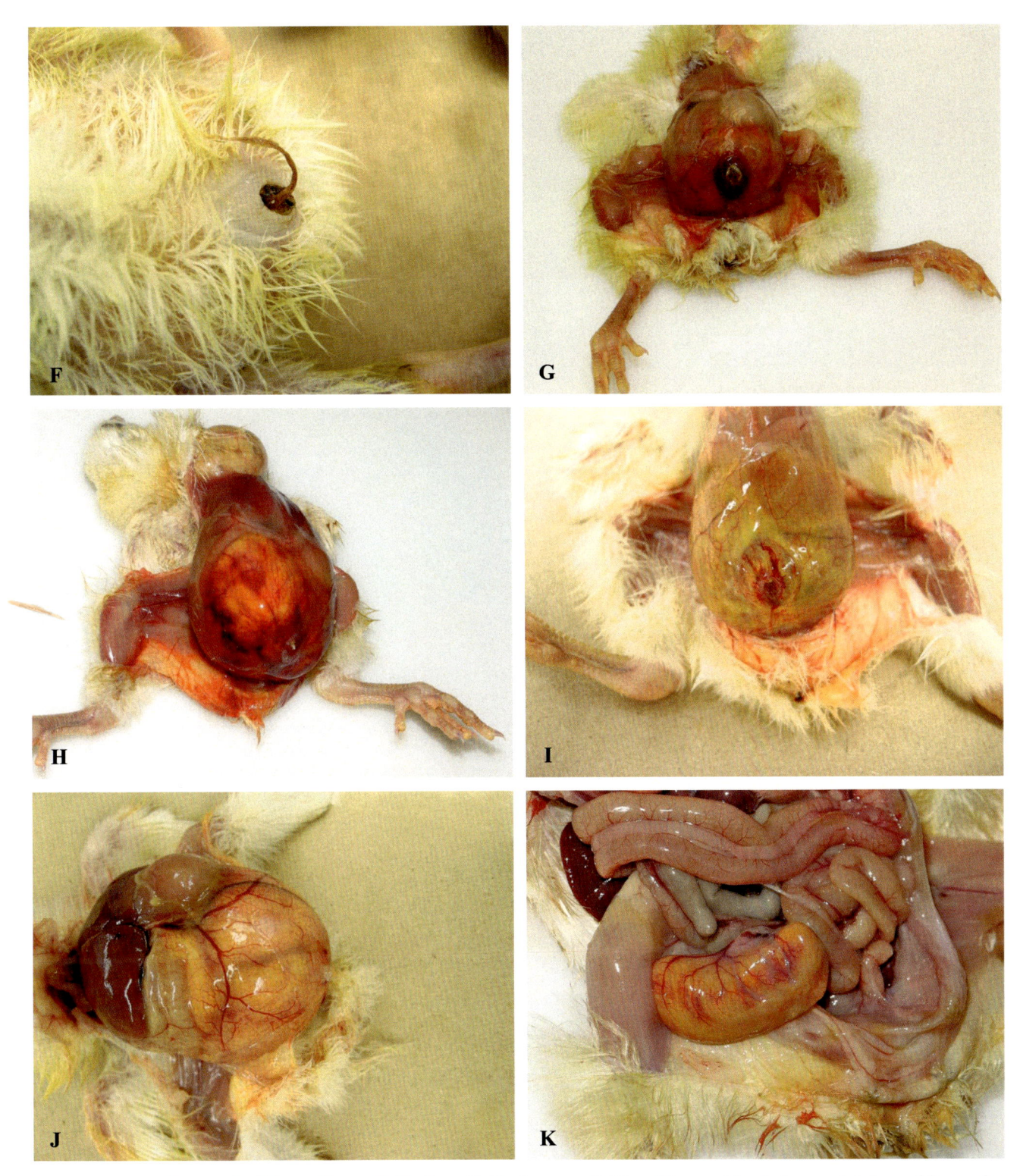

Unhealed navels, omphalitis, yolk sac infection. F. Turkey poult. Navel has not healed completely and has a dry string, which was the stalk that attached the yolk sac to the intestine in the embryo during development. **G, H.** Chicks. Omphalitis and yolk sac infection. Navels and areas around it are markedly reddened. Abdomens are distended by the inflamed yolk sacs. **I.** Chick. Omphalitis and yolk sac infection. Navel is open and inflamed. Abdomen is distended by an inflamed yolk sac. **J.** chick. Yolk sac infection. Inflamed yolk sac is very large and filling and distending the abdomen. There was no gross evidence of omphalitis. **K.** 4-day broiler chicken. Yolk sac is inflamed, wall is thickened, and it is filled with thick yolk.

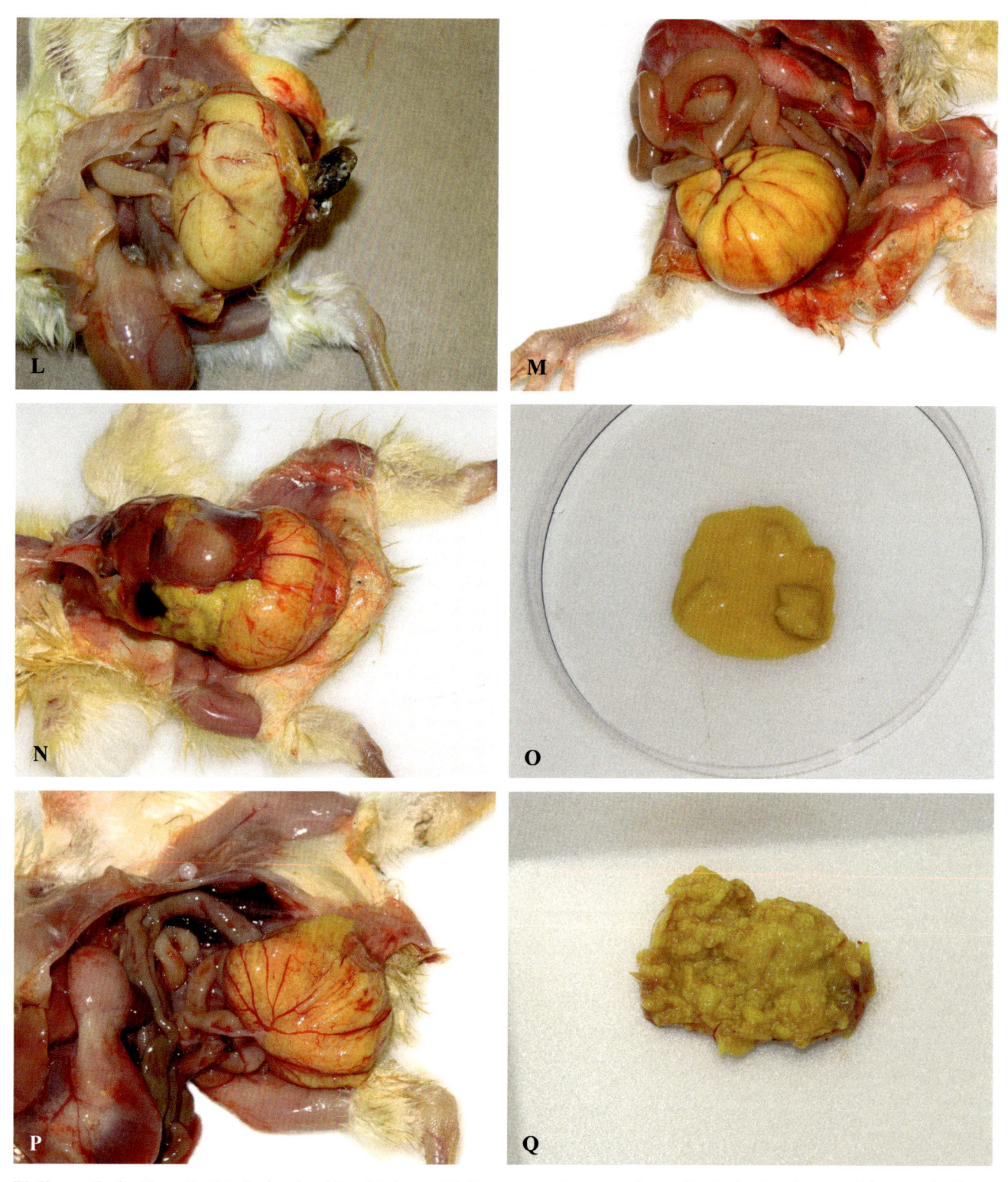

Yolk sac infection. L, M. 3-day broiler chickens. Yolk sacs are large and turgid. In L, fecal material extends from the navel into the yolk sac. **N.** 7-day broiler chicken. Yolk sac is large and infected. Infection extends into the body cavity causing diffuse, severe peritonitis. Blood vessels in the wall of the yolk sac are prominent. **O.** Contents of the yolk sac in N is thick and lumpy. **P.** 4-day broiler chicken. Infected yolk sac is distended with thick yolk. Blood vessels in the wall of the yolk sac are prominent. **Q.** Contents of the yolk sac in P is thick and curdled.

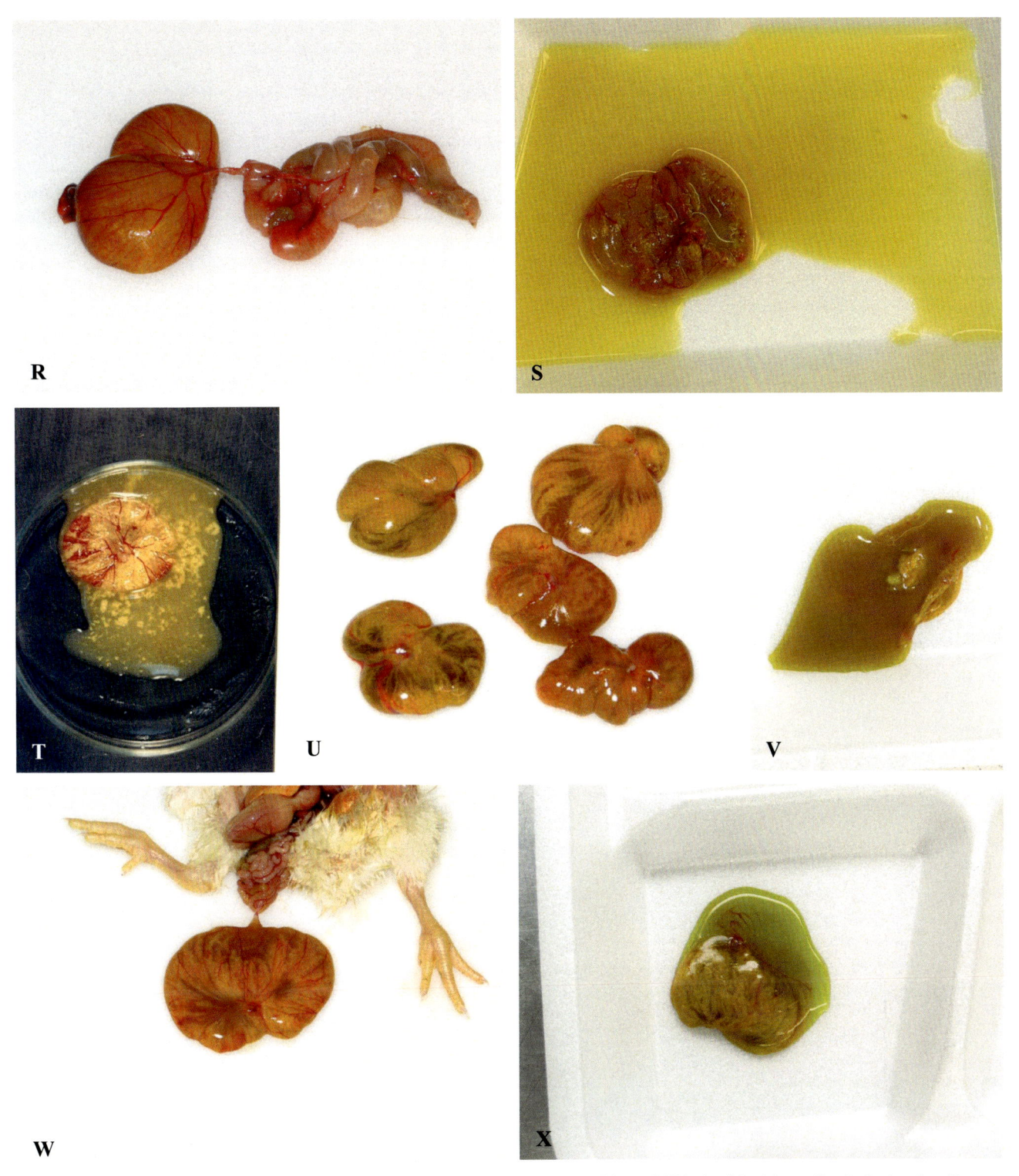

Yolk sac infection. R. 3-day broiler chicken. Yolk sac is large, turgid, anf filled with thin yolk. **S.** 3-day broiler chicken. Yolk sac wall is thickened and congested. The yolk is watery. **T.** 2-day broiler chicken. Infected yolk sac with thickend, congested wall. **Normal yolk sacs. U, V, W, X.** One- and 3-day broiler chickens. Yolk sacs are falccid and contained thick, viscous yolk that can be yellow, yellow-green, or green.

Neonatal Septicemia

Septicemia is a common cause of first-week mortality in young birds including chickens, turkey poults, ducklings, and goslings. Mortality usually begins within the first few days after hatching, peaks on days 4-7, and gradually declines during the next 2-3 weeks. Infection often follows omphalitis-yolksacculitis, but some affected birds have normal navels and yolk sacs. In the absence of omphalitis or yolksacculitis, the portal of entry for the causative bacteria becomes uncertain. Virulent organisms may be inhaled or ingested, or it is possible the birds became infected *in ovo* and were harboring bacteria in their yolk sacs when they hatched. Following infection, bacteria enter the blood circulation, which results in septicemia and death.

Cause. Bacteria, but *Escherichia coli* and *Pseudomonas aeruginosa* are most common. Other bacteria include *Enterococcus* and *Salmonella*.

Gross lesions. Pericarditis of varying severity with or without hepatic serositis is the hallmark lesion of neonatal septicemia. The spleen is often enlarged. In some cases, the only lesions are an enlarged liver that may be gray to green or congested, and an enlarged, black-red spleen. Sometimes, the enlarged, black-red spleen is the only lesion seen. Additionally, there may be yellow exudate in the body cavity (peritonitis), green discoloration of the proventriculus, and pulmonary congestion. Lungs and proventriculus darken and become almost black as decomposition progresses.

Severe generalized polyserositis with extensive adhesions of visceral organs or localized infections in the eye, brain, bones, or joints/tendons occur in birds that survive sepsis. Survivors are often stunted and unthrifty. Eye infections are generally unilateral. Infected eyes are swollen and opaque; hypopyon may be present. Those with encephalitis or meningoencephalitis show neurologic signs including twisting of the neck or lying on their side and paddling. Careful removal of cranial bones and *in-situ* examination of the brain reveals yellow discolored areas in the cerebral hemispheres or cerebellum. Osteomyelitis occurs in the proximal tibiotarsus and may be unilateral or bilateral. Birds with arthritis/synovitis of tendons, hock joints, or feet are lame and reluctant to move. Swelling of one or both hock joints or feet may be obvious or barely perceptible.

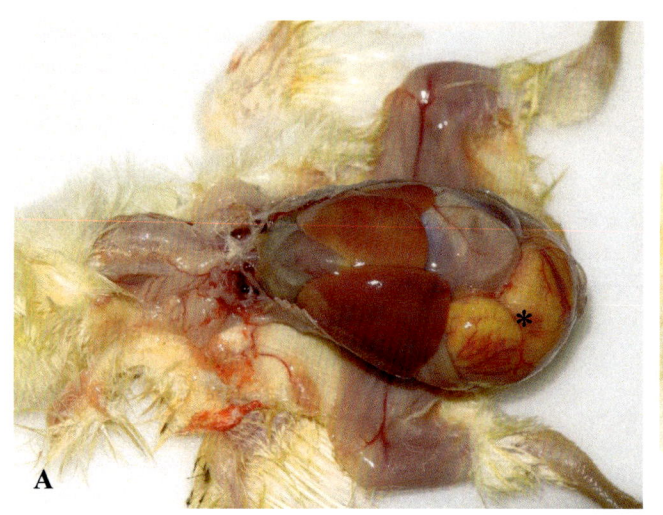

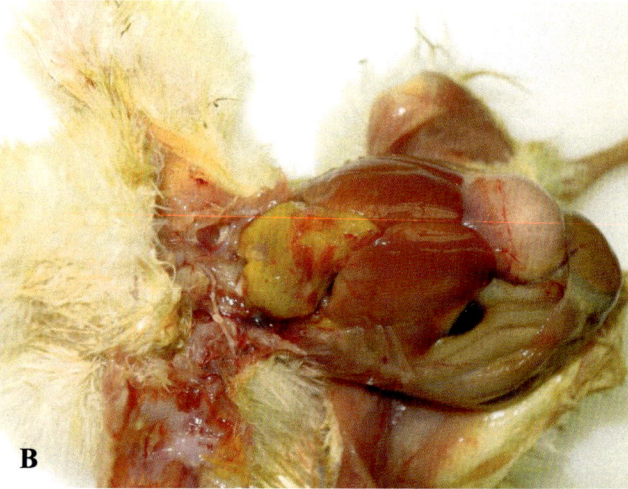

Septicemia caused by *E. coli* (colisepticemia). **A.** 4-day broiler. Early lesion of pericarditis characterized by mild turbidity, thickening, and yellow discoloration of the pericardium. Note the enlarged inflamed yolk sac (asterisk) that distends the abdomen. **B.** 6-day broiler breeder. Severe pericarditis characterized by accumulation of fibrinous exudate on the surface of the heart.

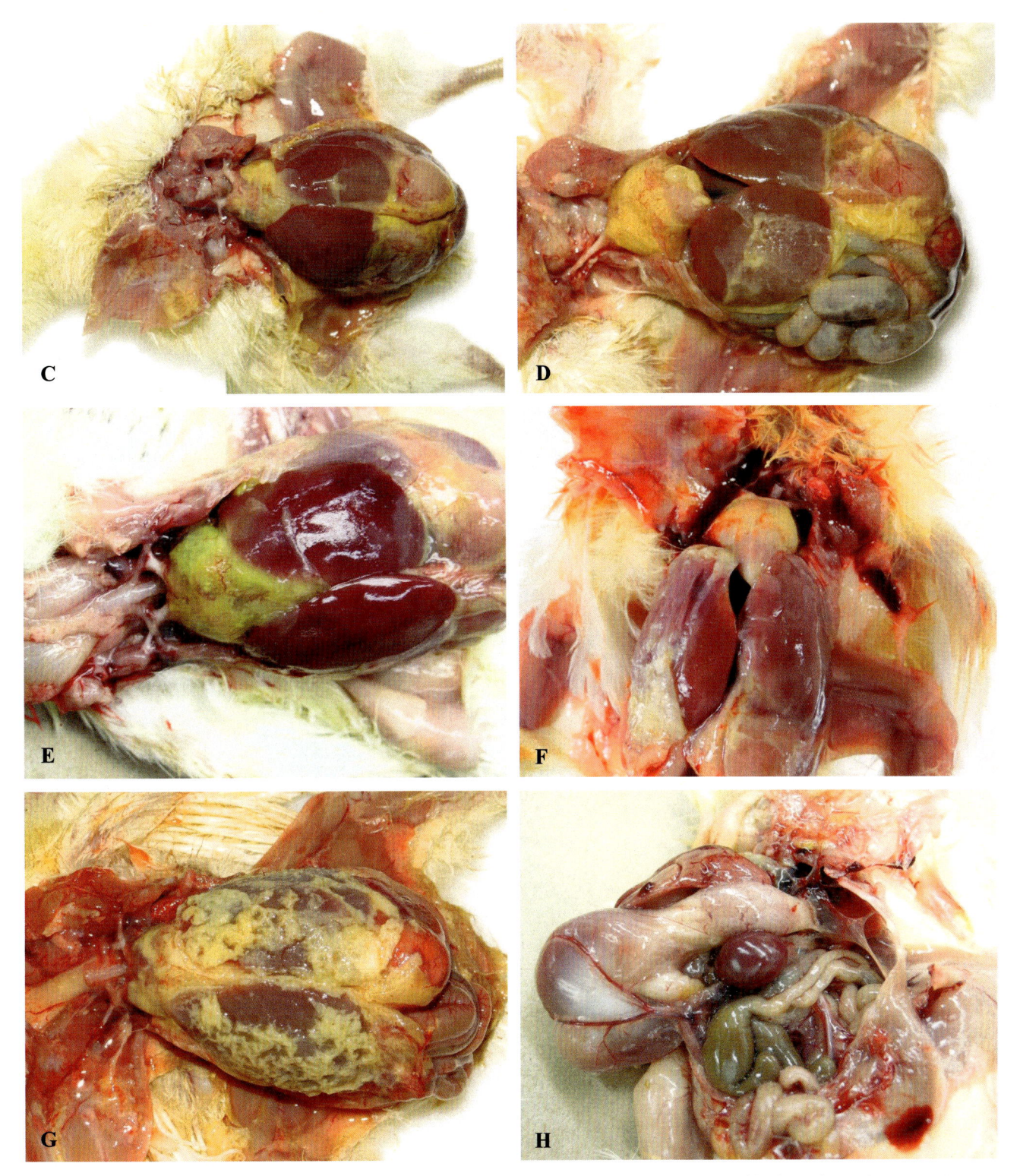

Septicemia caused by *E. coli* (colisepticemia). 4- to 9-day broiler chickens and broiler breeders. **C, D, E, F.** Pericarditis and hepatic serositis characterized by accumulation of fibrinous exudate on the surface of the heart and liver. In E and F, livers are notably enlarged. **G.** Severe, diffuse polyserositis in a bird that survived long enough for these lesions to develop. **H.** Spleen is enlarged. This bird also had severe pericarditis.

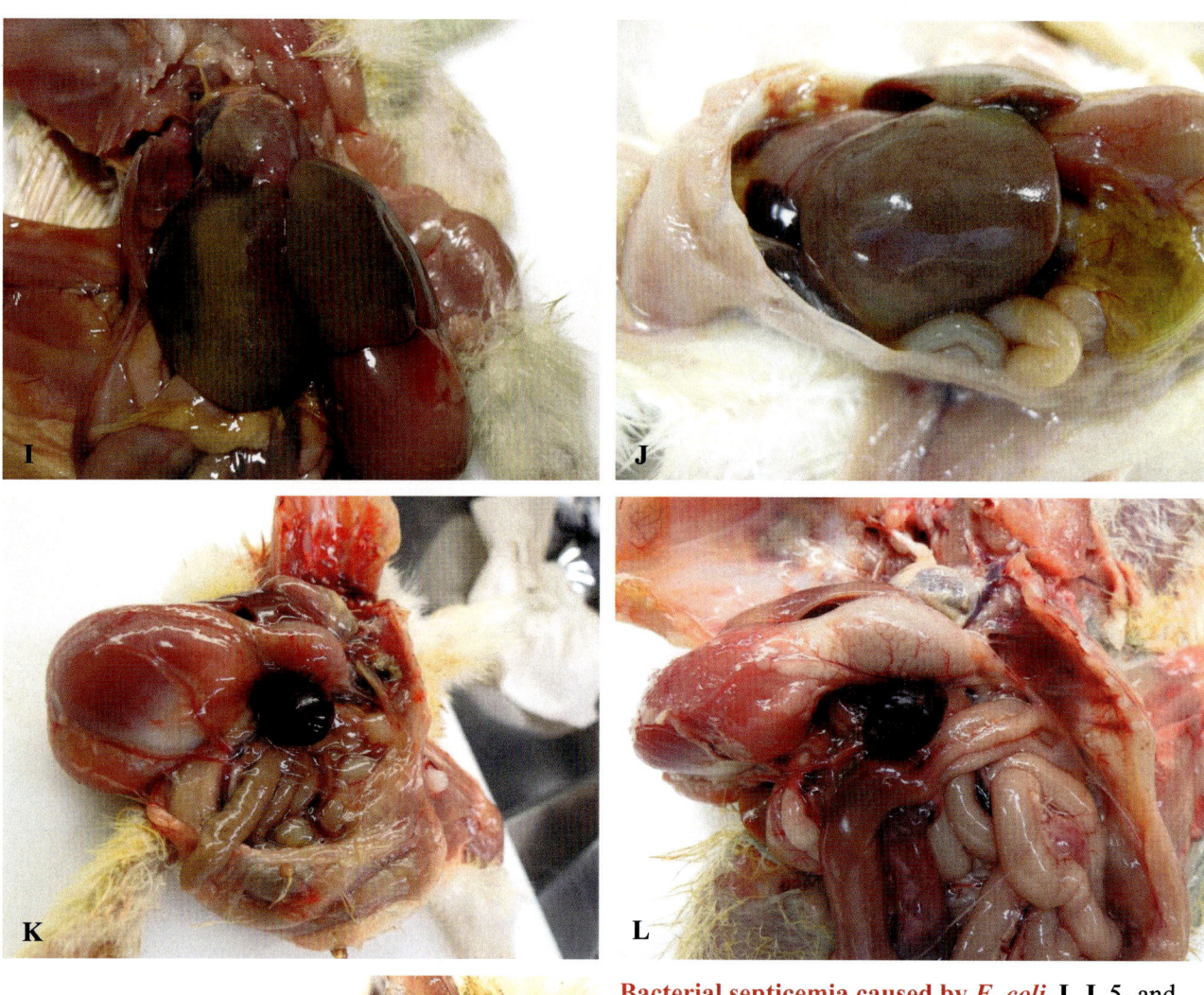

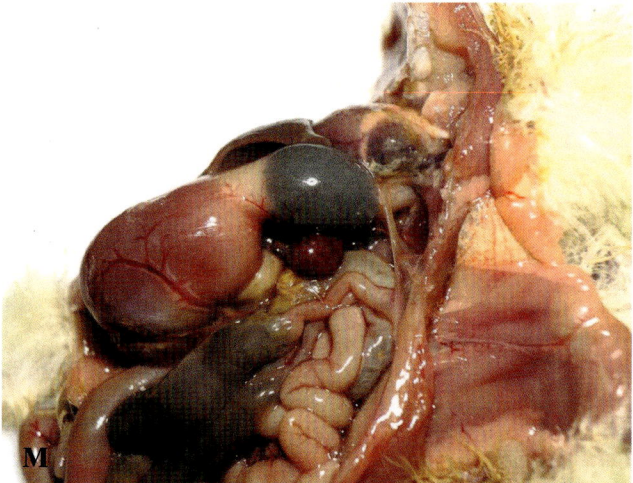

Bacterial septicemia caused by *E. coli*. I, J. 5- and 6-day broiler chickens. Enlarged, green livers. Bird in G also had mild pericarditis. **K, L.** 5- and 7-day broiler chickens. Enlarged, black-red spleen is a characteristic lesion of bacterial septicemia caused by *E. coli* or *Pseudomonas aeruginosa*. Sometimes, it is the only lesion found in septic birds. In both birds, the cause was *E. coli*. **M.** 6-day broiler chicken. Marked green discoloration of the proventriculus and dark red color of the spleen. This is the same bird in I.

Brain infection. N. 3-day broiler breeder pullet. *P. aeruginosa*. Severe meningoencephalitis. Cerebellum is enlarged and distorted. Yellow areas are due to necrosis and accumulation of exudate. **O.** 3-day broiler chicken. *E. coli*. Exudate in the lateral ventricles caused yellow discoloration of the posterior areas of the cerebral hemispheres (arrows). There also is mild yellowing of the posterior part of the cerebellum. **P, Q.** 5-day broiler breeder pullet. *E. coli*. **P.** Yellow discoloration of the cerebral hemispheres can be seen through the cranial bones (arrow). **Q.** Yellow areas in the cerebral hemispheres (arrows) are due to necrosis and accumulation of exudate. **R, S.** 5-day broiler chicken. *P. aeruginosa*. **R.** Cerebellum is enlarged and discolored light green. Note yellow area in the right cerebral hemisphere (arrow). **S.** Cut surface of the cerebellum in R showing a large yellow area of necrosis.

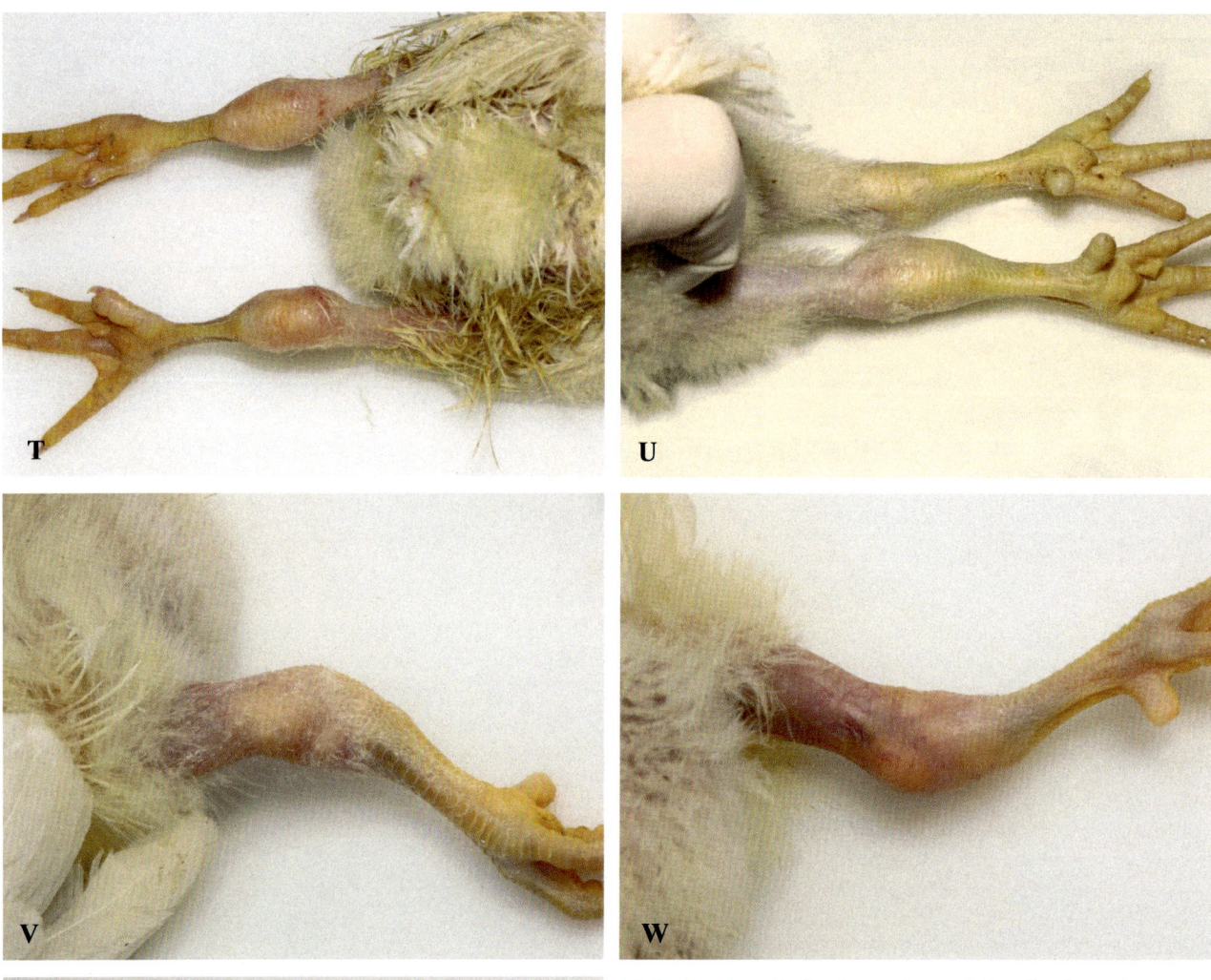

Joint/tendon infections. 2-week broiler breeders. Arthritis/tenosynovitis of hock joints/gastrocnemius tendons (**T, U, V, W**) and foot (**X**) caused by *Pseudomonas aeruginosa*. The hock joints and the foot are swollen. Clinical history indicated several birds in the flock were limping or could not stand. Note that the lesion is bilateral in T and unilateral in U.

Salmonella Enteritidis Infection in Broiler Chickens

Gross lesions. Gross lesions characteristic of systemic bacterial infection (septicemia) are most frequently seen in infected broiler chickens less than 2 weeks old, although lesions have been seen in broiler chickens as old as 28 days. Severe fibrinous pericarditis and hepatic serositis are the most common lesions. Hepatic serositis can be so severe that the yellow fibrinous exudate on the liver surface extends into the abdominal cavity and can be seen through the abdominal wall. Marked fibrin exudation reflects the severe damage to blood vessels caused by potent endotoxins of the *Salmonella*. Liver and spleen are usually enlarged (hepatomegaly, splenomegaly). Yellow exudate is present in the body cavity. In some cases, multiple pale foci consistent with necrosis are seen on the capsular surface of the liver. Infected yolk sacs are usually present. In most cases, the yolk is thick and inspissated rather than watery or flocculent. Occasionally, only concurrent yolksacculitis and pericarditis of varying severity are seen. *Salmonella* Enteritidis infection needs to be differentiated by isolation and identification from other systemic bacterial infections that cause polyserositis.

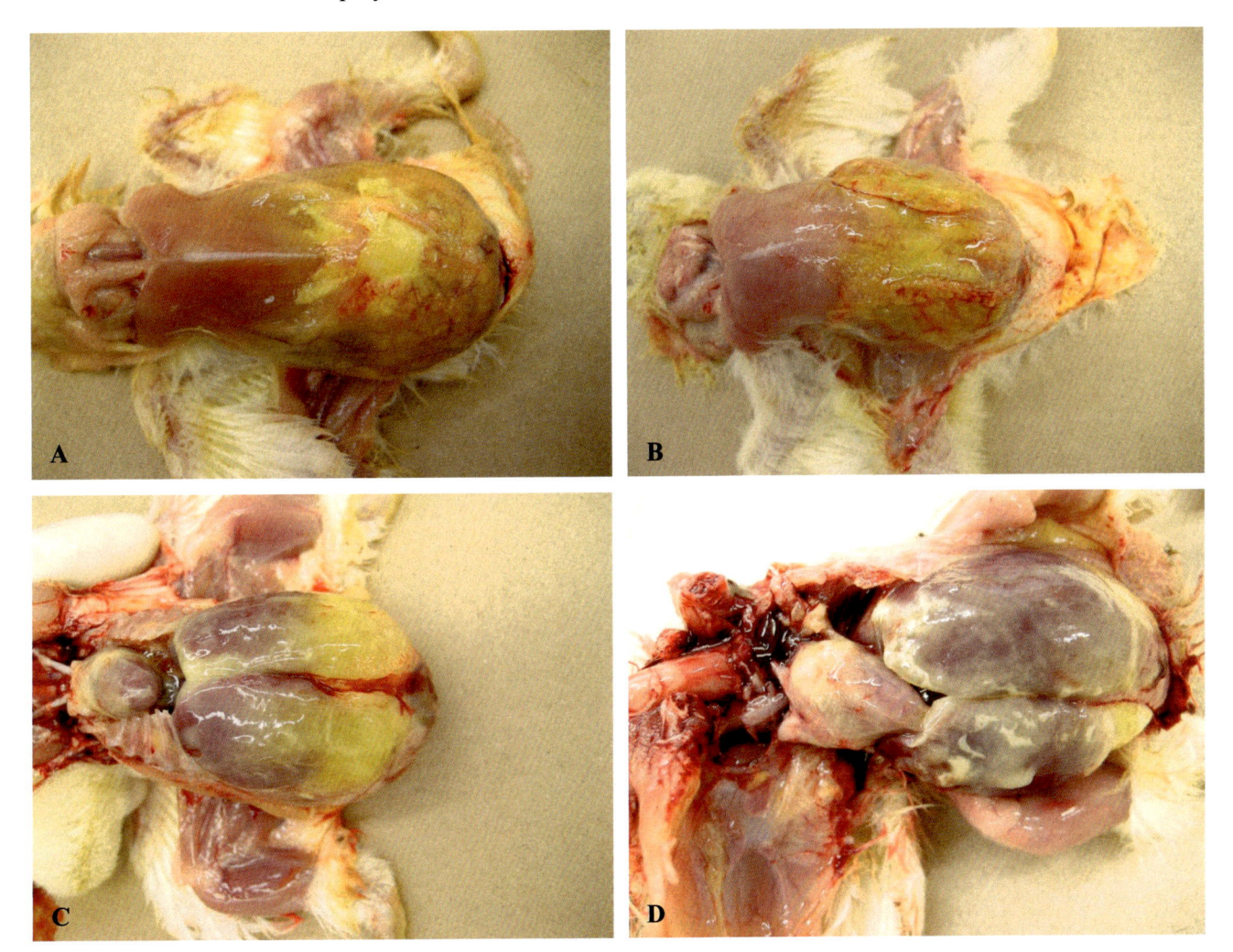

Salmonella **Enteritidis infection.** Broiler chickens (A, C. 11 days. B, D. 13-days). **A, B.** Fibrinous exudate is visible through the abdominal wall. **C.** Very severe fibrinous pericarditis and hepatic serositis. Fibrinous exudate on the liver surface extends into the abdominal cavity. **D.** Hepatomegaly and polyserositis.

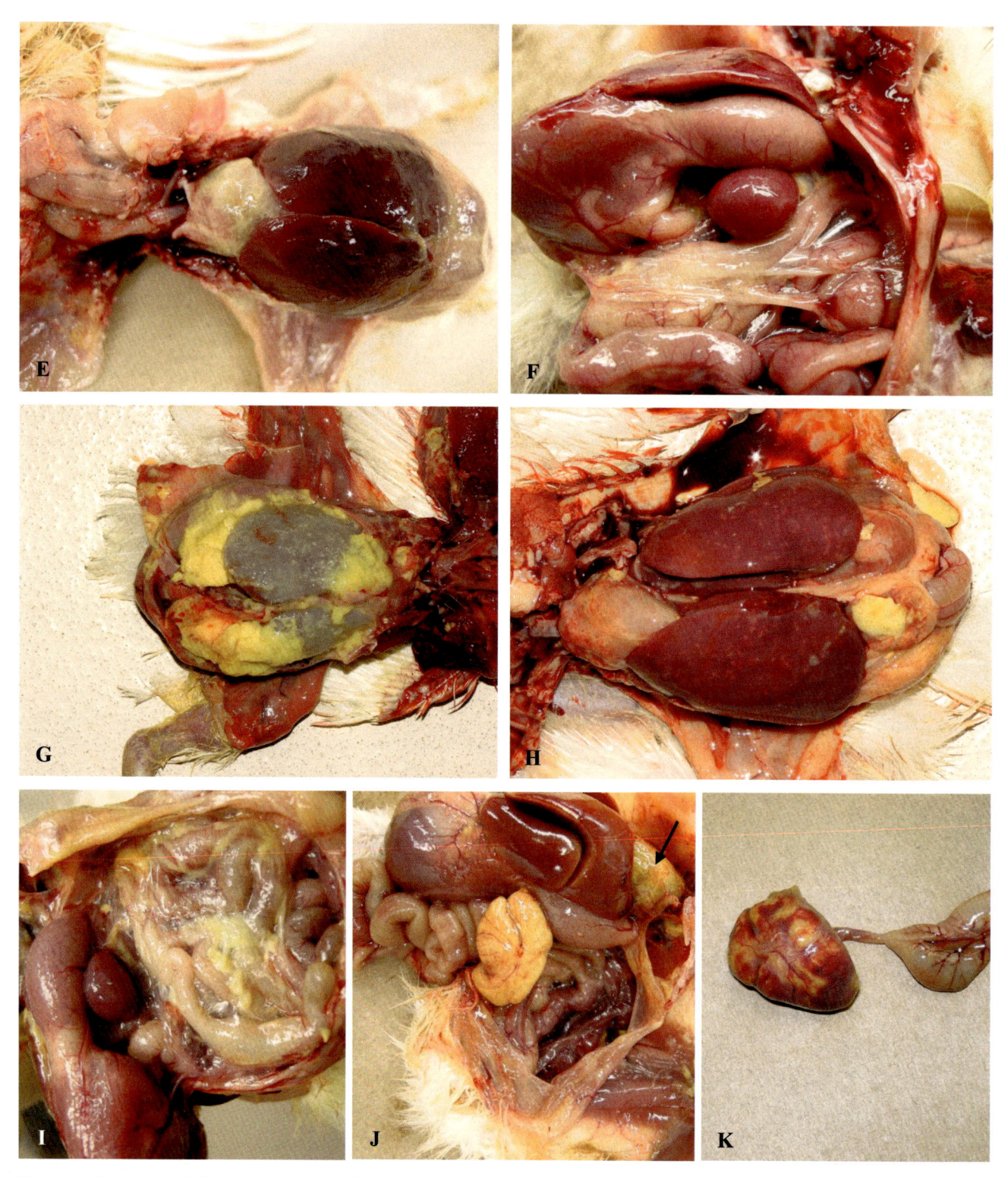

12 *Gross Pathology of Avian Diseases: Text and Atlas*

***Salmonella* Enteritidis infection.** Broiler chickens (E, F. 11 days. G, H. 28 days. I. 13 days. J. 6 days. K. 9 days). **E.** Marked pericarditis. Liver is enlarged and has a glossy surface caused by a thin layer of fibrinous exudate. **F.** Spleen is markedly enlarged; diffuse peritonitis. **G.** Abundant thick yellow fibrinous exudate covers the liver and extends into the body cavity. Liver is discolored. **H.** Enlarged liver with many pale foci. Pericardial sac is thickened (pericarditis). **I.** Fibrinous exudate in the body cavity (peritonitis, serositis). Spleen is mildly enlarged. **J, K.** Yolksacculitis; yolk is inspissated. The arrow in J points to pericarditis.

Colibacillosis with Tracheitis Caused by Infectious Bronchitis Virus in Broiler Chickens

Infectious bronchitis (IB) is a disease of chickens caused by a virus in the family Coronaviridae. IB virus has a tropism for epithelial cells in the respiratory tract, damages the trachea and air sacs, and predisposes birds to secondary bacterial infection, especially *Escherichia coli*. Septicemia and airsacculitis caused by *E. coli* are leading causes of broiler chicken condemnations at processing. Subacute to chronic tracheitis is a common lesion in broiler chickens with *E. coli* septicemia and airsacculitis, and IB virus is frequently detected in the tracheas of these birds. Recognizing the role of IB virus is crucial for developing a strategy to prevent septicemia and airsacculitis caused by *E. coli* in broiler chickens. IB virus is ubiquitous. Therefore, protecting broiler chickens against the virus through proper vaccination and biosecurity is critical.

Mucociliary blanket of the trachea. Ciliated epithelium, mucus, and mucous secreting cells in the respiratory tract comprise the mucociliary blanket (mucociliary escalator), which constitutes an important mechanism for entrapping and clearing particulate material from the respiratory tract. The wave-like, propulsive action of cilia moves entrapped particles through the mucous layer toward the pharynx where they can be swallowed or expelled. Damage to the respiratory mucosal epithelium impairs its functional capacity to clear inhaled particles. This may explain in part the increased susceptibility of birds to bacterial respiratory infection, particularly *E. coli*, following damage to the respiratory mucosa by environmental insults, such as ammonia and dust, or following infection with a respiratory virus. Defective clearance by the upper respiratory tract may be one of several factors enabling *E. coli* to colonize the damaged lower respiratory tract and, in some cases, invade the blood stream and cause septicemia.

Septicemia, airsacculitis, and tracheal lesions. Broiler chicken flocks affected with septicemia and airsacculitis caused by *E. coli* typically experience elevated mortality that may climb to hundreds of birds per day. Sick birds in the flock are lethargic; have ruffled feathers, and stand or sit with eyes closed. Necropsy of dead or sick birds reveals enlarged, dark, congested spleens, enlarged livers, and polyserositis including pericarditis, hepatic serositis (perihepatitis), airsacculitis, peritonitis, and pleuritis that ranges from mild to very severe. Severity of lesions is inversely related to *E. coli* virulence; the longer the bird survives, the more severe the lesions. Affected birds often have a characteristic odor and tissues become gray to green as they sit exposed to air. Cultures of pericardial sac and/or livers yield heavy pure growth of *E. coli*. Unilateral or bilateral bronchopneumonia, characterized by discoloration and consolidation of lung parenchyma, occurs in some birds. In severe cases, inflammation may extend from the body cavity through the abdominal wall, causing cellulitis. Stunting, poor feathering, synovitis/arthritis, and localized infections in a variety of tissues are found in chronically infected birds. The tracheal mucosa is typically thickened with excess mucoid gray-white or pale yellow exudate in the lumen. In some cases, the tracheal mucosa is reddened. Tracheas are best evaluated in freshly dead or euthanized birds as postmortem autolysis makes it difficult to evaluate the appearance of the tracheal mucosa.

Ancillary diagnostic tests. Whenever possible, tracheas of birds with septicemia and airsacculitis caused by *E. coli* should be examined by histopathology and tested for IB virus by PCR. Results of histopathology and virus testing need to be interpreted in conjunction with each other. Detection of IB virus in tracheas with minimal or no microscopic lesions should be interpreted cautiously with regard to the role of the virus in respiratory disease, colisepticemia, or airsacculitis. Alternatively, if there are tracheal lesions, but IB virus is not detected, then other respiratory viruses (e.g. avian paramyxovirus-1, infectious laryngotracheitis virus) or *Mycoplasma gallisepticum* need to be considered as possible causes of the tracheitis.

Isolation of IB virus in embryonated chicken eggs may be attempted on PCR-positive tracheas. Infectious bronchitis virus isolates can be genotyped to determine the virus strain. If IB is a recurring problem on broiler chicken farms, determining the serotype/genotype of the virus will be important in understanding the epidemiology of the infection and help in choosing the appropriate IB immunization program.

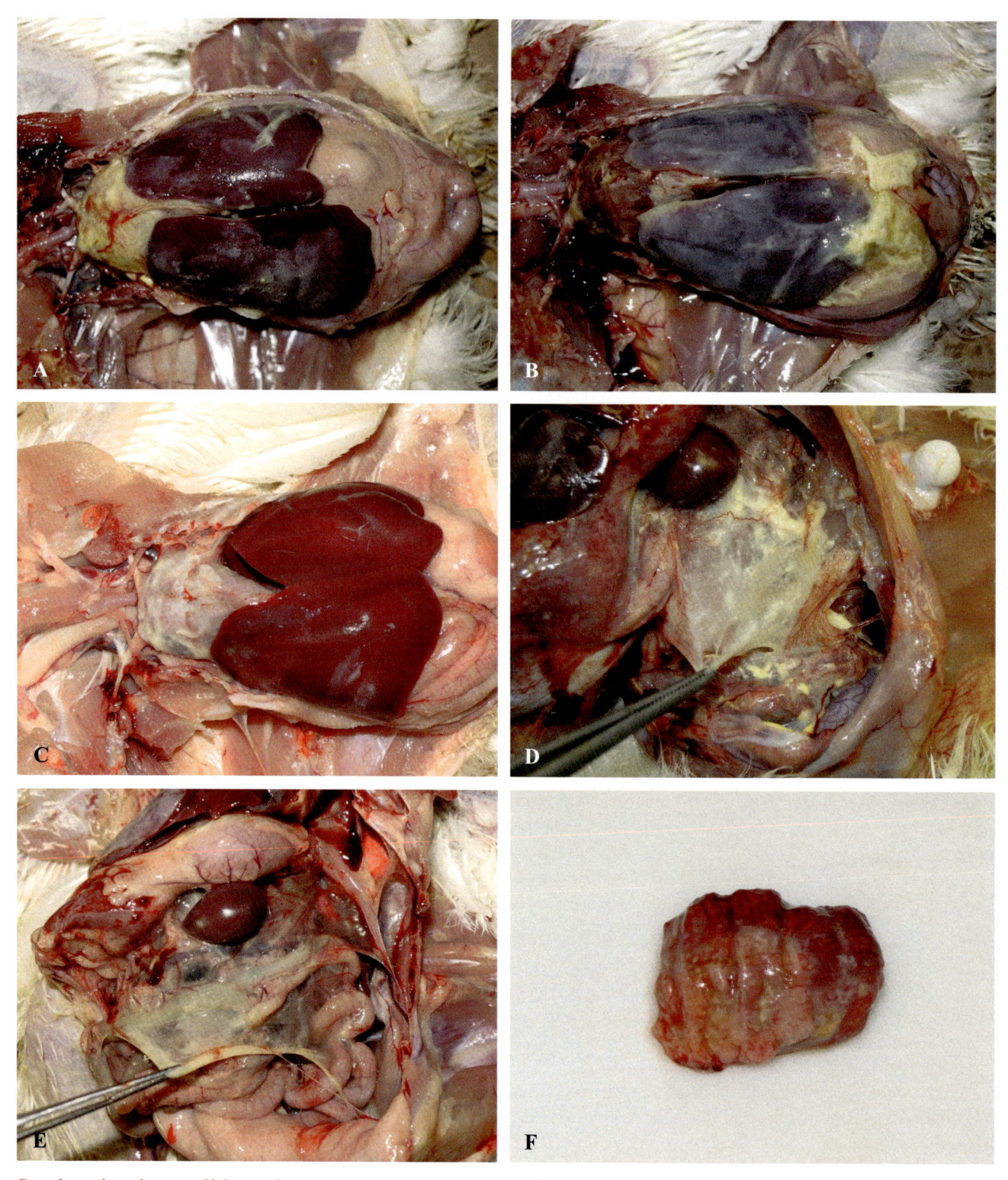

Septicemia, airsacculitis, and pneumonia caused by *E. coli*. 28- to 58-day broiler chickens. **A, B, C.** Pericarditis and hepatic serositis (perihepatitis) characterized by accumulation of fibrinous exudate on the epicardial surface of the heart and capsular surface of the liver. In **B**, thick exudate extends beyond the posterior margin of the liver. In **C**, there is mild hepatic serositis (thin layer of fibrin on liver surface) but the liver is enlarged. **D, E.** Airsacculitis and splenomegaly. Air sacs are markedly thickened by yellow exudate, and spleens are swollen and congested. **F.** Pneumonia characterized by discoloration and consolidation of lung parenchyma. In all the cases, there were histopathological lesions in tracheas, and infectious bronchitis virus was detected by PCR.

Swollen-Head Syndrome in Broiler Chickens

Cause. *Escherichia coli*, usually with concurrent infection with infectious bronchitis virus or avian metapneumovirus. All cases seen by the authors have been associated with infectious bronchitis virus. High ammonia levels intensify the disease.

Clinical signs and gross lesions. The disease is seen primarily in broiler chickens over 3 weeks of age. Clinical history indicates a respiratory disease in the flock. Mortality is increased and respiratory gurgling noises may be heard. Nasal sneezing (snicking) is the first clinical sign noted in affected birds. Initially, there is swelling of the conjunctiva, which this progresses rapidly to swelling and reddening of the eyelids and periorbital area. Affected birds are lethargic and, because of the conjunctivitis, keep their eyes closed. Periorbital swelling progresses to involve the face and sometimes the intermandibular area and wattles. Facial skin over the swollen area is usually reddened.

On postmortem examination, there is facial cellulitis characterized by notable thickening of the facial subcutis by gelatinous material or yellow caseous exudate. Exudate in air spaces of cranial bones and in middle ear also is present in some birds. Mucoid exudate may be present in the trachea and nasal chambers. Cultures of the facial subcutis typically yield pure heavy growth of *Escherichia coli*. Histopathology confirms the diagnosis of cellulitis. If possible, the tracheas of affected birds are examined histologically and tested by PCR for infectious bronchitis virus and metapneumovirus. Tracheitis is evident on histopathology. PCR results should always be interpreted within the context of the histopathology findings, and vice versa. As increased mortality in the flock is due to colisepticemia with airsacculitis, swollen-head syndrome is a manifestation of *E. coli* infection and a specific form of colibacillosis.

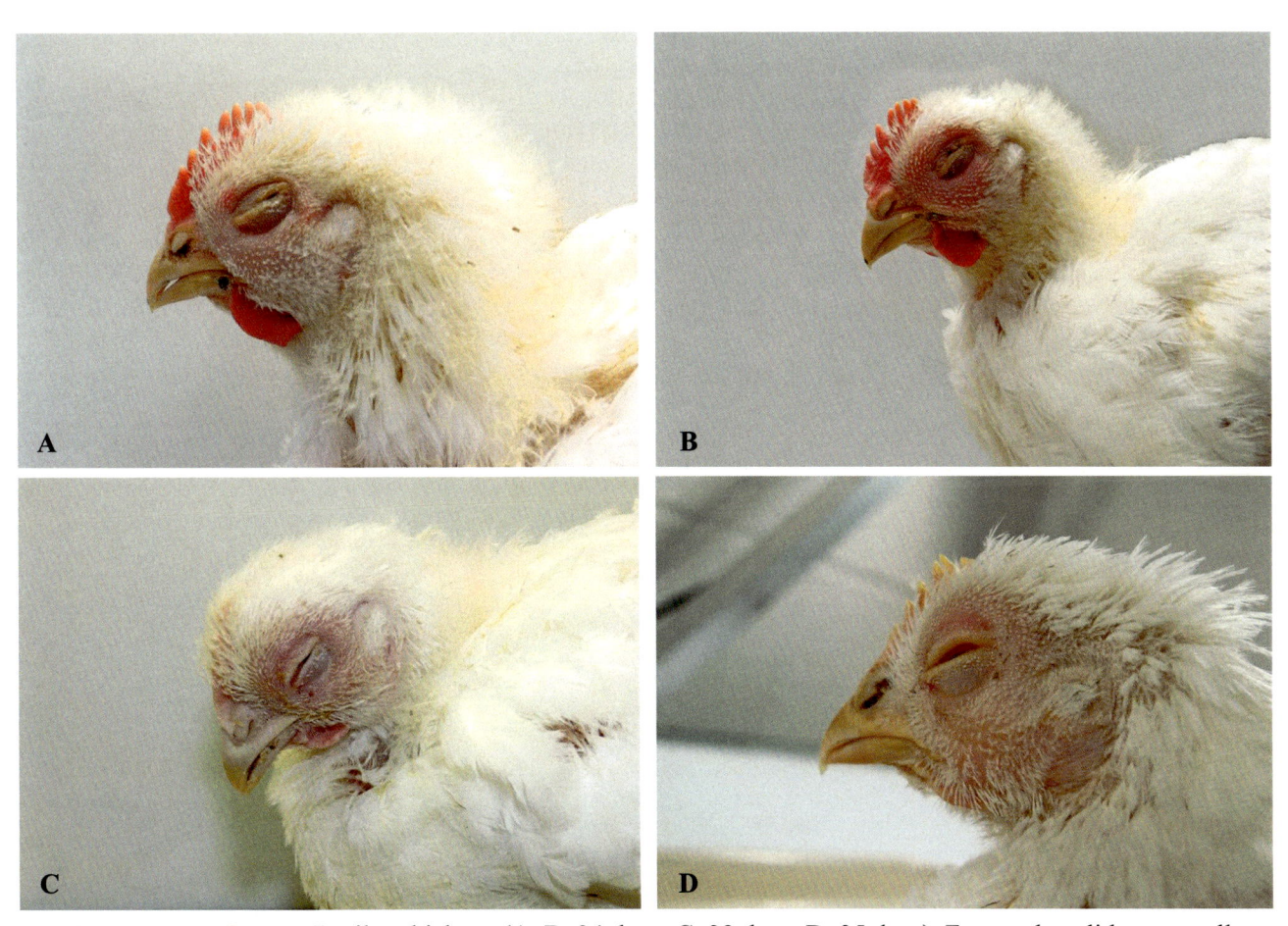

Swollen-head syndrome. Broiler chickens (A, B. 34 days. C. 29 days. D. 35 days). Face and eyelids are swollen due to cellulitis. Eyes are closed. There is acute conjunctivitis. Note reddening of the skin. In **D**, the swelling also involves the intermandibular area. In all these cases, *E. coli* was isolated from the facial subcutis, there was tracheitis, and infectious bronchitis virus was detected in tracheas by PCR.

Inflammatory Process (Cellulitis) in Broiler Chickens

Inflammatory process (IP) in broiler chickens refers to caseous cellulitis that involves the abdominal and sometimes inguinal areas. The condition is economically significant because affected birds are heavily trimmed or condemned when processed.

Cause, pathogenesis, and contributing factors. *Escherichia coli* is frequently isolated in pure culture from IP lesions. However, other bacteria including *Pseudomonas aeruginosa*, *Enterobacter*, and *Proteus* have also been isolated. The pathogenesis of IP is unclear, but it is likely that *E. coli* enters the skin through a scratch, reaches the subcutaneous tissues, and causes inflammation and development of the IP lesion. Scratches most likely result from the birds' sharp toe nails. Gravity is responsible for migration of lesions from the upper part of the body where scratches occur to the abdomen. Inguinal areas are relatively large spaces where exudate can accumulate. Factors implicated in increased IP include:

- *High stocking density*. Birds placed at higher stocking densities generally have more scratches and, therefore, more cellulitis. High density stocking is probably the most important predisposing factor to cellulitis.
- *Disturbance of the flock*. Frequent, unnecessary disturbance of the flock causes birds to jump on one another increasing the likelihood of scratches. Flighty birds are more likely to injure each other.
- *Low quality wood shavings and wet litter*. Inadequate airflow, poor gut health, high stocking density, and poor management of drinkers contribute to wet litter, which favors high bacterial growth and increases the probability that scratches will become infected.
- *Inadequate feeder space*. Crowding at feeders increases skin scratches.
- *High yield, fast growing broiler chickens*. Slower feather development makes their skin more prone to scratches. In feather sexable strains of broiler chickens, males feather slower than females and have a higher risk of skin scratches.
- *Season*. Higher rates of IP occur during winter.
- *Immunosuppression*. Impaired immunity increases susceptibility to infection and IP.
- *Impaired mobility, lameness*. Sitting birds are more likely to the scratched when other birds walk on them.

Gross lesions. Externally, loss of feathers and thickened, rough, yellow to yellow-brown discoloration of the skin is seen over affected areas in the abdominal or inguinal regions. Scratches and scabs may still be present or may have healed. Reflection of the abnormal skin reveals a sheet of yellow caseous exudate in the subcutaneous tissues, which adheres to the skin or abdominal wall. Exudate is soft initially but becomes dry and leathery with time. Lesions may be confined to the abdomen or extend to the inguinal region and outer thigh. In more severe cases, the back and flank can also be affected. Some birds may have fibrinous pericarditis and hepatic serositis, indicative of septicemia.

Less commonly, cellulitis develops over the abdomen centered around the umbilicus when there is severe chronic colisepticemia. Caseous exudate throughout the body cavity involving serous membranes is seen in these cases.

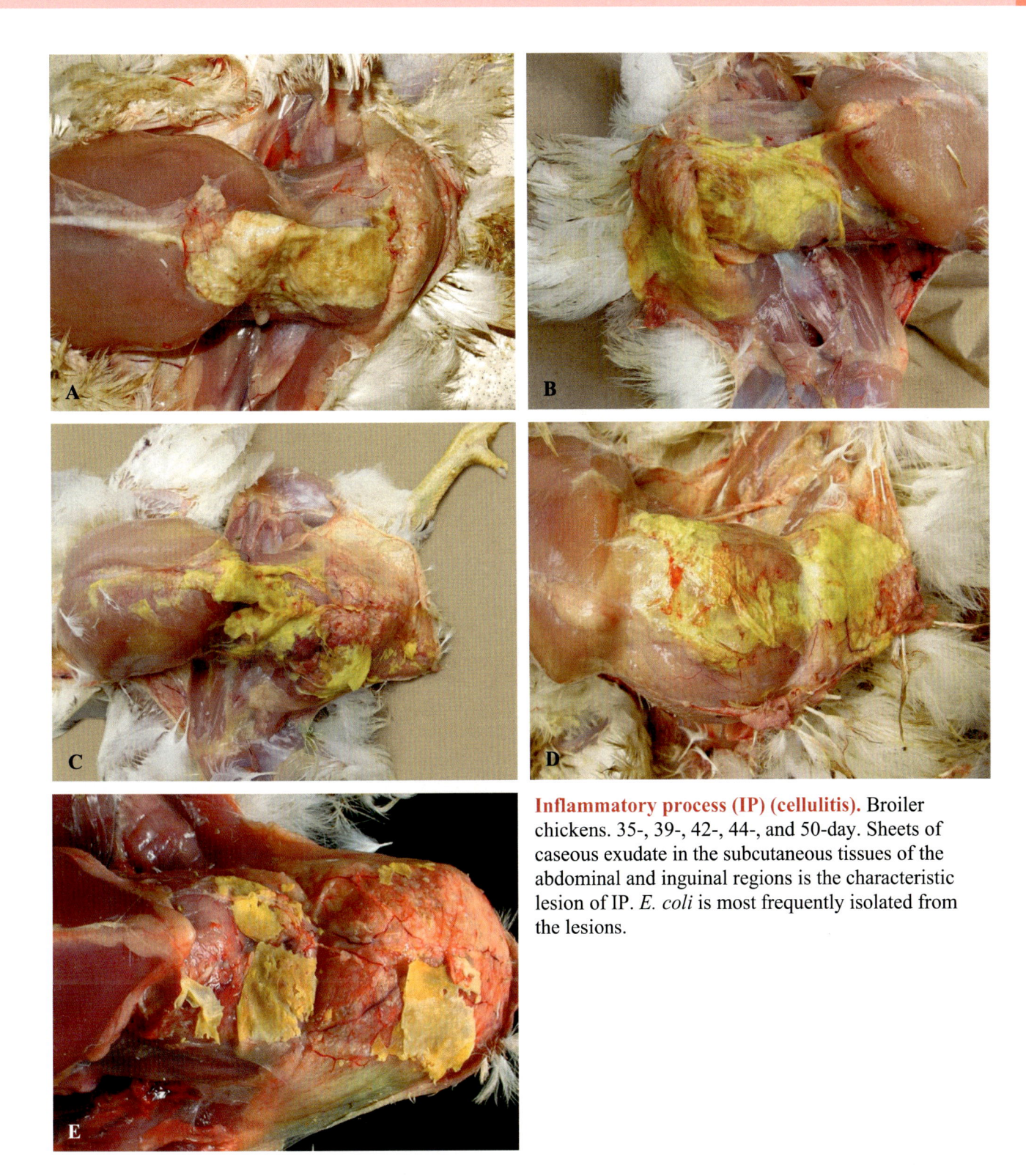

Inflammatory process (IP) (cellulitis). Broiler chickens. 35-, 39-, 42-, 44-, and 50-day. Sheets of caseous exudate in the subcutaneous tissues of the abdominal and inguinal regions is the characteristic lesion of IP. *E. coli* is most frequently isolated from the lesions.

Pasteurella multocida Infection (Fowl Cholera)

Gross lesions. Lesions of *Pasteurella multocida* infection (Fowl Cholera) in poultry vary in type, extent, and severity, depending on the species of bird, age, immune status, and stage of the disease. Domestic, captive, and wild birds are susceptible. Mortality can be high, especially in waterfowl. Older birds are more susceptible than young birds. In acute cases, lesions include those seen in other septicemic diseases. There may be increased pericardial fluid that becomes increasingly yellow and turbid or pericarditis. Livers are usually enlarged with rounded margins and pale; sometimes with foci that represent areas of necrosis. Spleens may become enlarged and diffusely pale or mottled. There is generalized hyperemia. There may be hemorrhages in skeletal muscles. Petechial and ecchymotic hemorrhages in visceral fat, intestinal serosa, mucosal surfaces, epicardium, myocardium, and endocardium are common. Oophoritis, regressed ovarian follicles, and yolk material in the body cavity occur in laying hens and breeders. Severe pleuritis, pneumonia, and pulmonary necrosis are seen in infected turkeys. Inflammation often extends via air sacs into pneumatic bones

Chronic fowl cholera in chickens and turkeys is characterized by localized, caseous lesions. There is swelling and induration of wattles, face, head, and/or eyelids due to subcutaneous and conjunctival cellulitis, sinusitis, otitis interna, or infection of cranial bones in chickens. Meningitis may occur. Torticollis and opisthotonos result from otitis interna and meningitis. Affected lung replaced with a necrotic sequestrum is a chronic lesion of *P. multocida* infection in turkeys. Arthritis and synovitis are sequelae that cause lameness, poor growth, and general unthriftiness.

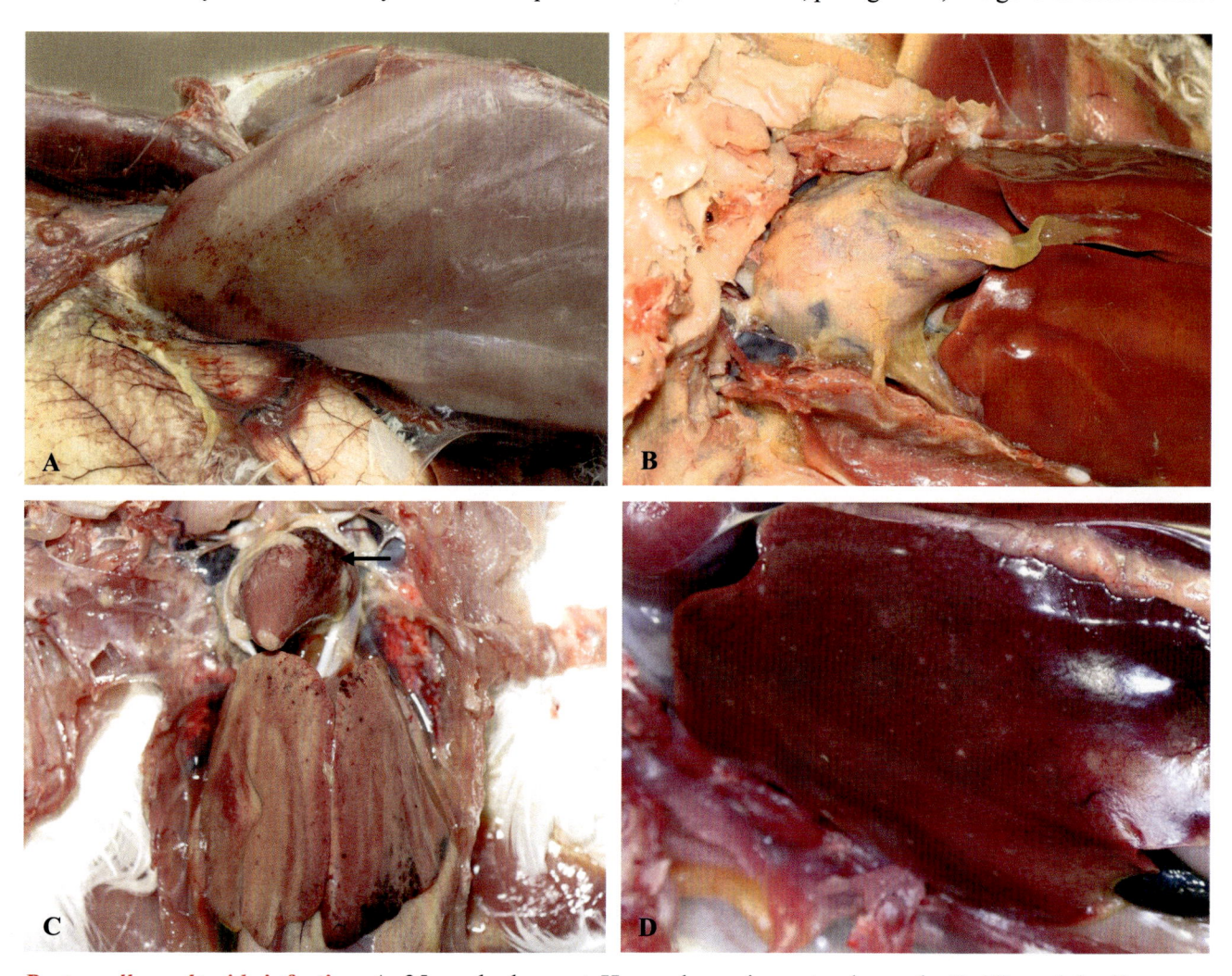

Pasteurella multocida infection. **A.** 25-week pheasant. Hemorrhages in pectoral muscle. **B.** 57-week broiler breeder hen. Pericarditis characterized by thickening and opacity of the pericardial sac. **C.** 16-week pheasant. Liver is pale and has areas of hemorrhage. There is hemorrhage in the myocardium (arrow). **D.** 25-week pheasant. White foci in the liver. Histologically, these were areas of necrosis.

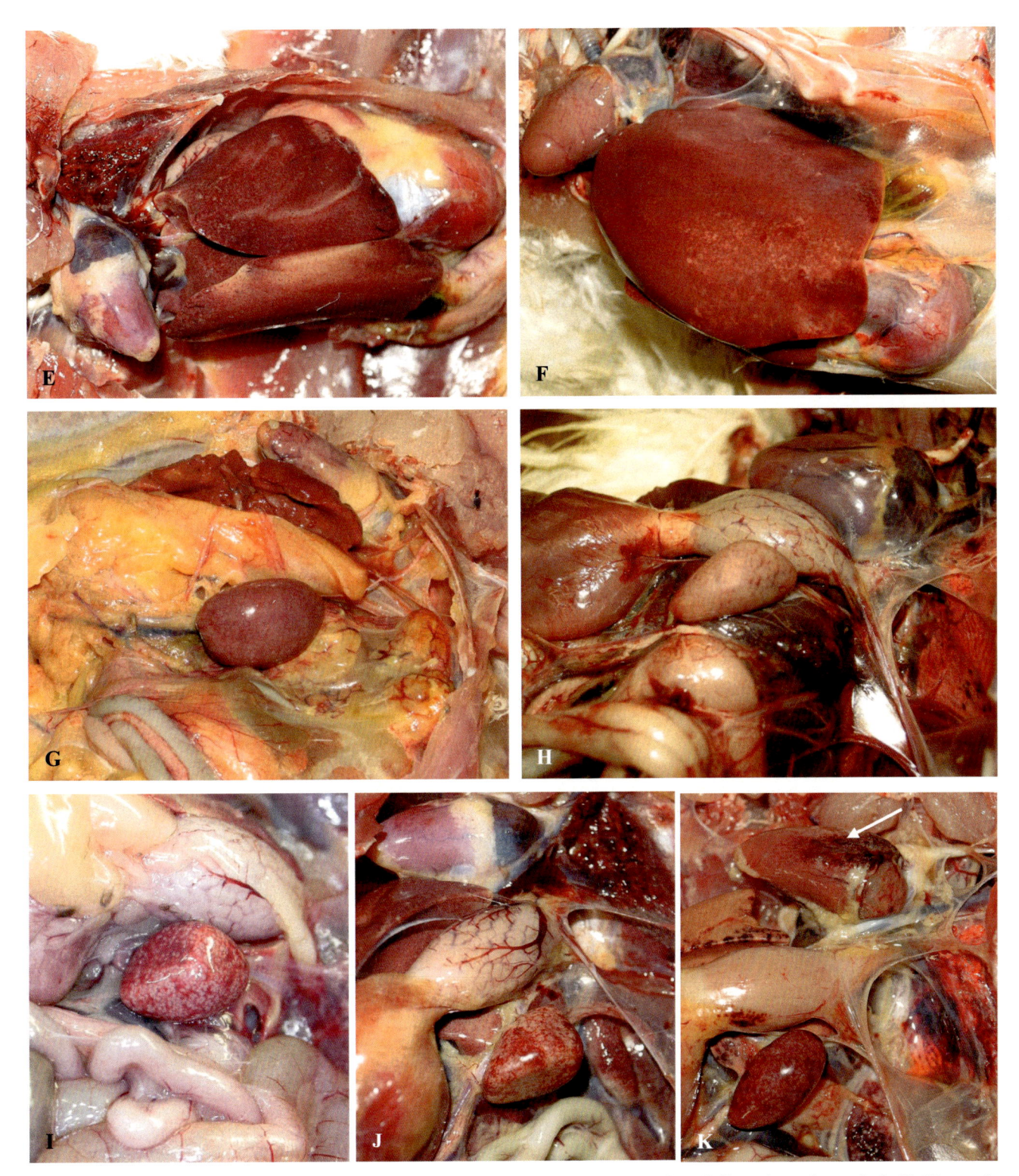

***Pasteurella multocida* infection. E, F.** 57-week broiler breeder hen. Liver is mildly pale and mottled. **G.** 32-week broiler breeder hen. Spleen is enlarged and pale and ovary is undergoing acute regression. **H, I, J, K.** Pheasants, (H. 22-week, I. 25-week. J, K. 16-week). Splenic lesions. In **H**, spleen is enlarged and diffusely pale due to necrosis. In **I, J, K**. spleens are enlarged and mottled due to necrosis with fibrin deposition in the ellipsoids. Myocardial hemorrhage in **K** (arrow).

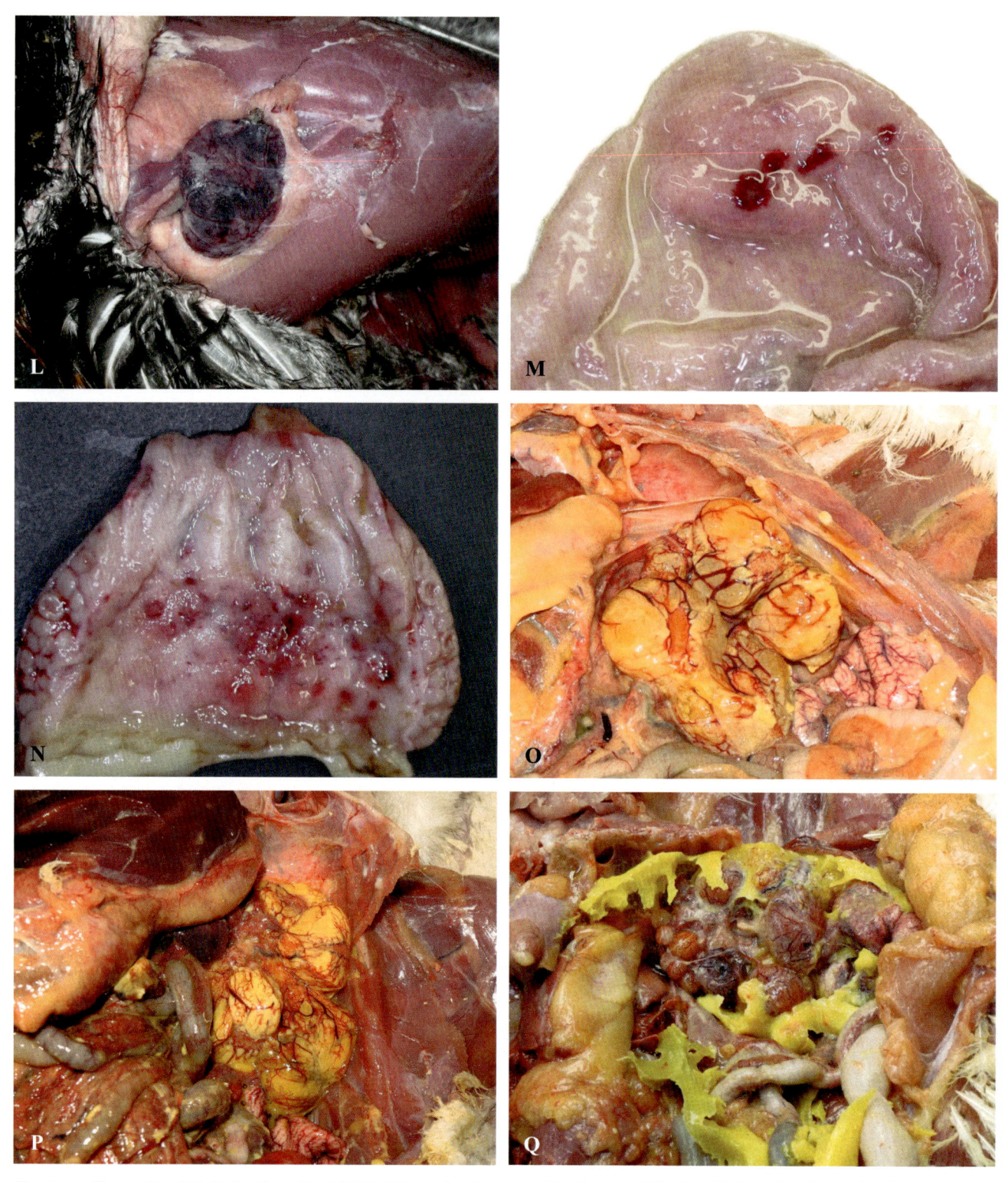

***Pasteurella multocida* infection. L, M. N.** 25-week pheasant. **L.** Crop is filled with blood. **M.** Foci of hemorrhage in the crop mucosa. **N.** Hemorrhages in the mucosal surface of the proventriculus. **O, P.** 32- and 49-week broiler breeder hens. Oophoritis. Walls of the yolk follicles are thickened due to accumulation of inflammatory exudate. **Q.** 32-week broiler breeder hen. Oophoritis, ovarian regression, and yolk peritonitis. Yolk follicles are inflamed and regressed. The large amount of inspissated yolk material in the body cavity.

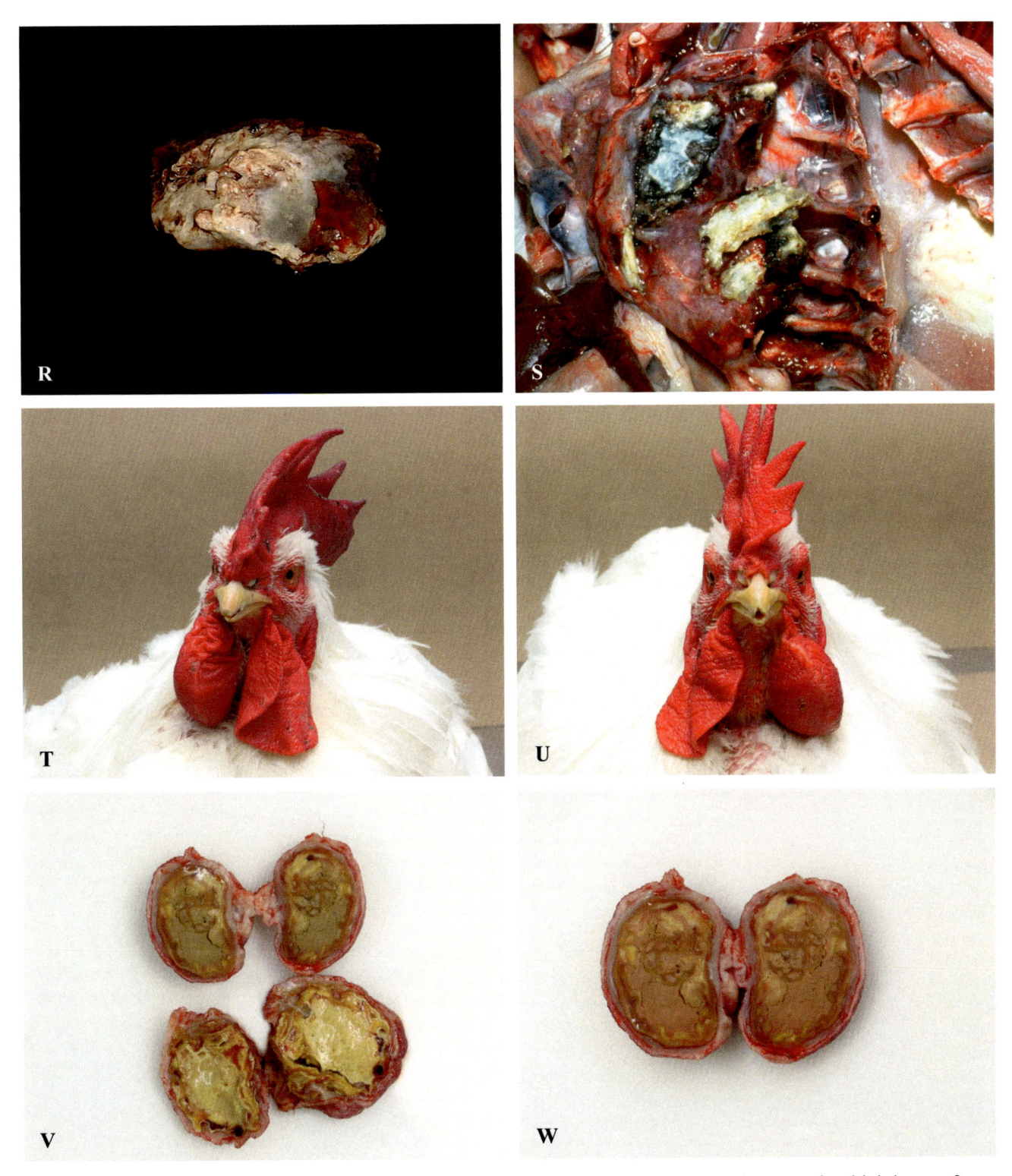

***Pasteurella multocida* infection. R.** Turkey breeder hen. Lung with pleuropneumonia. Note the thick layer of fibrinous exudate on the surface. **S.** Turkey. Chronic lung lesion. Necrosis leaves a residual small, black, necrotic lung (necrotic sequestrum). Only one lung was affected. This is typical of chronic *Pasteurella multocida* lesions. **T, U, V, W.** 51-week broiler breeder males with localized chronic lesions. **T, U.** Swelling and induration of the wattles. **V. W.** Cut surface of wattles showing accumulation of yellow caseous exudate.

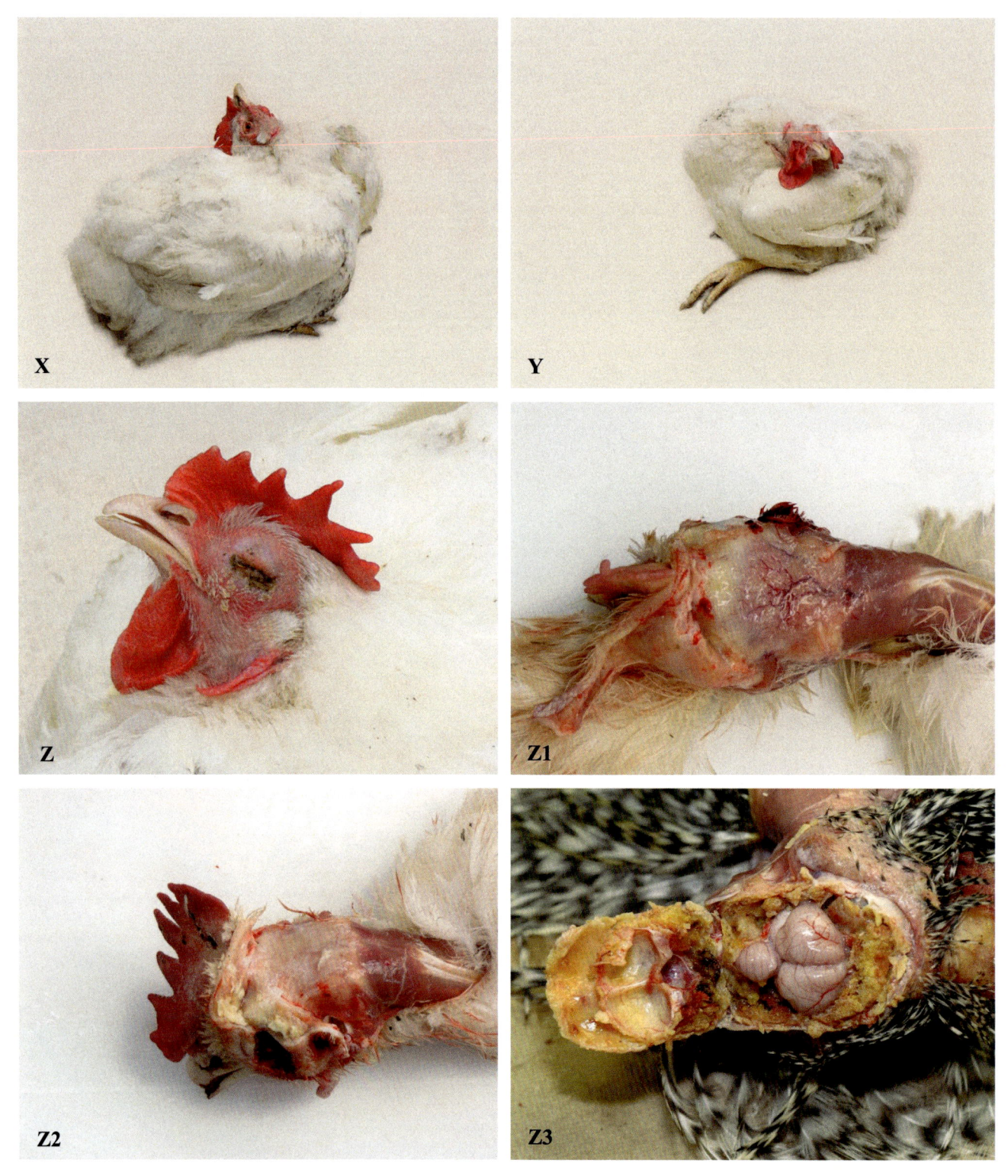

***Pasteurella multocida* infection.** 41-week broiler breeder males. **X, Y.** Opisthotonos due to infection of the calvarian (skull) bones and possibly meningitis and/or otitis interna. **Z.** Localized lesions characterized by swelling of the face and eyelids due to accumulation of caseous exudate in the facial and conjunctival subcutaneous tissue. **Z1, Z2.** Cellulitis involving the subcutaneous tissue of the head and face. Note the yellow exudate in the subcutis. **Z3.** 7-month hobby rooster. Yellow discoloration and necrosis of cranial bones. Cultures of cranial bones yielded pure growth of *P. multocida*. The bird was exhibiting head shaking and seizures.

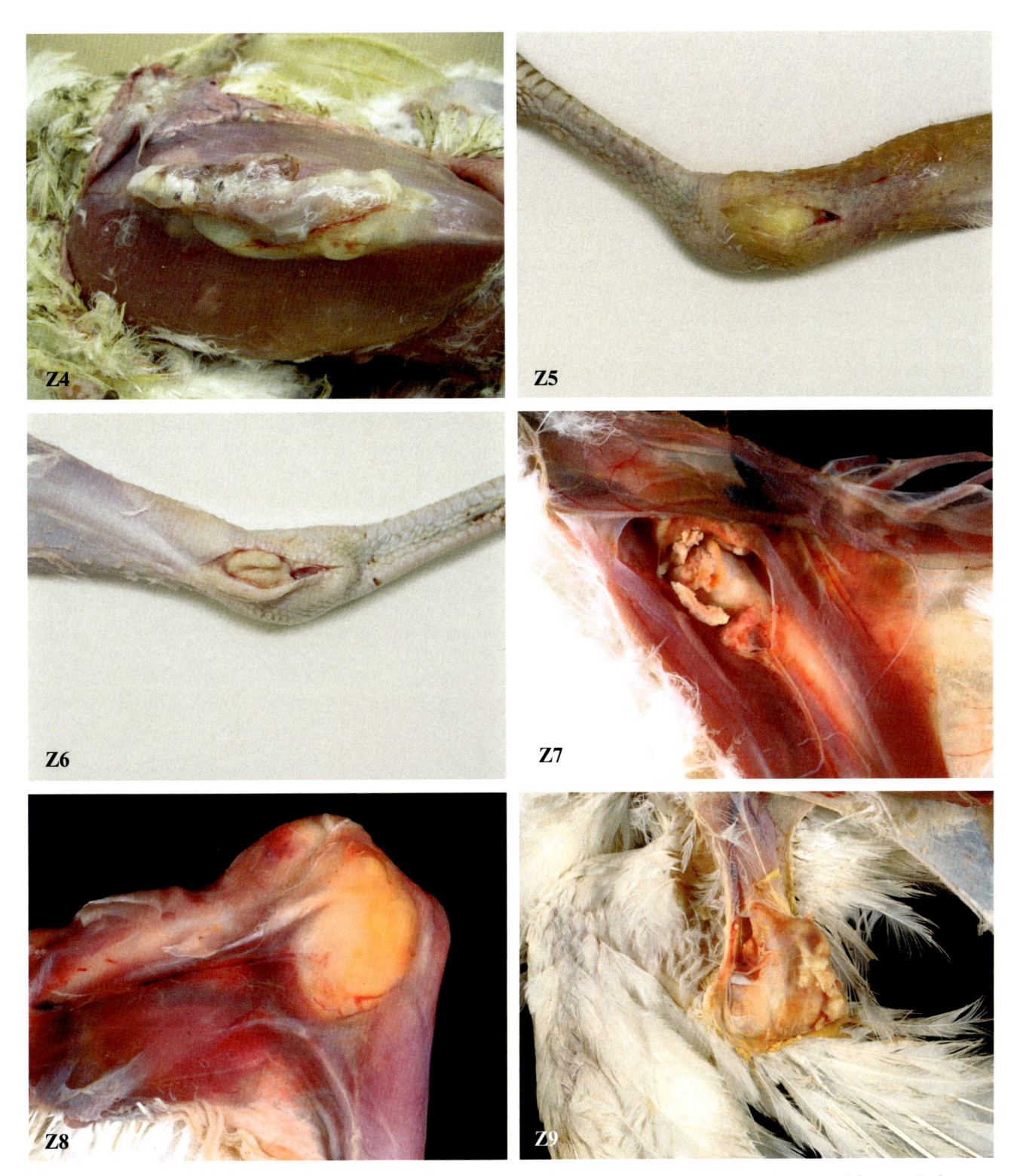

***Pasteurella multocida* infection. Z4.** 54-week broiler breeder hen. Severe synovitis of the sternal bursa. Culture of the lesion yielded pure growth of *P. multocida*. **Z5-Z9.** Pheasants (Z5, Z6. 14-week. Z7-Z9. 17- week). Chronic arthritis of hock joints (**Z5, Z6**), Coxofemoral (hip) joint (**Z7**), tibiofemoral joint (**Z8**), and wing joint (**Z9**). There is an accumulation of caseous exudate in the affected joints.

Erysipelas in Turkeys and Pheasants

Cause. *Erysipelothrix rhusiopathiae*. The organism is a Gram-positive rod found in soil. Turkeys, especially ones being raised on range, are most often affected, but the disease can occur in other wild and domestic birds. Males and older birds are most likely to develop the disease, but infections can occur at any age including neonates following toe trimming.

Clinical signs. In acute cases, birds are usually found dead without premonitory clinical signs or they are lethargic and droopy for a few hours before death. Mortality depends mainly on the immune status of the flock. Mortality is usually high in unvaccinated flocks but low in immunized flocks. Sporadic daily mortality may be seen in partially immune flocks.

Gross lesions. Gross lesions are consistent with septicemia. Hemorrhages resulting from blood vessel injury and thrombosis are present in skeletal muscles, coronary fat, myocardium, visceral fat, and sometimes proventricular mucosa, especially at the junction with the ventriculus (gizzard). Liver is enlarged and may have hemorrhages or pale foci of degenerating and necrotic hepatocytes. The spleen is almost always enlarged and either pale or dark. Typically, it is mottled with pale foci. Excess mucus may be in the small intestine (catarrhal enteritis), with hemorrhages in the intestinal mucosa. Lungs are congested and edematous. In breeder hens, ovarian follicles may be hemorrhagic. Chronic lesions in turkeys include vegetative valvular endocarditis, swelling and necrosis of the snood and sometimes dewlap, and arthritis. In pheasants, pasteurellosis caused by *Pasteurella multocida* is the main differential diagnosis as splenic lesions are similar in both diseases.

Public health significance. Humans are susceptible to infection with *E. rhusiopathiae*. Precautions must be taken during postmortem examination of birds suspected of having erysipelas. Infection in humans occurs in three forms: erysipeloid, generalized cutaneous infection, and septicemia. Erysipeloid is the most common form. Bacteria enter the skin through even very small wounds in the hands, particularly fingers, and rapidly causes localized, painful swelling in the area. More severe infections can result in sepsis and endocarditis.

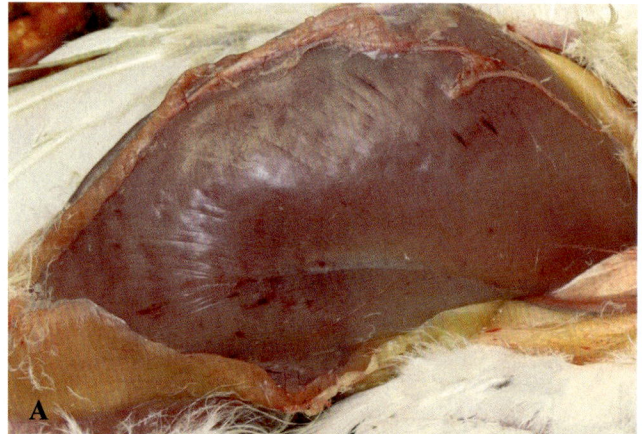

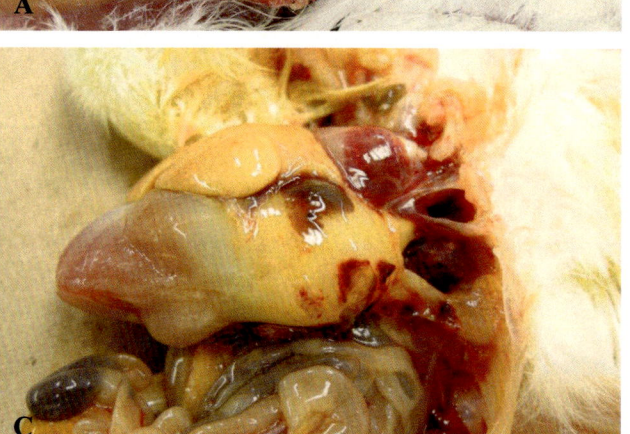

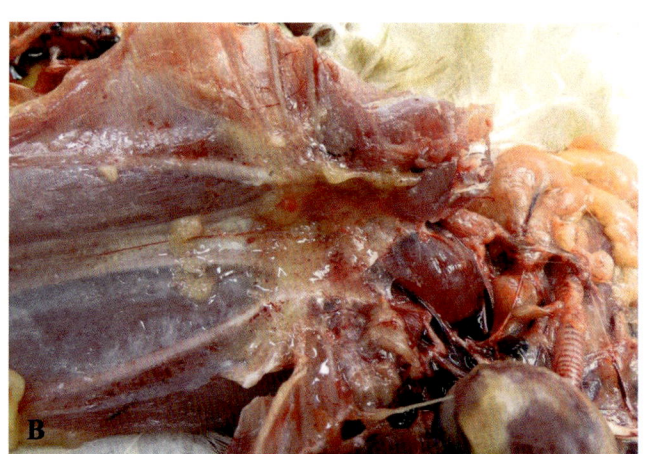

Erysipelas. Pheasants. **A.** Hemorrhages in breast muscle. **B.** Hemorrhages in the ventral surface of the keel bone. **C.** Hemorrhages in coronary fat.

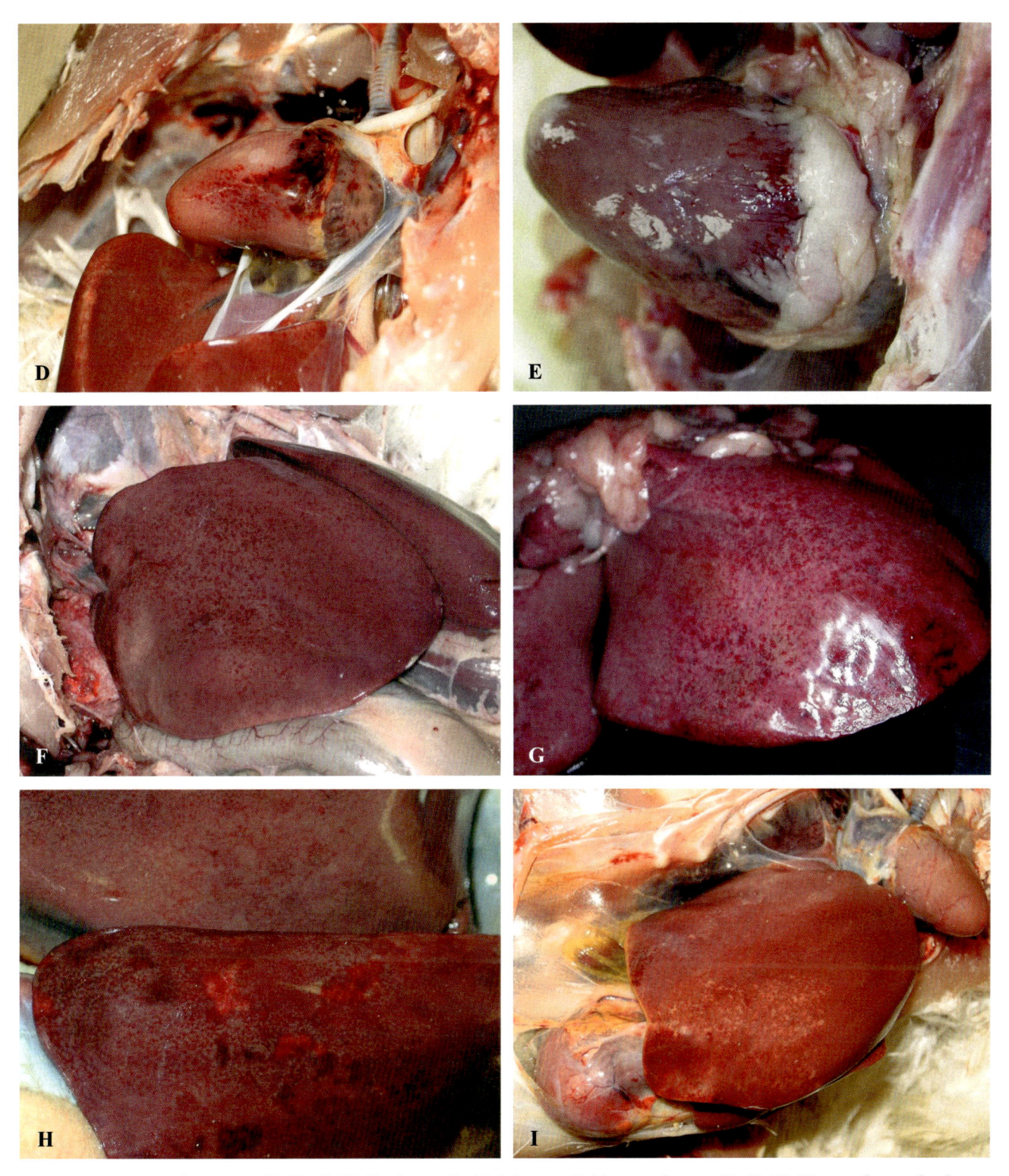

Erysipelas. D, I. Pheasants. **E, F, G, H.** Turkeys. **D, E.** Myocardial hemorrhages. **F, G, H.** Hemorrhages in the liver. The liver in **H** also has pale areas of necrosis associated with hemorrhages. **I.** A discolored area in the liver due to hepatocyte necrosis and degeneration.

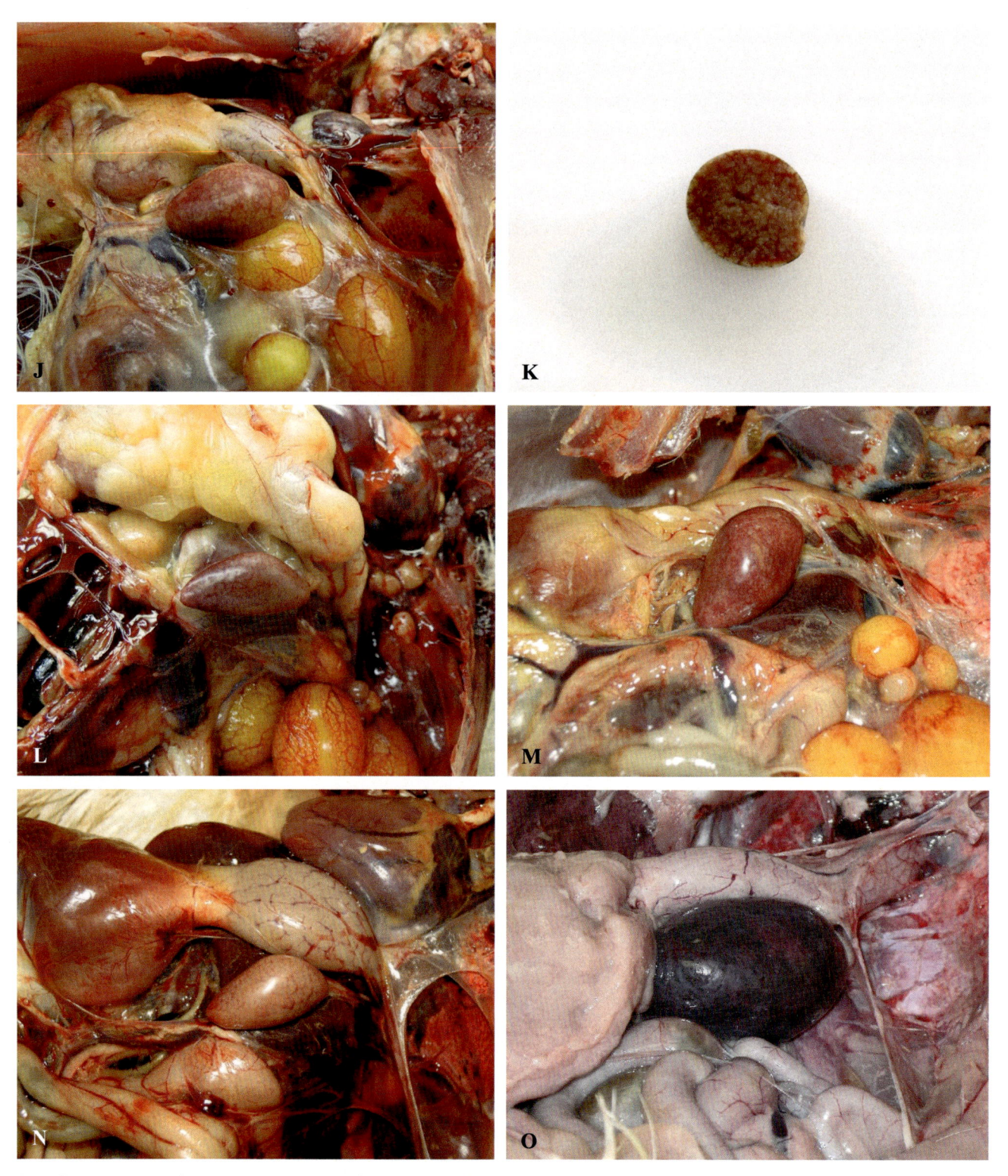

Erysipelas. J-N. Pheasants. **J, L, M.** Spleens are enlarged and mottled. **K.** Cut surface of the spleen in **J** showing multifocal to confluent yellow necrotic foci. **N.** Spleen is pale. **O.** Turkey. Spleen is purple-black and markedly enlarged.

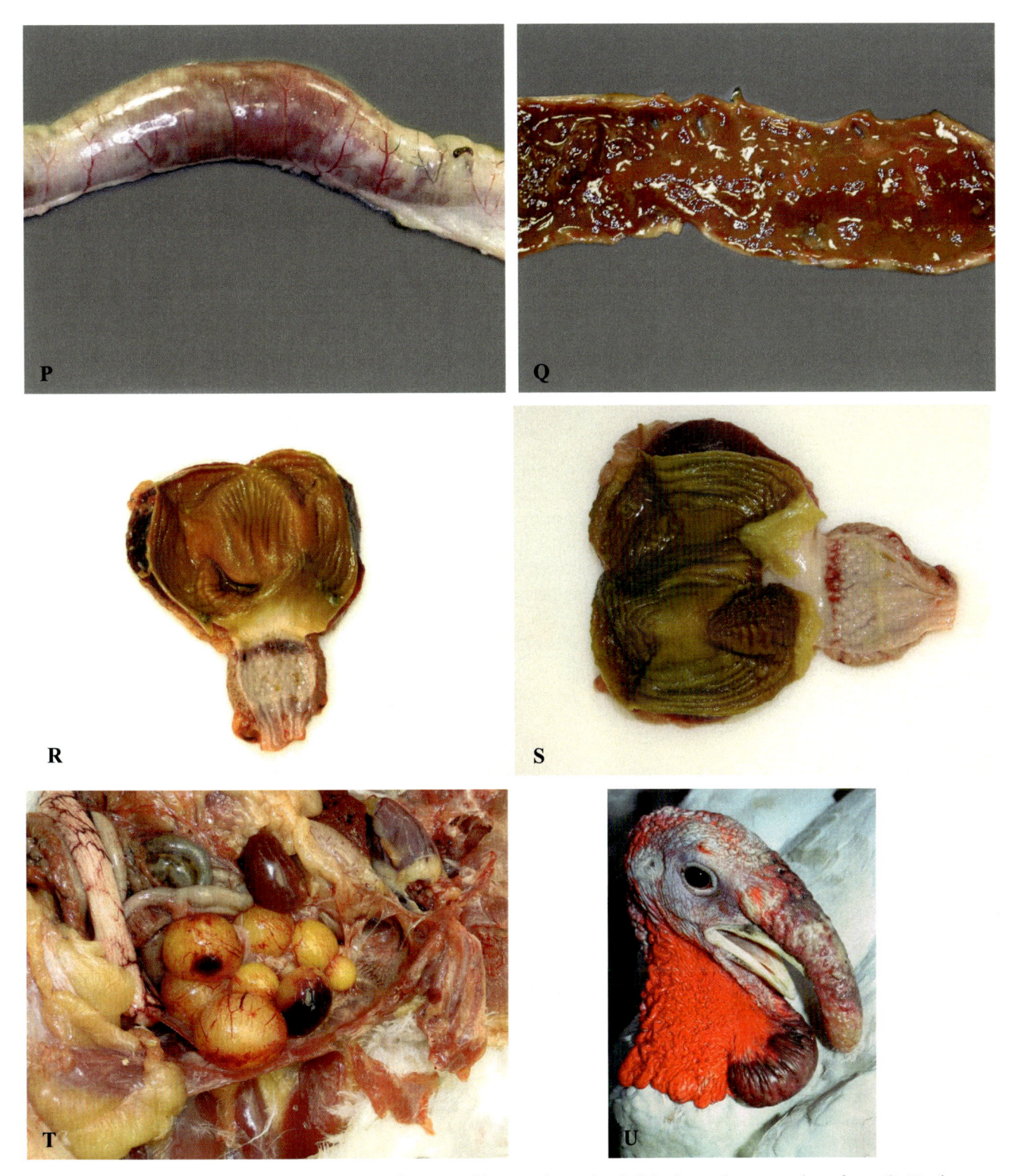

Erysipelas. P. Turkey, intestine. An area of mucosal hemorrhage is visible from the serosal surface. **Q.** Turkey. Blood-stained mucus covers the mucosal surface of the small intestine. **R, S.** Pheasants. A band of hemorrhage is located at the junction of the proventriculus and ventriculus. **T.** Pheasant. Hemorrhage in ovarian follicles. Note enlarged spleen. **U.** Turkey. Snood and margin of the dewlap are swollen and necrotic. This lesion is seen in some chronic cases. Lesions represent infarcts that occur when dermal vessels are thrombosed.

Riemerella anatipestifer Infection in Ducks

Riemerella anatipestifer infection is primarily a disease of ducks and geese. Turkeys are also susceptible and outbreaks have occurred in turkey flocks. *R. anatipestifer* has been isolated from other waterfowl, chickens, pheasant, quail, Guinea fowl, and partridge. Ducks become infected via the respiratory tract or through skin wounds, particularly on the feet.

Clinical signs. Ducks of all ages are susceptible. Typically, 1- to 8-week ducklings are highly susceptible. Mortality rates range from 5% to 75%, depending on age and other factors. Affected ducks may exhibit a range of clinical signs including listlessness, green diarrhea, ocular and nasal discharges, ataxia, tremors, and bobbing or jerking of the head. A characteristic clinical sign in affected ducklings is lying on the back and paddling the legs. Recumbency with backward retraction of the head and neck (opisthotonos) is seen in some ducks. In ducks with access to ponds, the first indication of infection may be abnormal swimming and a tendency to swim in circles. Neurologic ducks in ponds can drown. Neurological signs are not universally present as affected ducklings may appear weak, unable to walk or stand, or semi-comatose. Typically, these birds die within a few hours. Ducklings under 5 weeks of age die one to 2 days after onset of clinical signs. Older birds usually survive longer. Individual birds may recover but remain unthrifty. Localized chronic infections are common in older and breeder ducks.

Gross lesions. The most consistent lesions are fibrinous pericarditis and hepatic serositis characterized by yellow fibrinous exudate on the surface of the heart and liver. Airsacculitis is also frequently present. Other serosal surfaces may be involved. There is hepatomegaly and splenomegaly. The spleen may be mottled with multiple gray foci. Petechial hemorrhages are occasionally present on the epicardial surface of the heart. Yellow discoloration of the surface of the brain due to fibrinoheterophilic meningitis is seen in ducks with neurologic signs. Joints may be swollen and contain turbid exudate. Differential diagnoses include salmonellosis, colibacillosis, pasteurellosis, and chlamydiosis.

In chronic cases, fibrinoheterophilic exudate on serosal surfaces becomes caseated. Casts of caseous exudate are often present in the air sacs, especially thoracic air sacs. Nasal sinuses and joint cavities may be filled with caseous exudate. A mass of caseous exudate distending the oviduct is seen in some female ducks.

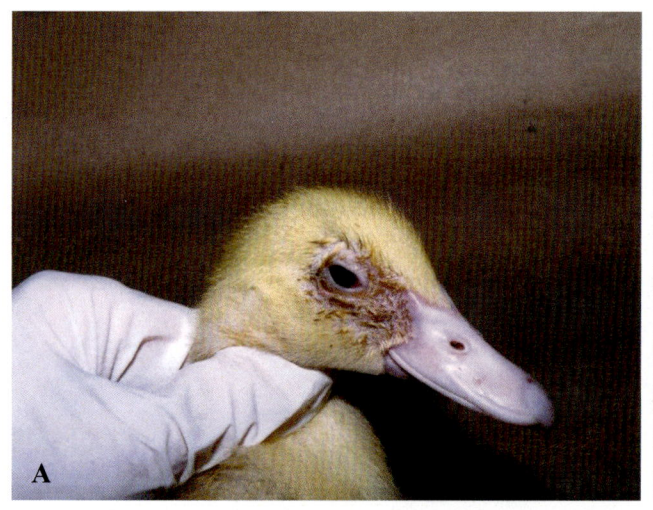

Riemerella anatipestifer infection. **A.** Matting of feathers around the eyes due to ocular discharge. **B.** This bird is sitting on its legs with retraction of the neck and head (opisthotonos). The bird had meningitis caused by *R. anatipestifer*. **C.** This duckling is showing neurological signs. *(Photo C courtesy of Dr. Takumi Chikuba and Mie Chuo, Livestock Hygiene Service Center, Japan).*

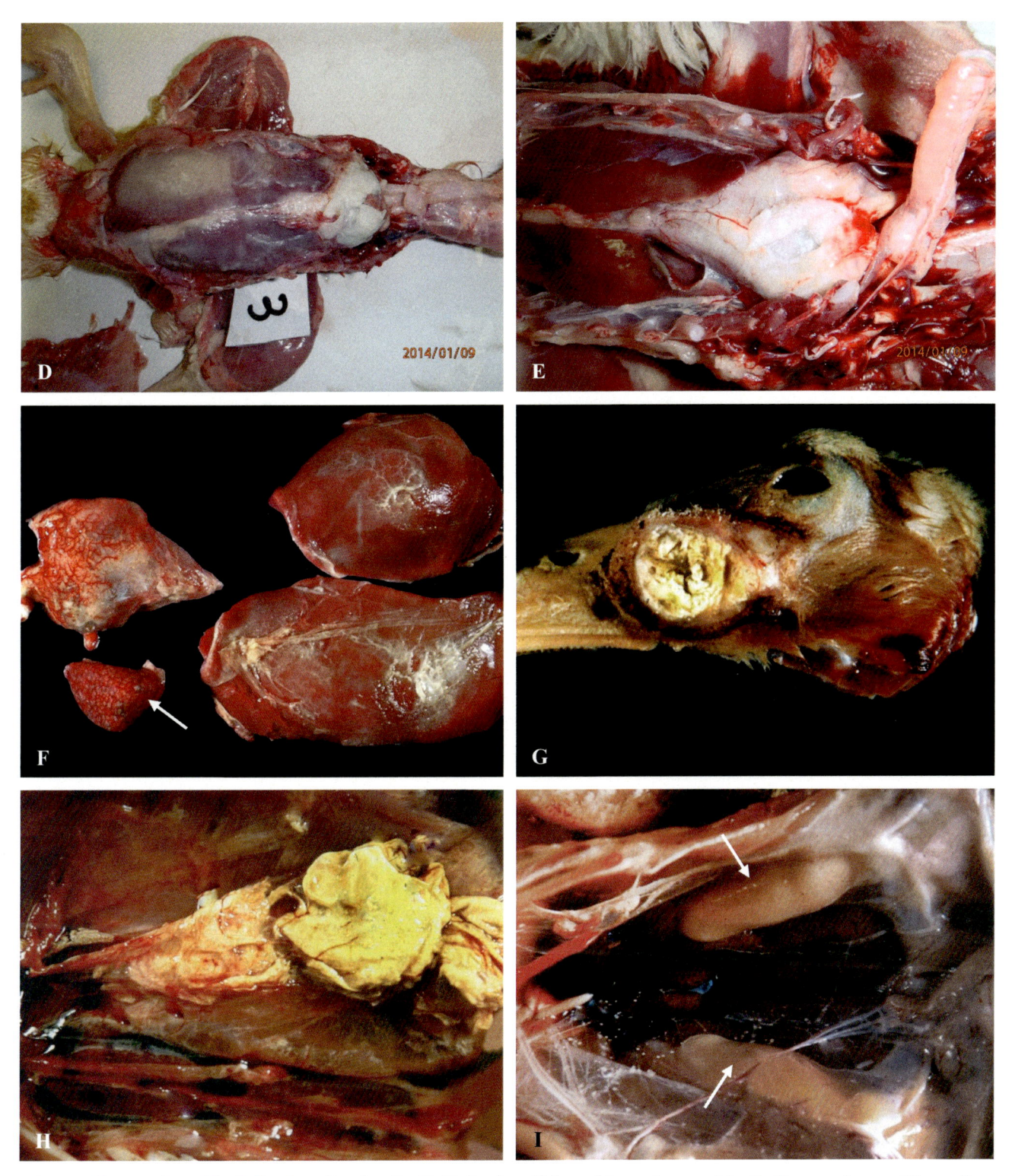

***Riemerella anatipestifer* infection.** Ducks. **D, E, F.** Pericarditis and hepatic serositis. In **F**, note the mottling of the spleen *(arrow)*. Ducks. **G, H, I.** Chronic *R. anatipestifer* infection. Accumulation of caseous material in the infraorbital sinus (**G**), air sacs (**H**), and coxofemoral joints (**I** - arrows). *(Photos D, E courtesy of Dr. Takumi Chikuba and Mie Chuo livestock hygiene service center, Japan. Photo F-I courtesy of Dr. Jarra Jagne and College of Veterinary Medicine, Cornell University, USA).*

Ornithobacterium rhinotracheale (ORT) Infection in Turkeys

Clinical signs and gross lesions. There is a sudden increase in mortality. Birds in affected flocks are inactive and some may be coughing or show respiratory distress and open-mouth breathing. Feed consumption and water intake are decreased. In breeders and laying birds, drops in egg production and increased poor quality eggs are seen. On necropsy, there may be blood in the mouth and tracheal lumen. Blood in the tracheal lumen must be differentiated from hemorrhagic tracheitis. The most consistent and prominent gross lesion is bilateral pleuritis and pneumonia. Pleuritis of varying severity is characterized by accumulation of white or yellow fibrinous exudate on the surface of the lungs. Pneumonic lungs are swollen, red, heavy, and firm (consolidated). Dense areas sink in formalin. Some lungs may have pale, yellow areas of necrosis or caseation. Fibrinous pericarditis is a common necropsy finding. Some birds have airsacculitis of variable severity, with thoracic air sacs being more affected than abdominal air sacs. Livers and spleens may be swollen and congested. The primary differential diagnoses, especially for lung lesions, are *Escherichia coli* and *Pasteurella multocida* infections. Bacterial culture is necessary to confirm the diagnosis.

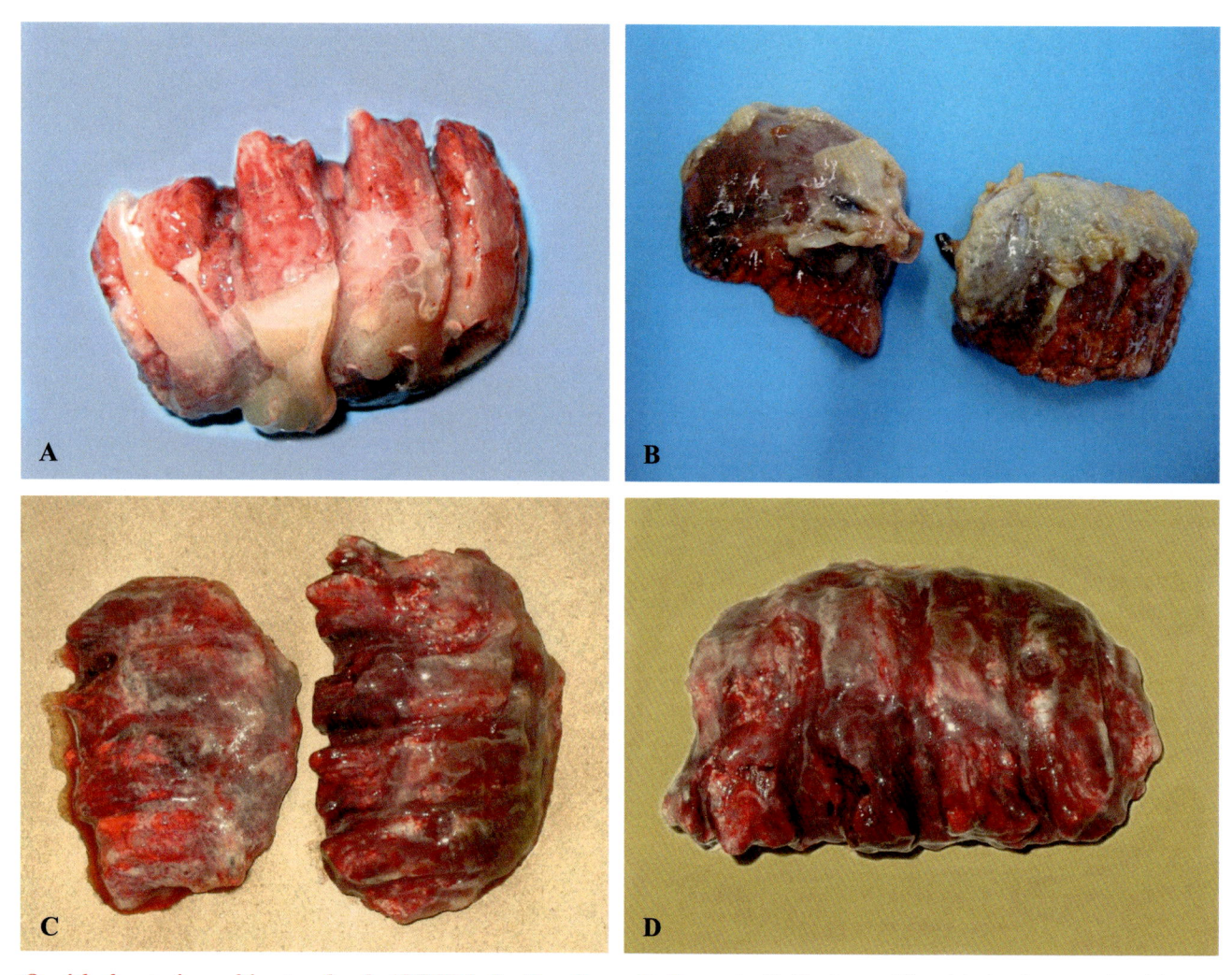

Ornithobacterium rhinotracheale (ORT) infection. Lung lesions. **A, B.** Turkeys. Pleuritis is characterized by fibrinous exudate on the pleural surface of the lungs. **C, D.** 55-week turkey breeder hen. **D** is a closer view of the lung on right in **C**. Pleuritis and pneumonia. Fibrinous exudate is on the surface. Lungs are red and firm and have pale areas of necrosis. Similar lesions are seen with *E. coli* and *P. multocida* infections. Bacterial culture is necessary to confirm a diagnosis of ORT. *(Photos A, B courtesy of Dr. Hafez M. Hafez, Germany).*

Bordetellosis in Turkeys

Cause. *Bordetella avium*. Young turkeys are most affected. Older turkeys and chickens become infected but do not develop significant clinical disease.

Gross lesions. Live birds exhibit excessive lacrimation, ocular and nasal discharge, mouth breathing, and intermandibular edema. In dead birds, ocular and nasal discharges are evident by staining and matting of the feathers in the periorbital area and on the shoulder feathers, and by the presence of crusted material in the nares. The nasal discharge can be expressed by applying slight pressure on the sinuses or bridge of the beak over the nostrils. Due to rubbing of the eyes, feathers on the shoulders become stained and crusted. The trachea is soft, reddened, and may be distorted or compressed dorso-ventrally. In-folding of the dorsal wall of the trachea into the tracheal lumen just below the larynx occurs in severe cases. Mucoid exudate is present in the lumen of the trachea. In the lungs, bronchial associated lymphoid tissue is hyperplastic. This can be seen as small nodules at the junction of secondary bronchi with the primary bronchus.

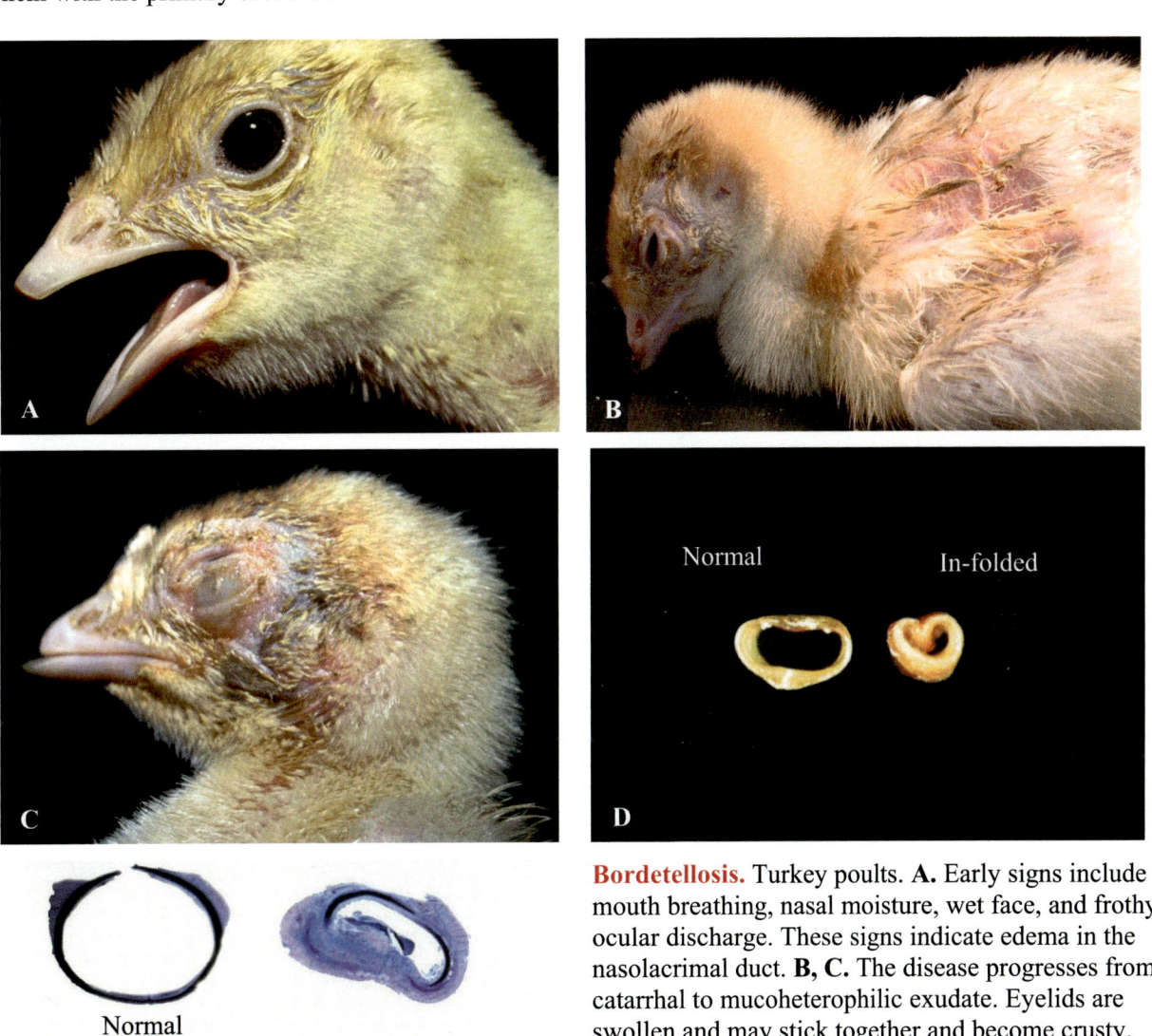

Bordetellosis. Turkey poults. **A.** Early signs include mouth breathing, nasal moisture, wet face, and frothy ocular discharge. These signs indicate edema in the nasolacrimal duct. **B, C.** The disease progresses from catarrhal to mucoheterophilic exudate. Eyelids are swollen and may stick together and become crusty. The bird wipes its nostrils on the wing or back. In **B**, note the matting of feathers on the shoulder. **D, E.** In-folding of the tracheal wall into the lumen. This occurs because of softening and distortion of tracheal rings, possibly due to a toxin produced by *B. avium*. (Photo B courtesy of Dr. Robert Porter, USA).

Infectious Coryza

Cause. *Avibacterium paragallinarum*.

Gross lesions. Lesions are characterized by facial edema, rhinitis, sinusitis, and conjunctivitis. Externally, there is swelling of one or both infraorbital sinuses (facial swelling beneath the eyes), facial puffiness (edema), adherence of eyelids, and sometimes serous to mucoid nasal and ocular discharges. Facial swelling is due to the accumulation of exudate in the nasal sinuses (sinusitis) and expansion of the subcutis by inflammatory exudate and edema. In advanced cases, or when secondary organisms are involved, exudate in the sinuses undergoes caseation, forming hard masses of caseous material. Infection is usually limited to the upper respiratory tract, but there may be excess mucus in the proximal trachea. Pneumonia and airsacculitis caused by *A. paragallinarum* or secondary bacteria are seen in some cases. In hobby chickens, *Mycoplasma gallisepticum* infection is the primary differential diagnosis.

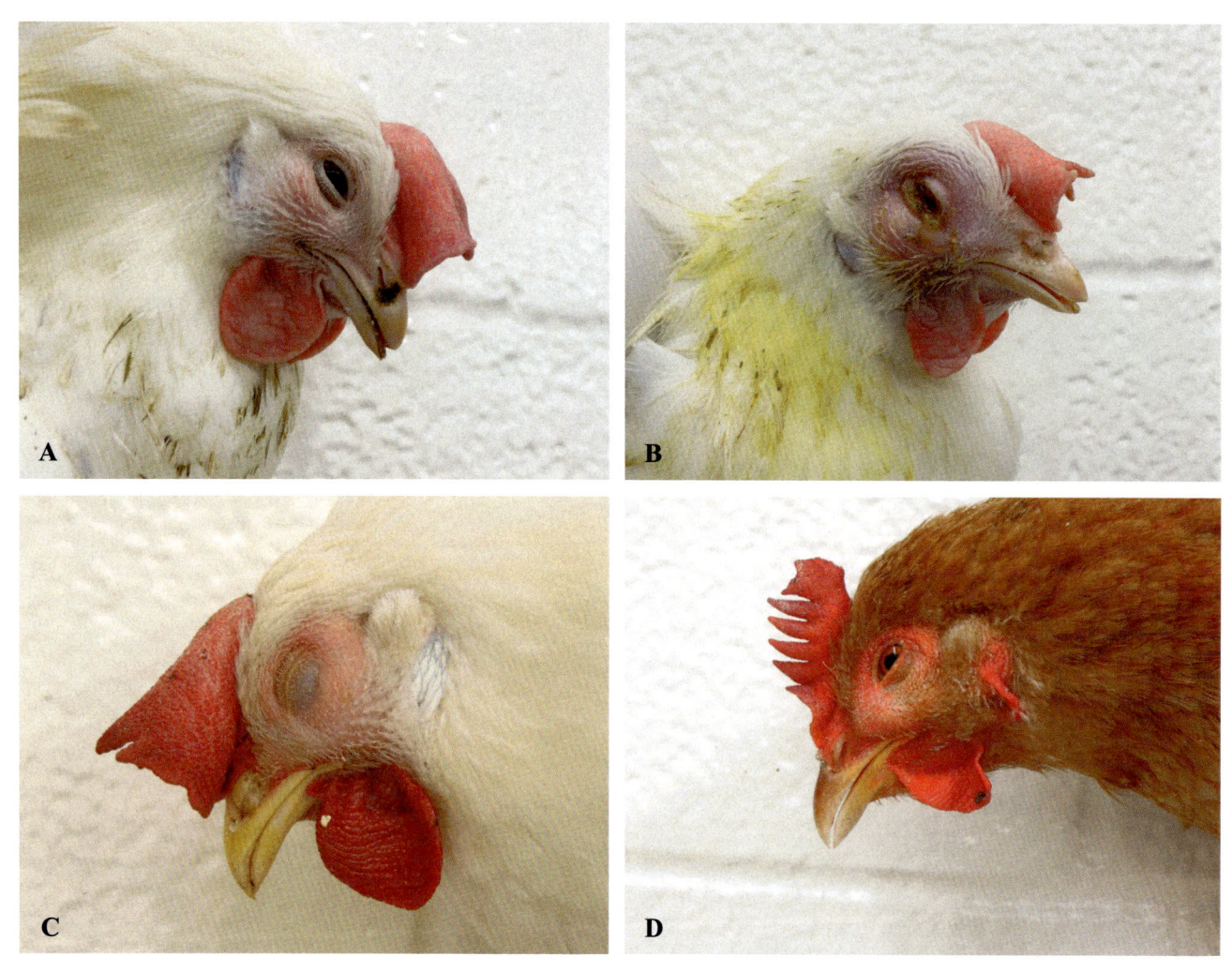

Infectious coryza. A, B. 21-week white Leghorn egg layers. Swelling of the face due to accumulation of exudate in the nasal sinuses (sinusitis). In **B**, there is conjunctivitis, with ocular discharge and adhering of the eyelids. A pure growth of *Avibacterium paragallinarum* was obtained from the swollen nasal sinuses. **C.** 7-month hobby chicken. **D.** One-year hobby chicken. Facial swelling beneath the eyes has resulted from accumulation of exudate in the nasal sinuses due to sinusitis. *A. paragallinarum* was isolated from nasal sinuses of both birds.

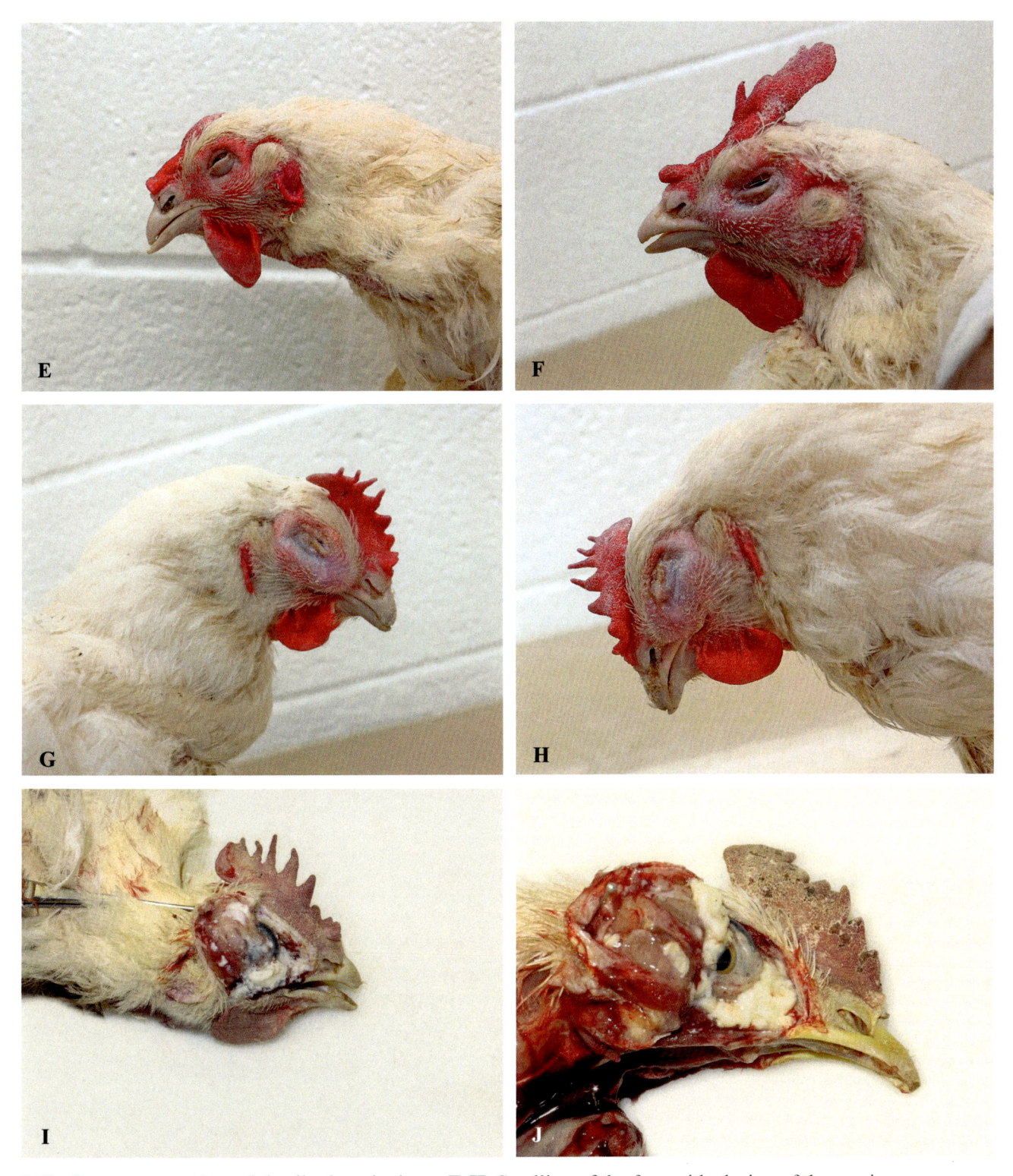

Infectious coryza. 45-week broiler breeder hens. **E-H.** Swelling of the face with closing of the eye is a characteristic lesion of infectious coryza. In **H**, note the mucoid discharge from the eye. Facial swelling is due to sinusitis and facial cellulitis and edema. **I, J.** Accumulation of large amounts of caseous exudate in the infraorbital sinuses. Cultures of exudate yielded a heavy growth of *Avibacterium paragallinarum*.

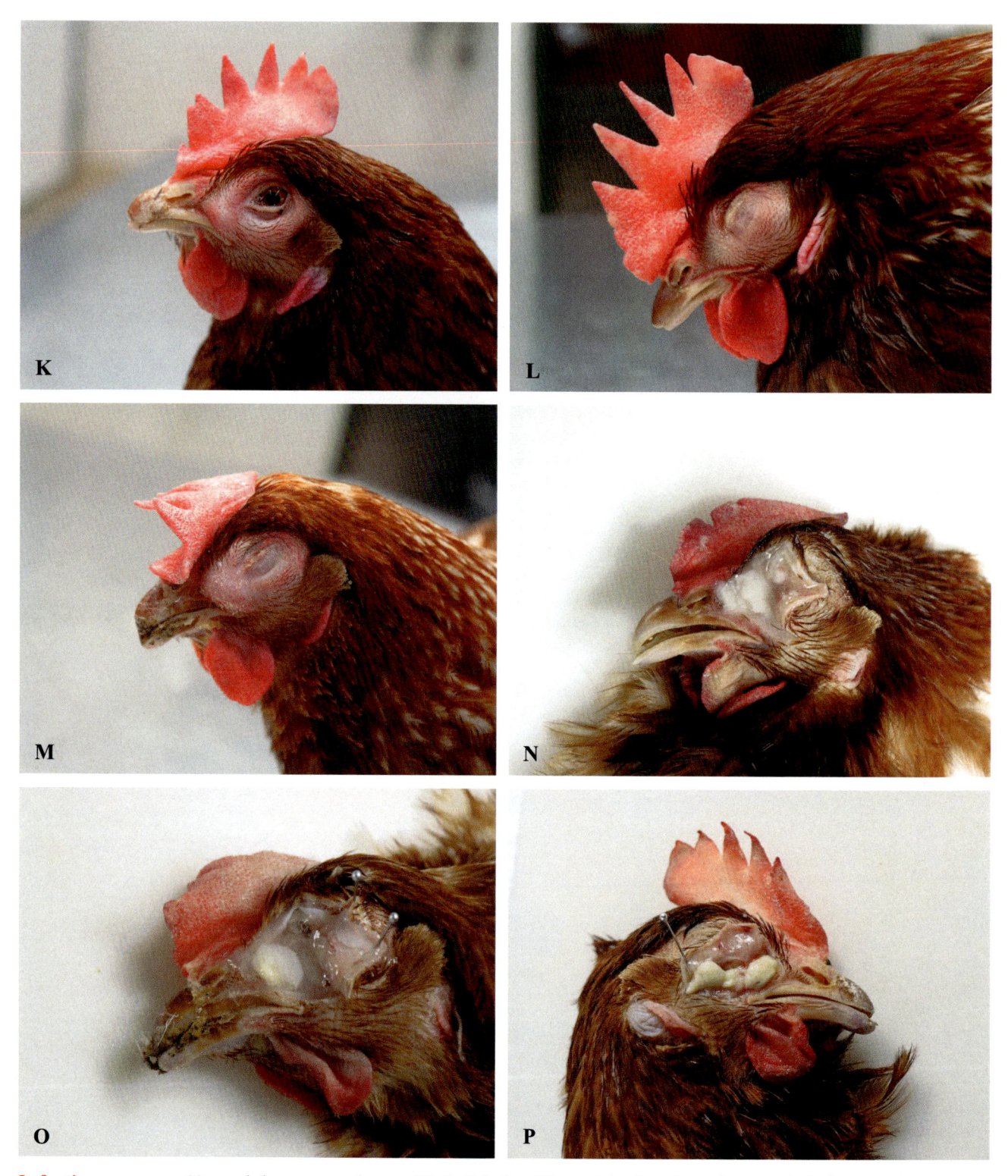

Infectious coryza. 41-week brown egg layers. **K, L, M.** Swelling of the face is a characteristic lesion of infectious coryza. In **K**, there is foamy lacrimation. In **L** and **M**, the eyes are closed. Facial swelling is due to sinusitis and facial cellulitis and edema. **N, O, P.** Accumulation of large amount of mucus and exudate in the infraorbital sinuses. In **P**, the exudate is caseous. Cultures of the exudate yielded a heavy growth of *Avibacterium paragallinarum*.

Bacterial Peritonitis, Salpingitis, and Salpingoperitonitis

All female birds producing eggs are susceptible, but commercial egg-laying and broiler breeder hens, ducks, and turkey breeders are most often affected. Infections follow septicemia, spread from affected air sacs, ascension of bacteria from the cloaca, or secondary to egg-binding. Salpingitis in immature birds results from extension of airsacculitis or septicemia usually caused by *Escherichia coli* secondary to infectious bronchitis virus infection.

Cause. *E. coli* is usually isolated from peritoneal and oviductal exudate. Less frequently, *Gallibacterium anatis* is isolated from salpingitis lesions. *Riemerella* is often isolated from salpingitis in ducks. Other bacteria may be isolated from advanced peritoneal or oviductal lesions.

Gross lesions. Abdomen is distended and the abdominal wall of dead birds may be green or blue-green. In peritonitis, fibrinoheterophilic exudate is present in the abdominal cavity between the intestinal loops, especially duodenum and pancreas, and on the surface of the ovary and intestine (intestinal serositis). Exudate varies in consistency, color, and quantity. Inspissated caseous exudate is present in chronic cases. Exudate often has a bad odor. Lesions become green or black because of iron released during red cell lysis reacting with H_2S as decomposition progresses. Ovary and oviduct are still functional in acute cases but become atrophied (regressed, involuted) later. Lesions of bacterial septicemia including pericarditis, airsacculitis, hepatomegaly with or without pale foci, and splenomegaly may occur. Masses can be free in the abdomen because of regurgitation from the oviduct or rupture of the oviduct wall. The laminated appearance of the mass on cut section will identify its oviductal origin.

An edematous or reddened oviductal mucosa, with or without creamy or mucoid exudate adhering to the surface, characterizes early salpingitis lesions. As lesions progress, exudate increases and mixes with ova and albuminous secretions as the hen continues to ovulate. Ultimately, the oviduct becomes thin-walled and distended with one or more compact masses of pale-yellow to white caseous material. Cut surface of the masses reveals concentric rings. One or more eggs, with or without shells, are located centrally in the mass if salpingitis began as egg-binding. Salpingoperitonitis refers to concurrent peritonitis and salpingitis. Hens with salpingitis or salpingoperitonitis usually have inactive ovaries. As with peritonitis, lesions suggestive of bacterial septicemia may be seen. Salpingitis can occur in cystic remnants of the right oviduct, but are generally smaller and less common.

Even though exudate in bacterial peritonitis resembles coagulated yolk, it must be distinguished from yolk peritonitis, which is milder, diffuse, not odorous, and does not yield high numbers of bacteria on culture. Exudate is yellow and fluid or viscous; it is not caseated. Yolk peritonitis is often seen when there is bursting atresia of follicles in acute ovarian regression. Bacterial salpingitis needs to be distinguished from oviduct obstruction caused by torsion or egg-binding. In the latter, material within the oviduct comes from ova and mucosal secretions. It is not caseated and there are no signs of inflammation. Cause of the obstruction is often apparent. Partially or fully formed eggs may be in the material in the oviduct. Small residual masses of protein secretions are occasionally free in oviduct and do not indicate early salpingitis.

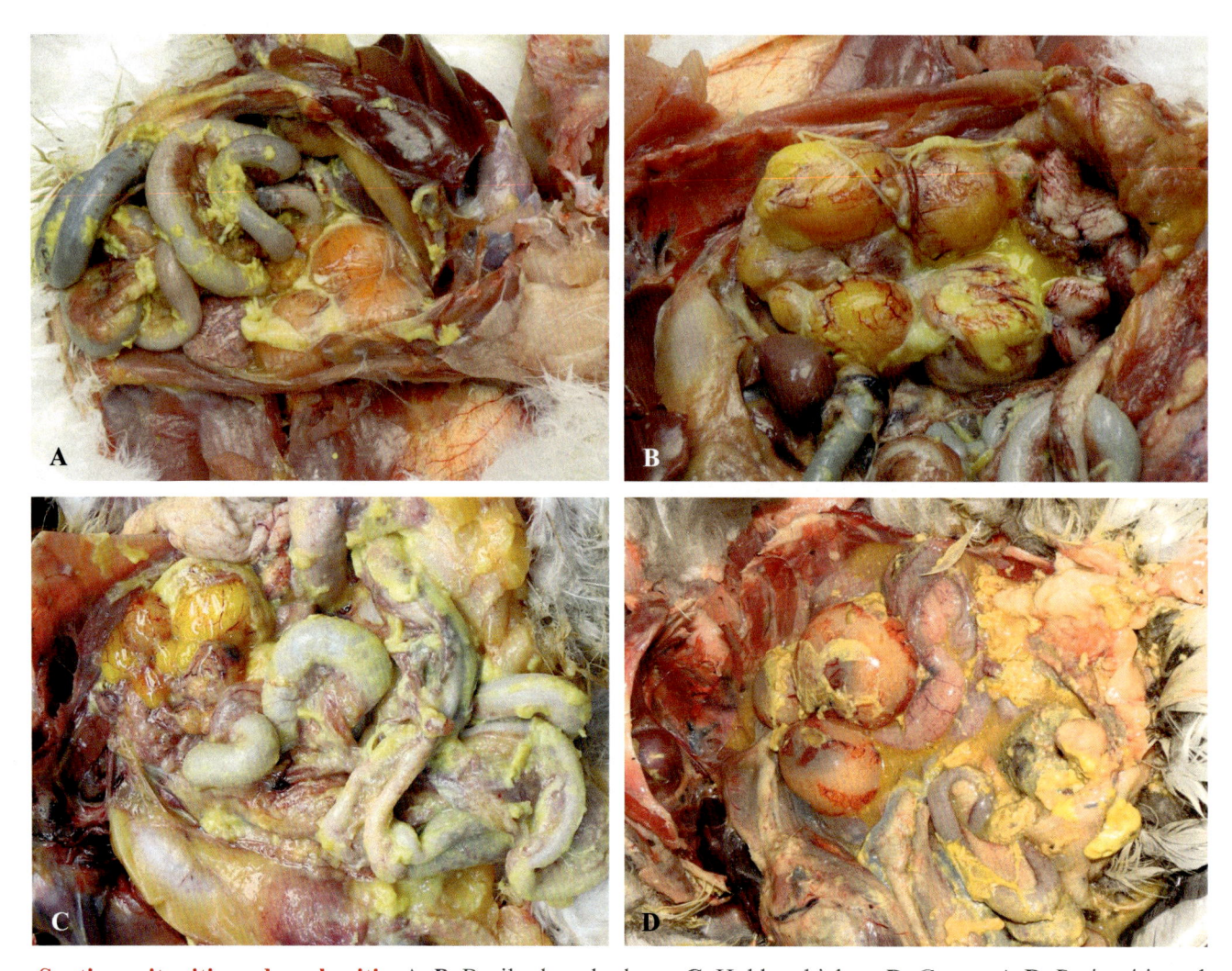

Septic peritonitis and oophoritis. **A, B.** Broiler breeder hens. **C.** Hobby chicken. **D.** Goose. **A-D.** Peritonitis and oophoritis are characterized by accumulation of thick yellow exudate in the abdominal peritoneal cavity and over the surface of the ovary.

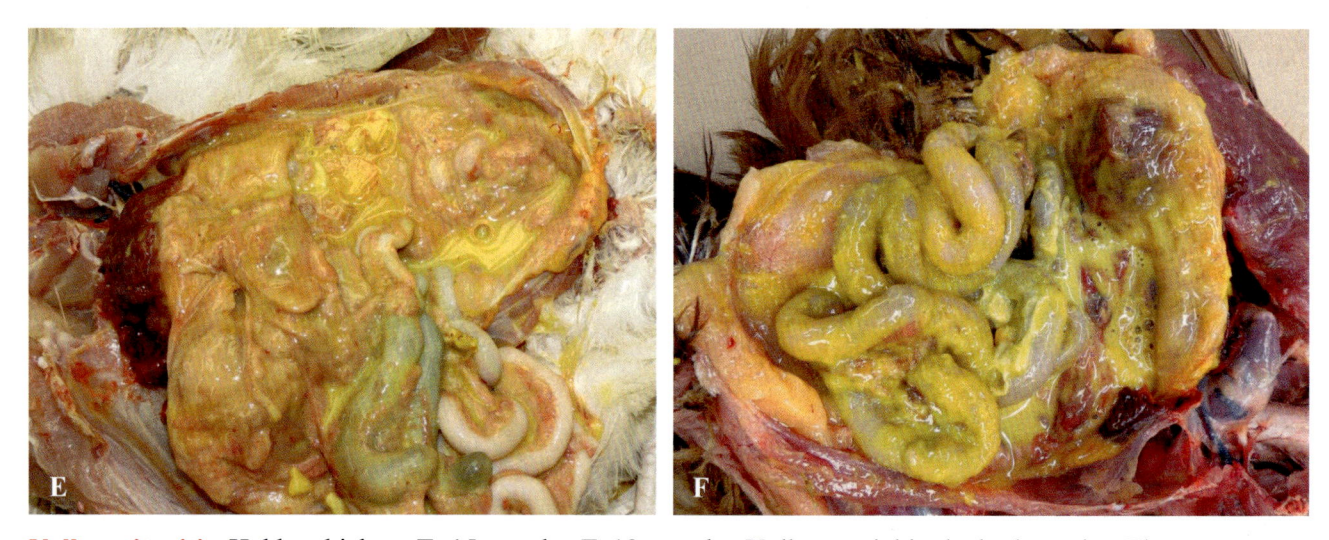

Yolk peritonitis. Hobby chickens **E.** 15-months. **F.** 18-months. Yolk material in the body cavity. The appearance of the yolk is different from the peritoneal exudate in septic peritonitis seen above.

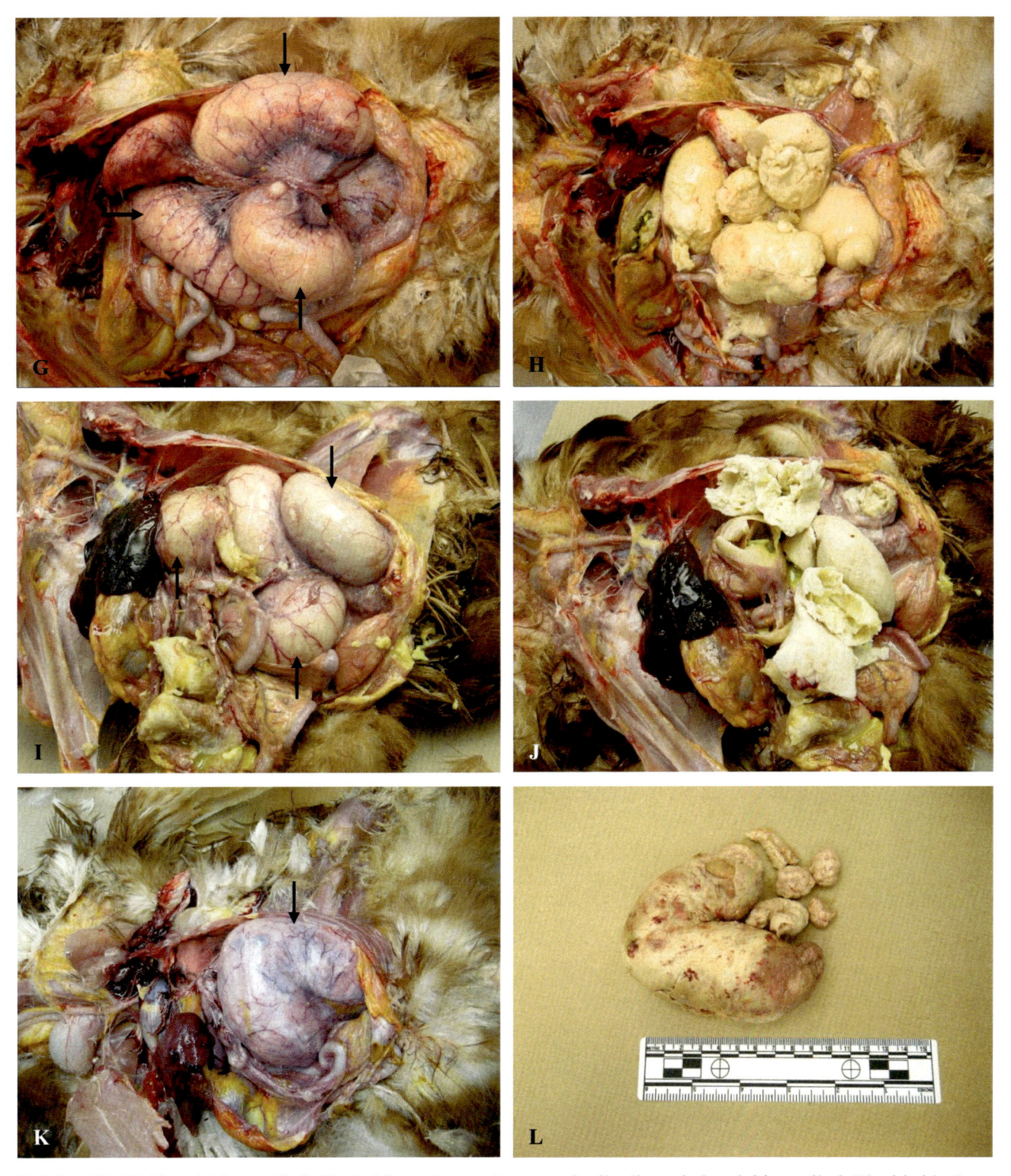

Gross Pathology of Avian Diseases: Text and Atlas 37

Salpingitis. Hobby chickens. **G, I, K.** Oviducts (arrows) are markedly distended and thin-walled. The bird in **I** also has peritonitis (salpingoperitonitis). **H, J.** Oviducts have been opened to show caseous exudate in the lumens. **L.** Large caseous mass was removed from the distended oviduct in K.

Salpingitis. M, N. Caseous masses in the oviducts of two different hobby chickens. Cut surfaces of oviduct masses have concentric rings of different colors that represent alternating layers of exudate and secretions from continued ovulations.

Orchitis, Epididymitis, Epididymo-orchitis

Inflammation of one or both testes (orchitis), epididymis (epididymitis), or both (epididymo-orchitis) occurs infrequently in broiler breeder roosters. Fewer males are kept and infection of the male reproductive tract is apparently more difficult compared to the female reproductive tract. Pathogenesis of infection in the male reproductive tract is the same as that of ascending salpingitis and oophoritis in the female. Virulent bacteria colonize the cloaca and ascend the ductus deferens to affect the epididymis and testis. Infections are usually unilateral and epididymo-orchitis occurs more frequently than infections in just the testis or epididymis. Bacteria, especially *Escherichia coli*, are responsible for male reproductive tract infections. *Staphylococcus*, *Salmonella*, and *Pasteurella* are less frequent causes. *Chlamydia* causes orchitis in turkeys and companion birds. Affected testes are swollen, hyperemic, abnormally shaped, and have multifocal discolored areas and hemorrhages. Fibrin may adhere to the surface of the testis. Affected epididymides are swollen and nodular. Cloacitis can occlude ejaculatory ducts in the urodeum and prevent semen from being expelled. Semen backs up into the ductus deferens, epididymis, and testis.

Lesions resulting from viral infections of the male reproductive tract are less well known. Infectious bronchitis virus has been associated with epididymitis and epididymal calculi in broiler breeders but the etiological role of the virus is controversial.

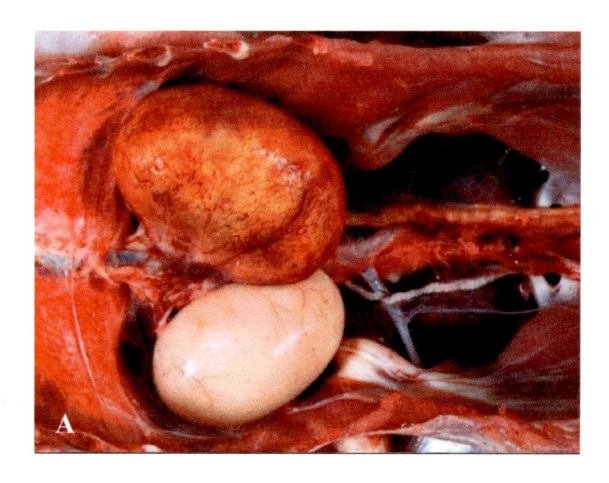

Orchitis. A. 26-week broiler breeder. Unilateral orchitis. Affected testis is swollen, discolored, and hyperemic. Inflammation extends along the ductus deferens. Contralateral testis and ductus deferens are normal.

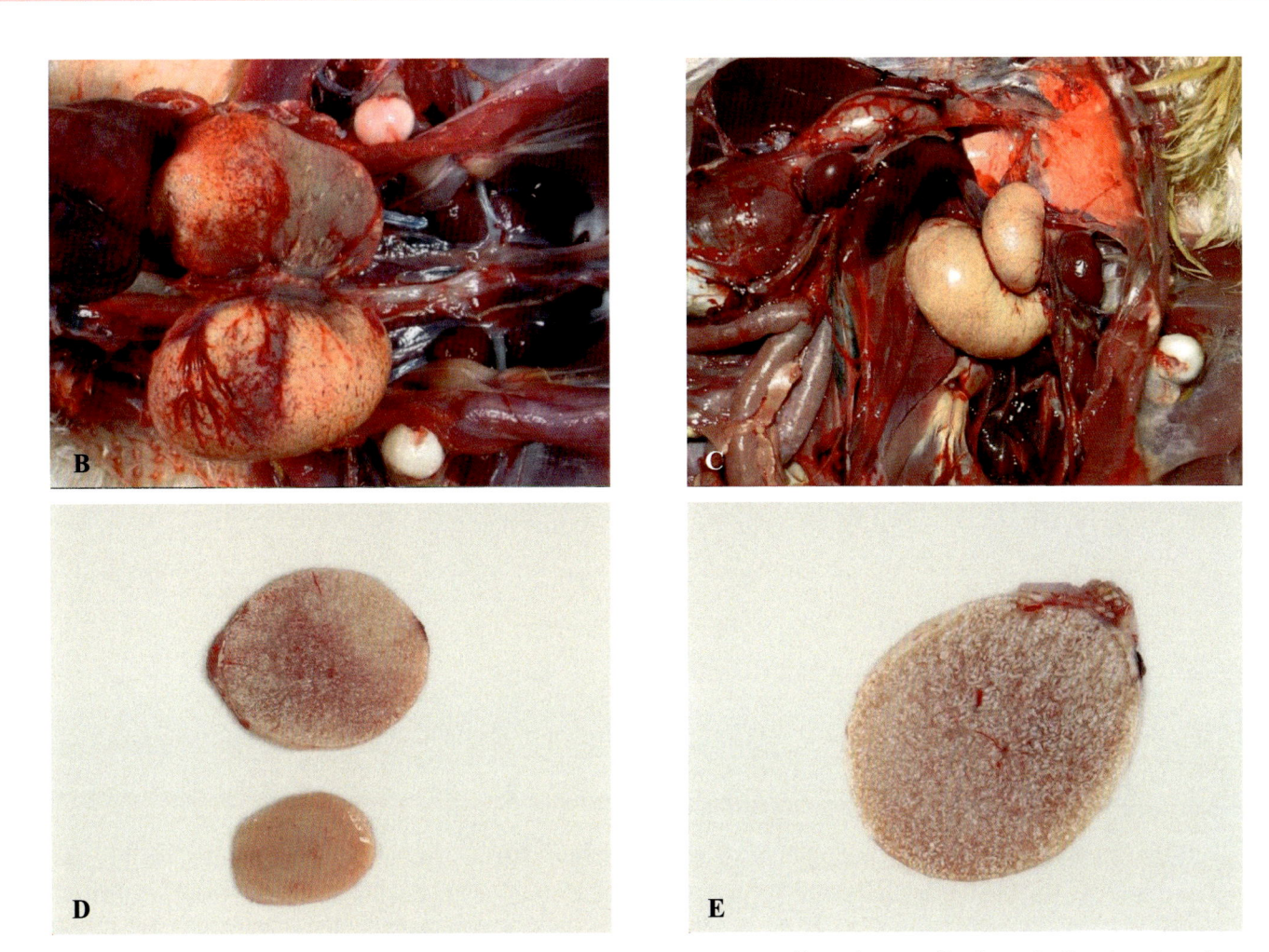

Orchitis. B. 28-week broiler breeder. Bilateral orchitis. Testes are swollen, abnormally shaped, discolored, and hyperemic. *E. coli* was isolated. **C, D, E.** 32-week broiler breeder. **C.** Unilateral orchitis. Right testis is swollen and misshapen. Right ductus deferens is distended with soft, yellow exudate. Left testis is normal. **D.** Cut surfaces of normal and affected testes. **E.** Close-up of the cut surface of the affected testis shows seminiferous tubules distended with exudate.

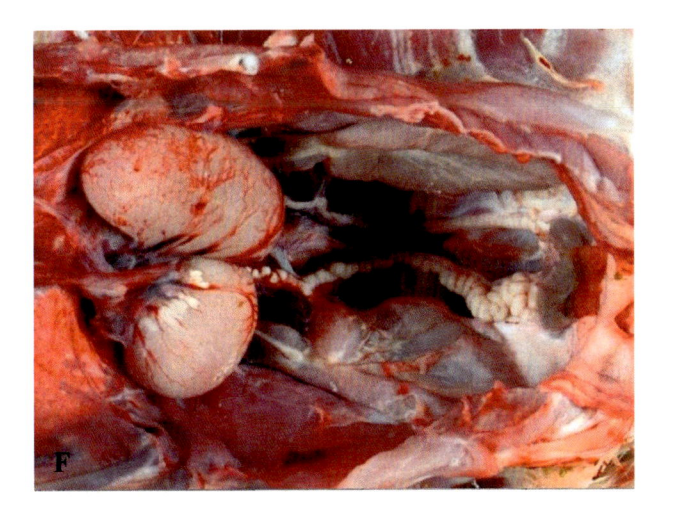

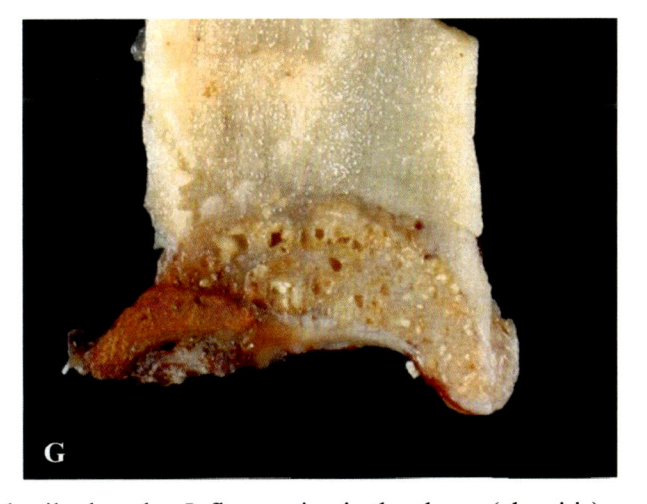

Epididymal obstruction, epididymal calculi. F. 62-week broiler breeder. Inflammation in the cloaca (cloacitis) has obstructed the opening of the right ductus deferens. Semen expands the ductus to the testis where it has accumulated in seminiferous tubules. The affected testis is undergoing early atrophy. Compare with the normal testis and ductus on the opposite side. **G.** 62-week broiler breeder, formalin-fixed tissue. Epididymal calculi and dilated epididymal tubules. Formation of epididymal calculi has been associated with epididymitis and infectious bronchitis virus infection.

Staphylococcal Tenosynovitis of the Gastrocnemius Tendon

Cause. *Staphylococcus aureus*.

Gross lesions. There is a discolored, firm swelling over and above one or both hock joints. Discoloration varies in intensity from barely discernible to notably yellow or yellow-orange. Deep longitudinal incision of the swollen area reveals exudate in the tissue around the gastrocnemius tendon. Exudate may be minimal or abundant and is viscous to caseous and usually pale yellow or yellow-gray. In some cases, masses of caseous exudate are present around the tendon. In chronic cases, a cord-like induration is felt in the area of the gastrocnemius tendon proximal to the hock joint. There may be subcutaneous edema in the area, causing thickening and discoloration of the skin, with accumulation of jelly-like, yellow material on the surface of gastrocnemius muscles. Hemorrhage and tendon rupture are not seen.

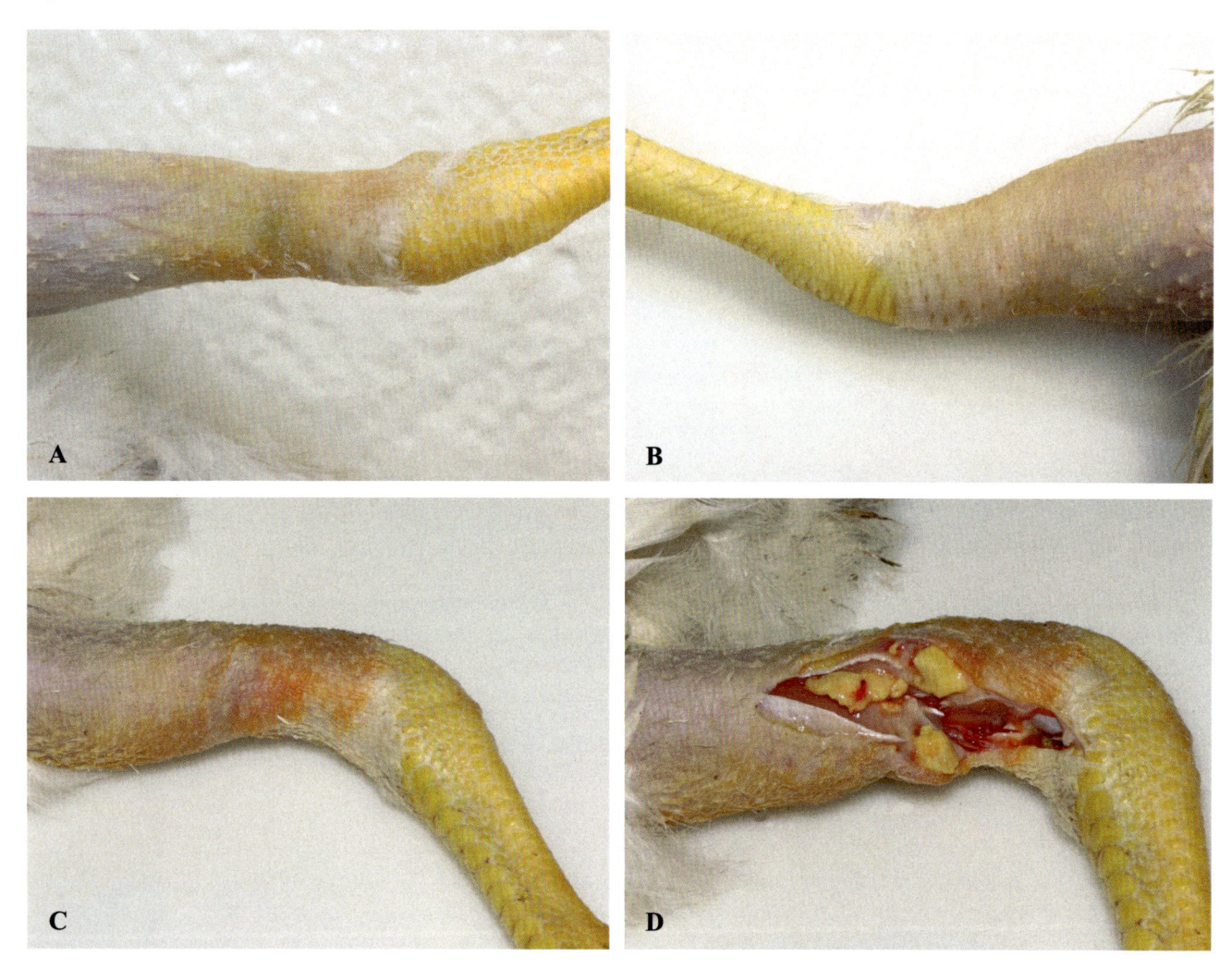

Tenosynovitis of the gastrocnemius tendons caused by *Staphylococcus aureus*. 18- to 24-week broiler breeder males and females. **A, B, C.** Swelling and discoloration over and above the hock due to tenosynovitis of the gastrocnemius tendon. **D.** Caseous masses are present in the swollen area. Histopathology of the gastrocnemius tendons shows fibrinoheterophilic tenosynovitis, usually with intralesional Gram-positive bacterial colonies.

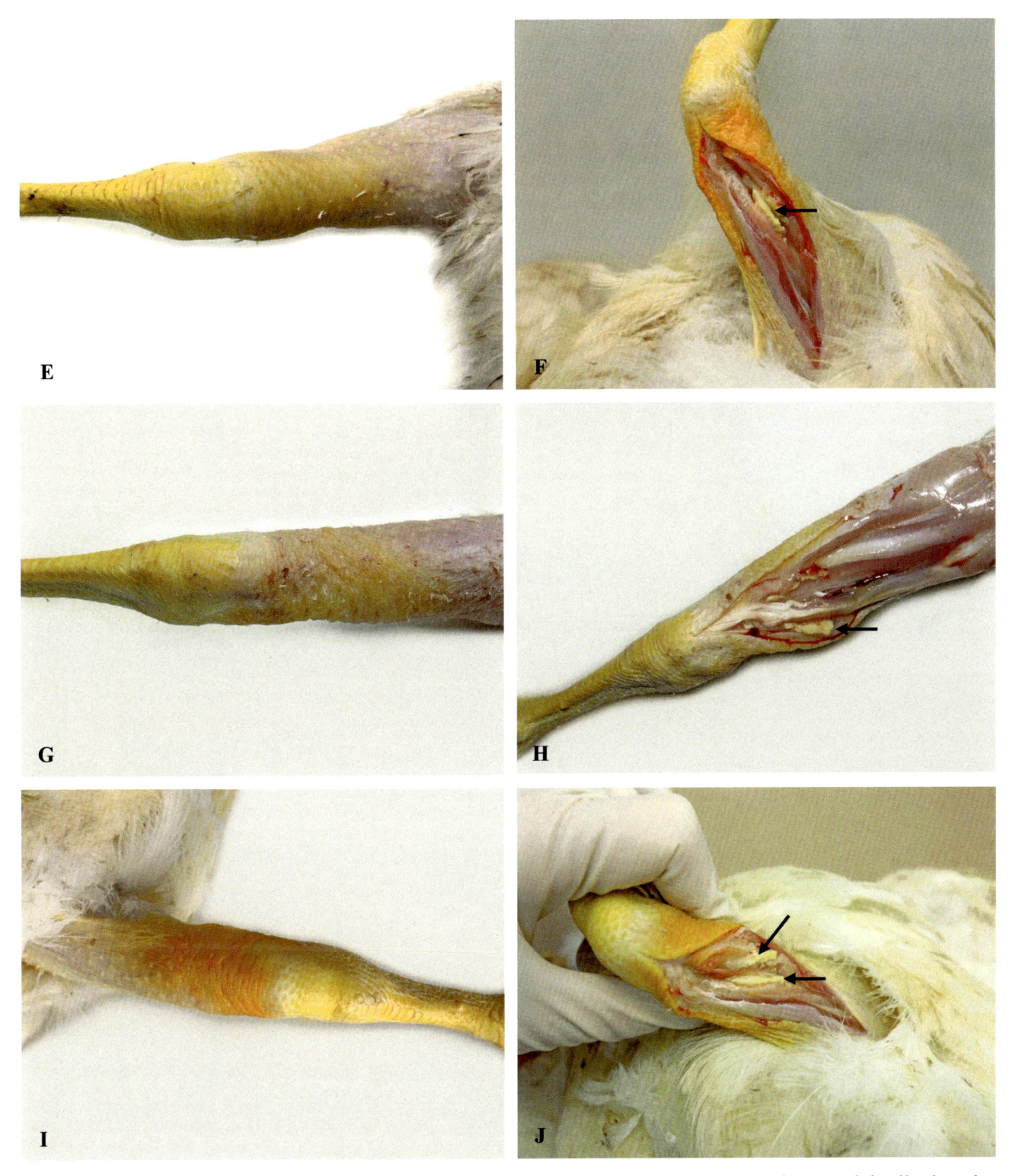

Tenosynovitis of the gastrocnemius tendon caused by *Staphylococcus aureus*. 20- and 25-week broiler breeder males and females. **E, G, I.** Swelling and yellow or yellow-orange discoloration over and above the hock joints due to tenosynovitis of gastrocnemius tendons. **F, H, J.** Yellow masses of soft caseous exudate (arrows) are present around the gastrocnemius tendons.

Bacterial Tenosynovitis of Foot Tendons in Broiler Breeders

Cause. Almost always *Staphylococcus aureus*.

Gross lesions. One or both feet may be involved, although in most cases, only one foot is affected. There is swelling in the foot, usually on the ventral surface and at the junction with the tarsometatarsal bone. The swelling is either soft, or firm and indurated. Soft swellings contain variable amounts of white, viscous exudate, which is evident on incision. Firm swellings may contain caseous material or be indurated and consist of fibrous tissue without grossly visible exudate. In rare cases, there is also swelling of one or more toes, which is probably due to arthritis in the interphalangeal joints.

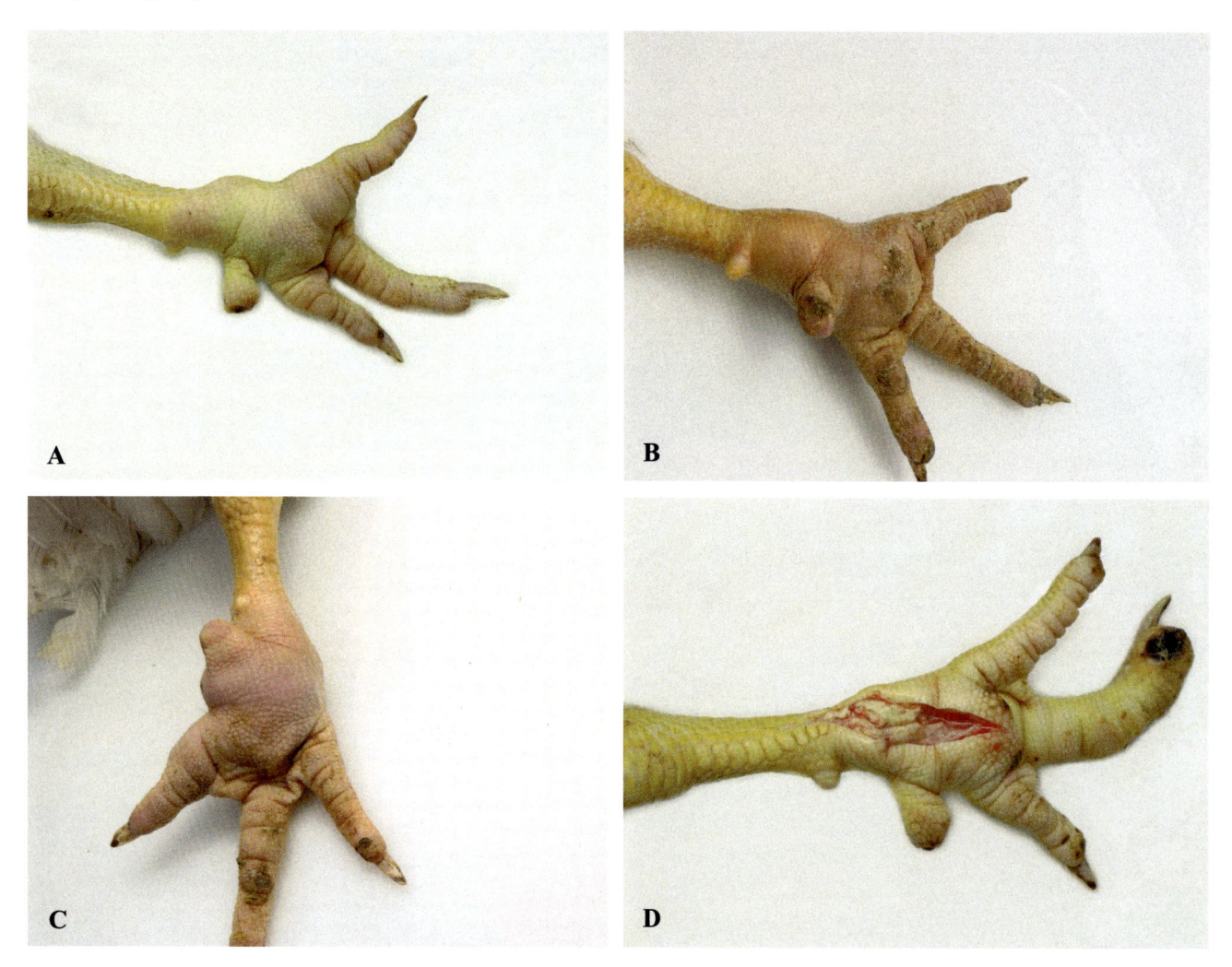

Tenosynovitis of foot tendons caused by *Staphylococcus aureus*. Broiler breeders, **A.** 31-week hen. **B.** 29-week male. **C.** 30-week male. **D.** 35-week hen. **A, B, C.** Swelling of the foot, mostly on the ventral surface and at the junction with the tarsometatarsus. Swelling is due to tenosynovitis of the foot tendons. **D.** Caseous material in the swollen area. The third toe is swollen, probably due to arthritis of interphalangeal joints.

Bacterial Osteomyelitis and Femoral Head Necrosis

Bacterial osteomyelitis is an important cause of lameness in broiler chickens and turkeys and carcass downgrading or condemnation at processing. It is likely the condition is under diagnosed. It is characterized by bacterial infection of cartilaginous tissues and bone marrow in the metaphyseal region, and sometimes the physis, of long bones. Infection is usually hematogenous because of sepsis, but direct infections of compound fractures or other injuries and spread from adjacent infected tissues also occur. Extension of airsacculitis into air sacs in pneumatic bones, especially the skull, is a feature of some diseases, most notably fowl cholera, but the bony tissue remains unaffected. This lesion is best referred to as intraosseous airsacculitis rather than osteomyelitis.

Cause. *Staphylococcus aureus* and *Escherichia coli* are isolated most frequently, but *Enterococcus* spp., coagulase-negative *Staphylococcus*, and other bacteria are sometimes involved. Osteomyelitis is often a sequela to colisepticemia. Spondylitis (vertebral osteoarthritis) caused by *Enterococcus cecorum* is discussed in a separate chapter. The capillary tips of metaphyseal blood vessels are lined by attenuated endothelium that is fenestrated and frequently discontinuous. It is thought that blood-borne bacteria extravagate and invade the cartilage matrix through gaps between endothelial cells of these capillaries. Slow blood circulation in the tips of metaphyseal blood vessels may play a role in the accumulation of blood-borne bacteria in this region and establishment of infection. Bacteria involved in hematogenous osteomyelitis typically have an affinity for binding to free cartilage. *Osteochondrosis dissecans* predisposes to osteomyelitis.

Gross lesions. Unilateral or bilateral lesions are most common in the proximal tibiotarsus and femoral head. Lesions are less frequent in the proximal tarsometatarsus, distal femur, distal tibiotarsus, and vertebrae. To find lesions, the proximal end of the tibiotarsus and femur are sliced longitudinally with a sharp knife. More than one cut through the bone may be necessary to find small lesions. Decalcification in acidic formalin aids in trimming suspect bones, but interferes with culturing. Very small, early lesions may not be visible and only detected microscopically. Gross lesions are yellow, dry, caseated tissue that extends from the growth plate into the metaphysis (metaphyseal osteomyelitis). Large lesions may also involve the physis (physeal bacterial chondritis). Lytic necrosis and disintegration of bone leave an open cavity. Spread of infection into adjacent joint and surrounding muscle can occur via transphyseal vessels or follow collapse of overlying articular cartilage into the lesion. Longstanding lesions are often surrounded by hard dense bone. Lesions may resolve after the growth plate fuses. Other lesions in affected birds include decreased weight, poor body condition, breast skin lesions (ulceration, sternal bursitis), abrasions, and broken or lost feathers on wing tips, green discoloration of the liver, and muscle atrophy in affected leg(s). Osteomyelitis can occur in conjunction with tibial dyschondroplasia. Lesions of osteomyelitis occurring concurrently with tibial dyschondroplasia develop around the periphery of the cartilage plug where abnormal vessels that fail to penetrate the cartilage are located.

Necrosis in the metaphysis of the femur may cause the bone to break when the coxofemoral (hip) joint is disarticulated during necropsy, leaving the femoral head in the acetabulum. This condition is referred to as femoral head necrosis although femoral head osteomyelitis is a better term. Unfortunately, the term femoral head necrosis, an aseptic degenerative process, is frequently used incorrectly for other skeletal lesions including osteopenia, osteochondrosis, and epiphyseal separation.

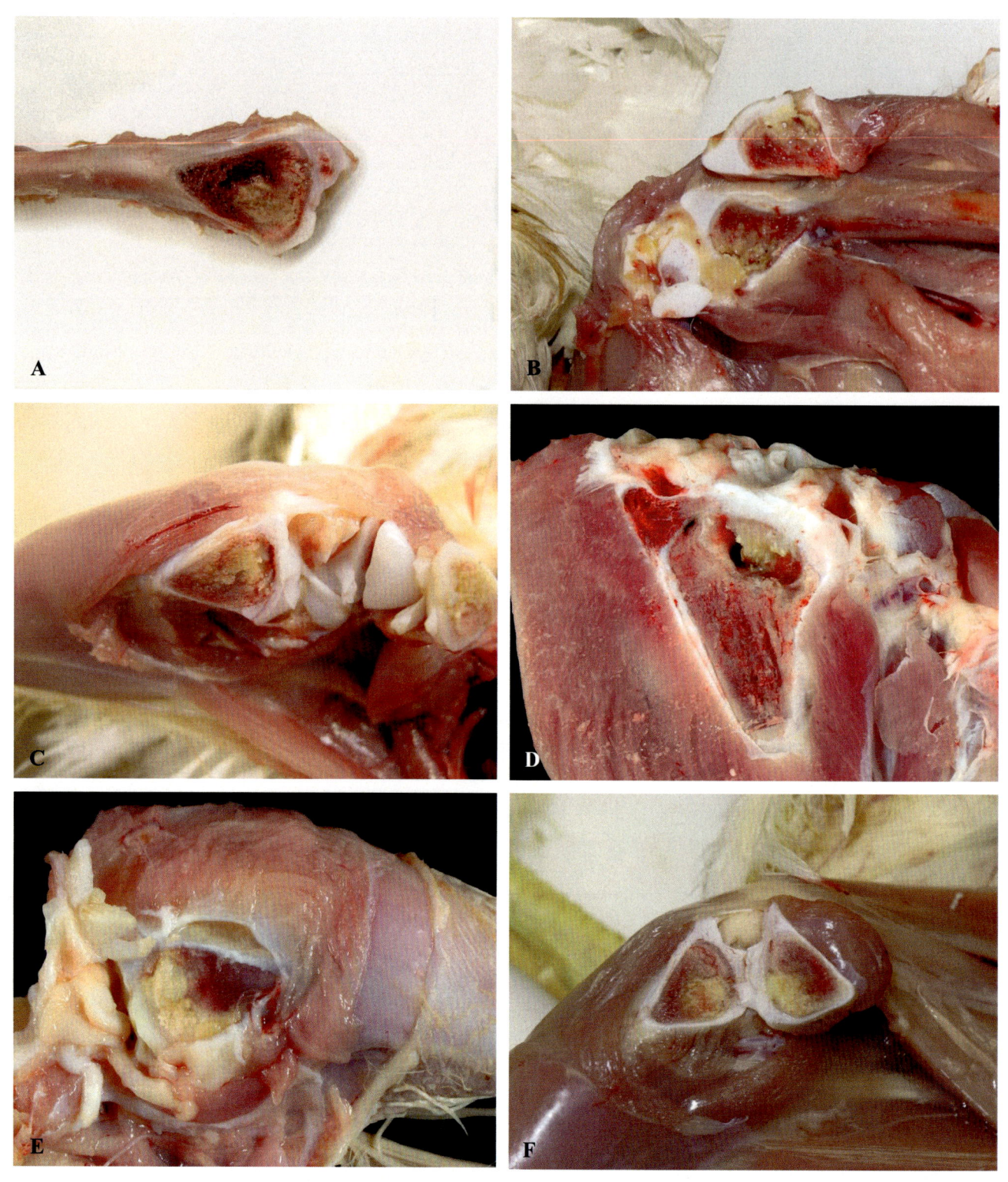

Osteomyelitis. A, B. Broiler chickens (A. 40-day. B. 58-day). In both **A** and **B**, dry, crumbly, yellow necrotic tissue in the metaphysis of the proximal tibiotarsus involves the physis (growth plate). In **B**, a fistulous tract extends from the lesion into adjacent tissue. **C.** Broiler chicken. Necrotic tissue extends from the physis into the metaphysis. **D.** Tom turkey, processing. Osteomyelitis in a tibial dyschondroplasia lesion. Lysis of bone has occurred and dense bone is being formed adjacent to the lesion. **E.** Broiler chicken. Large lesion of osteomyelitis extends across the physis and into the metaphysis. **F.** Broiler chicken. Yellow necrotic tissue in the metaphysis of the proximal end of the tibiotarsus.

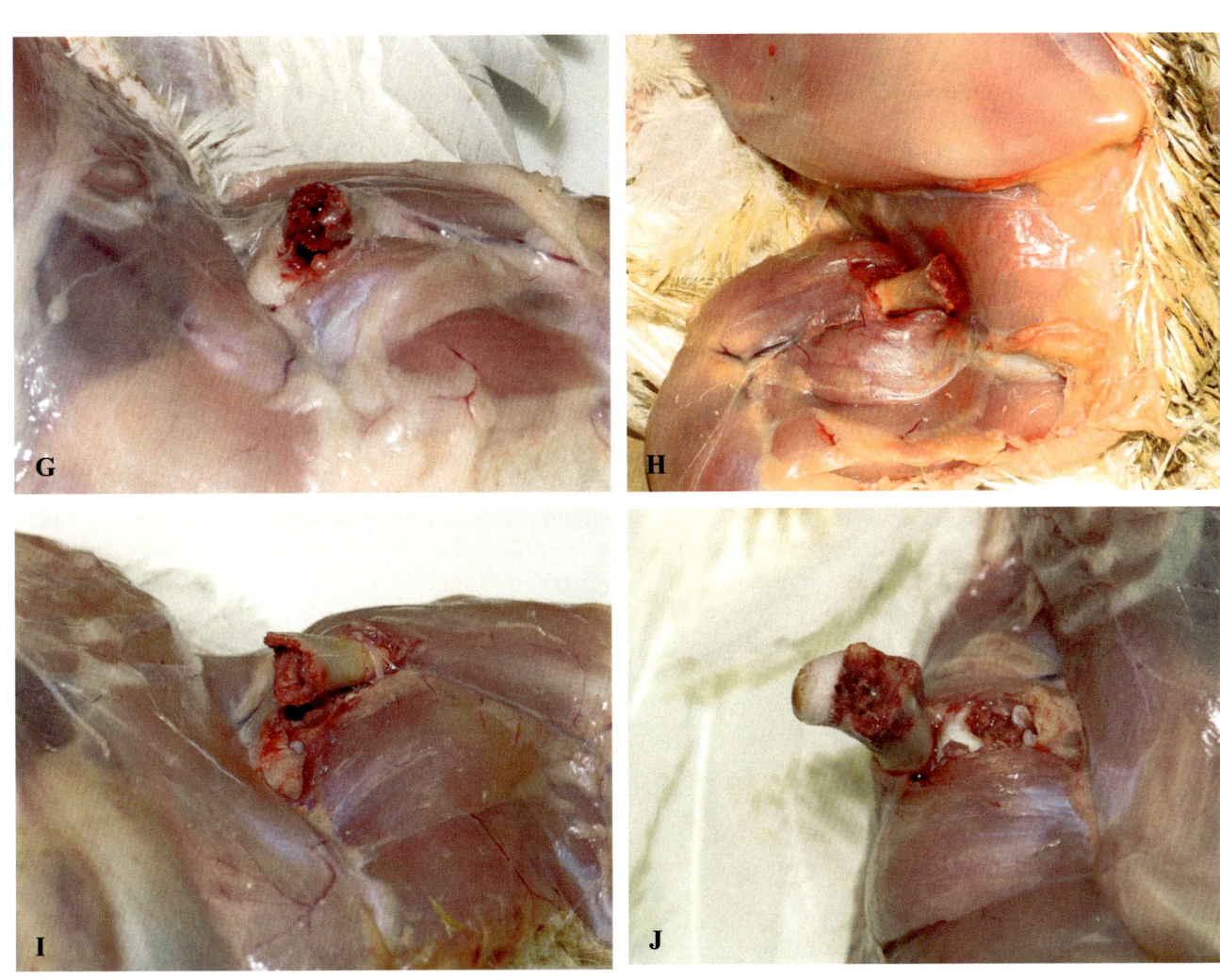

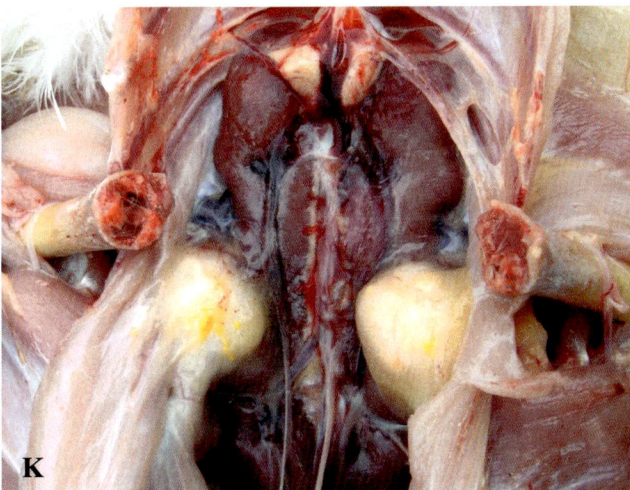

Gross Pathology of Avian Diseases: Text and Atlas   45

Femoral head osteomyelitis. G, H, I. Broiler chickens. Head of the femur remains in the acetabulum because the bone broke at the neck of the femur. **J.** Broiler chicken. Osteomyelitis has eroded the greater trochanter at the proximal end of the femur. **K.** Broiler breeder. Bilateral femoral head osteomyelitis. Round masses of necrotic bone and exudate extend into the body cavity and encroach on the kidneys. Both femurs have broken at the femoral necks because of osteomyelitis.

Spondylitis (Vertebral Osteoarthritis)

Cause. Outbreaks involving several broiler chickens or broiler breeders in a flock are caused by specific pathogenic strains of *Enterococcus cecorum*. Isolated sporadic cases of spondylitis in broiler chickens, turkeys, and other avian species result from infections with a variety of bacteria capable of causing systemic infections, most often *Staphylococcus aureus* or *Escherichia coli*. Spondylitis caused by *E. cecorum* occurs, for unknown reason, predominantly in males.

Clinical signs. Typically, birds sit on their hocks and tails with their feet and occasionally shanks slightly raised off the ground. They may flap their wings and push themselves backwards. This posture is the same as a bird with kinky back (spondylolisthesis), which has led to the erroneous use of this name for birds with spondylitis. Other birds are in ventral recumbency with their legs extended forwards or backwards or they lay on their sides with outstretched legs.

Gross lesions. **Gross lesions**. Necropsy reveals a marked bony swelling involving the articulating thoracic vertebra (T_4). In some birds, an irregular arrangement of the ribs is also seen. Enlargement in the spine is usually visible when the lungs are removed to expose the ribs and vertebral column. Less often, it is necessary to remove the cranial divisions of the kidneys to reveal the spinal lesions. Small bits of lung tissue often adhere to the lesion after the lungs are removed because of adhesions to the spinal lesion. A sagittal section through the center of the thoracolumbar vertebrae and spinal cord shows an area of necrosis filled with caseous exudate involving the body of T_4 and adjacent vertebrae in the notarium (lesion in the cranial articulation) or synsacrum (lesion in the caudal articulation). Infrequently, lesions are found in both cranial and caudal articulations. Expansion of the lesion dorsally into the vertebral canal compresses the spinal cord. Loss of bone in the vertebral bodies causes dorsal buckling of the spine (kyphosis), which further compresses the spinal cord. Necrosis of the vertebral body of T_4 is also evident on cross section of the vertebra.

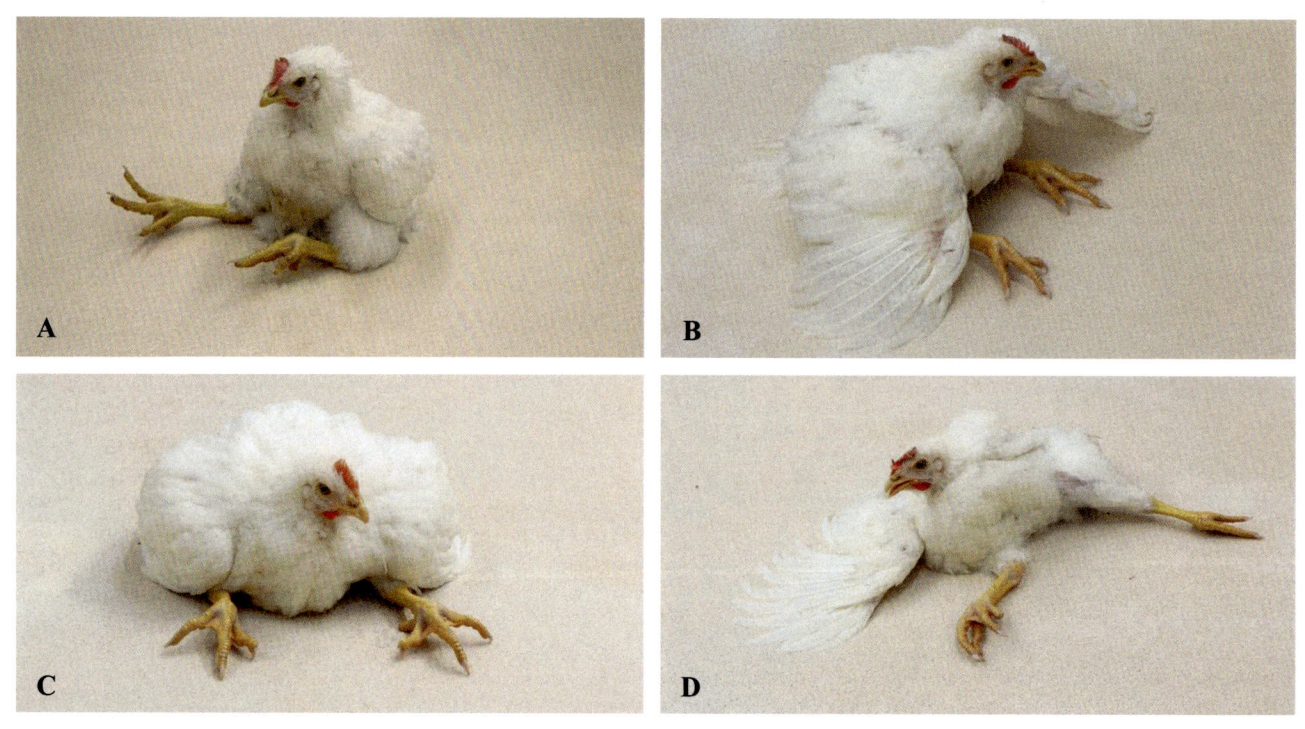

Spondylitis of caused by *Enterococcus cecorum*. A. 10-week broiler breeder male. The bird sits on the hock joints and tail, with the feet and leg off the ground. **B.** 55-day broiler chicken. The bird sits on the hock joints. The feet and legs are slightly off the ground. The bird tries to move with the wing support. **C.** 55-aday-old broiler chicken. The bird is in a lateral recumbency with the leg stretched to the front. The feet are off the ground. **D.** 37-day broiler chicken. The bird lay on side with the legs stretched to side.

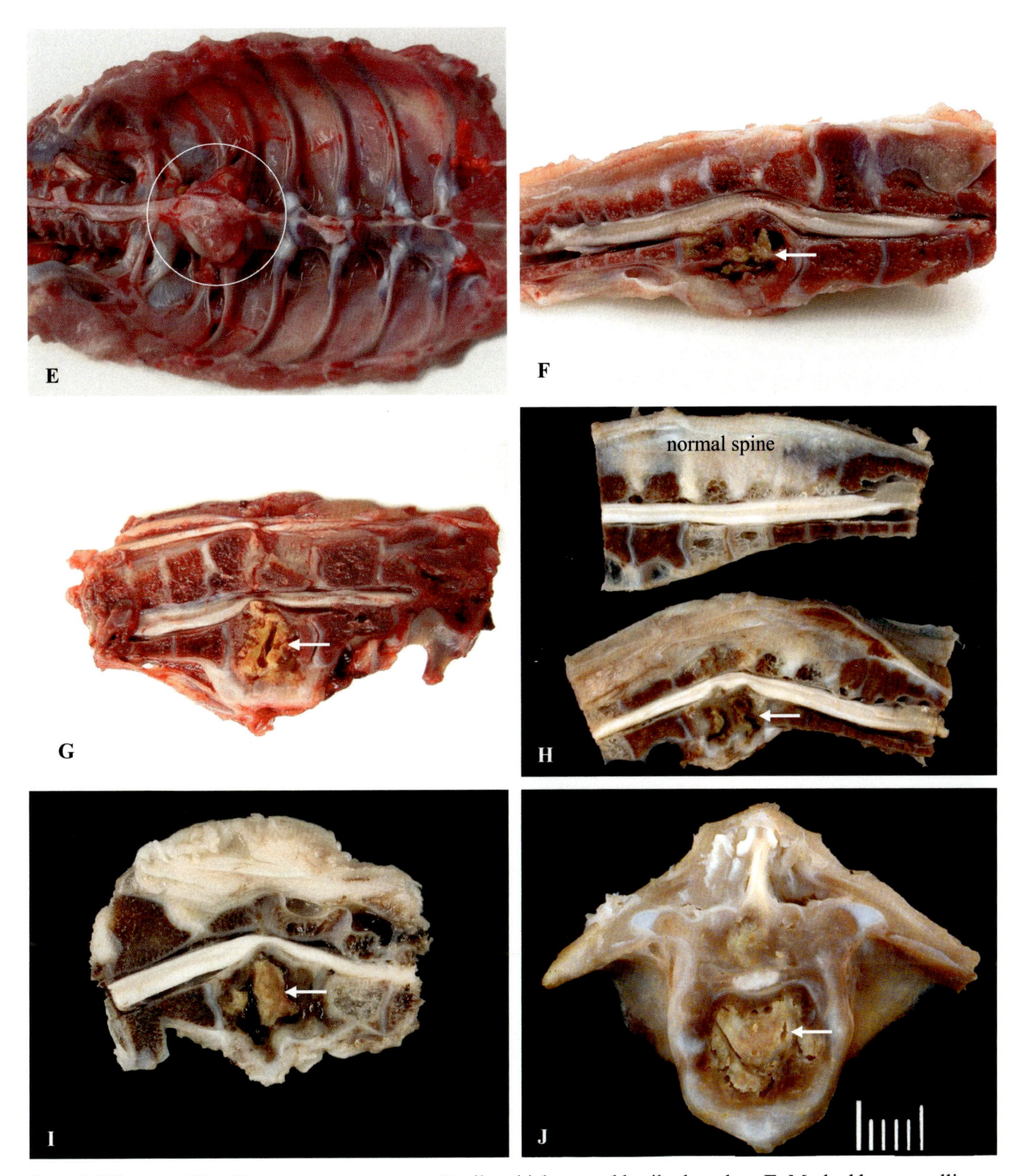

Spondylitis caused by *Enterococcus cecorum*. Broiler chickens and broiler breeders. **E.** Marked bony swelling (circle) in T$_4$ at the level of the last two ribs. **F-I.** Sagittal sections of fresh and formalin-fixed, decalcified thoracolumbar vertebral columns. Necrosis (arrows) in the body of T$_4$ and adjacent vertebrae. A large area of necrosis in the body of T$_4$ vertebra has caused deformity, dorsal displacement, and spinal cord compression. **J.** Cross section through the body of T$_4$ shows necrosis with caseous material (arrow) in the vertebral body and proliferation of cartilage and fibrous tissue around the lesion. *Enterococcus cecorum* was isolated from all these vertebral lesions.

Gangrenous Dermatitis (Clostridial Cellulitis, Blue Wing Disease)

Cause. *Clostridium septicum*, with other bacteria, especially *Staphylococcus aureus*, are isolated from the lesion. Other clostridial species and bacteria are less common. Chicken anemia virus predisposes to gangrenous dermatitis in young chickens. Wings are usually affected, which is the reason for the common name, "Blue Wing Disease".

Gross lesions. Chickens and turkeys are affected. Birds with gangrenous dermatitis decompose rapidly after death. Lesions of gangrenous dermatitis need to be differentiated from changes that result from postmortem decomposition. Areas consistently affected are the abdomen, breast, and inguinal regions. Wing tips are affected in young chickens with blue wing disease. Skin over the breast and abdomen is soft, featherless, swollen, and red to purple. Crepitation may be felt when the skin is palpated. Skin often sloughs or tears easily when rubbed. Removal of the skin reveals edema in the subcutaneous tissues that is often blood stained. Edematous fluid may have a gelatinous consistency and contain gas bubbles produced by *Clostridium*. Superficial breast muscle is either dark with pale streaks or appears cooked. Livers are frequently dark with pale blotches. Lungs are dark-red and edematous in some birds.

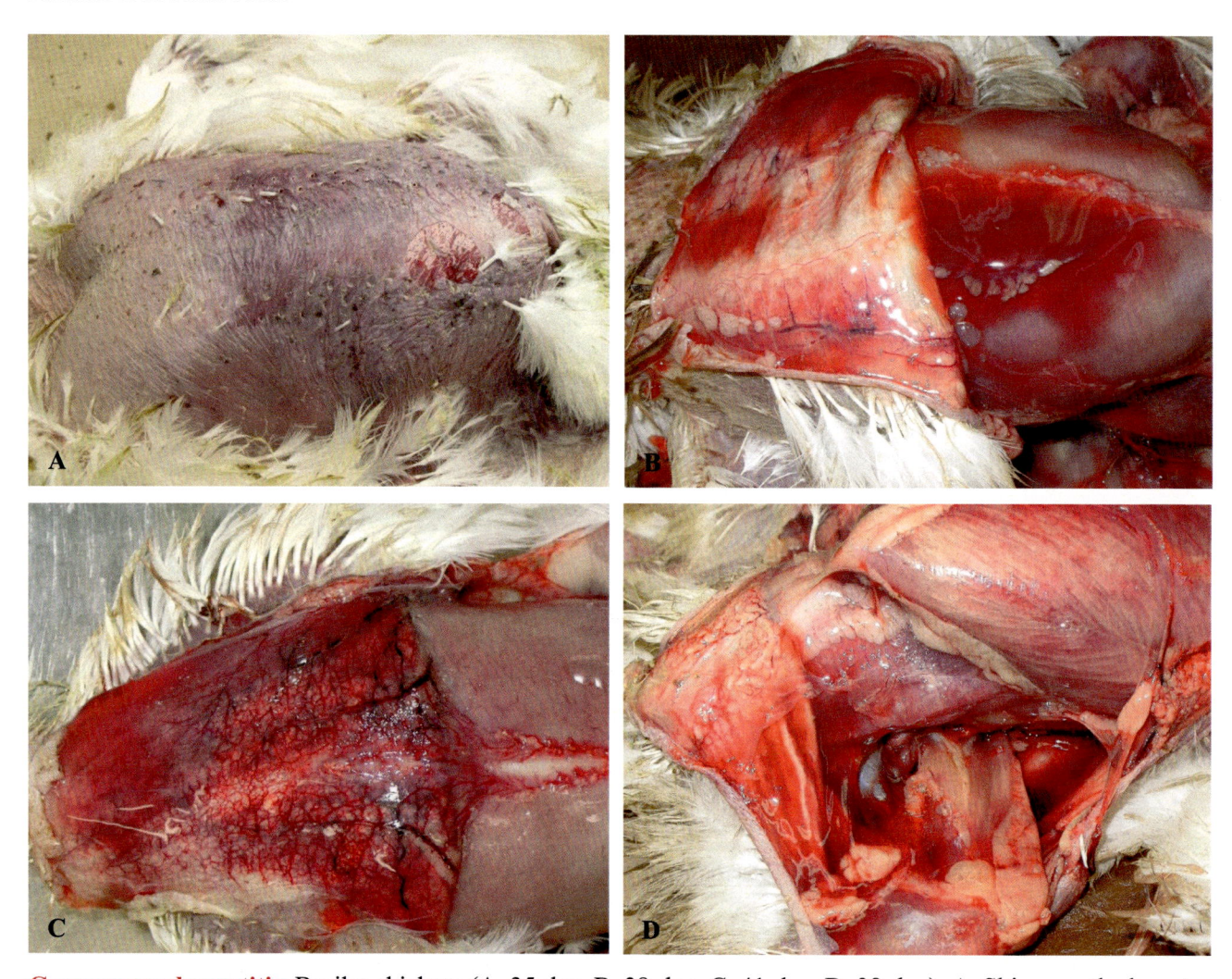

Gangrenous dermatitis. Broiler chickens (A. 35-day. B. 38-day. C. 41-day. D. 38-day). **A.** Skin over the breast and abdomen is purple, thickened, and featherless. **B.** Marked blood-stained subcutaneous edema over the breast. **C.** Subcutaneous tissue over the breast is edematous, severely congested, and possibly hemorrhagic. **D.** Severe blood-stained edema in the inguinal area. Note the congested, pale-streaked pectoral muscle.

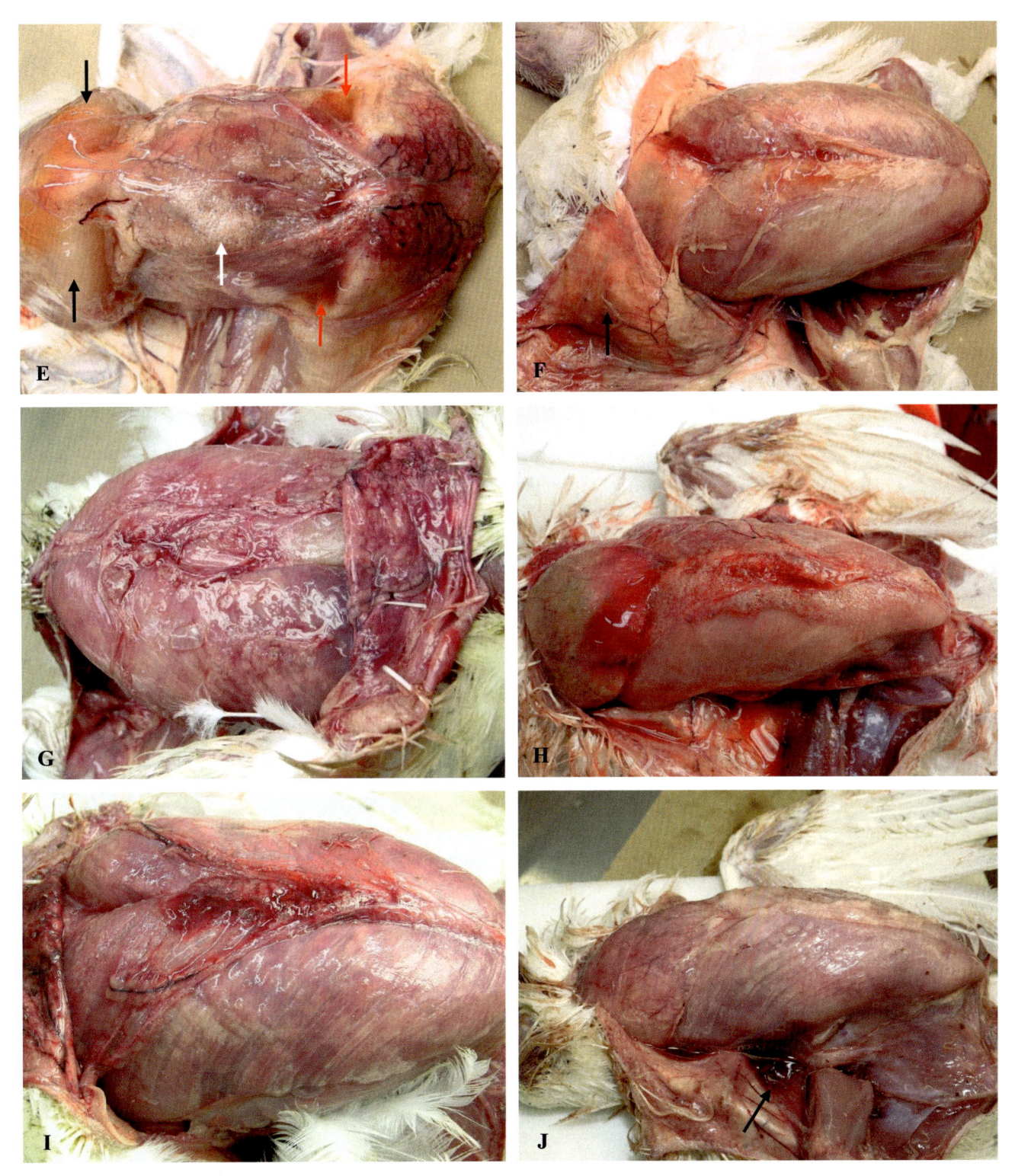

Gangrenous dermatitis. Broiler chickens (**E.** 41-day, **G**, **I.** 35-day) and broiler breeders (**F.** 5-week. **H**, **J.** 12-week). **E.** Subcutaneous tissue over the breast muscles is edematous (black arrows). Note frothy air bubbles over the breast muscles (white arrow). Red arrows: edema fluid. **F.** Subcutis is thickened (arrow), and there is blood stained subcutaneous edema over the pectoral muscles, which are necrotic. *Clostridium septicum* and *E. coli* were isolated. **G.** Severe subcutaneous edema and emphysema, with necrosis of the superficial pectoral muscles. **H.** Blood-stained edema with gas bubbles (emphysema) over the breast. **I.** Blood-stained subcutaneous edema, with marked necrosis of the superficial pectoral muscles. **J.** Blood-stained edema fluid in the inguinal area (arrow), with necrosis of the superficial pectoral muscle.

Necrotic Enteritis

Necrotic enteritis (NE) is an enteric bacterial disease of chickens, turkeys, and a few other avian species caused by *Clostridium perfringens*. The disease is characterized by damage to the intestinal mucosa by toxins produced by the causative bacteria. It has a worldwide distribution and causes considerable financial losses to broiler chicken producers due to mortality, treatment cost, and, in its milder, subclinical form, poor growth and feed utilization. The disease was first reported in chickens in 1961.

Cause. *Clostridium perfringens*, a Gram-positive, obligatory anaerobe, non-motile, rod-shaped, spore-forming bacterium. *C. perfringens* is divided into 5 toxinotypes (A, B, C, D, and E) based on 4 major toxins designated alpha (α), beta (β), epsilon (ε), and iota (ι). Most isolates from NE cases are type A, with a few cases caused by type C.

The organism is a natural inhabitant of the environment (used litter, soil, marine sediments, decaying vegetation, sewage) and intestinal tracts of healthy humans, animals, and insects. *C. perfringens* is part of the normal flora of the digestive tract of birds. Typically, it can be found in the crop, duodenum, jejunum, ileum, and ceca of healthy birds. It colonizes the intestines of broiler chickens within a few hours after hatching and the numbers of the organism increase gradually after initial colonization. The intestine of healthy birds contains large numbers of *C. perfringens*, up to 10^5 colony-forming units per gram of intestinal contents. The population of *C. perfringens* in the intestine is affected by nutritional and environmental factors and health status of the gut of the bird. Feed and litter contaminated with large numbers of *C. perfringens* have been convincingly implicated as sources of infection. It is difficult to prepare spore-free poultry feed by standard feed preparation procedures.

Natural hosts. Necrotic enteritis is most common in broiler chickens and young broiler breeder pullets. In commercially raised broiler chickens, clinical disease usually occurs between 2 and 5 weeks of age. The disease is also seen in turkeys (mostly young meat-type) and table-egg layers (mostly pullets kept on litter). It has also been reported in farmed ostriches, captive capercaillies, and free-living geese and crows. An NE-like disease caused by *C. perfringens* has occurred in quail.

Pathogenesis. Toxins produced by *C. perfringens* are responsible for damaging the intestinal mucosa, enterotoxaemia, and death of the bird. Disease occurs when *C. perfringens* overgrows in the intestinal tract and produces potent toxins that severely damage the intestinal mucosa. Toxins absorbed from the intestinal tract produce a toxemia, which is responsible for death of the bird. Thus, NE is a type of enterotoxaemia. α-toxin produced by type A and C and β-toxin produced by type C have been considered to be the principal virulence factors. However, the amount of alpha toxin produced in vitro by *C. perfringens* isolated from NE lesions is not significantly different from the amount produced by isolates from the intestines of healthy birds. The intestinal level of alpha toxin is not correlated with intestinal lesions, and an α-toxin-deficient mutant of *C. perfringens* is equally capable of causing NE lesions. The search for an alternative virulence factor in *C. perfringens* lead to the discovery of NetB toxin.

NetB toxin belongs to the α-hemolysin family of pore-forming, membrane damaging toxins. NetB causes pores in the cell membrane by disrupting the phospholipid bilayer, which results in an influx of ions and osmotic lysis of cells. The *NetB* gene has been identified in certain strains of *C. perfringens*. The gene encodes a 323-amino acid protein; it is located on a 42-kilobase locus (NE-Loc1) in an approximately 85-kilobase plasmid. Several studies have shown that *NetB* gene is strongly associated with NE-derived strains *C. perfringens*. The gene distinguishes *C. perfringens* strains that are capable of inducing NE from strains that do not cause the disease.

In birds with NE, a single clone dominates the *C. perfringens* population in the intestine. This clonal population usually carries and expresses the *NetB* gene. In healthy chicks, the *C. perfringens* population is mixed and contains only a low percentage of *NetB* expressing clones. However, events leading to the multiplication and colonization of *NetB*-positive strains, with subsequent production of toxin and damage to the intestinal mucosa, are uncertain. Simple infection with NetB-positive strains is not sufficient to induce disease. Predisposing factors likely play a major role in development of the disease.

NE-causing strains may possess other virulence factors that are responsible for the disease. Genomic analysis has shown that, in addition to the NE-Loc-1, two other smaller loci (NE-Loc-2 and NE-Loc-3) also are associated with NE strains of *C. perfringens*. Other virulence factors, whose genes are clustered at discrete loci, may be involved in the disease, but further studies are needed to determine if additional toxins, hydrolytic enzymes, or both contribute to the complex pathogenesis of the disease.

Clinical signs. Typically, NE has a short clinical course. Birds in the flock are usually found dead without premonitory clinical signs. Some birds may appear listless and lethargic for a few hours before death. Birds affected with the mildest, subclinical form of NE, do not die but show reduced weight gains and higher feed conversion ratios, with increased condemnations at processing due to cholangiohepatitis. Mortality rates in broiler chicken flocks due to NE are generally less than 10%, but can be as high as 50%.

Gross lesions. Lesions in the intestinal tract are usually confined to the jejunum and ileum, but ceca and colorectum may be involved. They are most common between the distal end of the duodenum and Meckel's diverticulum. Lesions vary in appearance depending on the severity of infection, stage of the disease, presence or absence of coccidiosis, and freshness of the carcass. When birds have NE, it is best to examine euthanized or fresh dead birds for lesions. Once the intestine starts to decompose after death, NE lesions tend to be less obvious and difficult to identify. The jejunum and ileum may be dilated and flaccid, have a thin, friable wall, and filled with gas or contain green or red-tinged fluid admixed with debris. In mild cases, the intestinal mucosa has a granular or roughened appearance. In severe cases, the mucosa is markedly thickened, discolored green, brown, or red–brown, and roughened or velvety. A green, red, brown, or pink pseudomembrane often covers and loosely adheres to the mucosa; sloughed pieces of the membrane may be in the intestinal lumen. Infrequently, multifocal necrosis in the liver and an enlarged, inflamed gall bladder due to cholecystitis may be seen.

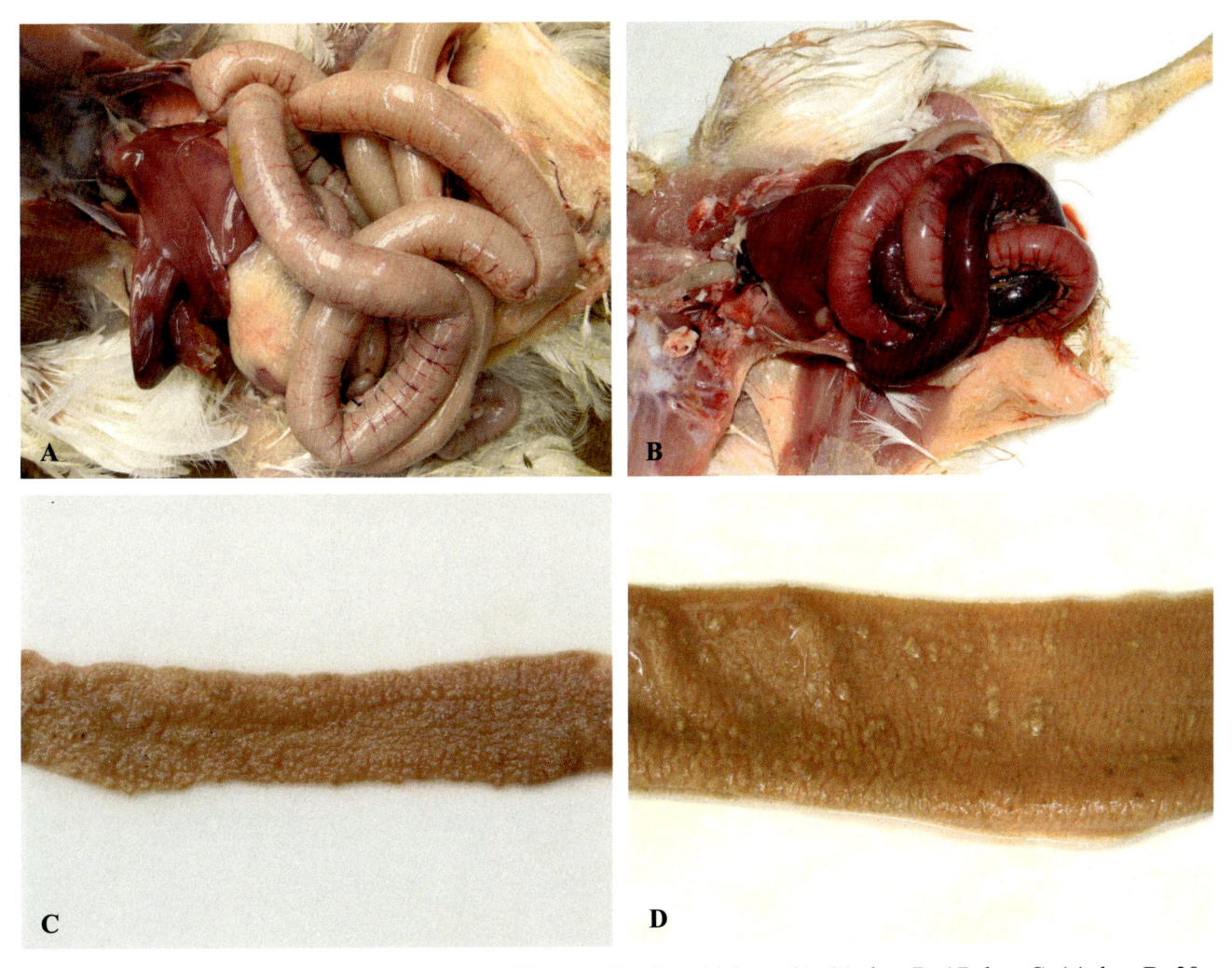

Necrotic enteritis caused by *Clostridium perfringens*. Broiler chickens (A. 31-day, B. 17-day, C. 14-day. D. 29-day). **A.** Jejunum and ileum are dilated. Only birds that have been euthanized or died very recently can be evaluated for this lesion as the changes seen here can also result from postmortem decomposition. **B.** Jejunum and ileum are dilated and a segment is hemorrhagic. This lesion is unusual in birds with necrotic enteritis. The bird was negative for coccidiosis. **C.** Mucosa of the jejunum/ileum is thickened and has a granular appearance. **D.** Mucosa of jejunum/ileum is thickened and has a "velvety" appearance.

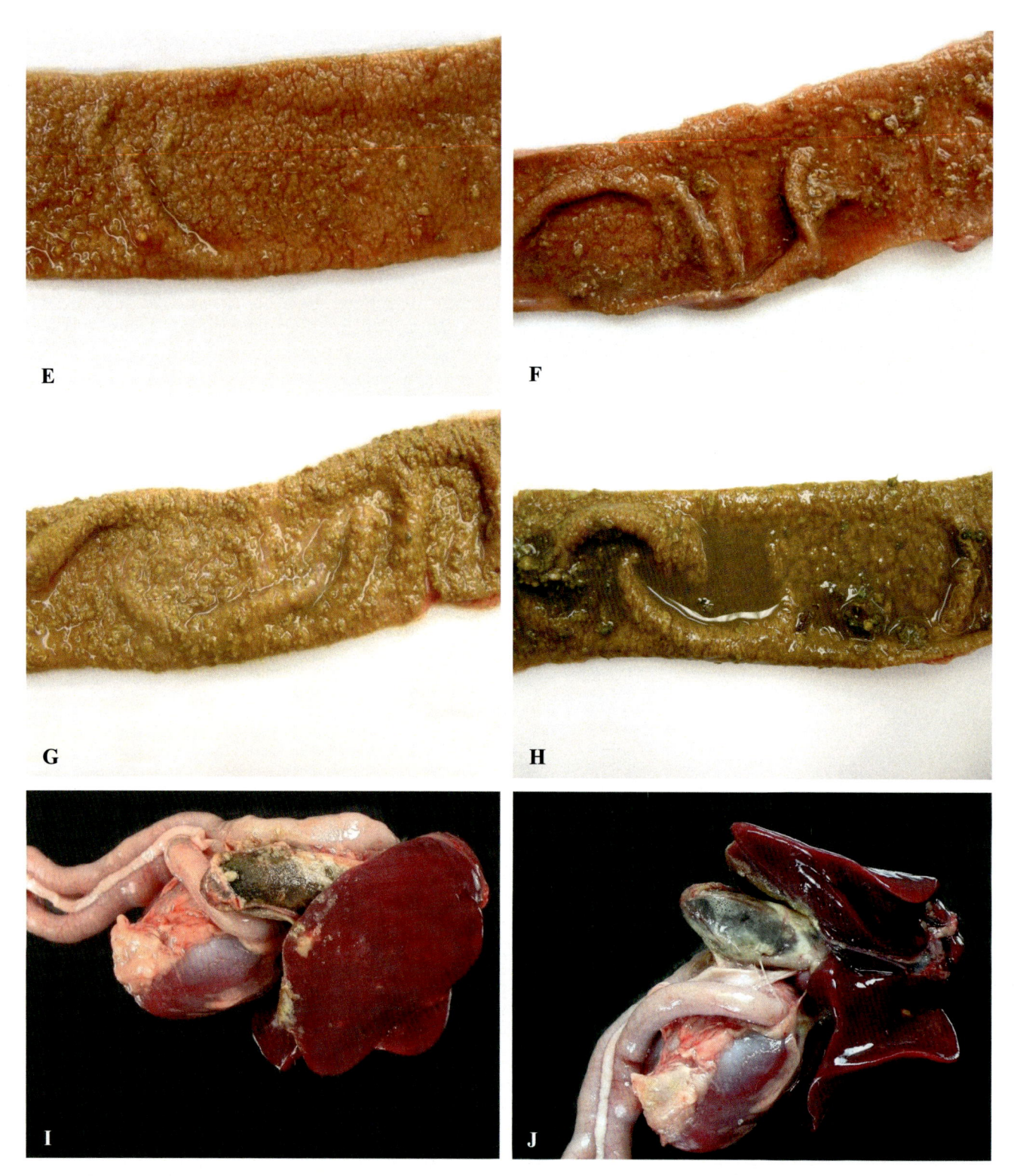

Necrotic enteritis caused by *Clostridium perfringens*. Broiler chickens (E, F. 31-day. G. 38-day. H. 35-day. I, J. 28-day). **E, F.** Mucosa of jejunum/ileum is discolored, thickened, and irregular because of diffuse necrosis. In **F**, blood-tinged fluid is admixed with necrotic debris in the lumen. **G, H.** The mucosa is roughened because of necrosis. In **H**, green fluid is admixed with debris in the lumen. **I, J.** Chickens with necrotic enteritis. Gallbladders are distended with thick, opaque walls, and exudate on the serosal surface. Bile is discolored. Culture of bile yielded a pure growth *Clostridium perfringens*. Note the yellow (necrotic) areas in the livers.

Ulcerative Enteritis in Quail

Cause. *Clostridium colinum*.

Clinical signs and gross lesions. Mortality is increased. Affected birds appear sick, stop eating, lose weight, and become emaciated. Droppings are abnormally watery and feathers around the vent are matted with feces. Ulcers are present in the intestinal mucosa, especially the ileum, ceca, and anterior part of the rectum. They are usually visible through the serosal surface as pale areas that are circular, lenticular, or irregular and are firm to touch. On the mucosal surface, multiple small, shallow or deep ulcers are a characteristic finding. Small ulcers may coalesce to form large necroulcerative lesions covered with a necrotic pseudomembrane. Ulcers may be hemorrhagic or have a raised border. Deep ulcers perforate the intestine and cause severe peritonitis and intestinal adhesions. Small grey to yellow foci are sometimes seen in the liver. Spleen may be enlarged and congested or mottled.

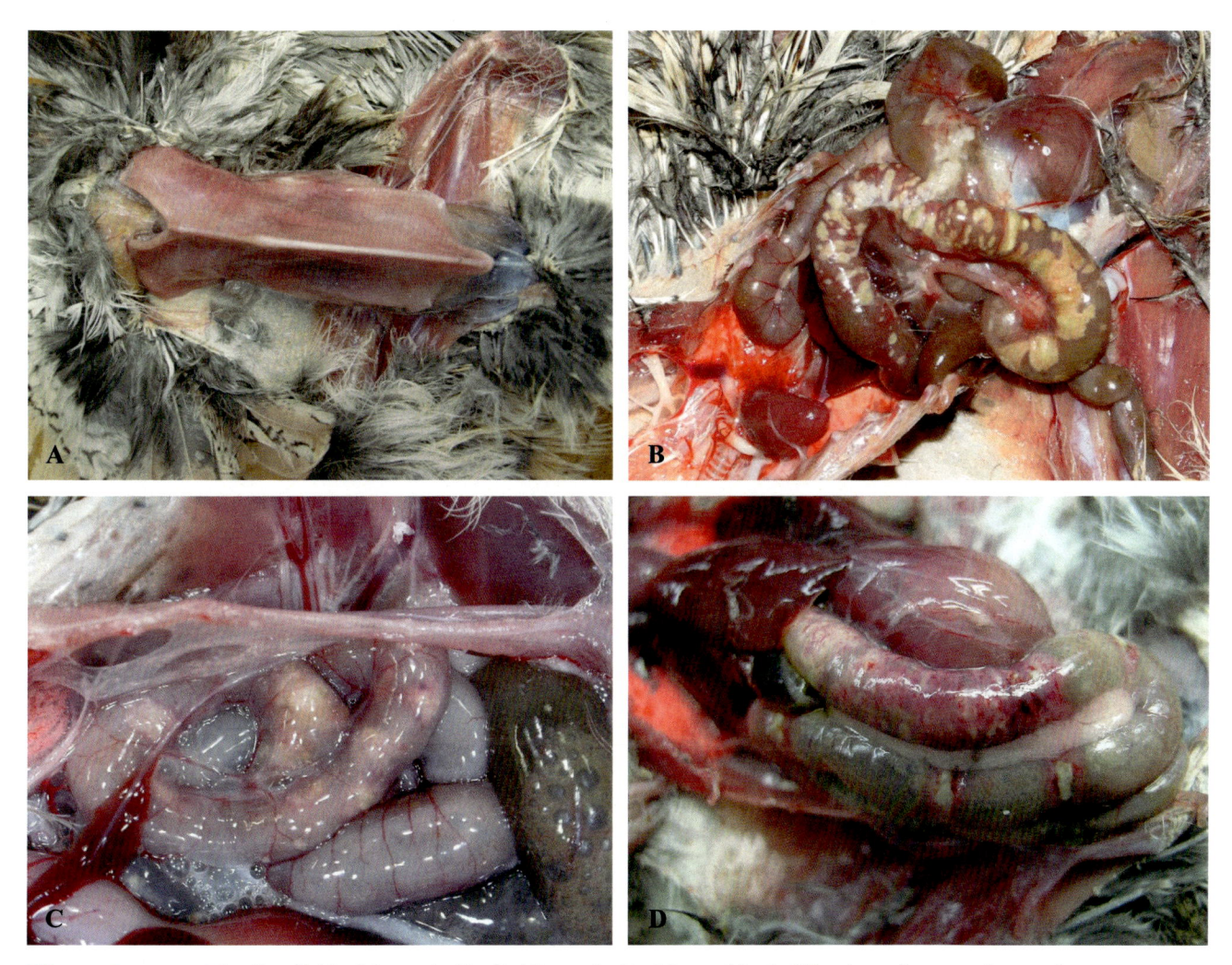

Ulcerative enteritis. Quail (A. 16-week. B, C. 10-week. D. 12-week). **A.** Wasting of pectoral muscles (emaciation). **B, C.** Mucosal ulcers in the jejunum and ileum are visible through the serosal surface. In **C**, the gray frothy exudate around the intestine indicates peritonitis. **D.** Discrete and confluent deep ulcers are in the wall of duodenum.

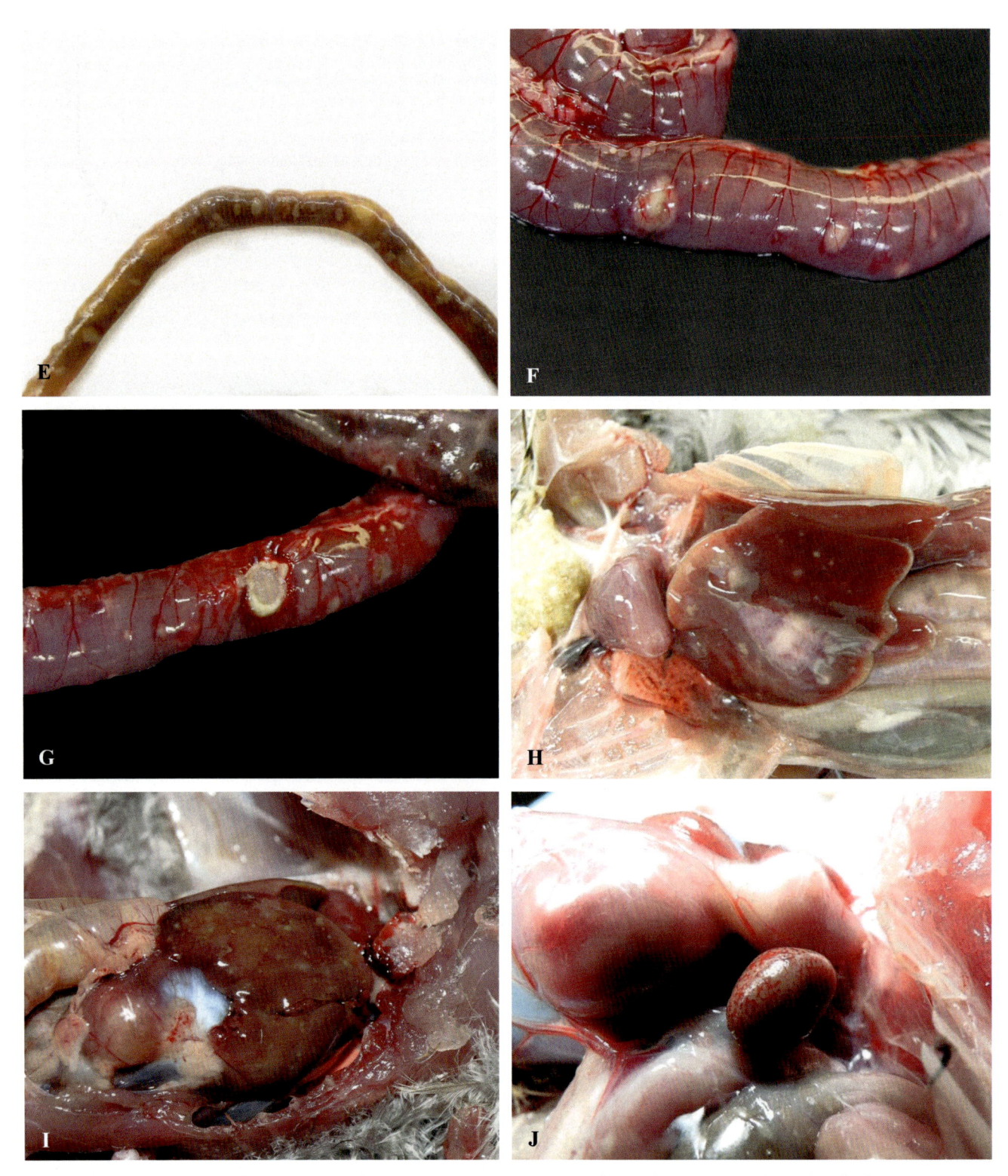

Ulcerative enteritis. Quail (E, J. 8-week. F, G. 20-week. H. 16-week. I. adult). **E, F.** Ulcerative lesions are seen through the serosal surface of the small intestine. **G.** Large perforating ulcer and several small, deep ulcers in the intestinal wall. **H, I.** Foci of necrosis in the liver. **J.** Spleen is enlarged and mottled brown and red.

Focal Duodenal Necrosis in Table-Egg Layers

Focal duodenal necrosis (FDN) is a recently recognized disease of table-egg laying chickens. The disease affects caged, cage-free, and organic flocks of white and brown strains of egg layers.

Cause. Cause of the disease is unknown, but type A *Clostridium perfringens* has been implicated.

Clinical signs. Peak egg production may be 2% to 3% below standard or flocks may show a post-peak drop of one to 10%. Affected flocks have reduced egg weight (as much as 2.5 grams per egg). Clinical signs may be absent or affected birds may have a pale comb and weight loss. Flock livability is not affected. Because clinical signs are vague and nonspecific, affected birds may not be detected, and the disease is probably under diagnosed. Birds from 15 weeks of age until the end of lay can be affected.

Gross lesions. Multiple patches of superficial mucosal necrosis (erosions) are present in the duodenum and less frequently the upper part of the jejunum. Severe lesions are visible as dark spots on the serosal surface. Lesions in the mucosa consist of red, green, gray-green, or brown-gray foci that vary in size from 3-15 mm and have an irregular outline. Some lesions may be covered with a yellow diphtheritic membrane. The duodenum often contains gas and may smell like rotten eggs. Contents of the duodenum are usually green to pale brown.

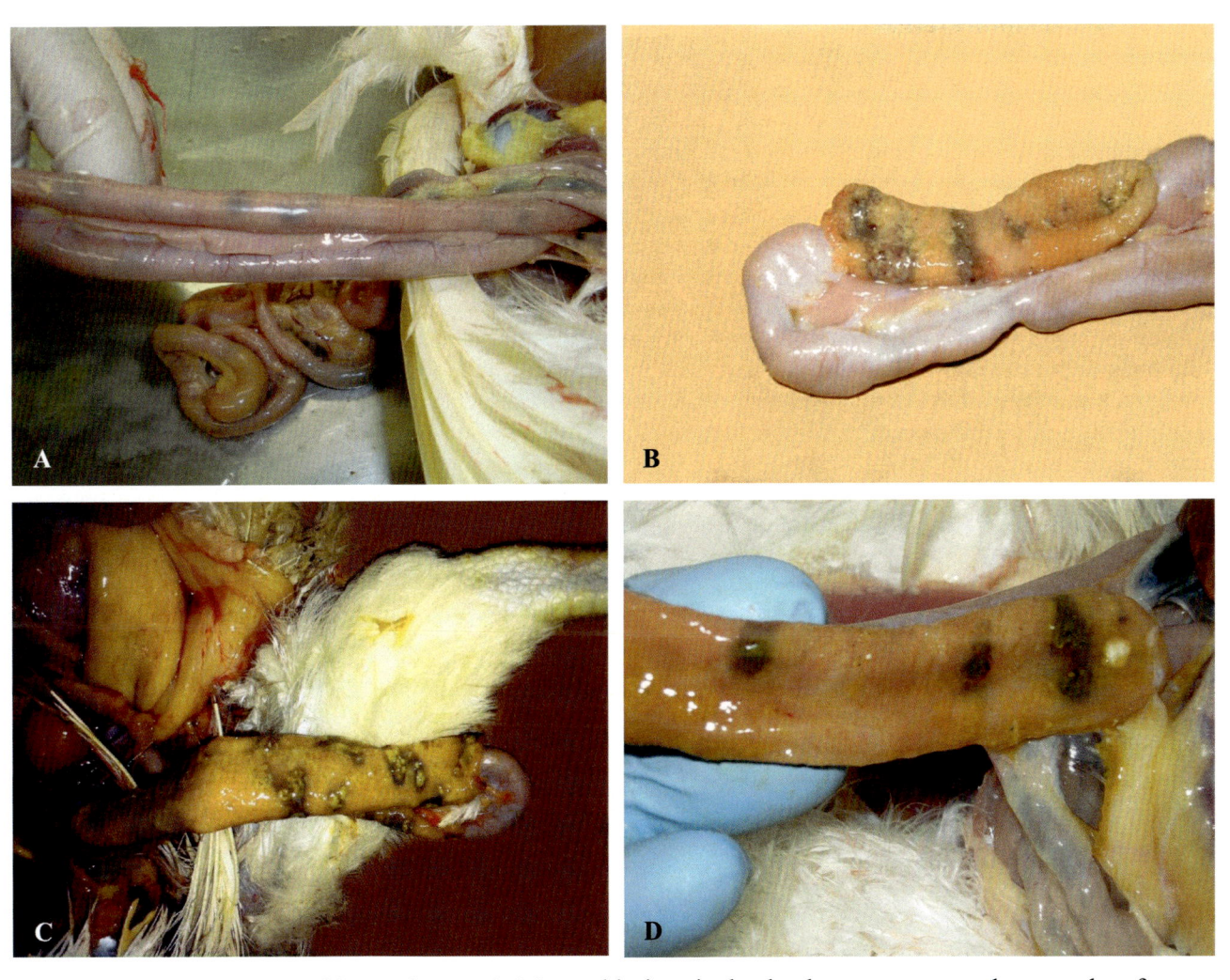

Focal duodenal necrosis. Table-egg layers. **A.** Mucosal lesions in the duodenum appear on the serosal surface as dark spots. **B, C, D.** Surface of the duodenal mucosa has multiple foci of necrosis. Note the color and shape of the foci. In **C**, necrotic patches are covered with yellow diphtheritic membranes. *(Photos courtesy of Dr. Eric Gingerich, USA).*

Avian Mycobacteriosis

Avian mycobacteriosis has a worldwide distribution and affects all species of birds and any organ system. Previously referred to as "tuberculosis", the term mycobacteriosis is preferred as infections in birds are rarely caused by *Mycobacterium tuberculosis* and to avoid confusion with tuberculosis in people. Diagnosis is confirmed by demonstrating acid-fast bacteria in granulomatous lesions that are not mineralized and may or may not be caseated, or by molecular methods. Culture and identification for some mycobacteria are possible but require special procedures. Classic tubercles are not formed in birds.

Cause. *Mycobacterium avium* subsp. *avium* is the most common cause of mycobacteriosis in small poultry flocks. Mycobacteriosis in commercial, intensively-reared poultry is extremely rare. In companion birds and zoological collections, mycobacteriosis is usually caused by *M. genavense.* Infrequently, other mycobacterial species, including *M. tuberculosis*, infect birds. *Mycobacterium avium* and *M. intracellulare* are so closely related that they can only be distinguished by molecular methods. Often the organisms are grouped together and simply referred to as the *M. avium-intracellulare* complex (MAIC). Four subspecies of *M. avium* (*M. avium* subsp. *avium*, *M. avium* subsp. *silvaticum*, *M. avium* subsp. *paratuberculosis*, and *M. avium* subsp. *hominissuis*) are recognized by nucleic acid hybridization and growth characteristics.

Gross lesions. Affected birds are older as the disease develops slowly. Typically, they are in poor body condition being thin to emaciated. There is marked atrophy of skeletal muscles, particularly pectoral muscles, and absence of subcutaneous and visceral fat. Occasionally granulomatous lesions occur as tumor-like nodules in the skin and subcutaneous tissues. Cutaneous lesions may occur anywhere, but are most often located near the eye. Retrobulbar lesions cause proptosis of the eye. Internally, gross lesions of mycobacteriosis are variable and depend on the species of bird and route of entry (ingestion or inhalation). A lesion pattern characteristic of mycobacteriosis is the presence of discrete white, gray, yellow, or tan nodules of various sizes in multiple organs and tissues. Liver, spleen, lung, intestinal wall, air sacs, mesentery, and bone marrow are frequent sites for lesions. In the intestine, nodules usually protrude from the serosal surface and may have the appearance of a tumor-like mass. Lack of uniformity with possible necrotic areas on the cut surface helps differentiate granulomas from tumors. In the liver, spleen, and lung, nodules are either slightly raised above the surface or embedded in the parenchyma. In severe cases, most of the liver and spleen parenchyma is replaced by multifocal to coalescing yellow or white-to-tan variably sized nodules. In some avian species, most notably psittacines, canaries, and finches, lesions in the liver, spleen, and intestine are usually diffuse rather than nodular, and mycobacteriosis may not be suspected initially. With such lesions, the liver appears enlarged and is either diffusely pale white or mottled with numerous tan-brown or pale-white miliary foci. The spleen may be mildly to markedly enlarged and either diffusely pale or mottled with pale foci. Regionally diffuse lesions in the intestinal wall cause tubular thickening of the affected segment of the intestine. Miliary foci along the intestinal mucosa represent the gross appearance of villi greatly expanded by macrophages and giant cells that contain acid-fast bacteria. This form of avian mycobacteriosis is referred to as the acute or fulminant form of the disease. Gray-cheeked parakeets (*Brotogeris pyrrhopterus*) are especially prone to fulminant mycobacteriosis, which may affect young birds only a few months old.

Lesions caused by *Mycobacterium* sp. occur in other organs and tissues, including heart, upper digestive tract, gonads, oviduct, skeletal muscle, and nasal sinus. In some sites, such as thoracic inlet, air sacs, and heart, nodules may appear as a large, irregular mass resembling a tumor.

Amyloidosis can accompany mycobacteriosis. Liver and spleen are diffusely enlarged, pale, firm, and have a waxy appearance, especially on cut surfaces. Granulomas of mycobacteriosis are also usually present in the affected tissues.

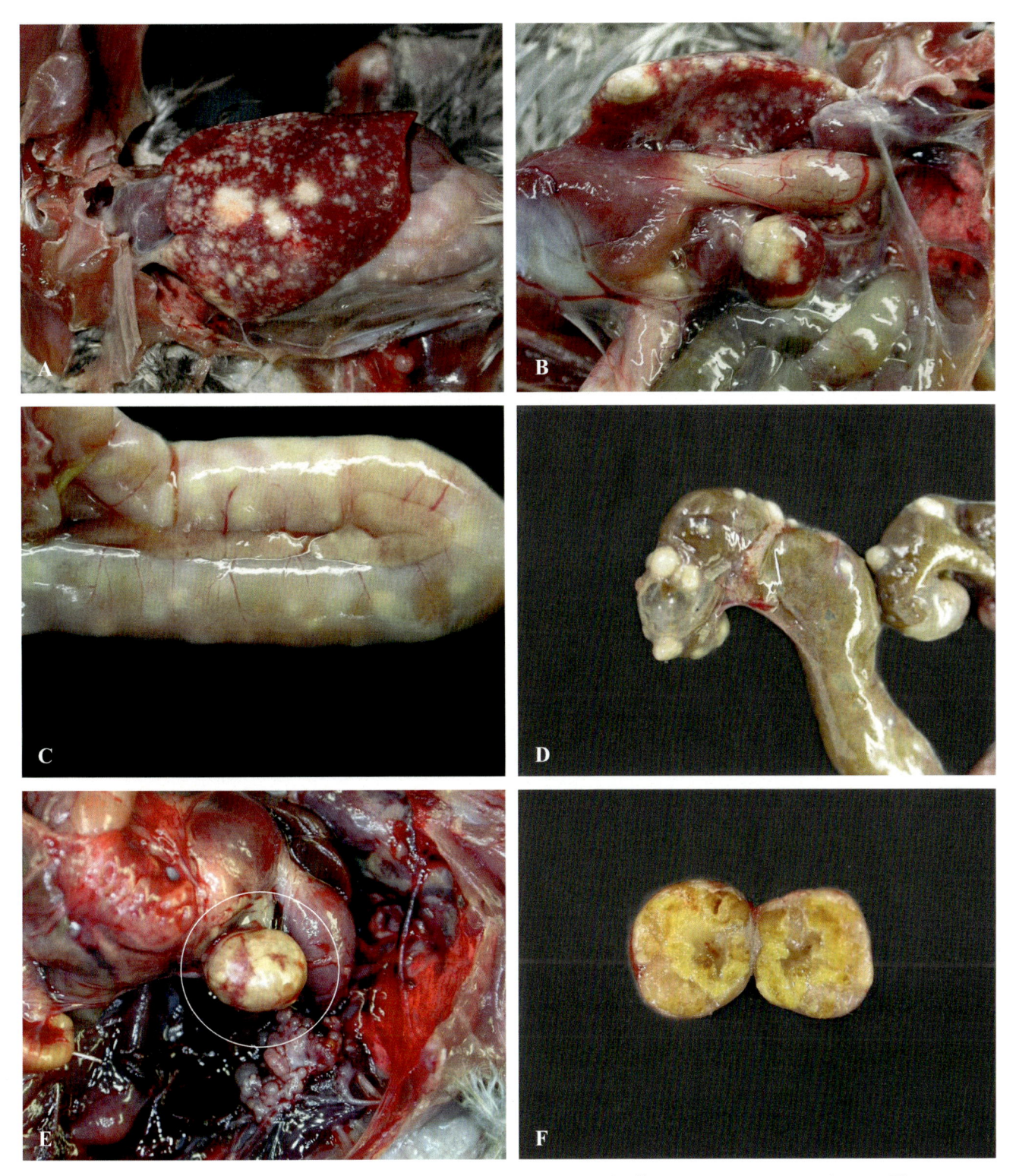

Mycobacteriosis. A-D. 6.5-year quail. **A.** Numerous white areas in the liver are caseous granulomas. These are either embedded in the parenchyma or slightly raised above the surface of the liver. **B.** The pale-yellow area in the spleen is a large caseous granuloma. **C.** Several white subserosal nodules visible through the serosal surface of the duodenum are caseous granulomas in the intestinal wall. **D.** White nodule in the cecal wall at the tips of the ceca. **E, F.** 3-year quail. **E.** Spleen (circle) is almost totally replaced by caseous material. **F.** Cross section of the spleen in E showing large areas of caseous necrosis. There is no mineralization.

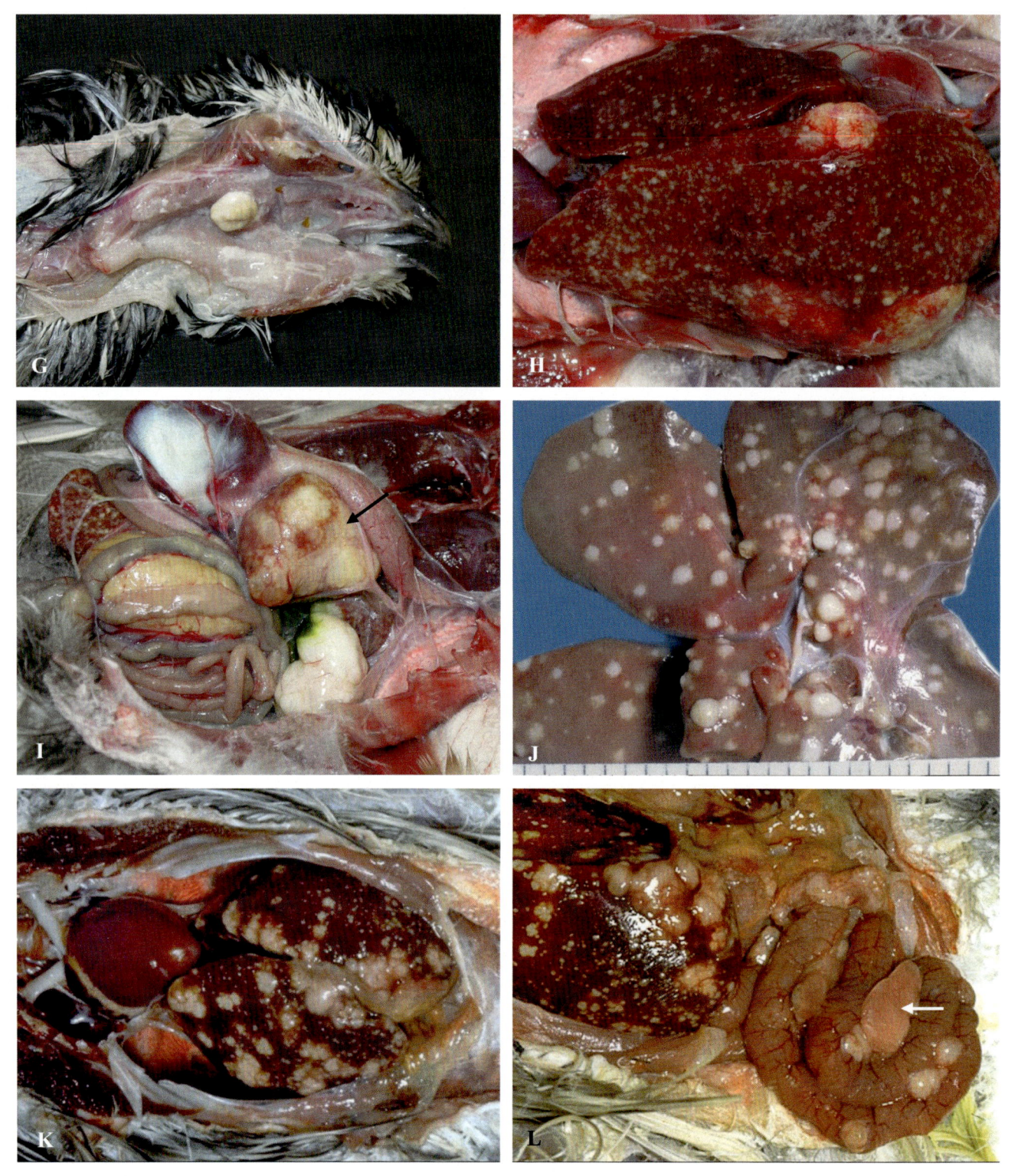

Mycobacteriosis. G. 3-year quail. Caseous nodule in the oropharynx. Mycobacteriosis was confirmed by histopathology. **H, I.** Duck. **H.** Liver is enlarged and has two caseous nodules and numerous, nearly confluent yellow foci that are either embedded in the parenchyma or slightly raised above the surface. **I.** Spleen is replaced by a large caseous mass with nodular surface (arrow). Note compression of the adjacent proventriculus by the mass. **J.** Chicken. Numerous white nodules protrude from the liver surface. Lesions resemble lymphoid tumors but are granulomas. **K, L.** Adult falcon. **K.** Multifocal, white, variably sized nodules and spots on the liver surface. These nodules and spots are caseous granulomas with large numbers of acid-fast bacilli detected on histopathology. **L.** Nodules on the serosal surface of the duodenum. Arrow: pancreas.

Mycoplasma gallisepticum Infection in Turkeys (Infectious Sinusitis)

Mycoplasma gallisepticum causes sinusitis in turkeys. Infrequently, *M. synoviae* also can cause sinusitis. Infectious sinusitis is characterized by facial swelling, usually bilateral, below and anterior to the eyes due to accumulation of exudate in the infraorbital sinuses. Infection of the sinuses causes inflammation of the sinus mucosa and hypersecretion of mucus. Exudate is usually mucoid and somewhat gray and opaque, but if the mycoplasmal infection is complicated by bacteria, it becomes thick and yellow. Sinus swelling may be severe enough to cause closure of the eyes. There is nasal discharge, dry, crusty material in the nostrils and on the skin around them, and dried exudate on the shoulder feathers on the same side as the swollen sinuses. Pressure on the swollen sinus will force exudate out of the nostril and choana, which helps differentiate a sinus distended by trapped air from one that is inflamed and filled with exudate.

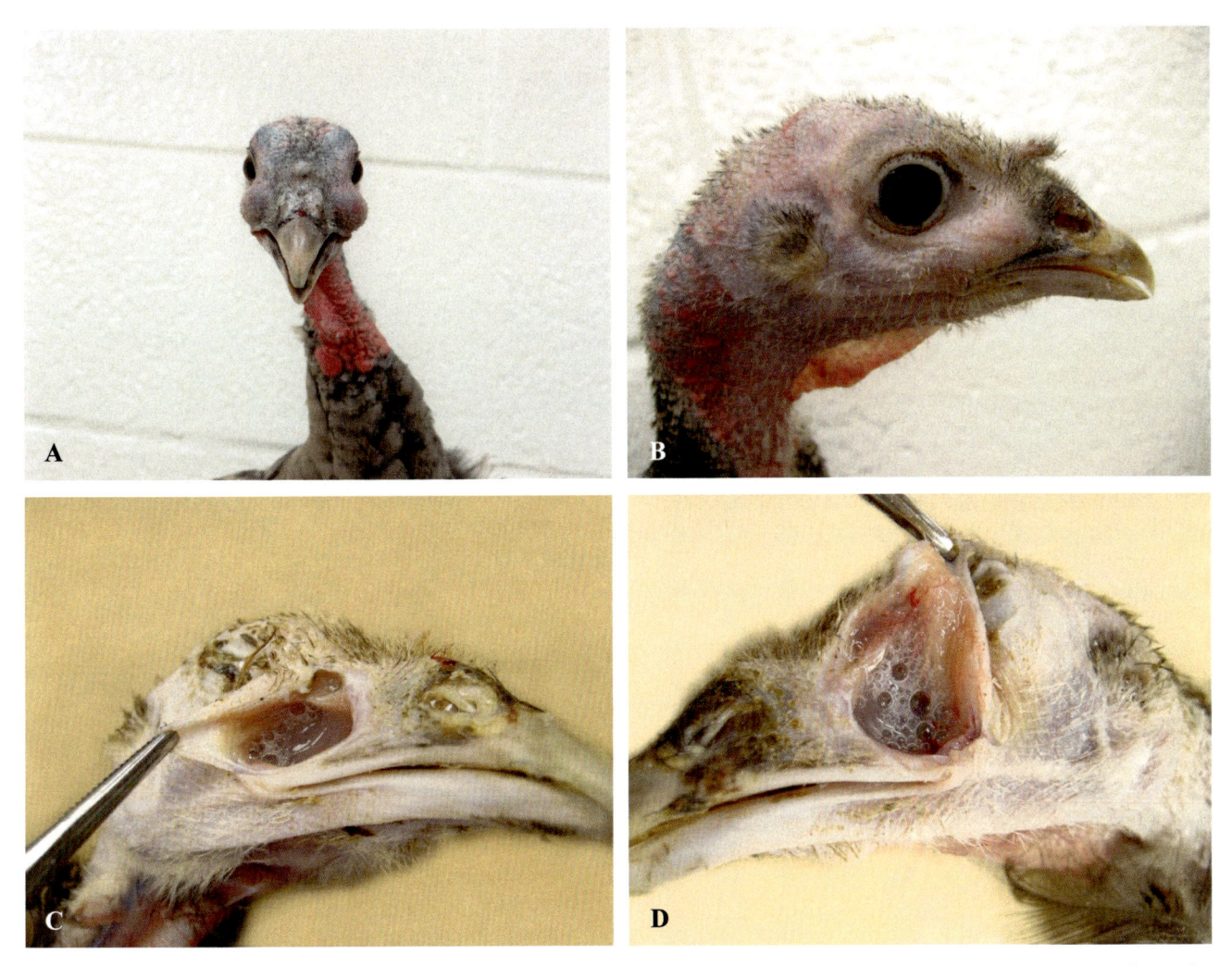

***Mycoplasma gallisepticum* infection (Infectious Sinusitis) in turkeys.** **A.** 6-month turkey. Bilateral swelling of the infraorbital sinuses results in facial swelling beneath the eyes. **B, C, D.** 3-month turkey. **B.** Swelling of the infraorbital sinus results in facial swelling below and anterior the eye. **C, D.** Mucoid, frothy, gray, somewhat opaque exudate in the infraorbital sinuses.

Mycoplasma gallisepticum Infection in Hobby Chickens

Clinical signs and gross lesions. Clinical signs and gross lesions vary in severity. Tracheal respiratory sounds (gurgling, rales, etc.) are heard when the affected bird is breathing. Difficult breathing (dyspnea), facial (sinus) and eyelid swelling, conjunctivitis, excessive lacrimation, and nasal and ocular discharges are seen in infected birds. One or both eyes may be partially closed or completely shut. In severe cases, eyelids are sealed shut. Dry, crusty material adheres to the feathers and skin around the eyes and to the feathers on the shoulders where the birds wipe their faces. Secondary bacterial infection of nasal sinuses results in more severe facial swelling, with accumulation of caseous material in one or both sinuses. On postmortem examination, the tracheal mucosa may be thickened and dull, and clear mucus or yellowish mucoid material is often found in the tracheal lumen. Sinusitis in hobby chickens can also be caused by *Pasteurella* (fowl cholera) or *Avibacterium* (infectious coryza). Cultures help differentiate the diseases, however, concurrent mycoplasmal and bacterial infections can occur.

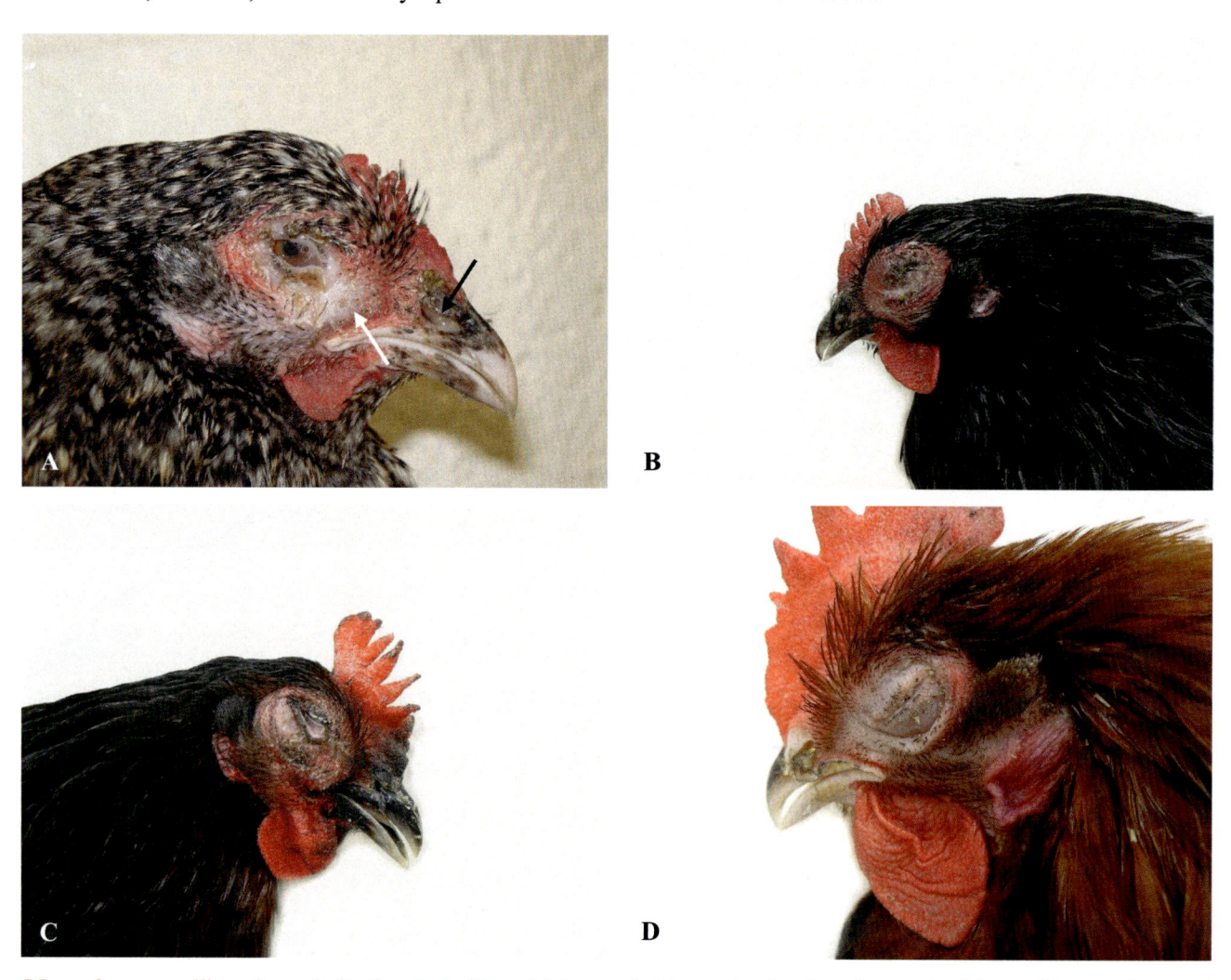

Mycoplasma gallisepticum **infection in hobby chickens. A.** Excessive lacrimation and mild swelling of the nasal sinus (white arrow). Mucoid material is in the nostril (nasal discharge) (black arrow). **B.** Eyelids are completely sealed shut and face is swollen. Dry, crusty material sticks to the skin around the eye. **C.** Excessive lacrimation is evident, face and eyelids are swollen, and eye is partially closed. **D.** Eyelids are swollen and closed.

Mycoplasma synoviae Infection

Only one serotype of *Mycoplasma synoviae* (MS) is recognized, but there is considerable variation among isolates in tissue tropism, pathogenicity, and virulence. Arthrotropic strains cause "infectious synovitis" in chickens and turkeys. Other strains have a tropism for the respiratory tract and cause airsacculitis. Some strains have a tropism for the oviduct (salpingotropic strains). Strains isolated from air sac lesions are more likely to cause airsacculitis, while strains isolated from synovitis lesion are more likely to cause synovial lesions.

Gross lesions.
Infectious synovitis. The disease is characterized by infection of the synovium of appendicular joints and tendon sheaths. Hock joints and gastrocnemius and digital flexor tendons are most commonly involved, but lesions may occur in other joints. Clinical signs in affected birds include lameness and swelling of hock joints and foot pads. On post-mortem examination, viscous creamy to gray exudate is present in the hock joint and around the gastrocnemius and digital flexor tendons. There is edema of soft tissues around the joint and tendons. Exudate is caseous in chronic cases. The sternal (keel) bursa may be infected, resulting in inflammation, accumulation of yellow exudate in the bursal lumen, and thickening of the bursal wall. In chronic cases, the gastrocnemius tendon becomes thickened, fibrotic, and may rupture. The main differential diagnosis is reoviral tenosynovitis.

Respiratory disease. In chickens and turkeys, infection of the upper respiratory tract (trachea and nasal sinuses) is usually asymptomatic. Air sac lesions caused by MS vary in severity, depending on the strain and presence or absence of concomitant infection with viruses or bacteria. MS by itself generally causes only mild airsacculitis. However, more severe air sac lesions are seen when there is coinfection with respiratory viruses, particularly field or vaccine strains of infectious bronchitis virus or avian paramyxovirus type 1. Poor air quality and cold temperatures exacerbate air sac lesions. Secondary *Escherichia coli* infections can result in severe fibrinoheterophilic airsacculitis, mortality due to septicemia, and increased condemnations at processing. Rarely, swollen sinuses containing mucoid exudate occurs in infected turkeys. The combination of a few turkeys with swollen sinuses and several birds with swollen feet is highly suggestive of MS infection.

Eggshell apex abnormalities. Certain strains of MS have a tropism for the oviduct. Infection results in the production of eggs with abnormal shells at the apex (wide end) of the egg. So far, the condition has been seen in white and brown table-egg layers. Shell abnormalities are confined to a circular area extending approximately 2 cm from the apex. The shell in the affected region is roughened, dark, thin, semi-translucent, and sharply demarcated from the normal part of the shell. The abnormal shell is prone to cracks and breakage. The percentage of affected eggs may reach 25%. After onset, production of eggs with defective shells continues throughout the production cycle. Economic losses result from downgrading and breakage of affected eggs at the farm and egg packaging station. Scanning electron microscopy of the abnormal shell has identified an absence of the mammillary knob layer and part of the palisade layer.

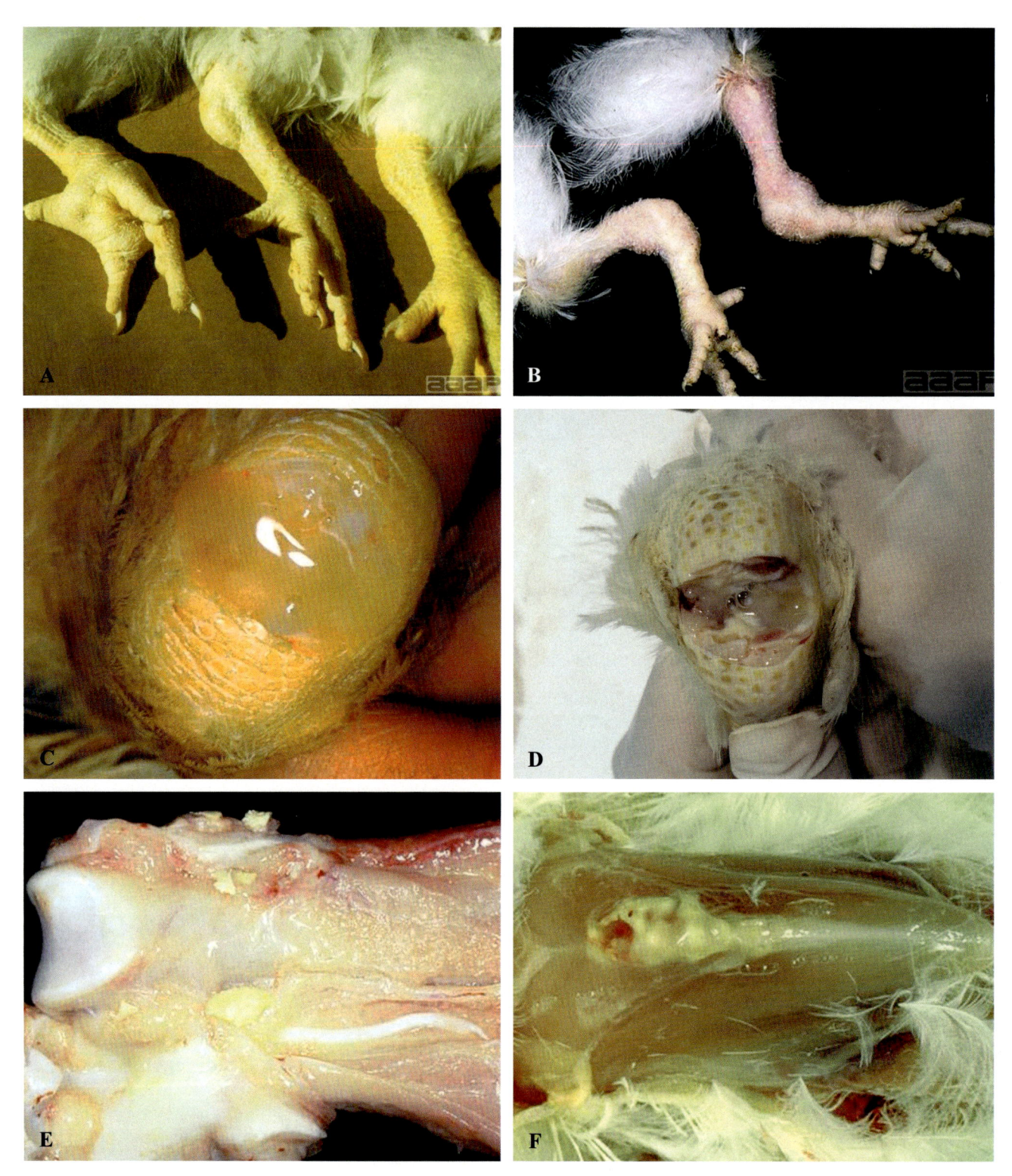

Synovitis caused by *Mycoplasma synoviae*. **A.** Chicken. Swelling of footpads is a characteristic lesion of *M. synoviae* infection. **B.** Chicken. Swelling of joints, tendons, and foot pads due to inflammation of synovial membranes. **C, D.** Chicken. Hock joint is swollen and contains viscous, yellow-gray exudate. **E.** Turkey. Caseous material around leg tendons due to tenosynovitis. Surrounding tissues are edematous. **F.** Turkey. Exudate in the sternal bursa (sternal bursitis). *(Photos A, B, C, E, F courtesy of AAAP. Photo D courtesy of Dr. Salvatore Catania, Italy).*

Eggshell apex abnormalities caused by salpingotropic *Mycoplasma synoviae*. G-K. Brown-egg layers. Circular, dark, roughened, well-demarcated areas extend from the apex of the egg. The area is thin and prone to cracks and breakage. *(Photos courtesy of Dr. Salvatore Catania, Italy).*

Mycoplasma iowae Infection

Mycoplasma iowae consists of a number of different mycoplasma strains that infect primarily turkeys and are vertically transmitted. Decreased hatchability due to late embryo mortality has been the characteristic manifestation of infection, but that is rarely seen today. Current strains have been associated with a low incidence of skeletal and joint lesions in poults including chondrodystrophy, vertebral and leg deformities, and tenosynovitis. The extent to which *M. iowae* contributes to these lesions is largely unknown. Lack of information about the prevalence and economic significance of the organism makes it difficult to determine if the expense and effort necessary to eradicate *M. iowae* from turkey breeders is justified.

Host. Turkeys are the primary natural host of *M. iowae*, although occasional isolations have been made from chickens, geese, Amazon parrots, and wild and exotic birds. Clinical disease associated with *M. iowae* infection occurs in Grey partridge. Pathogenicity of *M. iowae* for turkeys is well established, but little is known about its significance at the commercial production level, or in chickens and other birds.

Transmission. *Mycoplasma iowae* is vertically transmitted (i.e., infected turkey hens pass the organism through eggs to poults). The oviduct is the primary site of infection, although it also has been found in the ovary, cloaca, and phallus. Following experimental infection of breeder hens, most infected eggs are laid by only a few birds, while the majority of birds produce only a few infected eggs. The pattern of egg transmission in a naturally infected flock (*M. iowae*-positive flock) has been characterized as (1) most hens never transmit the organism, (2) a few hens lay one or 2 infected eggs, and (3) a small percentage of hens consistently lay infected eggs, usually producing several infected eggs in succession. Oviductal infection, egg transmission, and embryonic mortality decrease with time after the initial infection. During their second laying cycle, egg transmission is low. The number of microorganisms in infected embryos may also vary with the phase of transmission. Early and late in the transmission cycle, the burden of infection may be low, allowing infected embryos to hatch. Turkey embryos experimentally infected with a low dose of *M. iowae* hatched and were a source of infection for other poults.

Horizontal transmission among poults may occur in the hatchery. Because *M. iowae* is enterotropic, organisms are shed in the meconium, which can lead to oral infection. Venereal transmission is considered important for spreading *M. iowae* naturally. Turkey breeder hens inseminated with semen from toms infected with *M. iowae* produce infected embryos that fail to hatch. Although infected toms can infect clean hens, hen to hen infection during artificial insemination may be the most important means by which *M. iowae* infection spreads within the flock. Horizontal transmission from hen to hen can occur either directly or indirectly through the hands of the insemination crew. Before the start of egg production and artificial insemination, only a few birds in the flock may be *M. iowae*-positive, but following artificial insemination, most hens in the flock become positive. It has been suggested that horizontal transmission among hens is necessary, even essential, for maintenance of the infection of hens, thus ensuring egg-transmission and infection in successive generations.

Clinical disease and lesions. Embryonic mortality and poor poult quality are primary manifestations of vertical infection of turkeys with *M. iowae*. Embryos die during late incubation, typically between days 18 and 24. Decreased hatchability in affected turkey flocks averages 2% to 5%. Embryonic mortality and decreased hatchability due to *M. iowae* infection can vary widely from minimal to significant and be of variable duration. Extent of hatchability loss depends on virulence of the *M. iowae* strain, rate of egg transmission (i.e., number of hens transmitting mycoplasmas into eggs), and dose of the organism. Other factors related to egg-incubation conditions may also influence the rate of embryonic mortality in hatches from *M. iowae*-positive flocks. There is evidence that high temperatures during incubation can exacerbate mortality of *M. iowae*-infected embryos. It is important to realize that considerable variation exists among *M. iowae* strains in their pathogenicity for turkey embryos. Some isolates are more embryo lethal, causing death of the embryo with marked lesions, particularly stunting and edema, while others have little to no effect on embryo viability.

Lesions in natural and experimental *M. iowae* infected embryos include stunting, edema (particularly around the head), hemorrhage, excess urates in ureters, poor feathering, abnormal feathers (clubbing of down), hepatomegaly, splenomegaly, and hemorrhage in the chorioallantoic membrane. Although airsacculitis has been described in culled day-old poults naturally infected with *M. iowae*, air sac lesions could not be convincingly attributed to *M. iowae*, as infection with other mycoplasmas, especially *M. meleagridis*, has not been ruled out. However, turkey poults inoculated directly into their air sacs with *M. iowae* develop lesions of varying severity. Histologically, there is exudative and cellular airsacculitis characterized by fibrinous exudate and infiltrates of heterophils and mononuclear inflammatory cells.

Different leg deformities have been described in poults naturally or experimentally infected with *M. iowae*. Chondrodystrophy (shortening and thickening of bones) is the most obvious lesion. *Mycoplasma iowae* has been isolated from cloacas, air sacs, and joints of 17-day commercial poults with leg problems that included chondrodystrophy, valgus deformity, excess clear fluid in joint cavities, curled toes, and splayed legs. *M. iowae* has been associated with chondrodystrophy in meat-type turkeys at 3 to 7 weeks of age. Birds with chondrodystrophic lesions constituted 17.3% of the culled birds and mortality in the flock. Poor growth and lameness were noted in affected birds.

Gross lesions of chondrodystrophy are characterized by deformities in bones of the legs and vertebral column including shortening, thickening, and bowing of tarsometatarsi (shank bones); enlarged hock joints; slight widening of the growth plate in proximal tibiotarsi; shortening of the vertebral column; marked deformity of the posterior segment of the thoracic vertebrae (due to deformity of the articulating thoracic vertebra and caudal articulation of the notarium); uneven spacing between ribs; and twisting (rotation) of the neck.

Experimentally, when day-old turkey poults were inoculated via air sacs and foot pads with *M. iowae*, poor feathering and uneven growth were apparent in some poults by the second week of age. From the second to third week of age, most of the inoculated poults showed one or more of the following skeletal abnormalities: chondrodystrophy, rotated tibia, splayed leg, deviated toes, excess fluid in joint cavities, pitted articular cartilage, and wrinkled, sigmoid folding, and/or ruptured digital flexor tendons. Excess joint fluid was the most common abnormality. Histologically, there was evidence of mild lymphocytic tenosynovitis in digital flexor tendons. Day-old poults that were inoculated orally with a strain of *M. iowae* showed only a mild clinical disease (poor feathering, slight growth depression) compared with poults inoculated via the air sacs and foot pads with the same strain. In the same study, most of 60 turkey embryos inoculated via yolk sac with *M. iowae* at 21 days of incubation failed to hatch. Those that did hatch exhibited weakness, poor growth, abnormal feathering, and poor appetite. Fourteen of the 18 poults that hatched died within the first week after hatching and 2 more poults died by 16 days of age. The two poults that survived into the third week developed chondrodystrophy. Chickens inoculated with strains of *M. iowae* into air sacs and foot pad at one day of age developed marked gross and histologic lesions in the digital flexor tendons.

Findings in naturally and experimentally infected poults indicate that *M. iowae* is most pathogenic for turkey embryos, and that skeletal deformities, particularly chondrodystrophy, occur only in poults infected in ovo or during the first few days after hatching. At a commercial level, *M. iowae* is not recognized as an important cause of tenosynovitis and leg deformities in turkeys (or chickens). Clinical disease, adverse effect on production, or lesions do not occur in mature hens and toms due to infection with *M. iowae*.

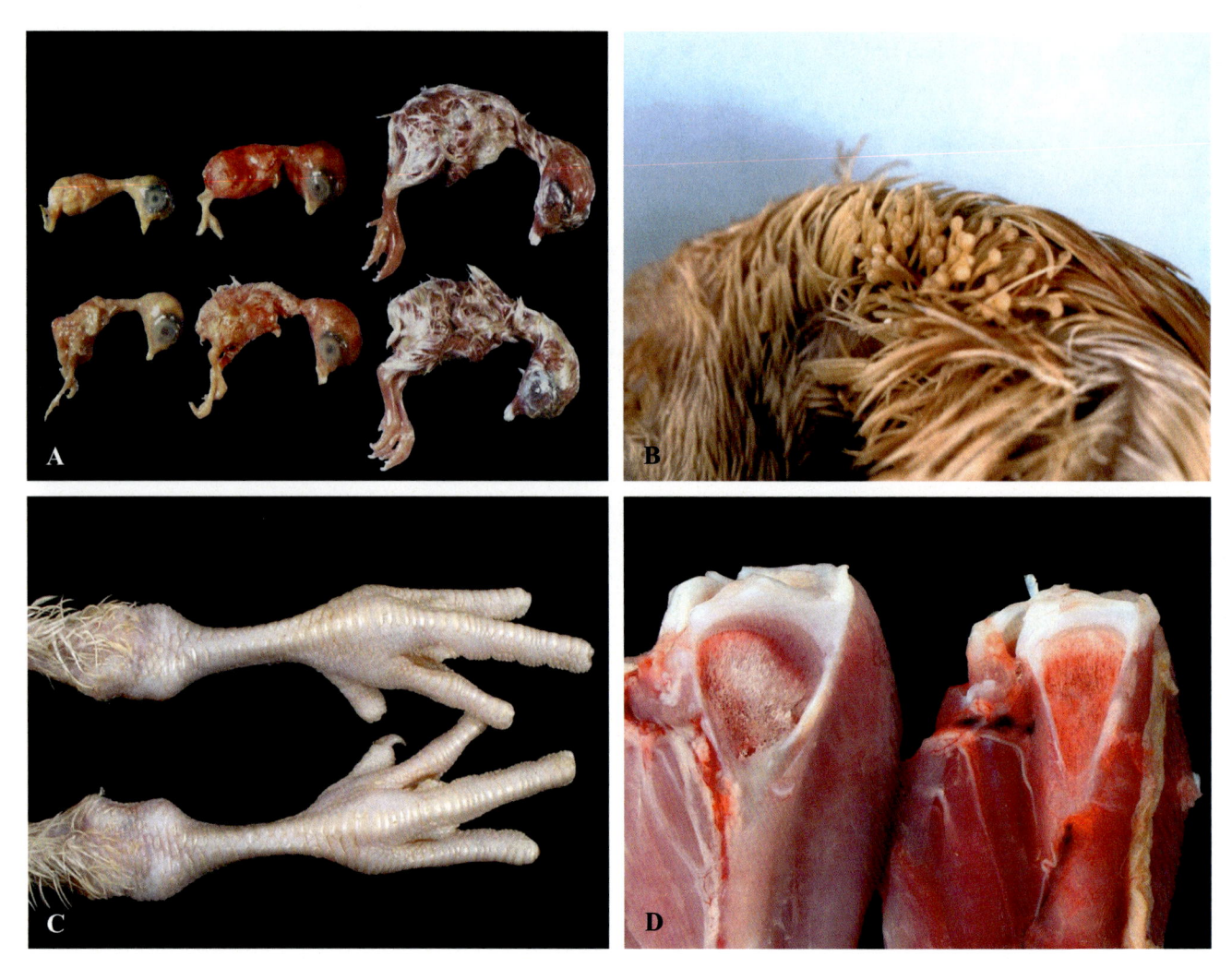

***Mycoplasma iowae* infection in turkeys.** **A.** Reduced hatchability due to late embryo mortality caused by *M. iowae*. **B.** Distended feather tips result in "clubbed down", a lesion often seen late in development or at hatching in *M. iowae* infected embryos. However, clubbed down is not specific for *M. iowae* infection. Other causes include high incubation temperatures and B-vitamin deficiencies. **C.** Chondrodystrophy. 18-day turkey. In chondrodystrophy, appositional growth exceeds longitudinal growth. Legs of chondrodystrophic poults are short, thick, and have prominent joints. Poults infected with *M. iowae* typically show chondrodystrophy, but not all poults with chondrodystrophy are infected with *M. iowae*. Other causes of this lesion include genetics, high incubator temperatures, and malnutrition. Bowing of legs or other angular deformities are often seen in chondrodystrophic limbs. **D.** Chondrodystrophy. 28-day turkey. Proximal tibiotarsus from a chondrodystrophic poult (left) is markedly thickened, has a "U" shape, and thickness of the growth plate is not uniform. In contrast, the proximal tibiotarsus from an unaffected bird (right) is uniform and has normal thickness, and the bone has a "V" shape. *(Photos A, B courtesy of Dr. Colin Baxter-Jones).*

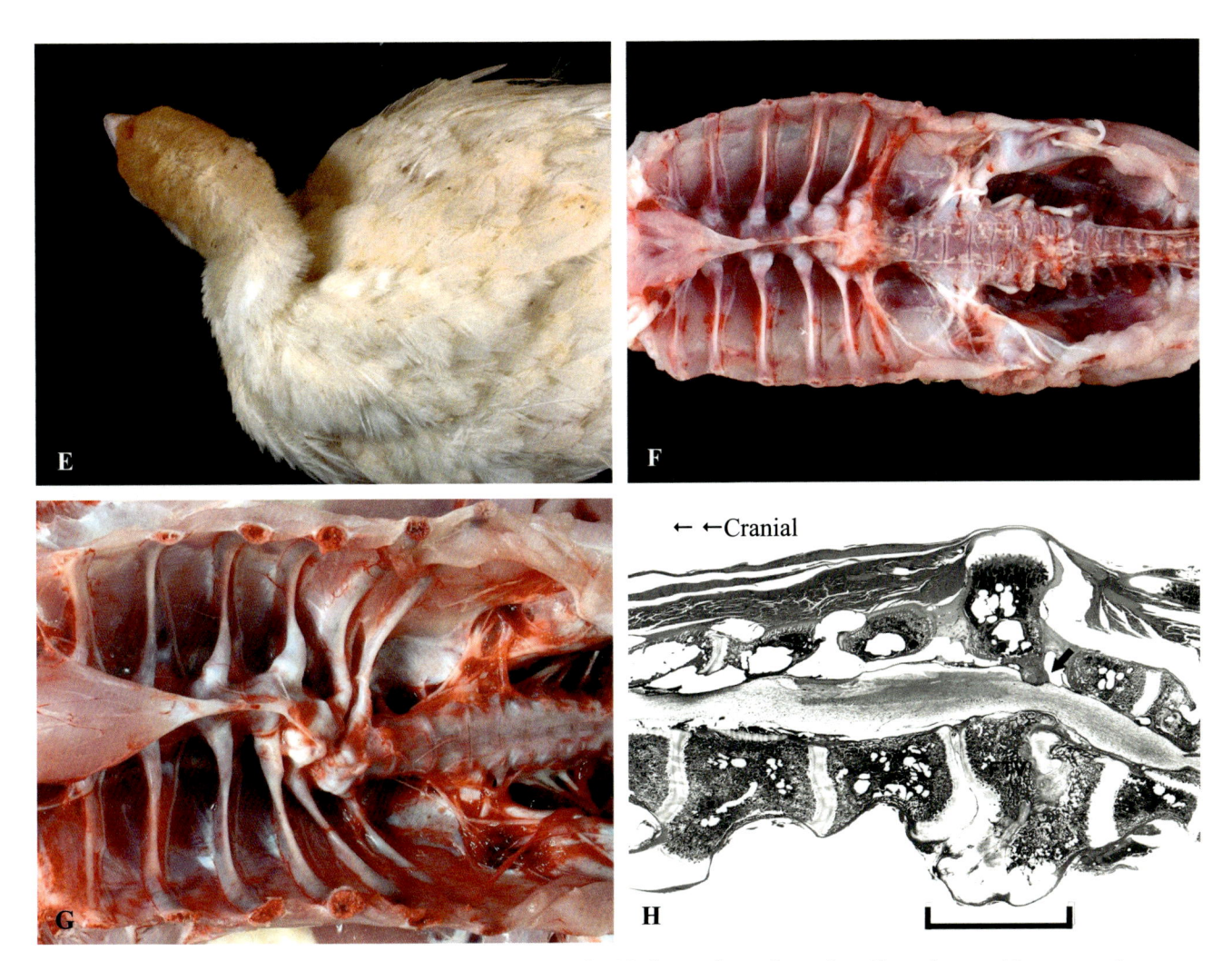

***Mycoplasma iowae* infection in turkeys. E.** Wry neck. 30-day turkey. Occasionally turkeys with wry neck occur in flocks with *M. iowae* infected birds. The neck is rotated and permanently held to one side. *M. iowae* has been isolated from intervertebral spaces in the affected part of the neck. **F.** Spinal chondrodystrophy. 28-day turkey. Chondrodystrophy of the spine is characterized by thickening and deformity of the free thoracic vertebra, which lies between the notarium cranially and synsacrum caudally. *M. iowae* can be isolated from the intervertebral joint spaces of a high percentage of these lesions. In contrast to chondrodystrophy of the legs, spinal chondrodystrophy is specific for *M. iowae* infection and is not known to have other causes. **G.** Spinal chondrodystrophy. 45-day turkey. Lesions of spinal chondrodystrophy likely persist for the life of the turkey. Typical lesions have been identified in 18-week tom turkeys. How long *M. iowae* remains in the lesion is unknown. Severe deformity of the back can result in scoliosis as seen here. **H.** Spinal chondrodystrophy. 26-day turkey (left is cranial). In the spinal chondrodystrophic lesion (bracket), the free thoracic vertebra (FTV) and cranial vertebra of the synsacrum are markedly distorted and compressed. Masses of proliferating cartilage extend along the ventral vertebral body and fill the caudal articulation between the FTV and synsacrum. Cartilage forming the cranial articulation is mildly thickened. There is moderate kyphosis (arching of the spine) due to loss of bone in the vertebral bodies and the vertebral deformity has resulted in compression of the spinal cord (arrow).

Avian Chlamydiosis

Cause. *Chlamydia psittaci*. *Chlamydia* is a Gram-negative, obligate, intracellular bacterium. According to a recent classification, *Chlamydia* is the only genus in the family *Chlamydiaceae*. Currently, there are 12 species in the genus. *C. psittaci*, the cause of avian chlamydiosis, is an important zoonotic organism. It has a worldwide distribution and wide range of avian hosts. Infections have been reported in most orders of birds. Infection is particularly frequent in wild Columbiformes (pigeons, doves). Among captive pet birds, infection is common in psittacines but infrequent in passerines. Information about the prevalence of *Chlamydia* infection in free-living birds of prey of prey is limited.

Based on sequencing and analysis of the outer membrane protein A (*ompA*) gene, *C. psittaci* can be divided into 7 avian genotypes (A to F and E/B) and 2 mammalian genotypes (M56 and WC). Certain genotypes tend to be predominant in certain types of birds (see table). Genotype A is predominantly found in psittacine and passerine birds. It is considered the major genotype in human infections. *C. psittaci* isolates from pigeons, doves, and passerines mainly belong to genotype B. Genotype C is associated with chlamydiosis in ducks and geese. Genotype D has been isolated most frequently from turkeys, seagulls, and budgerigars. However, zoonotic infection of processing plant employees from chickens infected with this serotype has occurred. Genotype E isolates are obtained from ratites and pigeons. Genotype F is rare, but has been isolated from psittacines and turkeys. Genotype E/B has been found mainly in ducks, but also affects pigeons and turkeys. The mammalian genotypes, M56 and WC, have been isolated from muskrats and hares (M56) and cases of enteritis in cattle (WC).

Chlamydia psittaci Genotypes Commonly Found in Different Types of Birds

Type of birds	Genotype	Type of birds	Genotype
Columbiformes	B, E	Waterfowl	C, E/B
Psittacines	A	Turkeys	D
Passerines	A	Chickens	B
Ratites	E		

A new *Chlamydia* was detected for the first time in domestic poultry in France. Infection of chicken flocks with this *Chlamydia* has now been reported from several European countries, Australia, and China. The organism has been isolated from pigeons in Italy, France, and Germany. A *Chlamydia* species isolated from songbirds and waterfowl is closely related to the isolate from pigeons in France. Based on gene sequencing and analysis of 11 recent *Chlamydia* isolates from France, Germany, and Italy, two new *Chlamydia* species, *C. avium* and C. gallinacea have been proposed. *C. avium* comprises pigeon and psittacine strains, while *C. gallinacea* infects chickens, guinea fowl, turkeys, ducks, and probably other birds. The pathogenic and zoonotic potential of these *Chlamydia* species for birds and humans is uncertain. Mammalian species of *Chlamydia* are also occasionally isolated from birds.

Developmental cycle of *Chlamydia*. *Chlamydia* has a biphasic life cycle and is present in two forms: an infectious elementary body and a replicating, non-infectious reticulate body. When an elementary body contacts a susceptible cell, it attaches to a specific receptor on the cell membrane, enters the cell by endocytosis, and is enclosed within a membrane-bound compartment known as the inclusion. The elementary body undergoes exponential multiplication by binary fission in the cytoplasmic compartment and develops into a reticulate body. Some reticulate bodies transform back to elementary bodies, which are released from the cell by extrusion or cell lysis. These infect other cells or are shed into the environment and are transmitted to another host. Infection occurs through inhalation, digestion, or direct contact with an infected host. Vertical and trans-eggshell penetration infects embryos and newly hatched birds.

Asymptomatic infection. Asymptomatic infection in captive and wild birds is common and considered the normal *Chlamydia*-host relationship. Birds may remain infected for months or years without any clinical signs. The rate of subclinical infection varies among avian species and geographical location. Wild doves and pigeons are the major bird reservoir of *C. psittaci* across Europe. A high prevalence of asymptomatic infection has also been demonstrated in some wild passerines. Asymptomatic birds shed the organisms regularly or intermittently in droppings, nasal discharges, lacrimal fluid, and oropharyngeal mucus and are a potential source of infection for humans and other birds. Stress can trigger shedding of quiescent organisms. In feral pigeons, shedding in droppings is higher during the breeding season compared to the nonbreeding season. Different wild birds, e.g., gulls, herons, egrets, house sparrows, grackles, etc. are reservoirs of *C. psittaci*. High seropositive rates are found in birds of prey. *C. psittaci* strains in asymptomatically infected birds can be highly pathogenic for other birds and possibly humans.

Clinical signs and gross lesions in clinical disease.
Pigeons. Clinical signs include lethargy, anorexia, diarrhea, weight loss, nasal and ocular discharges, swelling of the eyelids, and conjunctivitis. There is fibrinous pericarditis, hepatic serositis, and airsacculitis. The liver and spleen may be enlarged and discolored. Airsacculitis may be the only lesion seen in some birds.

Ducks and geese. Chlamydiosis in ducks is usually severely debilitating and fatal. Ducklings exhibit anorexia, severe weight loss, trembling, and ataxia. There is watery green diarrhea and ocular and nasal exudation. Birds becomes emaciated and die. Clinical signs have been minimal or absent in some outbreaks in Australia and Europe.

Turkeys. Birds infected with virulent strains show clinical signs of anorexia, weight loss, respiratory distress, and yellow-green mucoid droppings, with severe drops in egg production in breeder flocks. Gross lesions include severe pneumonia; marked fibrinous pericarditis and airsacculitis; severe vascular congestion of mesenteric blood vessels; enlargement and discoloration of the liver; fibrinous hepatic serositis and peritonitis; enlargement, dark discoloration, and white mottling of the spleen. Pneumonia is more common in young turkeys than adult turkeys. Orchitis and epididymitis caused by *C. psittaci* affects toms.

Chickens. Chickens are generally resistant to infection with many strains of *C. psittaci*. Natural infection is usually subclinical and transient. However, clinical disease with pericarditis, hepatic serositis, and airsacculitis can occur.

Psittacine birds. The clinical manifestation of chlamydiosis in psittacine birds is quite variable. Birds may die acutely without premonitory clinical signs, or may show mild-to-severe lethargy accompanied by anorexia, muscle wasting, and weight loss. Soiling of feathers around the vent with yellow, yellow-orange, or green droppings is common in acute cases. Internally, the liver is usually enlarged and diffusely pale, green-brown, or orange-tan depending on the degree of hepatocellular degeneration and necrosis, lipidosis, vascular congestion, and bile stasis. Punctate to irregularly shaped necrotic foci that are usually light-yellow tan in color are seen in the liver. The spleen is frequently enlarged, firmer than normal, and dark red (congested) or gray-tan to light yellow-tan. Fibrinous exudate may be present in air sacs and on the epicardial surface of the heart, capsular surface of the liver, and other serosal surfaces. Enlarged kidneys with punctate white to yellow-tan foci are seen in some cases.

Zoonotic potential. Chlamydiosis caused by *C. psittaci* is a zoonotic disease. All genotypes should be considered potentially transmissible to humans and causes of disease. In humans, the disease is called psittacosis because infection is often attributed to direct or indirect contact with infected captive psittacines. However, poultry (particularly ducks), doves and pigeons, and wild and captive passerines also are potential sources of infection. Asymptomatic carriers or actively infected birds shed organisms in the droppings and respiratory secretions. Zoonotic transmission usually occurs through inhalation of aerosolized organisms. People should take hygienic precautions when handling sick or dead wild birds and when cleaning wild bird feeders. Areas heavily contaminated with wild bird droppings need to be thoroughly wet before cleaning to minimize aerosolization and inhalation of infective material. Infection in humans ranges from inapparent to mild flu-like symptoms (fever, chills, headache, muscle aches, malaise, and dry cough) to severe pneumonia with dyspnea. Complications include myocarditis, pericarditis, and endocarditis.

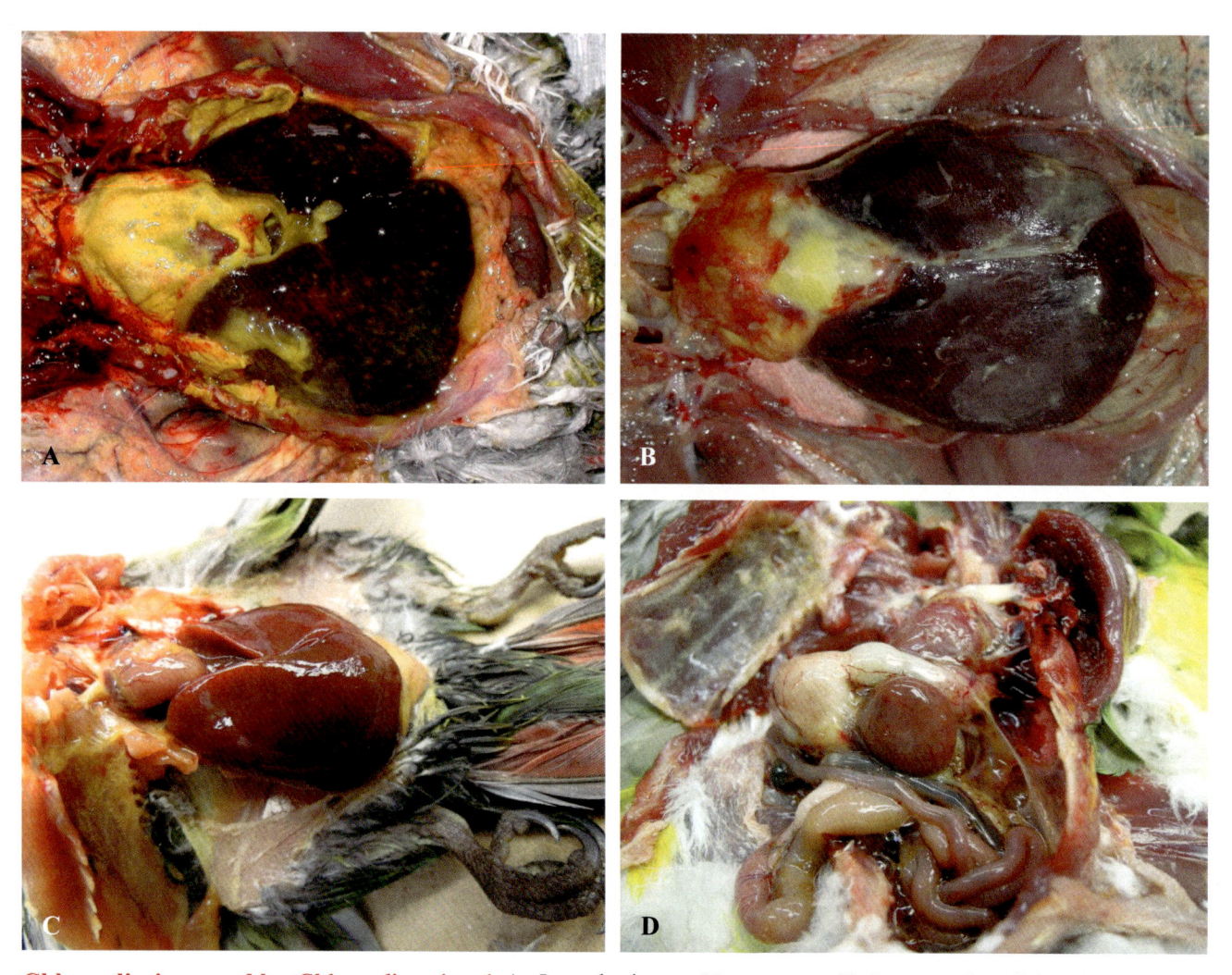

Chlamydiosis caused by *Chlamydia psittaci*. A. 5-week pigeon. Very severe fibrinous pericarditis. Liver is enlarged, discolored, and has numerous yellow foci representing areas of necrosis. **B.** Pigeon. Very severe pericarditis and hepatic serositis. **C.** 2-month green-cheeked conure. Liver is markedly enlarged and has an enhanced reticular pattern. **D.** 16-year Senegal parrot. Marked enlargement of the spleen. In **A**, **C**, and **D**, chlamydiosis was confirmed by an antigen-capture ELISA. In **D**, chlamydiosis was confirmed by PCR. *(Photo B courtesy of Dr. Peter Wencel, Poland).*

Newcastle Disease in Chickens

Cause. Newcastle disease (ND) is caused by a paramyxovirus in the family *Paramyxoviridae* (Order *Mononegavirales* → Family *Paramyxoviridae* → Genus *Avulavirus* → Species *Newcastle disease virus* [NDV]). There are 12 serotypes of avian paramyxoviruses designated APMV-1 to APMV-12. Newcastle disease is caused by virulent strains of APMV-1. Previously these strains were designated as velogenic or mesogenic and had tropisms for either visceral organs or the nervous system. Infections with mild strains, previously designated as lentogenic viruses, are no longer called Newcastle disease, but are referred to as APMV-1 infection. Mild strains have a tropism for the respiratory system. In the US, Newcastle disease is called Exotic Newcastle disease, as virulent APMV-1 strains are not present whereas mild APMV-1 strains are endemic. Ranikhet disease is the name used in India for ND. ND occurs in many parts of the world, especially developing regions, where it causes devastating losses, especially small poultry flock owners. ND, along with highly pathogenic avian influenza, is one of the most important diseases of poultry worldwide.

Clinical signs. ND appears suddenly and spreads rapidly through the flock. Affected birds initially exhibit dullness followed by severe depression, rapid respiration, weakness, and prostration. Profuse watery, green, or bloody diarrhea is a common feature. Edema of the face and neck, corneal edema, hemorrhage of conjunctival-associated lymphoid tissue, and multifocal mucosal hemorrhage and necrosis in the cloaca are common clinical signs. Birds surviving the acute stage of the disease often develop neurologic signs characterized by torticollis and opisthotonos. Mortality is usually greater than 90% in unvaccinated flocks. Very severe drops in egg production and thin-shelled eggs occur in laying hens.

Gross Lesions. Hemorrhages in the mucosa of the proventriculus and necrohemorrhagic and ulcerative lesions in the intestinal mucosa are characteristic ND lesions. Proventricular hemorrhages are either diffuse, involving the papillae, or at the junctions with the esophagus and gizzard. Intestinal lesions occur primarily in gut-associated lymphoid tissues, including Peyer's patches and cecal tonsils. Depending on the stage of the disease, lesions in the intestine may be hemorrhages, necrotic foci, bleeding ulcers, ulcers covered with diphtheritic membranes, or ulcers filled with necrotic debris. Lesions seen less frequently include hemorrhages in the gizzard mucosa beneath the koilin, multifocal necrosis and hemorrhage in the cloaca, necrotic foci in the colorectum and cloaca, and petechial hemorrhages in subcutaneous tissues, myocardium, and coronary and mesenteric fat. Tracheal lesions are not consistently seen, but consist of hemorrhagic tracheitis or frothy exudate in the tracheal lumen. Other lesions include hemorrhage and necrosis of conjunctival-associated lymphoid tissue in the conjunctivae of the lower eyelids, corneal edema, peritracheal edema (especially at the thoracic inlet), hemorrhages in the proventriculus and gizzard serosa, and mottling of serosal and cut surfaces of the spleen with necrotic foci. In laying hens, there is acute ovarian regression, hemorrhages in follicles (especially in the stigmata), and watery yolk in the body cavity.

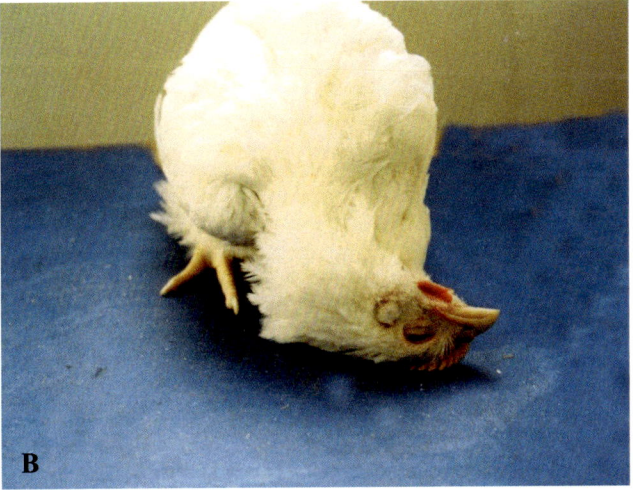

Newcastle disease. A, B. Torticollis and opisthotonos in chickens that survived the infection.

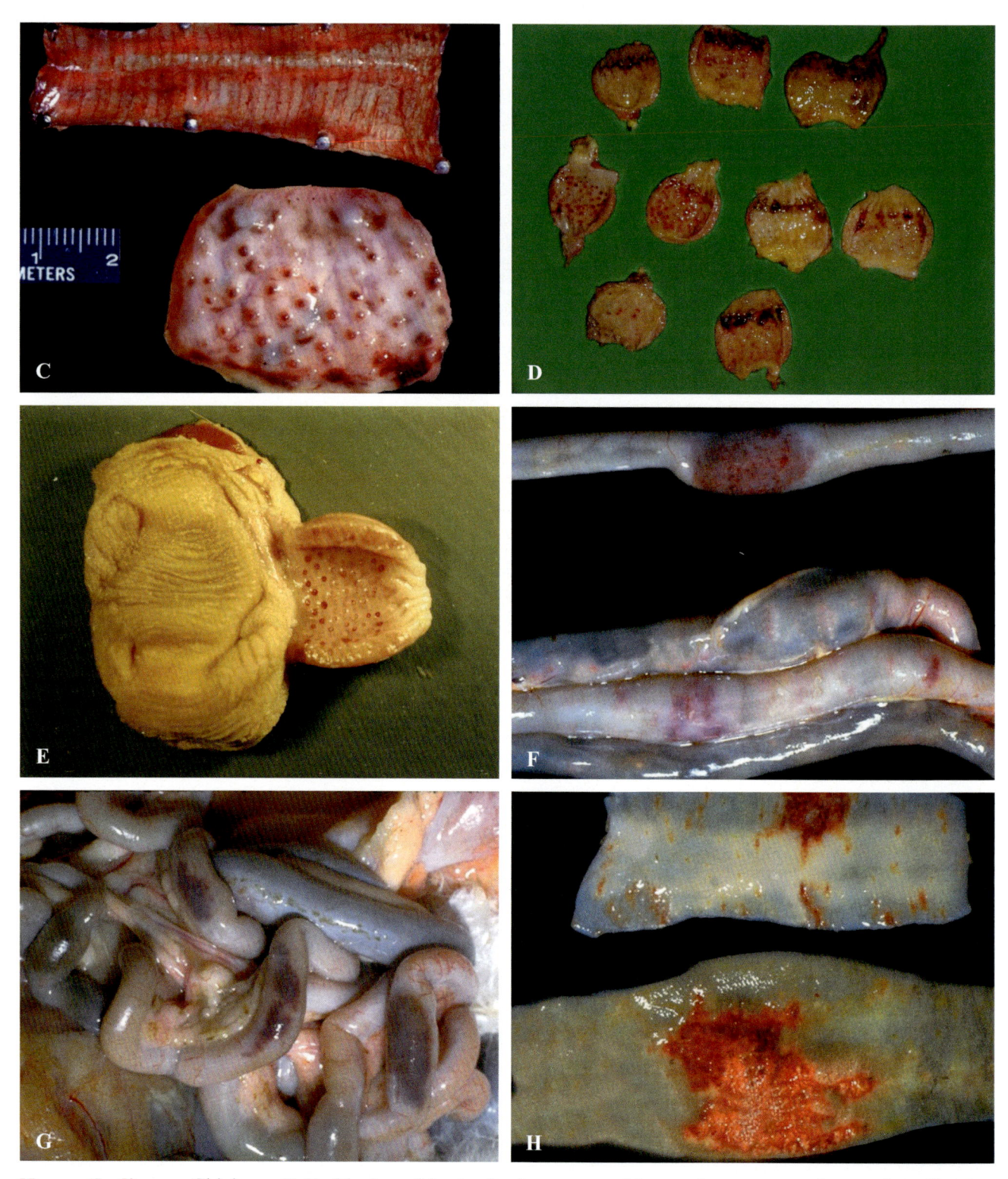

Newcastle disease. Chickens. **C.** Reddening of the tracheal mucosa and hemorrhages centered around papillae in the proventricular mucosa. **D.** Hemorrhages in the mucosa of proventriculi. Note the different location, extent, and severity of the hemorrhages. **E.** Hemorrhages in the papillae of the proventriculus. **F, G.** Hemorrhages are seen through the intestinal serosa. **H.** Large and several small mucosal ulcers are in the small intestine mucosa. Note the diphtheritic membrane covering the large ulcer *(Photo D courtesy of Dr. M. Asok Kumar, India)*.

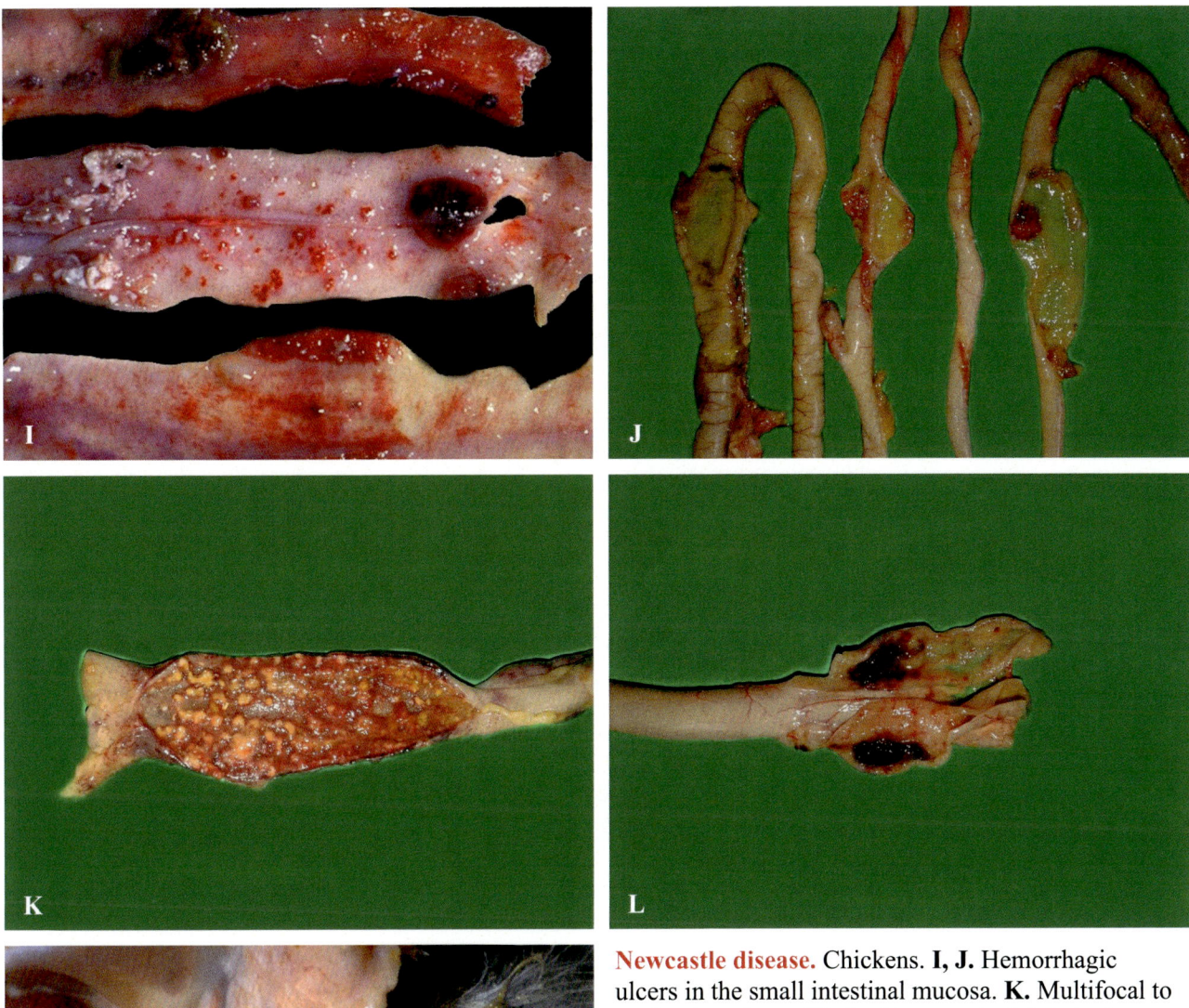

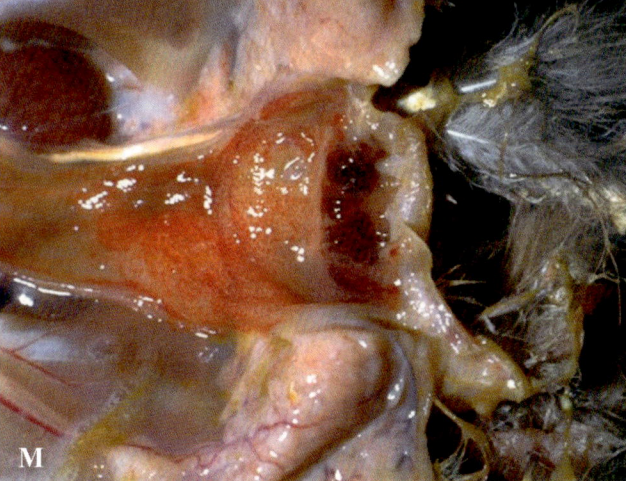

Newcastle disease. Chickens. **I, J.** Hemorrhagic ulcers in the small intestinal mucosa. **K.** Multifocal to coalescing ulcers filled with necrotic debris in the colorectum mucosa. **L.** Cecal tonsils are severely hemorrhagic. **M.** Cloaca is hemorrhagic. *(Photo J, K, L courtesy of Dr. M. Asok Kumar, India).*

Infectious Laryngotracheitis (ILT)

Infectious laryngotracheitis (ILT) is a highly contagious respiratory viral disease of chickens that has a worldwide distribution and can cause significant financial losses during periodic outbreaks. The disease was first described in 1925 in a flock of chickens in Rhode Island in the United States. However, other reports indicate that it likely existed earlier.

Cause. Herpesvirus (order *Herpesvirales* → family *Herpesviridae* → subfamily *Alphaherpesvirinae* → genus *Iltovirus* → species *Gallid herpesvirus 1*).

Hosts. Chickens are the primary natural host, and all ages are susceptible. Pheasants and peafowl are susceptible to ILT virus; these species can sometimes be naturally infected by contact with chickens actively shedding the virus. Natural infection in turkeys can occur but is rare.

Incubation period, carriers, and shedding. In natural infection, the incubation period is 6 to 12 days. Infected birds shed the virus before clinical signs are seen. Virus shedding continues for only a few days after infection. Experimentally, birds inoculated intratracheally shed virus until day 6 post-inoculation. Latent infection is a major feature of ILT virus. Following exposure to either a field strain or vaccine virus, birds become persistently infected carriers. The principal sites of ILT virus latency are the trigeminal ganglia and trachea. Persistently infected birds are asymptomatic but shed virus intermittently. Shedding of latent virus may be spontaneous or follow stresses such as onset of lay, handling, transport, crowding, or respiratory challenges.

Clinical signs and gross lesions. Severity of clinical signs and mortality rates vary widely among outbreaks and are influenced by several factors including: virulence of the virus strain, immune status of the flock, initial exposure dose, age of the birds, and adverse environmental factors. Most outbreaks of ILT in broiler chickens are in flocks over 40 days of age, although outbreaks have occurred in flocks as young as 3 weeks.

Usually birds in one area of the house suddenly show clinical signs. From there, the disease spreads relatively slowly through the rest of the flock. Mildly affected flocks may have slight respiratory disease and conjunctivitis. Excessive lacrimation (watery or weeping eyes) is a characteristic sign in birds with conjunctival lesions. In severe cases, eyelids may be closed or are adhered together, with dry, crusty, ocular discharge sticking to the eyelids and skin around the eyes. Gurgling respiratory sounds are usually heard in the flock. Some birds may exhibit open-mouth breathing (gasping), coughing, or intermittent shaking of the head. The head and neck are usually fully extended. Expulsion of bloody mucus is a characteristic clinical sign that occurs in birds with severe tracheal damage. Bloody mucus occurs on and around the beak or in the oral cavity. Spots of dried bloody exudate may be found in the bird's environment on side walls and equipment when flocks are severely affected. In some layer flocks, there may be no change in egg production, while in other flocks, egg production drops 5% to 15%. Eggshells and internal quality are unaffected.

Lesions in the larynx and trachea of infected birds vary in type, reflecting the severity and stage of infection. Very early in the infection, the appearance of the tracheal and laryngeal mucosa is usually unremarkable. As lesions advance, the mucosa may develop a somewhat dull, roughened appearance, and the tracheal lumen may contain yellow mucoid exudate. In some acutely infected birds, the laryngeal and tracheal mucosa is notably reddened or hemorrhagic. Tracheal lumen may contain free blood, casts of blood clots, bloodstained frothy or mucoid exudate, or caseous material that may form casts. A diphtheritic membrane (pseudomembrane) is occasionally present in the larynx or upper trachea. Caseous material may partially or completely occlude the tracheal lumen or laryngeal glottis, resulting in death from suffocation. In other acutely infected birds, the tracheal mucosa may be only slightly reddened with small to copious amounts of yellow mucoid exudate in the tracheal lumen. Similar mucoid exudate also can be found in the mouth and around the glottis in some birds. In birds in the subacute to chronic stages of infection, the tracheal mucosa often appears thickened. It is common to find lesions in one or both lungs of infected birds. Affected lungs are red and reveal white or yellow exudate within bronchi and openings of air sacs on cut section.

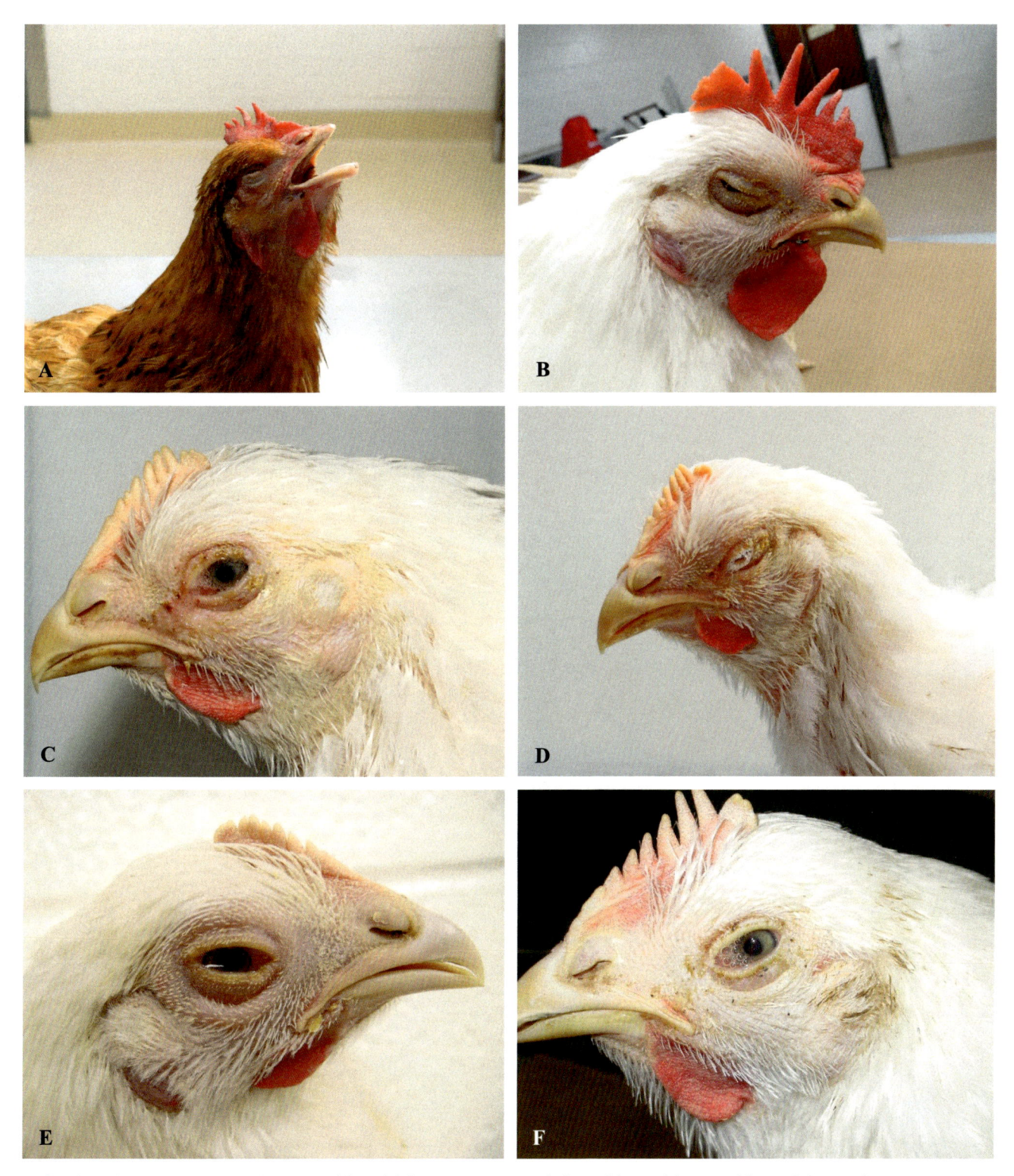

Infectious laryngotracheitis. A. Hobby chicken. Open-mouth breathing with stretching of the neck. **B-F.** 42- to 60-day broiler chickens. Swelling of eyelids and excessive lacrimation ("watery eyes") due to conjunctivitis are characteristic clinical signs in birds with conjunctival lesions, In **D**, eyelids are adhered with crusty, dry ocular discharge sticking to the eyelids.

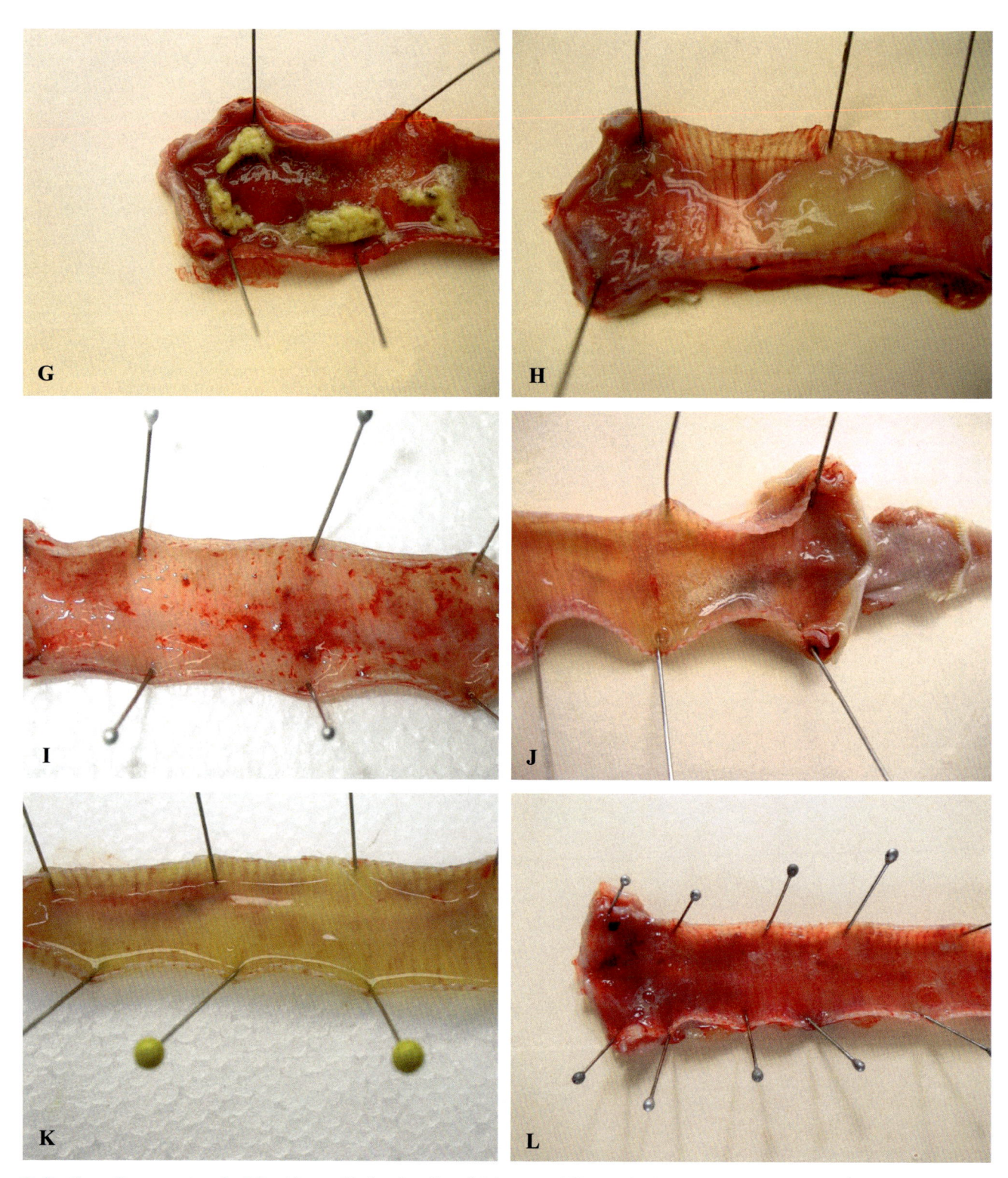

Infectious laryngotracheitis. 42- to 63-day broiler chickens. Different lesions are present in the larynges and tracheas. **G.** Reddened mucosa. Caseous exudate in the larynx and tracheal lumen. **H.** Thick, yellow exudate fills tracheal lumen. **I.** Hemorrhages in tracheal mucosa and mucoid exudate on surface. **J, K.** mucoid, yellow exudate fills the lumen. **L.** Marked reddening of the mucosa with gray exudate in the lumen.

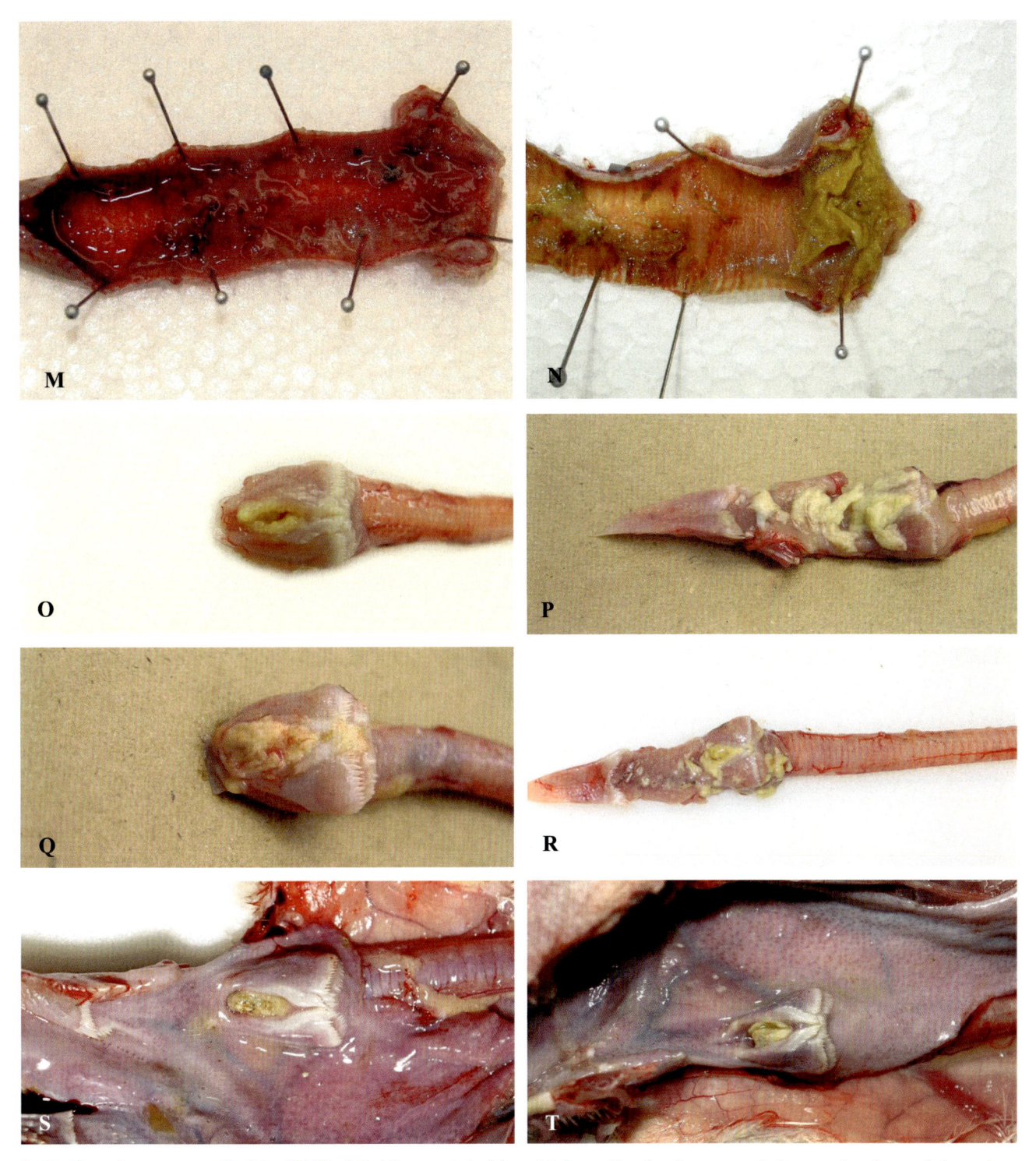

Infectious laryngotracheitis (ILT). M. 18-month hobby chicken. Tracheal mucosa is hemorrhagic, and there is blood in the lumen. **N.** 5-month hobby chicken. Layer of caseous material on the surface of the larynx. **O, P, Q, R, S, T.** Broiler breeders (**O**. 5-week, **S**. 40-week, **T**. 55-week) and adult hobby chickens (**P, Q, R**). In this lesion of ILT, the larynges are occluded by caseous material. Diagnosis of ILT was confirmed by histopathology and PCR. The lesion can be mistaken for diphtheritic wet pox.

Avian Influenza

Cause. Avian influenza is caused by *Influenza A virus*, which is the only species in the genus *Influenza virus A* of the family *Orthomyxoviridae*. The genome of the virus is composed of 8 segments of single-stranded RNA with a total length of 13,500 nucleotides (13.5 kbp). The genome codes for 8 different proteins that have different functions. Virions are usually spherical and range in size from 80 to 120 nm. The virus has a lipid envelope acquired from the host cell. A characteristic feature of influenza virus is the presence of approximately 500 spikes of rod- and mushroom-shaped glycoprotein on the surface. Rod-shaped projections are hemagglutinin (H) protein; mushroom-shaped projections are neuraminidase (N) protein. About 80% of the spikes are H, the remaining 20% are N. H is the receptor-binding and membrane fusion protein that enables the virus to attach and fuse with a cell membrane.

Infection is initiated by the hemagglutinin binding to host cell sialic acid receptors. Virus enters the cell by endocytosis where the viral membrane fuses with endosomal membranes. Ribonucleoprotein of the virus is released from the endosome into the cell cytosol and transported to the nucleus where transcription of RNA occurs. Messenger RNA (mRNA) is transported back to the cell cytosol and translated to proteins. Viral proteins and ribonucleocapsids are transported to an assembly site on the plasma membrane where virus particles bud and are released into the outside environment. After budding, the new virions are still attached to the cell surface. Neuraminidase enzymatically cleaves sialic acid releasing the virus from the cell surface. Antibodies against N do not neutralize the virus but rather block neuraminidase activity preventing release and spread of new virus particles in infected tissues. H is the major surface protein (antigen) eliciting antibodies that have virus-neutralizing activity.

Hemagglutinin protein consists of approximately 560 amino acid residues. Cleavage of the precursor H protein (H_0) by cellular proteases into two subunits (H_1 and H_2) is essential for fusion between viral and endosomal membranes. The N-terminal end of the H_2 subunit contains a sequence of hydrophobic amino acids called a fusion peptide. During entry of influenza virus into cells, the fusion peptide inserts into the endosomal membrane and causes fusion of viral and cell membranes, which permits the influenza viral genome to enter the cytosol. The cleavage occurs at the cleavage site of H_0. The types of cellular proteases that can cleave H_0 protein depend on the amino acid motif at the cleavage site. A cleavage site with only one basic arginine or lysine is cleaved only by trypsin-like proteases found in respiratory and intestinal epithelial cells and respiratory secretions, which limits tissue tropism. On the other hand, a cleavage site with multiple basic amino acids is recognized and cleaved by several proteases present in different visceral organs, including nervous and cardiovascular tissues, which permits highly pathogenic viral strains to replicate in and cause damage to many organs and tissues.

Virus subtypes and pathotypes. Based on the structure of H and N proteins, *influenza A virus* is classified into subtypes. Currently, there are 18 known H subtypes (H1-H18) and 11 known N subtypes (N1-N9). Different combinations of H and N glycoproteins affect wild and domestic birds. Based on pathogenicity, avian influenza (AI) viruses are classified into two subtypes based on their virulence as highly pathogenic (HPAI) or low-pathogenicity (LPAI). HPAI viruses have an intravenous pathogenicity index (IVPI) in 6-week chickens greater than 1.2 or cause at least 75% mortality in 4- to 6-week chickens following intravenous inoculation. Additionally, H5 and H7 viruses are considered highly pathogenic if the amino acid motif at the HA cleavage site is like that in other highly pathogenic AI viruses. Although, all documented HPAI outbreaks have been caused by H5 or H7 subtypes, not every H5 and H7 virus is highly pathogenic.

Emergence of new variants and strains. Emergence of new variants or strains of *influenza A virus* occurs through either antigenic drift or antigenic shift.
- Antigenic drift arises from point mutations in the H or N genes, which result in minor changes in the structure of H or N proteins. Immune pressure in infected hosts likely plays a role in gene mutation.
- Antigenic shift results from reassortment of genetic material when a host cell is infected with two or more different viruses with different genomes.

The segmented nature of the influenza virus genome makes genetic exchange possible. If a cell is infected at the same time with *influenza A virus* of two different H or N subtypes, RNAs of both viruses are copied in the nucleus. When virus particles are assembled at the cell membrane, some RNA segments in the new viruses may originate from either of the infecting viruses. Exchanging RNA segments coding for H or N protein results in emergence of a virus with a different H and N combination. Genetic reassortment also may involve RNA segments coding for proteins other than H and N.

Clinical signs and gross lesions. Highly pathogenic virus.
Chickens. The rapidity of viral spread through the flock and level of mortality depend on the management system. In flocks reared on the floor, virus spreads quickly through the flock. Mortality may reach 100% within a few days. Most of the birds in the flock are listless, reluctant to move, and quiet. There is a severe drop in feed consumption and water intake. In broiler breeders, there is an extreme drop, or even cessation, of egg production. Clinical disease progresses rapidly, and numerous birds in the flock are recumbent, appear paralyzed, and some exhibit head tremor. Severe prostration is followed by death. Birds that survive longer may exhibit more prominent neurologic signs including inability to stand, opisthotonos, and torticollis.

In caged table-egg layers, infection spreads more slowly; it may take 2 weeks or more for the disease to go through the entire flock. Clinical signs include severe drops in feed and water consumption and an extreme drop in egg production. Birds are recumbent and have flaccid, cyanotic combs; some are gasping and exhibit head tremors. Prostration precedes death. Eggs have thin shells and there is loss of pigmentation in brown eggs.

On necropsy, external examination reveals swelling of the head, face, and upper part off the neck due to subcutaneous edema. Conjunctivitis and edema cause the eyelids to be swollen. Comb, wattle, lower legs, and feet are cyanotic and may have hemorrhages. Internally, there are hemorrhages in skeletal muscles, subcutaneous and visceral fat, serosal and mucosal surfaces, and epicardium of the heart. Mucosal hemorrhages are commonly present in the proventriculus, ventriculus (gizzard), and cecal tonsils. Multifocal pale lesions occur frequently in the pancreas. Microscopically, pancreatic lesions represent acinar necrosis and hemorrhage. The tracheal mucosa is hemorrhagic and may contain caseous exudate; lungs are usually red and edematous.

Turkeys. Highly pathogenic influenza is a fulminant disease in turkeys. Birds may be found dead without premonitory clinical signs. The disease spreads very rapidly in the flock affecting 90-100% of the birds within 2-3 days from the onset of clinical signs. The initial clinical signs are sudden onset of a dramatic drop in feed consumption associated with marked listlessness. This is followed quickly by neurologic signs including head tremors, leg weakness, and incoordination. Birds become recumbent and paralyzed, flapping their wings as they attempt to move. Some birds lie on their side and paddle their legs. Many birds are found dead lying on their legs. Due to the peracute nature of the disease, gross lesions may be absent in dead birds. When lesions are present, hemorrhages in the intestine, proventriculus, ventricular mucosa, and cecal tonsils are seen. The pancreas is commonly involved and appears hemorrhagic. Petechial hemorrhages may be present on the epicardium. The spleen is often enlarged and spotted.

Waterfowl. Waterfowl and other aquatic and shore birds are natural reservoirs of avian influenza virus. They play a role in the perpetuation and ecology of the virus. In these birds, AI viruses, which can be any combination of H and N subtypes are highly adapted, typically replicate in the intestinal epithelial cells, and cause no clinical disease. These viruses are of low virulence for chickens, turkeys, and other types of poultry, usually causing subclinical infection or mild respiratory diseases and a drop in egg production. However, low-pathogenicity H5 and H7 subtypes can mutate and became highly pathogenic after circulating in domestic poultry.

However, since 2002, outbreaks of highly pathogenic H5N1 have occurred in waterfowl in different countries. Mortality and clinical signs have been associated with these outbreaks. Clinical signs in ducks, geese, and swans are predominantly neurologic and consist of depression, lack of coordination, paralysis, body and head tremors, torticollis, and opisthotonos. Birds die within a few days after onset of clinical signs. Gross lesions consist of pulmonary congestion and edema, red-brown mottling of the pancreas, bloody duodenal contents, petechial hemorrhages in coronary fat and myocardium, multifocal hepatic necrosis, and thickening of air sacs. Histopathological lesions are present in different organs and tissues, including the brain.

Clinical signs and gross lesions. Low-pathogenicity virus.
Chickens. Infection may be inapparent unless complicated by other pathogens. Feed and water consumption decrease and birds in the flock are notably quiet and lethargic. Gurgling respiratory noises, snicking, and coughing are heard in the flock. In broiler breeder and table-egg layers, there is a drop in egg production and eggs may be misshapen with loss of pigmentation of brown eggs. Facial and eyelid swelling, with excessive lacrimation, has occurred in flocks infected with H9N2 viruses. Gross lesions are generally mild and limited to hyperemia of tracheal mucosa and pulmonary congestion.

Turkeys. Turkeys are more susceptible to avian influenza than chickens. Different subtypes, particularly H1, H3, H5, H6, H7, and H9, have caused infections in turkeys in different countries. Mortality varies from very low to extremely high, depending on age, concurrent viral or bacterial infection, air quality, and husbandry. Clinical disease is more severe and mortality is substantially higher in young birds. Clinical signs include lethargy, anorexia, respiratory noises, swelling of infraorbital sinuses, and conjunctivitis. Green to yellow diarrhea may be present in young birds.

In turkey breeders, respiratory signs are generally mild and include coughing, rales, facial edema, and swelling of infraorbital sinuses. Lesions are mostly found in the respiratory tract and consist of sinusitis, tracheitis, and airsacculitis. Sinusitis is manifested grossly by accumulation of mucoid to yellow exudate of variable amount and consistency in the infraorbital sinuses. Trachea may be reddened due to vascular congestion and sometimes-mucosal hemorrhage. It may contain yellow exudate that can be caseous and copious causing occlusion of the lumen. Airsacculitis may be present, but it is usually caused by secondary bacterial infection. Pancreas may be enlarged and have pale foci of necrosis or red foci of hemorrhage. In turkey breeders, drops in egg production can be severe and are accompanied by production of misshapen, thin-shelled, white eggs. Acute regression of ovarian yolk follicles and free, watery yolk in the body cavity are usually seen. The oviduct mucosa is frequently edematous and contains mucoid to yellow inflammatory exudate.

Subtypes infecting birds and humans. Nine N subtypes (N1-N9) of 6 H subtypes (H5, H7, H9) are known to infect birds and humans.

- Most of the N subtypes of the H5 subtype found in wild birds and poultry are low-pathogenicity AI viruses, but occasionally highly pathogenic strains occur. The H5N1 reported in different parts of the world is highly pathogenic causing high mortality in birds and severe, even fatal, illness in people.
- Most of the N subtypes of the H7 subtype detected in wild birds and poultry have low pathogenicity. Infection of humans with H7 is uncommon, but has affected people who have been in direct contact with infected birds. Infection in people is generally mild and consists of conjunctivitis and upper respiratory tract infection.
- All the H9 subtypes identified worldwide in wild birds and poultry are of low pathogenicity. H9N2 virus has been identified in poultry flocks in Asia, Europe, the Middle East, and Africa. In humans, sporadic cases of H9N2 infections have generally caused mild upper respiratory tract illness.

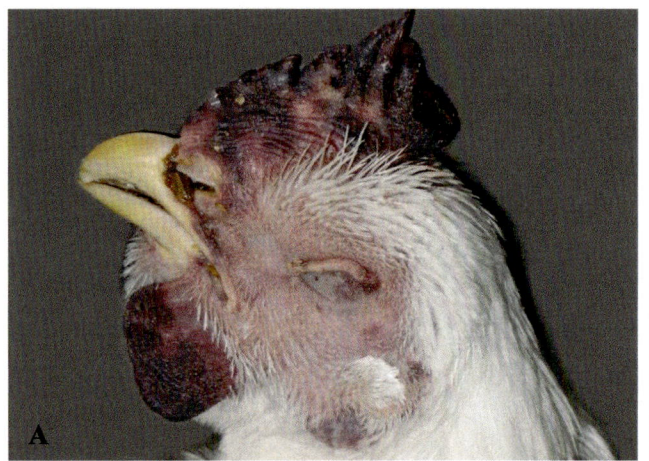

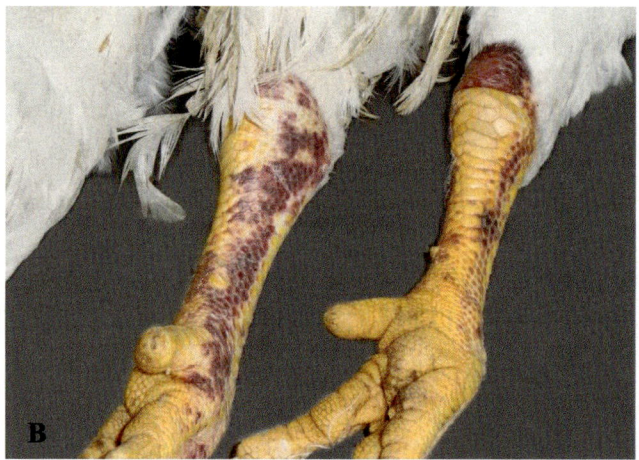

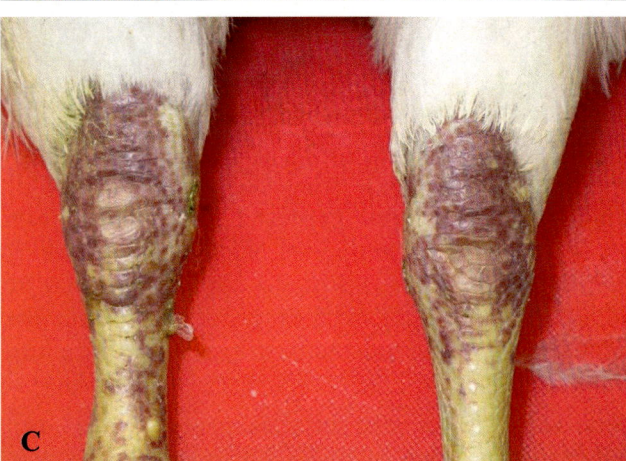

Avian influenza (highly pathogenic virus). Chickens. **A.** Comb and wattles are cyanotic with hemorrhages. **B, C.** Hemorrhages in the legs. **C** is a broiler breeder infected with H5N1 (*Photos A, B courtesy of Dr. Yugendar Reddy Bommineni, USA. Photo C courtesy of Dr. Avishai Lublin, Israel*).

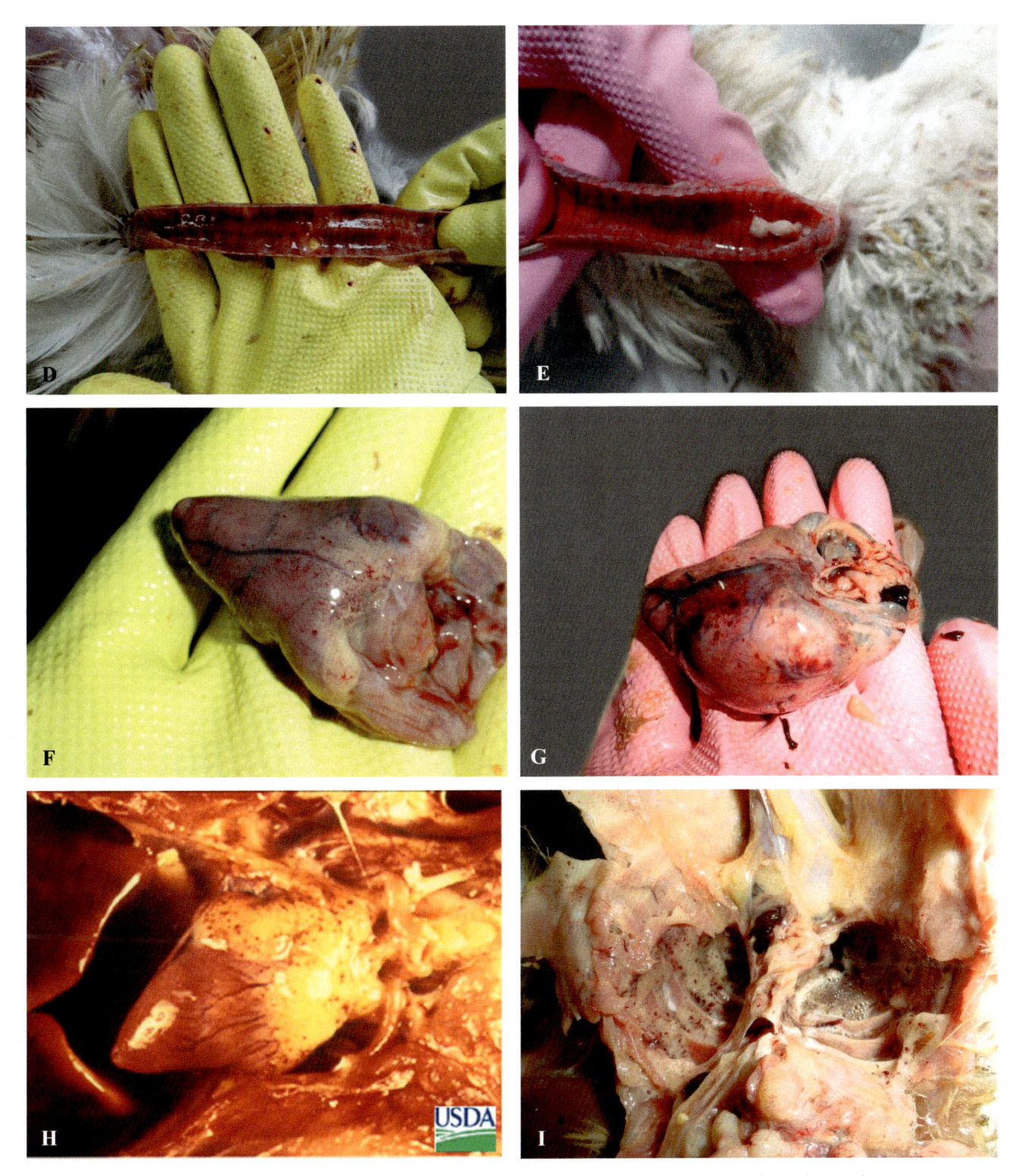

Avian influenza (highly pathogenic virus). Chickens. **D, E.** Tracheas are hemorrhagic and contain caseous exudate. **F, G.** Petechial and ecchymotic hemorrhages in the coronary fat and myocardium. **H.** Petechial hemorrhages in the coronary fat. **I.** Petechial hemorrhages in the thoracic wall. (*Photos D, E, F, G, I courtesy of Dr. Yugendar Reddy Bommineni, USA. Photo H courtesy of USDA, Dr. David Swayne, USA*).

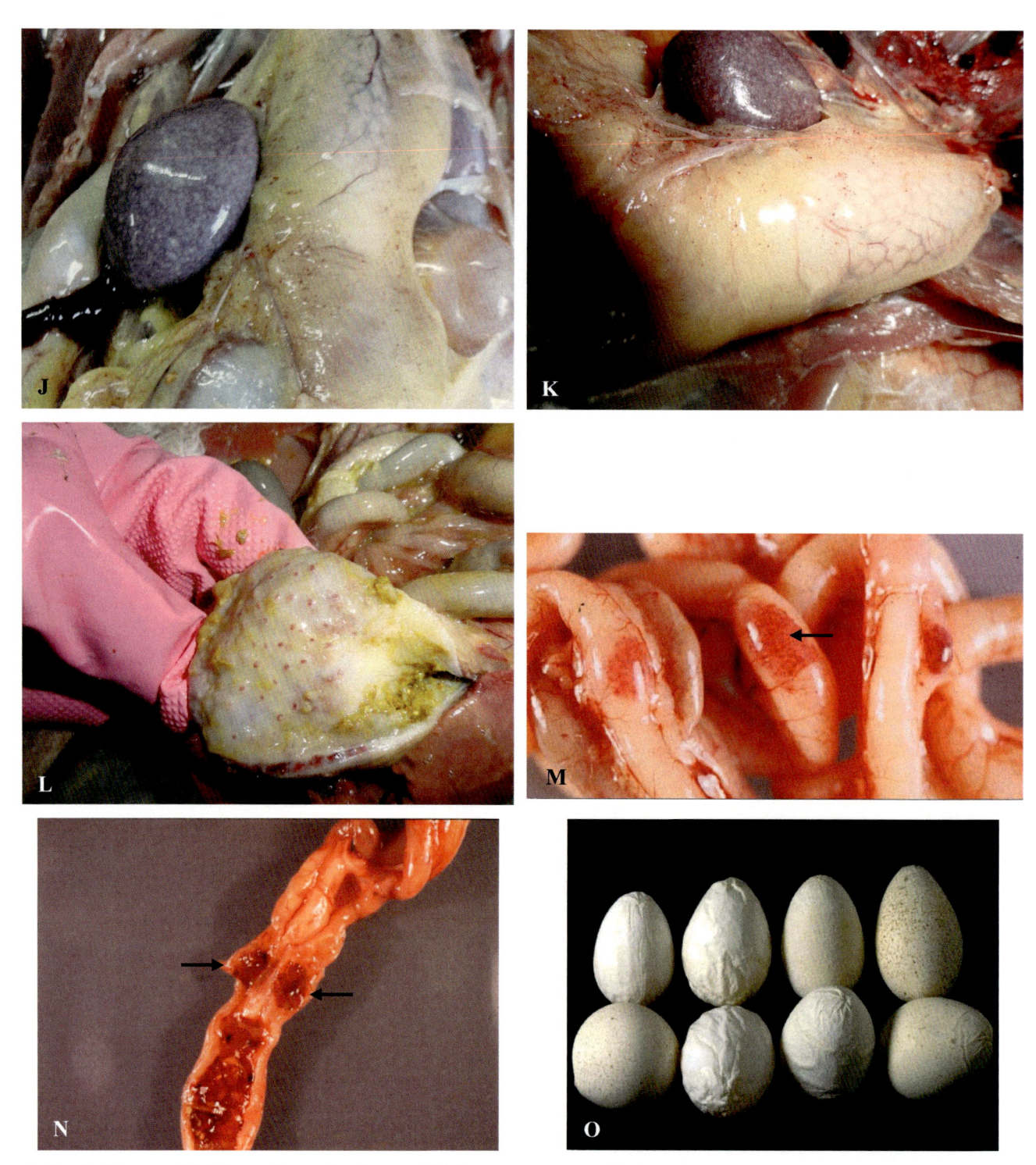

Avian influenza (highly pathogenic virus). Chickens. **J, K.** Petechial hemorrhages in visceral fat and on the serosal surface of the proventriculus. Spleen is enlarged and markedly mottled. **L.** Hemorrhages in the papillae of the proventricular mucosa. **M.** Hemorrhage in cecal tonsils and small intestine mucosal lymphoid aggregates is seen as red areas through the serosal surface. Arrow: cecal tonsil. **N.** Cecal tonsils (arrows) are hemorrhagic and there is a focal area of necrosis and hemorrhage in the intestinal mucosa. (*Photos J, K, L courtesy of Yugendar Reddy Bommineni, USA. Photos M, N courtesy of USDA, Dr. David Swayne, USA*). **Avian influenza (low-pathogenicity virus).** **O.** Eggs from turkey breeder hens infected with low pathogenic avian influenza virus. Many eggs had no shells, just membranes ('skins'). Only other clinical sign in the flock was a mild respiratory disease.

Infectious Bursal Disease (IBD)

Cause. A virus in the family *Birnaviridae* → genus *Avibirnavirus* → species *infectious bursal disease virus* causes infectious bursal disease (IBD). Infectious bursal disease virus (IBDV) is lymphotropic, with a predilection for differentiating B-lymphocytes in the bursa of Fabricius. It induces B-cell apoptosis, necrosis, and bursal atrophy, with concomitant suppression of humoral immunity. Two serotypes, designated 1 and 2, are recognized. Antigenically, they have only 30% similarity. The two serotypes can be differentiated by virus-neutralization, but not by enzyme-linked immunosorbent assay (ELISA) or immunofluorescent antibody tests. Serotype 2 strains infect chickens and turkeys but do not cause clinical disease or immunosuppression. Two major antigenic groups of serotype 1 virus are recognized: standard (classic) and variant strains. Antigenic variation among strains and emergence of new strains result mostly from antigenic drift (random genetic mutation), but random homologous recombination of the virus genome can occur. Presence of different variants has implications for vaccine development and immunization against the disease, as vaccine strains may not provide full protection against infection with field isolates. Very virulent IBDV (vvIBDV) strains are endemic in some parts of the world. Antigenically, vvIBDV are similar to classic strains but have one or more modified neutralizing epitopes that have developed via gene mutation. vvIBDV strains replicate faster and cause more severe damage to the bursa of Fabricius compared to variant strains.

Clinical signs. Results of infection depend on age and breed of chicken, level of immunity, and virulence of the virus. Young chickens, especially egg-laying birds, between 3 and 6 weeks of age are most susceptible to clinical disease. The incubation period is 2-3 days. Following infection with virulent strains, there is a sudden increase in mortality and decrease in feed consumption in the flock. Clinical signs exhibited by birds are not specific and include lethargy, disinclination to stand or walk, ruffling of feathers, huddling, mild trembling, and white or watery diarrhea. Prostration often precedes death. Mortality varies considerably, depending largely on the virulence of the IBDV strain. Some strains of vvIBDV can cause mortality rates of 90% to 100%. Variant viruses produce mild clinical signs or inapparent disease with little to no mortality. Bursal lesions and immunosuppression occur with variant viruses even in the absence of clinical disease.

Gross lesions. Gross lesions vary in severity and depend largely on the virulence of the virus strain. Birds infected with vvIBDV strains have the most severe disease and lesions. Lesions are consistently found in the bursa of Fabricius, which becomes swollen and covered by colorless or yellow, gelatinous material. Mucosal folds are swollen and edematous and may be diffusely or focally reddened. The bursal lumen often contains turbid, off-white exudate. In some cases, bursas are diffusely hemorrhagic, in which case, birds may void blood in the droppings. Other lesions include hemorrhages in leg and thigh muscles, hemorrhages in the proventriculus mucosa (usually at the junction with the gizzard), occasional hemorrhages on serosal surfaces, swollen kidneys and spleen, and general pallor of visceral organs. As the disease progresses, bursas become small, flaccid, discolored, and have shrunken, necrotic folds.

Subclinical infections. Chickens infected before 3 weeks of age do not exhibit clinical signs but develop subclinical infections characterized by microscopic lesions in the bursa of Fabricius and immunosuppression. Economic losses associated with subclinical infection in young chickens are mostly due to the severe, prolonged immunosuppression and increased susceptibility to bacterial infections. Some variant strains of IBDV can cause subclinical infections with transient immunosuppression in chickens over 3 weeks of age. In broiler chickens, this can cause economic losses due to poor feed conversion and longer time to reach market weight. With subclinical infection, there is necrosis and loss of follicular B-lymphocytes without an inflammatory response. Atrophied bursas without other gross lesions are typical of infection with mild variant viruses.

Predisposing infection with IBDV should be considered in any outbreak of bacterial disease in broiler chickens. Presence of an atrophied bursa alone is inadequate for a diagnosis of IBD as any stress or bacterial disease, including colibacillosis, can cause non-specific atrophy of the bursa.

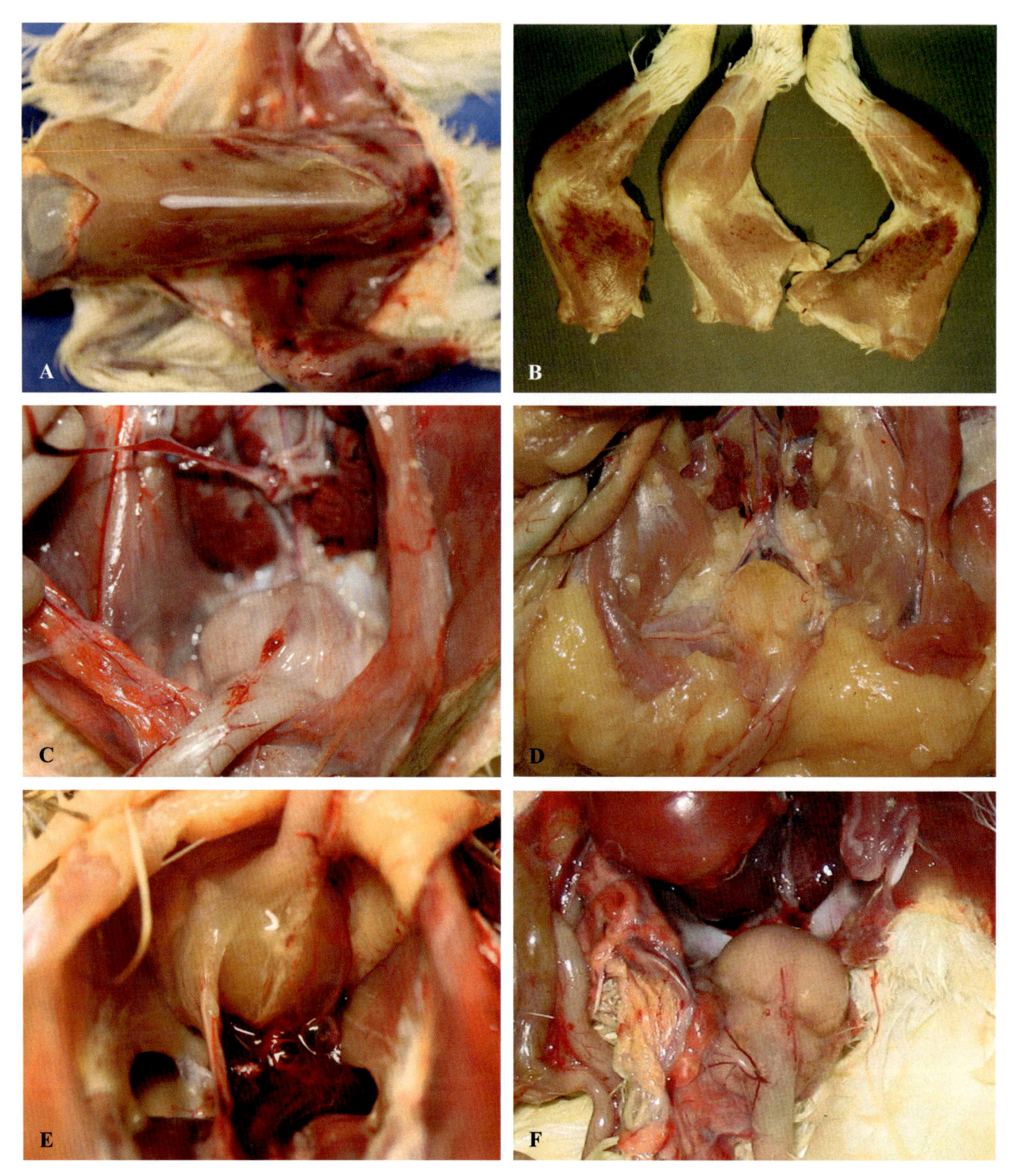

Infectious bursal disease. Chickens. **A, B.** Hemorrhages in the breast and thigh muscles. **C-F.** Bursas of Fabricius are enlarged and covered with colorless or yellow gelatinous material. *(Photos A, C, D, E courtesy of Dr. Rocio Crespo, USA)*.

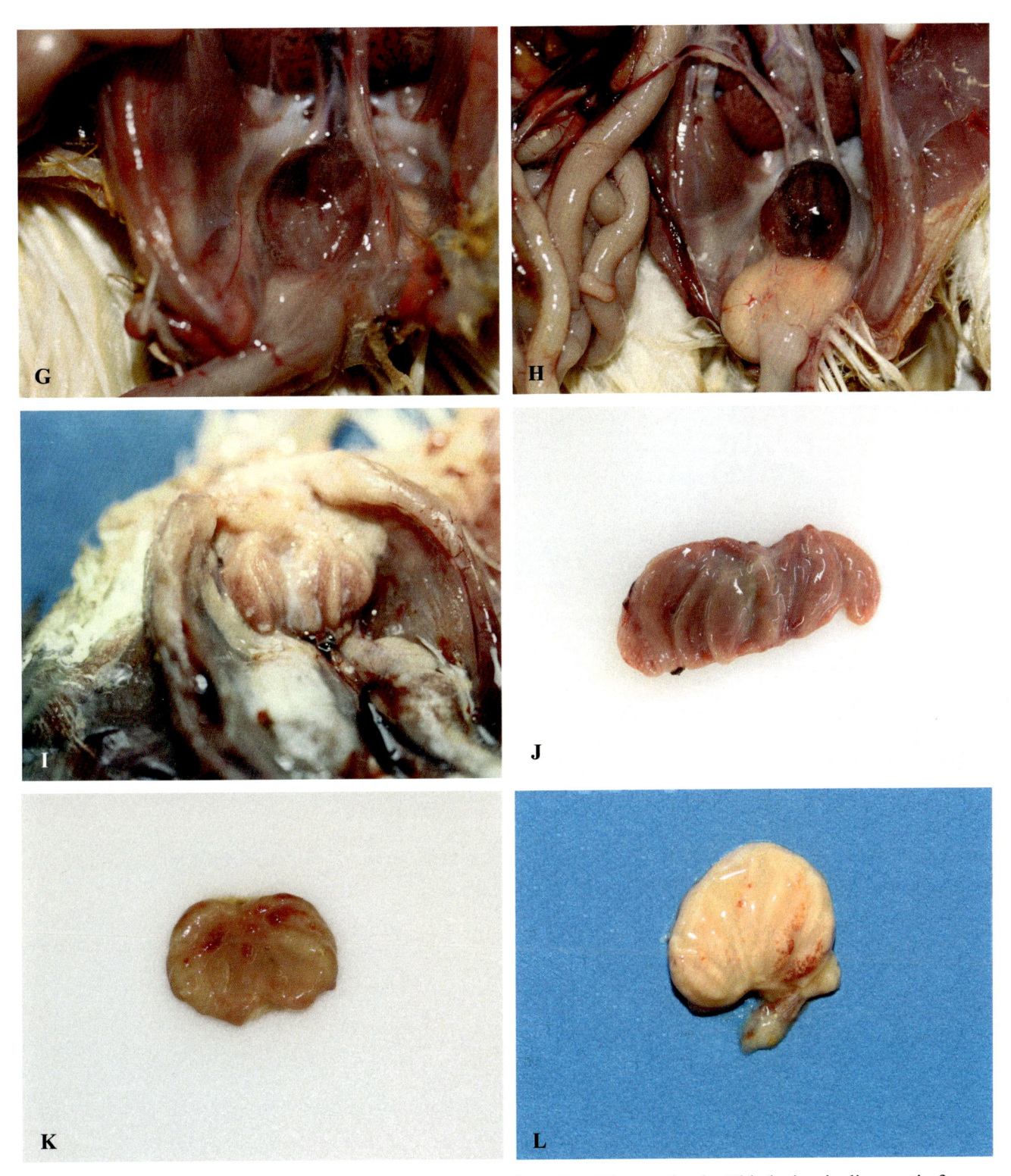

Infectious bursal disease. Chickens. **G, H.** Bursas are enlarged and hemorrhagic. This lesion is diagnostic for infectious bursal disease (IBD) caused by very virulent strains of IBD virus. **I, J, K, L.** Opened bursas showing swelling or atrophy of mucosal folds, accumulation of exudate in the lumen, necrosis, and areas of hemorrhage. *(Photos G, H, K courtesy of Dr. Rocio Crespo, USA).*

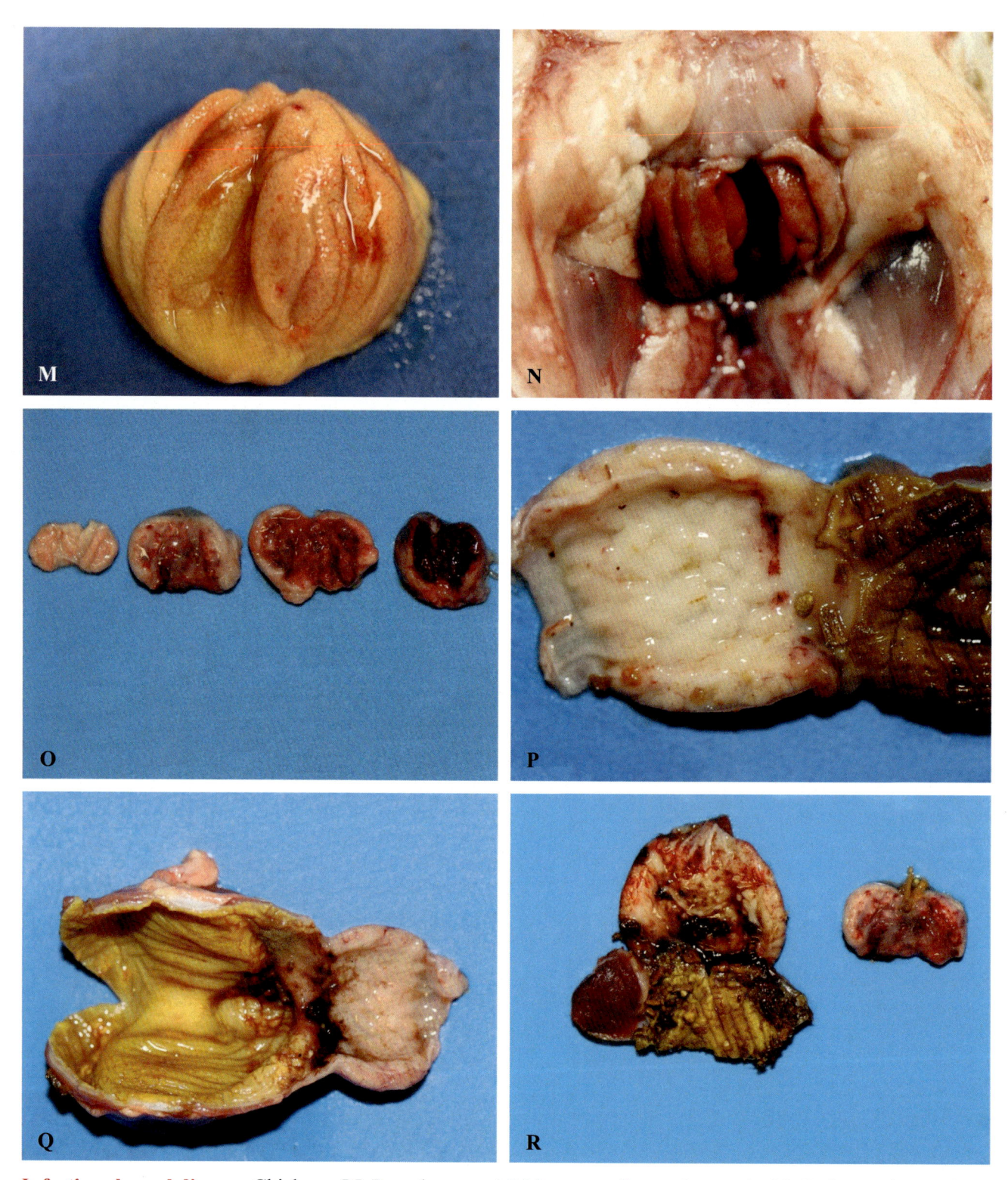

Infectious bursal disease. Chickens. **M.** Bursal mucosal folds are swollen and necrotic. **N, O.** Severe hemorrhage in the bursas of Fabricius. This lesion is diagnostic for infectious bursal disease (IBD) caused by very virulent strains of IBD virus. **P, Q, R.** Hemorrhages in the proventriculus at the junction with the gizzard. In **R**, note blood in the proventriculus lumen. *(Photos M, O, P, Q, R courtesy of Dr. Rocio Crespo, USA).*

Inclusion Body Hepatitis and Hepatitis-Hydropericardium Syndrome in Chickens

Cause. *Aviadenovirus* in the *Adenoviridae* family. The International Committee on Taxonomy of Viruses separates the genus *Aviadenovirus* into 12 species: *Duck aviadenovirus B, Falcon aviadenovirus A, Fowl aviadenovirus A-E, Goose aviadenovirus A, Pigeon aviadenovirus A,* and *Turkey aviadenovirus B-D*. Based largely on cross-neutralization assays, fowl adenoviruses are further divided into 12 serotypes, designated as FAdV-1 to 8a and FAdv-8b to 11. There are several strains of each serotype. Inclusion body hepatitis is caused by FAdv-D and FAdv-E strains. Hepatitis-hydropericardium syndrome is mainly caused by FAdv-C serotype 4.

Clinical signs and gross lesions. Inclusion body hepatitis (IBH) occurs mostly in broiler chickens between 2 and 4 weeks of age, while hepatitis-hydropericardium syndrome (HHS) usually affects slightly older broiler chickens between 3 and 6 weeks of age. Generally, HHS is more severe and causes greater morbidity and mortality than IBH. Affected birds become lethargic and die within 48 hours or recover. With both IBH and HHS, livers are enlarged, yellow or pale tan, and are typically mottled with pinpoint or larger red foci. In some cases, the liver is only mildly discolored with pinpoint red foci. Mottling is due to degeneration and necrosis of hepatocytes. Kidneys may be enlarged and pale. Pericardial effusion (hydropericardium), characterized by an accumulation of several mL of clear, straw-colored fluid in the pericardial sac, is the characteristic lesion of HHS. Yellow discoloration of the skin, anemia, and hemorrhages in skeletal muscles and other organs described in the disease were more likely due to simultaneous infection with infectious anemia virus.

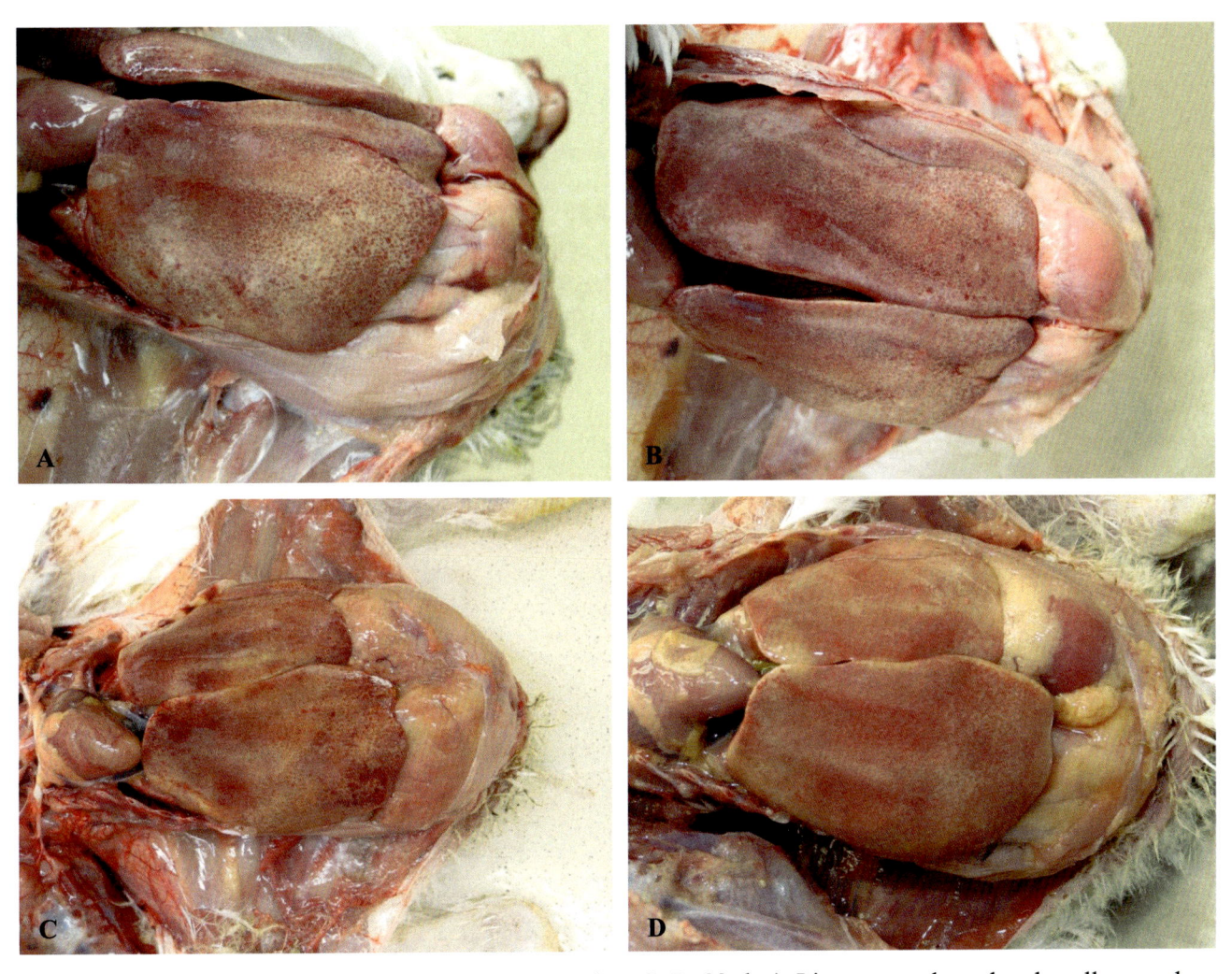

Inclusion body hepatitis. Broiler chickens (**A, B.** 27-day. **C, D.** 23-day). Livers are enlarged, pale yellow, and mottled with red foci that are pinpoint or larger size. Inclusion body hepatitis in these cases was confirmed by histopathology.

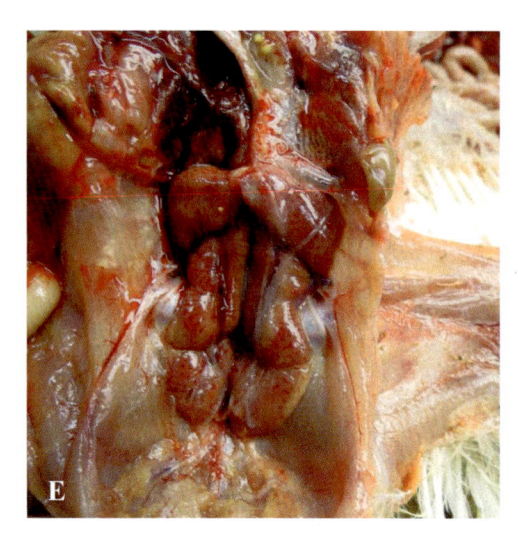

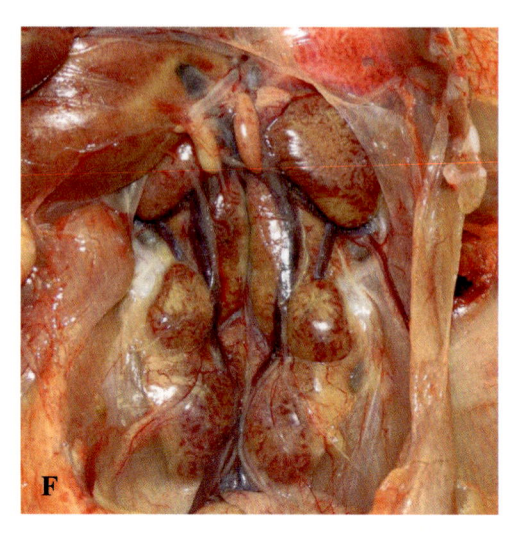

Inclusion body hepatitis. E, F. Broiler chickens (E. 14 days. F. 26 days) Kidneys of broiler chickens affected with inclusion body hepatitis are swollen and pale.

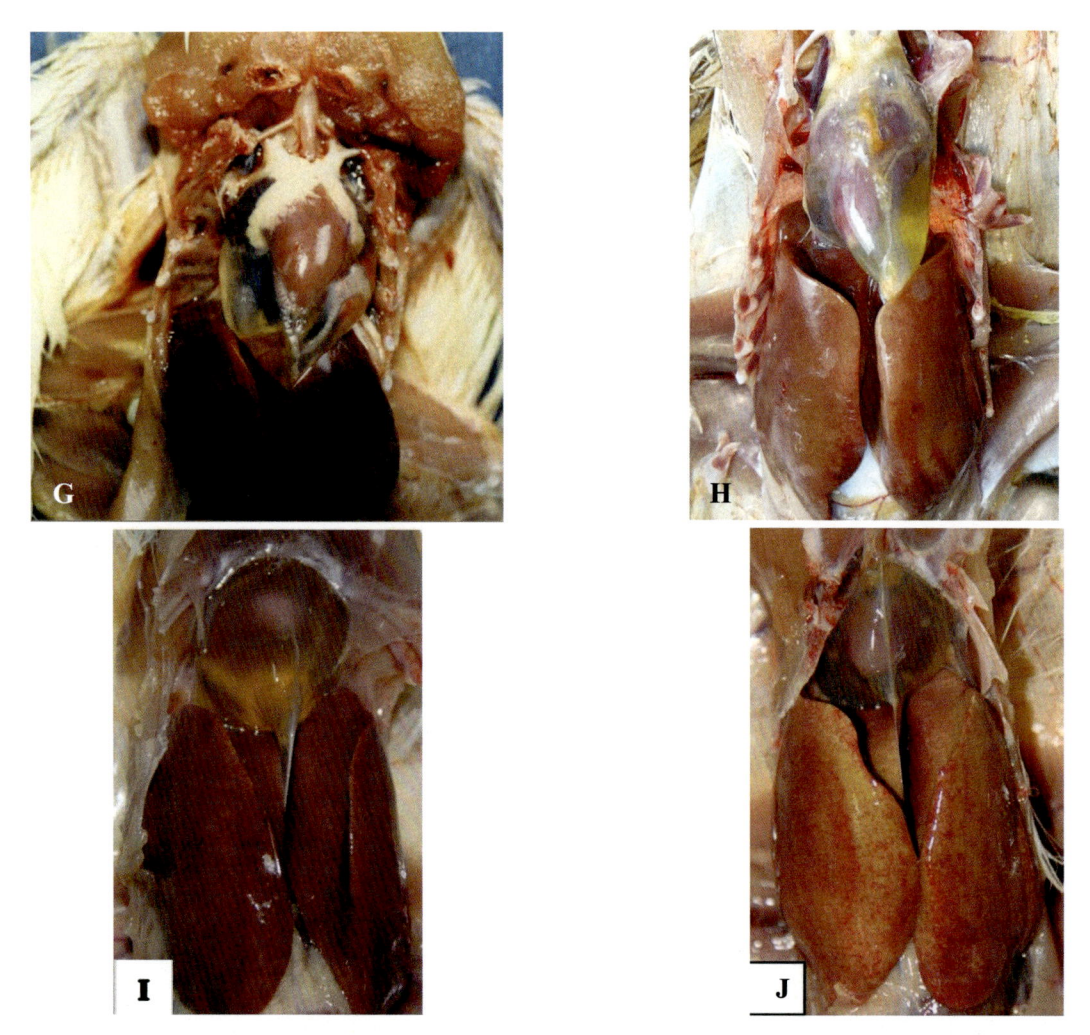

Hepatitis-hydropericardium syndrome. G-J. Pericardial sac is distended with clear straw-colored fluid. Livers are swollen and mottled with red foci. *(Photo H courtesy of Dr. Jun Zhao, China. Photos I and J Source: Pathogenicity and Complete Genome Characterization of Fowl Adenoviruses Isolated from Chickens Associated with Inclusion Body Hepatitis and Hydropericardium Syndrome in China. Authors: Jing Zhao et al. Published in PLOS ONE, July 13, 2015. License: Creative Commons attribution license).*

Hemorrhagic Enteritis in Turkeys

Cause. Adenovirus. The species is *turkey siadenovirus A* in the genus *Siadenovirus* of the family *Adenoviridae*. Previously, the virus was classified as Type II adenovirus. Hemorrhagic enteritis only affects turkeys, but marble spleen disease in pheasants is caused by a closely related virus. Turkeys are generally between 4 and 8 weeks when they become infected with the virus.

Pathogenesis. In experimentally infected turkeys, viral antigen is detected by immunoperoxidase staining in lymphoid cells in the duodenal lamina propria, bursa of Fabricius, and cecal tonsils one day post-infection (PI). After initial replication at these sites, the virus enters the blood stream and spreads to other organs and tissues. Virus antigen is found in the spleen as early as day 2 PI, and high levels of virus are detected in the spleen and cecal tonsils on day 3 PI. In the spleen, the highest virus titer occurs on day 4 PI, which coincides with the appearance of microscopic lesions in the duodenum. Numerous intranuclear inclusion bodies can be seen between days 3 and 5 PI. Lymphoid cell necrosis begins between days 4 and 5 PI, and marked lymphoid depletion occurs by days 6 to 7 PI. Interestingly, intestines with marked microscopic lesions (epithelial degeneration and sloughing and hemorrhage) have few virus-positive cells in the lamina propria and no virus-positive cells in the villous epithelium. Intestinal lesions probably do not result from direct damage to mucosal epithelium or vascular endothelial cells, but are caused by immune-mediated injury.

Clinical signs and gross lesions. Clinical signs progress rapidly over a 24-hour period. Affected birds become lethargic and may have bloody droppings that frequently adhere to the skin and feathers around the vent. Blood loss may cause dead turkeys to appear pale. Characteristic gross lesions are found in the small intestine and spleen. Intestinal lesions are most pronounced in the duodenal loop but may extend to the jejunum or even ileum in severe cases. The intestinal mucosa is reddened and there may be blood in the lumen. In severe cases, intestines of dead birds are distended, discolored black-red, and are filled with blood and tissue debris. The spleen is characteristically enlarged, friable, and mottled or marbled gray or white. Infection can be subclinical. Moderate enlargement, and sometimes mottling of the spleen, may be the only lesion in subclinically infected birds and birds that survive the acute stage of infection. It is common for septicemia to follow hemorrhagic enteritis because of viral-induced immunosuppression.

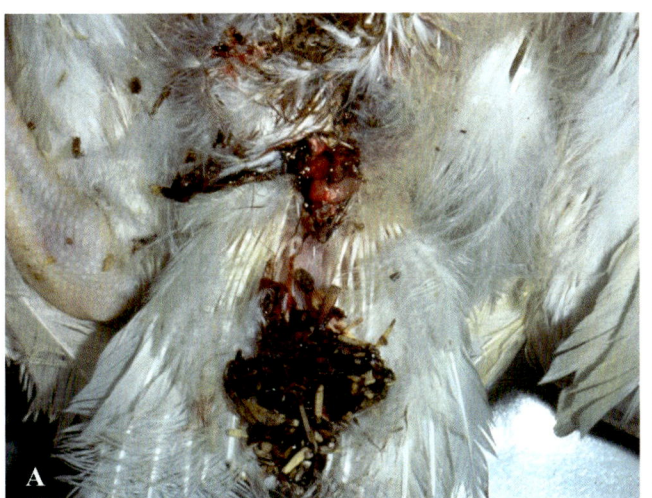

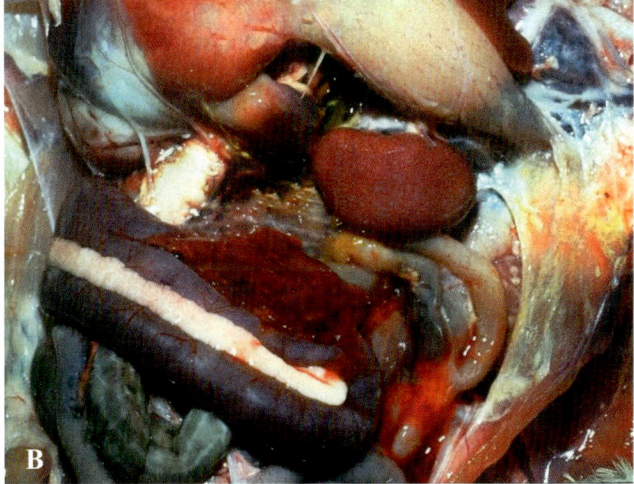

Hemorrhagic enteritis. 12-week turkey. **A, B.** Blood stained fecal material adheres to the feathers around the vent, and the vent is stained with blood. **B.** Duodenum is filled with blood and tissue debris. Spleen is markedly enlarged and has multiple white foci. The combination of intestinal and splenic lesions is characteristic of the disease; however, often only splenic lesions are seen.

Chicken Infectious Anemia

Chicken infectious anemia (CIA) is an immunosuppressive viral disease of young chickens. It is characterized by aplastic pancytopenia, i.e. anemia, leukopenia, and thrombocytopenia, due to reduced production of all three blood-cell lineages (erythrocytes, leukocytes, and thrombocytes) in the bone marrow.

Cause: *Gyrovirus* (family *Anelloviridae* → genus *Gyrovirus* → species *chicken anemia virus*).

Transmission. Vertical transmission is the most important route of infection. Susceptible (seronegative) breeder hens that become infected during the laying period develop viremia and shed the virus into the eggs between 8 and 14 days after infection. Field observations suggest spread of infection in a broiler breeder flock may take 3 to 6 weeks, depending on the number of houses, size of the flock, and level of biosecurity. Egg transmission in individual hens stops around 14 days post-infection when antibodies to the virus are detected. Vertically infected chicks shed the virus in the feces, and horizontal transmission occurs in the flock by the fecal-oral route. Age resistance to clinical disease is a feature of CIA. Chickens over 2-3 weeks of age can still be infected, but do not develop clinical disease (subclinical infection). However, they become viremic, seroconvert, shed the virus, and recover with the development of antibodies.

Clinical signs and gross lesions. Vertically infected, susceptible chicks show clinical signs between 14 and 21 days of age. Signs are not specific and include lethargy, depressed weight gain, ruffled feathers, general pallor, and increased mortality. Anemia is the only specific feature of the disease. Anemic birds have hematocrit values below 20%. Surviving chickens recover from anemia a few weeks after infection. In natural outbreaks, mortality occurs between 12 and 28 days; commonly peaking between days 17 and 21. Mortality is usually around 5% to 10%, but can be up to 50%. Clinical signs and mortality are enhanced by concurrent infections with infectious bursal disease virus and Marek's disease virus. The protective effects of age and maternal antibodies can be overcome by dual infection with these viruses.

Thymic and bone marrow atrophy are the most consistent and characteristic findings in acutely infected chicks. Thymic lobes are severely atrophied and may even be difficult to find. Bone marrow (best evaluated in femurs) becomes pale or yellow and changes in consistency from spongy to fatty. There is variable atrophy of the bursa of Fabricius. Blood is thin and bright red. Skeletal muscle and visceral organs are pale. Hemorrhages in muscle, subcutaneous tissue, legs, feet, and gizzard mucosa may be associated with severe anemia. Subcutaneous hemorrhage and serosanguineous edema cause blue-red discoloration of the skin. This lesion is particularly seen in the wings ("blue wing disease"), but occurs to a lesser extent in other areas including head, thorax, abdomen, and thighs. Skin bruising and secondary bacterial infections lead to dermatitis and cellulitis. Because of damage to lymphoid tissues, chickens are more susceptible to other diseases e.g. inclusion body hepatitis, coccidiosis, and clostridial cellulitis (gangrenous dermatitis). Immunosuppression also results in poor responses to vaccines (vaccine failure).

Chicken infectious anemia. 20-day broiler chickens. **A, B.** Hemorrhage in the wings is a characteristic lesion of chicken infectious anemia. **C, D, E.** Bluish discoloration of the wing web **(C)** and abdomen **(D, E)** due to severe subcutaneous hemorrhages and serosanguineous edema. Secondary bacterial cellulitis, especially caused by *Clostridium* spp. and *Staphylococcus aureus*, is common in affected birds and may contribute to the lesion. **F.** Hemorrhage in a foot.

White Chick Syndrome

Egg production drops in breeder hens, a severe decrease in hatchability, and hatching of weak chicks with pale white feathers characterize white chick syndrome.

Cause. The syndrome is caused by a chicken astrovirus in the genus *Avastrovirus* of the family *Astroviridae*. The virus does not belong to any of the three species (*astrovirus* 1, 2, and 3) of the genus *Avastrovirus*, and it could represent a new species in the genus. The virus spreads horizontally from house to house on a broiler breeder farm.

Clinical signs. Breeder flocks become infected at 30 to 40 weeks of age. There is a sudden drop in egg production, ranging from 3% to 20%. The egg production drop usually lasts one to 2 weeks after which production returns to normal. In some cases, the drop may be less apparent or even absent. Eggshell quality is unaffected. Hatchability of eggs produced during the egg production drop is reduced. Severity of the reduction in hatching varies considerably but can be as high as 60% to 70%. Embryonic mortality occurs between middle to late incubation. Unhatched eggs may also have fully developed chicks that are too weak to hatch. During this period, the number of weak, small, white chicks is high. Most affected chicks die within 24 hours.

Gross lesions. Affected chicks are small and have pale white feathers. Livers are characteristically green, varying from light to dark color, and they may be mottled or have pale areas of necrosis. Dead-in-shell and failure-to-hatch embryos have enlarged, firm, tan or bronze green livers, sometimes with foci or areas of necrosis. Other lesions in infected embryos include splenomegaly, enlarged kidneys, and watery bile.

White chick syndrome. A, B, C. Feather color of normal and affected chicks. **D.** White feathers in affected chicks. *(Photo A courtesy of Dr. Kasia Domanska-Blicharz, Poland. Photo B courtesy of Dr. Benjamin Schlegel, Canada. Photos C, D courtesy of Dr. Kathleen Long, Canada).*

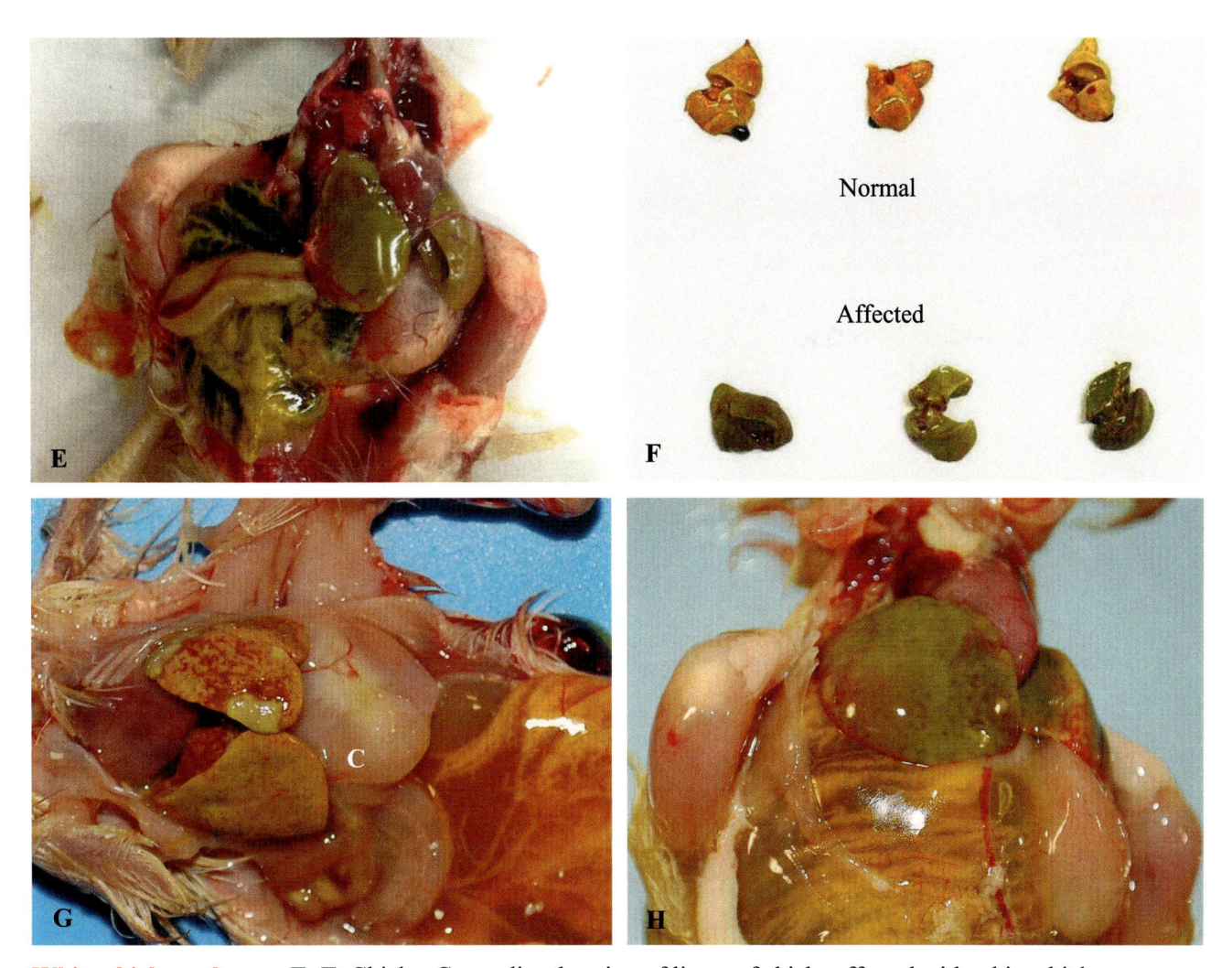

White chick syndrome. E, F. Chicks. Green discoloration of livers of chicks affected with white chick syndrome. **G, H.** Chick embryos. Livers are enlarged, discolored tan or green, and have multiple foci consistent with necrosis. (*Photos E, F courtesy of Dr. Phil Stayer, USA. Photos G, H courtesy of Dr. Marina Brash, Canada*).

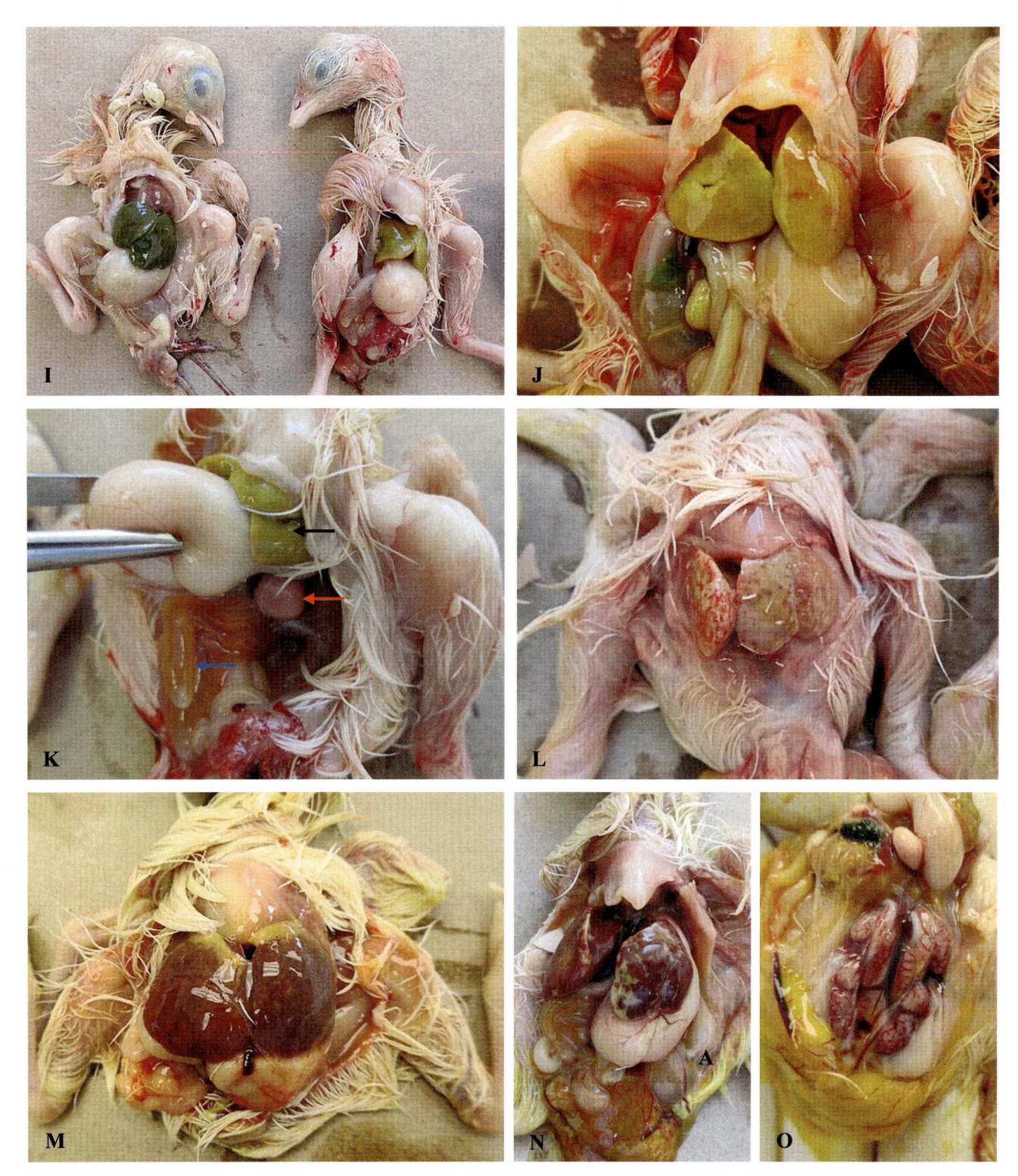

94 Gross Pathology of Avian Diseases: Text and Atlas

White chick syndrome. Dead-in-shell chick embryos inoculated with white chick syndrome astrovirus. **I, J.** Green discoloration of the liver. In I, the liver is enlarged. **K.** Green discoloration of the liver (black arrow), splenomegaly (red arrow), and watery bile in the gallbladder (blue arrow). **L, M.** Livers are enlarged and may have necrosis. **N.** The liver has pale green necrotic areas. **O.** Marked swelling and paleness of the kidneys. *(Photos courtesy of Dr. Jack Rosenberger, USA).*

Avian Hepatitis E Virus Infection in Chickens

Avian hepatitis E virus infection is a disease of broiler breeders and table-egg layers. Infections may be subclinical or associated with low mortality and mild to moderate decreases in egg production. Clinical disease caused by avian hepatitis E virus is referred to as hepatitis-splenomegaly (HS) syndrome (first recognized in Canada in 1991) and big liver and spleen (BLS) disease (first recognized in Australia in 1980). From mid-1993 to 2001, a disease similar to HS syndrome was referred to as necrotic hemorrhagic hepatitis-splenomegaly syndrome, necrotic hemorrhagic hepatomegalic hepatitis, hepatitis-liver hemorrhage syndrome, or chronic fulminating cholangiohepatitis.

Cause. Avian hepatitis E virus (HEV) is an RNA virus in the family *Hepeviridae*. The family includes two genera: *Orthohepevirus* and *Piscihepevirus*. *Orthohepevirus*, which includes all mammalian and avian HEVs, is divided into four species: *Orthohepevirus A*, *B*, *C*, and *D*. Infection in chickens is caused by *Orthohepevirus B*.

In 2001, a virus was first isolated in the USA from bile of chickens with HS syndrome. Based on genome organization and significant nucleotide sequence identities with human and swine hepatitis E viruses, the isolated virus was classified as avian HEV to distinguish it from mammalian HEVs. Avian HEV shares common antigenic epitopes and approximately 50% nucleotide sequence identity with mammalian HEV. HS syndrome virus isolated in the USA shares about 80% nucleotide sequence identity with BLS disease virus isolated in Australia in 1999 indicating HS syndrome and BLS disease are caused by related strains of avian HEV. Based on phylogenetic analysis of genomic sequences, avian HEV is classified into 4 genotypes: genotype 1 (Australia, Korea), genotype 2 (North America), genotype 3 (Europe), and genotype 4 (Hungary, Taiwan). Despite variations in nucleotide sequences, there is only a single serotype of HEV.

Clinical signs and gross lesions. Although subclinical HEV infection is common in chicken flocks in the USA and probably other countries, clinical disease associated with infection is relatively infrequent.

Hepatitis-splenomegaly syndrome. Disease in broiler breeders and table egg layers usually occurs between 30-72 weeks of age with the highest incidence between 40 and 50 weeks. Clinically, the syndrome is characterized by above-normal mortality for several weeks. Weekly mortality usually increases by 0.3% but may reach or exceed 1%. In some cases, increased mortality is associated with a drop in daily egg production of up to 40%. Hatchability of fertile eggs is not affected. In the USA, infection with avian HEV has been associated with "primary feather drop syndrome" in which flocks show delayed sexual maturity, fail to reach peak production, and molt primary feathers.

At necropsy, dead birds are in good body condition. Livers are enlarged, slightly pale, somewhat friable, and mottled or stippled with white, red, yellow, or tan foci. Some birds have subcapsular hemorrhages or hematomas in the liver, occasionally associated with rupture of the liver capsule. Blood clots loosely adhering to the surface of the liver may be present. Small to moderate amounts of fresh clotted blood or serosanguineous fluid in the abdominal cavity is found in some birds. Spleens are frequently mildly to markedly enlarged and their capsular and cut surfaces may show pale foci. Ovaries of clinically affected hens are typically regressing.

Big liver and spleen disease. Although chickens of all ages are susceptible to infection, clinical cases have only occurred in hens > 24 weeks of age. As with HS syndrome, weekly mortality may increase to up to 1% and daily egg production decease by up to 20% (usually 4% to 10%). A sudden, rapid drop in egg production may be the first indication of avian HEV infection in a flock. The egg production drop usually lasts 3-6 weeks with another 3-6 weeks before production returns to a near-normal level. Decreased egg production is more evident if the flock becomes infected after peak production. If the flock is affected during the first few weeks of production, delayed sexual maturity and low peak production are initial signs of infection. Eggs are small with thin, poorly pigmented shells, but hatchability is usually not affected. Individual birds in affected flocks are lethargic, anorexic, have pale combs and wattles, and soiled feathers around the vents (pasty vents). Many birds in the flock exhibit loss of primary feathers resembling molting.

Birds found dead or showing clinical signs are usually in good body condition, but the crop is empty indicating anorexia. Marked enlargement of the spleen (splenomegaly) is most common and may be the only lesion in affected birds. Spleens are usually 2-3 times normal size and show mottling of the capsular surface and numerous white foci on the cut surface. Many birds with splenomegaly also have enlarged livers, which may have subcapsular hemorrhages. Ovaries are usually regressing, with blood clots frequently present within flaccid yolk follicles.

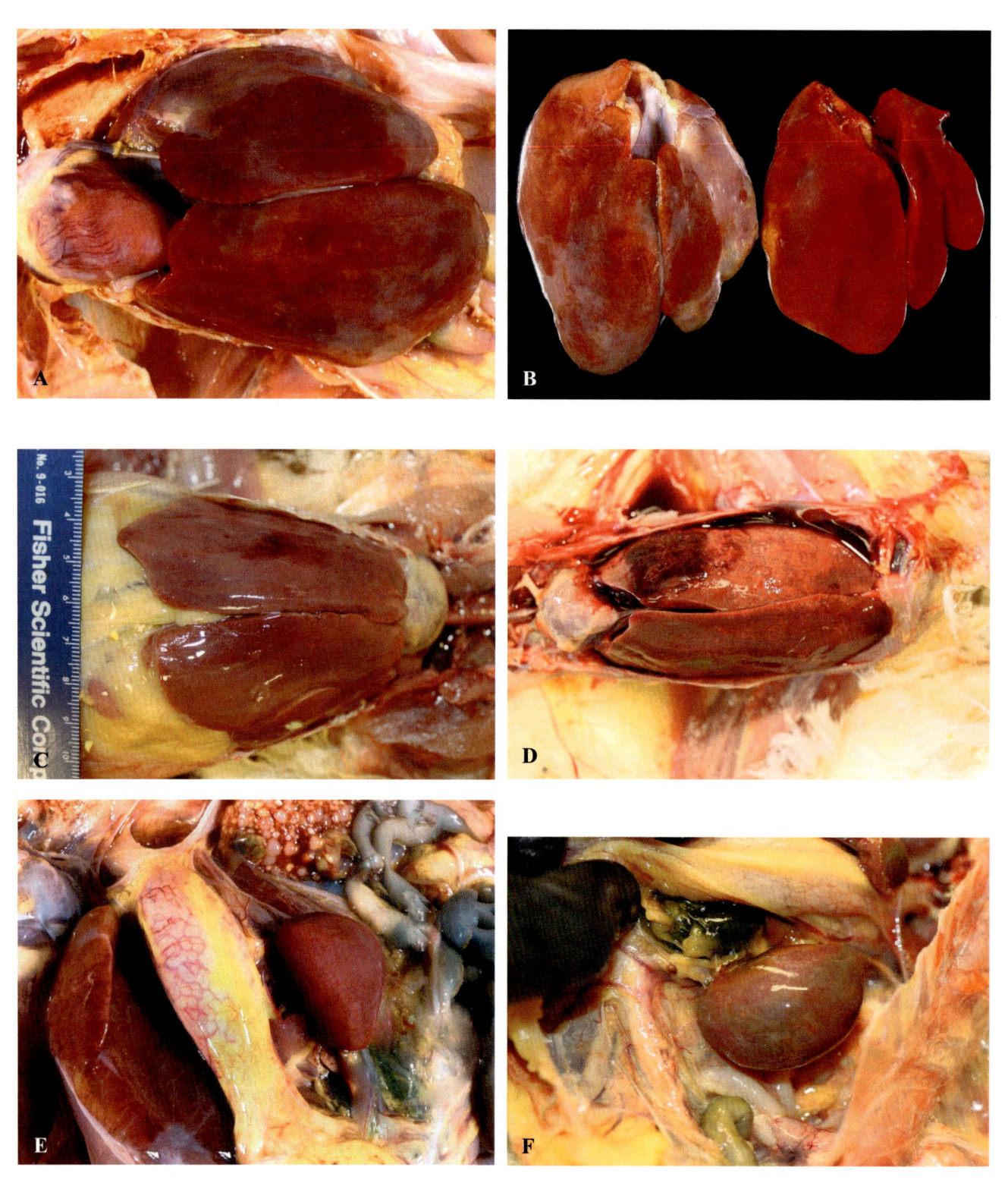

Avian hepatitis E virus infection. Table-egg layers. **A.** Liver is enlarged, has rounded margins, and is faintly mottled with fine spots. **B.** Affected liver from **A** on left compared with unaffected liver from another hen in the flock. **C.** Liver with barely visible pinpoint pale foci of necrosis. **D.** Liver with multifocal to coalescing necrosis and hemorrhagic area. **E, F.** Enlarged spleen. *(Photos C, D, F. courtesy of Dr. Rocio Crespo, USA).*

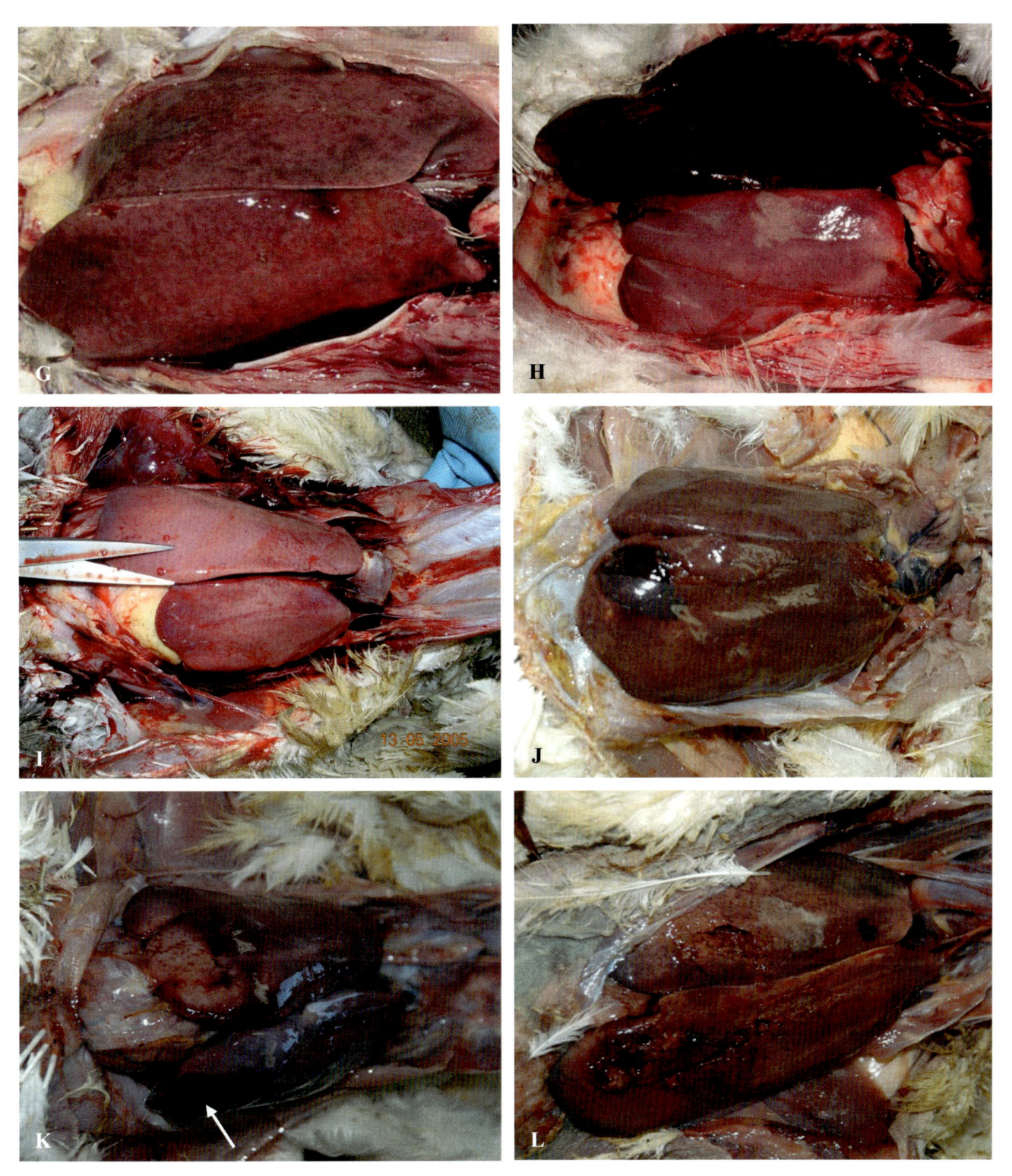

Avian hepatitis E virus infection. Broiler breeders. **G, H, I.** Livers are enlarged and mottled. In **H**, a large blood clot is on the liver surface. **J.** Liver is mottled and has a subcapsular hematoma. **K.** Liver is enlarged and has rounded margins, with a subcapsular hematoma (arrow). **L.** Liver is enlarged, friable, and mottled. *(Photos G, H, K courtesy of Dr. Michael Hess, Austria. Photos I, J, L courtesy of Dr. Chris Morrow, Australia).*

Viral Tenosynovitis in Chickens

Cause. Reovirus (family *Reoviridae* → subfamily *Spinareovirinae* → genus *Orthoreovirus* → species *avian orthoreovirus*). Clinical disease also occurs in turkeys.

Clinical signs and gross lesions. Affected birds sit on their hocks, are reluctant to move, stand stiff, and exhibit stiff gaits when forced to walk. Severely affected birds are in ventral recumbency with one or both legs extended to the side. Birds with ruptured tendons are unable to bear weight on the affected leg(s). Gross lesions are minimal in some cases. Varying degrees of swelling of the digital flexor tendons is usually evident visually and on palpation of the posterior aspect of the tarsometatarsus. Shanks are thickened in some birds because of swelling of the digital flexor tendons. Swelling may be unilateral or bilateral in the area over and just above the posterior aspect of the hock joint where the gastrocnemius tendon crosses over the joint and extends into the gastrocnemius muscle. Careful examination of the gastrocnemius and digital flexor tendons may reveal pale yellow fluid around the tendons, with yellow discoloration and thickening of peritendinous tissues. Hock joints may contain a small amount of yellow fluid. Internally, the spleen is slightly to moderately enlarged in some birds.

As the infection progresses, the gastrocnemius tendon becomes firm and thickened because of fibrosis, which causes a hard area just above the posterior aspect of the hock joints. Rupture of the tendon, usually just above the hock, results in subcutaneous hemorrhage and green discoloration of the overlying skin.

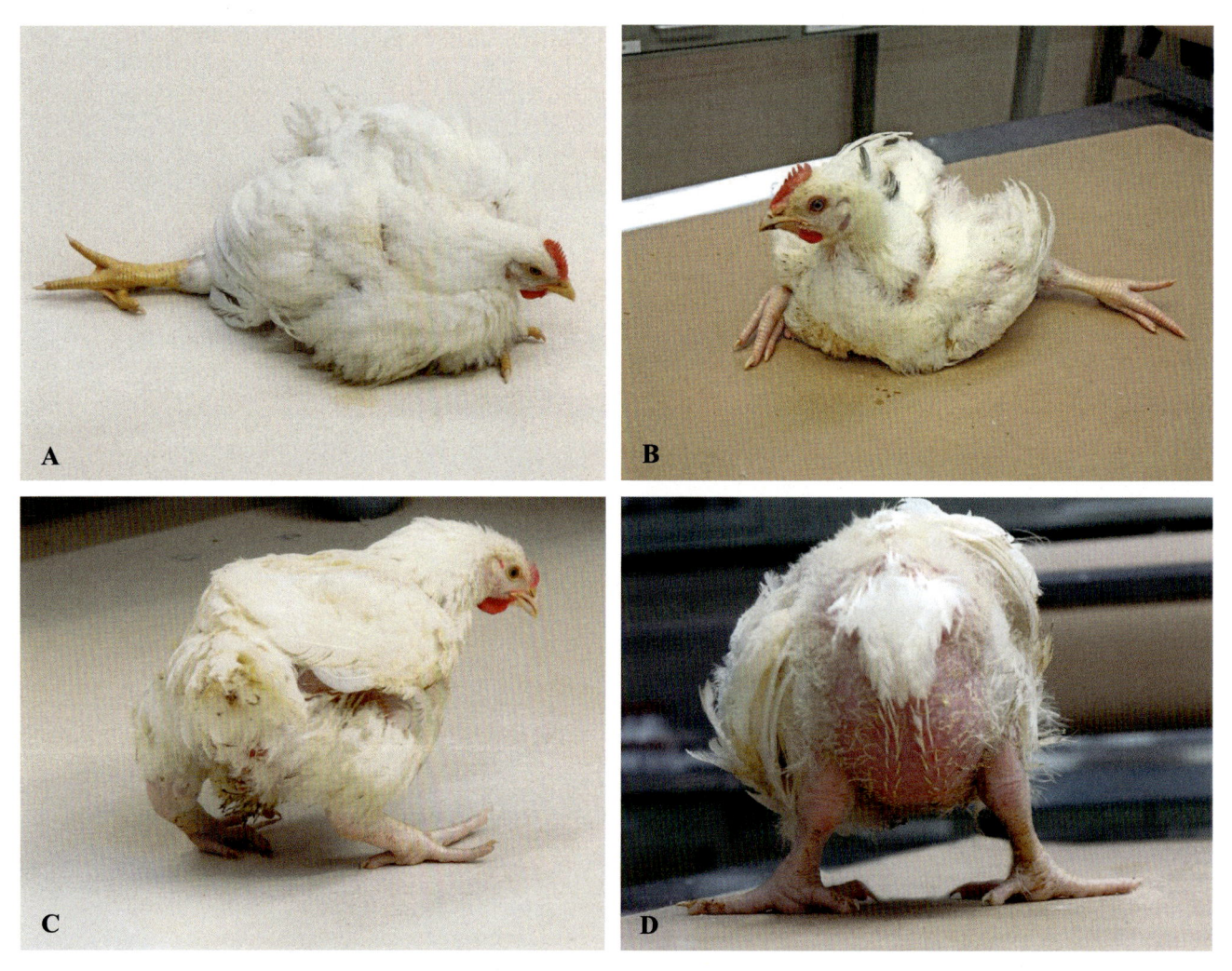

Reoviral tenosynovitis. 40- to 55-day broilers. **A, B.** Birds are in ventral recumbency with one leg extended to the side. **C, D.** Birds are standing stiff and reluctant to move. There is redness and swelling of the hock joints in D.

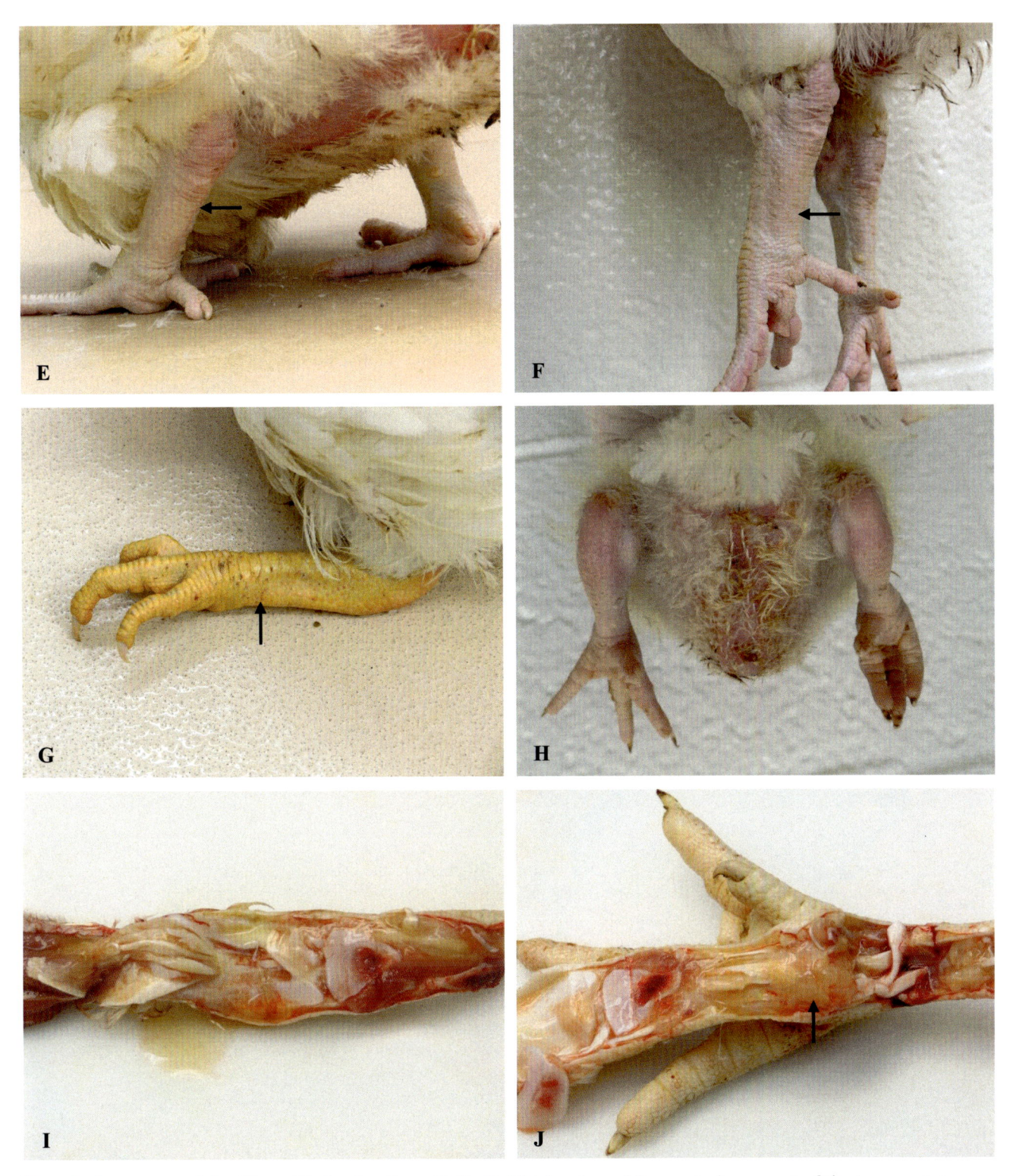

Reoviral tenosynovitis. 40- to 55-day broilers. **E, F, G.** Thickening of the posterior aspect of the tarsometatarsus (arrows) due to tenosynovitis of the digital flexor tendons. This is a characteristic feature of tenosynovitis of the digital flexor tendons. **H.** Swelling and redness of the posterior aspect of the hock joint due to tenosynovitis of the gastrocnemius tendon. **I, J.** The skin on the tarsometatarsus is reflected to show pale-yellow fluid around digital flexor tendons and thickening of peritendinous tissues (arrow).

Avian Pox

Cause. Avian pox viruses in the genus *Avipoxvirus* in the family *Poxviridae*. The genus includes the viruses *Fowlpox, Canarypox, Juncopox, Mynahpox, Peacockpox, Penguinpox, Pigeonpox, Psittacinepox, Quailpox, Sparrowpox, Starlingpox,* and *Turkeypox*. Only birds are infected. Most birds are susceptible to some type of avian pox virus. Often pox viruses are named for the species in which the virus is found, but the viruses are generally not host specific.

Clinical signs and gross lesions. Extensive cutaneous infections are debilitating. The diphtheritic form is fatal when upper airways are occluded by lesions. A severe systemic form involving the lungs and air sacs causes high mortality in canaries and finches.

Cutaneous form ('dry pox'). Lesions are proliferative. Initial lesions are small firm papules or nodules that increase in size and change to vesicles and pustules and later form dark crusty plaques and scabs, which eventually drop off leaving a healed lesion. Early lesions are difficult to recognize, and a few encrusted lesions may be confused with injury caused by pecking or other trauma. In some avian species, the lesion may occur in the form of firm masses or cauliflower–like growths resembling tumors. Virulent strains cause ulcerative dermatitis rather than proliferative lesions. Most lesions occur on unfeathered areas of the head (corners of the mouth, base of the beak, nares, eyelids) and on the comb, wattles, ear lobes, dewlap, legs, and feet. Infrequently, lesions are in feathered areas. Large lesions on eyelids cause closure of the eyes. Involvement of the conjunctiva is common.

Diphtheritic form ('wet pox'). Extension of cutaneous lesions into the mouth or nasal cavity or spread of the virus via nostrils or eyes to the oral cavity results in the diphtheritic form of pox. Diphtheritic lesions can form in the absence of cutaneous lesions, but this is uncommon. Yellow caseous necrotic plaques in the mouth, at the base of the tongue, oropharynx, and larynx are typical lesions of diphtheritic avian pox. Extension down the esophagus to the crop rarely occurs. The larynx may become markedly thickened, a lesion that is difficult to differentiate from lesions of infectious laryngotracheitis. Thickening of the larynx may result in almost total occlusion of the glottis and death of the bird. Infection may extend to the nasal vestibules or as far as the anterior chamber of the nasal cavity.

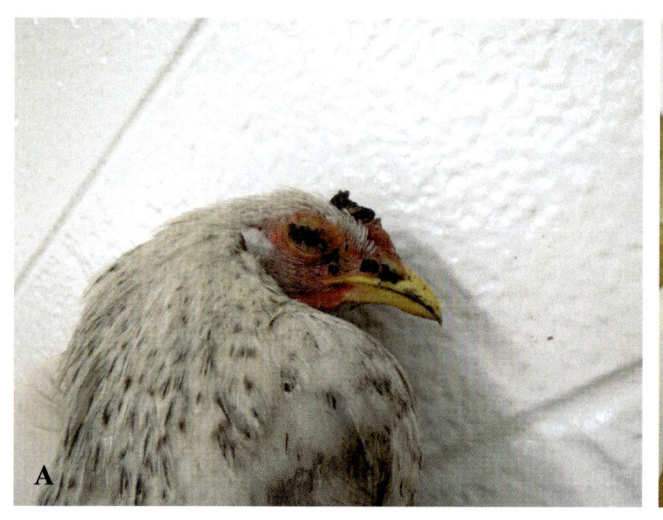

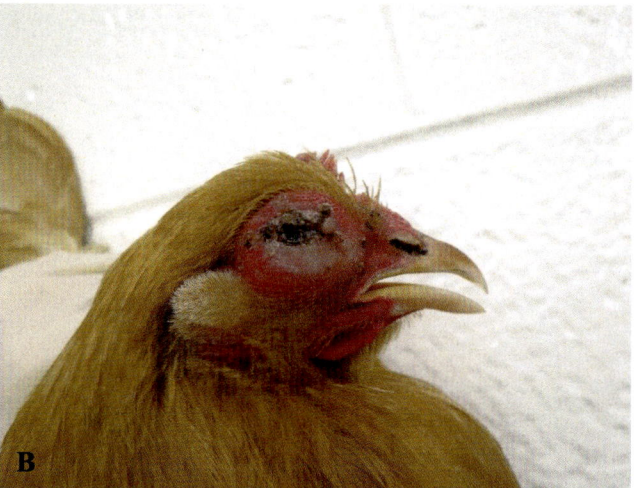

Cutaneous pox. Hobby chickens. **A.** Scabby lesions on the comb, face, and eyelid. Eye is closed because of the eyelid lesions. **B.** Severe scabby lesions involving and causing sticking of the eyelids. The cause of swelling of the infraorbital sinus was uncertain in this case.

Gross Pathology of Avian Diseases: Text and Atlas 101

Cutaneous pox. **C, D.** 12-week broiler breeder pullets. Scabby or reddish nodules in the skin around the beak and on the lower eyelid . **E, F.** Turkey breeder toms. Scabby nodular wart-like lesions on the head, face, snood, and dewlap. **G.** Hobby chicken. Severe proliferative lesion on the plantar surafce of the feet and posterior aspect of the hock joints. **H.** Sandpiper. Large, scabby nodules on the tibiotarsus and hock joint.

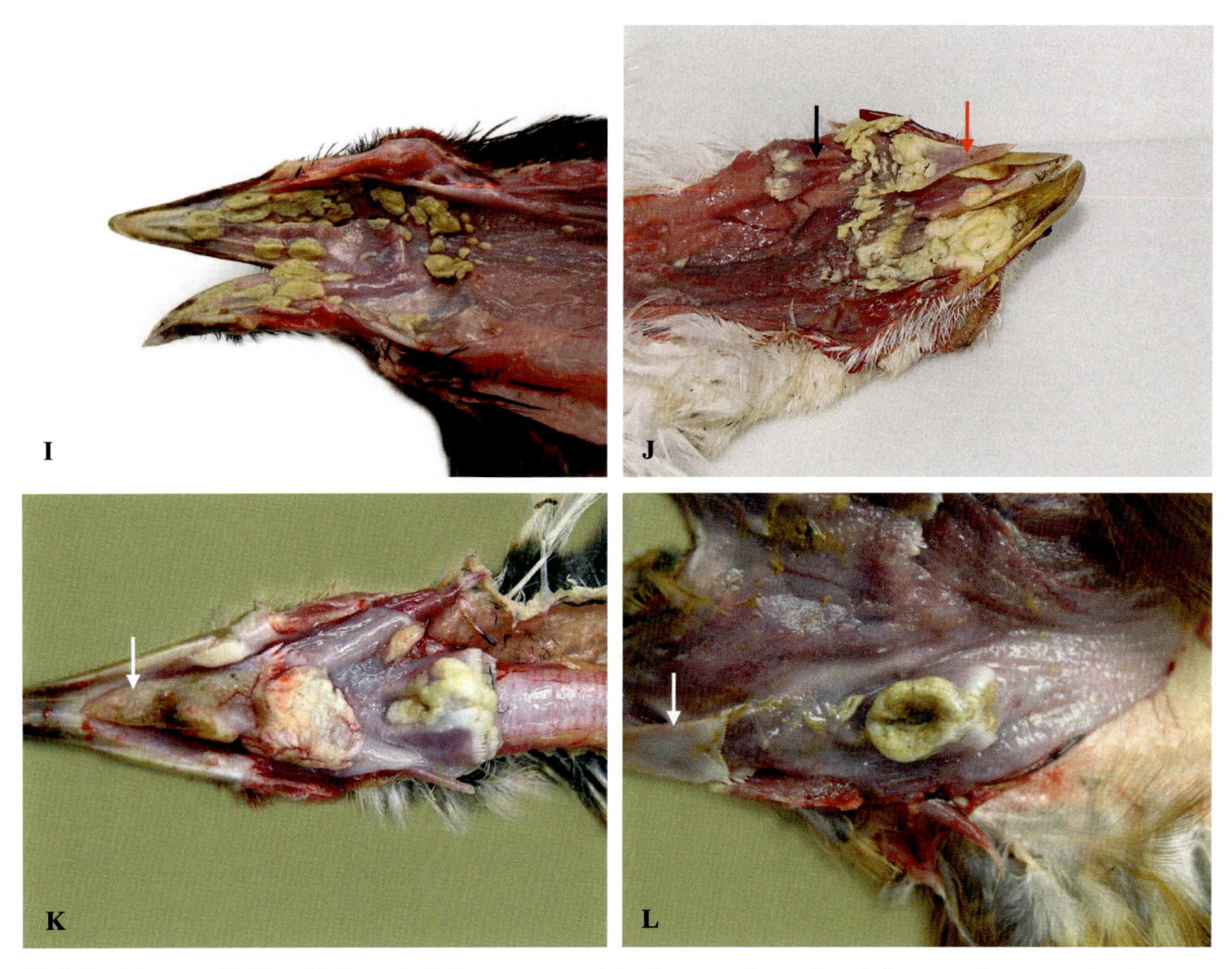

Diphtheritic pox. Hobby chickens. **I, J.** Caseous material adheres to the oral and pharyngeal mucosa. Lesions involve the posterior area of the tongue, and caseous material occludes the choanal opening. Black arrow: tracheal opening (glottis). red arrow: tongue. **K, L.** Proliferative lesions in the larynx almost completely occludes the glottis. In **K**, a large caseoproliferative lesion is also present in the pharynx just behind the tongue. Arrows: tongue.

Turkey Viral Hepatitis

Cause. Turkey viral hepatitis (TVH) is caused by a virus in the family *Picornaviridae*. Only turkeys are known to be affected. The disease is usually seen in poults between 3 and 6 weeks of age.

Gross lesions. Lesions of turkey viral hepatitis (TVH) are found in the liver and sometimes in the pancreas. Liver lesions consist of few to many small pale foci on the capsular and cut surfaces. Lesions in the pancreas are less frequent and consist of roughly circular or patchy, pale areas that can be focal or involve large areas of a pancreatic lobe. Lesions in the liver develop first followed by pancreatic lesions, therefore, it is not often that both lesions are seen together in the same bird. However, if multiple birds are examined from an affected flock, both liver and pancreatic lesions are usually found.

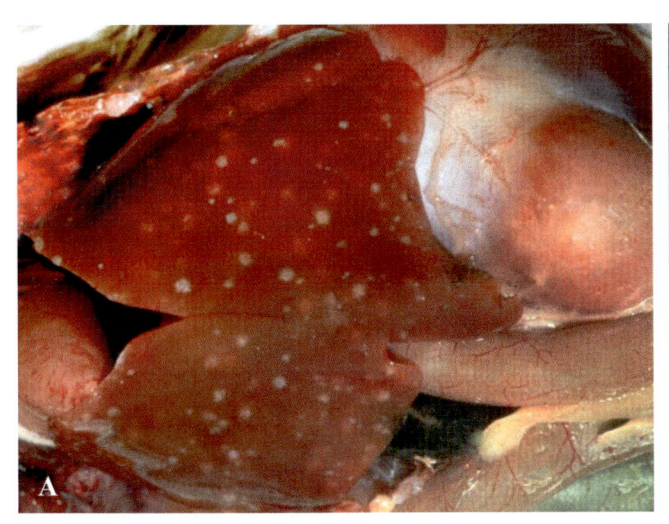

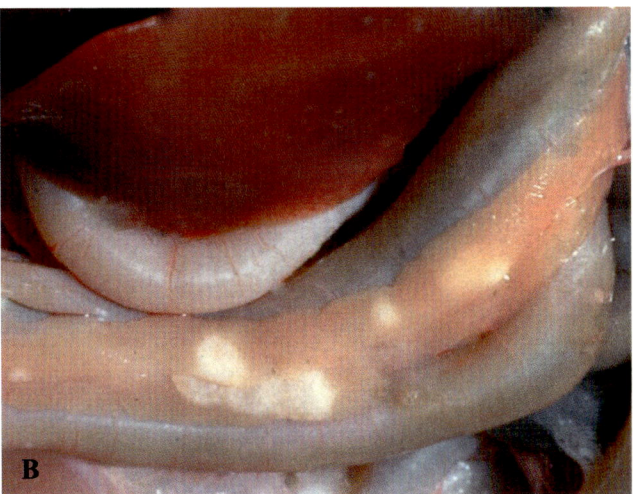

Turkey viral hepatitis. 4-week turkey. **A.** Pale foci are visible on the capsular surface of the liver. **B.** Pale, patchy areas are seen in the pancreas (arrows). Histologically, pale foci in the liver and pancreas are necrotic lesions containing a characteristic pleocellular infiltrate.

Duck Viral Enteritis

Cause. Herpesvirus (order *Herpesvirales* → family *Herpesviridae* → subfamily *Alphaherpesvirinae* → genus *Mardivirus* → species *anatid herpesvirus 1*). Disease occurs in ducks, geese, and swans of any age. Transmission is fecal-oral or fecal-cloacal via contaminated water.

Clinical signs. Sick birds show weakness, dehydration, thirst, diarrhea that may be bloody or green colored, and nasal-ocular discharges. High mortality is often the first indication of the disease. Mortality among free-living waterfowl crowded on wildlife refuges can number in the thousands. Moderate to marked drops in egg production occur in affected breeder ducks.

Gross lesions. Gross lesions reflect vascular and mucosal damage. Blood or bloody fluid is often located in various body cavities or gastrointestinal tract. Subcutaneous edema, especially of the neck, may occur. Petechial, ecchymotic, or brush hemorrhages occur in the heart, abdominal fat, ovary, and other visceral organs. Specific lesions are present in the oral cavity, esophagus, small intestine, cecum, large intestine, and cloaca. In the esophagus, lesions consist of linear, multifocal to coalescing, elevated, ulcerative areas along esophageal folds that are covered with yellow to green diphtheritic membranes. Hemorrhagic annular bands are seen in the small intestine of ducks, and a band of hemorrhage is often located at the esophageal-proventricular junction. Intestinal lesions in swans are discoid rather than annular. Hemorrhagic bands correspond to necrosis and hemorrhage of gut-associated lymphoid tissues. Lesions in the large intestine and cloaca consist of yellow to green exudate and necrotic debris adhering to areas of mucosal necrosis. Ceca have multifocal elevated, debris-filled mucosal ulcers or diffuse mucosal necrosis with necrotic debris in the lumen. Necrosis surrounding salivary gland duct openings beneath the tongue is seen in chronic infections. Liver is often pale and blotchy with numerous pinpoint red foci.

Duck virus enteritis. Muscovy duck. **A, B.** Esophageal lesion. The lesion consists of mucosal necrosis covered with yellow to green diphtheritic membranes. Note the lesion extending along the longitudinal axis of the mucosal folds. **C, D.** Hemorrhages in the epicardium and myocardium. In **D**, myocardial hemorrhage is extensive and petechial hemorrhages are in the fat in the coronary grove at the base of the heart. **E.** Petechial hemorrhages in mesenteric fat. **F.** a hemorrhagic annular band (circle) in the small intestine.

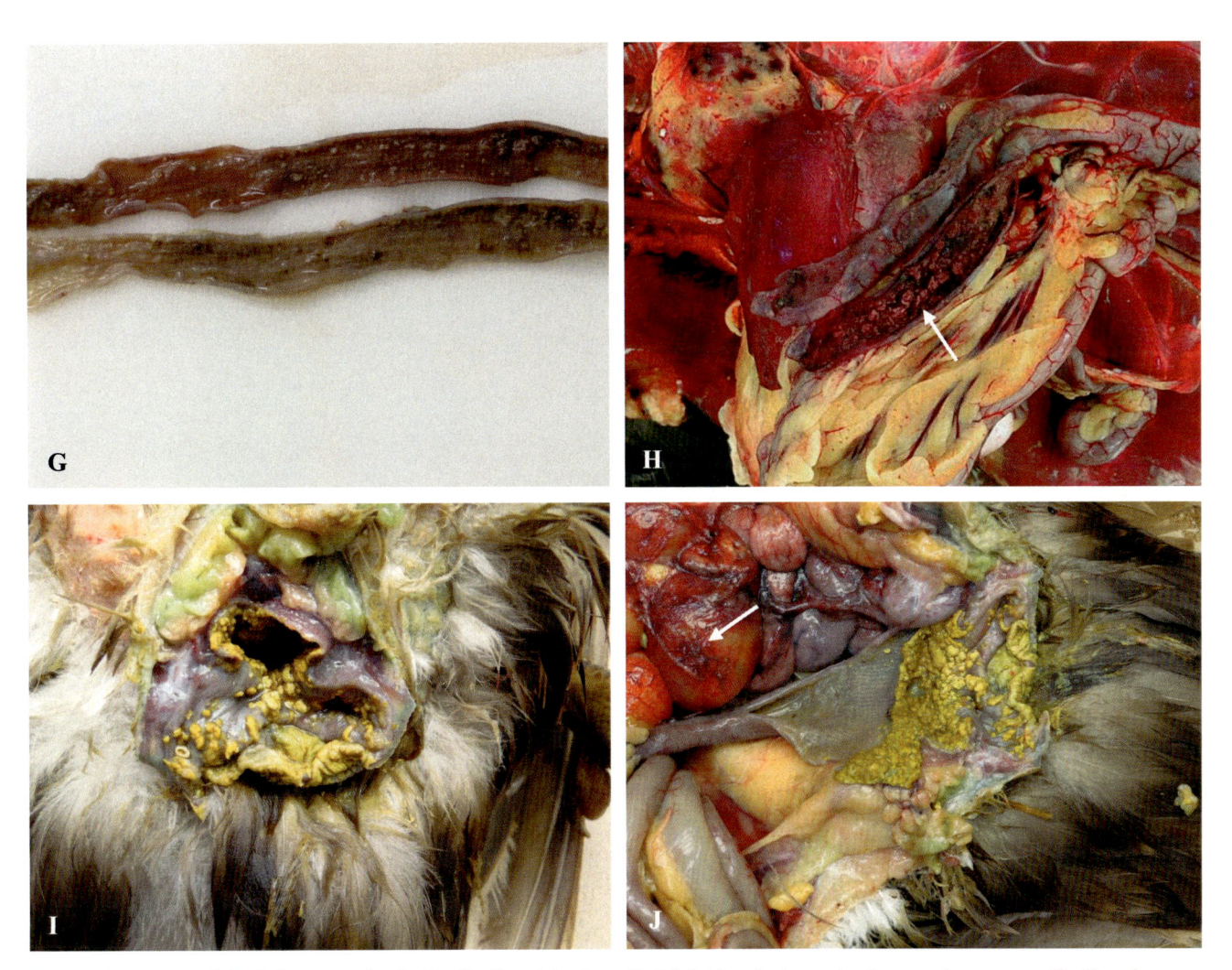

Duck virus enteritis. Muscovy duck. **F, G.** Cecal lesion. **F.** Multifocal ulcers in the cecal mucosa. **G.** Cecal mucosa is necrotic and hemorrhagic, and there is blood stained necrotic debris in the lumen (arrow). **H, I.** Cloacal lesions. Diphtheritic membranes cover underlying mucosal necrosis; in **I**, note hemorrhage in an ovarian follicle (arrow).

Duck Viral Hepatitis Type A

Cause. *Avihepatovirus A* (order *Picornavirales* → family *Picornaviridae* → genus *Avihepatovirus* → species *avihepatovirus A*).

Clinical signs. Clinical disease occurs only in young ducklings less than 6 weeks of age. Pekin ducks are very susceptible. The disease is highly contagious and characterized by sudden onset, high morbidity and mortality, and rapid spread within the flock. Mortality may reach 90% in ducklings less than one week of age. In ducklings between 4 and 5 weeks of age, mortality is low to negligible. Lethargy is the earliest clinical sign in affected ducklings. They appear weak, are reluctant to move, and have their eyes partially closed. The disease progresses quickly. Ducklings fall on their sides and exhibit spasmodic contractions (kicking) of the legs; they usually die within an hour in a typical opisthotonus ("arched-back") position. In severe outbreaks, high mortality occurs within a short time period.

Gross lesions. Liver is enlarged and pale-pink, pale-yellow or red, and spotted with hemorrhagic foci or blotched with dark and pale areas. In some cases, the spleen is enlarged and mottled. Kidneys may be enlarged and pale.

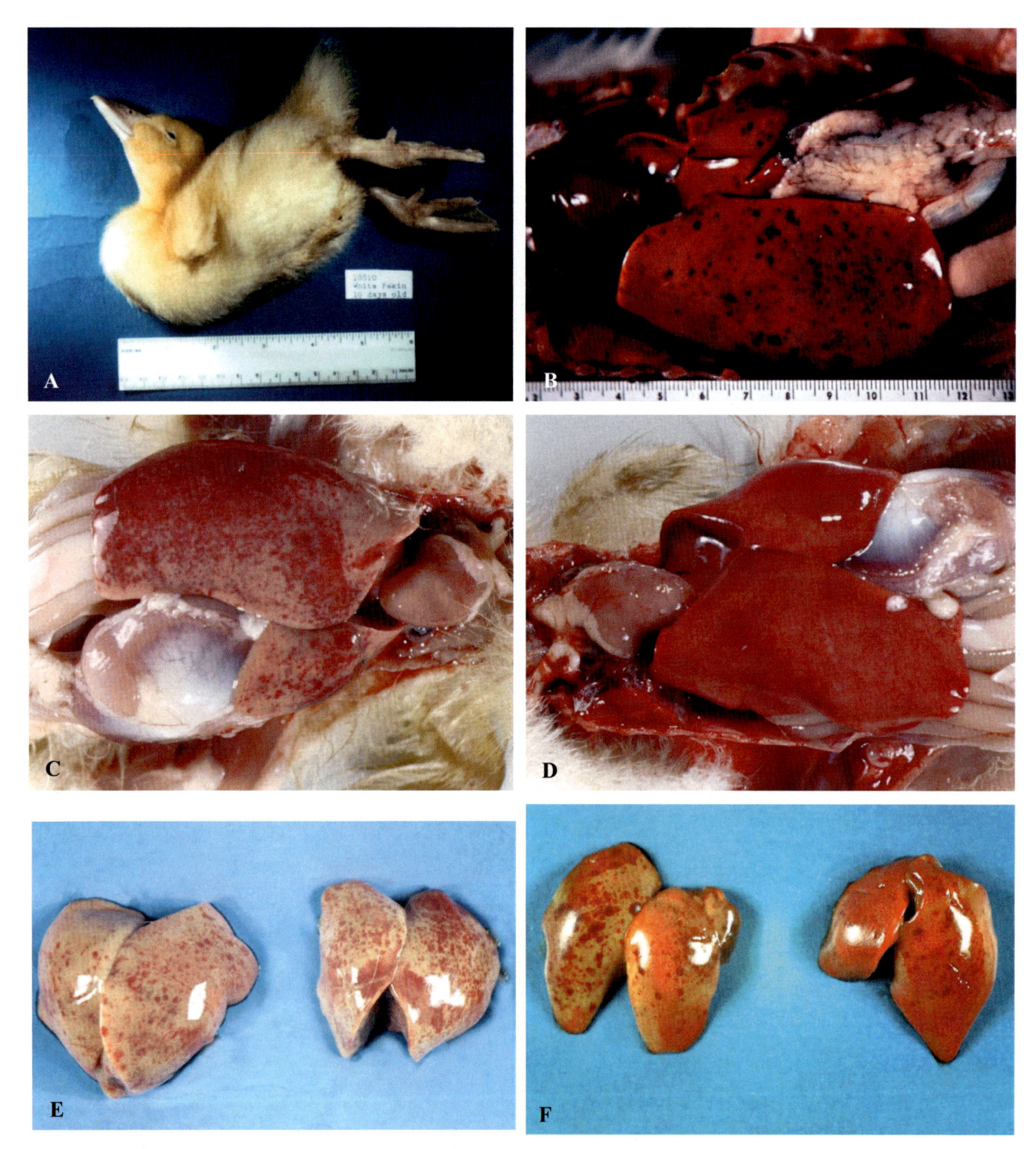

Duck viral hepatitis type A. Ducklings. **A.** Dead duckling in typical opisthotonos position. **B.** Liver is red and has hemorrhagic spots. **C.** Liver has pale-pink and red areas. Pale discoloration is due to necrosis and degeneration of hepatocytes. **D.** Liver is lightly pale and has pinpoint dark foci. **E.** Liver is pale beige with brownish spots. Pallor is due to extensive necrosis and degeneration of hepatocytes. **F.** Liver is pale yellow with hemorrhagic spots. *(Photos courtesy of Dr. Jarra Jagne and College of Veterinary Medicine, Cornell University).*

Paramyxovirus Infection in Pigeons (Pigeon Paramyxovirus)

Cause. Infection is caused by Newcastle disease virus (NDV) (also known as avian paramyxovirus 1 [APMV-1]), which belongs to the genus *Avulavirus* in the family *Paramyxoviridae*. The genome of the virus has six open reading frames, which code for six nucleocapsid proteins: nucleoprotein (NP), phosphoprotein (P), matrix protein (M), fusion protein (F), hemagglutinin-neuraminidase (HN), and RNA-dependent polymerase protein (L).

APMV-1 isolates belong to a single serotype but are genetically diverse. Based on genome length and nucleotide sequences, APMV-1 strains are classified into two distinct classes, I and II. Class I comprises a single genotype. Class II is separated into 15 genotypes (I-XV), based on genotypic and phylogenetic relationships. Class I strains are usually avirulent and found worldwide, typically in shorebirds and waterfowl. Class II strains circulate in wild birds and poultry and contain the most virulent genotypes. Sub-genotypes are present among the two classes. The amino acid motif at the cleavage site of the F protein is the main molecular determinant of virulence. Virulent strains have at least three arginine or lysine residues between positions 113 to 116 and a phenylalanine residue at position 117. However, factors related to other genes and proteins of the virus may also play a role in the virulence of a specific virus strain.

Pigeon paramyxovirus 1 (PPMV-1) is an antigenic and host variant of Newcastle disease virus that has a strong affinity for pigeons. The virus seems to arise from cross-species transmission from chickens to pigeons. Phylogenetic analysis based on partial nucleotide sequences of the F protein gene of several PPMV-1 isolates place the virus in genotype IX of class II APMV-1. The amino acid motif of the F protein cleavage site of PPMV-1 has a pattern consistent with virulent NDV. However, there is considerable genetic diversity among PPMV-1 isolates.

Host. PPMV-1 infects Columbiformes (pigeons and doves). Despite possessing the virulence signature at the F protein cleavage site, PPMV-1 is not consistently virulent for chickens. Pathogenicity for chickens following experimental infection is determined by virus strain, age of the birds, route of inoculation, and dose of the virus. Consequences of experimental inoculation range from mild respiratory disease to neurologic disease with mortality. Because some strains of PPMV-1 replicate poorly in chickens, it is possible that variants with different replicative and pathogenic potential in chickens exist among the genetically diverse PPMV-1 strains. Natural outbreaks of PPMV-1 infection with clinical disease in commercial poultry occurred in Great Britain. Contamination of feed with pigeon droppings and carcasses of pigeons that had died were considered the main sources of most of these outbreaks. Because of these outbreaks, there is concern that PPMV-1 may spread from pigeons to commercial poultry flocks and cause serious clinical disease. From a biosecurity standpoint, pigeons should be considered a potential source of virulent NDV.

Clinical signs. All ages are susceptible. Birds may be found dead without premonitory clinical signs. In a pigeon loft, the first sign is usually watery, green diarrhea. Birds become lethargic and anorexic. Some birds show neurologic signs including head tremor, ataxia, disorientation, circling, torticollis, opisthotonos, and paresis of legs and wings. Nervous signs either develop early, even preceding onset of diarrhea, or occur later in birds that survive virus infection. Mortality varies, but can be as high as 100%.

Gross lesions. Lesions may be absent. Kidney lesions are prominent in some outbreaks. Kidneys are enlarged, have white speckles and spots, and may be pale. In some birds, the pancreas has pale white areas. No lesions are present in tracheas.

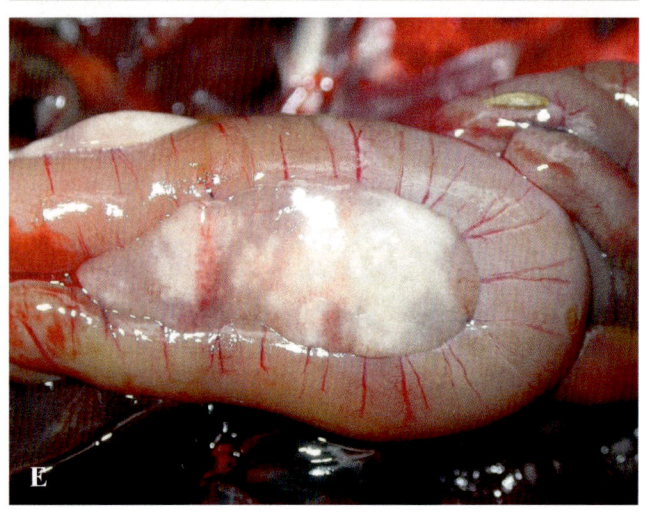

108   *Gross Pathology of Avian Diseases: Text and Atlas*

Pigeon paramyxovirus 1 (PPMV-1) infection. A. Pigeon is lethargic and reluctant to move. **B.** Watery diarrhea is an early clinical manifestation of PPMV-1 infection. **C.** Neurologic signs (torticollis) are exhibited by this infected pigeon. **D.** Pale areas in the pancreas. **E.** Coalescing white areas in the pancreas. *(Photos B, C, E courtesy of Dr. Peter Wencel, Poland).*

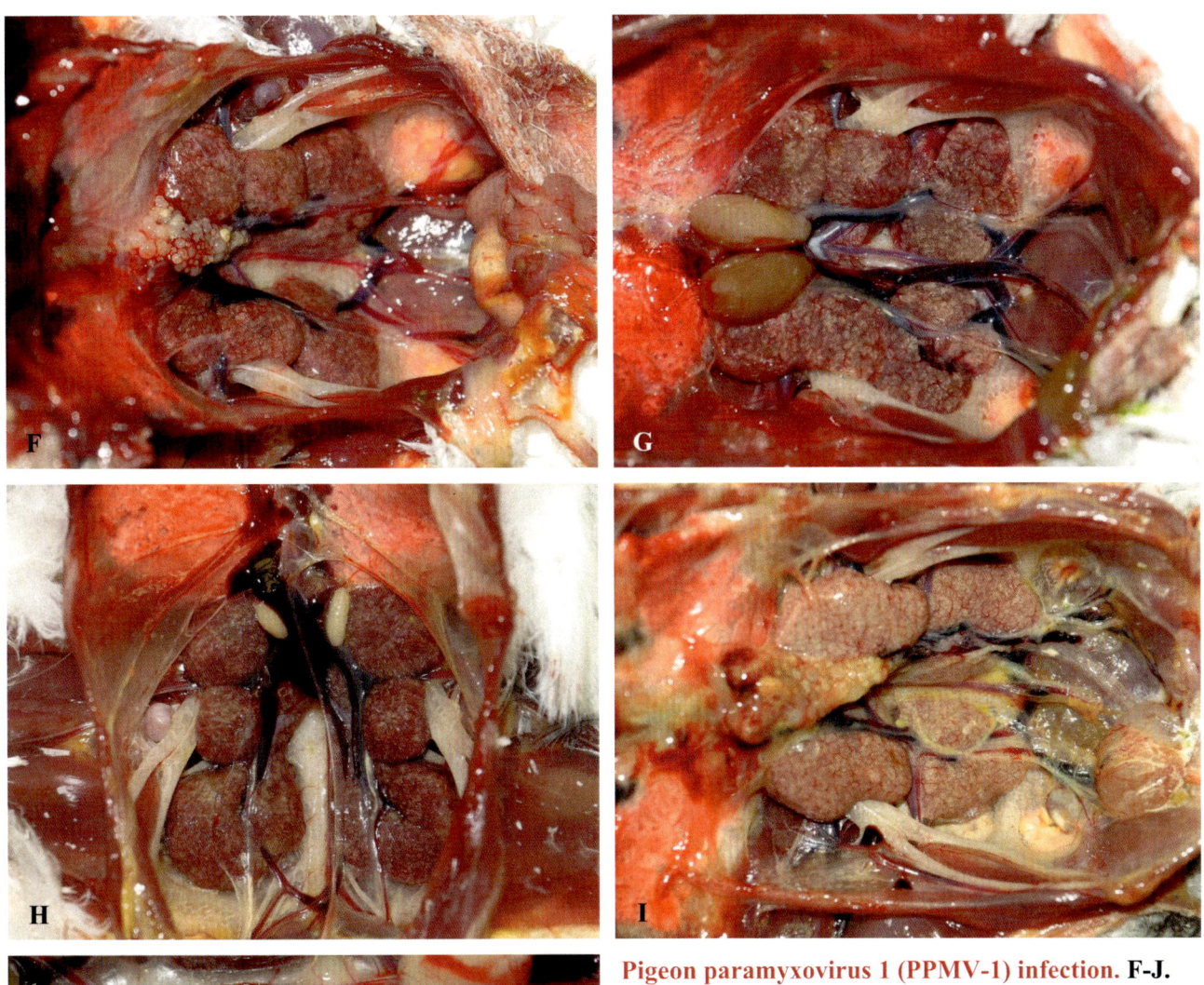

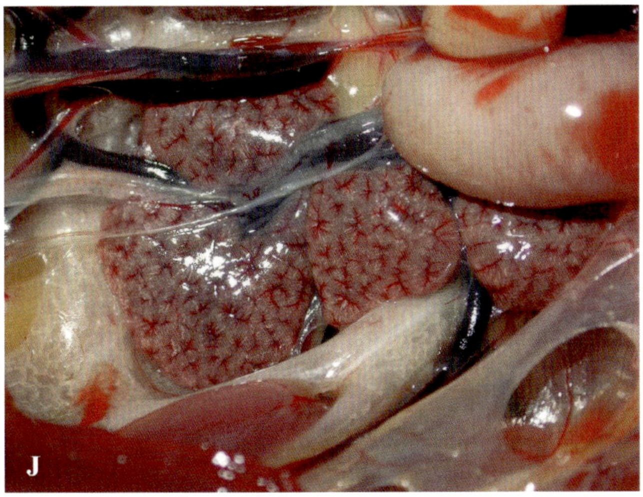

Pigeon paramyxovirus 1 (PPMV-1) infection. F-J. Kidneys are enlarged and have characteristic white speckles and spots. Kidneys in **H** are pale. **F-I** are kidneys of pigeons from a loft with high mortality due to PPMV-1 infection. PPMV-1 was detected in cloacal swabs by PCR. *(Photo J courtesy of Dr. Peter Wencel, Poland).*

Herpesvirus Infection in Pigeons

Cause. Herpesvirus (order *Herpesvirales* → family *Herpesviridae* → subfamily *Alphaherpesvirinae* → genus *Mardivirus* → species *Columbid herpesvirus 1* [CoHV-1]) infects pigeons and causes "herpesviral inclusion body disease" in pigeons, falcons, and owls. Based on nucleotide sequences, herpesvirus infections in pigeons, falcons, and owls are all caused by CoHV-1, which is distinct from other avian herpesviruses.

Epidemiology. Adult birds are asymptomatic, latently-infected carriers that shed virus intermittently, especially during reproduction. The virus is not egg-transmitted, but squabs are exposed soon after hatching to virus shed by adults. Virus in the pharynx is readily transmitted to squabs during feeding. Squabs with protective levels of maternal antibodies do not develop clinical disease, but they become asymptomatic carriers. Squabs experimentally infected by "pharyngeal painting" persistently shed high amounts of virus for 7-10 days. Appearance of lesions coincided with peak virus shedding 3 to 4 days post-inoculation. During periods of stress, e.g., after weaning or learning to fly, young birds may develop clinical disease due to activation of latent virus. This explains why clinical signs develop in young birds shortly after stressful events. In addition, immunosuppression caused by damage to the bursa of Fabricius by circovirus or other infectious agents may trigger activation and shedding of latent virus.

Clinical signs. Young birds between 2 and 10 weeks of age that lack adequate protective immunity typically develop clinical disease 5 to 7 days after exposure. Sick birds exhibit mucoid nasal discharge and unilateral or bilateral conjunctivitis. Food may be retained in the crop for a prolonged period causing crop distension and anorexia. Dyspnea occurs in birds with laryngeal lesions. Depending on the level of immunity and virus strain, mortality varies among infected flocks, and the severity of the infection varies among birds within the flock. Conjunctivitis may be the only clinical sign in mildly infected birds. Birds that survive recover in 1 to 3 weeks but become asymptomatic carriers.

Gross lesions. Lesions generally are found in the oral and pharyngeal mucosa, which is reddened and has a confluent to multifocal thin, loose, yellow diphtheritic membrane. In severe cases, the oral and pharyngeal mucosas have small foci of necrosis and ulceration. Lesions are sometimes also found in the mucosa of the esophagus, larynx, or trachea. Secondary bacterial infection is common and results in sinusitis, airsacculitis, or septicemia. Infection may become generalized following transient viremia during which the virus spreads to other organs. With systemic infection, the liver may have multiple, small, white foci caused by degeneration and necrosis of hepatocytes, or it can be enlarged and pale yellow. Microscopically, presence of typical intranuclear inclusion bodies is diagnostic.

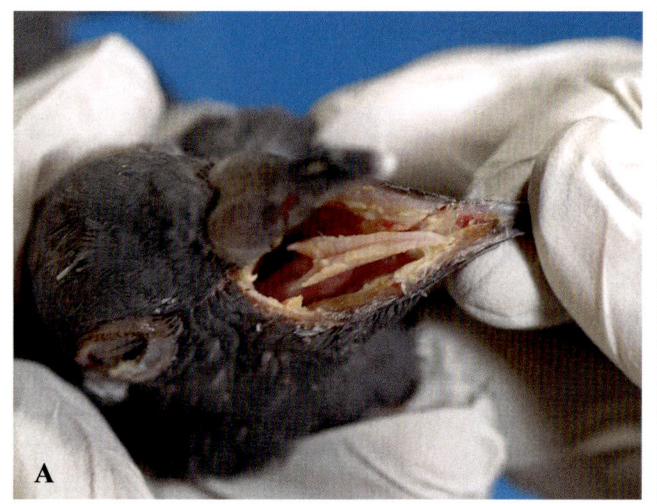

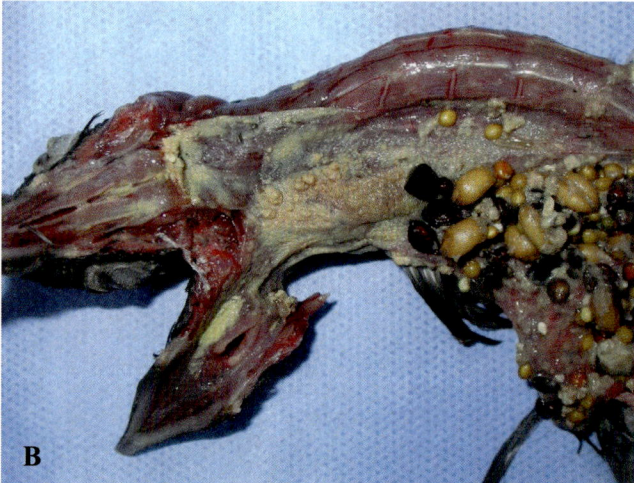

Columbid herpesvirus 1 infection. Pigeons. **A.** Necrotic lesions in the oral mucosa. **B.** Oral and esophageal mucosa is covered with a yellow diphtheritic membrane. Food has remained in the crop. *(Photo A wixsite.com/pigeon viral diseases. Photo B courtesy of Dr. Peter Wencel, Poland).*

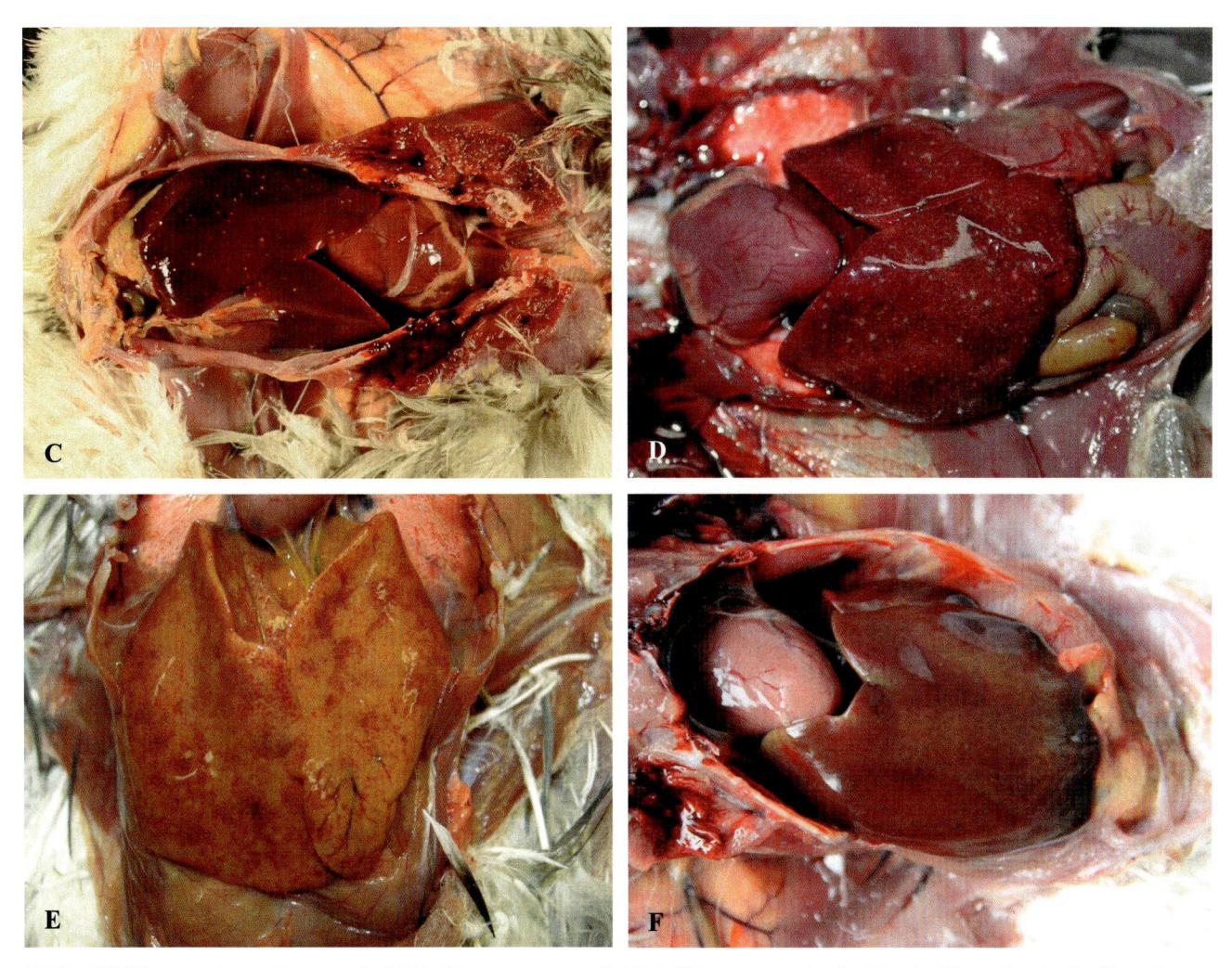

***Columbid herpesvirus 1* systemic infection, pigeons. C, D.** Miliary necrotic foci in the liver. In **D**, the liver is enlarged. **E.** 3-week pigeon. Liver is enlarged, pale yellow, and mottled. **F.** Liver is enlarged and has discolored areas. *(Photo C courtesy of Dr. Arnaud Van Wettere, USA. Photo D courtesy of Dr. Peter Wencel, Poland. Photo F courtesy of Dr. Jingliang Su, China).*

Pacheco's Disease

Pacheco's disease is a highly contagious, often fatal, viral disease of psittacine birds. The disease was first reported from Brazil in 1930. Psittacine species susceptible to infection include parrots, macaws, cockatiels, cockatoos, parakeets, conures, lovebirds, rosellas, and lories. New World parrots (macaws, Amazon parrots, and some species of conures) are more likely to develop fatal disease than Old World parrots. Most cases are diagnosed in Amazon parrots followed by macaws, conures, and African gray parrots. Clinical disease typically follows a stressful event. Parrots of all ages are susceptible.

Cause. Herpesvirus (order *Herpesvirales* → family *Herpesviridae* → subfamily *Alphaherpesvirinae* → genus *Iltovirus* → species *Psittacid herpesvirus 1*). Based on gene sequencing and phylogenetic analysis, psittacid herpesvirus 1 (PsHV-1) is classified into four genotypes designated 1 to 4. Three serotypes have been identified by virus-neutralization. Usually, virus serotype can be predicted by genotype. Genotypes 1 and 4 correspond to serotype 1, genotype 2 corresponds to serotype 2, and genotype 3 corresponds to serotype 3. It is believed that PsHV-1 genotypes co-evolved with and adapted to several species of Neotropical parrots and do not cause disease in their host species. However, acute fatal disease occurs in birds infected with genotypes to which they are not evolutionarily adapted. Because of virus-species adaptation, Pacheco's disease is a disease of captive psittacines when latently infected species are commingled with susceptible species. Patagonian conures and Nanday parakeets (also known as Nanday conures) are notorious asymptomatic carriers and natural hosts in the wild. They are resistant to clinical disease but harbor the virus. Old World species are less likely to develop clinical disease or become asymptomatic carriers.

The outcome of the infection depends on virus genotype, species of bird infected, and bird's overall health. Birds that survive infection become chronic carriers and remain persistently infected; intermittently shedding virus throughout their lives. The following table shows examples of the possible origins of different PsHV-1 genotypes in wild psittacines.

Psittacid herpesvirus 1 infections: Possible host-adaptation and clinical disease

Virus genotype	Adapted host	Pacheco's disease
Genotype 1	Red-shouldered macaws	Amazon and African gray parrots
Genotype 2	*Aratinga* sp. (conures)	Amazon parrots
Genotype 3	Hyacinth macaws	Amazon and African gray parrots, macaws, conures
Genotype 4	Patagonian conures	Amazon and African gray parrots, macaws, conures

Clinical signs and gross lesions. Well-fleshed birds may die acutely without premonitory clinical signs. Other birds may exhibit subtle or obvious clinical signs shortly before death. Clinical signs are non-specific and include watery green diarrhea, lethargy, anorexia, frequent prolonged closing of eyes, and preference for the cage floor over a perch. Gross lesions may be absent in very acute cases. In less acute cases, lesions are found in the liver, which becomes swollen and slightly to markedly discolored with petechial hemorrhages and pinpoint pale foci of necrosis. Some birds show only subtle diffuse mottling of the liver due to centrilobular necrosis. The spleen may be enlarged and hemorrhagic or mottled. Other lesions include swollen kidneys, epicardial hemorrhages, and enteritis.

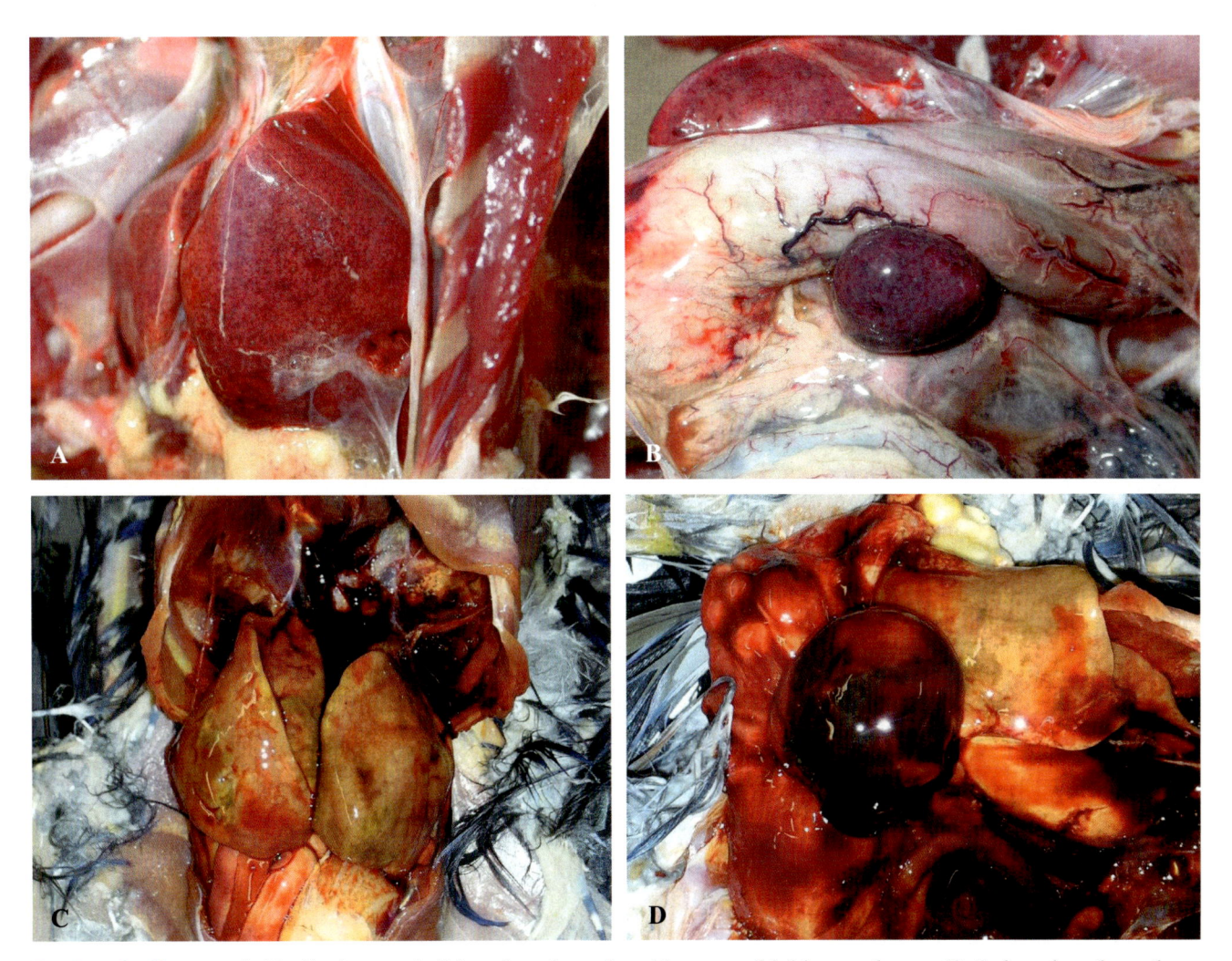

Pacheco's disease. A, B. Cockatoo. **A.** Liver is enlarged and has petechial hemorrhages. **B.** Spleen is enlarged and purple. **C. D.** African gray parrot. **C.** Liver is enlarged and discolored. **D.** Spleen is markedly enlarged and hemorrhagic. *(Photos C, D courtesy of Dr. Hafez M. Hafez, Germany).*

Proventricular Dilatation Disease in Psittacines

Initially affecting macaws and called 'macaw wasting disease', proventricular dilatation disease (PDD) is now known to occur in at least 28 different captive and free-living psittacine species.

Cause. Proventricular dilation disease in psittacines is caused by avian bornavirus (order *Mononegavirales* → family *Bornaviridae* → genus *Bornavirus* → species *psittaciform 1 bornavirus*). The virus was originally isolated from parrots and named parrot bornavirus (PaBV), which is distinct from mammalian bornaviruses. Several genotypes of PaBV isolates are recognized. Currently, genotypes 1-4 and 7 belong to *psittaciform 1 bornavirus*, genotype 5 is classified as *Psittaciform 2 bornavirus*, and one genotype is yet to be classified. Genotypes 2 and 4 are most commonly isolated.

Transmission. Infected birds shed the virus in droppings; infection of other birds occurs via the oral route. Subclinically infected birds may shed virus intermittently for years. The virus is also vertically transmitted. It has been suggested that birds infected *in ovo* may develop immunological tolerance and become persistent asymptomatic carriers and shedders of the virus. This may explain why only some birds develop clinical disease despite widespread infection.

Clinical signs. Clinical signs in psittacines affected with PDD include chronic weight loss, progressive decrease in feed consumption and activity, crop stasis, intermittent regurgitation, and passage of loose droppings containing undigested seeds. Affected birds become emaciated and eventually die from starvation. The virus may affect the central nervous system causing neurologic signs including inability to fly or perch, tremors, ataxia, seizures, and blindness. The same bird may have concurrent gastrointestinal and nervous signs.

Gross lesions. The hallmark gross lesion in birds with PDD is dilation of the proventriculus, which becomes thin walled and distended with food. The degree of proventricular dilation ranges from mild to severe. Dilation of the ventriculus (gizzard) and/or intestine may also be noted. The duodenum contains partially digested food that is often heavily bile stained. There is severe emaciation evidenced by wasting of pectoral muscles and loss of subcutaneous, abdominal, and visceral fat.

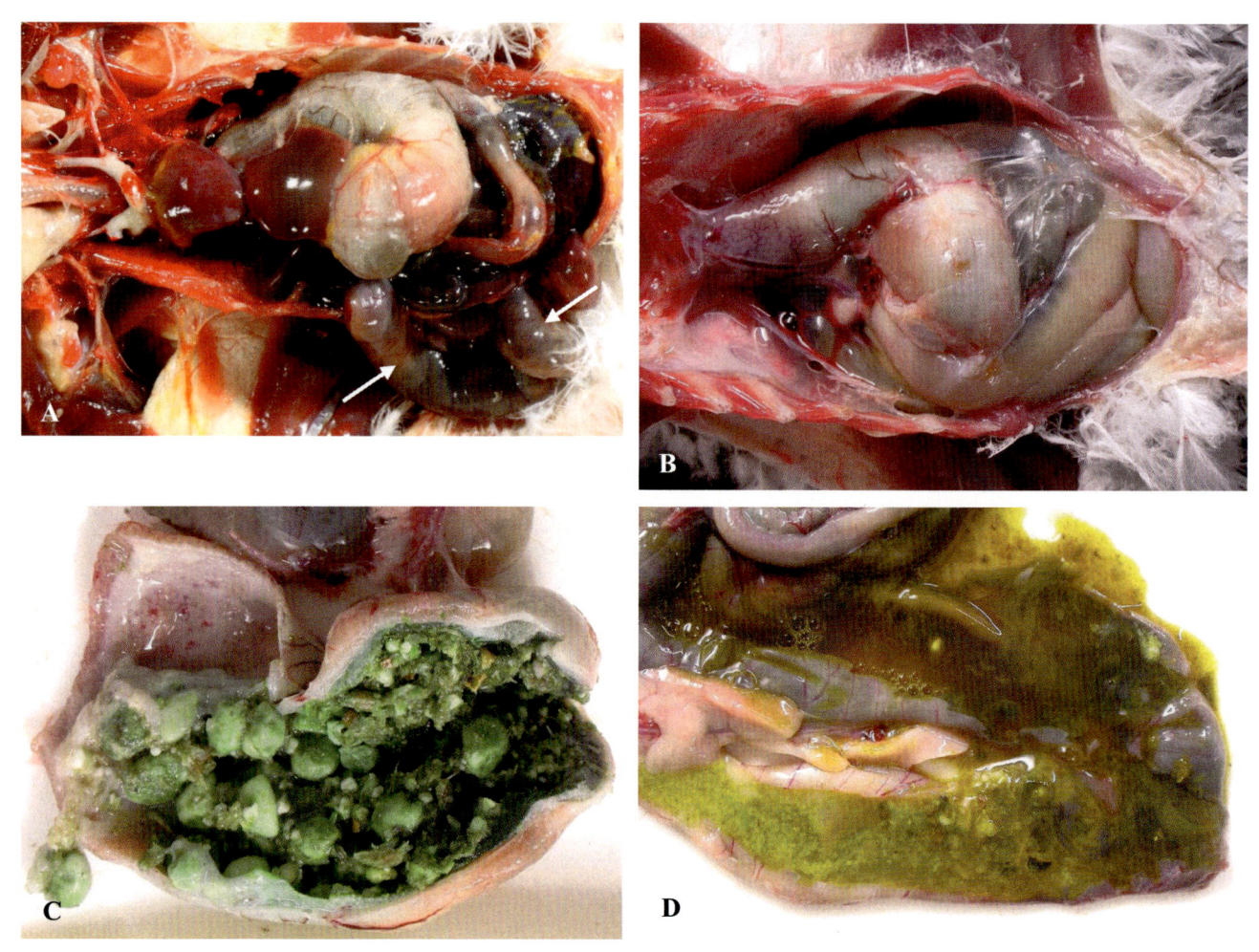

Proventricular dilatation disease. **A.** Cockatoo. Proventriculus is thin walled and markedly enlarged. Note also the distended duodenum (arrows). **B, C, D.** 8-year male African gray parrot. **B.** Enlarged proventriculus, gizzard and duodenum. **C.** Proventriculus is thin walled and filled with undigested food that is heavily stained with bile. **D.** Duodenum is filled with partially digested, bile stained food. (*Photo A. courtesy of Dr. John Edward, USA. Photos B, C, D. courtesy of Dr. Gerry Dorrestein, Netherlands*).

Polyomavirus Infection in Budgerigars and Other Psittacine Birds

Cause. *Aves polyomavirus 1* in the genus *Gammapolyomavirus* of the family *Polyomaviridae*. The recently classified species *Serinus canaria polyomavirus 1* in the same genus causes fatal disease in canaries

Hosts and susceptibility. Avian polyomavirus infection is an important cause of disease in psittacine pet birds. It is responsible for significant economic losses for aviculturists and pet store owners. Polyomavirus infects most species of psittacine birds, but they vary considerably in their susceptibility to clinical disease. Macaws, conures, eclectus parrots, budgerigars, lovebirds, and ring-necked parakeets are highly susceptible. Clinical disease is infrequently reported in cockatiels, lories, Amazon parrots, hawk-headed parrots, and caiques. Cockatoos, Quaker parrots, and African gray parrots are generally considered resistant to clinical disease, although, like most psittacines, they are susceptible to infection.

In conures, avian polyomavirus can cause clinical disease and death in young birds under 6 weeks of age. Infection is asymptomatic when birds are over 6 weeks of age. Infected birds shed virus for 4-8 weeks (rarely up to 16 weeks). In macaws, clinical disease occurs in birds under 14 weeks of age, after which infections are asymptomatic. Virus is known to be shed for up to 14 weeks in blue-and-gold macaw nestlings that survive infection, 10 weeks in red-fronted macaws, and less than 6 weeks in hyacinth macaws. In eclectus parrots, avian polyomavirus causes clinical disease and death in birds infected under 14 weeks of age. Cockatoos of any age are highly susceptible to infection but resistant to clinical disease; virus shedding lasts for 4-8 weeks. Polyomavirus infection in lovebirds is distinct in that birds up to one year of age can be affected and die from the disease.

Clinical signs and gross lesions in budgerigar fledgling disease. Disease and death occur in nestling budgerigars (1-3 weeks of age), with up to 100% mortality. Adult budgerigars typically are resistant to clinical disease, but seroconvert and shed virus for up to 90 days. Nestling budgerigars may die suddenly, usually between 10 and 15 days of age (range 10-28 days), without premonitory clinical signs. Other nestlings may exhibit clinical signs for 24-48 hours before death. Signs are not specific and include lethargy, anorexia, and crop stasis. In some cases, polyomavirus infects the brain and nestlings show neurologic signs including head tremor, ataxia, paresis, and paralysis. Lack of development of downy feathers is a prominent feature in infected budgerigars that survive up to 28 days of age. Normally, budgerigars hatch without feathers, but down begins to appear by 12 days of age, and feathering is almost complete by about one month of age.

Gross lesions in birds that die from the disease include distension of the abdomen due to ascites; subcutaneous and muscle hemorrhages; myocardial pallor and hemorrhages; enlargement, discoloration, and mottling of the liver; enlargement of the spleen; pericardial effusion (hydropericardium); enlargement and pallor of the kidneys; necrosis, ulceration, and hemorrhage in the esophagus and crop mucosa; necrotic debris in the crop lumen; and hemorrhage and swelling in the tissues around the esophagus. Infected budgerigars may survive the infection and never become outwardly ill. Some nestlings that survive do not develop primary and secondary wing feathers or tail feathers. These budgerigars have been referred to as runners or creepers because of their inability to fly. However, it is important to keep in mind that beak and feather disease virus may cause similar poor feathering.

Lesions in other psittacines. Lesions in other psittacine birds are more or less similar to those in budgerigars.

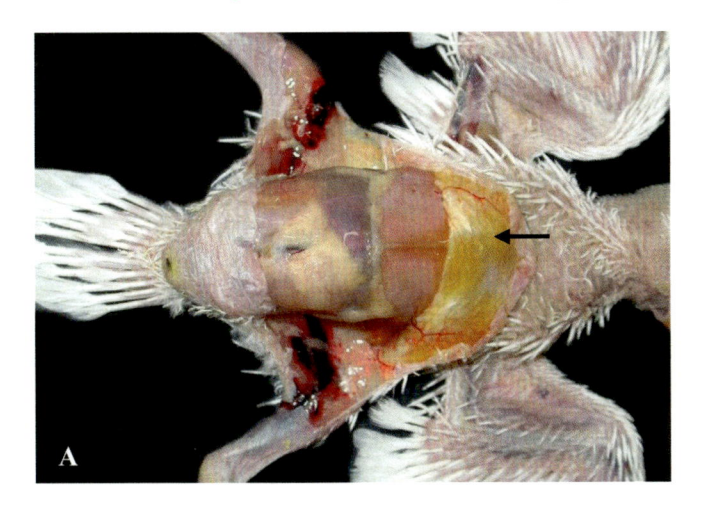

Polyomavirus infection. Fledgling ring-necked parakeet. **A.** Hemorrhages in the subcutis and skeletal muscle in the inner thigh. There is subcutaneous edema (arrow).

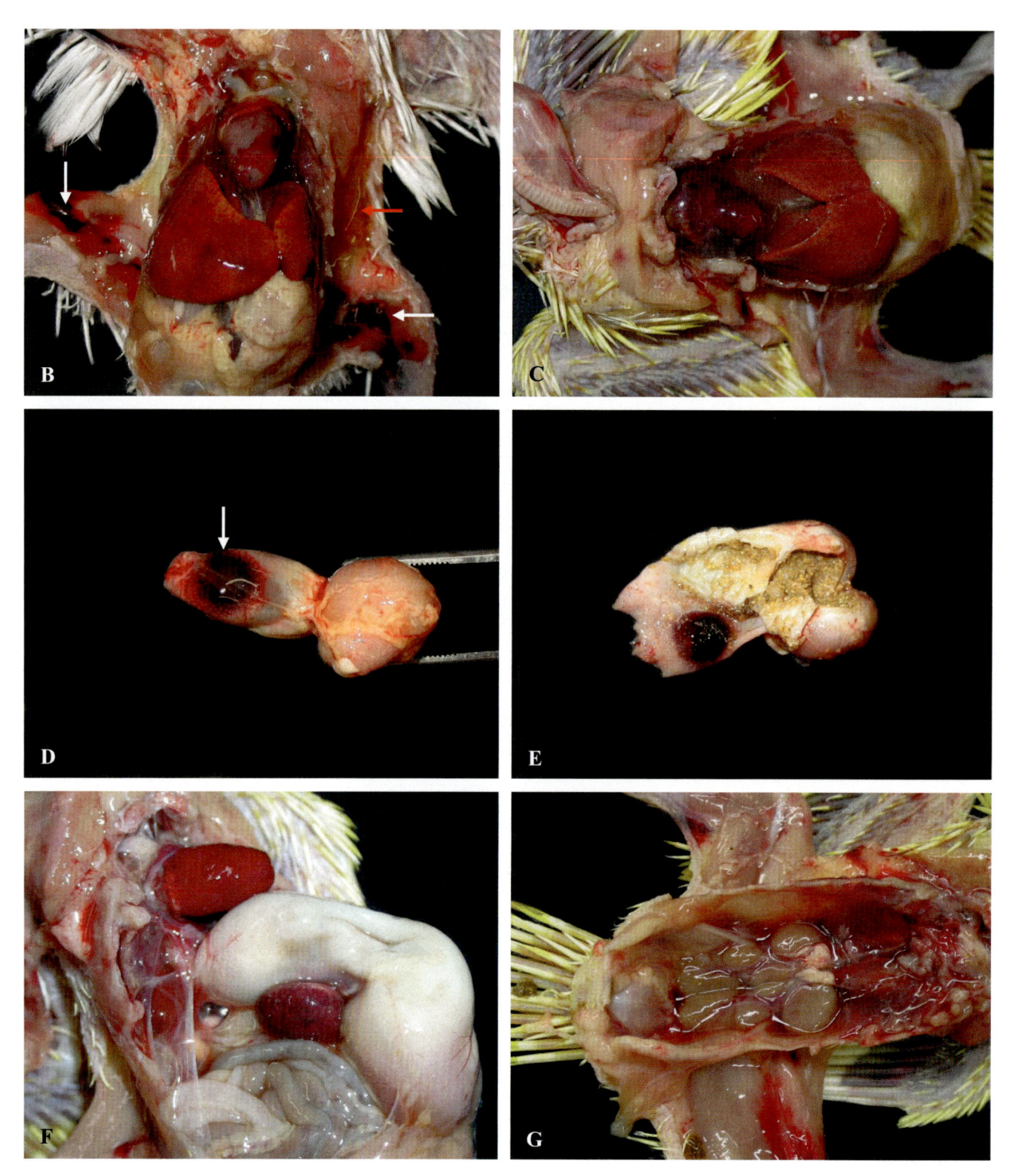

Polyomavirus infection. B, C. Liver is enlarged, pale, and mottled. Note the hydropericardium and myocardial hemorrhages. In **B**, note the subcutaneous hemorrhages (white arrows) and edema (red arrow). **D.** Hemorrhagic area is visible through the serosal surface of the proventriculus (arrow). **E.** Focal hemorrhage in the proventricular mucosal surface (the area in **D**). **F.** Spleen is enlarged and mottled. **G.** Kidneys are swollen and pale tan.

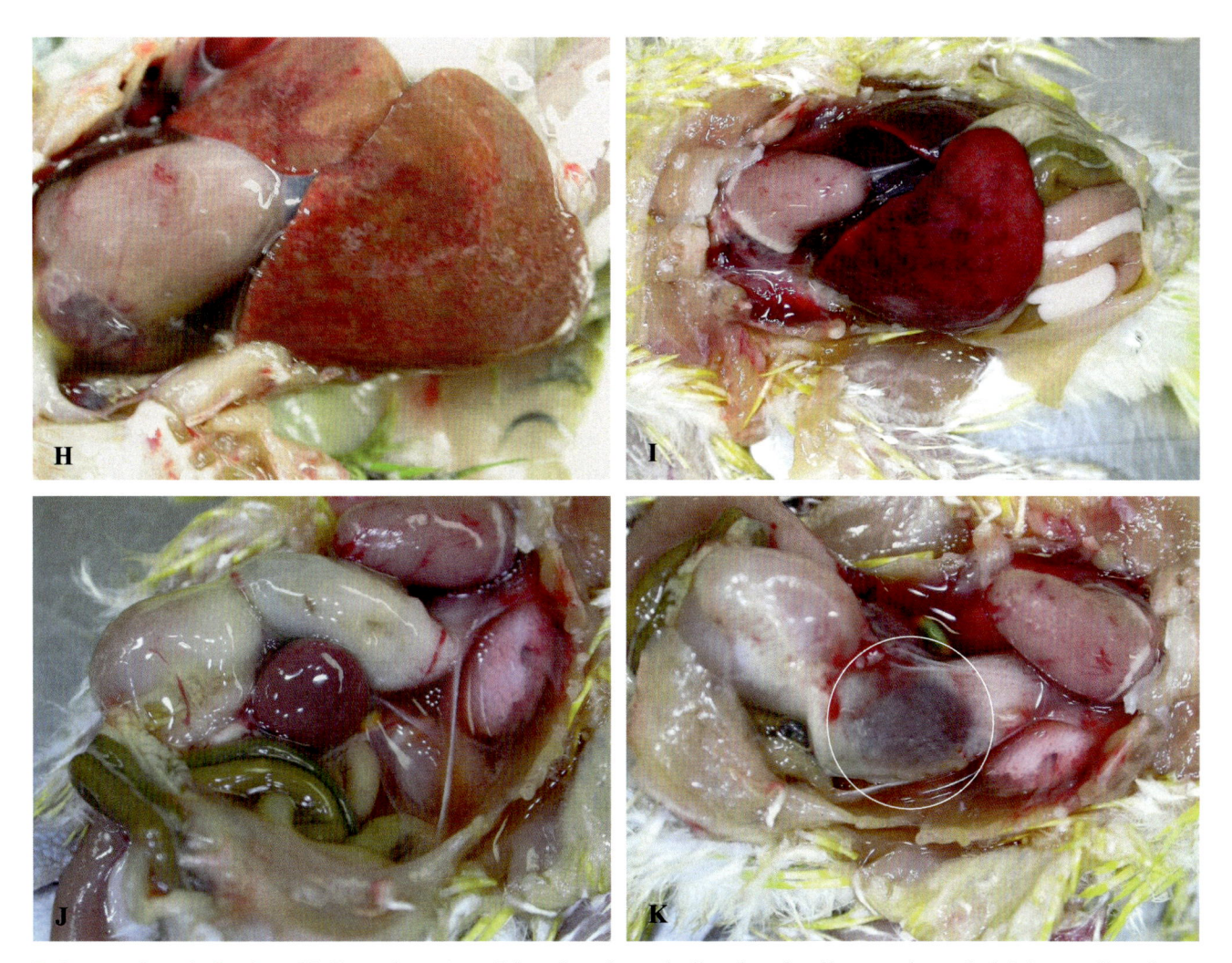

Polyomavirus infection. H. 7-week macaw. Liver is enlarged, discolored yellow, and mottled. Myocardium is pale with a small focal hemorrhage. **I, J, K.** Lovebird. **I.** Liver is enlarged and has multifocal hemorrhages. Myocardium is pale and has foci of mild hemorrhages. **J.** Spleen is markedly enlarged. **K.** Hemorrhagic area is visible through the serosal surface of the proventriculus (circle).

Psittacine Beak and Feather Disease

Psittacine beak and feather disease (PBFD) is a viral disease that affects most species of wild and captive parrots. It was first recognized and described in 1975 in Australia, but is now known to have a worldwide distribution. New World psittacines are inherently more resistant to PBFD infection and disease compared to Old World species. Cockatoos, African grey parrots, lovebirds, lories, lorikeets, eclectus parrots, and budgerigars are most frequently affected. African grey parrots and cockatoos are particularly susceptible and develop severe disease. Younger birds are more severely affected, especially with the acute form of the disease. All ages are susceptible to infection, but clinical disease is seen mostly in birds under 2 years of age. As the immune system develops, birds become more resistant to infection, and the disease tends to be less severe. Birds over 3 years rarely develop clinical disease, but cases can occur in older birds if they are heavily exposed to the virus. Latent carriers may develop clinical disease following a stressful episode.

The virus is highly contagious. It is present in the droppings and feather dander of acutely and latently infected carrier birds. Infection occurs through inhalation of virus or ingestion of contaminated food and water. The virus can also be transmitted through contact with contaminated surfaces such as hands, utensils, food dishes, clothing, and nesting materials. The incubation period can be as short as 3-4 weeks, or up to several years.

Cause. Beak and feather disease virus in the genus *Circovirus* of the family *Circoviridae* is the cause. The virus targets rapidly proliferating cells in feather follicles, bone marrow, and lymphoid cells in the bursa of Fabricius and thymus.

Clinical disease and gross lesions. The clinical manifestation and appearance, and severity of lesions vary considerably depending on the species of bird, age of bird when exposed, dose of virus, and state of the immune system. Young birds cannot mount a good immune response, which is why the disease is more severe and fatal in them. Three forms of PBFD are recognized: peracute, acute, and chronic. A non-clinical carrier state, without signs of disease also occurs.

Peracute form. This form occurs in very young birds. Affected birds die suddenly without premonitory clinical signs. Other birds exhibit clinical signs of lethargy, crop stasis, regurgitation, diarrhea, anorexia, and die within 1-2 weeks. Usually no gross lesions are seen. African grey parrots, cockatoos, and lovebirds are most affected.

Acute form. This form occurs in fledglings developing their first feathers. Loss of powder down is a common manifestation and useful early indicator of viral infection. When birds with gray or black beaks are infected, the beak becomes shiny and black instead of its normal white, powdery appearance. Feather abnormalities are seen in birds when the first feathers are still developing. Changes in feathers include breaking, bending, hemorrhage in quills, and premature shedding of feathers. Feathers may be abnormally colored, e.g., pink to red body feathers in African grey parrots. Because the virus attacks bone marrow and lymphoid cells, infected birds become severely immunocompromised and highly susceptible to secondary bacterial and fungal infections, especially pneumonia. As with the peracute form, African grey parrots, cockatoos, and lovebirds are most often affected.

Chronic form. This form occurs in older birds and is characterized by feather dystrophy and deformities of the beak and claws. Feather dystrophy results from infections of feather pulp and epithelial cells of feather follicles. Dystrophic (abnormal) feathers do not appear until after the first molt following infection, which could be up to 6 months, and then continue with successive molts. Abnormalities in feathers include retention of the sheath, blood in the rachis, brittleness, breaking, having a constricting band near the base of the quill, failure to grow after emergence from feather follicles, and short, clubbed, or curly feathers that may look like stubble. Feather color changes in some birds. As feather follicles are damaged, lost feathers are not replaced, and feather loss becomes increasingly obvious. Feather loss in cockatoos typically develops in the following order: powdery down (often noticed over the flank), contour feathers in most feather tracts, primary and secondary feathers of the wings, tail feathers, and finally crest feathers. Eventually, the skin becomes bare without feather dander. White cockatoos look disheveled, grubby, and untidy. In lorikeets, there is simply loss of tail and primary flight feathers but, after a few months, affected birds regrow lost feathers. Parrots in the genus *Neophema* lose feathers when handled.

Beak and claws become shiny and black instead of having a white, powdery appearance. This is due to the absence of feather dander that accumulates and keep the beak and claws clean during preening. Beak lesions are inconsistent among species of parrots; cockatoos being most severely and consistently affected. The beak, especially the maxillary part, may overgrow, become deformed, and be very fragile. Focal areas of necrosis inside the beak cause irregular, sunken, soft areas on the beak's surface. Splitting or breaking the beak exposes underlying sensitive tissue that causes pain and reluctance to eat. Nails may overgrow and become deformed and brittle. Birds with the chronic form of PBFD may live for months to years before dying, usually of a secondary infection.

Carrier state. Birds that survive infection with PBFD virus may or may not be able to eliminate the virus from the body. Most birds with a healthy immune system are capable of eliminating the virus after a transient period of infection. Birds that cannot eliminate the virus become life-long asymptomatic carriers that shed the virus intermittently in feather dander and droppings. Carriers are an important source of infection for other birds. Old World psittacines such as eclectus parrots, cockatoos, and African grey parrots have a higher rate of subclinical infection than New World psittacines. Budgerigars and lovebirds tend to have high rates of subclinical infection, which needs to be considered when introducing these birds into a house with more susceptible birds such as cockatoos and African grey parrots.

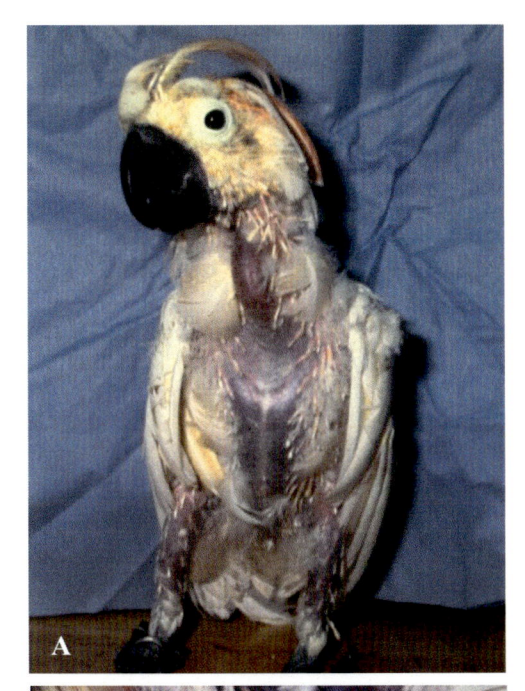

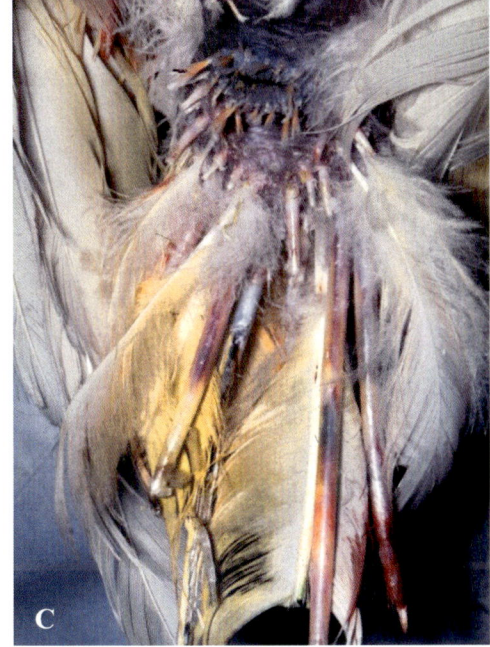

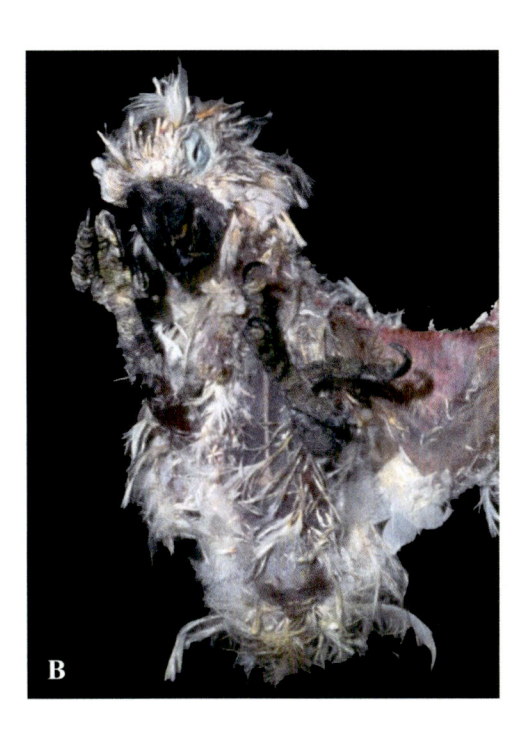

Psittacine beak and feather disease. Moluccan cockatoos. **A, B.** Loss of feathers. **C.** Retention of feather sheaths with blood in rachis. (*Photos courtesy of Dr. David Pass, Western Australia*).

Cutaneous and Mucosal Papillomas

Both cutaneous and mucosal papillomas occur in companion birds. Cutaneous papillomas are found in wild finches, canaries, African gray parrots, Amazon parrots, macaws, and cockatoos. Mucosal papillomas affect New World parrots; predominantly macaws, in which they occur most frequently, conures, Amazon parrots, and hawk-headed parrots. Mucosal papillomas are most common in the cloaca (cloacal papillomas) but occasionally occur in the oral cavity/oropharynx and larynx, and rarely in esophagus, crop, proventriculus, gizzard, and conjunctiva. Mucosal papillomas in Amazon parrots are usually in the cloaca, whereas macaws and conures typically have papillomas in the cloaca as well as in the oral cavity/oropharynx. Mucosal papillomatosis is most severe in macaws, especially green-winged macaws. In these birds, lesions may occur in the oral cavity, esophagus, crop, or even gizzard. Concurrent biliary and pancreatic duct carcinomas are more common in parrots with mucosal papillomas.

Cause of cutaneous papillomas. Cutaneous papillomas in finches, canaries, African gray parrots, and Cuban Amazon parrots are believed to be caused by papillomaviruses. Typical virus particles have been identified by electron microscopy in nuclei of affected epithelial cells. Papillomaviruses from an African gray parrot and a finch have been cloned, purified, and characterized. In cockatoos and macaws, cutaneous papillomas may be caused by herpesviruses, based on finding eosinophilic intranuclear inclusion bodies that contain herpesvirus virions in the lesions.

Cause of mucosal papillomas. The cause of mucosal papillomas is uncertain. Clinical observations and epidemiological data suggest they are infectious. Herpesvirus sequences have been detected by *in situ* hybridization in cloacal papillomas in parrots. Using PCR, DNA sequencing, and phylogenic analysis, genotypes 1, 2, and 3 of *Psittacid herpesvirus 1* (PsHV-1), which causes Pacheco's disease, were found in mucosal papillomas in New World parrots. Genome of genotype 2 of PsHV-1 was detected by PCR in choanal and cloacal swabs from African Gray parrots with oral (choanal) mucosal papillomas and lymphohistiocytic, mildly hyperplastic cloacitis. Furthermore, cloacal papillomas developed in parrots that survived Pacheco's disease. It is likely that PsHVs-1 plays a role in the development of mucosal papillomas in parrots. No evidence of a virus has been identified in cloacal papillomas in cockatiels or cockatoos.

Gross lesions of cutaneous papillomas. Cutaneous papillomas occur as benign, proliferative, wart-like lesions on the unfeathered parts of the skin. They commonly occur on the legs and feet, toes, eyelids, face, corner of the beaks, neck, base of the tail, and wing.

Gross lesions of cloacal papillomas. Lesions of cloacal papillomas vary in extent and severity. In the early stages, the cloacal mucosa has a diffuse, cobblestone appearance. As lesions progress, papillomas enlarge and appear as broad-based, fleshy, firm, pink or red, wart-like proliferative masses attached to and protruding from the mucosal surface of the dorsal wall of the cloaca. Cloacal papillomas may look like and be mistaken for a cloacal prolapse. Large masses cause considerable discomfort, straining, and difficulty in defecation. Ulceration and bleeding result in blood in the droppings.

Gross lesions of other mucosal papillomas. Oral lesions usually occur along the choanal margin and in oropharynx, larynx, and base of the tongue. Papillomas are raised, white to pink, and often have cauliflower-like surface. Lesions often regress spontaneously and disappear entirely. Secondary bacterial infections are common, exacerbate the lesions, and delay regression.

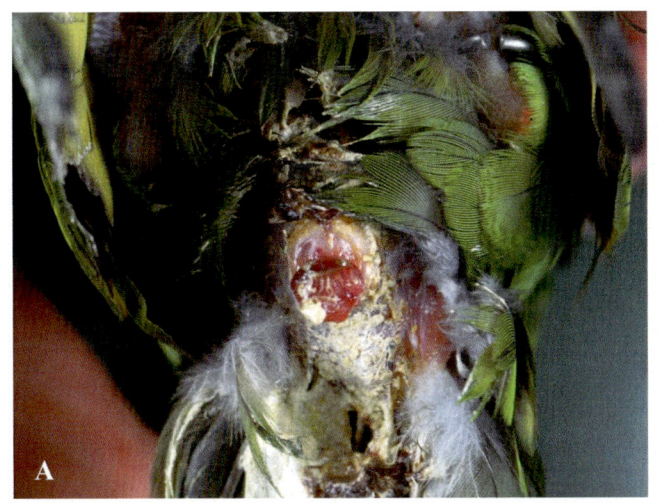

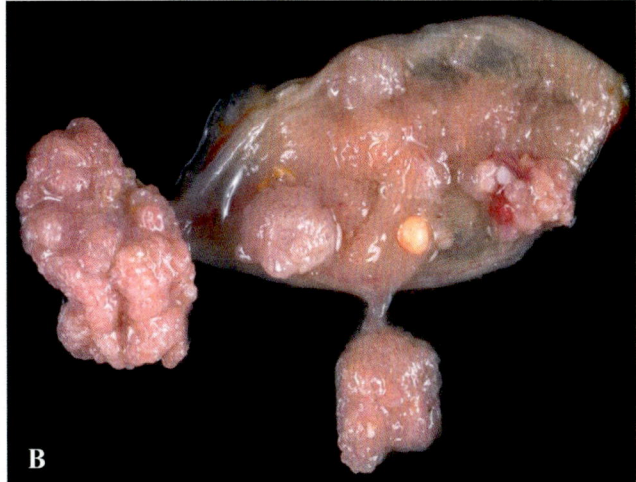

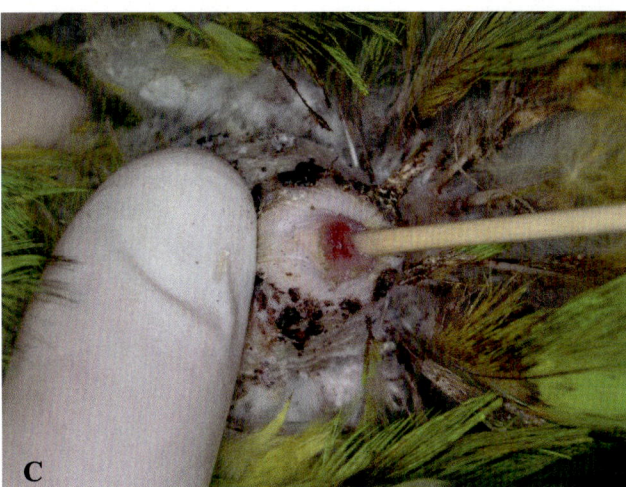

Papillomas. **A, B.** 3-year conure. **A.** Papilloma protrudes from the mucosal surface of the cloaca. Note the red color of the papilloma. **B.** Multiple papillomas in the cloacal mucosa. **C.** 40- to 50-year Mexican red-headed Amazon parrot. Papilloma (red lesion) in the cloacal mucosa. The bird had bloody droppings. (*Photo C courtesy of Dr. Lauren Powers, USA*).

Marek's Disease

Cause. Marek's disease is caused by *Gallid herpesvirus 2* of the genus *Mardivirus* in the subfamily *Alphaherpesvirinae*. Strains of *Gallid herpesvirus 2* (Marek's disease virus [MDV]) vary widely in pathogenicity from nearly avirulent to very virulent. Based on their virulence, MDV strains are divided into pathotypes designated as mild (mMDV), virulent (vMDV), very virulent (vvMDV), or very virulent plus (vv+MDV).

Clinical signs and gross lesions of the neural (classical) form. Affected chickens show leg weakness and lameness that progress to paraplegia and paralysis. Flexing of the toes is frequently noted. When walking, the bird may hobble or have one leg held stiffly in front. Drooping of wings is seen in some birds due to damage to the brachial plexus. Paraplegic birds sit on their legs or are in lateral or sternal recumbency with legs extending backwards or to the side. The classic posture of a chicken with neural form of Marek's disease is stretching one leg forward and the other leg backward (hurdler's position). Crop stasis and labored breathing are associated with involvement of the vagus nerve. Diarrhea results from involvement of nerves supplying the intestinal tract.

Sciatic nerves and plexuses show variable degrees of enlargement, depending on the severity and duration of the lesion. Obviously swollen nerves are firmer than normal, have a round contour, and usually are yellow to gray-white color. In some cases, sciatic nerves are not enlarged but show loss of striations. Thickening of the sciatic nerve may be more or less uniform and extend along the entire nerve, segmental and fusiform shaped, confined to the sciatic plexus, or affect only one of the spinal nerve roots that form the plexus. Sciatic nerves and plexuses on one or both sides may be affected. When involvement is unilateral, it is possible to compare the appearance of the affected nerve with the opposite unaffected nerve. In addition to the sciatic nerve and plexus, the brachial plexus, vagal nerves, and Remak's nerve (*n. intestinalis*) innervating the large intestine also should be examined for thickening. Other spinal nerve plexuses may be affected but are difficult to examine grossly.

Clinical signs and gross lesions of the acute (visceral) form. Clinical signs are not specific and may include lethargy, weight loss, and anorexia. Gross lesions include firm, gray to white nodular tumors (lymphomas) in different organs and tissues. Liver, spleen, and one or more divisions of the kidneys may be diffusely enlarged and mottled or diffusely discolored. Diffuse thickening of the proventricular wall is a common lesion. Ovary or testes and one or both lungs are frequently involved. Ovary may be replaced by a large white tumor. Lungs become enlarged, firm, and gray. In young birds, the bursa may show enlargement of one or more plicae (folds). Multiple lymphomas in skeletal muscles occasionally occur.

Gross ocular lesions (ocular form). In healthy chickens, the color of the iris is red, orange, or yellow depending on the breed. The normal pupil is sharply circular with a well-defined margin. In Marek's disease, early lesions are characterized by patchy or diffuse gray discoloration and distortion of the iris with indentation of its margin. Gradually, the shape of the pupil changes from circular to ovoid, elliptical, or pear-shaped. Over time, the pupil is reduced and may become pin-head size or totally effaced. Eventually, the pupil becomes unresponsive to light.

Gross cutaneous lesions (cutaneous form). Involvement of the skin is another manifestation of Marek's disease. It is the most common form of the disease in young chickens. Cutaneous lesions are associated with feather follicles, which become enlarged and nodular. Lesions (nodular feather follicles) may be few and scattered or numerous and almost coalescing. Enlarged feather follicles are firm and white in color. Reddening of the lower legs is another manifestation of the cutaneous form of Marek's disease. Scales on the legs are elevated and may separate because tumor develops beneath them and pushes the scales outward. Ulceration of the legs is seen in severely affected birds.

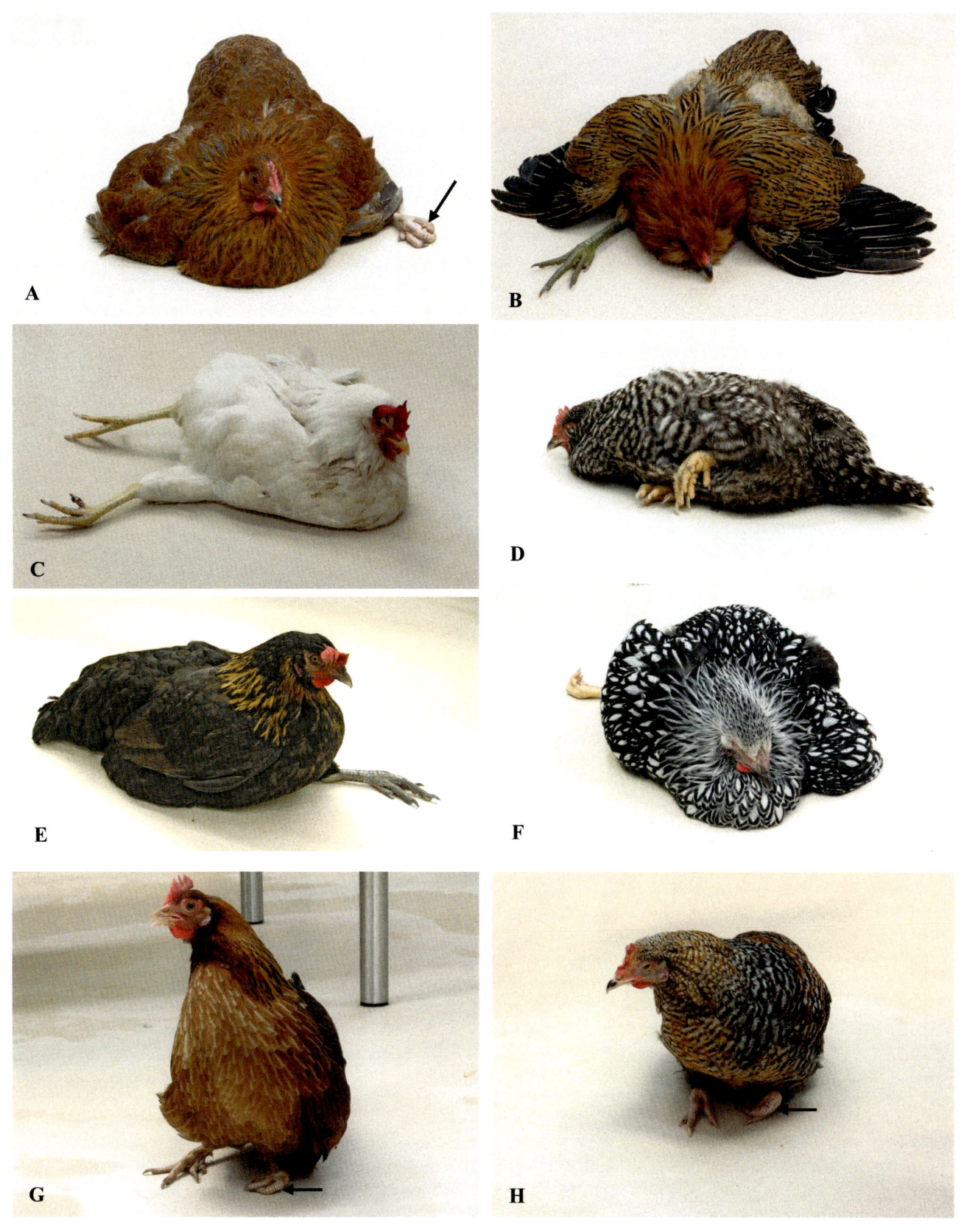

Marek's Disease - Neural form. **A-H.** 5- to 12-month hobby chickens exhibit different postures. Note the toe clutching (arrows) in figures A, G, H. Note drooping of the wings in figures A and B. These postures are due to damage to the sciatic and brachial nerves and plexuses.

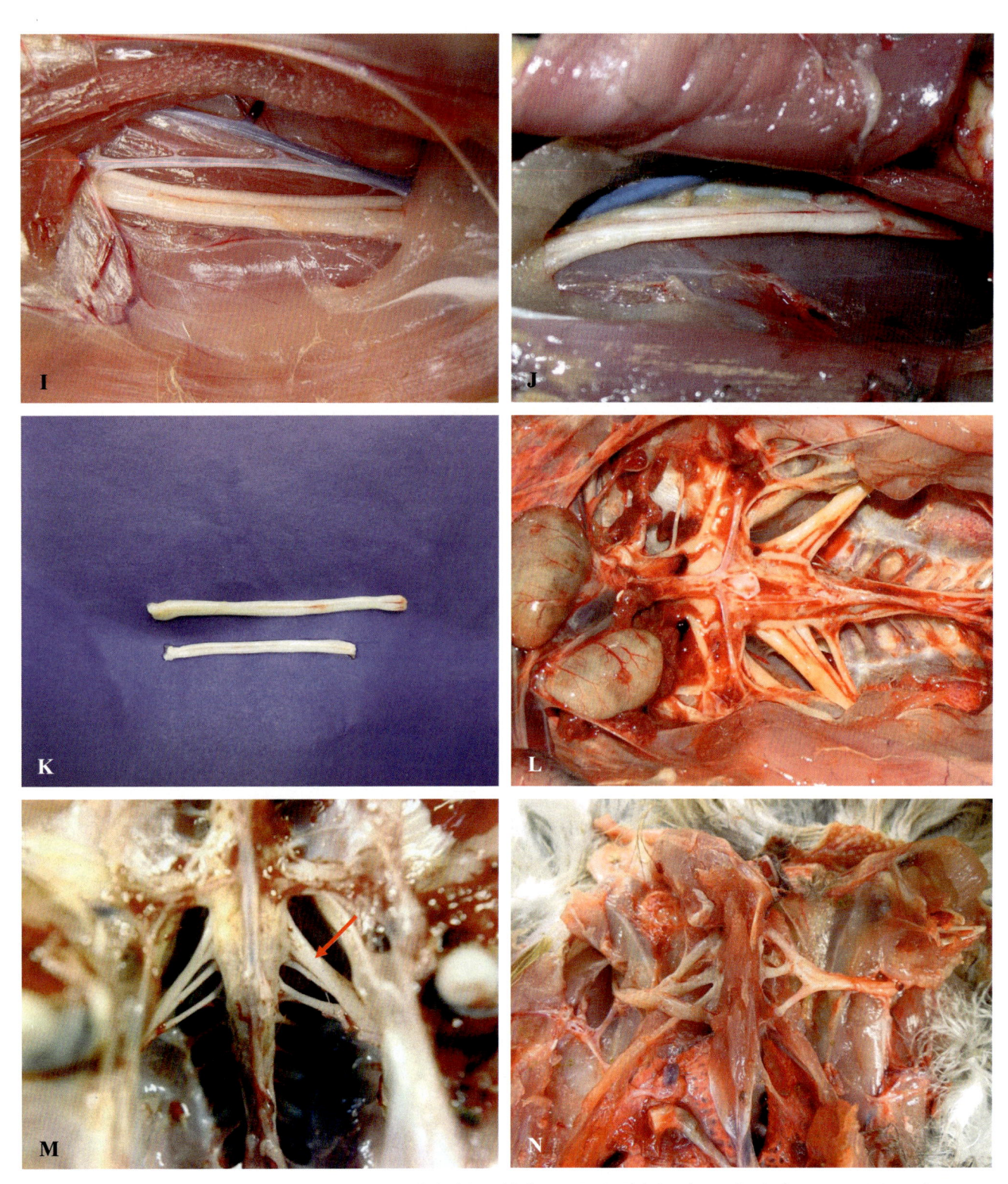

Marek's Disease - Neural form. 5 to 12-month hobby chickens. **I, J.** Thickening of sciatic nerves. Note the round contour of the thickened nerves. **K.** Left and right sciatic nerves of a lame chicken were removed to demonstrate the thickening in one of them. **L, M.** Thickening of the sciatic plexus. In **M**, note that the thickening is evident in particularly one nerve of the plexus (arrow). **N.** Thickening of the brachial plexus on both sides. The bird had drooping wings.

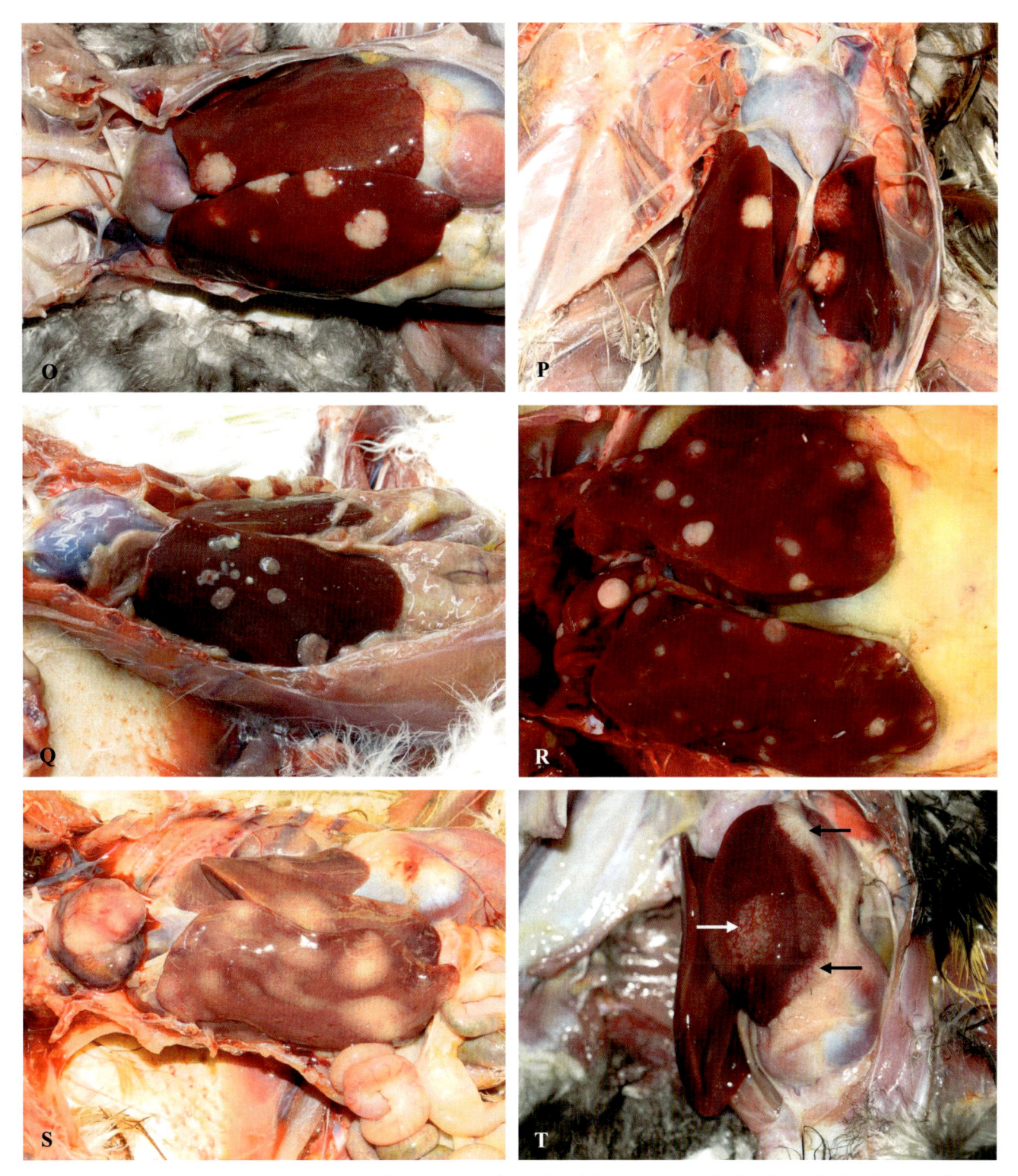

Marek's disease - Visceral form. 13-week to 12-month hobby chickens (**O, P, Q, S, T**), and a broiler breeder (**R**). **O-S.** Lymphomatous nodules in the livers. Nodules are off-white and slightly or notably raised from the surface. **T**. A single slightly raised nodule (white arrow), with off-white discoloration of areas at margin of the left lobe (black arrows) due to infiltration of neoplastic lymphocytes.

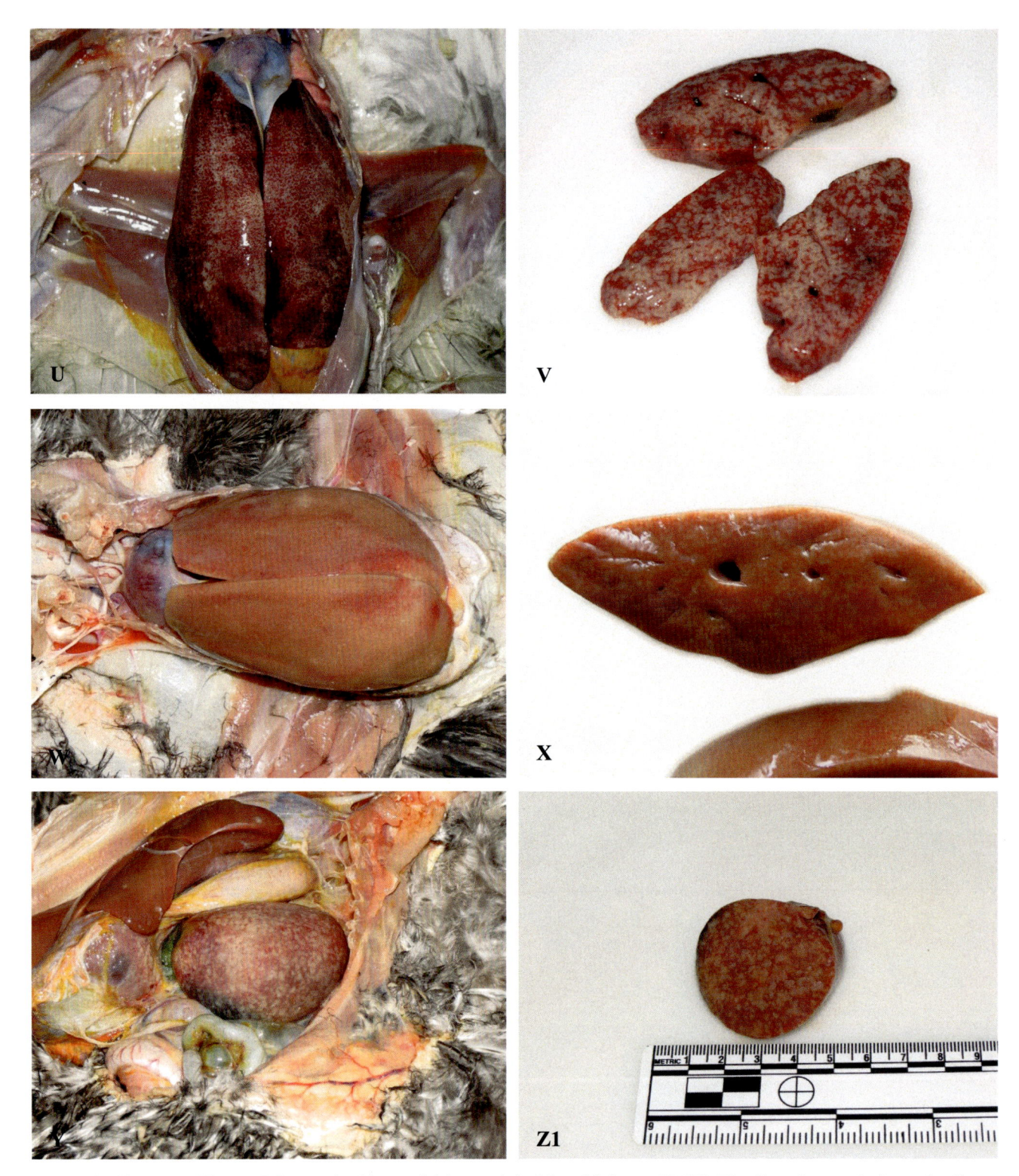

Marek's disease - Visceral form. 6-, 11-, and 16-month hobby chickens. **U, W.** The liver is mottled, markedly enlarged, and discolored. **V, X.** Cut surface of the livers in **U** and **W**, respectively. **Y, Z1.** Spleen is markedly enlarged and its capsular and cut surfaces are mottled with numerous off-white spots.

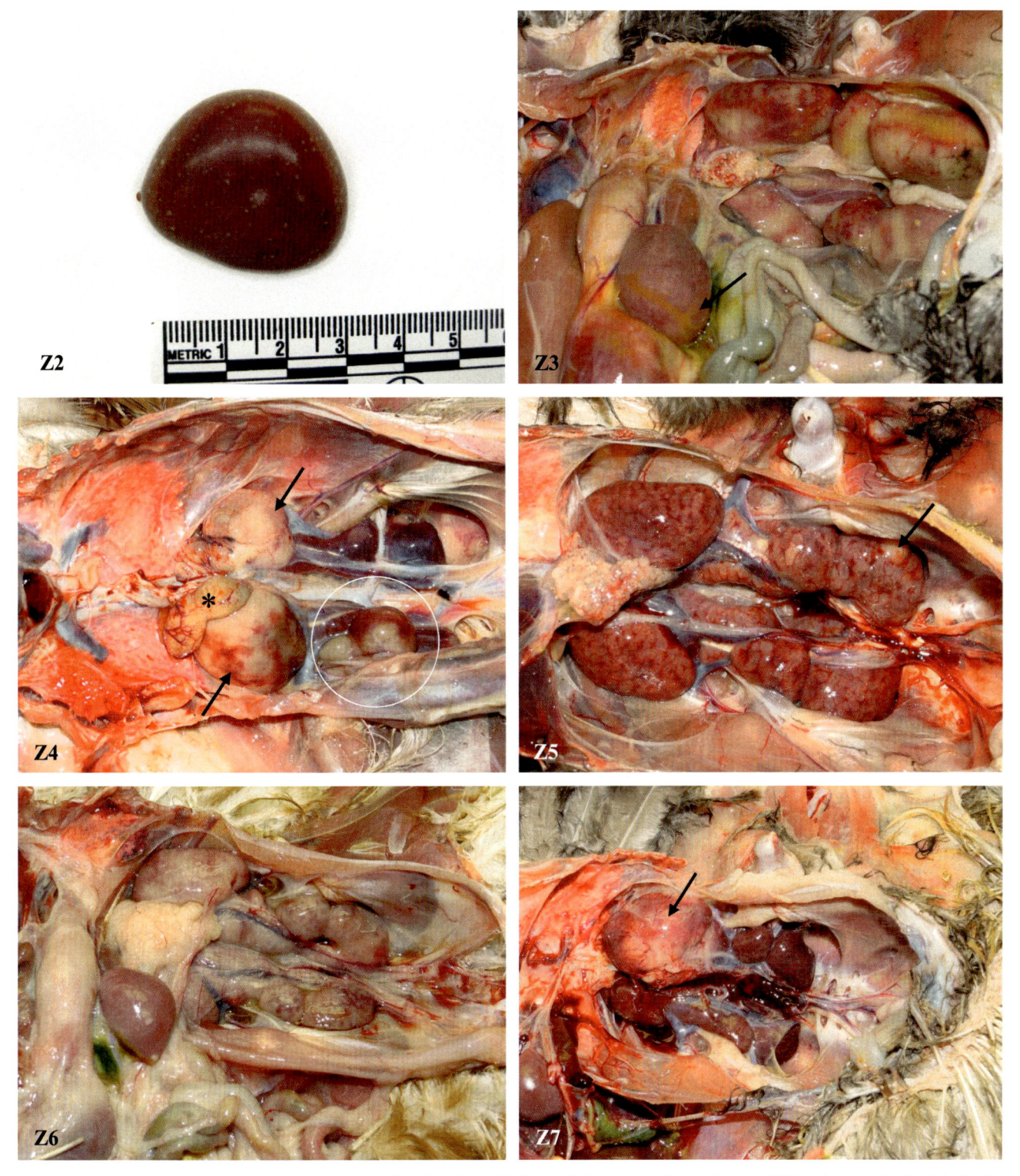

Marek's disease - Visceral form. Z2. 63-day broiler chicken. Spleen is enlarged and diffusely mottled with foci. **Z3.** 11-month hobby chicken. Spleen (arrow) is markedly enlarged and discolored. Divisions of both kidneys are enlarged and discolored white. **Z4.** 4-month hobby rooster. Anterior division of both kidneys is replaced by lymphoid tumor (arrows). Off-white areas are in the middle division of the right kidney (circle). Asterisk: right testis. **Z5.** 9-month hobby chicken. Kidneys are enlarged and pale. A white nodule is in the posterior division of the left kidney (arrow). Histologically, the kidneys had marked interstitial lymphoid cell infiltrates. **Z6.** 3-month hobby chicken. Kidneys are diffusely enlarged and discolored off-white. **Z7.** One-year hobby chicken. A lymphoid tumor (arrow) involves just the anterior division of the left kidney (arrow).

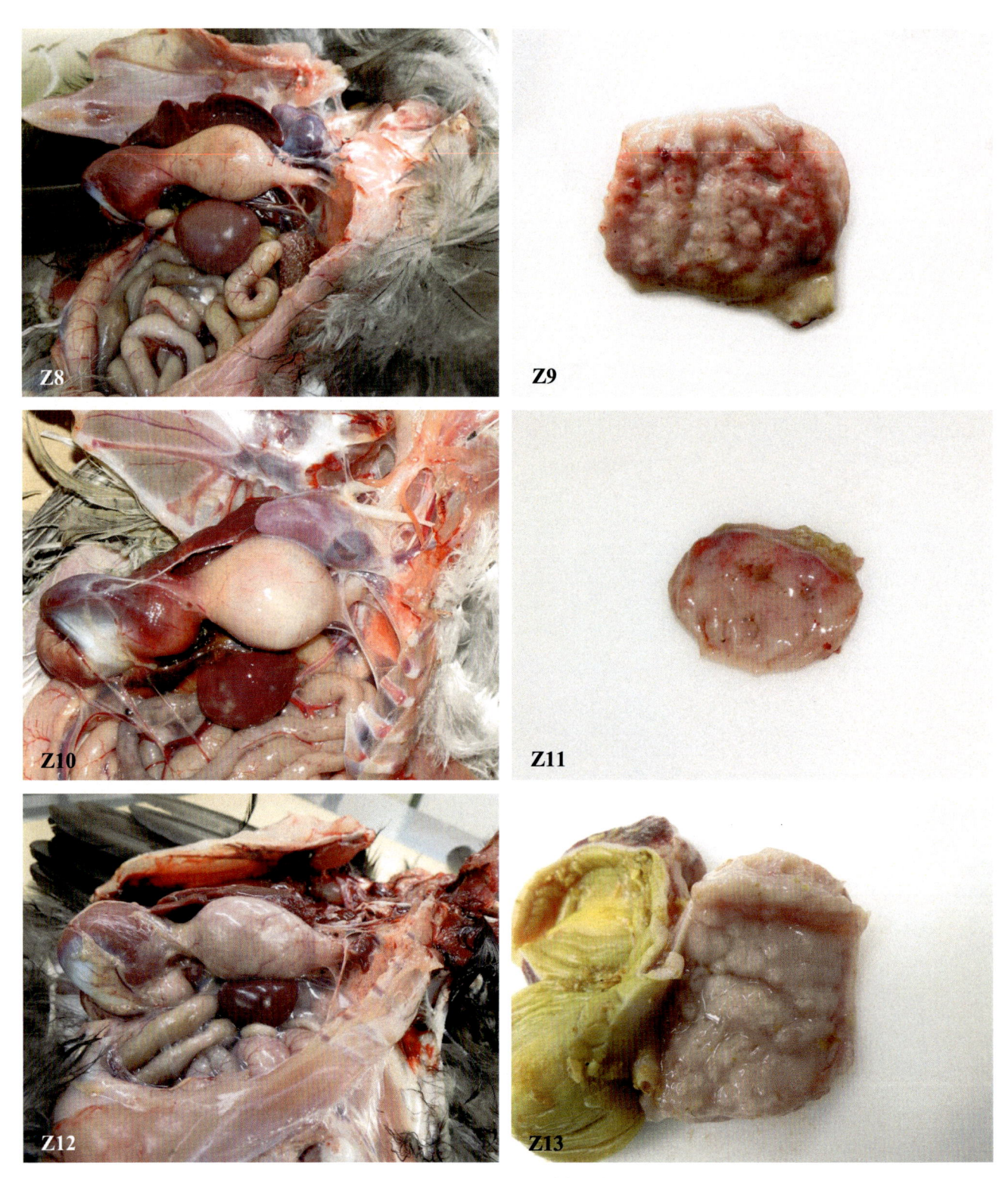

Marek's disease - Visceral form. Proventricular lesions. Hobby chickens (**Z8, Z9** One-month; **Z10, Z11** 8-week; **Z12, Z13** 5-month). **Z8-Z13.** Proventriculi are distorted and have thickened, firm walls. Mucosa is markedly thickened and nodular. Papillae are no longer evident in Z11. Note splenic enlargement in Z8 and Z10. Spleen in Z10 is spotted.

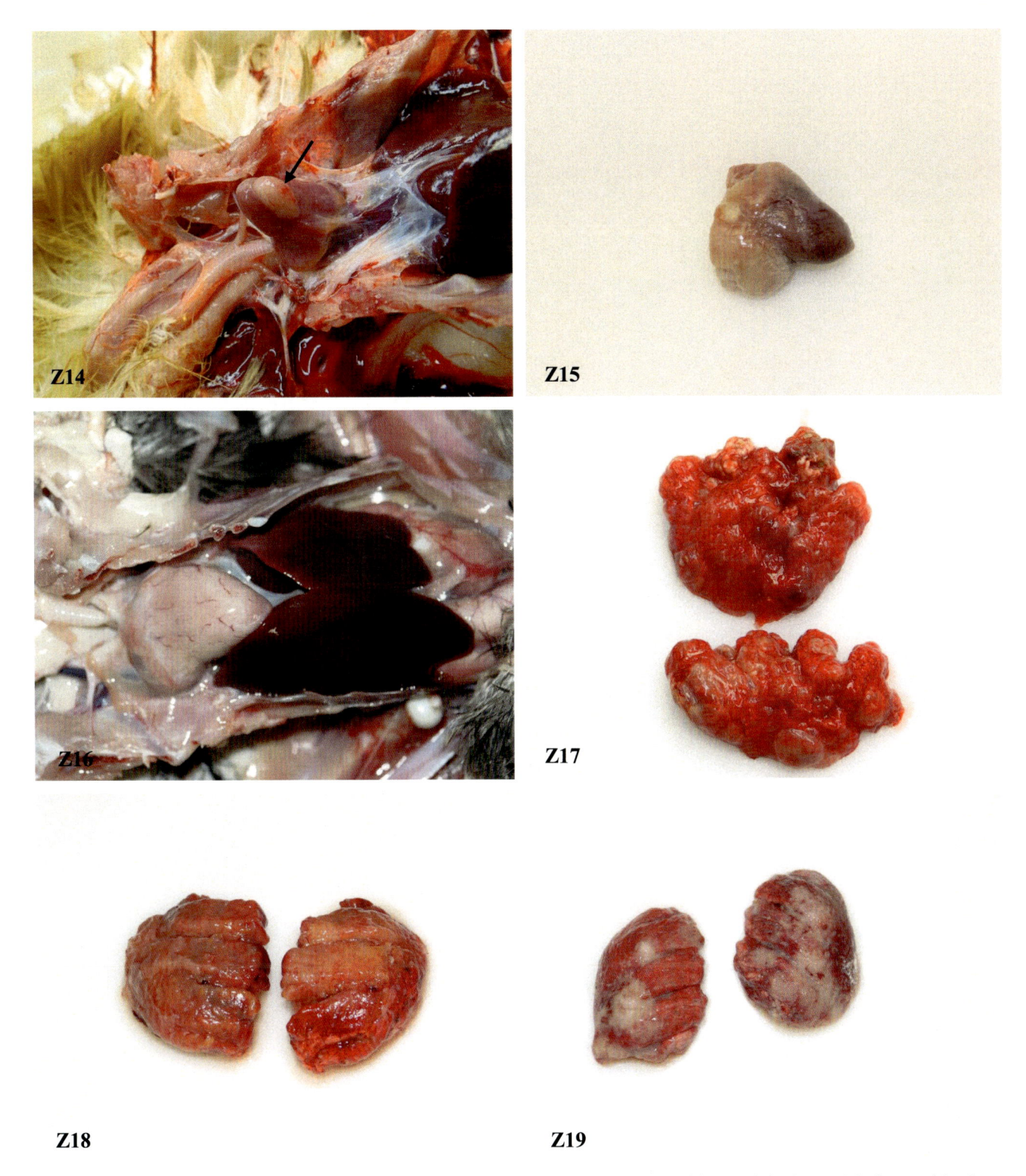

Marek's disease - Visceral form. Hobby chickens. **Z14.** 5-month. An off-white nodule (arrow) is located in the myocardium. **Z15.** One-year. Lymphoid tumor involving the auricles and coronary fat of the heart. **Z16.** 6-month. Diffuse white discoloration of the heart due to massive infiltration of the myocardium with neoplastic lymphoid cells. **Z17.** 9-month. Nodular tumors in the lungs. **Z18.** 6-month. Lungs are firm and have a rough, discolored pleural surface; they adhered to the wall of the thorax. **Z19.** 3-month. Off-white, slightly raised areas in the lung are lymphoid infiltrates that efface and replace the lung parenchyma.

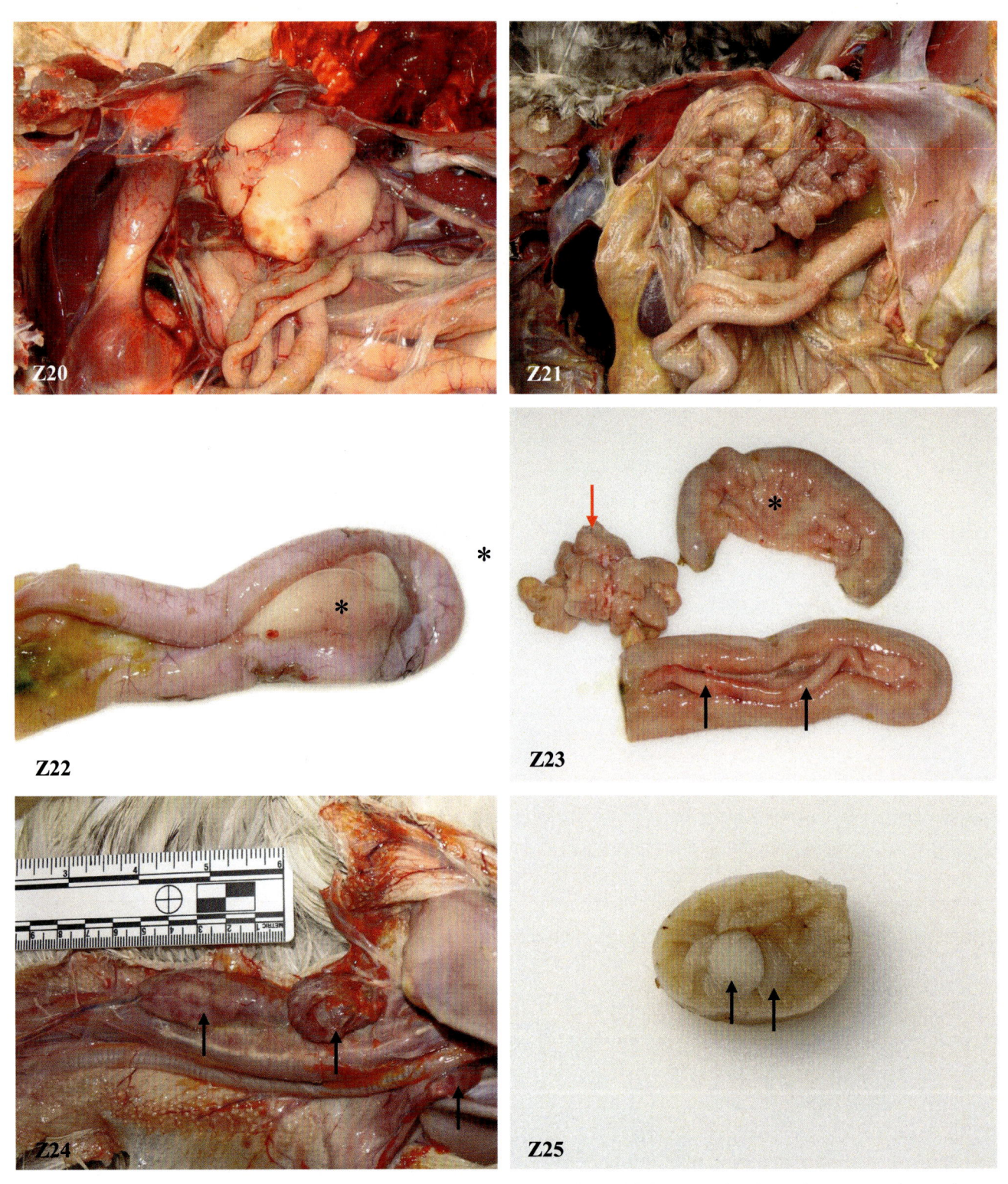

Marek's disease - Visceral form. Hobby chickens. **Z20.** 5-month. Solid, irregularly shaped tumor replaces the ovary. **Z21.** One-year. Ovarian follicles are off-white and have thick walls. **Z22.** 9-month. Pancreas (asterisk) is thickened due to infiltration of lymphoid cells. **Z23.** Adult. Thickening of the pancreas (black arrows) and mesentery (asterisks) due to infiltration of lymphoid cells. Ovary (red arrow) is distorted and off-white due to massive infiltration of lymphoid cells. **Z24.** 16-month. Thymic lobes (arrows) are markedly enlarged. **Z25.** 13-week. Bursa of Fabricius has swollen mucosal folds (plicae) (arrows). Histologically, interfollicular tissue in the folds was densely infiltrated by lymphoid cells that partially or completely effaced most of the lymphoid follicles.

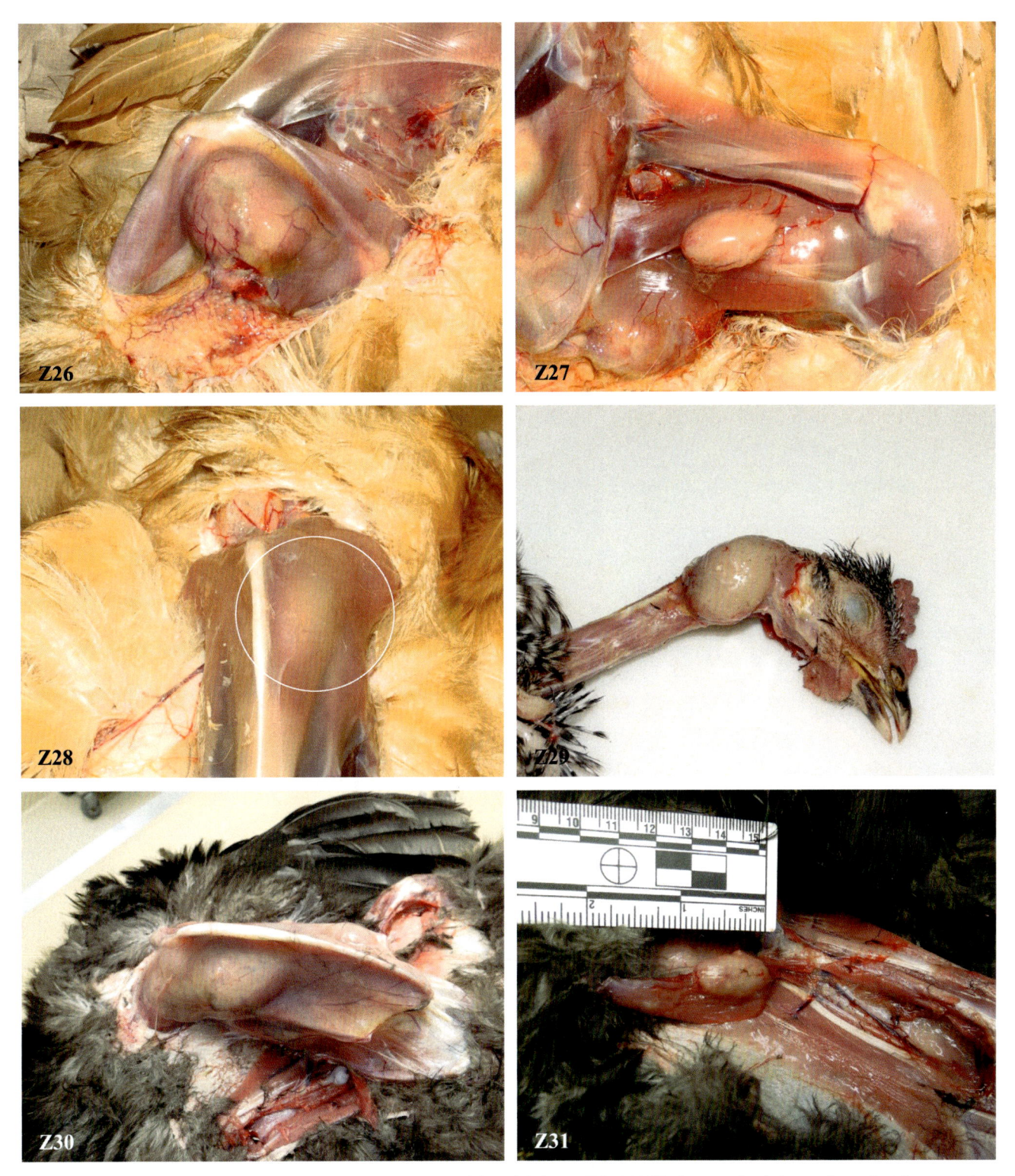

Marek's disease. Skeletal muscle lymphomas. Hobby chickens **Z26**, **Z27**. 5-month. A large lymphoid tumor is seen on the outer and inner aspects of the left thigh. **Z28**. 5-month. A tumor (circle) is embedded within the left pectoral muscle. **Z29**. One-year. A lymphoid tumor is in the anterior part of the neck. **Z30, Z31.** 9-month. **Z30**. There is a large lymphoid tumor in the left pectoral muscles. **Z31**. A lymphoid tumor is associated with a muscle in the inner aspect of the thigh; arrow: sciatic nerve.

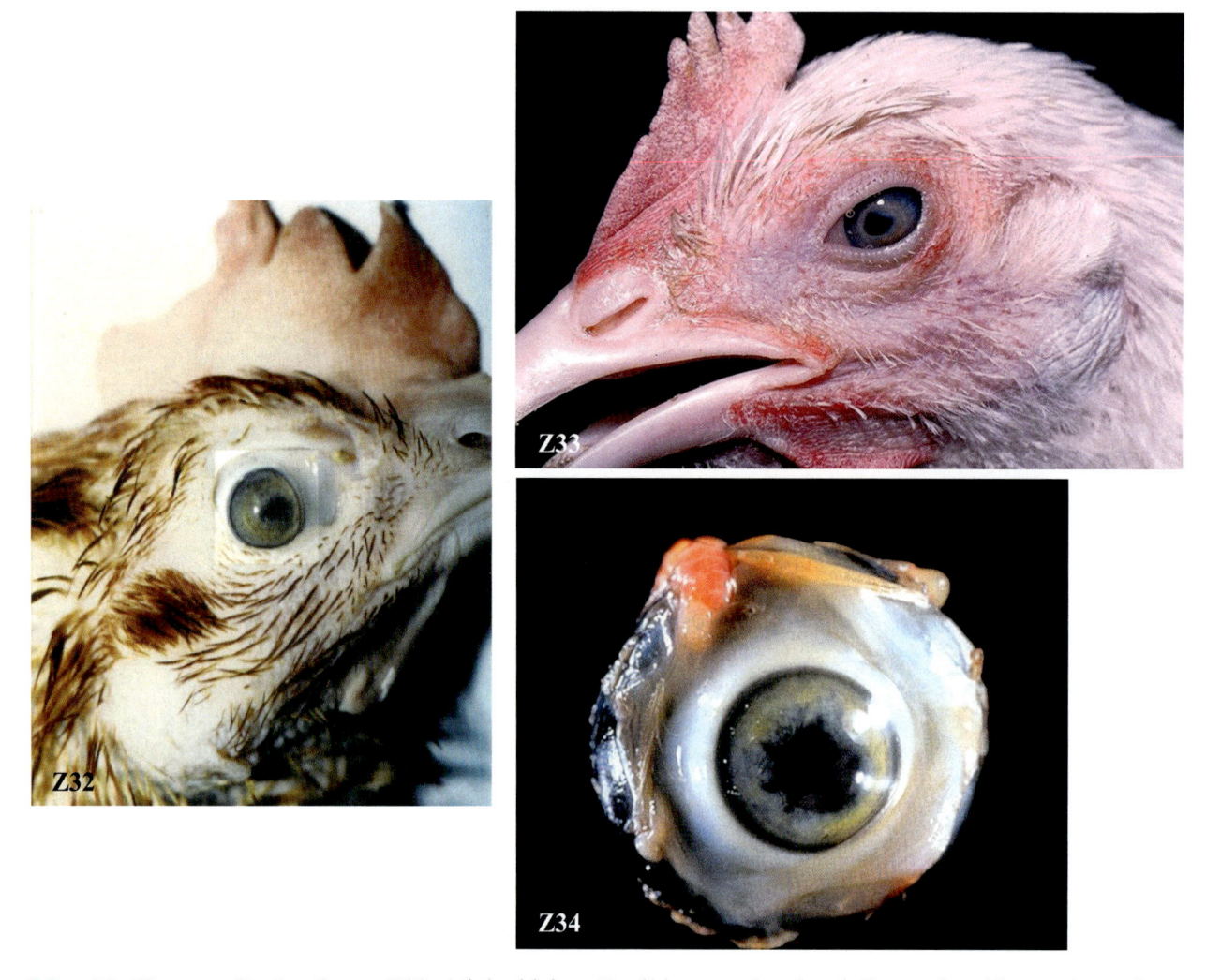

Marek's disease - Ocular form. Z32. Adult chicken. Pupil is constricted and distorted and has an irregular margin. **Z33.** Broiler breeder. Discoloration of the iris, with distortion and constriction of the pupil. **Z34.** 27-week broiler breeder. Yellow areas are remaining normal iris while the white to gray areas are lymphocytic infiltrates. Lymphocytic infiltrates in the iris have caused a marked irregular, distorted pupil.

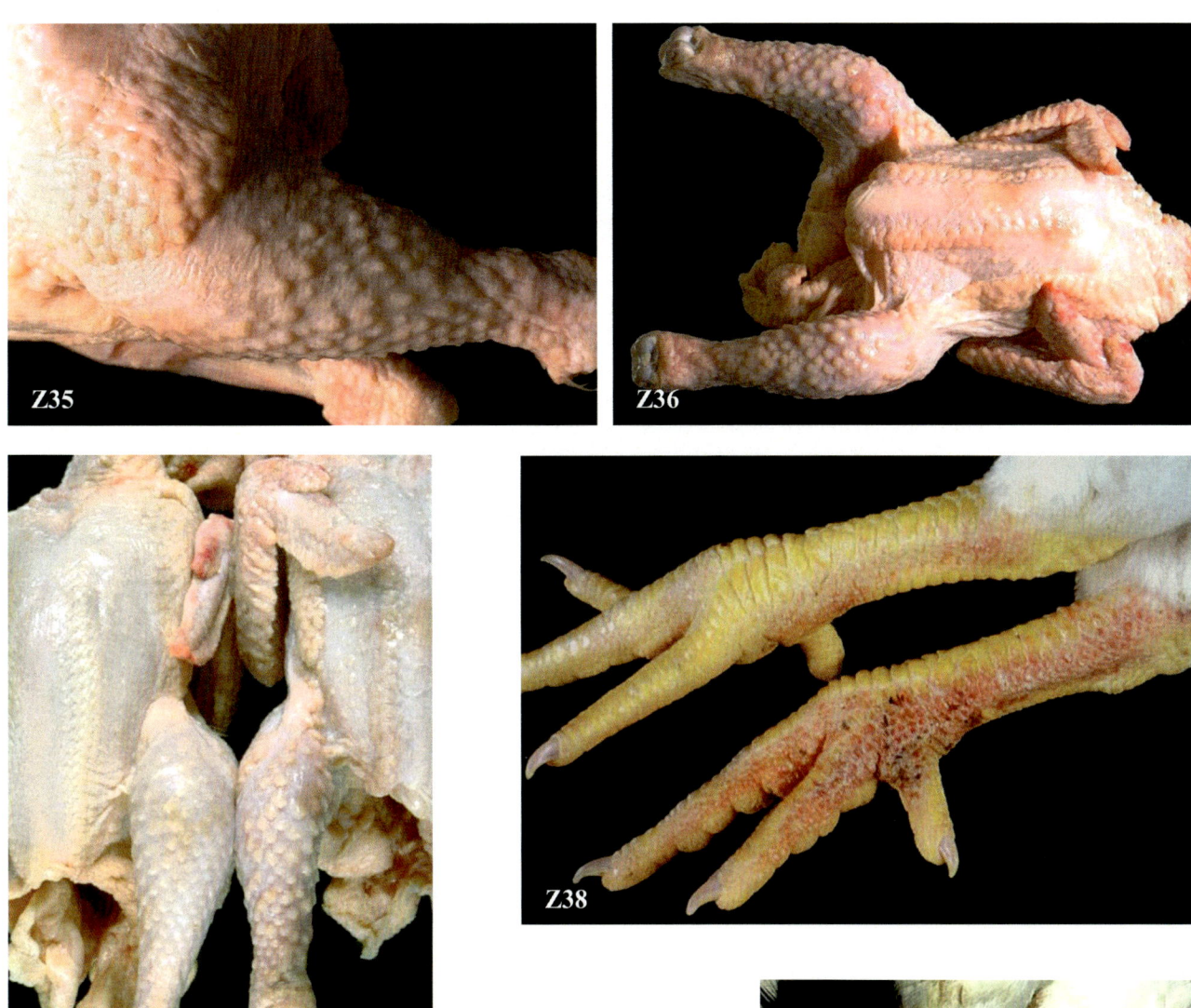

Gross Pathology of Avian Diseases: Text and Atlas 133

Marek's disease - Cutaneous form. Broiler chickens. **Z35-Z37.** Enlargement of feather follicles due to infiltration of lymphoid cells. In **Z37**, normal carcass (left) and affected carcass (right) are shown for comparison. **Z38, Z39**. Reddening and ulceration of the skin on the shanks is another manifestation of the cutaneous form of Marek's disease.

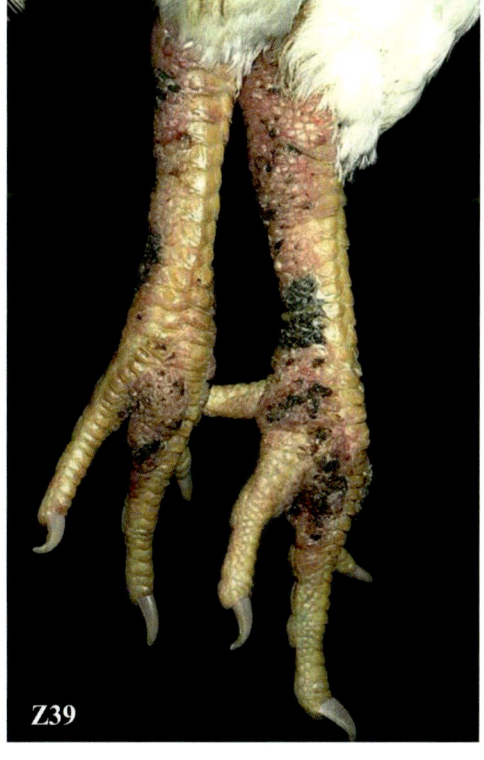

Lymphoid Leukosis

Cause. Lymphoid leukosis (LL) is caused by viruses in the *Alpharetrovirus* genus of the family *Retroviridae*. Viruses that cause LL belong to a group of viruses known as "Avian leukosis/sarcoma" viruses (ALSVs). In chickens, ALSVs are classified into 6 subgroups designated A to J. Viruses in these subgroups are oncogenic and cause several different types of neoplasia in chickens. Lymphoid leukosis is caused by viruses in subgroups A and B. Subgroup A occurs more frequently than subgroup B. Avian leukosis/sarcoma viruses are mostly transmitted vertically.

Gross lesions. Gross lesions are almost invariably found in the liver, spleen, and bursa of Fabricius. Other frequently involved organs include kidneys, gonads, lungs, heart, and mesentery. The liver is markedly enlarged (hence the common name 'big liver disease'), usually diffusely discolored off-white, and may have few to numerous, often almost coalescing off-white foci. In some cases, liver tumors may be multi-nodular. The spleen is often enlarged, off-white, mottled, and occasionally has small off-white tumors on the serosal surface. The bursa of Fabricius is usually enlarged and may have nodular tumors on the serosal or mucosal surface. Kidneys may be diffusely enlarged and off-white or have white nodular areas. Lymphoid leukosis needs to be differentiated from Marek's disease.

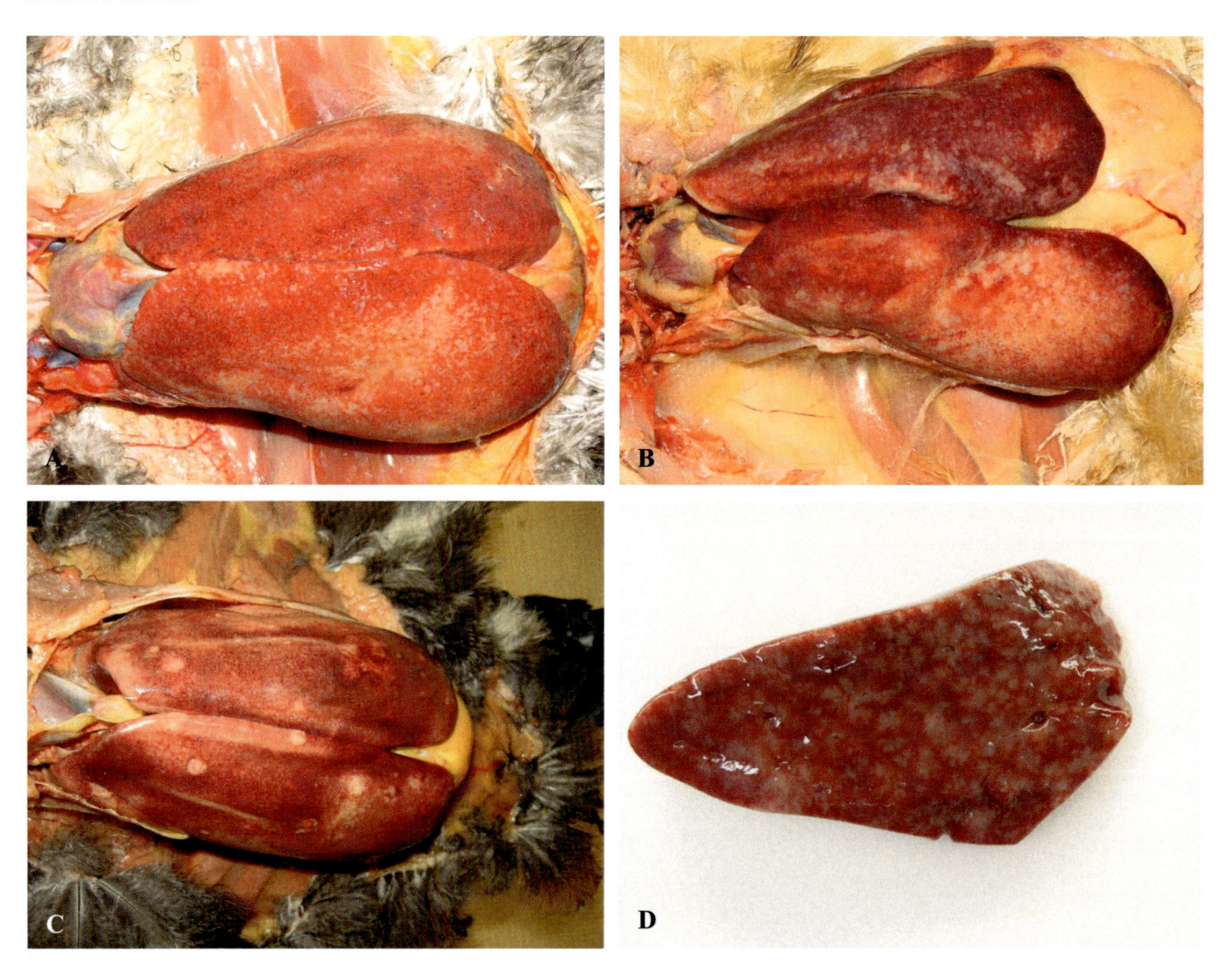

Lymphoid leukosis. 8- to 12-month hobby chickens. **A, B, C.** Livers are markedly enlarged, off-white, and pale. **D.** Cut surface of the liver in C has multifocal pale areas due to lymphoid cell infiltration.

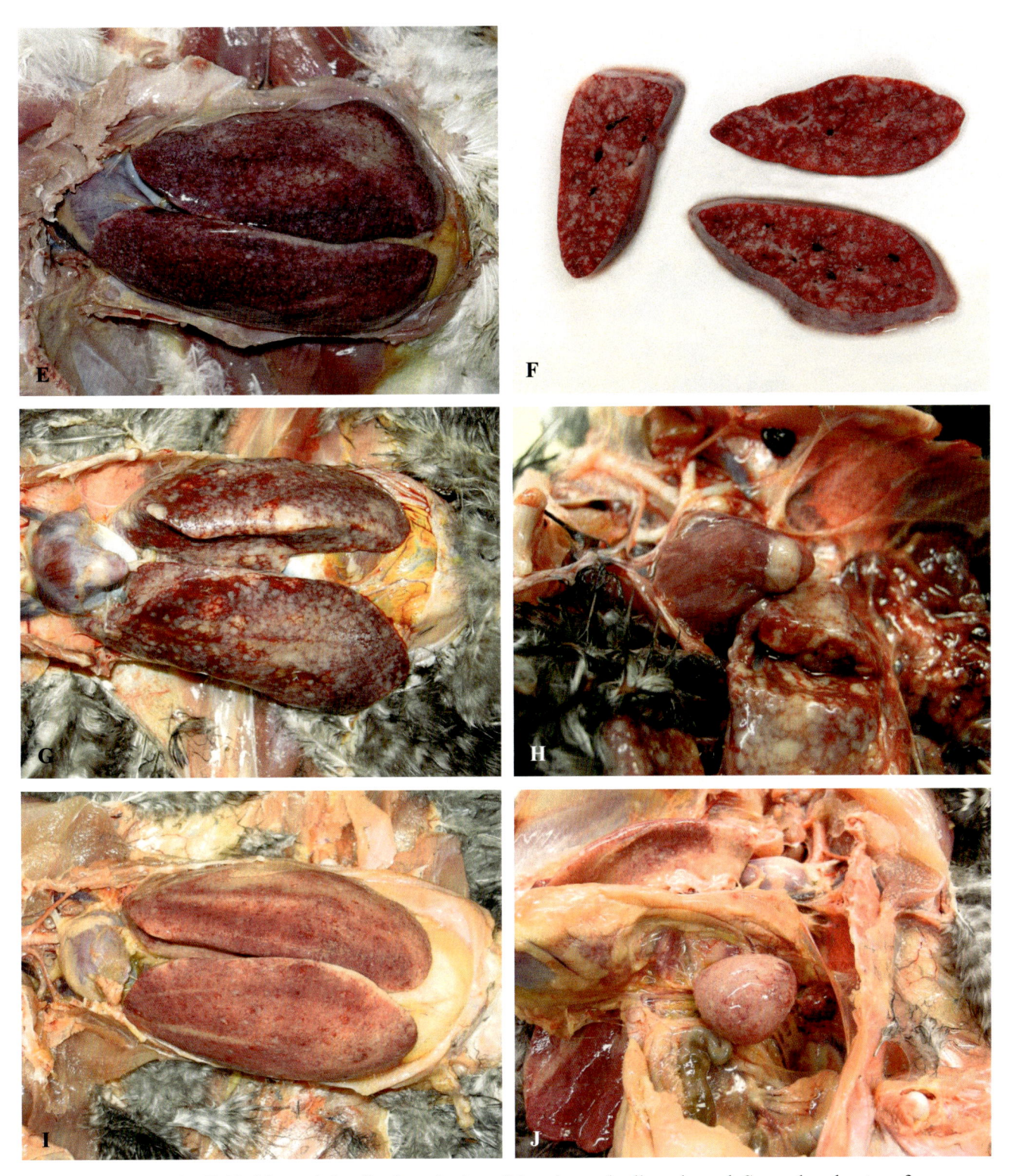

Lymphoid leukosis. E, F. 33-week broiler breeder hen. Liver is markedly enlarged. Serosal and cut surfaces are diffusely mottled with off-white foci. **G, H.** 24-week hobby chicken. **G.** The liver is enlarged and has numerous, almost coalescing white foci. **H.** A nodular tumor is located at the apex of the heart (arrow). **I, J.** 22-week hobby chicken. **I.** Liver markedly enlarged, pale, and has white spots. **J.** Spleen is enlarged and pale white.

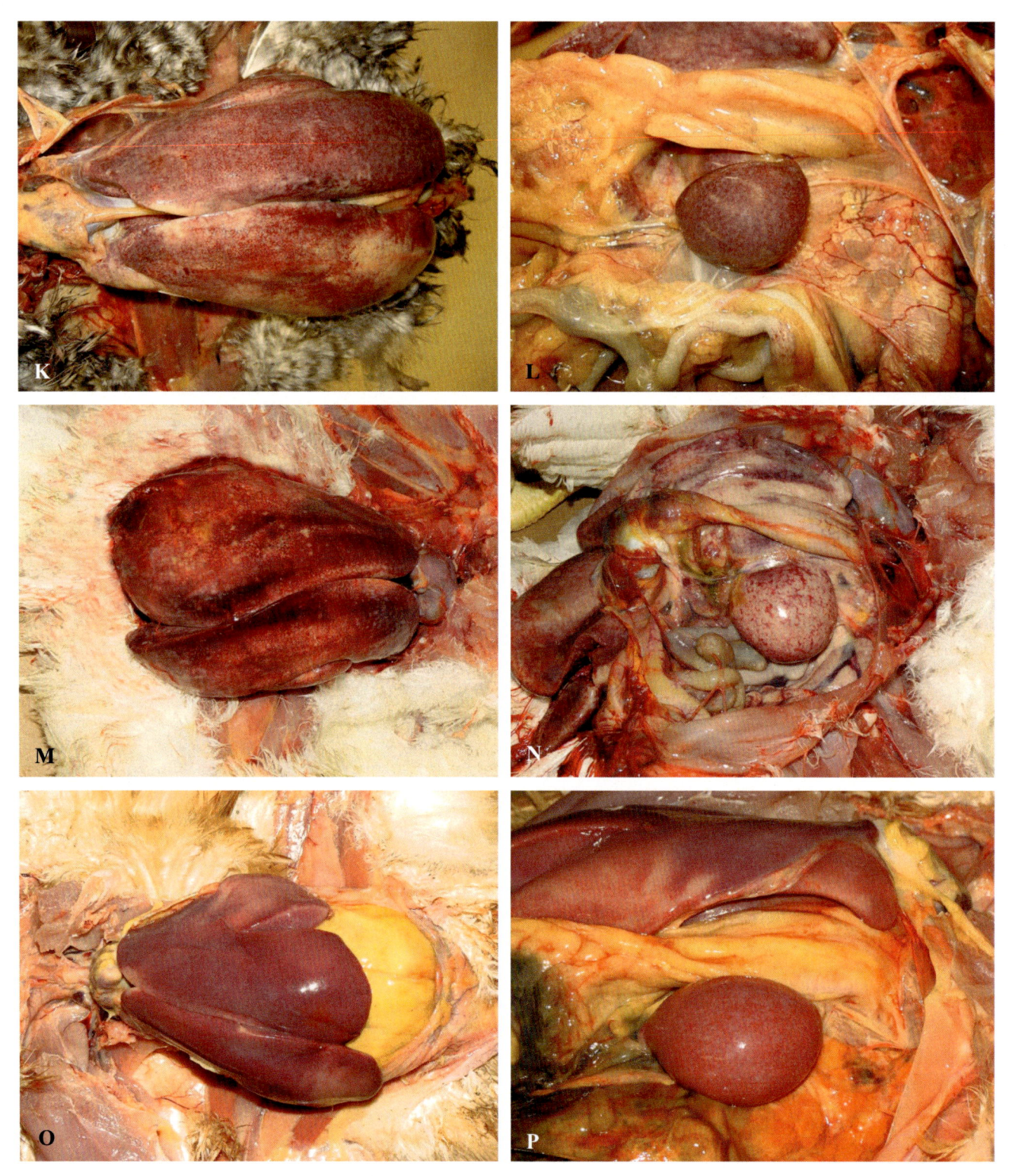

136 *Gross Pathology of Avian Diseases: Text and Atlas*

Lymphoid leukosis. K. L. One-year hobby chicken. **K.** Liver is markedly enlarged and discolored (asterisk: heart). **L.** Spleen is enlarged and mottled. **M, N.** 28-week broiler breeder hen. **M.** Liver is enlarged, discolored, and mottled with off-white spots. **N.** Spleen is enlarged and diffusely pale. **O, P.** 8-month hobby chicken. Liver (**O**) and spleen (**P**) are uniformly enlarged and pale.

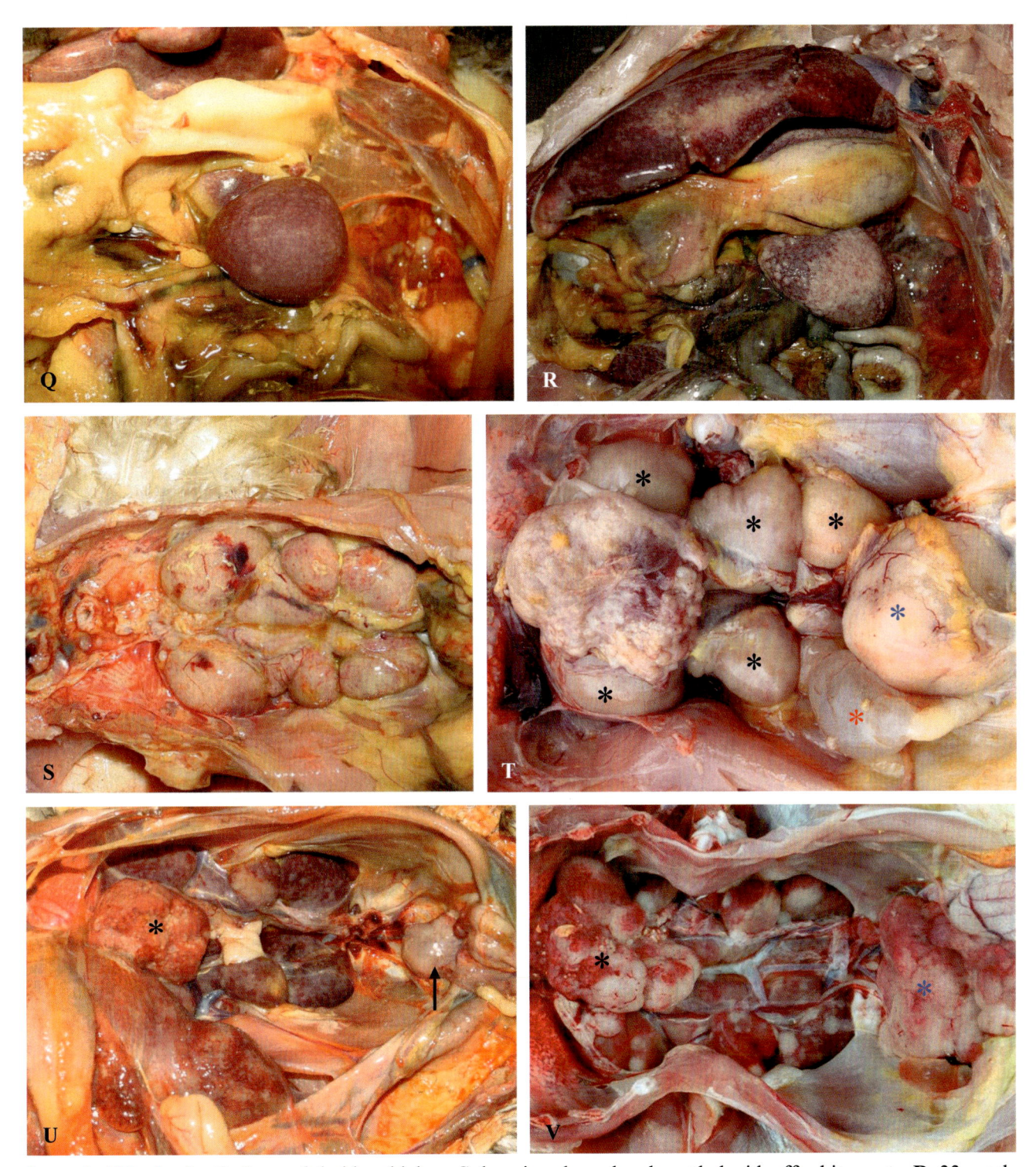

Lymphoid leukosis. Q. 8-month hobby chicken. Spleen is enlarged and mottled with off-white spots. **R.** 33-week broiler breeder hen (same bird in **E** and **F**). Spleen is diffusely off-white with slightly raised foci. **S.** 7-month hobby chicken. Kidneys are markedly enlarged and off-white. **T.** 67-week broiler breeder hen. Kidneys (black asterisks) are markedly enlarged and off white. Bursa (blue asterisk) is markedly enlarged. Note the cystic right oviduct (red asterisk). **U.** 10-month hobby chicken. Bursa is enlarged (arrow). Kidneys have white areas. Ovary (asterisk) is inactive and appears as a tissue mass. **V.** 44-week broiler breeder hen. Kidneys are enlarged and have white foci. Ovary has been replaced by a large tissue mass (black asterisk). A tumor is located at the site of bursa of the Fabricius (blue asterisk).

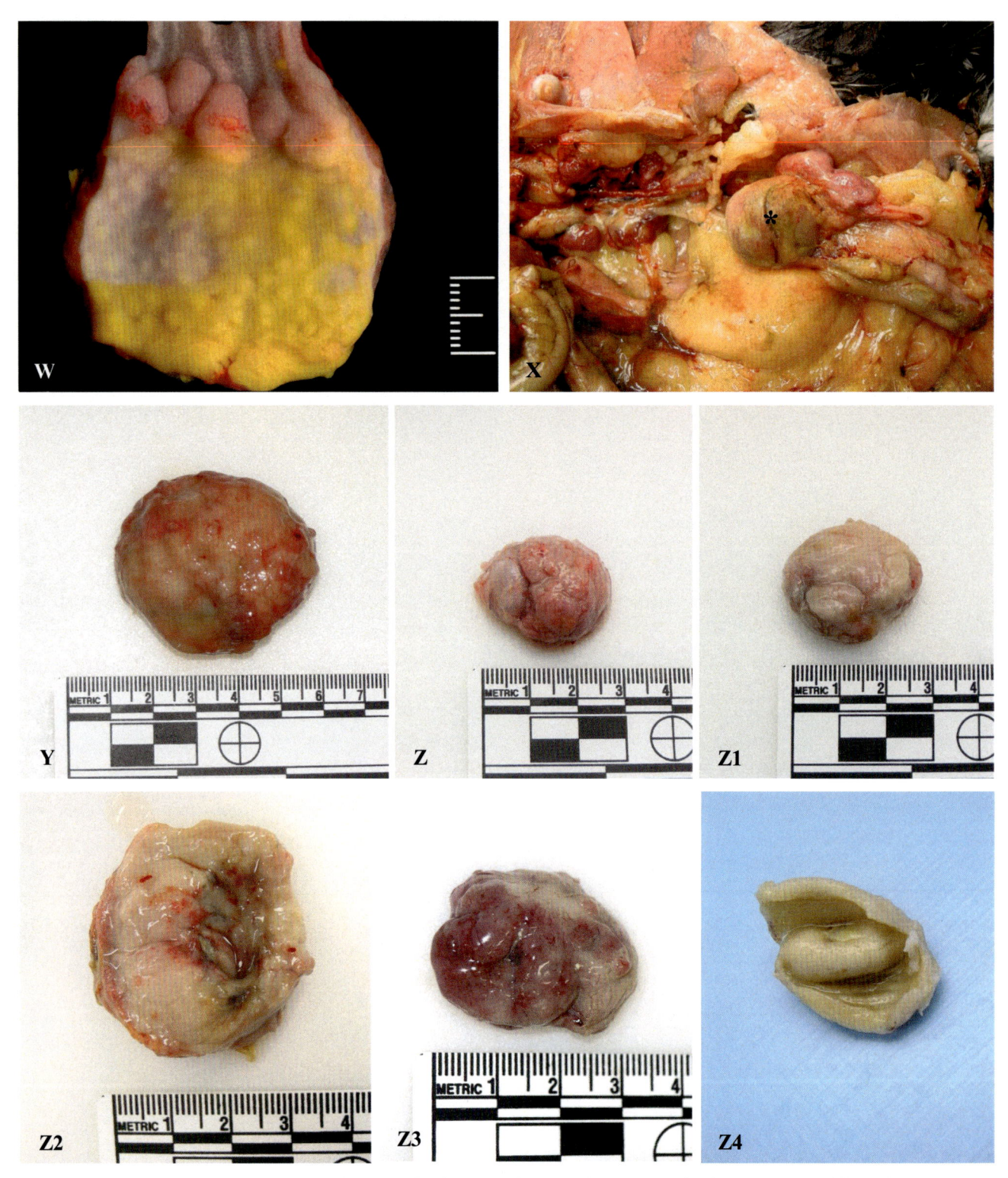

Lymphoid leukosis. W. 44-week broiler breeder hen. Nodules at the proventricular-esophageal junction are lymphoid tumors that likely involve lymphoid tissue in this area. **X.** 8-month hobby chicken. Bursa of Fabricius (asterisk) is enlarged. **Y-Z3.** 6- to 12-month hobby chickens (Y-Z2) and 33-week broiler breeder hen (Z3). Bursas are markedly enlarged and have thickened, irregular serosal surface. **Z4.** 22-week hobby chicken. A mucosal fold (plica) is markedly enlarged due to neoplastic transformation of lymphoid follicles.

Myelocytic Leukosis (Myelocytomatosis)

Cause. Myelocytic leukosis (ML) is caused by viruses in the *Alpharetrovirus* genus of the family *Retroviridae*. These viruses belong to the "Avian leukosis/sarcoma" group of viruses (ALSVs) and cause a variety of leukoses, sarcomas, and other neoplasms in chickens. ALSVs are classified into 6 subgroups (A-E, J) based on envelope type. Myelocytic leukosis is usually caused by subgroup J (ALV-J) viruses. Infection with ALV-J occurs both vertically and horizontally. Target cells are myelomonocytic cells in the bone marrow. Neoplasia caused by ALV-J following natural infection only occurs in chickens.

Gross lesions. Myelocytic tumors (myelocytomas) characteristically occur on the surface of bones and cartilage, although visceral organs can also be involved. Myelocytomas often develop on the inner surface of the sternum, at costovertebral junctions, and on the flat bones of the skull and mandible. Tumors may occur in the beak, larynx, and trachea when ossification with formation of bone marrow occurs. Myelocytomas are usually nodular, firm, and buff-colored. Organs heavily infiltrated with myelocytes are enlarged and pale white. The liver in particular becomes markedly enlarged, firm, and has diffuse pale white spots representing myelocytic infiltrates that may create a finely pebbled irregular surface. Other tissues often involved include spleen, kidney, ovary, and bone marrow. Infrequently, birds have numerous tumor nodules resembling disseminated carcinomas in organs and on serosal surfaces. Gross diagnosis is readily confirmed by microscopic examination of stained touch impressions of tumors and identifying high numbers of monomorphic myelocytes with characteristic eosinophilic cytoplasmic granules.

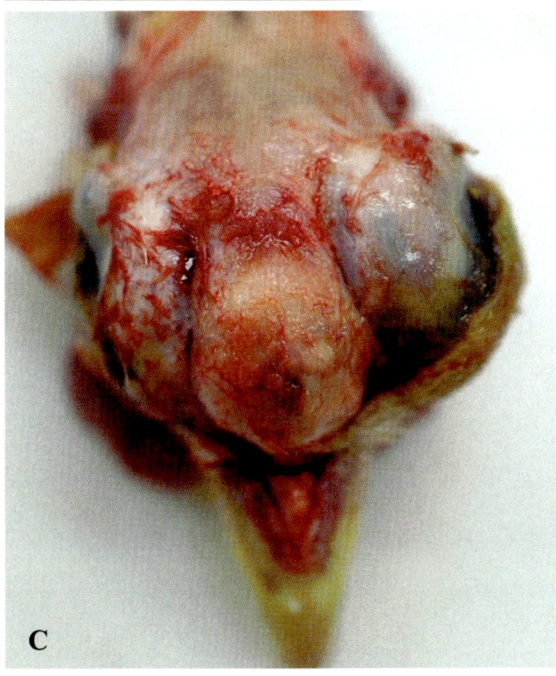

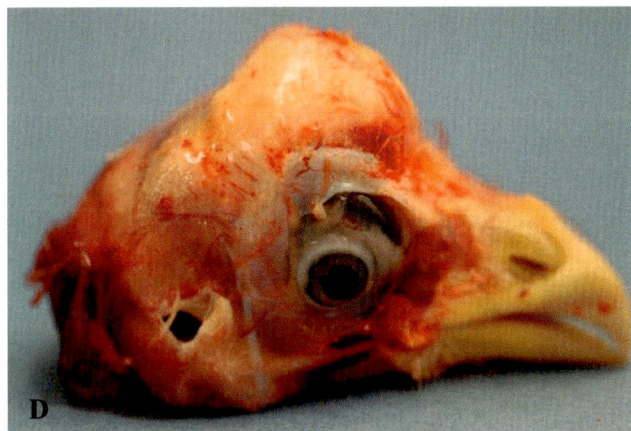

Myelocytic leukosis. Chickens. **A, B.** Swelling in skull (**A**) and above the eye (**B**) due to myelocytic tumors in cranial bones. **C, D.** Myelocytic tumors in cranial bones. *(Photos courtesy of Dr. Guillermo Zavala, USA).*

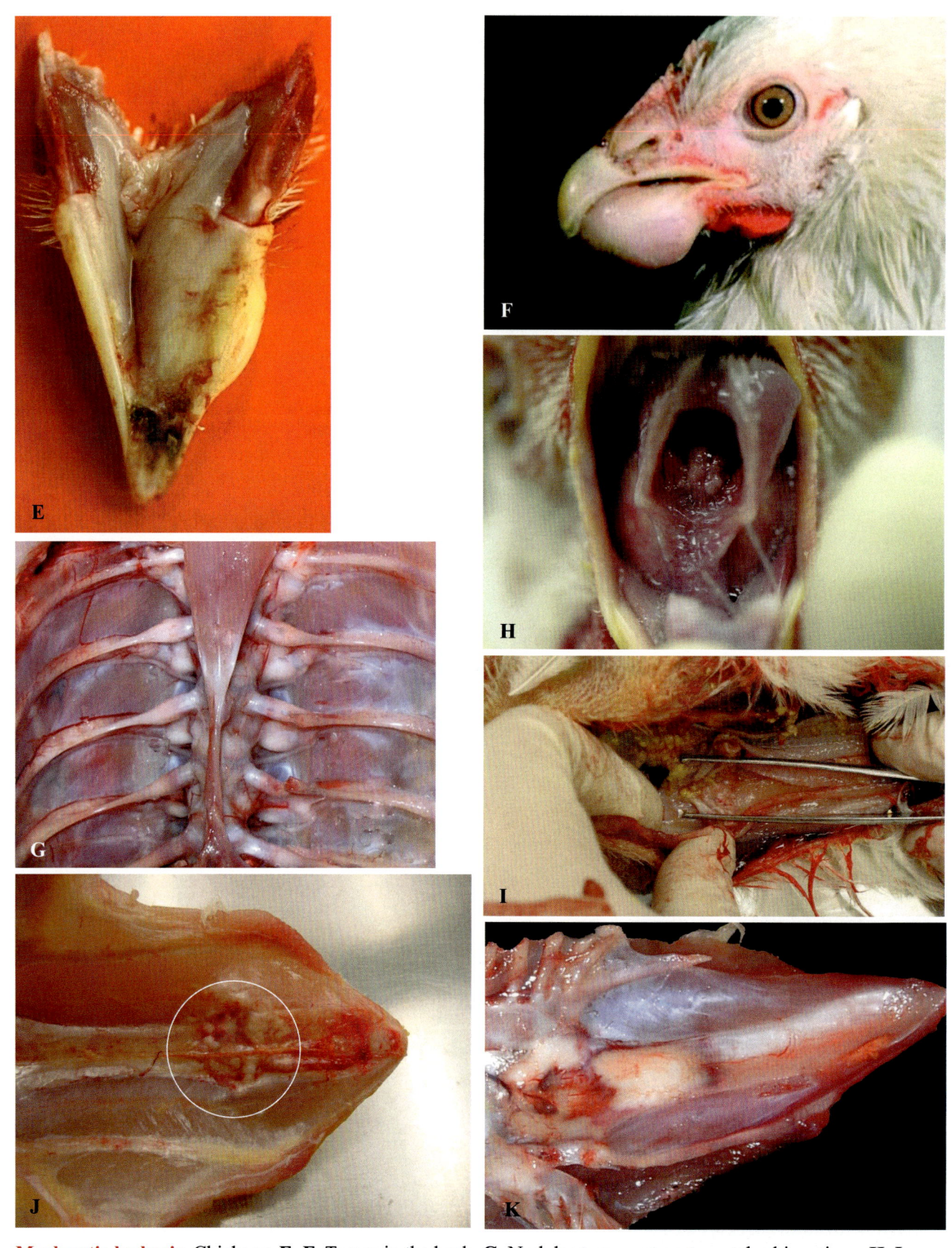

Myelocytic leukosis. Chickens. **E, F.** Tumor in the beak. **G.** Nodular tumors at costovertebral junctions. **H, I.** Nodular tumors in the larynx **J, K.** Tumor in the inner surface of the sternum. Circle in **J**: tumor nodules. *(Photos E, H, I, J, courtesy of Dr. Guillermo Zavala, USA).*

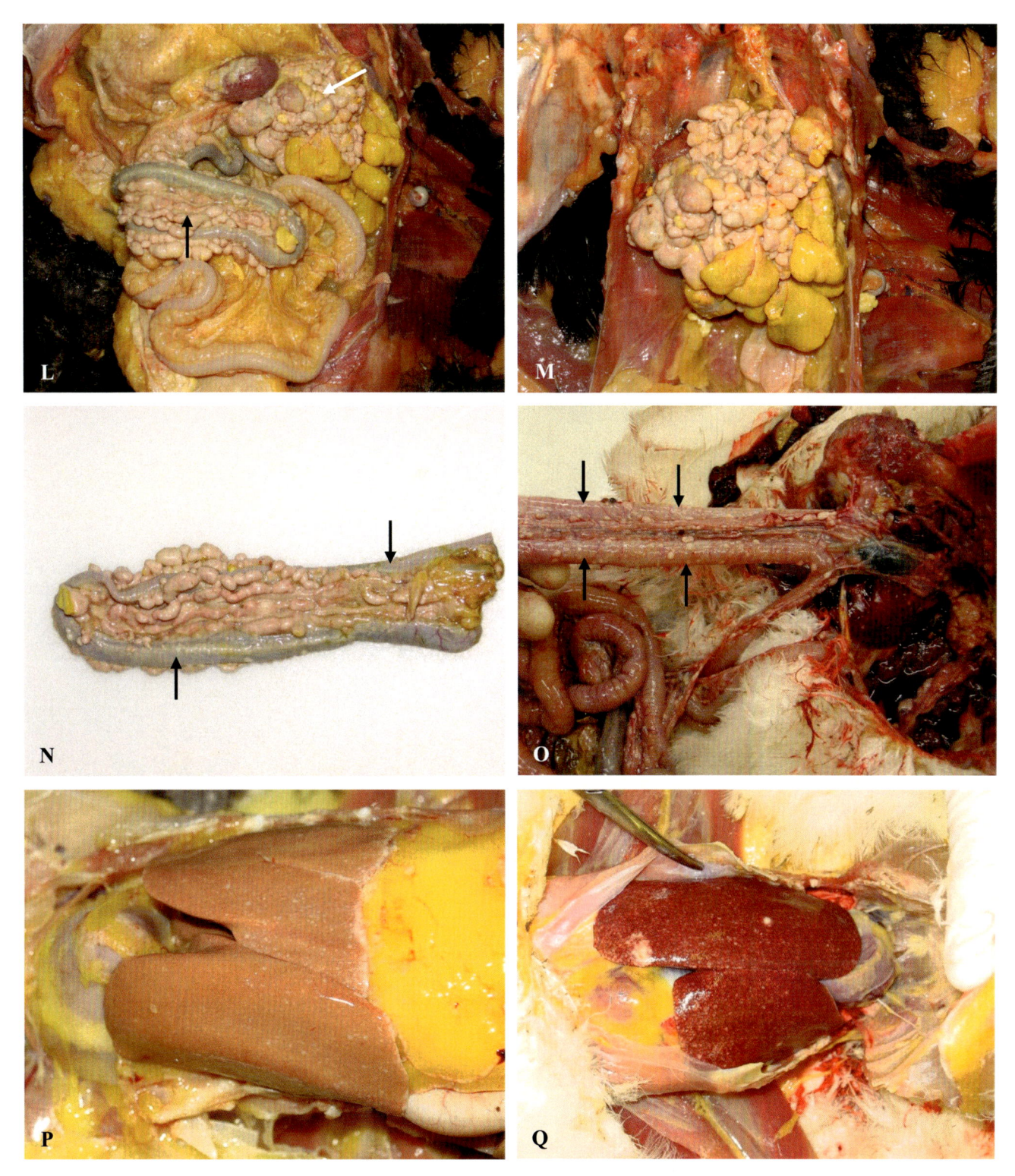

Myelocytic leukosis. L, M, N. 3-year hobby hen. **L.** Nodular tumors in the ovary (white arrow) and pancreas (black arrow). **M.** Close view of the nodular tumor in the ovary in **L**. Tumors may be mistaken for ovarian adenocarcinoma. **N.** Nodular tumors involving the pancreas. Arrows: duodenum. **O.** Many small nodules in the wall of duodenum. Arrows: duodenum. **P.** 16-month hobby hen. Liver is pale and diffusely mottled with white spots. The bird was anemic due to effacement of bone marrow by myelocytes. **Q.** Liver is enlarged and heavily spotted with white foci. *(Photos O, Q courtesy of Dr. Guillermo Zavala).*

Nephroblastoma in Chickens

Cause. Avian leukosis/sarcoma virus.

Gross Lesion. Nephroblastoma in chickens is usually unilateral and varies in appearance from multifocal, gray or pink small renal nodules to large solitary yellow lobulated masses that replace renal tissue. The tumor is not pedunculated but connected to the kidney by a prominent fibrous stalk. Large tumors are often cystic and consist of multiple large thin-walled cysts filled with yellow fluid. In heavily keratinized nephroblastomas, white to yellow, firm granules or spherical bodies composed of keratin are present within the cysts. Nephroblastomas can also occur in the ovary.

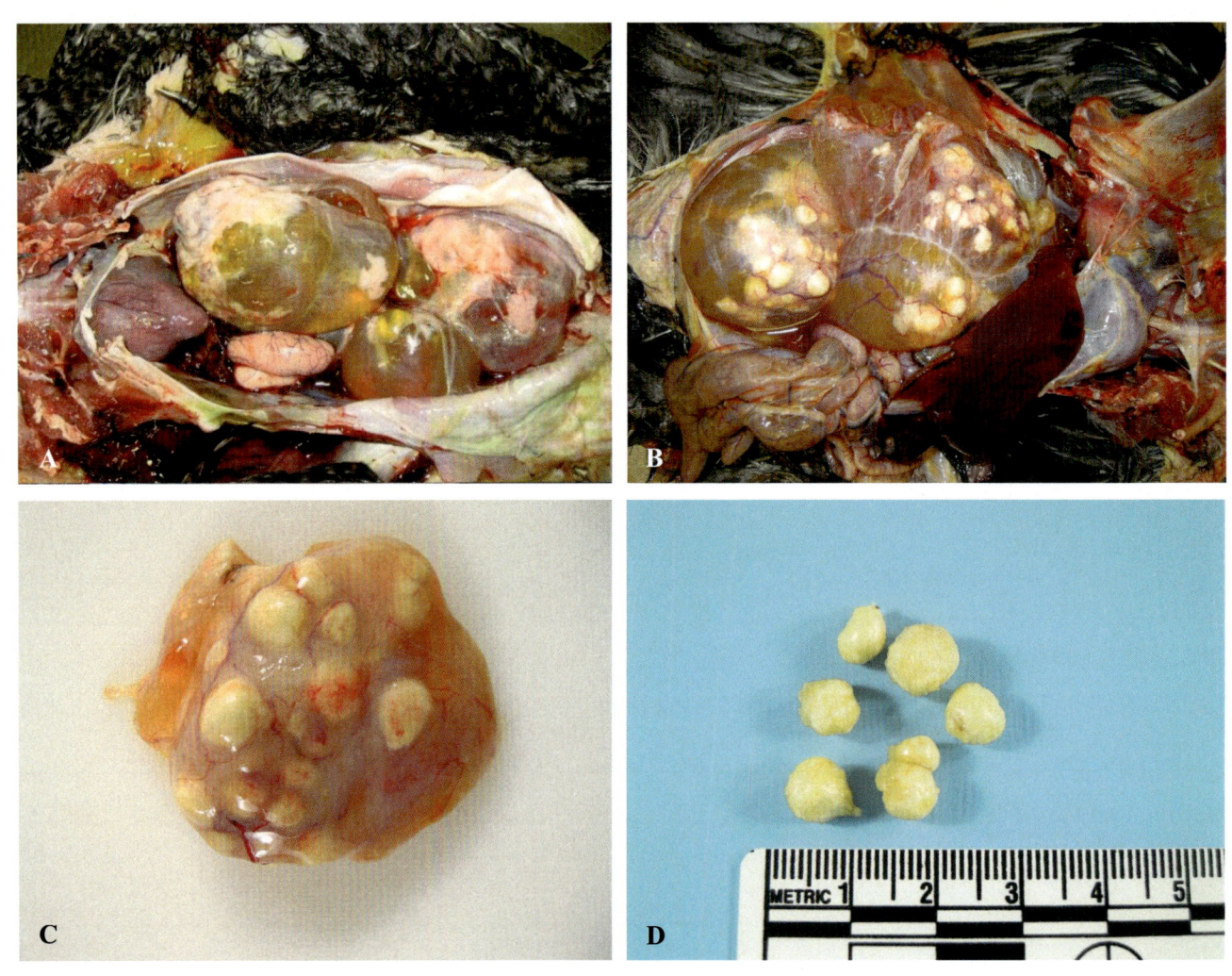

Nephroblastoma. A. 9-month hobby rooster. Large, multicystic tumor replaces the left kidney and occupies much of the body cavity. Cysts are thin-walled and filled with clear, yellow fluid. There are areas of dense tissue in cyst walls. **B, C, D.** 3.5-year hobby rooster. Occupying the body cavity and displacing visceral organs are four, thin-walled cysts. Cysts are associated with the right kidney, most of which, except for a small part of the anterior division, has been replaced by tumor. Cut surfaces of cysts are gelatinous, yellow, and multilocular. Lobules are filled with clear, yellow fluid and contain few to several yellow to white spherical bodies composed of keratin. In **D**, keratin bodies removed from a cyst. *(Photo A courtesy of Dr. David Drum, USA).*

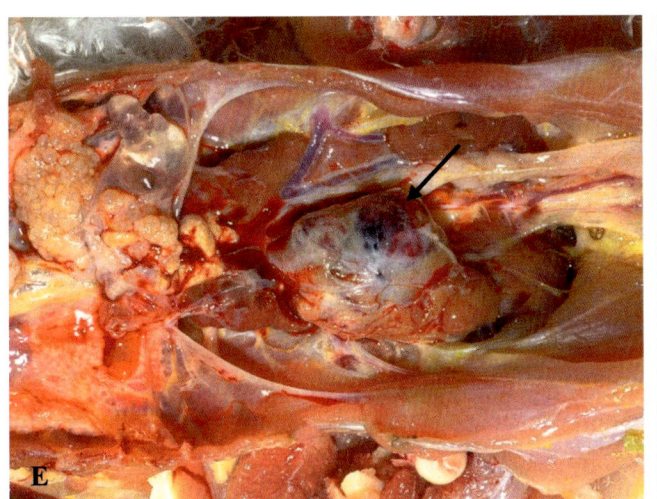

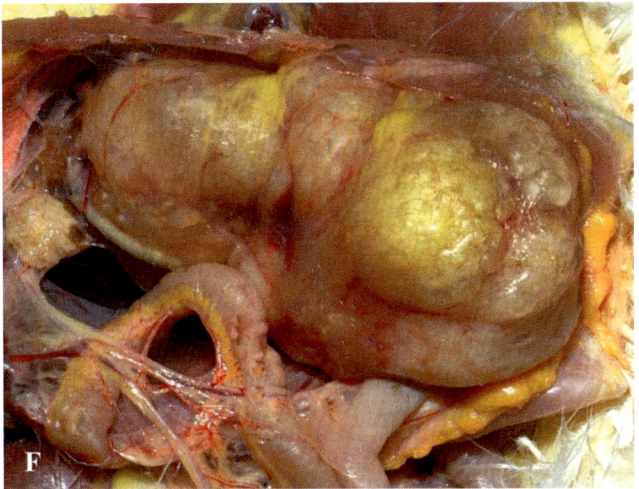

Nephroblastoma. E. 2-year chicken. Incidental finding. Multilobulated cystic tumor (arrow) replaces the middle division of the right kidney. Note regressed reproductive tract and ovarian cysts. **F.** 14-week broiler breeder. Large tumor replaces the left kidney and fills the abdominal cavity.

Third-eyelid Aspergillosis

Cause. *Aspergillus* spp.

Gross Lesions. Gross lesions consist of accumulations of caseous exudate under the 3rd eyelid. Lesions result from colonization and infection of the 3rd eyelid conjunctiva by *Aspergillus* spp., usually *A. fumigatus*.

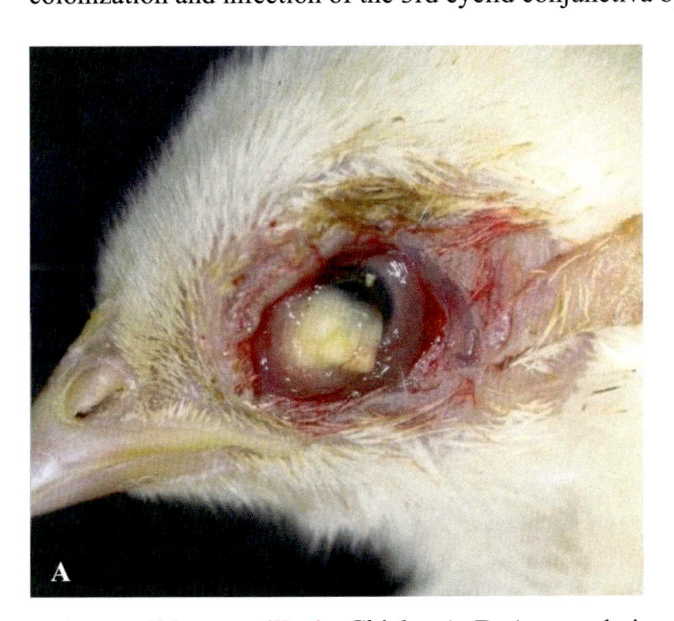

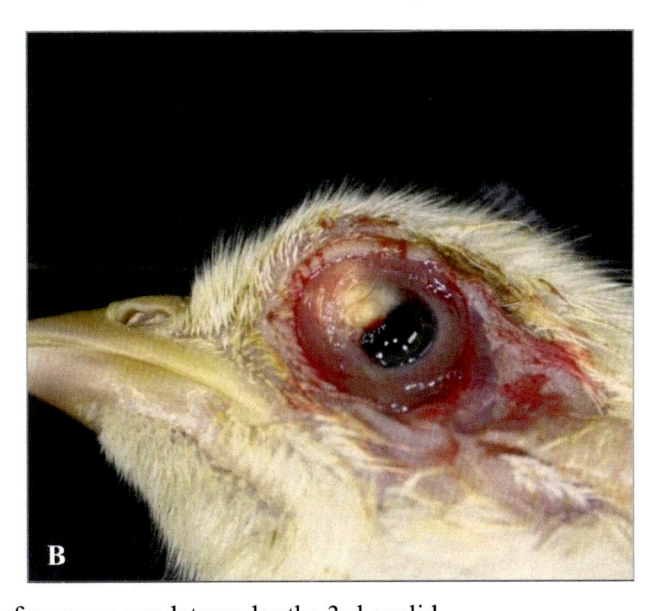

Third-eyelid aspergillosis. Chicks. **A, B.** Accumulation of caseous exudate under the 3rd eyelid.

Mycotic Keratitis Caused by *Aspergillus*

Cause and pathogenesis. *Aspergillus* spp., mostly *A. fumigatus*, is the most frequent fungus isolated from ocular lesions. Injury to the cornea is considered the key predisposing factor. Tiny pieces of wood shavings or large dust particles either directly implant fungal conidia into the corneal stroma or abrade the outer epithelial surface, allowing invasion by fungi. A moldy, dusty house environment or prolonged exposure to high ammonia levels are the main risk factors.

Gross lesions. Lesions vary in appearance depending on the stage and severity of infection. They may be confined to the cornea or the inflammatory process and fungal hyphae spread through Descemet's membrane into the eye causing exudate to accumulate in the anterior chamber (hypopyon). In some cases, there is diffuse, marked gray and yellow opacity of the cornea. In other cases, severe damage results in perforation of the outer surface of the cornea with accumulation of white to yellow exudate on the surface of the eye. The entire surface may be covered with a discoid shaped mass of caseous exudate. Often, eyelids are swollen due to edema.

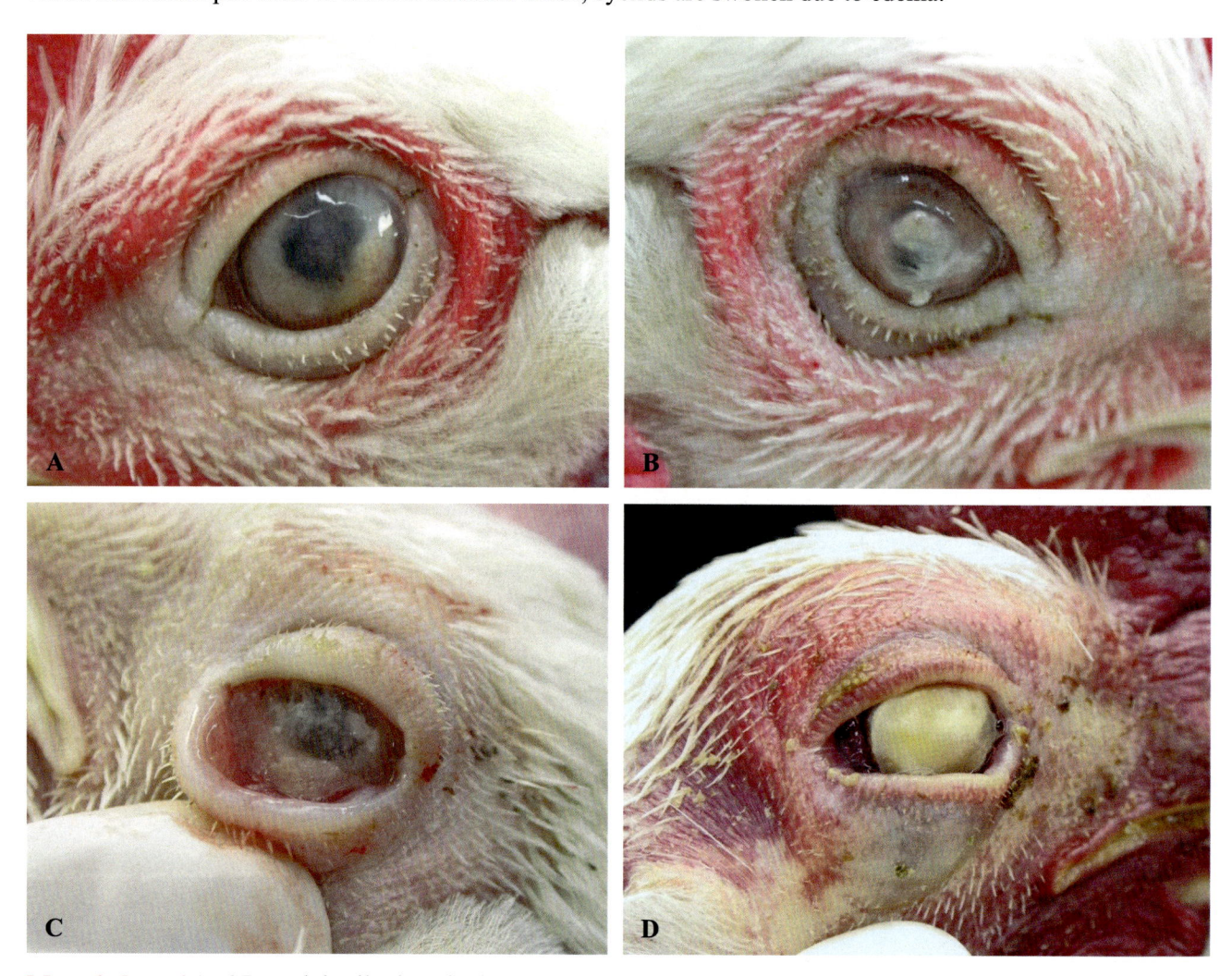

Mycotic keratitis. 27-week broiler breeder hens. **A.** Diffuse, marked gray and yellow opacity of the cornea due to keratitis. **B, C.** Cornea is opaque. Severe damage to the cornea has resulted in an accumulation of exudate on the surface. **D.** The corneal surface of the eye is covered with a discoid mass of caseous exudate. Note eyelid swelling. *A. fumigatus* was isolated and mycotic keratitis was confirmed by histopathology.

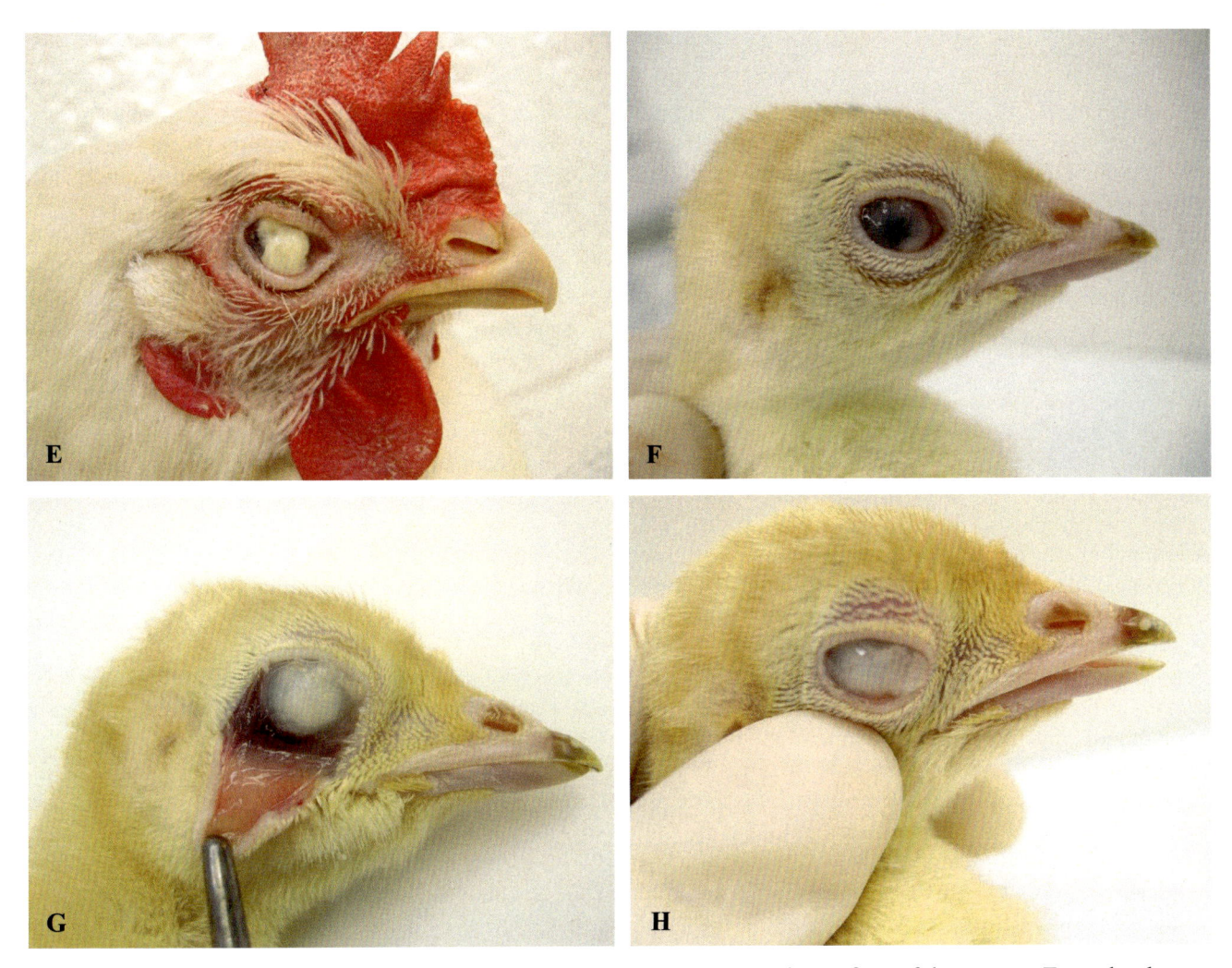

Mycotic keratitis. E. 32-week broiler breeder hen. Caseous exudate on the surface of the cornea. Fungal culture was not done, but the diagnosis of mycotic keratitis was confirmed by histopathology. **F, G.** One-week turkey poults. **F.** Gray opacity of the cornea is due to keratitis and there is hypopyon in the anterior chamber. **G.** Severe keratitis has resulted in marked white opacification and thickening of the cornea. In the turkey poults, *A. fumigatus* was isolated and mycotic keratitis was confirmed by histopathology.

Respiratory Aspergillosis

Cause. *Aspergillus fumigatus,* which produces abundant small spores that are readily inhaled and lodge in the lower respiratory tract, is the most common cause of respiratory aspergillosis. Young birds exposed to high numbers of spores in the hatchery or after placement on the farm are usually affected. Aspergillosis in older birds, including breeders, is usually caused by *A. flavus.* Spores of this species are much larger and tend to lodge in the upper respiratory tract. Infrequently, the disease is caused by other *Aspergillus* species including *A. niger, A. glaucus,* and *A. terreus.* Environments rich in organic material that alternate between wet and dry predispose to the disease. Litter that was previously wet and allowed to dry puts newly hatched birds at high risk of developing the disease. Impaired local and systemic immunity due to concurrent respiratory disease or uncompensated stress are other important predisposing factors.

Gross lesions. Lesions vary in extent and severity depending on the level of exposure to *Aspergillus* spores. Typically, a few to many firm, pale yellow or white, nodules are present in the lung parenchyma of young chicks and poults that have respiratory aspergillosis caused by *A. fumigatus*. Similar lesions can result from staphylococcal infection. Lesions in air sacs consist of yellow to white plaques (fungal plaques), small pale yellow nodules, and/or clumps and sheets of soft yellow caseous exudate. Plaques are common at the ostia of the caudal thoracic and abdominal air sacs. Even small plaques at these sites can block return flow of air from the air sacs into the lungs and cause death. Plaques may have green to brown fungal growth on the surface. Touch impressions of these lesions reveals hyphae and, occasionally, conidiophores and spores. In chronic, severe cases in older birds, air sacs may be covered with fungal growth that has a fluffy, cotton-like appearance.

Syringeal aspergillosis is characterized by occlusion of the lumen of the syrinx and one or both extra-pulmonary primary bronchi by yellow caseous exudate, with damage to the wall of the syrinx and bronchi. Usually there is also involvement of intrapulmonary primary and secondary bronchi in the lungs (bronchial aspergillosis). External examination of affected lungs reveals firm, white to yellow areas around the hilus of the lung. Cut surfaces of affected lungs, especially in the area around the hilum, show dense white, caseous exudate distending and occluding bronchial lumens. Gray to green areas of fungal growth may be evident in the exudate.

Respiratory and disseminated aspergillosis caused by *A. flavus* occurs in broiler breeders. Firm, yellow to white nodules resembling tumors ('aspergillomas') occur in lungs, air sacs, myocardium, liver, kidney, spleen, peritoneal surfaces, proventriculus, ventriculus, intestine, muscle, bone, and eyelids.

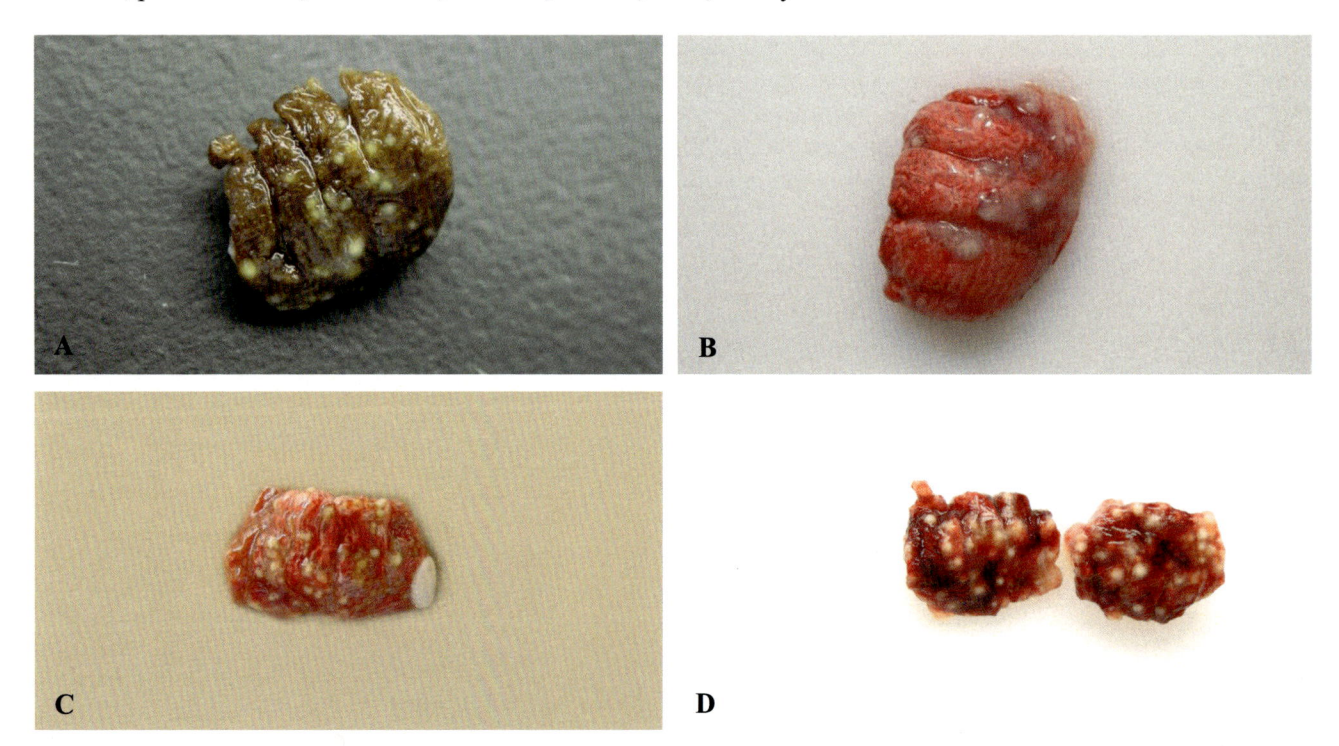

Pulmonary aspergillosis. 5- and 7-day broiler chickens (A, C), 3-week broiler breeder pullet (B), and 46-week quail (D) Yellow to gray caseous nodules in the lungs are characteristic of aspergillosis. Aspergillosis in young chicks and poults is usually caused by *A. fumigatus*.

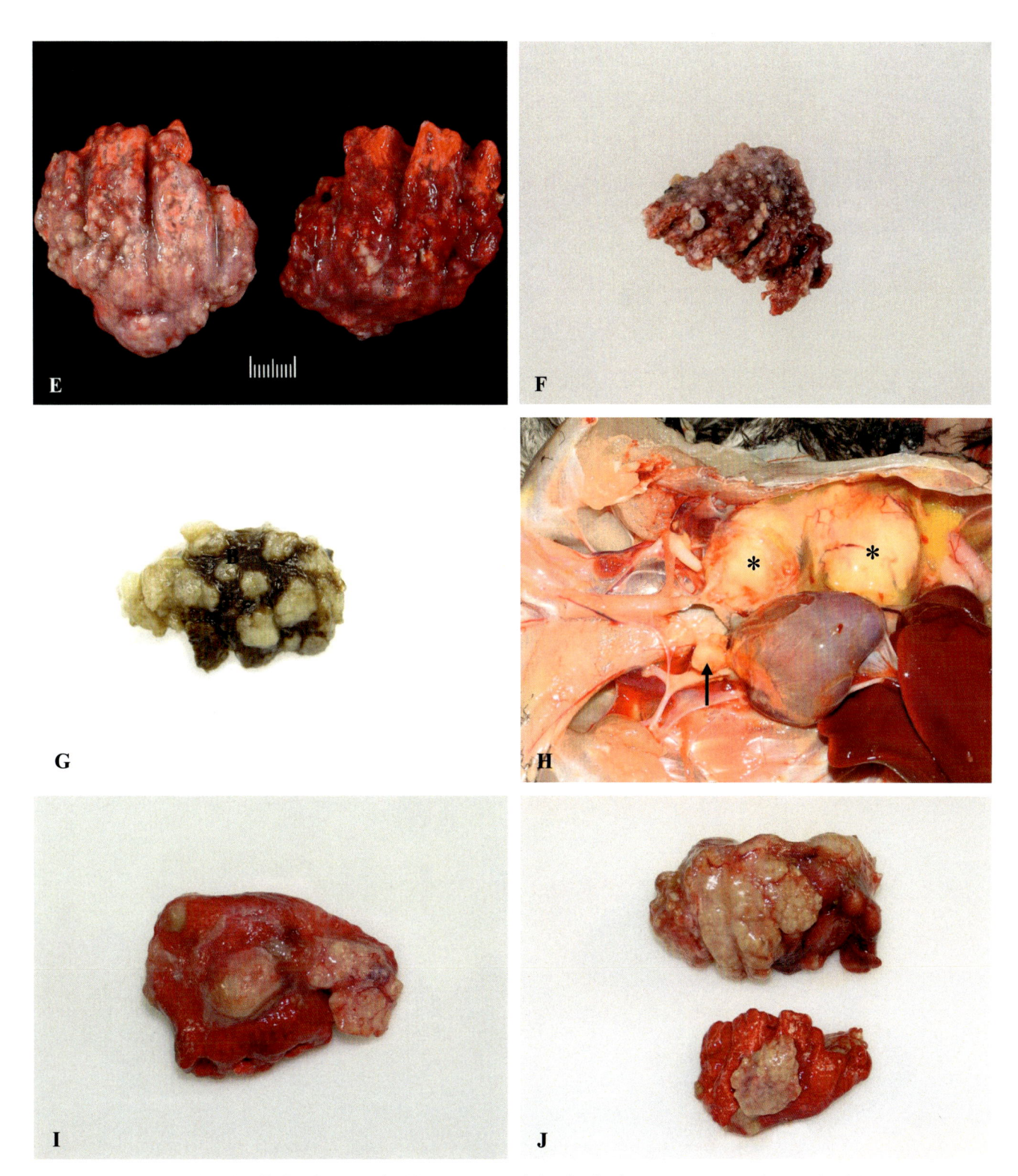

Pulmonary aspergillosis. E. Turkey poult. Numerous nodules in the lungs. **F.** Lung of an owl with many small pale nodules, which proved to be fungal granulomas caused by *A. fumigatus*. **G.** 5-week broiler breeder pullet. Tumor-like fungal granulomas in the lung. **H-J.** Lung lesions in 6-month hobby chicken caused by *A. flavus*. Tumor-like lesions in the lungs are exuberant mycotic granulomas. In **H**, note the large tumor-like lesion in the left lung (asterisks) and small nodule at the base of the heart (arrow). These nodules are sometimes referred to as 'aspergillomas'.

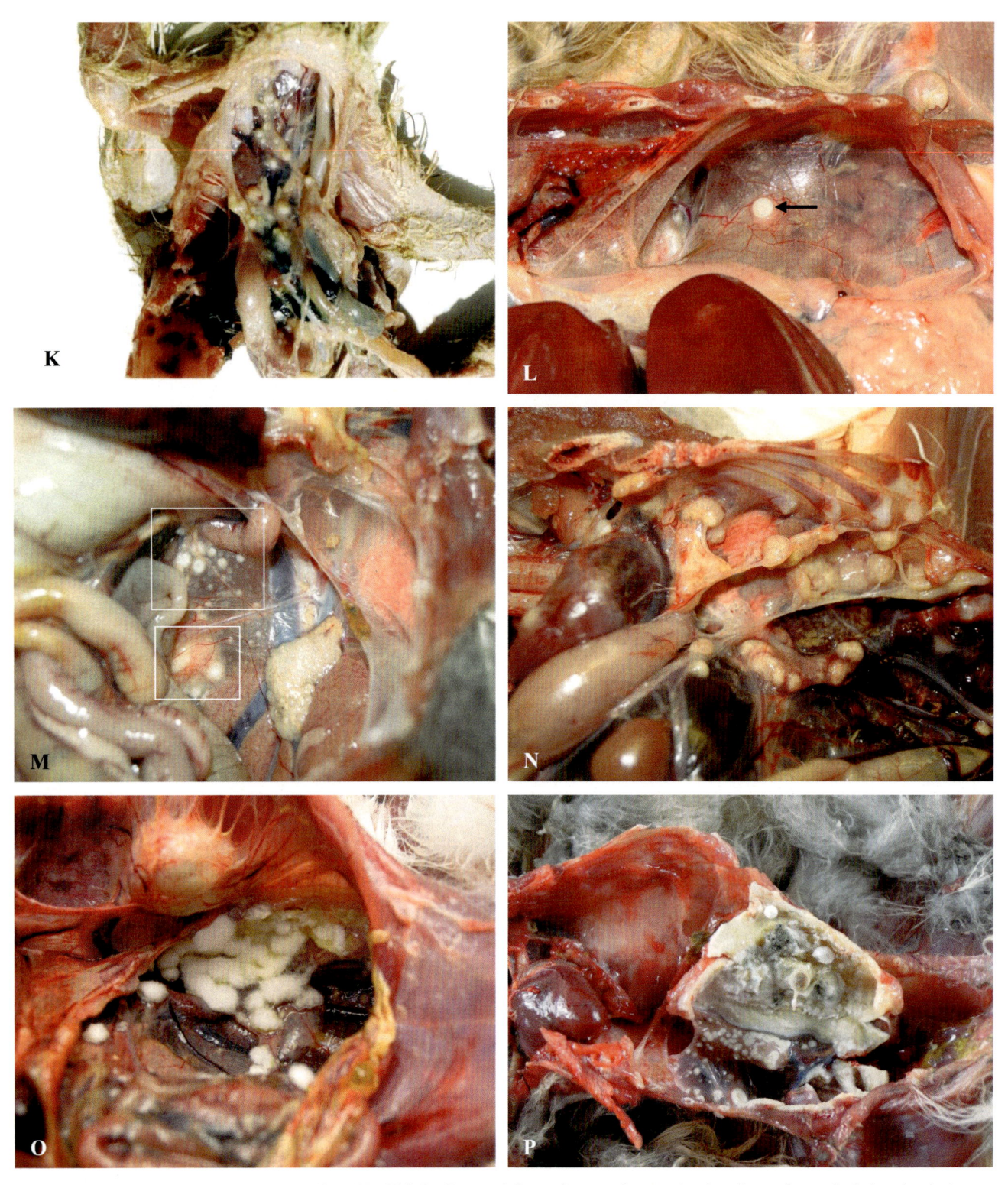

Air sac lesions caused by *Aspergillus*. **K.** Chick. Several fungal granulomas in the thoracic and abdominal air sacs. **L.** Owl. White fungal plaque (arrow) in the thoracic air sac and next to the lung at the air sac ostium. **M.** Owl. Several fungal plaques (triangles) in the thoracic air sac. **N.** 5-week broiler breeder pullet. Tumor-like fungal granulomas caused by *A. flavus* in the thoracic air sac. **O.** Duck. Cottony, fluffy growth of *A. fumigatus* in the abdominal air sac. **P.** Owl. Heavy fungal growth in the thoracic air sacs. The appearance and gray-green color of the lesions are characteristic of mycotic infection.

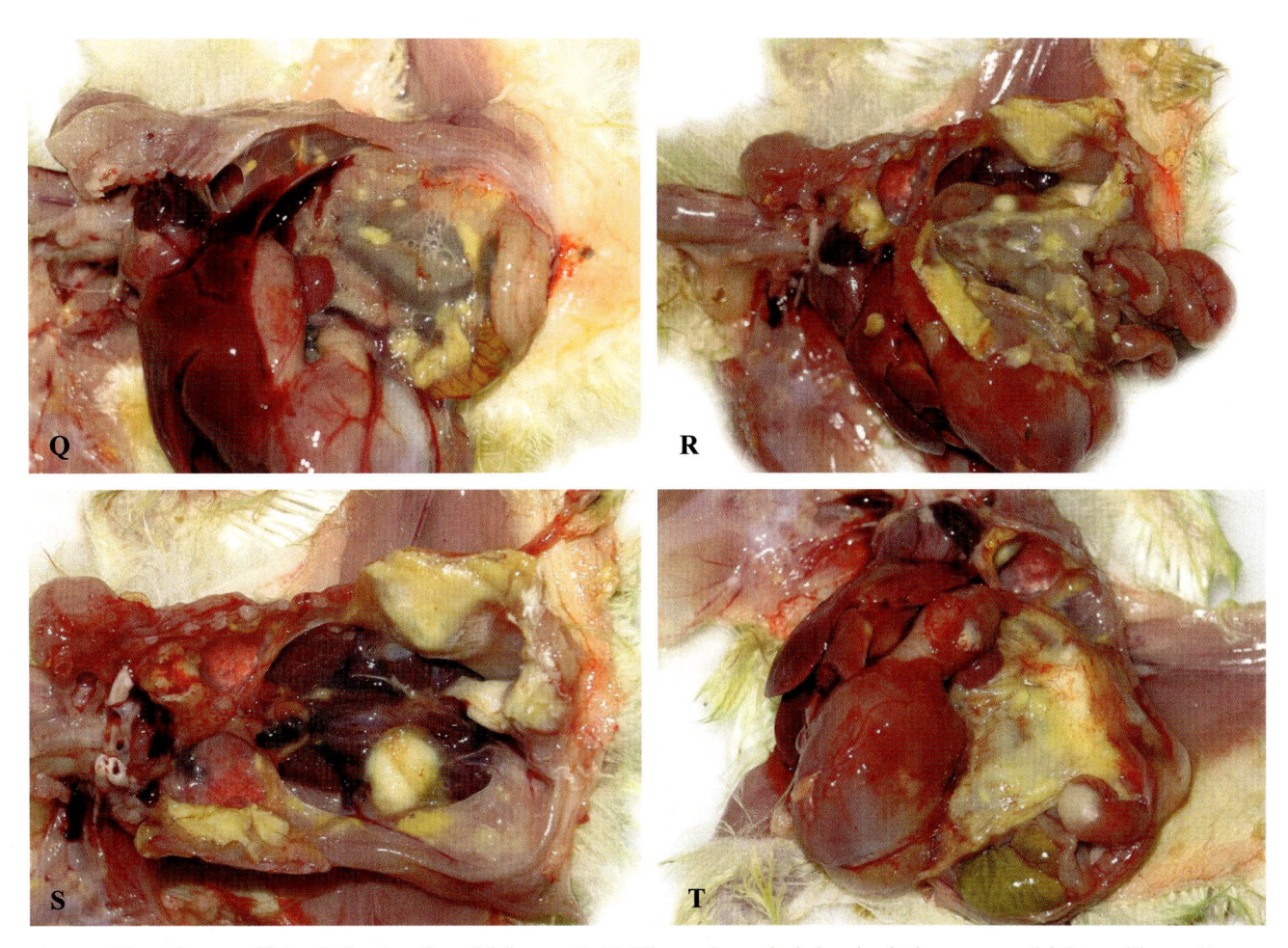

Aspergillus **airsacculitis.** 6-day broiler chickens. **Q-T.** Thoracic and abdominal air sacs are thickened by yellow caseous exudate. Interclavicular air sacs are also involved. Mycotic airsacculitis was confirmed by histopathology. *A. fumigatus* was isolated from lesions. Mycotic caseous granulomas were in the lungs of some birds.

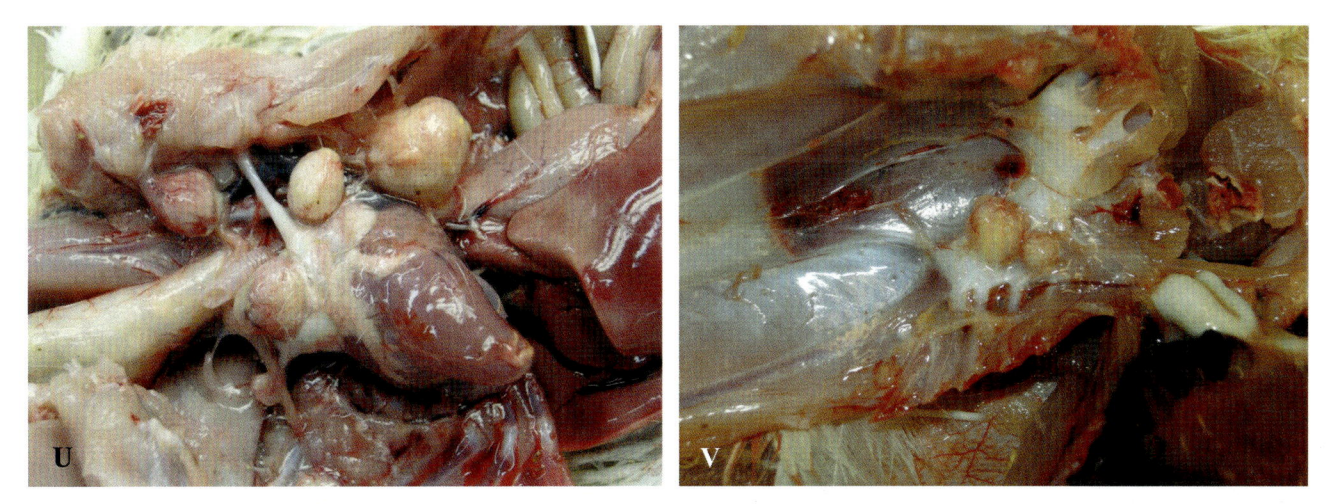

Aspergillus **granulomas in air sacs.** 5-week broiler breeder pullets. **U.** Large tumor-like firm nodules at the base of the heart. **V.** Tumor-like nodules in the anterior part of the inner surface of the keel. In both **U** and **V**, nodules were located in the interclavicular air sac around the base of the heart and on the inner surface of the keel. Neoplasia was suspected and the nodules were not cultured. Histologically, each nodule consisted of coalescing granulomas with intralesional fungal hyphae. The histomorphological features of the granulomas were suggestive of *A. flavus* infection. These exuberant granulomas are sometimes referred to as 'aspergillomas'.

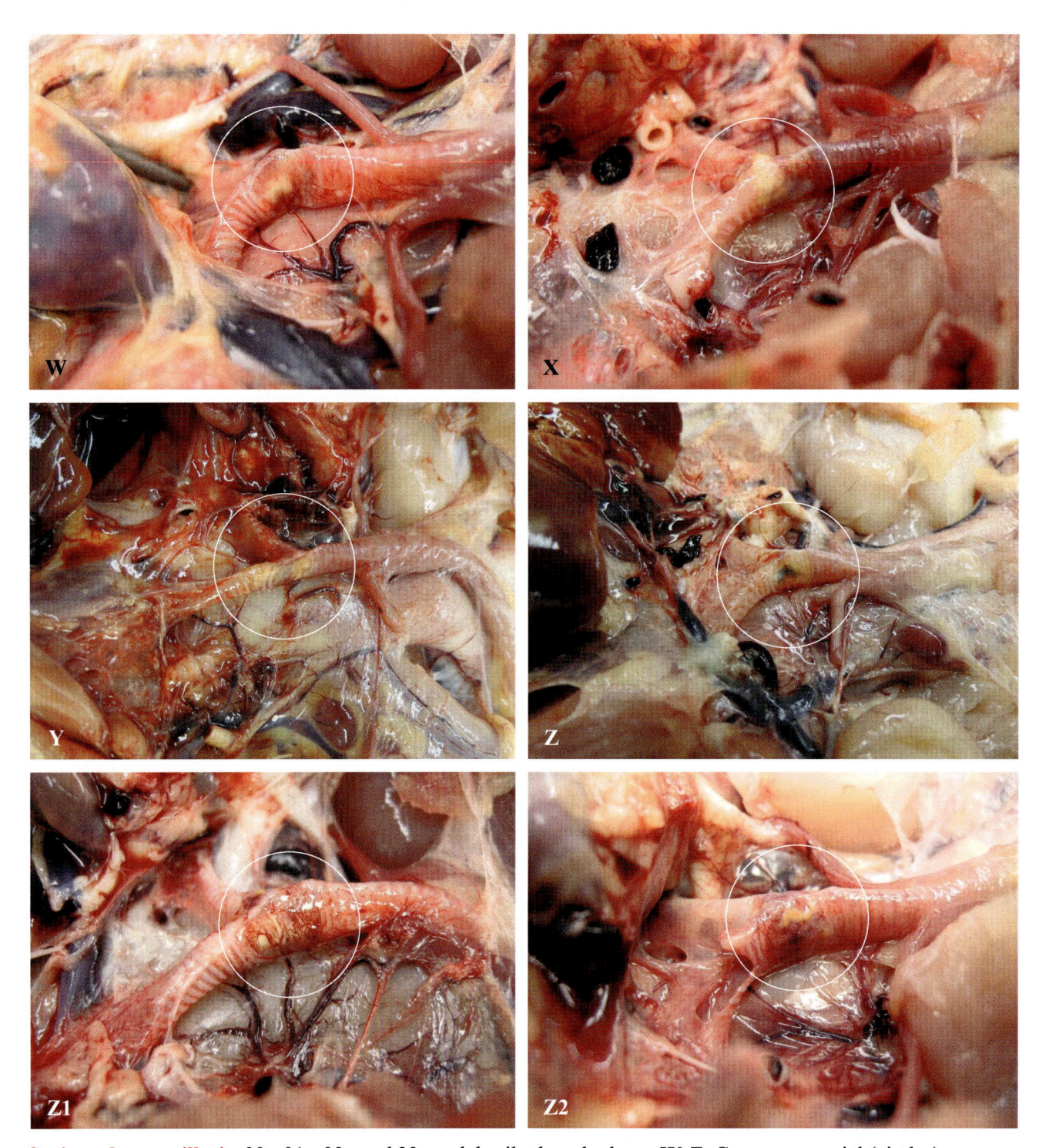

Syringeal aspergillosis. 29-, 31-, 32-, and 33-week broiler breeder hens. **W-Z.** Caseous material (circles) occludes the syrinx. In **Y**, exudate is also present in the right primary bronchus. In **Z**, green fungal growth is seen through the wall of the syrinx. *Aspergillus* infects the syrinx and causes severe damage, resulting in the accumulation of caseous debris. **Z1, Z2.** Circled area in the syrinx is colonized and infected by *Aspergillus* sp. In **Z1**, the wall of the syrinx is perforated and caseous exudate extends through it.

Z3 Z4

Z5 Z6

Intrapulmonary bronchial aspergillosis. **Z3-Z6**. 29- and 31-week broiler breeder hens. Caseous exudate distends and occludes the lumen of intrapulmonary bronchi. Histologically, fungi were abundant in the caseous exudate.

Crop Candidiasis (Crop Mycosis, Thrush)

Most species of birds are susceptible to crop candidiasis. Among poultry, turkeys are most often affected. The disease is sporadic and typically follows a predisposing factor that increases susceptibility of the bird to infection. Candidiasis is usually an incidental finding, but occasionally flocks have high mortality. Lethal infections occur in hummingbirds.

Cause. *Candida* spp. with *C. albicans* being the cause in the majority of cases.

Clinical signs and gross lesions. Clinical signs are not specific. Typically, affected birds are unthrifty or show signs of the predisposing factor. An empty thickened crop can often be palpated. The mucosal surface of the crop is thickened and usually rugose or has raised white areas or ulcer-like plaques. The mucosa may have a "Turkish towel" appearance. In some cases, pseudomembranes form and appear as multifocal to confluent white curd-like material adhering to the mucosal surface. Clumps of white debris may be present in the lumen. In severely affected birds, lesions may involve the oropharynx, esophagus, and proventriculus.

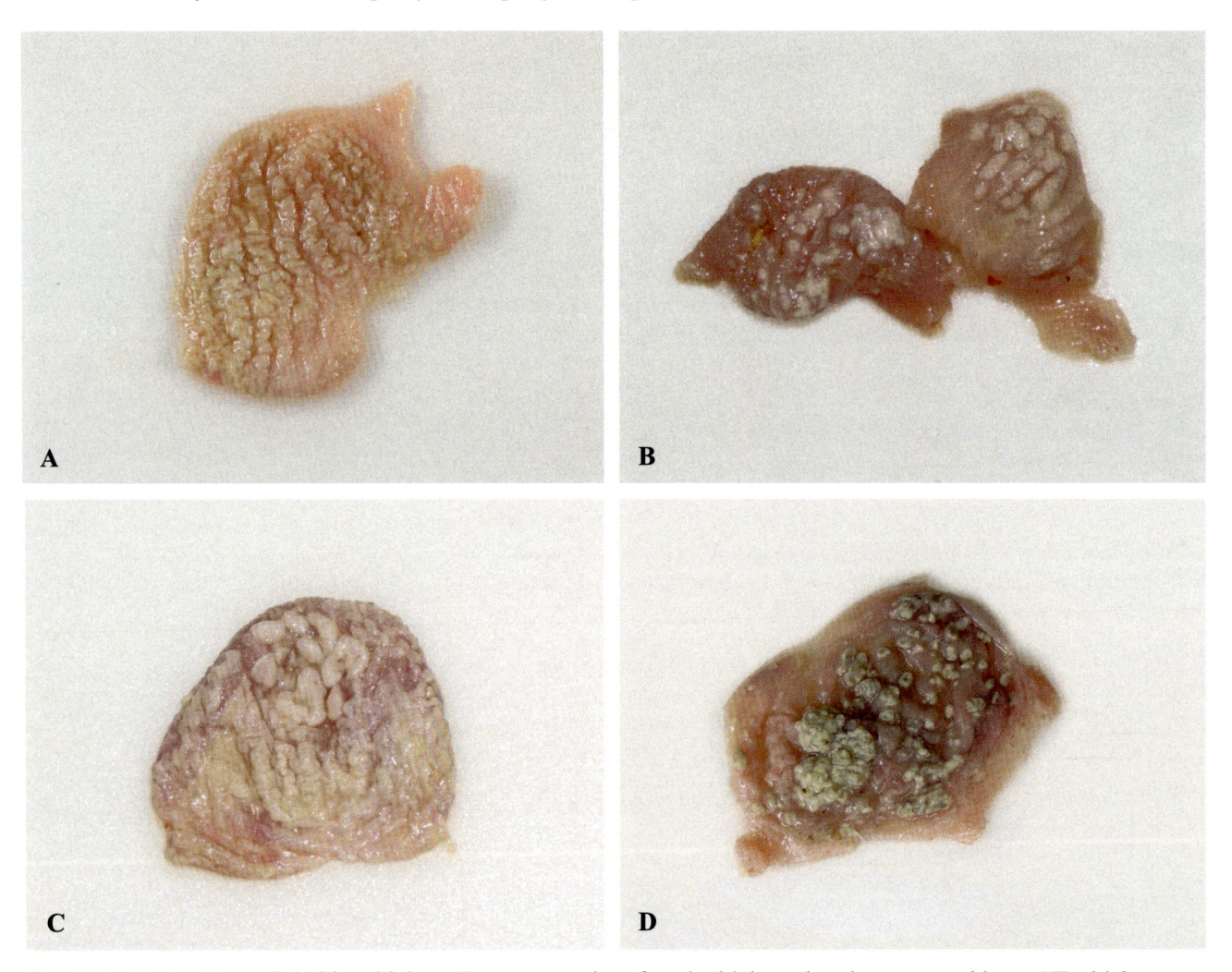

Candidiasis. A. 10-week hobby chicken. Crop mucosal surface is thickened and rugose and has a "Turkish towel" appearance. **B.** 20-day broiler breeder pullet. Raised, white areas are in the mucosal surface. **C.** 12-week hobby chicken. Mucosal surface is rugose and covered with a white, pseudomembrane. **D.** 13-week broiler breeder pullet. Green, ulcer-like plaques of varying sizes and thickness.

Comb Candidiasis

Cause. Comb candidiasis is caused by *Candida albicans*. Broiler breeders in humid environments are most frequently affected. It is common to find at least a few affected birds in most broiler breeder flocks. Males are more affected than females, but this may be due to easier recognition of lesions on their larger combs. The infection is incidental and not known to cause clinical disease. Production issues have erroneously been attributed to this disease.

Gross lesions. Lesions are found on the unfeathered areas of the head and upper neck. They are most common on the comb, but may also occur on the wattles, ear lobes, facial skin, and skin of the upper neck beneath the beak. Lesions are characterized by a white adherent dusting in diffuse or dense patches in the affected areas. Lesions typically extend to the tips of the comb and often are roughly circular with a sharply demarcated border. Small, irregular dark brown to black scabs may be present in some lesions.

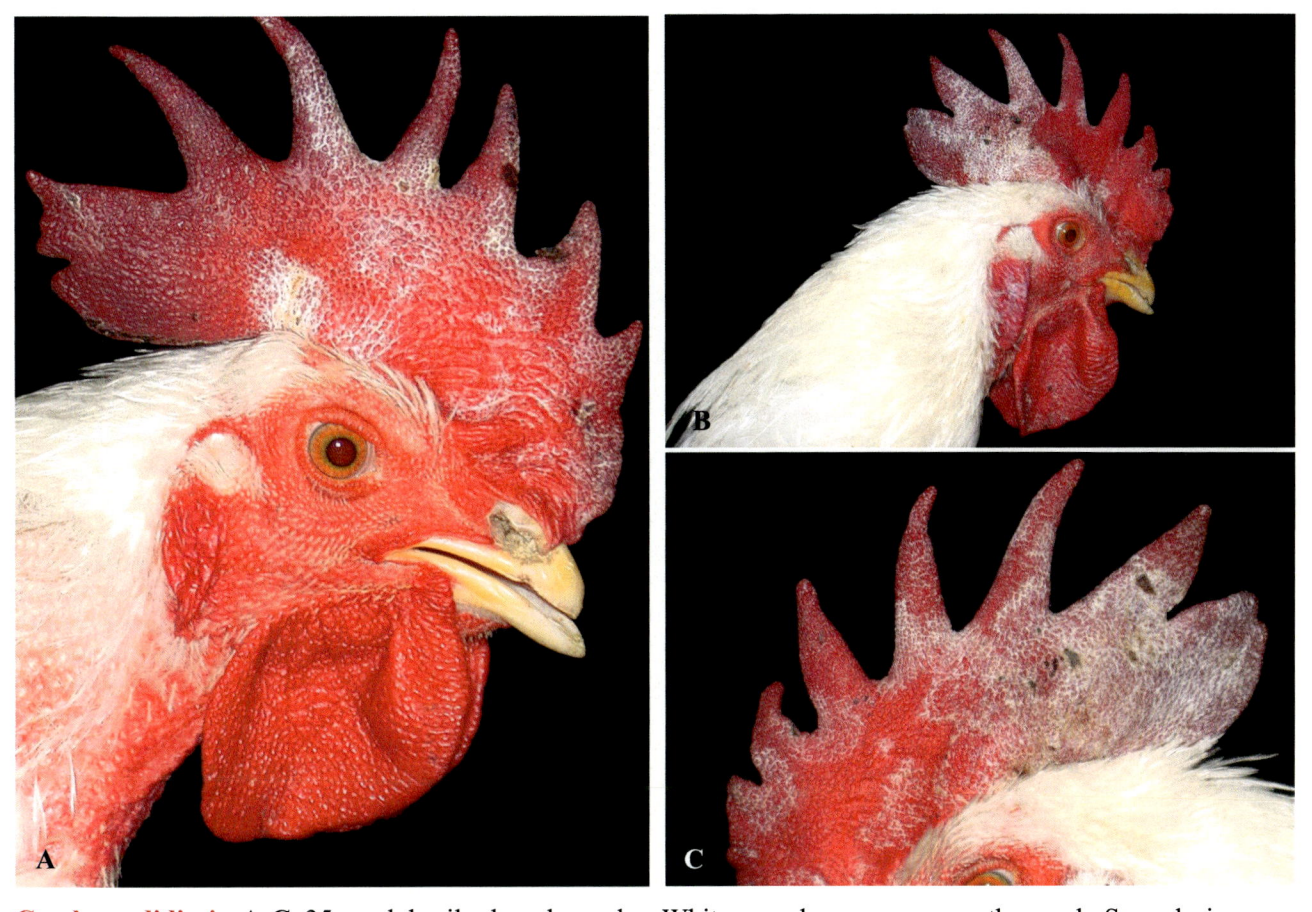

Comb candidiasis. A-C. 35-week broiler breeder males. White, powdery areas are on the comb. Some lesions have sharp margins and are roughly circular.

Intestinal Coccidiosis in Chickens

Cause. Species causing gross lesions in the intestinal tracts of chickens are *Eimeria acervulina*, *E. maxima*, *E. necatrix*, and *E. tenella*. *Eimeria necatrix* and *E. tenella* are the most pathogenic and can cause high mortality. Lesions vary with the severity of infection. Coccidiosis caused by other species commonly affects most domestic and captive birds. The disease in free-living birds is rare, as they are not exposed to high numbers of infective oocysts. Microscopic examination of mucosal scrapings or stained cytologic touch impression smears of the mucosa reveals oocysts and other developmental stages of the protozoa. Damage to the intestinal mucosa caused by coccidia can predispose to necrotic enteritis, which often occurs concurrently with coccidiosis. Blood in the intestinal lumen serves as a substrate for bacterial proliferation, which can be massive and complicate the disease.

Eimeria acervulina. Intestinal lesions caused by *E. acervulina* are primarily located in the duodenum, but may extend into the upper jejunum. The mucosa of the duodenum may be thickened and white or contain white to gray, transverse patches or short bands. Transversely oriented lesions are sometimes referred to as a "ladder rung" arrangement. The white discoloration is caused by numerous developmental stages of *E. acervulina* clustered together in the epithelial cells of villi. Hemorrhage is not a feature of coccidiosis caused by *E. acervulina*.

Eimeria maxima. Intestinal lesions caused by *E. maxima* are primarily located in the jejunum and ileum, but may extend into the duodenum. Characteristically, the mid small intestine is mildly dilated and contains excess orange mucus, or distended with fluid and thick bloody mucus that covers the mucosa. The mucosa is either diffusely reddened or has foci of hemorrhage.

Eimeria necatrix. Coccidiosis caused by *E. necatrix* occurs most frequently in older birds. Affected birds may have bloody droppings. Lesions usually occur in the same location as *E. maxima* and are characteristic or even diagnostic. The jejunum and most of the ileum are markedly dilated and filled with bloody fluid mixed with tissue debris. Red and white spots seen from the serosal surface of the dilated segment are sometimes referred to as a "salt and pepper" pattern. Microscopic examination of mucosal scrapings reveals clusters of large meronts (schizonts) containing merozoites. Finding large meronts but not oocysts in mucosal scrapings is a diagnostic feature of infection with *E. necatrix*. Oocysts of *E. necatrix* develop in the ceca rather than in the small intestine.

Eimeria tenella. *E. tenella* can cause high mortality. Bloody droppings may be seen. Lesions are confined to the ceca (cecal coccidiosis), which becomes distended with blood mixed with necrotic and sloughed epithelial debris. Diffuse reddening or multifocal red spots or patches, sometimes with white spots, are seen from the serosal surface. The cecal mucosa is thick and corrugated. Overtime, the luminal content gradually desiccates creating a dry, compact white mass ("cecal core"). Cecal cores too large to exit the cecum via the narrow opening at the ileocecal junction remain for long periods; smaller cores pass in the droppings. Many degenerate coccidial oocysts are usually present in cecal cores. Comb and visceral organs become pale because of blood loss.

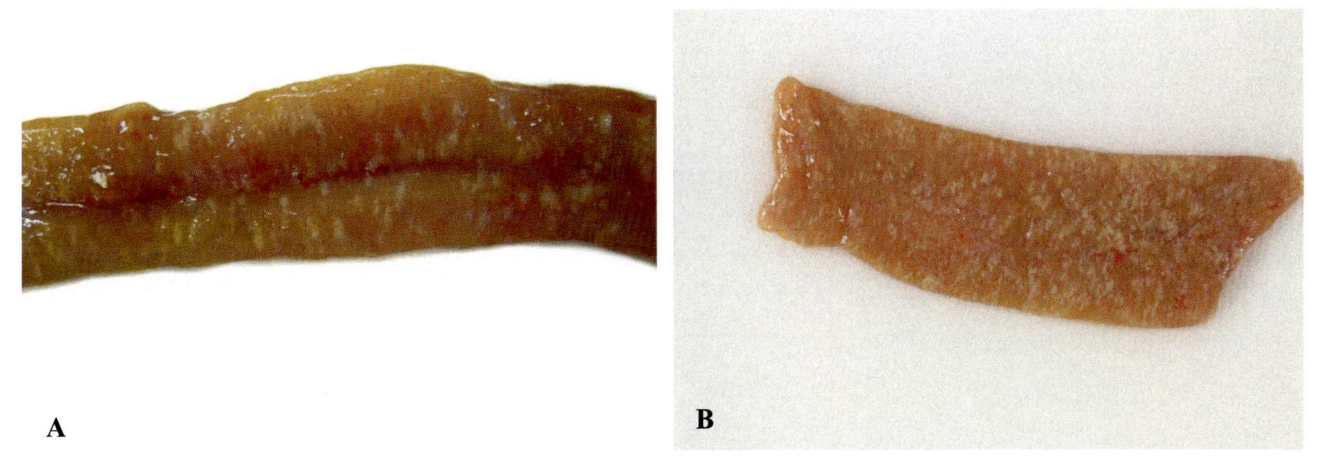

Coccidiosis. (*Eimeria acervulina*). Duodenum. **A, B.** Broiler chicken (A.17-day) and hobby chicken (B. 26-week). Transversely oriented white patches and short bands in the mucosa are characteristic lesions of *E. acervulina*.

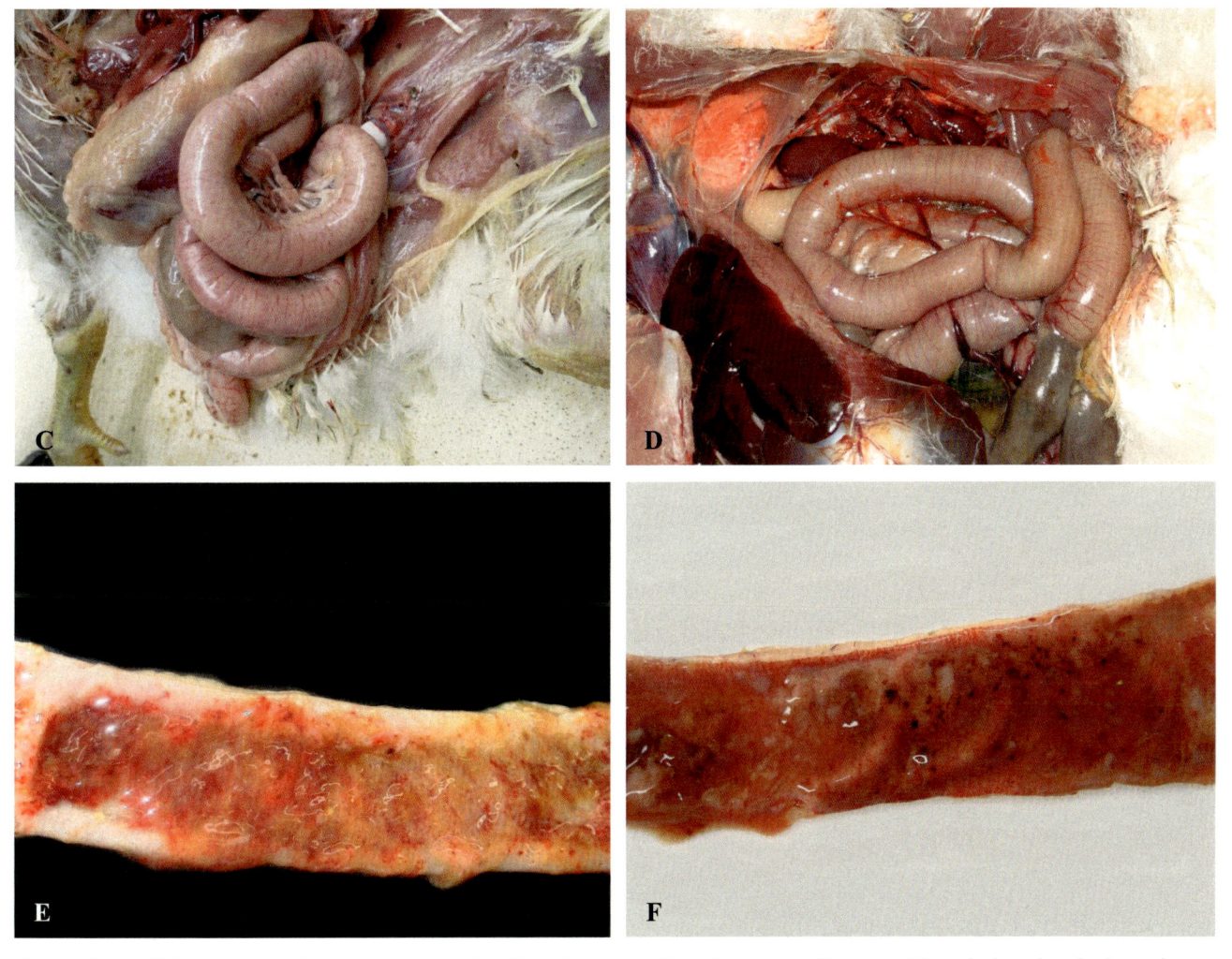

Coccidiosis (*Eimeria maxima*). C. 35-day broiler chicken. Dilated jejunum/ileum with red pinpoint foci on the serosal surface. **D.** 22-week broiler breeder male. Dilation of the jejunum/ileum. **E.** 28-day broiler chicken. Mucosa is covered with orange mucus and has red foci and patches (congestion, hemorrhages). **F.** 39-day broiler chicken. Thick layer of red-orange mucoid material covers the mucosa, which has hemorrhagic foci.

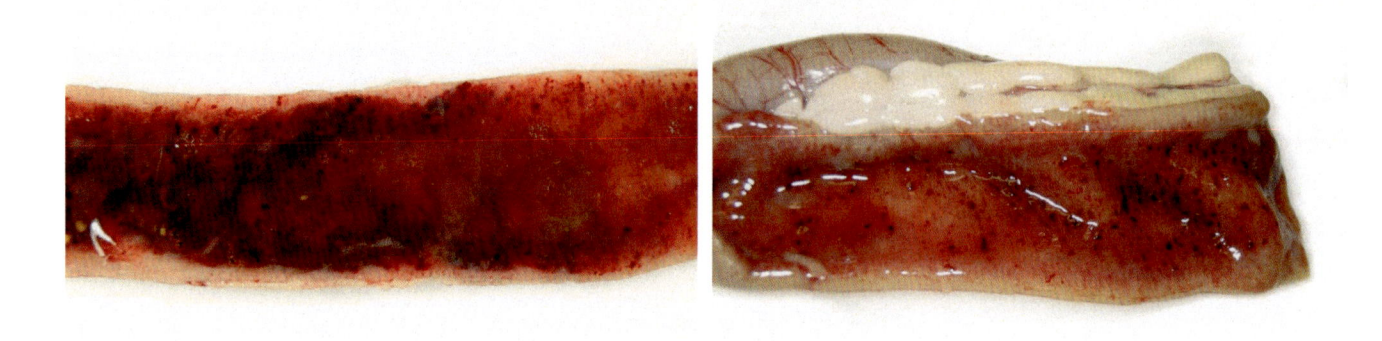

Coccidiosis (*Eimeria maxima*). G, H. 35-day broiler. Mucosa of the jejunum/ileum (G) and duodenum (H) has petechial hemorrhages and is covered with a thick layer of blood-stained mucus.

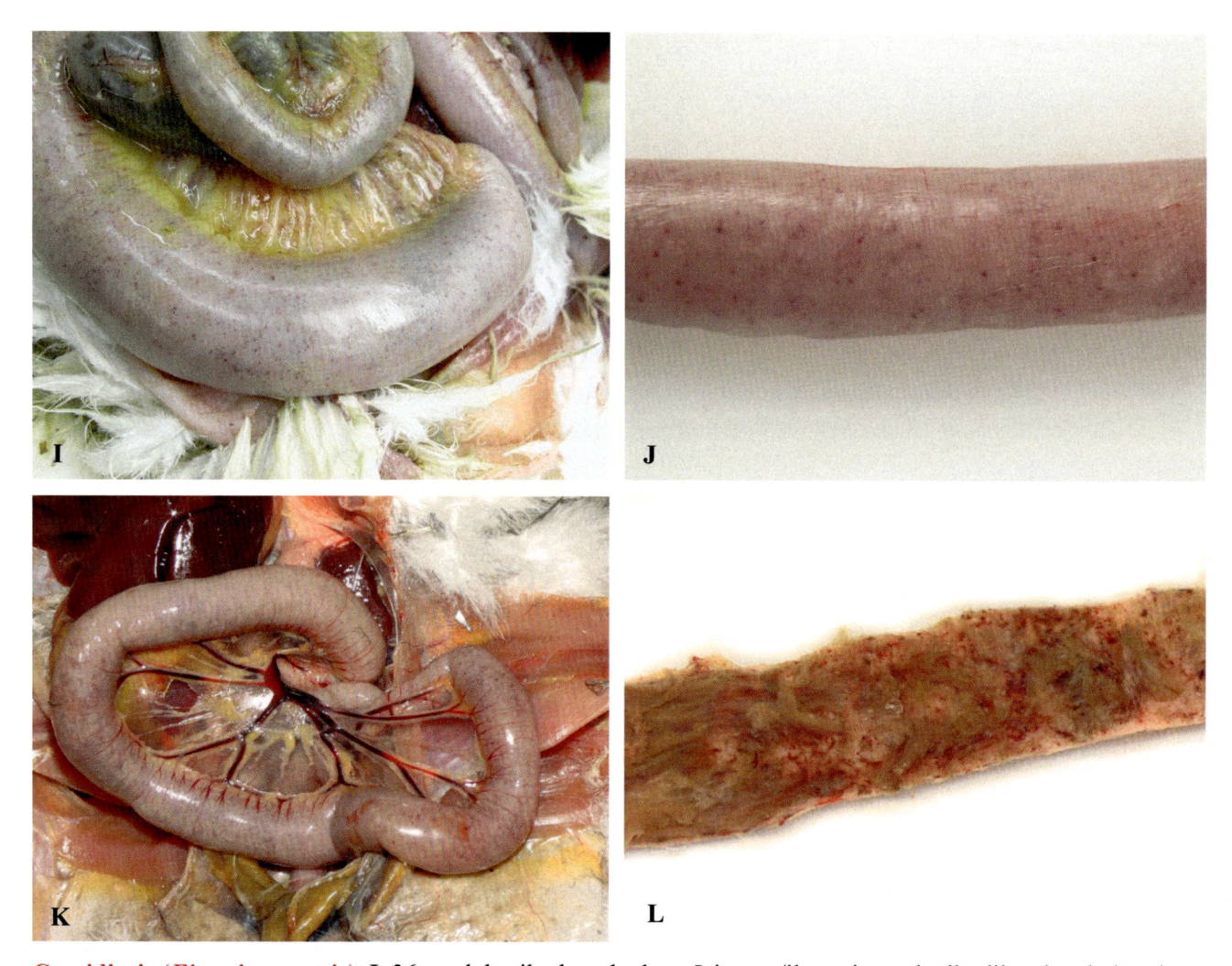

Coccidiosis (*Eimeria necatrix*). I. 36-week broiler breeder hen. Jejunum/ileum is markedly dilated and pinpoint foci are seen on the serosal surface. **J.** 4-week hobby chicken. Jejunum/ileum is markedly dilated and has red and white foci ("salt and pepper appearance") visible through the serosa. **K, L.** 12-week hobby chicken. **K.** The jejunum/ileum is distended with blood, with mottling of the serosal surface. **L.** The mucosal surface has hemorrhages and is covered with a thick layer of mucoid material.

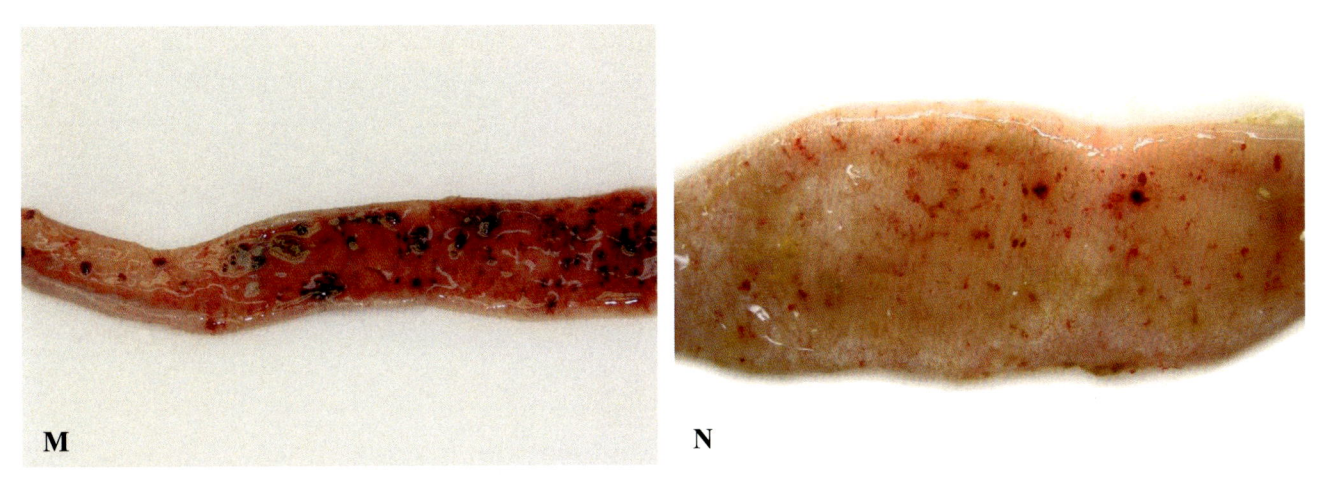

Gross Pathology of Avian Diseases: Text and Atlas   157

Coccidiosis (*Eimeria necatrix*). M. 7-week hobby chicken. Bloody mucoid debris is on mucosal surface of the jejunum/ileum. **N.** 7-week broiler breeder pullet. Mucosa of the jejunum/ileum is thickened and contains petechial hemorrhages

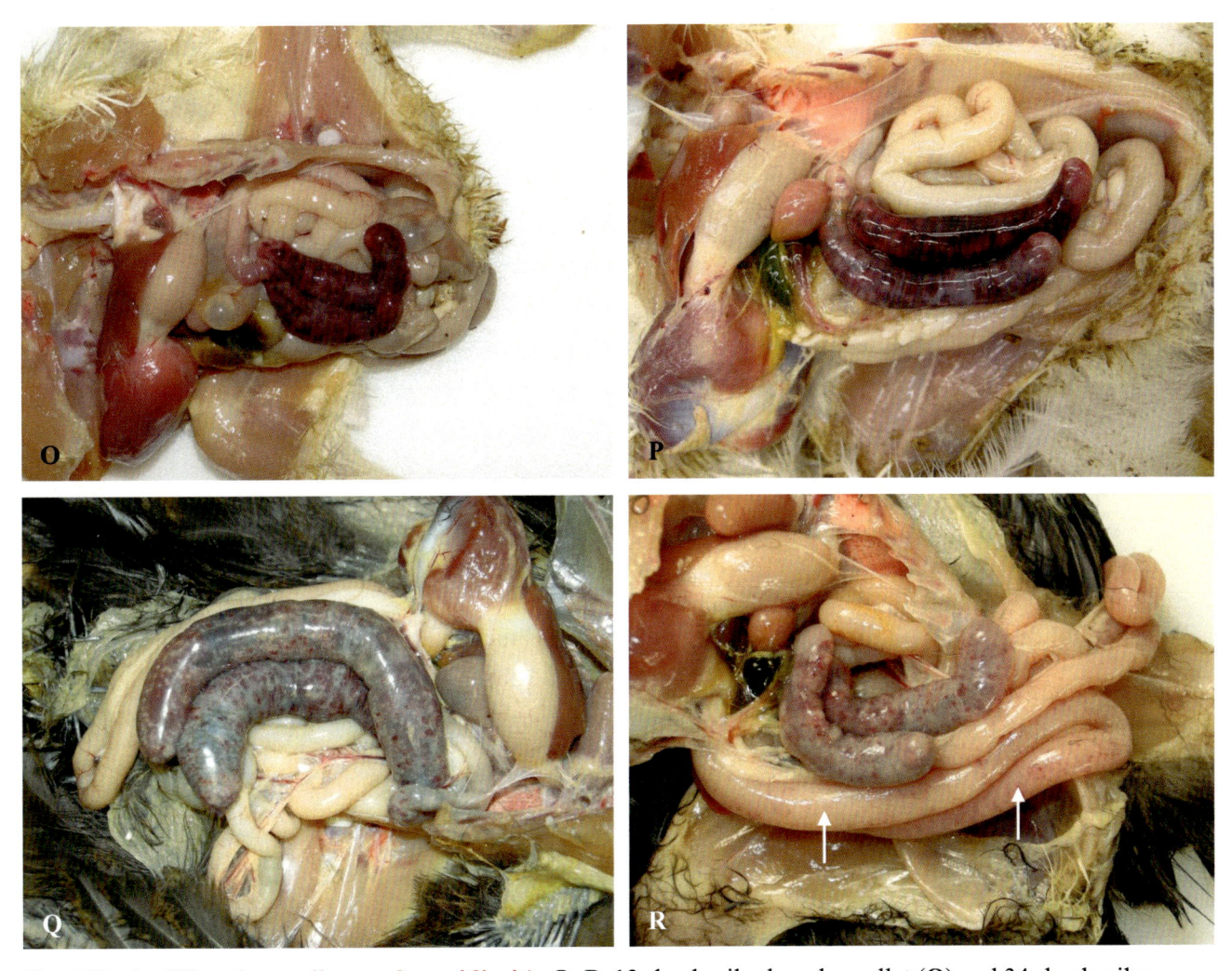

Coccidiosis. (*Eimeria tenella*, cecal coccidiosis). O, P. 13-day broiler breeder pullet (**O**) and 34-day broiler chicken (**P**). Ceca are hemorrhagic and distended with blood and tissue debris. In **P**, note the pallor of the spleen. **Q, R.** Hobby chickens (**Q**. One-month. **R**. 3-week). Ceca are distended with blood and tissue debris. Red and white spots are seen from the serosa. Bird in **R** also had *E. maxima* (note the red spots in duodenum - arrows).

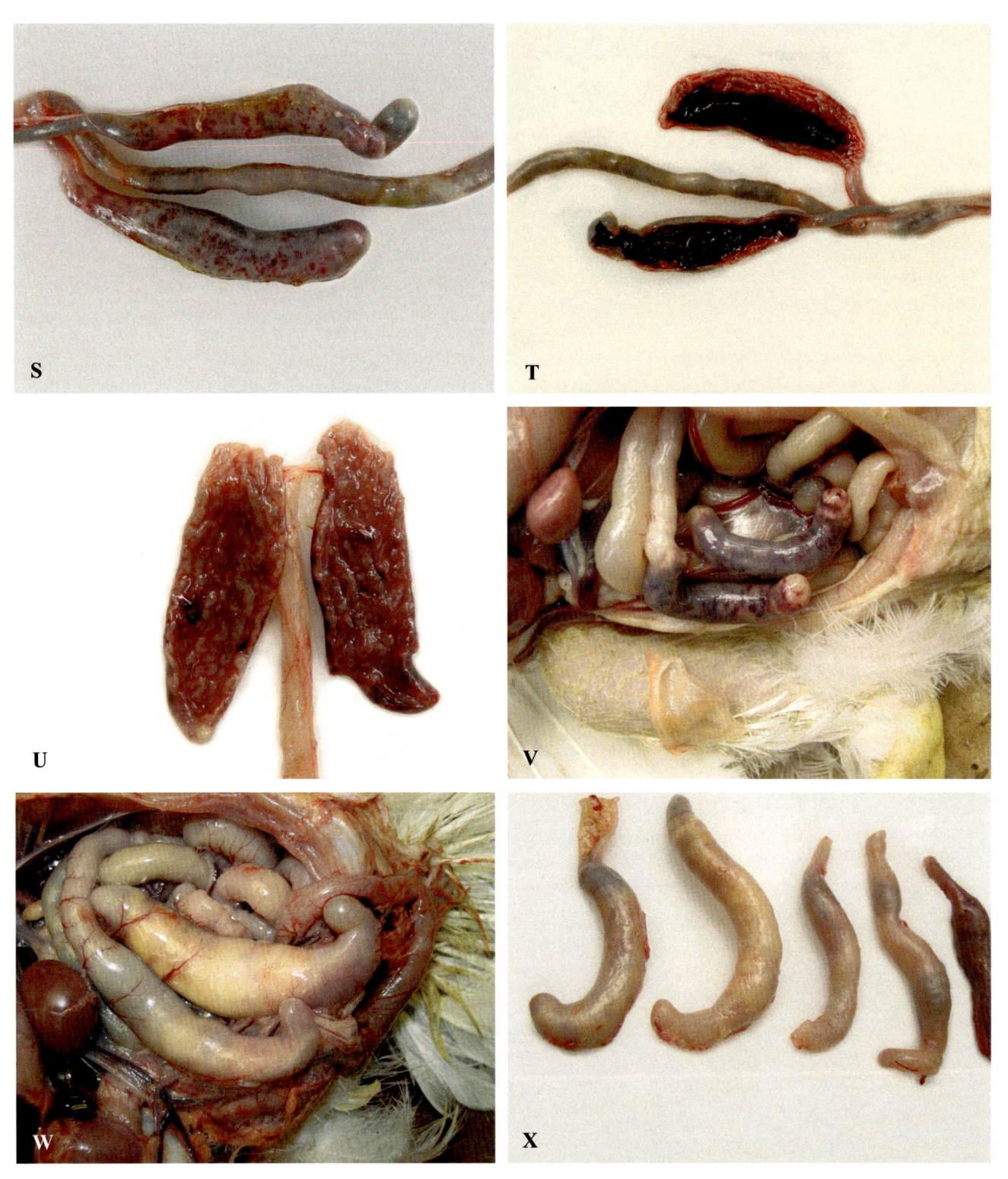

Coccidiosis. (*Eimeria tenella*, cecal coccidiosis). S, T. 6-week broiler breeder pullet. **S.** Ceca are distended with bloody fluid. Hemorrhages are seen from the serosal surface. **T.** Clotted blood fills both ceca. Mucosa is thickened and corrugated. **U, V.** 34-day broiler chickens. **U.** Mucosa is thickened and corrugated. Both ceca are filled with blood. **V.** Ceca are distended with white caseous debris mixed with blood. Hemorrhages are seen from the serosal surface. **W, X.** 6-week broiler breeder males. Caseous debris fills and distends the ceca. Caseous material in the ceca is referred to as a "cecal core".

Renal Coccidiosis in Geese

Cause. *Eimeria truncata* affects geese and is best known. Several different *Eimeria* species infect the kidneys of other waterfowl and aquatic birds. Terrestrial birds including owls and woodcocks are also susceptible to renal coccidiosis. Young and stressed birds are more likely to develop clinical disease. High mortality can occur in commercial geese.

Gross lesion. Lesions are usually not seen when infection is mild. In severe infections, kidneys are markedly enlarged, tan to brown or beige, and mottled with white foci and streaks. Smears of kidneys reveal *Eimeria* oocysts and stages of the protozoan.

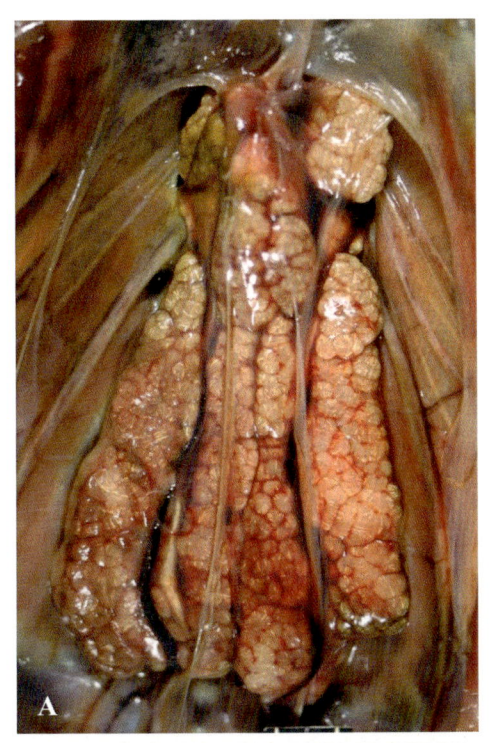

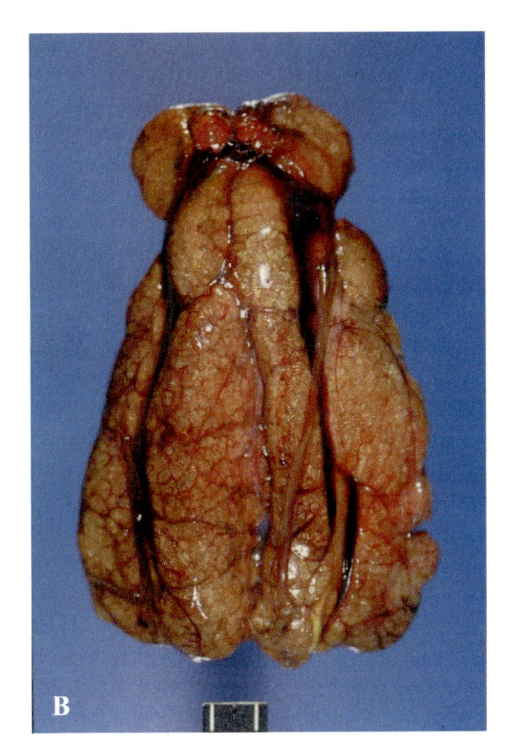

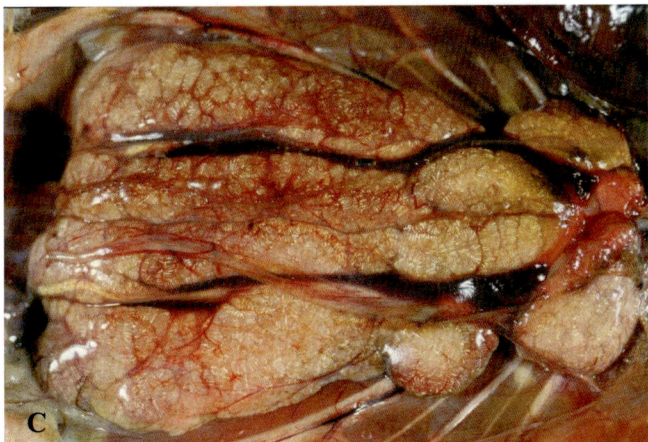

Renal coccidiosis caused by *Eimeria truncata*. Geese. **A-C.** Kidneys are markedly swollen and discolored due to severe tubular necrosis and urate deposition. *(Photos courtesy of Dr. Richard Chin, USA).*

Histomoniasis (Blackhead)

Cause. The parasitic ameboflagellate protozoan *Histomonas meleagridis*. Concurrent *E. coli* infection contributes to mortality.

Clinical signs and gross lesions. Turkeys, chickens (primarily broiler breeders), quail, peafowl, Guinea fowl, and other gallinaceous birds are susceptible. Clinical signs consist of inactivity, somnolence, anorexia, retraction of the head, weight loss, and passing bright yellow ("sulfur-colored") droppings. Some birds are cyanotic, which is the reason for the common name 'blackhead'. Icterus is seen in birds with marked liver damage. Mortality is variable but can be high. Birds that recover are underweight and in poor condition; recovered flocks lack uniformity. Gross lesions of histomoniasis occur primarily in the ceca. Liver lesions are also found in most infected turkeys and broiler breeders, but may not be found in other types of birds. Guinea fowl in particular develop severe cecal lesions, but not liver lesions, and do not die from the disease. Affected broiler breeders may have ascites and an enlarged liver that can be seen through the wall of the distended abdomen.

Liver. Variably sized, circular to oval, focal areas of necrosis are the primary lesions in the liver. Both lobes are usually involved, but the number of necrotic areas can vary from few to numerous and, in severe cases, may be nearly confluent. Necrotic lesions are highly variable in appearance, depending on the stage and severity of infection, freshness of the carcass, and presence or absence of concurrent bacterial infection. Lesions are often described as circular, usually dark-red, slightly depressed areas surrounded by a narrow, pale yellow rim ("target-like" lesions). However, lesions that appear differently are common in affected birds in the same flock. Variably sized white areas and/or nodules resembling tumors are unusual lesions that may occur in the livers of chronically infected turkeys.

Ceca. Lesions vary with the stage of infection. Initially, the cecal wall is thickened and hyperemic. As lesions progress, the mucosa becomes multifocally to diffusely ulcerated and the lumen contains necrotic debris that may or may not be hemorrhagic. Later, the lumen becomes distended with yellow or white caseous material ("cecal cores") and, as the luminal mass expands, the cecal wall becomes thin. Areas of necrosis and mucosal ulceration may be visible through the serosal surface of the thin cecal wall. Perforation of deep ulcers, or leakage of cecal contents through severely damaged cecal walls, results in generalized peritonitis and possible bacterial septicemia.

Other organs. Lesions in lungs, kidneys, spleen, and mesentery are sometimes recognized as pale or discolored, flat or slightly raised areas. However, lesions in sites other than the liver and ceca are not consistent features of histomoniasis in either chickens or turkeys. When the liver is severely damaged, the kidneys can take on a green color because of bile accumulation in tubular epithelium.

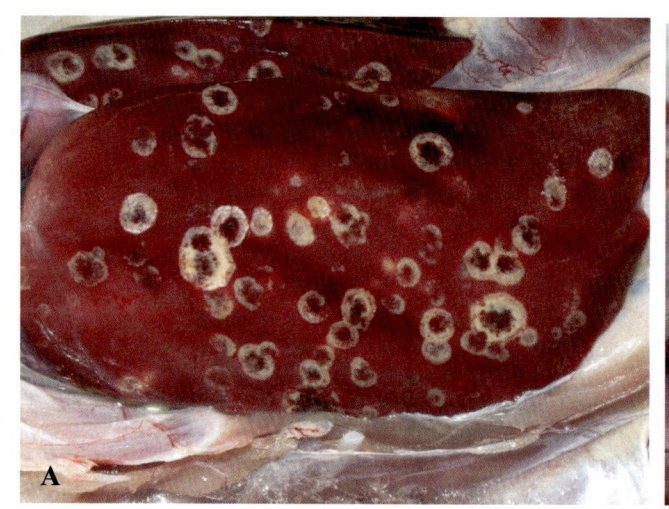

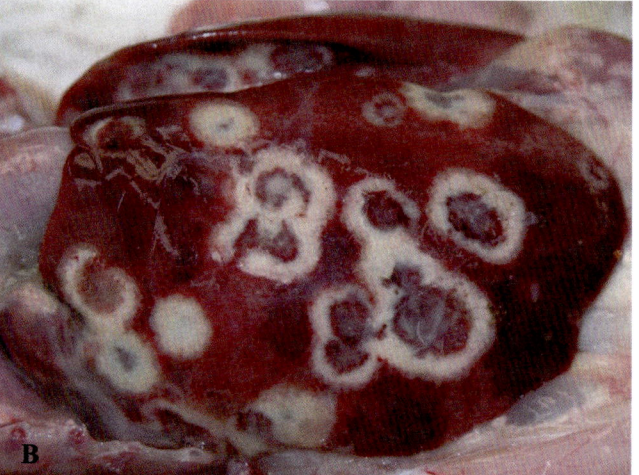

Histomoniasis. Liver lesions. Broiler breeders (A. 38-week. B. 24-day). **A, B.** Target-like lesions in livers are characteristic of histomoniasis. Lesions are depressed in the center and have a pale white to yellow margin.

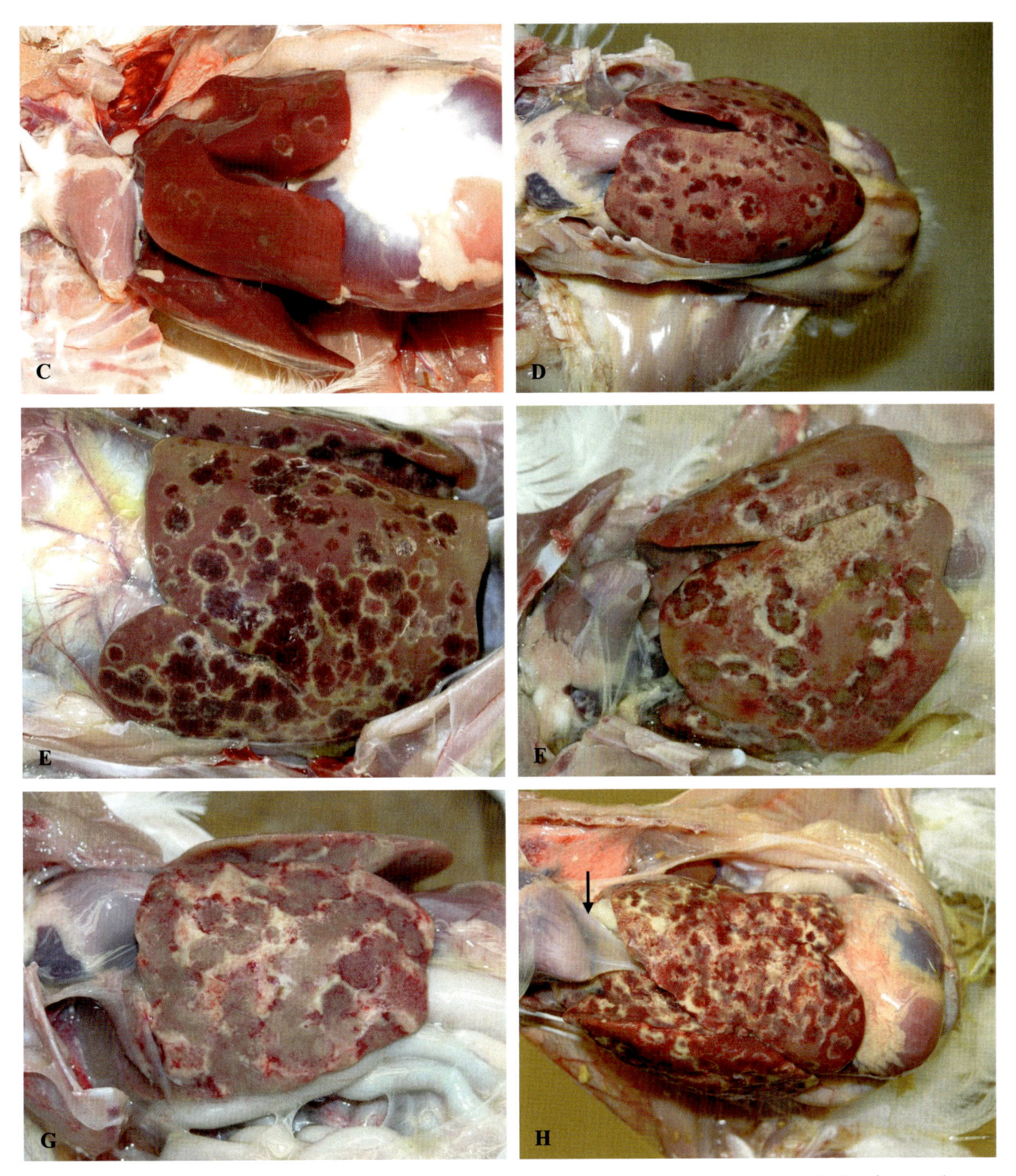

Gross Pathology of Avian Diseases: Text and Atlas 161

Histomoniasis. Liver lesions. Broiler breeder pullets (C. 4-week. D. 22-day. E. 38-week. F, G. 25-day. H. 6-week). **C, D.** Target-like lesions in livers are characteristic of histomoniasis. Lesions are depressed in the center and have a pale white to yellow margin. **E-H.** Necrotic lesions of various morphological appearance are seen. Lesions have a depressed, dark center surrounded by a white or yellow margin. Note the increased pericardial fluid (pericardial effusion) in **H** (arrow).

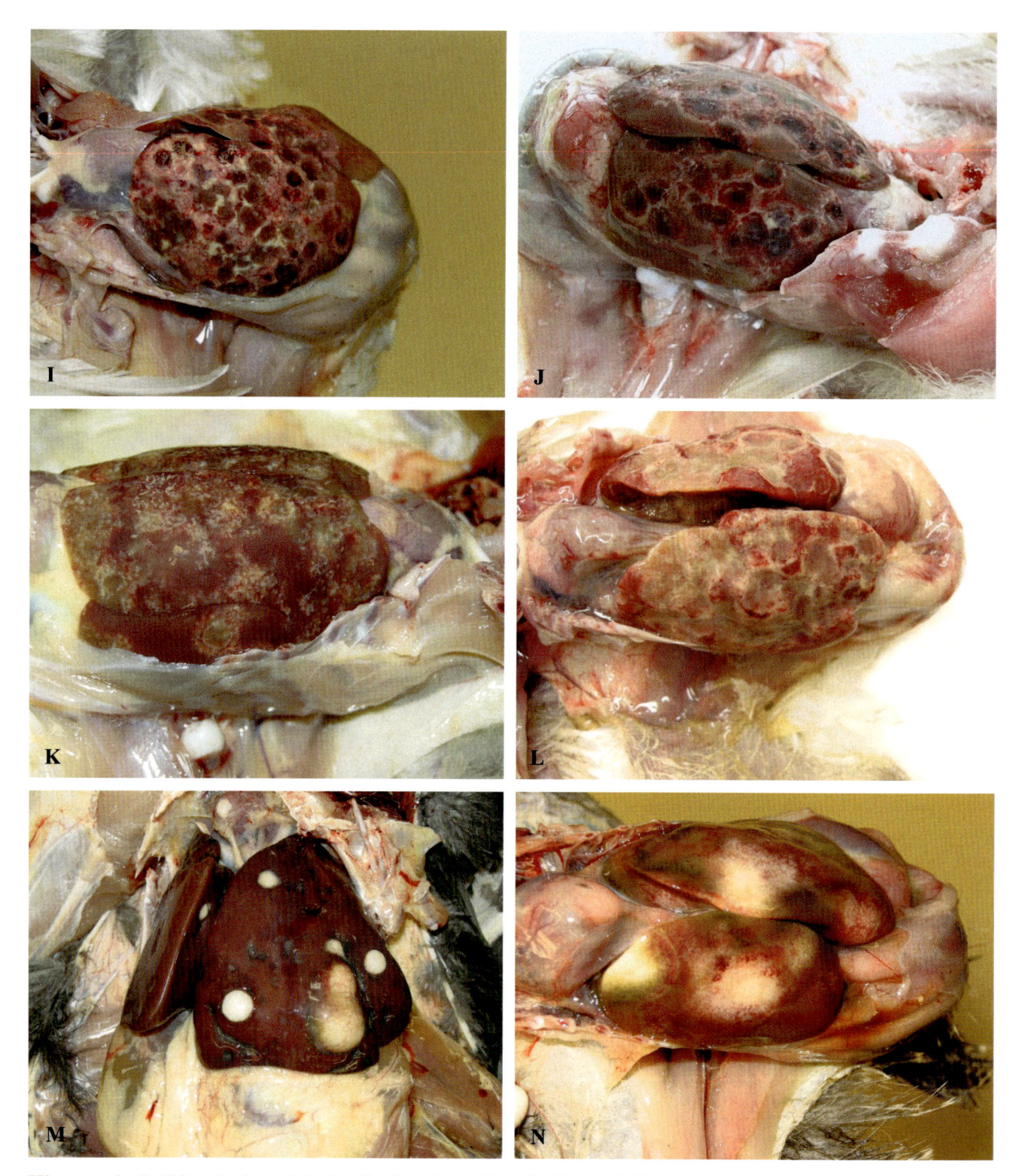

Histomoniasis. Liver lesions. I-L. Broiler breeder pullets (I. 22-day. J, K, L. 25-day). Note the appearance of the liver lesions. Lesions in **I** and **J** have depressed, dark centers surrounded by a white or yellow margin. Histomoniasis lesions in livers of birds with concurrent secondary bacterial infection (septicemia) tend to be more severe but less distinct. Culturing severely damaged livers for bacteria is warranted. **M, N.** Bronze turkeys (M. 20-week. N. 6-week). Chronic lesions of histomoniasis resembling neoplasia. Liver in **M** is from the same turkey as cecal lesions in **W** and **X**.

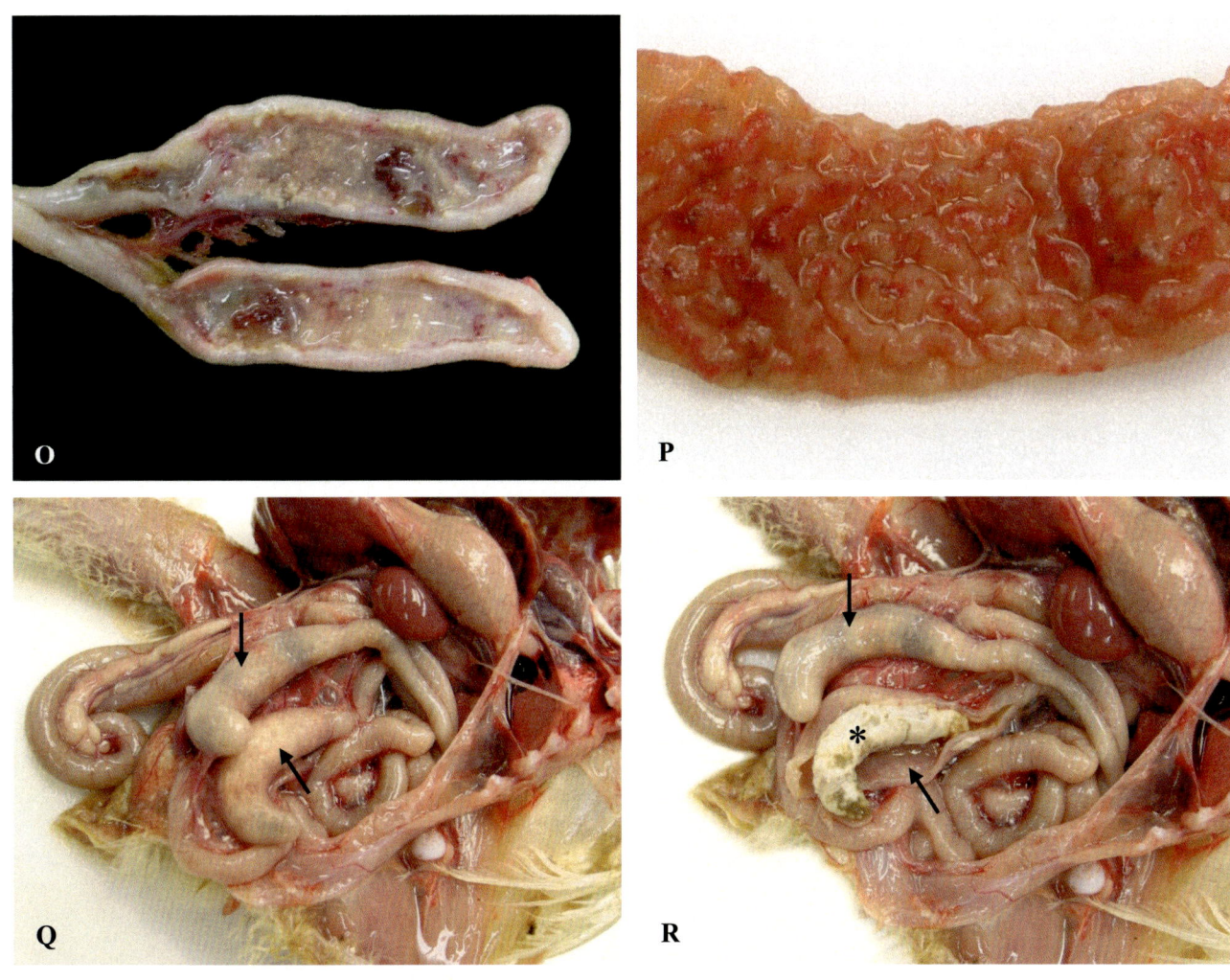

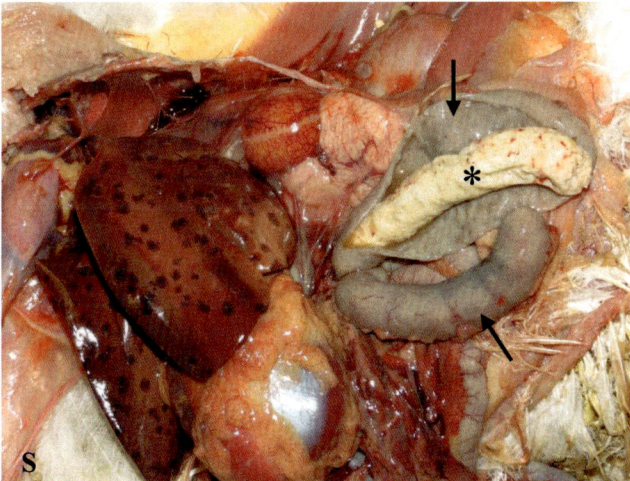

Histomoniasis. Cecal lesions. Broiler breeders (O. 4-week. P. 30-week. Q, R. 3-week, S. 24-week). **O.** Ceca have thickened walls and necrotic mucosa. **P.** Cecal mucosa is thickened and corrugated. This is a chronic lesion of histomoniasis (confirmed histologically) caused by persistent inflammatory infiltrates in the cecal wall. **Q, R, S.** Ceca (arrows) are distended with dense, white caseous material ("cecal core" - asterisk). Cecal coccidiosis needs to be ruled out by microscopic examination of wet smears of the caseous material. Note the liver lesions in **S**.

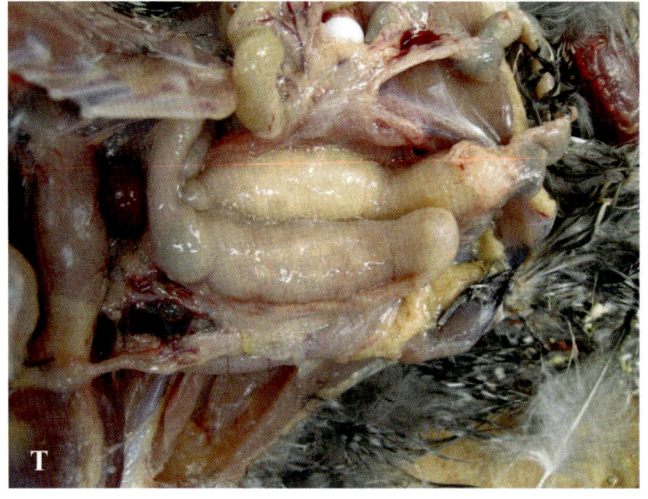

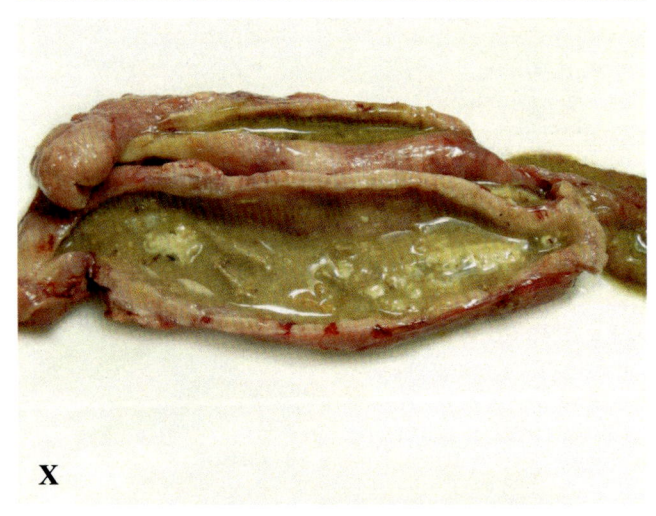

Histomoniasis. Cecal lesions. T, U, V. 6-week Guinea fowl. Both ceca are distended with light-yellow caseous material that has resulted from caseation of necrotic debris sequestered in the cecal lumen. **W, X.** 20-week hobby bronze turkey. Ceca are markedly distended. Walls of ceca are thickened and cecal lumens are filled with green fluid mixed with necrotic debris. Ceca are of the same turkey with neoplasm-like lesions in the liver in **M**.

Trichomoniasis

Cause. *Trichomonas gallinae*, a flagellated protozoan. The organism varies in shape from ovoid to pyriform and measures 12.5-20 µm in length. It has a fin-like undulating membrane that extends along two-thirds of the body. There are four whip-like, 11-13 µm anterior flagella, each arising from a separate basal body at the anterior pole. A fifth recurrent flagellum, which also arises from a basal body at the anterior pole, passes posteriorly and is closely attached to the undulating membrane. It does not have a free-trailing portion and only extends along two-thirds to three-fourths of the cell surface. The nucleus is ovoid, 2.5-3 µm in length, and located posterior to the basal bodies of the flagella. The organism is surrounded by a single membrane that forms pinocytotic vesicles or small food vacuoles, which take up nutrients. Pseudocyst stages have been described *in vitro*. During formation of the pseudocyst, the organism becomes spherical, invaginates, and internalizes its flagella. Pseudocyst formation is reversible. It is believed pseudocysts form under stressful environmental conditions, but their role in the epidemiology of the disease or pathogenicity of the organism is uncertain. There are wide variations in virulence among strains of *T. gallinae*. Some strains are nonpathogenic, while other strains are highly virulent and cause severe disease.

Hosts. Trichomoniasis primarily affects Columbiformes (pigeons, doves), but also occurs in raptors (hawks, falcons) and owls. Trichomoniasis is an important disease in mourning doves (*Zenaida macroura*) in North America. The disease is commonly known as canker in Columbiformes and frounce in raptors. Adult pigeons and doves frequently carry the trichomonads without developing lesions, but they transmit the organisms to their squabs when feeding them. Among captive birds, infection occurs in canaries, Gouldian finches, zebra finches, cockatiels, and Amazon parrots. Trichomoniasis is recognized as an important cause of mortality in wild finches in some parts of the world, e.g., United Kingdom. Infection with *Trichomonas* has been associated with morbidity and mortality in house finches, mockingbirds, and corvids in North America. Chickens, turkeys, waterfowl, and possibly other poultry are susceptible to natural infection but rarely develop clinical disease.

Gross lesions. Lesions are usually found in the oral cavity and pharynx, but esophagus and crop may also be involved. The appearance and severity of the lesion depend on the virulence of the strain and stage of infection. Early and mild lesions consist of white to yellow spots in the oropharyngeal mucosa. Lesions enlarge and appear as white or yellow caseous plaques or caseo-necrotic nodules. Individual lesions coalesce to form large firm caseo-necrotic masses that may block the oropharynx and prevent the bird from swallowing. Severe lesions are easily palpated. Lesions in the esophageal mucosa and inner surface of the crop consist of multifocal caseo-necrotic plaques and nodules or may appear as raised, roughly rounded, yellow, button-like areas with a central cone-shaped caseous spur. In some cases, the crop lining is covered with a yellow membrane that may continue into the proventriculus. Lesions in the oropharynx may extend externally to the beak and eye and may even invade deep tissues, extending into the sinus and through tissues in the neck. From the sinus, the lesion may even penetrate through the base of the skull into the brain and cause encephalitis.

In free-living finches, lesions are primarily found in the crop and esophageal mucosa. Necrotic lesions are only occasionally found in the oropharynx. Lesions vary in appearance and severity consisting of tiny yellow nodules, diffuse, slight to marked mucosal thickening with yellow-orange discoloration of the surface, or masses of white, yellow, or orange caseo-necrotic debris overlying areas of ulceration and necrosis.

Gross lesions in budgerigars include thick clumps of yellow necrotic material in the oral cavity, pharynx, and esophagus. A white necrotic lesion may be found in the oral cavity and extend into the infraorbital sinuses. Sinusitis, characterized by distension of one or both sinuses with caseous exudate, is seen in zebra and Gouldian finches.

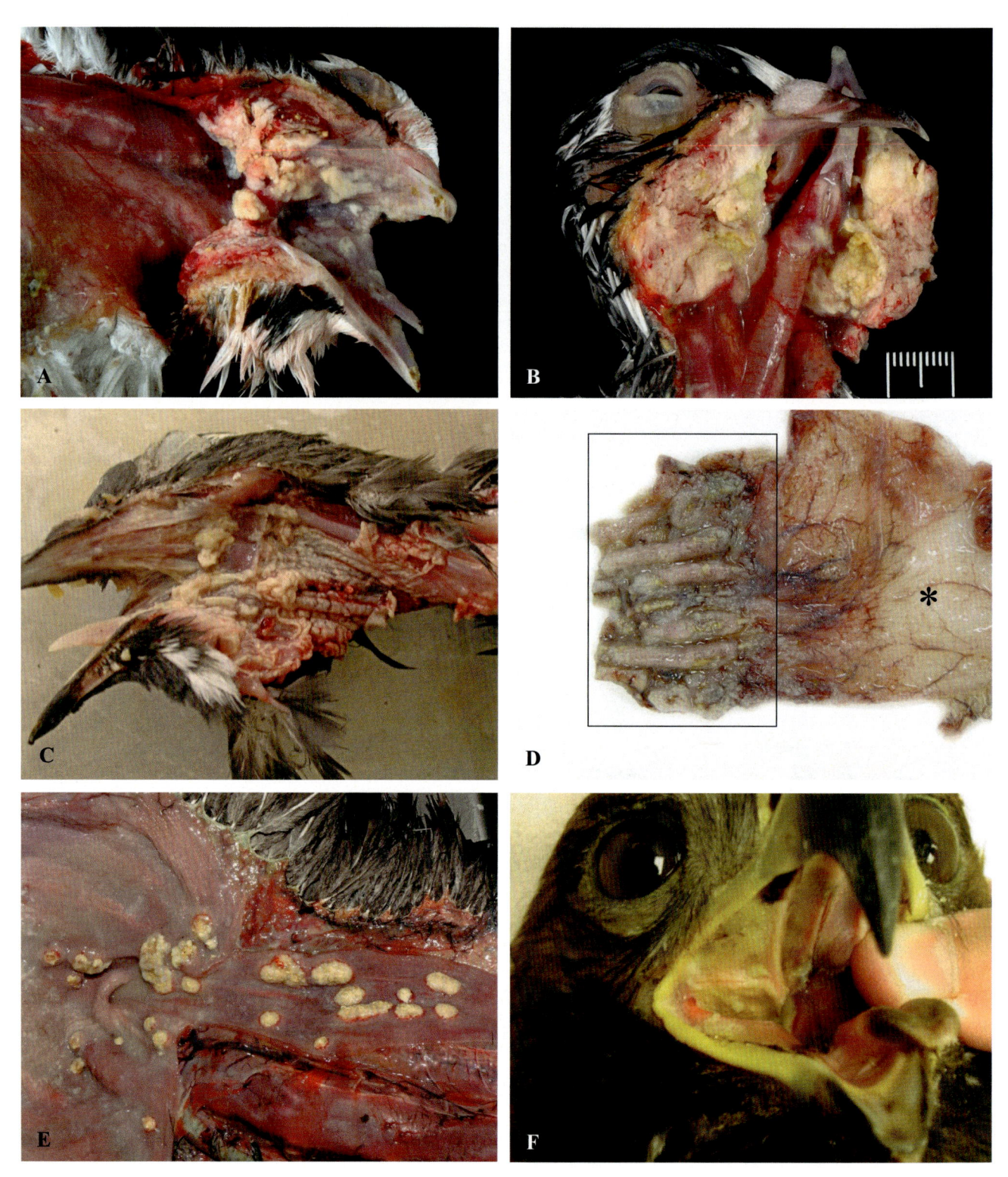

Trichomoniasis. A, B, C. Pigeons. Mass of caseous material occupying the oropharynx and destroying its wall. In **C**, the lesion extends down into the esophagus from the oropharynx. **D.** Pigeon. Esophageal mucosa (boxed area) is thickened, ulcerated, and has adhering necrotic debris. Asterisk. Crop. **E.** 6-month bronze turkey. Mucosa of the esophagus and anterior part of the crop has multiple yellowish nodular lesions consisting of caseous debris filling mucosal ulcers. **F.** Golden eagle. Caseo-necrotic lesion in the oral cavity. *(Photo F courtesy of Dr. Arnaud Van Wettere).*

Spironucleosis (Hexamitiasis)

Cause. *Spironucleus* spp. (formerly *Hexamita* spp.). *Spironucleus* is a parasitic flagellated intestinal protozoan. The organism is broadly pyriform or ovoid and bilaterally symmetrical. It has two S-shaped nuclei and six anterior and two posterior flagella. Each nucleus is located on one side of the broad anterior end of the body. All 8 flagella originate from the broadly rounded end. Six flagella (3 on each side) emerge anteriorly, and two flagella pass posteriorly through the body in two canals (cytopharyngeal or flagellar pockets) and emerge as posterior (recurrent) flagella.

The life cycle of *Spironucleus* includes alternate motile trophozoites and non-motile cystic stages. Trophozoites multiply by binary fission and become more spherical before they divide. *Spironucleus* cysts are ovoid to round, and each usually has two recently divided, unemerged flagella, and 2-4 nuclei. Cysts are shed in the feces; infection of new hosts occurs by ingestion of cysts.

Hosts. Spironucleosis caused by *Spironucleus meleagridis* occurs in turkeys, quail, pheasants, partridge, and peafowl. Spironucleosis caused by *Spironucleus columbae* is an important disease of pigeons. Clinical disease caused by *Spironucleus* spp. occurs in parrots, especially cockatiels; other captive birds, and free-living birds. Infection is often fatal in young birds, whereas older birds are subclinical carriers. The disease is most common when older and younger birds are kept together.

Clinical signs and gross lesions. Affected birds are lethargic and profoundly depressed, have ruffled feathers, and usually stand with their eyes closed. They become emaciated, dehydrated, and have loose watery droppings. There may be soiling and matting of feathers around the vent with fecal material. Breast muscles are severely atrophied and dry. Skin over the breast adheres tenaciously to underlying muscle. The small intestine, especially jejunum, is thin-walled and distended with foamy, watery, or slightly mucoid contents.

Wet smears and cytology. In euthanized and recently dead birds, microscopic examination of a drop of intestinal fluid or wet-mount of mucosal scrapings taken from duodenum and jejunum reveals flagellated organisms with characteristic rapid darting movement. The organism can also be identified in smears stained with Romanowsky-type stains. In stained smears, trophozoites of *Spironucleus* appear as slender-, sausage-, or pyriform-shaped organisms with average size of 7 x 3.5 µm. Flagella may or not be discernible, depending on the quality of staining. Paired nuclei are usually not distinguishable, but rather appear as a darkly stained triangular-shaped region in one end of the organism.

Cysts (encysted trophozoites) are predominantly found in smears of mucus from the intestine of infected birds. They are ovoid to round with an average size of 5.5 x 4.5 µm. Most cysts have two adjacent nuclei, but three or four nuclei may be identified in some cysts. The two cytopharyngeal canals can occasionally be seen, and the enclosed flagella within them may be visible as faintly stained transverse bands.

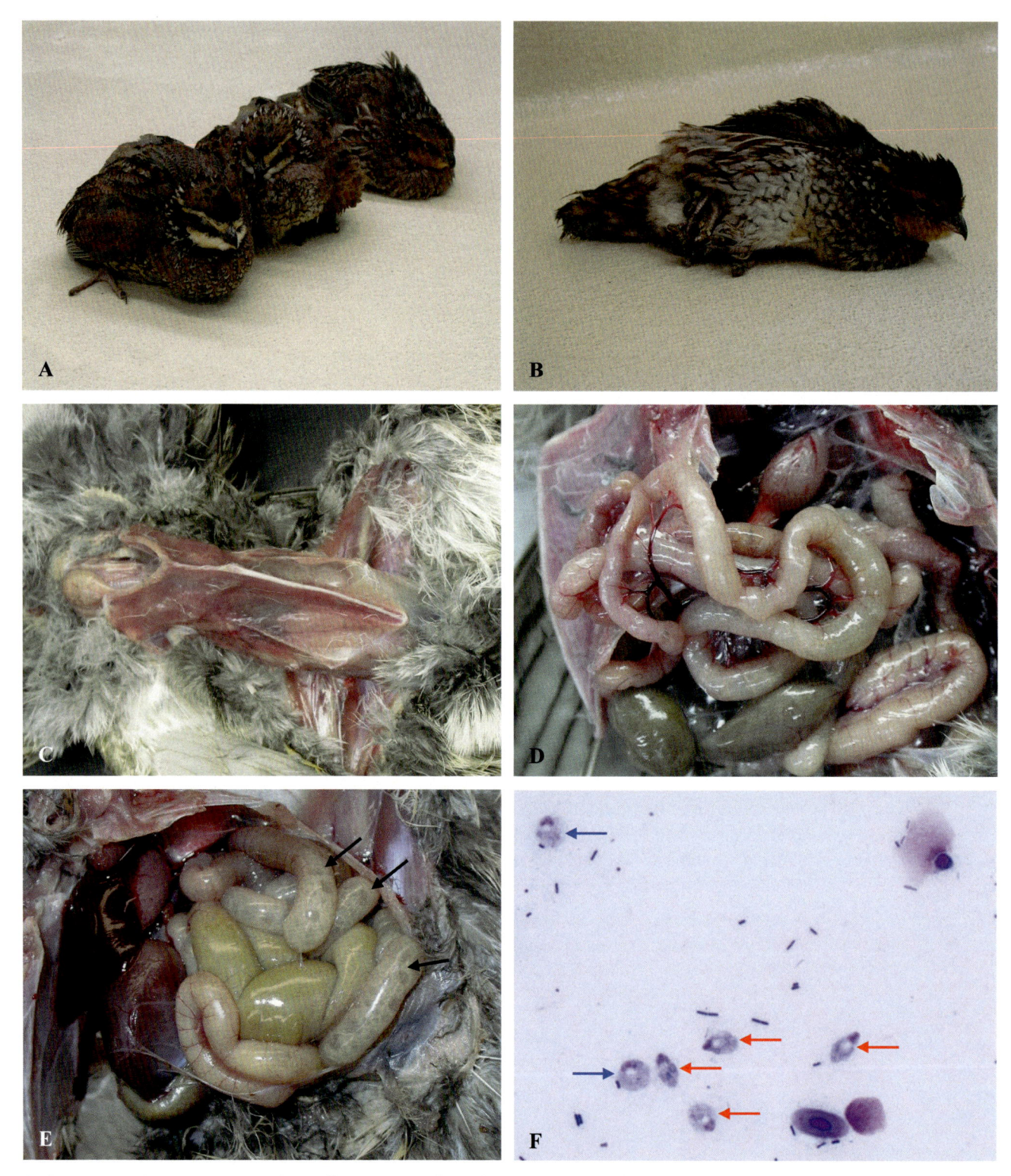

Spironucleosis. A, E. 17-week quail. **A, B.** Quail are lethargic, weak, listless, and have ruffled feather. **C.** Severe atrophy of pectoral muscles. **D, E.** Small intestine is thin-walled, distended, and filled with watery fluid. In **E**, note the frothy appearance of the fluid (arrows). **F.** Chukar partridge. Stained smear of intestinal fluid showing trophozoites of *Spironucleus*. Trophozoites (red arrows) are pyriform in shape. Paired nuclei are not distinguishable but appear as a darkly stained area at one end of the organism. Flagella also are not visible with this stain. Round *Spironucleus* organisms (blue arrows) are trophozoites that become spherical before dividing.

Sarcocystis rileyi Infection in Ducks

Sarcocystis are coccidian protozoan parasites with an obligate two-host life cycle. Sexual reproduction takes place in definitive hosts, while asexual reproduction takes place in intermediate hosts. In North America, the striped skunk (*Mephitis mephitis*) is the definitive host of *S. rileyi*. There is strong evidence that the red fox (*Vulpes vulpes*) and raccoon dog (*Nyctereutes procyonoides*) serve as definitive hosts of *S. rileyi* in Europe. Ducks are the intermediate hosts. Species of ducks most commonly affected are mallard, northern pintail, northern shoveler, teal, American black duck, gadwall, and American wigeon. Geese and swans are infrequently affected. Numerous other *Sarcocystis* species infect a wide variety of other avian species. Sarcocysts of other species are often not visible grossly.

Life cycle. Sexual development (gamogony) occurs in the epithelial cells of the intestine of the definitive host; infective oocysts develop and are shed in the feces. Oocysts have a thin, delicate wall and contain two sporocysts, each containing 4 sporozoites. Intermediate hosts become infected when they ingest oocysts in contaminated food or water. In the digestive tract of the intermediate host, the fragile walls of the oocyst and sporocysts break releasing the sporozoites. Sporozoites migrate through the intestinal epithelium and undergo asexual multiplication (merogony) in endothelial cells of blood capillaries and vessels in the intestinal lamina propria to develop into meronts (schizonts) that contain large numbers of merozoites. Merozoites released when meronts mature and rupture spread hematogenously to different organs and tissues. They develop again into meronts predominantly in endothelial cells of blood capillaries. This cycle repeats itself over several generations of merozoites in blood capillaries and venules. Eventually, merozoites invade skeletal and cardiac myocytes where they form sarcocysts. Mature sarcocysts, the stage of the parasite that is macroscopically visible, are surrounded by a wall and filled with bradyzoites.

Gross lesions. Sarcocysts are commonly found in breast muscles, but also occur in other skeletal and cardiac muscle. Cysts are white to yellow-white in color, resemble grains of rice, and run in parallel streaks through the skeletal muscle.

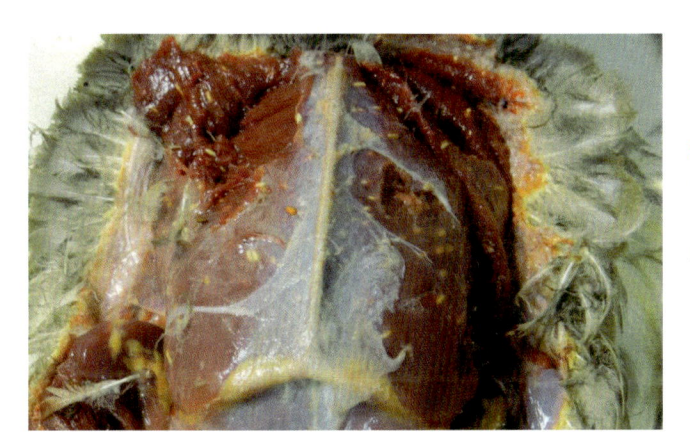

Sarcocysts. Mallard duck. The yellow-white, rice grain-like lesions in the pectoral muscles are sarcocysts of *Sarcocystis rileyi*. (Photo courtesy of Dr. Heather Wyss, USA)

Sarcocystis falcatula Infection

Opossums, especially the Virginia opossum (*Didelphis virginiana*), are the definitive hosts of *S. falcatula*. The intermediate host range is broad and includes Psittaciformes, Passeriformes, and Columbiformes. Galliformes and Anseriformes are resistant. Sarcocystosis is prevalent among old world psittacines. Cockatoos, cockatiels, eclectus parrots, and African gray parrots are especially susceptible and develop acute fatal illness. American and Neotropical (Mexico and South and Central America) parrots are resistant to the disease as adults, but it may be fatal in young birds. The life cycle is similar to that of *S. rileyi*. Merogony occurs most frequently in the lungs.

Gross lesions. Red edematous lungs are the most common lesions in affected birds. Other lesions include enlargement of the spleen, ascites, and hydropericardium.

Crop Capillariasis

Cause. *Capillaria* spp. *Capillaria* infect a number of avian species including poultry and wild birds. Gallinaceous birds, especially quail, are most affected. Some species of the parasite infect the intestinal tract while others infect the upper digestive tract. The latter are most virulent. Depending on species, the life cycle of the parasite may be direct or indirect (earthworms are intermediate hosts).

Clinical signs and gross lesions. Severely affected birds are weak, anorexic, emaciated, and may die. Lesions are mainly found in the crop and lower part of the esophagus. In severe cases, upper esophagus and mouth may be involved. The wall of the crop becomes thickened, and the surface of the crop mucosa is rough, rugose, or macerated, and may be covered with flocculent material or necrotic debris. In heavy infections, small, thread-like worms can be seen embedded in the thickened crop mucosa.

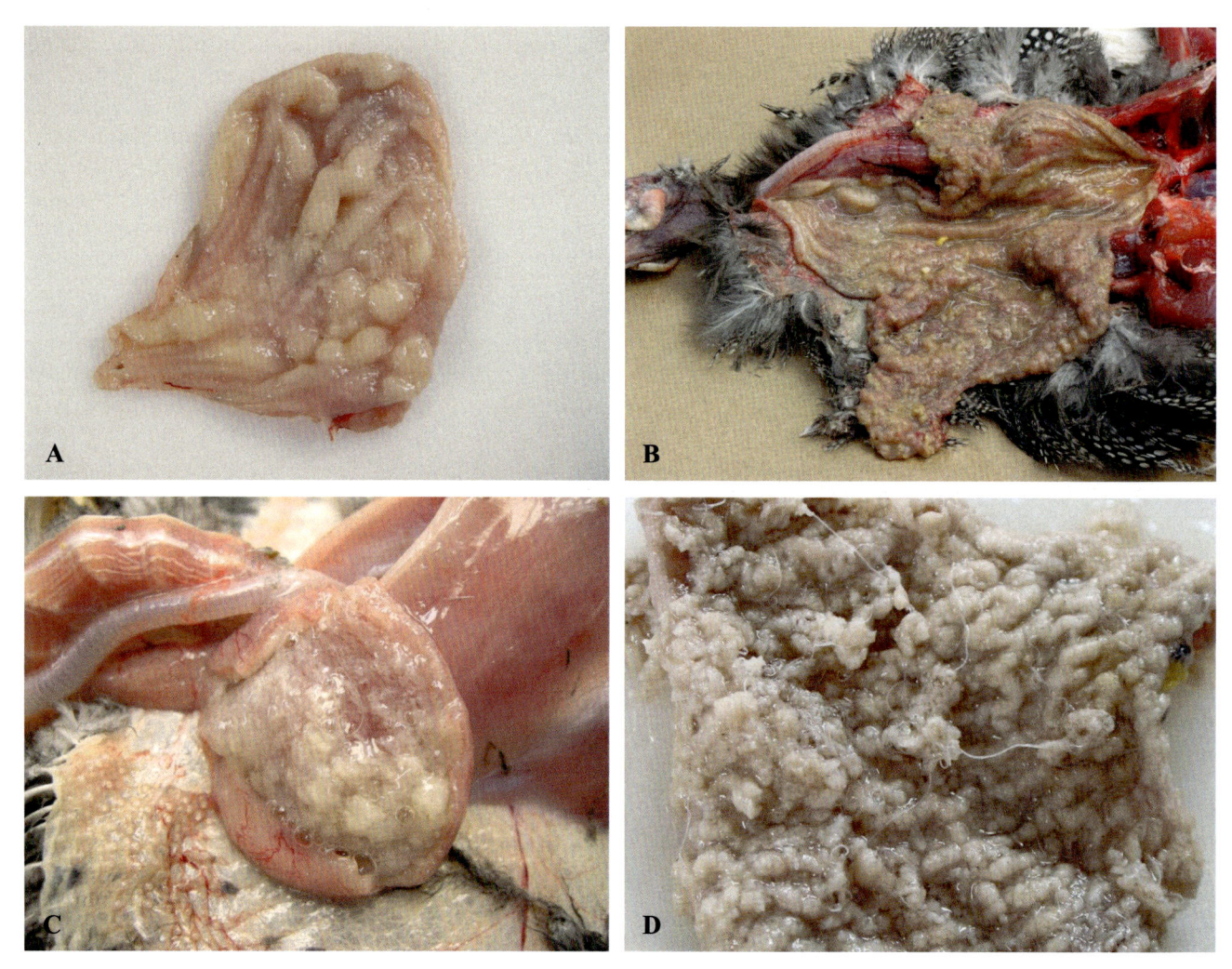

Crop capillariasis. A. One-year peacock. Nodular and linear thickening of the mucosal surface of the crop. **B.** Juvenile Guinea fowl. Thickening and marked irregularity of the mucosal surface of the crop. **C.** 17-week quail. Thick layer of flocculent material covers the mucosal surface of the crop. **D.** 5-year Guinea fowl. Remarkable thickening and rugosity of the mucosal surface of the crop. Thread-like, white *Capillaria* nematodes are seen embedded in the surface.

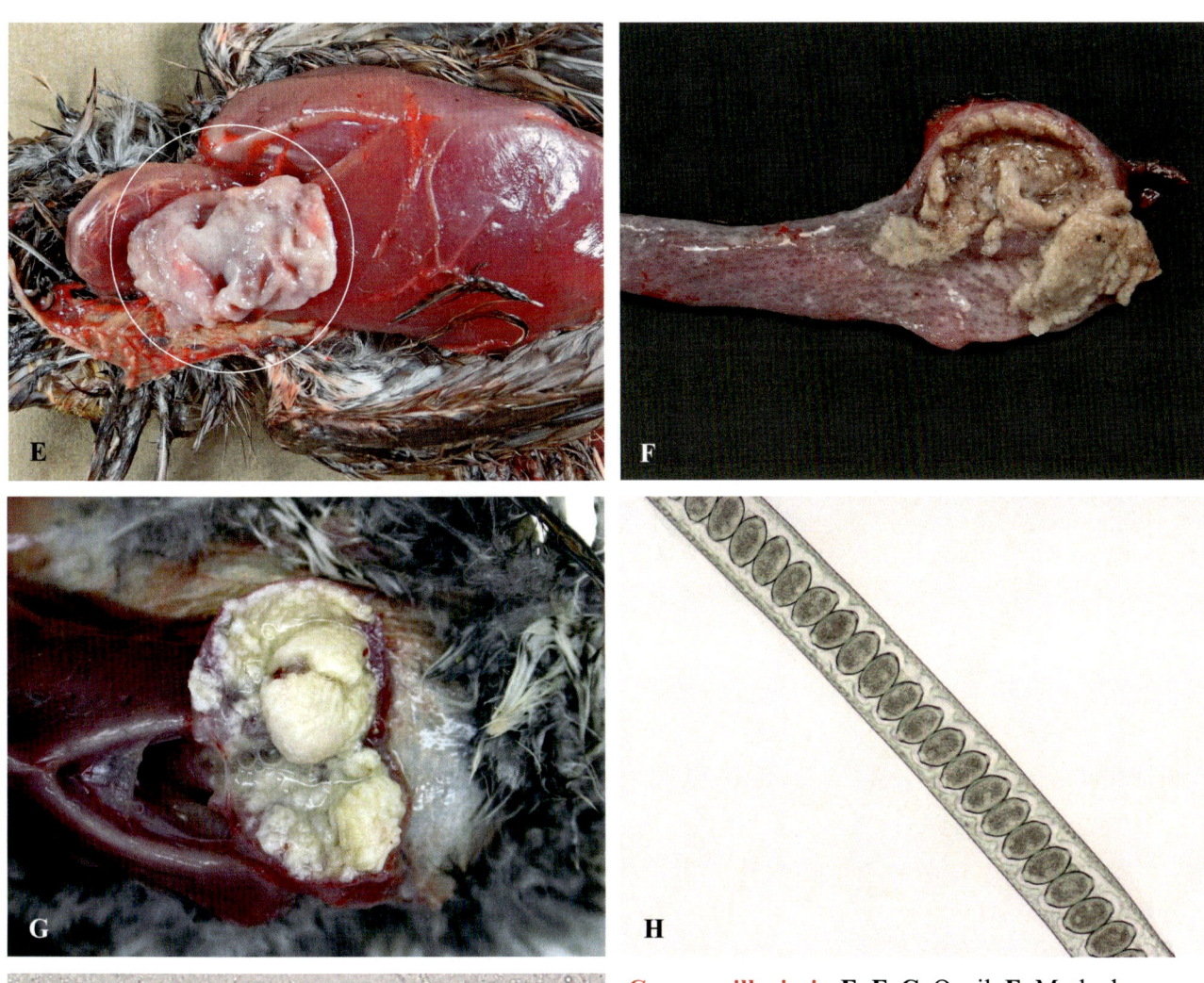

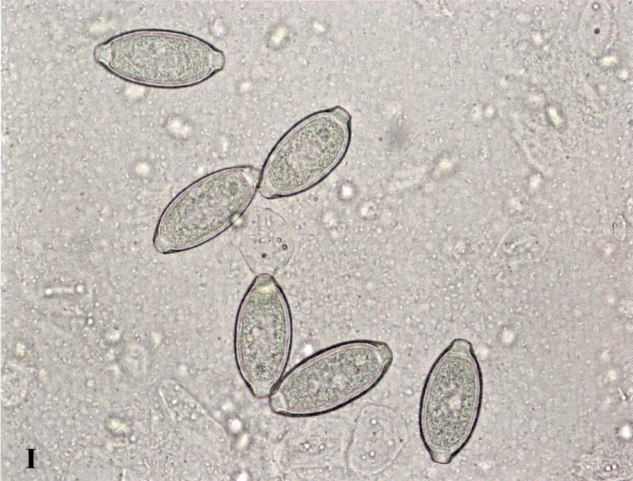

Crop capillariasis. **E, F, G.** Quail. **E.** Marked thickening of the crop mucosa. Circle: crop. **F.** Layer of necrotic debris covers the mucosal surface of the crop. **G.** White caseous material fills the crop. **H.** Female *Capillaria* filled with eggs. **I.** *Capillaria* eggs have characteristic thick walls and bipolar plugs with prominent, relatively acute 'shoulders'.

Cheilospirura hamulosa Infection of Ventriculus

Cheilospirura hamulosa is a spirurid nematode that infects the ventriculus (gizzard) of Galliformes including chickens, turkeys, quail, pheasants, Guinea fowl, peafowl, and grouse. The nematode is small and pink. Males are 16-19 mm long, and females are 19-25 mm long. The parasite has an indirect life cycle that requires an intermediate host (grasshoppers, beetles, weevils, and sandhoppers) for development to the infective stage. Embryonated eggs shed in the droppings of infected birds are ingested by an intermediate host and hatch in the intestine. Larvae migrate into the body cavity, molt twice, penetrate into the muscles, and become infective. When birds ingest an infected intermediate host, larvae reach the ventriculus and penetrate the koilin layer, where they undergo two molts during the following 22-24 days. In about a month, worms begin to penetrate through the mucosa into the ventricular muscle layer. The prepatent period is 76-120 days.

Gross lesions. *Cheilospirura hamulosa* infection usually does not result in clinical disease. Grossly, the ventriculus is enlarged with a thickened wall. A yellow swelling may be visible externally. Ulceration, sloughing, and thickening of the koilin layer, mostly in the caudal region of the gizzard occur. Later, proliferative changes are seen. Detachment of the koilin layer from the mucosal surface reveals small, pink worms associated with the inner surface of the koilin layer and mucosa. Some worms partially penetrate the gizzard muscle. A magnifying lens helps in visualizing parasites. The mucosal surface of the gizzard is thickened, lacks papillae, and has small foci of ulceration with hemorrhage where penetration of parasites has occurred. In the muscular layer, there may be pale foci representing caseous granulomas and an intense inflammatory reaction around parasites.

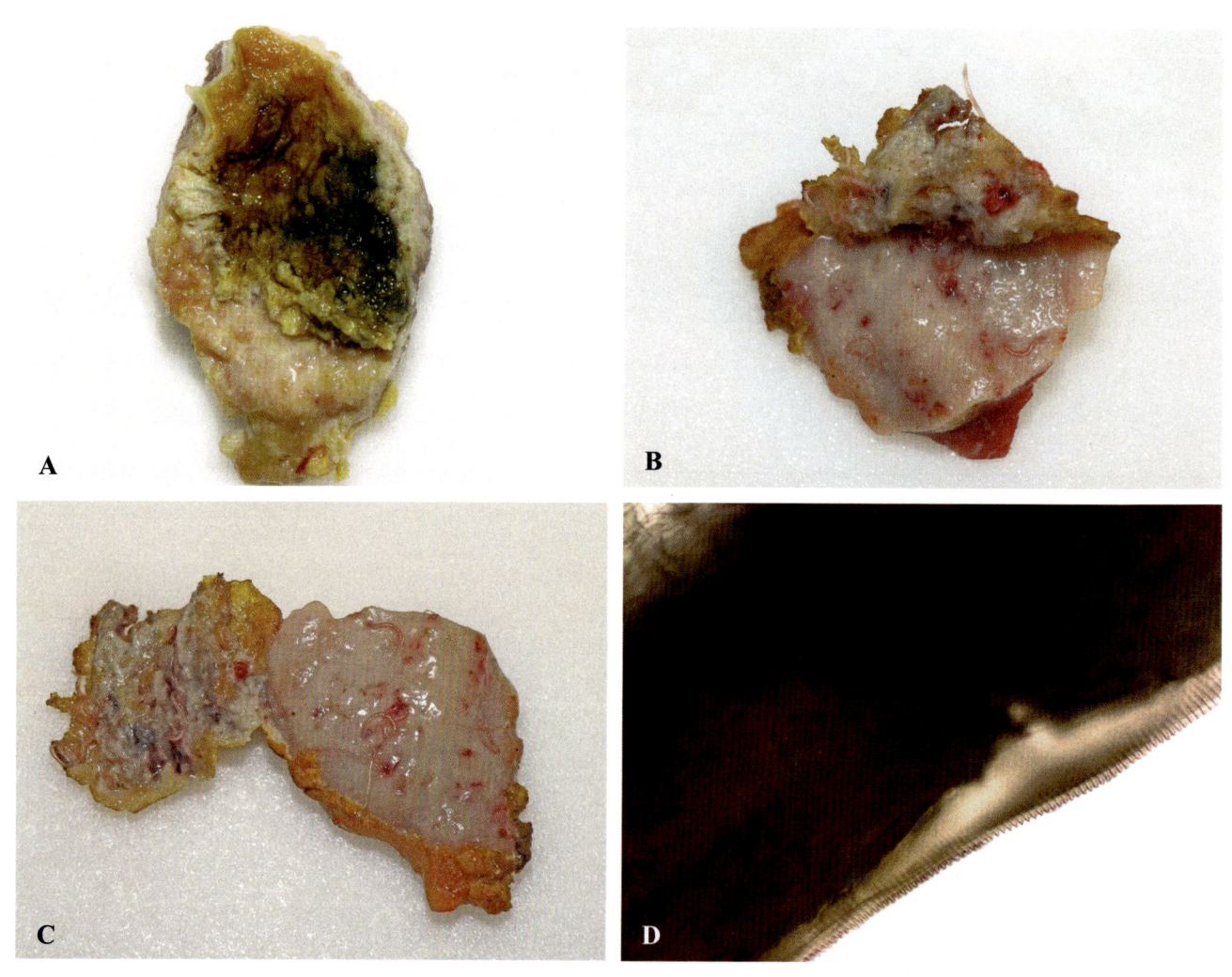

Cheilospirura hamulosa **infection of ventriculus.** Hobby chicken. **A.** Ulceration and sloughing of the koilin layer. **B, C.** Koilin is detached to show the small, pink worms associated with the mucosa and inner surface of the koilin. Mucosa is thickened and has small foci of ulcers with hemorrhage. Some worms penetrate the mucosa and may be difficult to remove. **D.** A characteristic feature of *Cheilospirura* spp. is the cuticular spines on its surface.

Tetrameres spp. Infection of Proventriculus

Cause. Nematode species in the genus *Tetrameres* infect the proventriculus of chickens, turkeys, quail, Guinea fowl, ducks, geese, pigeons, and nearly 300 species of wild birds. *Tetrameres* species of greatest importance in poultry include *T. americana* in chickens, pigeons, turkeys, ducks, quail, and grouse, *T. fissipina* in ducks, geese and other poultry, *T. crami* in ducks, and *T. pattersoni* in quail. *Tetrameres* spp. are found worldwide but are most common in birds in tropical and subtropical regions. Free-range chickens, especially in some areas of Africa, have high rates of infection. *T. americana* also is a common parasite of captive and wild pigeons. *Tetrameres* spp. have indirect life cycles. The intermediate host depends on the species and includes grasshoppers, cockroaches, earthworms, and small aquatic crustaceans in the order *Amphipoda* (Class: Crustacea).

Gross lesions. Lesions are found in the proventriculus. A few or several dark-red spots are seen through the serosal surface. When the proventriculus is opened, the mucosa appears thickened, and nodules resembling blood clots are associated with mucosal papillae that are raised above the mucosal surface. Cut surface of the proventriculus shows dark-red, globular bodies in the wall that are easy to remove. Each globular body is a gravid *Tetrameres* female residing within the center of a greatly distended proventricular gland. Occasionally, two parasites will be located in a single gland. Under a dissecting microscope, females are dark-red, globular-shaped worms with longitudinal furrows on their surface. Males are very small and have a filiform shape. Generally, males are not seen grossly because of their small size. *Tetrameres* represents an extreme example of sexual dimorphism among parasites. Eggs are embryonated when laid.

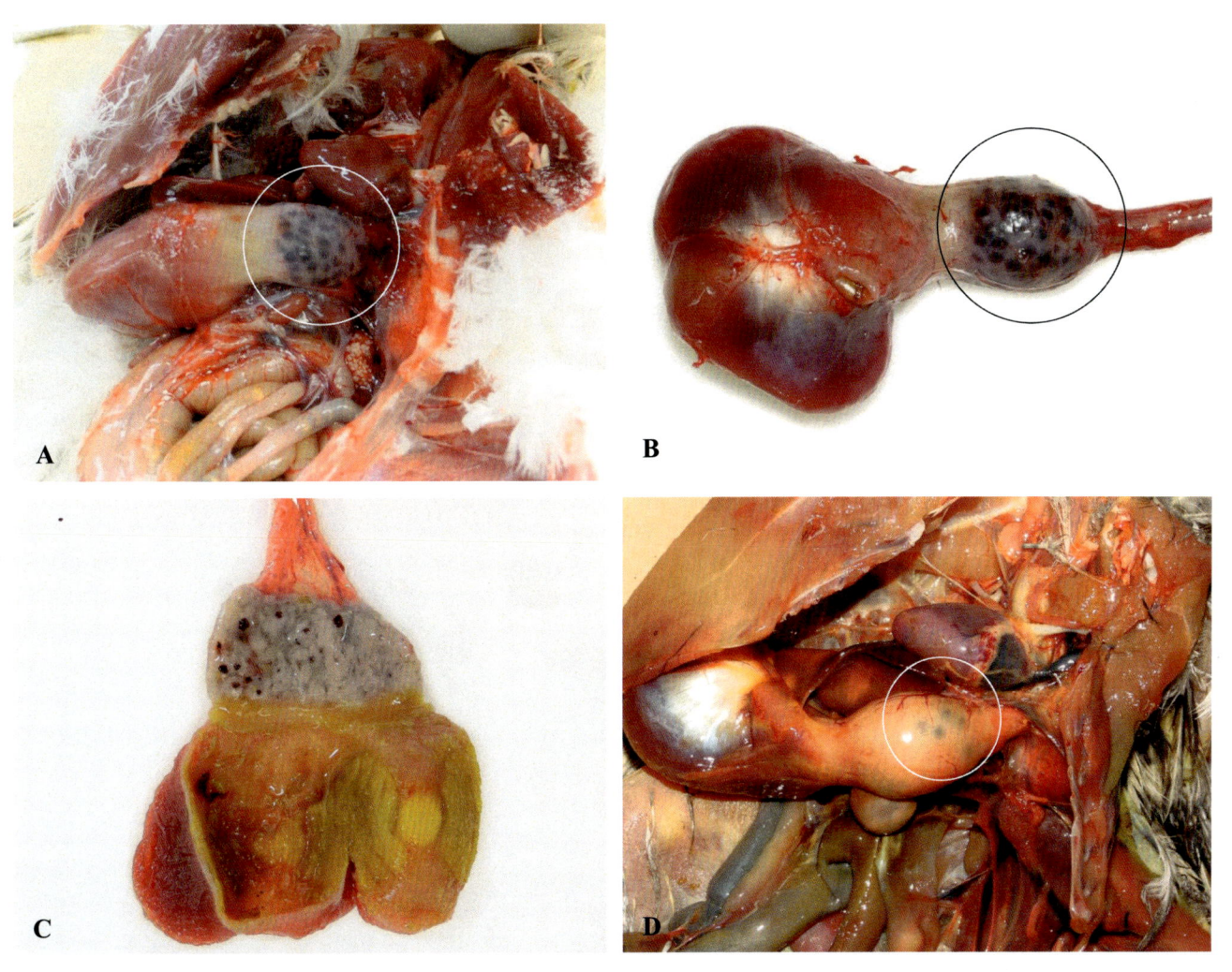

Tetrameres sp. (likely *T. americana*) infection of proventriculus. **A, B, C.** Pigeon. **A, B.** Dark-red spots are visible through the proventriculus serosal surface. Circles: proventriculus. **C.** Small blood clot-like nodules are project from the proventriculus mucosal surface and are associated with mucosal papillae. **D.** Jungle fowl. Few red spots (circle) are visible through the serosal surface of the proventriculus.

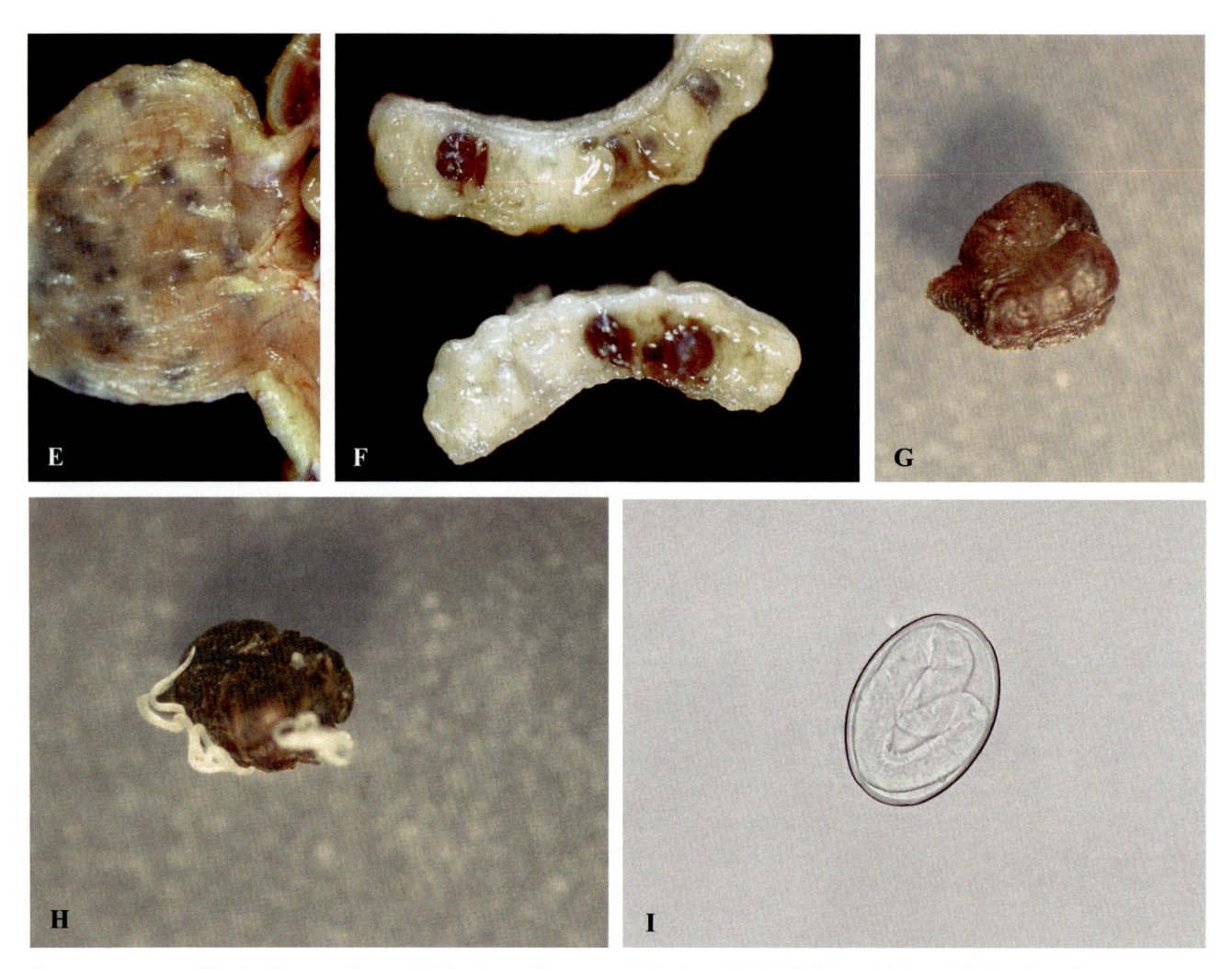

Tetrameres sp. (likely *T. americana*) infection of proventriculus. **E, F.** Hobby chicken. **E.** Dark-red spots are visible through the proventricular serosal surface. **F.** Cut surfaces of the proventriculus. Blood clot-like globular bodies are within the wall and project from the surface. Globular bodies are *Tetrameres* females residing within greatly distended proventricular glands. **G.** *Tetrameres* female as seen under a dissecting microscope. The female is dark-red and globular in shape and has longitudinal furrows on its surface. **H.** *Tetrameres* female with a male associated with it. The male is white and filiform. **I.** Embryonated egg of *Tetrameres*. The egg is from a gravid female. Eggs are embryonated when laid.

Hadjelia truncata Infection in Pigeons

Cause. The parasitic nematode *Hadjelia truncata* is a spirurid found in the gizzard of several species of birds including pigeons, magpies, cuckoos, blackcaps, nightjars, rollers, shrikes, and hoopoes. It is only known to be pathogenic for pigeons. The body of the nematode is straight and very thin. Females are 12-16.5 mm long and 229 μm wide; males are 6.5-9 mm long and 151 μm wide. *H. truncata* has an indirect life cycle, with certain beetles, including darkling beetles (*Alphitobius diaperinus*) and their larvae (lesser mealworms), serving as intermediate hosts. Eggs containing first-stage larvae are passed in the bird's droppings. They are ingested by beetles in which they develop into infective third-stage larvae.

Gross Lesions. Affected pigeons are emaciated. The gizzard is markedly thickened and distorted. At the anterior part of the gizzard (junction with proventriculus), the koilin layer is thickened, rough, irregular, pitted, discolored green or brown, and has multifocal rounded cavities and erosions. In these areas, the koilin layer is fragile and easily detached from the underlying epithelium. Numerous thread-like nematodes (*H. truncata*) are located between the koilin layer and epithelium in the lesions.

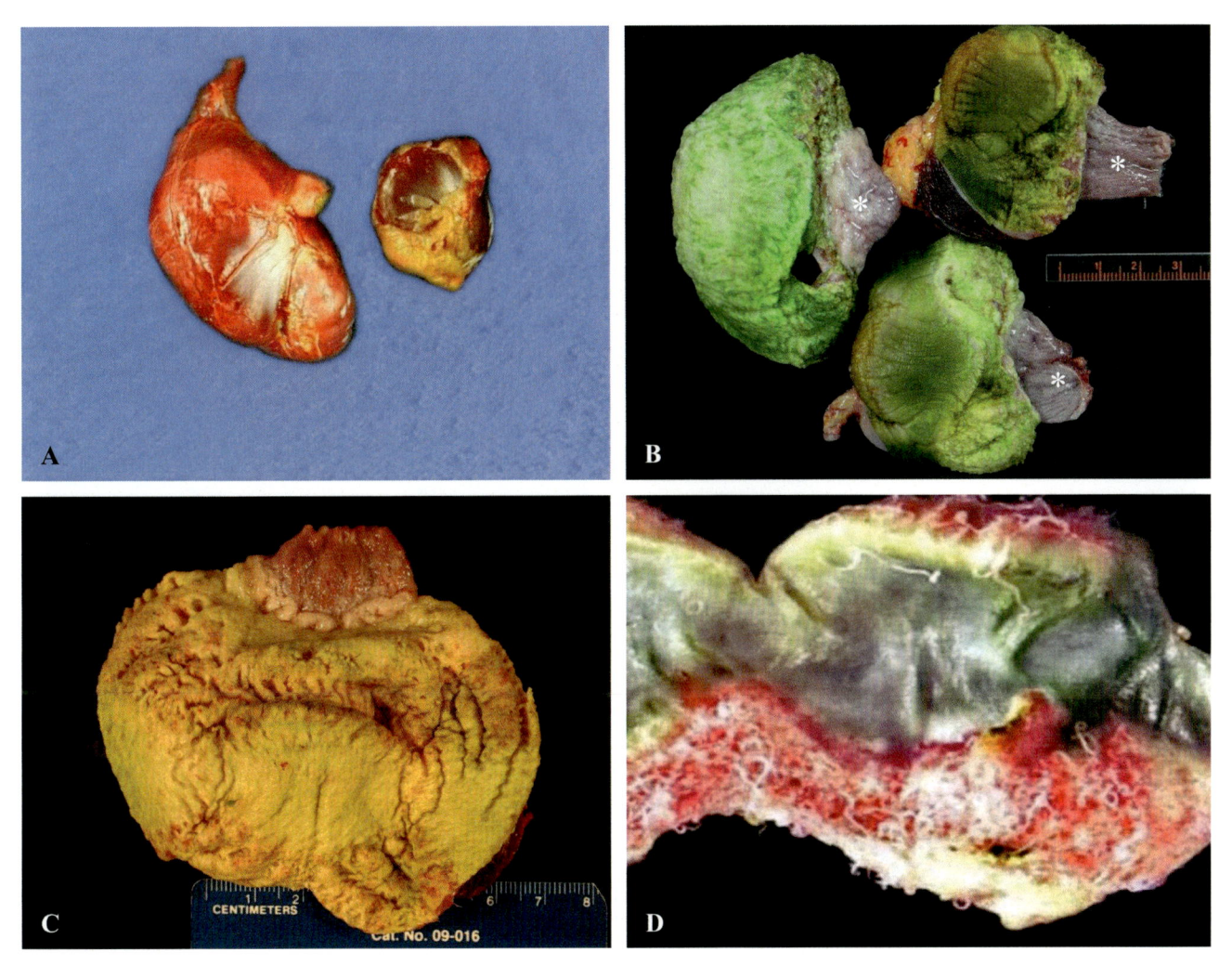

Hadjelia truncata **infection.** Pigeons. **A.** Gizzard on the left is infected with *H. truncata*. It is enlarged and has a distorted shape compared to the uninfected gizzard on the right. **B, C.** The koilin layer, especially in the anterior part of the gizzards (arrows in B), is thickened, pitted and roughened and has small round cavities and erosions. In **B**, note the green discoloration of the koilin. Asterisks in B: proventriculus. **D.** Numerous thread-like nematodes are located between the koilin and underlying epithelium. *(Photos courtesy of Dr. CG Santíes-Cué, USA)*.

Eustrongylidosis (Verminous Peritonitis)

Cause. Eustrongylidosis is caused by the nematodes *Eustrongylides tubifex*, *E. ignotus*, and *E. excisus*. Wading, fish-eating birds are the definitive hosts. The parasite has a complex, indirect life cycle that involves two intermediate hosts. Four developmental stages of the parasite are required from egg to sexually mature worm. Eggs of *Eustrongylides* spp. are shed in the feces of infected birds. After shedding, first stage larvae develop within the eggs. Eggs containing first-stage larvae are consumed by oligochaetes (aquatic worms). Within the aquatic worms, first-stage larvae are released and develop into second- and third-stage larvae. Small fish ingest infected oligochaetes and serve as the second intermediate host. Within fish, third-stage larvae encyst and develop into fourth-stage larvae. Birds become infected when they ingest fish infected with fourth-stage larvae. Paratenic (transport) hosts include predatory fish, amphibians, and reptiles that consume infected small fish. After ingestion of infected fish, fourth-stage larvae penetrate the walls of the gizzard and proventriculus within 3-5 hours. Maturity and egg shedding occurs 10-17 days and 14-23 days, respectively, post-infection.

Hosts. Wading birds infected with *Eustrongylides* spp. include herons, egrets, spoonbills, ibis, pelicans, mergansers, loons, and cormorants. Infection with *Eustrongylides* sp. also occurs in birds of prey. Mortality in young birds is often high and may be confused with starvation.

Gross lesions. Gross lesions of eustrongylidosis are characteristic and diagnostic. Infected birds are emaciated and have a mass of tortuous, intertwining, tubular tunnels in the serosal surface of the gizzard. Residing within these tunnels are large, red *Eustrongylides* nematodes. Tunnels are often encased by fibrous tissue and have openings into the lumen of the organs so eggs can pass into the alimentary tract and out of the bird in its feces. Perforation of the gizzard wall by parasites results in severe bacterial peritonitis characterized by accumulation of fibrinonecrotic material on peritoneal surfaces. There are extensive adhesions among abdominal visceral organs in chronic cases. Free *Eustrongylides* may be found in peritoneal cavities. Adult *Eustrongylides* nematodes are dark, up to 15 cm in length, and 4-5 mm in diameter. In chronic, resolving infection, lesions are less remarkable and appear as raised yellow or tan-colored fibrotic tunnels containing dead or disintegrating worms. Worm structures may not be recognizable in old lesions. As lesions resolve, tunnels gradually develop into irregularly shaped, firm nodules on the surface of the gizzard. Lesions of *E. tubifex* and *E. excisus* in mergansers and cormorants, respectively, consist of nodules or cyst-like lesions that contain parasites in the proventricular mucosa.

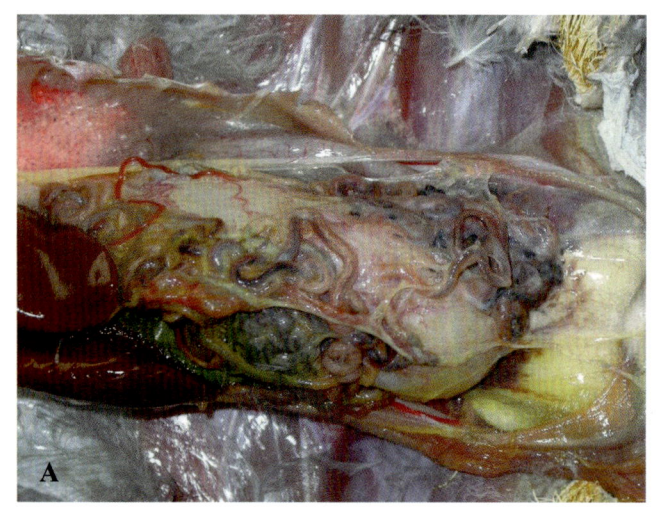

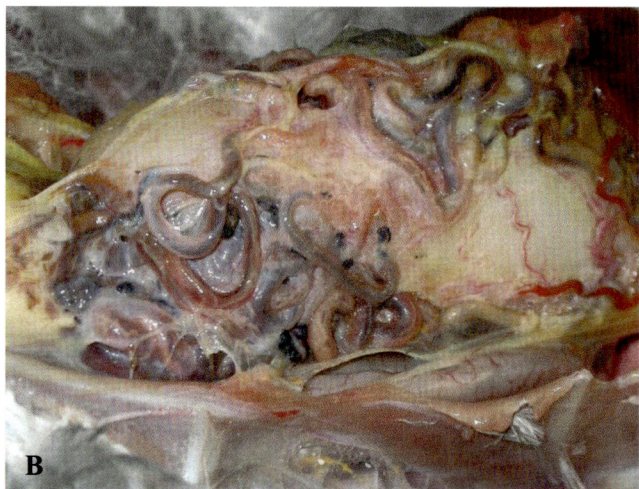

Eustrongylidosis. Great blue heron (*Ardea herodias*). **A, B.** Large *Eustrongylides* nematodes in the body cavity and peritoneal walls. There is severe peritonitis. Lesions are diagnostic for eustrongylidosis.

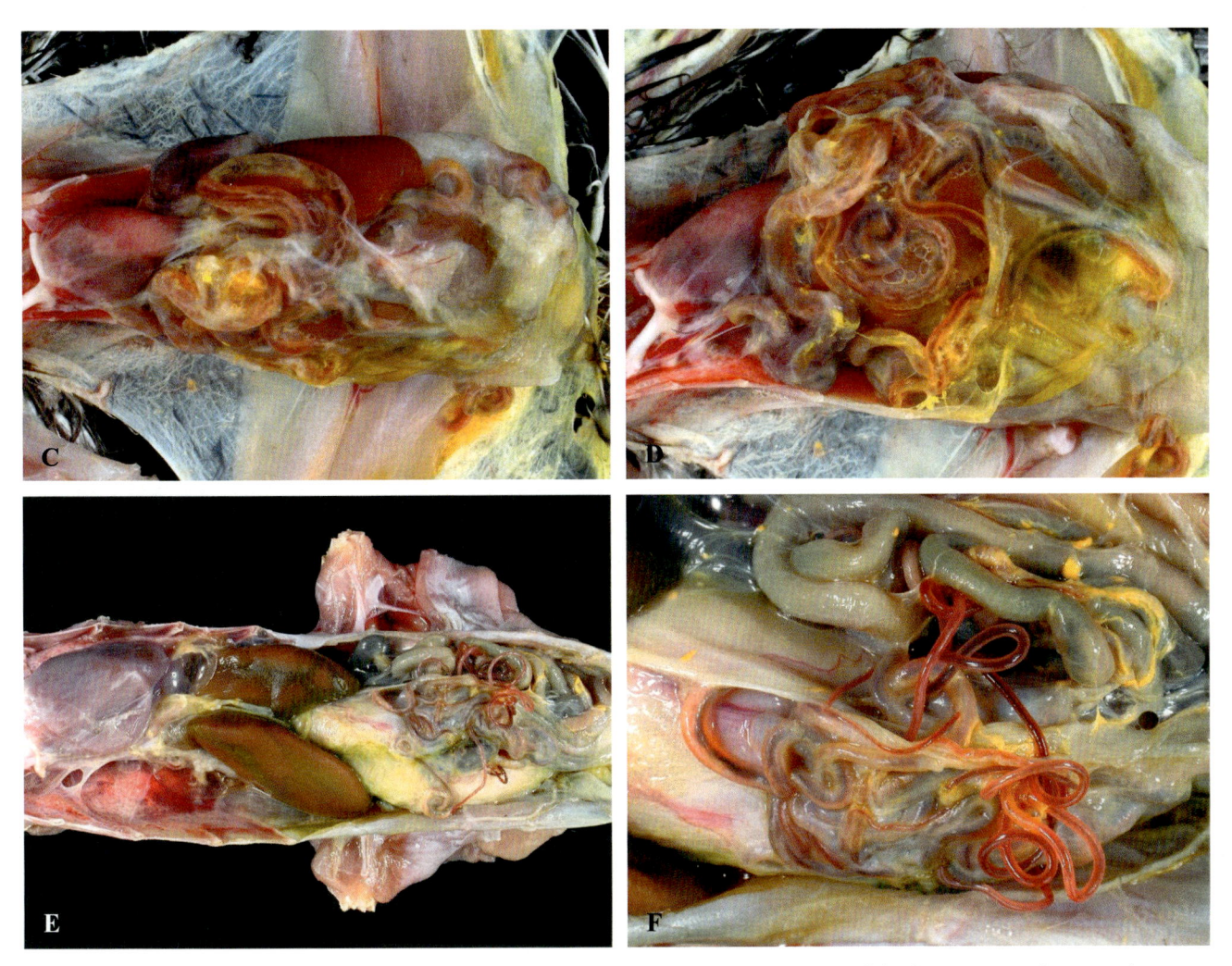

Gross Pathology of Avian Diseases: Text and Atlas   177

Eustrongylidosis. C, D. Green heron, (*Butorides virescens*), juvenile, eustrongylidosis. Large, red worms have penetrated the wall of the stomach and are located in the serosa and body cavity where they have caused peritonitis. Heron is emaciated as the heart lacks fat in the coronary groove and there is no stored fat in the body cavity. **E, F.** Great blue heron, (*Ardea herodias*), immature adult, eustrongylidosis. Heron is emaciated but has a swollen, green-discolored liver. Numerous large red worms are embedded in the serous membranes and free in the body cavity. Parasites have caused a mild, diffuse, chronic peritonitis.

Ascaridiasis

Cause. Many species of large roundworms in the genus *Ascaridia* infect a variety of poultry and wild, game, pet, and aviary birds. This section describes ascaridiasis in poultry, pigeons, and game birds. *A. galli* infects a wide host range of birds including chickens, turkeys, ducks, geese, doves, and peafowl. *A. dissimilis* usually occurs in confinement-raised commercial turkeys. *A. columbae* infects pigeons and doves. *A. numidae* is found in Guinea fowl. *A. compar* occurs in grouse, partridge, pheasant, and quail.

Life cycle. *Ascaridia* species have a direct life cycle, i.e., they do not need an intermediate host to complete their life cycle. Adult females lay thousands of non-embryonated eggs in the intestine of infected birds each day, which are voided into the environment in feces. Under optimal conditions of temperature and humidity, two larval stages (first- and second-stage larvae) develop within the eggs outside the host. *Ascaridia* eggs are relatively resistant to many adverse environmental conditions because of the thick eggshell that protects the embryo and developing larvae. When birds ingest infective eggs, second-stage larvae are released, usually in the proventriculus and duodenum. These continue down the intestine where they molt and develop into third-stage-larvae, which penetrate into the intestinal mucosa. Third-stage larvae return to the lumen and develop into fourth-stage larvae, which continue to grow to adult, starting the life cycle over. In heavy infections, third-stage larvae are impeded from developing further and remain in the intestinal wall, causing further tissue damage. Larval ascaridiasis occurs when the bird is exposed to high numbers of infective eggs at one time. Numerous larvae simultaneously penetrate the mucosa causing clinical disease and occasional mortality. Under field conditions, various stages of development (second-stage, third-stage, and fourth-stage larvae, immature adult, and mature adult) are usually present in the bird at the same time. Examination of intestinal mucosal scrapings is required to detect larvae in the wall of the intestine. Late fourth-stage larvae are visible in the lumen, but microscopic examination is necessary to see small, third-stage larvae. Generally, second-stage larvae of *A. galli* and *A. dissimilis* develop into mature adults in about 28-30 days, while maturation of *A. columbae* takes about 35-40 days.

Aberrant migration of larvae from the intestine to other tissues occurs with several *Ascaridia* spp., particularly when there is a heavy worm burden. Adult *Ascaridia* may enter bile ducts and reach the gall bladder or even intrahepatic bile duct. They may also stray into pancreatic ducts. Adult roundworms are occasionally found in avian eggs because they migrate into the oviduct of the bird. Larvae of *A. dissimilis* migrate to the liver. The route by which they reach the liver is uncertain, but experimental infections indicate migration is via the hepatic portal blood circulation. Larvae trapped in the liver eventually die and trigger an intense inflammatory reaction that appears as a small white spot on the surface of the liver. Occurrence of larvae-induced lesions in the liver of turkeys is named "hepatic foci". The condition can be a serious problem, which still occasionally occurs in commercial meat-type turkey flocks in the US. Larvae of *A. columbae* may be found in the intestinal mesentery, lung, liver, and kidneys. Larvae die and cause granulomatous lesions in the tissues. Small lesions may only be identified histologically.

Effect of the parasite on the host. In commercial poultry, infection with *Ascaridia* is a common problem in broiler breeders and turkeys, where it may adversely affect weight gain and feed conversion during the growing period. Infections of broiler chickens is uncommon. Ascaridiasis is also very common in small hobby flocks. Harmful effects are caused by both adult worms in the intestinal lumen and larvae in the intestinal wall. Adult worms may represent only 10% of the real burden of *Ascaridia* infection; the other 90% are mainly tissue bound third- and fourth-stage larvae that require microscopic examination to see. Although broiler breeders and turkeys of all ages are susceptible, infection tends to be most severe in younger birds.

The effect depends on the number of larvae and adult worms in the intestine. Since migration of larvae into and from the wall of the intestine can cause severe mucosal damage, this may predispose birds to secondary infection with opportunistic bacteria. In turkeys, necrotic enteritis caused by *Clostridium perfringens* has been associated with heavy migration of *Ascaridia* larvae into the intestinal mucosa. Hepatic foci caused by aberrant migration of larvae to the liver is an economically significant problem for the commercial turkey industry as livers with hepatic foci are condemned at processing. Giblets are simultaneously removed resulting in decreased carcass weight. Further, when there is a high incidence of hepatic foci, the speed of the processing line may be reduced to permit increased scrutiny by inspectors.

Gross lesions. Heavily infected birds are in poor body condition or emaciated. Adult worms are easily recognized in the small intestine as large, thick, yellow to white worms. Females are considerably larger than males. Immature adults are smaller than mature adults. Worms are found in different parts of the small intestine, from the duodenum to ileum. There may be only a few, or a tangled mass of worms. With heavy infection, the small intestine become distended. If the parasites are numerous in the duodenum, they may stray into the gizzard and bile ducts. They can be found even in the gall bladder or under the capsule of the liver. It is common to find other intestinal parasites in birds infected with roundworms.

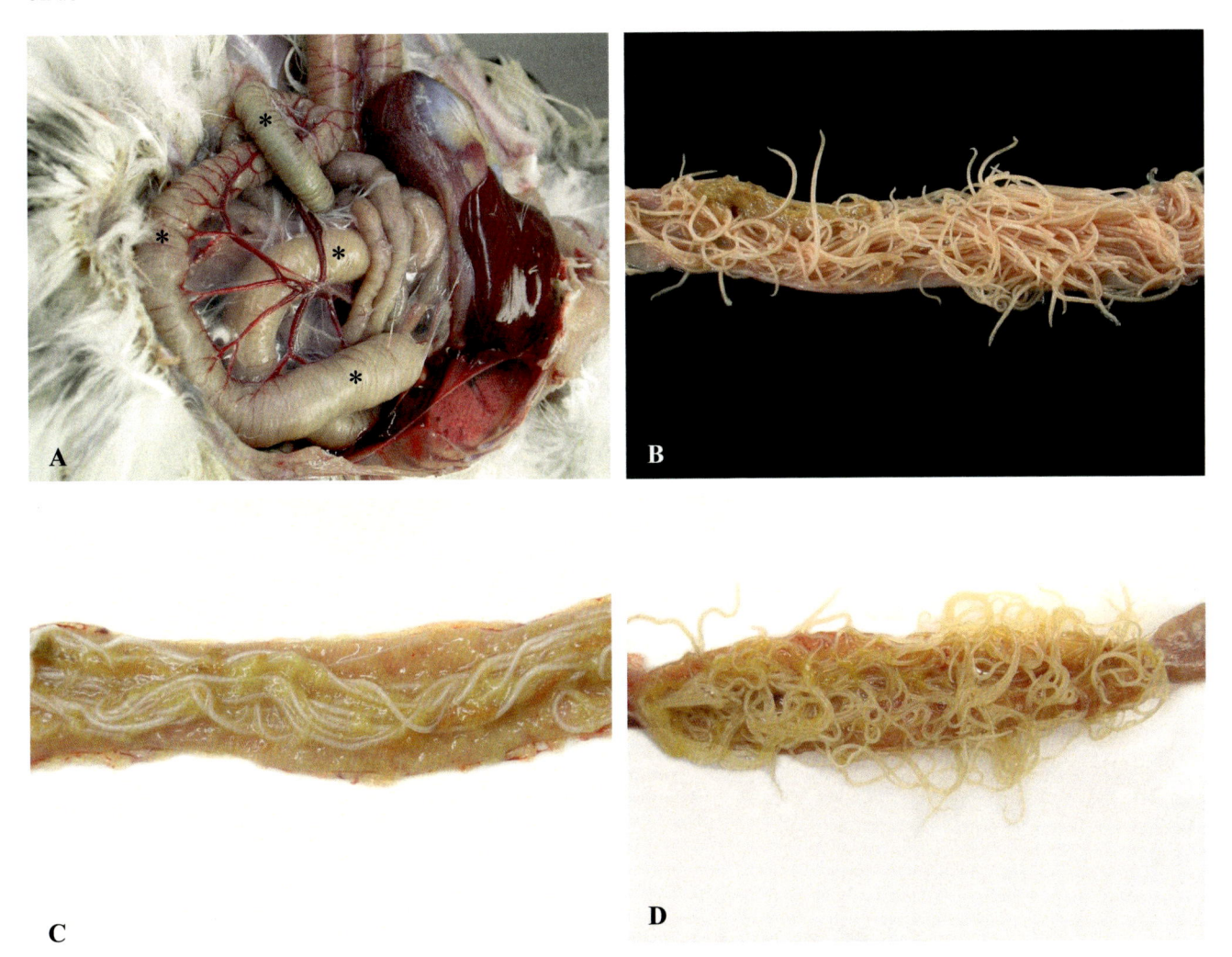

Ascaridiasis. A, B, C. Hobby chickens (A and B are same bird). **D.** 40-day broiler chicken. **A.** The small intestine (asterisks) is distended and turgid. **B, D.** A tangled mass of *Ascaridia galli* fills the lumen of the small intestine. **C.** Several roundworms are in the lumen of the small intestine. The mucosa looks thickened.

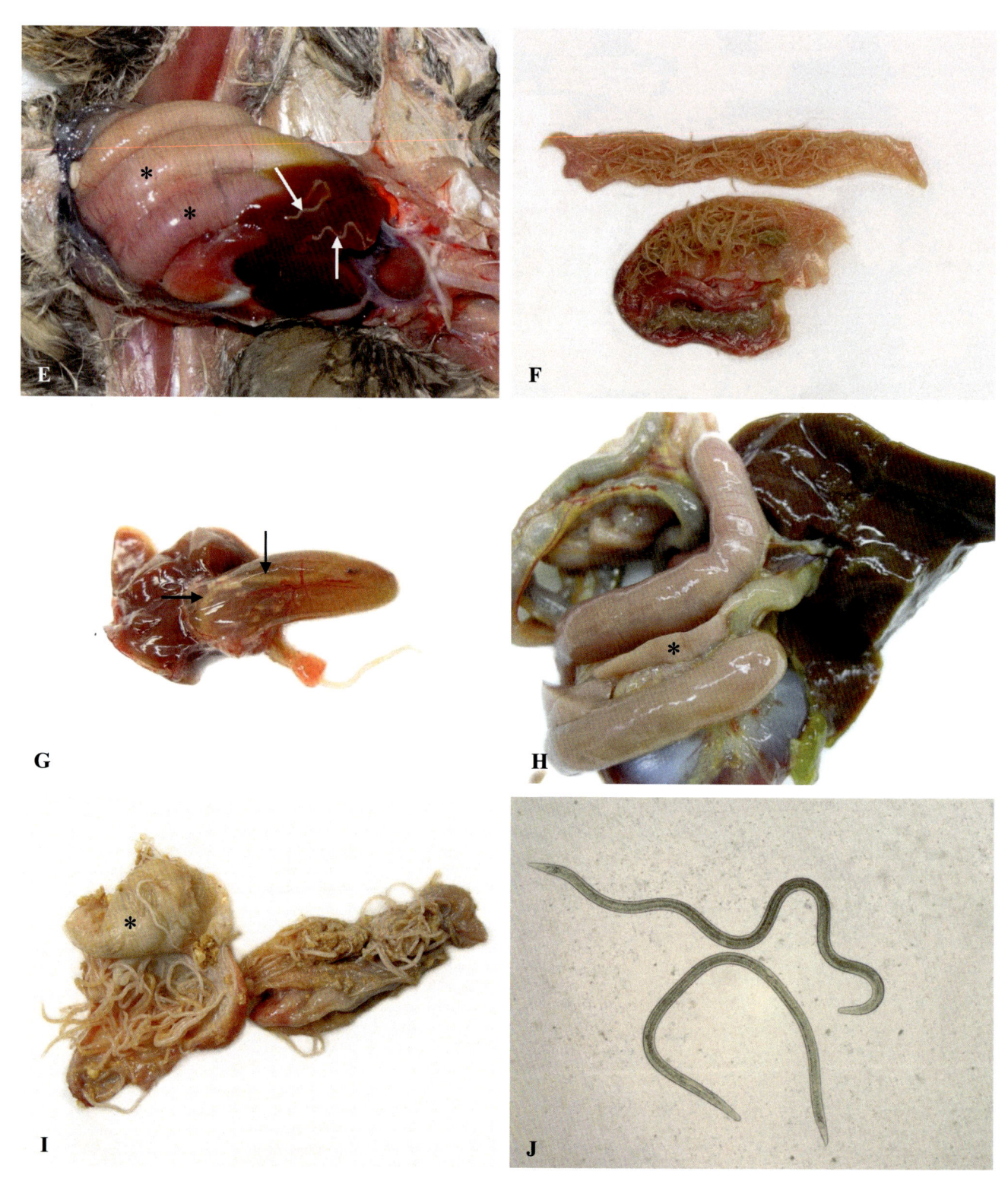

Ascaridiasis. E, F, G. 9-week chukar. **E.** Duodenal loop (asterisks) is distended and turgid. Two roundworms (*Ascaridia* sp.) (arrows) are seen beneath the capsule of the liver. The worms likely reached the liver via the bile duct. **F.** Numerous *Ascaridia* sp. form a tangled mass in the lumen of the duodenum. **G.** A single *Ascaridia* is in the lumen of the bile duct and gallbladder. Arrows identify the nematode seen through the wall of the gall bladder. **H.** 5-month pigeon. Duodenal loop is distended and turgid because it is filled with *Ascaridia* sp. (most likely *A. columbae*). A nematode is distending the bile duct (arrow). Asterisk: pancreas. **I.** Quaker parrot. Numerous *Ascaridia* sp. are in the duodenum and beneath the koilin layer of the gizzard. Asterisk: gizzard koilin layer. **J.** *Ascaridia* larvae in a mucosal scraping of small intestine from a broiler breeder.

Heterakis isolonche Infection in Pheasants

The parasitic nematode *Heterakis isolonche* causes nodular typhlitis in different species of pheasants. Due to the appearance of lesions in the cecal wall, the disease has also been called "verrucous typhlitis". Adult worms are small, round, and less than 15 mm. The life cycle is direct. Non-embryonated eggs pass out in the droppings of infected pheasants. Second-stage larvae develop within the eggs. Eggs with second-stage larvae are infective and can survive in the environment for several months to a few years depending on ambient conditions. Annelid worms (earthworms) may ingest infective eggs and act as mechanical vectors (paratenic hosts). Pheasants become infected after consuming infective eggs containing second-stage larvae either directly or indirectly via infected earthworms. Larvae released from eggs in the gizzard migrate to the cecum. They penetrate the cecal mucosa and reach the submucosa where they incite a marked proliferative response that results in nodule formation. The disease is considered an example of neoplasia resulting from a nematode infection.

Gross lesions. There is nodular thickening and discoloration of the serosal surface of the ceca. Protruding from the cecal mucosal surface are a few to many discrete to coalescing white-gray, light pink, or dark-brown nodules, usually 1-3 mm in diameter that usually extend to the submucosa. The mucosa of severely affected ceca may have a cobblestone appearance. Worms are commonly found within nodules.

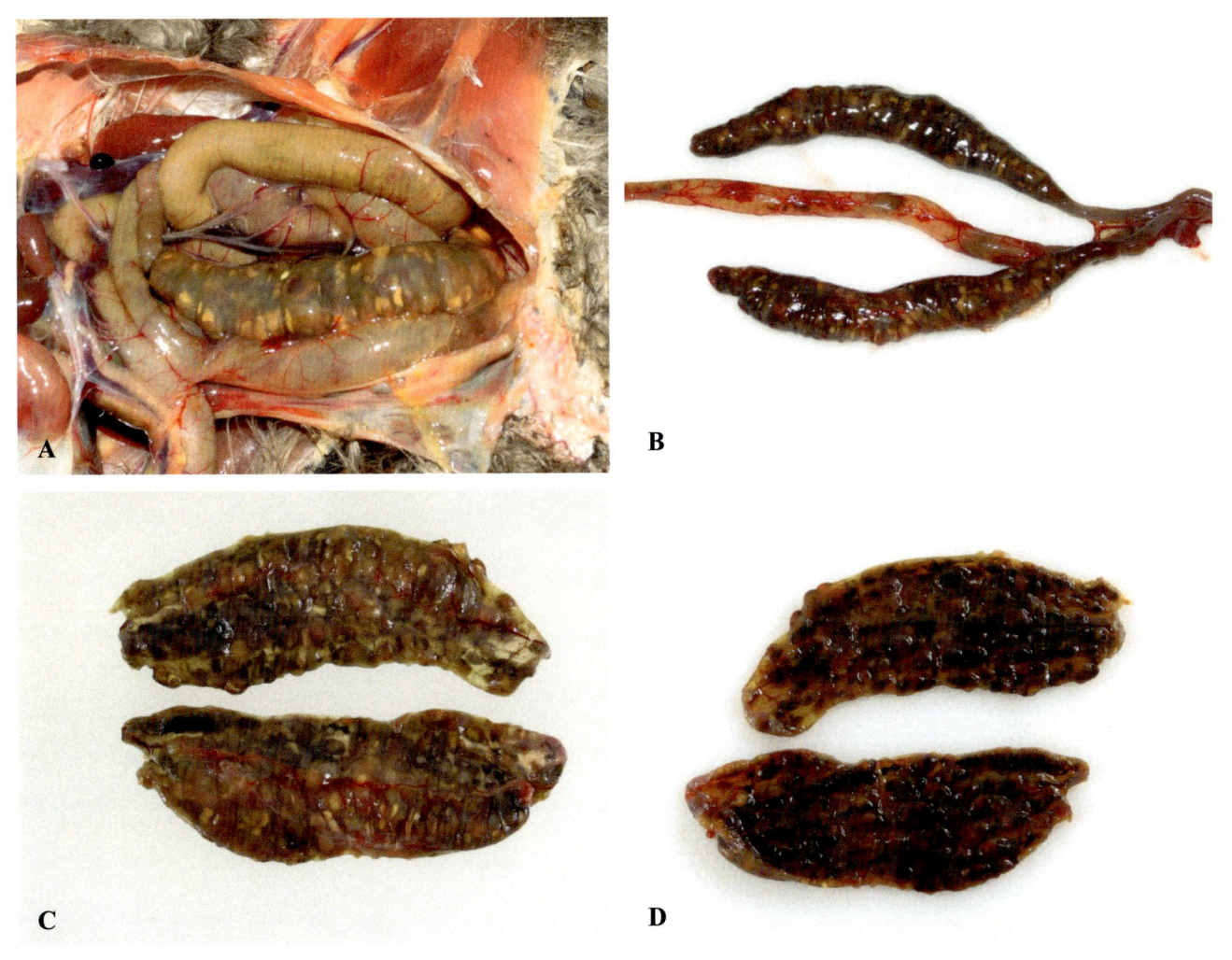

***Heterakis isolonche* infection.** Golden pheasant. **A, B, C.** Nodular thickening of the serosal surface of the ceca. Yellow or dark, small, variably shaped foci and nodules are seen through the thickened serosal surface. **D.** Cecal mucosas have several small dark nodules. Residing within some nodules are the causative nematode *H. isolonche*.

Syngamus trachea Infection

Syngamus trachea is a nematode that has a worldwide distribution and infects the trachea and bronchi of chickens, turkeys, geese, Guinea fowl, pheasants, peafowl, emus, quail, and several free-living birds. Young birds and pheasants are particularly susceptible to infection. Wild birds serve as reservoirs and have been implicated in outbreaks on game bird and poultry farms. Worms are bright red, which is responsible for the common name, "redworms". The male is 2-6 mm long, and the female is 5-20 mm long. The most distinctive feature of this nematode is that males and females are joined together in permanent copulation, forming a Y shape. Worms attach to the tracheal mucosa and feed on blood. Males permanently attach to the mucosa while females detach and reattach to feed.

Life cycle. Non-embryonated eggs are laid in the trachea. Gaping and coughing by the bird due to irritation bring the eggs up to the oropharynx where they are swallowed and shed in the droppings. In moist soil under optimal temperatures between 24 and 30°C, eggs embryonate and develop to 3rd stage larvae. Eggs become infective and hatch in 42 days at 17°C, 25 - 28 days at 19°C, about 16 days at 21°C, 13-14 days at 25°C, and 9 days at 27°C. Development does not occur below 15°C; temperatures above 30°C kill the embryo. Hatched larvae are susceptible to desiccation.

Earthworms serve as paratenic hosts and play an important role in perpetuating the parasite. They ingest larvae, which enter the body cavity, invade the body musculature, and are encapsulated. Encapsulated larvae in earthworms can remain infective for as long as 4 years. Other invertebrates that may serve as transport hosts include snails, slugs, house fly larvae, and possibly beetles and ants. Birds become infected directly by ingesting larvae or indirectly by eating infected paratenic hosts. Larvae penetrate the wall of the esophagus, crop, or duodenum and are carried via the blood stream to the lungs. Experimentally, larvae are seen in lung interstitial tissue and atria as early as 4 hrs and 24 hrs, respectively. Larvae molt and develop to adults in 4-5 days: most worms reach the trachea within 11 days. Females become fertile and start to produce eggs in 14 days.

Clinical signs and gross lesions. In severely infected young birds, mucus and worms in the tracheal lumen cause the bird to stretch out their neck, open their mouth, and gasp for air. This "gaping" posture gives rise to the common term "gapeworm" for *S. trachea*. Head shaking and coughing are seen in younger birds. Severely affected birds stop eating and drinking, deteriorate, and eventually die. Older birds may only exhibit occasional coughing.

Points of attachment of males to the mucosa are hemorrhagic. In pheasants, the anterior end of males may penetrate the mucosa provoking inflammatory and fibrotic responses, which results in formation of small, pale mucosal nodules that may be visible on the serosa. Nodules are composed mostly of connective tissue around the anterior end of males. In some cases, males penetrate deeply, reaching and causing mechanical damage to the cartilaginous tracheal rings. The large, bright red worms in a "Y" configuration are diagnostic for *S. trachea*. Excess mucus often accompanies presence of the parasite.

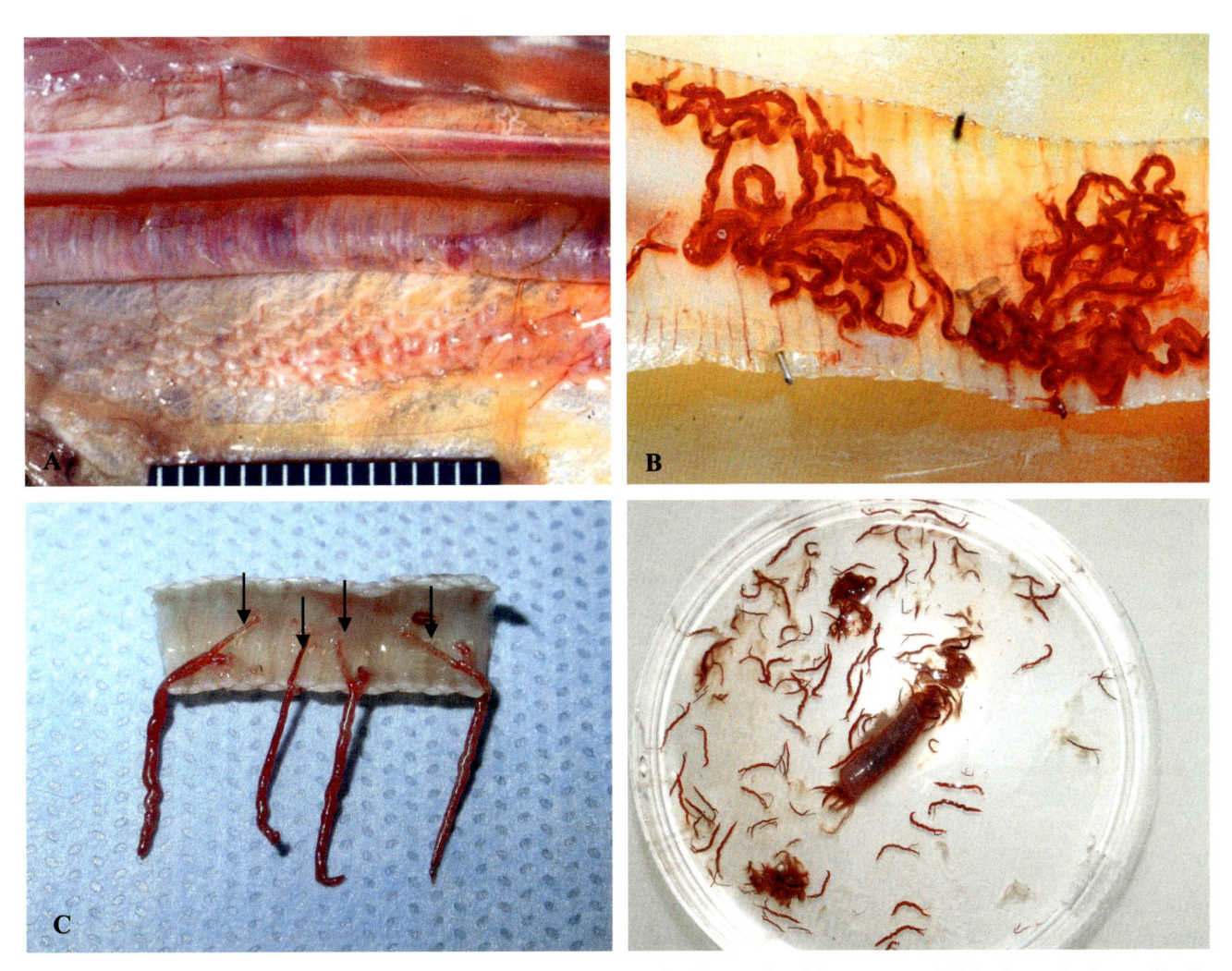

Syngamus trachea **infection. A.** Chicken. Bright red worms in the tracheal lumen are visible through the wall of the trachea. **B.** Chicken. Red worms are associated with the tracheal mucosa. **C.** Peacock. Several worms are attached to the tracheal mucosa. The "Y" shape at the anterior end is formed by males and females in permanent copulation. Males (arrows) are attached to the mucosa. Note excess mucus in the tracheal lumen. **D.** Large numbers of *Syngamus* sp. washed out of the trachea of an ivory gull. *(Photo C courtesy of Dr. Peter Wencel, Poland. Photo D.* Syngamus trachea *in Ivory gull by Tom Pennycott, University of Edinburgh. Royal (Dick) School of Veterinary Studies is licensed under CC BY 4.0).*

Cestodiasis in Chickens

Cestodiasis is a tapeworm infection. Tapeworms (cestodes) are flattened, ribbon-shaped worms with a body consisting of 3 parts: scolex (head), neck, and a chain of segments called proglottids. They lack an alimentary canal obtaining nutrients by direct absorption from the intestinal tract through a specialized integument. Each segment contains male and female reproductive organs. The scolex attaches to the intestinal mucosa. New proglottids are formed from the neck and push the old segment posteriorly, thus creating a chain of segments (strobila). The strobila may be loosely divided into immature, mature, and gravid (egg-filled) segments. One or more gravid segments occurs at the posterior end of the worm. Gravid segments detach from the worm and are shed in the feces. The life cycle requires intermediate hosts including beetles, slugs and snails, earthworms, houseflies, or ants. In the gravid segments, fertile eggs become embryonated. The embryo has six hooks and is called an onchosphere or hexacanth. Eggs or entire proglottids are ingested by the intermediate host. Embryos are released, penetrate through the gut wall, and enter the body cavity where they develop into cysticercoids. Birds become infected when they eat an infected intermediate host. Cysticercoids reach the intestine of the final host, attach to the mucosa, and begin formation of the strobila. The prepatent period (time from ingesting cysticercoid to egg production) is generally 1-3 weeks.

Tapeworms are mostly found in free-range and hobby chickens as they have ready access to intermediate hosts. They occur in the duodenum and/or jejunum-ileum. Some are only a few mm long, while others are several cm long. It is common to find multiple types of tapeworms in the same bird.

Davainea proglottina. This is a small tapeworm (<4 mm long) with up to 9 proglottids. It occurs in the duodenum, especially the ascending part. Proglottids can be seen protruding from the mucosal surface when the opened duodenum is placed into water. Examination using a dissecting microscope aids in recognizing the proglottids. Intermediate hosts are slugs and snails of different genera. Cysticercoids develop into adult worms in 1-2 weeks. *D. proglottina* is one of the most pathogenic tapeworms in chickens, especially young birds. Heavy infections cause duodenal enteritis, weight loss, and emaciation.

Amoebotaenia cuneata. This is another small tapeworm (<4 mm long) that parasitizes the duodenum. It usually has 25-30 proglottids. Worms appear as white projections among villi in the mucosal surface, especially when the duodenum is placed into water and examined under a dissecting microscope. Intermediate hosts are earthworms that belong to different genera. Infection is usually not associated with clinical disease.

Hymenolepis cantaniana. This tapeworm is up to 2 cm long. It infects the duodenum and jejunum. Dung beetles serve as intermediate hosts. Infection is usually not associated with clinical disease.

Hymenolepis carioca. This slender, thread-like, delicate worm measuring 3 to 8 cm is found in the duodenum and jejunum. Beetles of several genera serve as intermediate hosts, but dung and ground beetles are most common. Infection is usually not associated with clinical disease.

Ralleitina cesticillus. This is a long tapeworm (up to 15 cm) that is found in the duodenum and jejunum. The scolex is deeply embedded in the mucosa. Beetles of several genera are intermediate hosts. Infection is usually not associated with clinical disease.

Ralleitina tetragona. This long tapeworm (up to 25 cm) is found in the distal small intestine. Intermediate hosts are ants of several genera. *R. tetragona* is mildly to moderately pathogenic.

Ralleitina echinobothrida. This is a robust tapeworm that can grow to 34 cm. It is among the most pathogenic cestodes producing nodular intestinal disease in chickens. Scolices are deeply embedded in the mucosa of jejunum and ileum. They provoke a granulomatous reaction in the intestinal wall that results in formation of nodules protruding from the serosal surface. Several genera of ants serve as intermediate hosts.

Choanotaenia infundibulum. This is a long tapeworm (up to 23 cm) that is extremely white and infects the jejunum. Intermediate hosts are houseflies and beetles of several genera. *C. infundibulum* is moderately pathogenic. Heavy infections depress the growth of young birds.

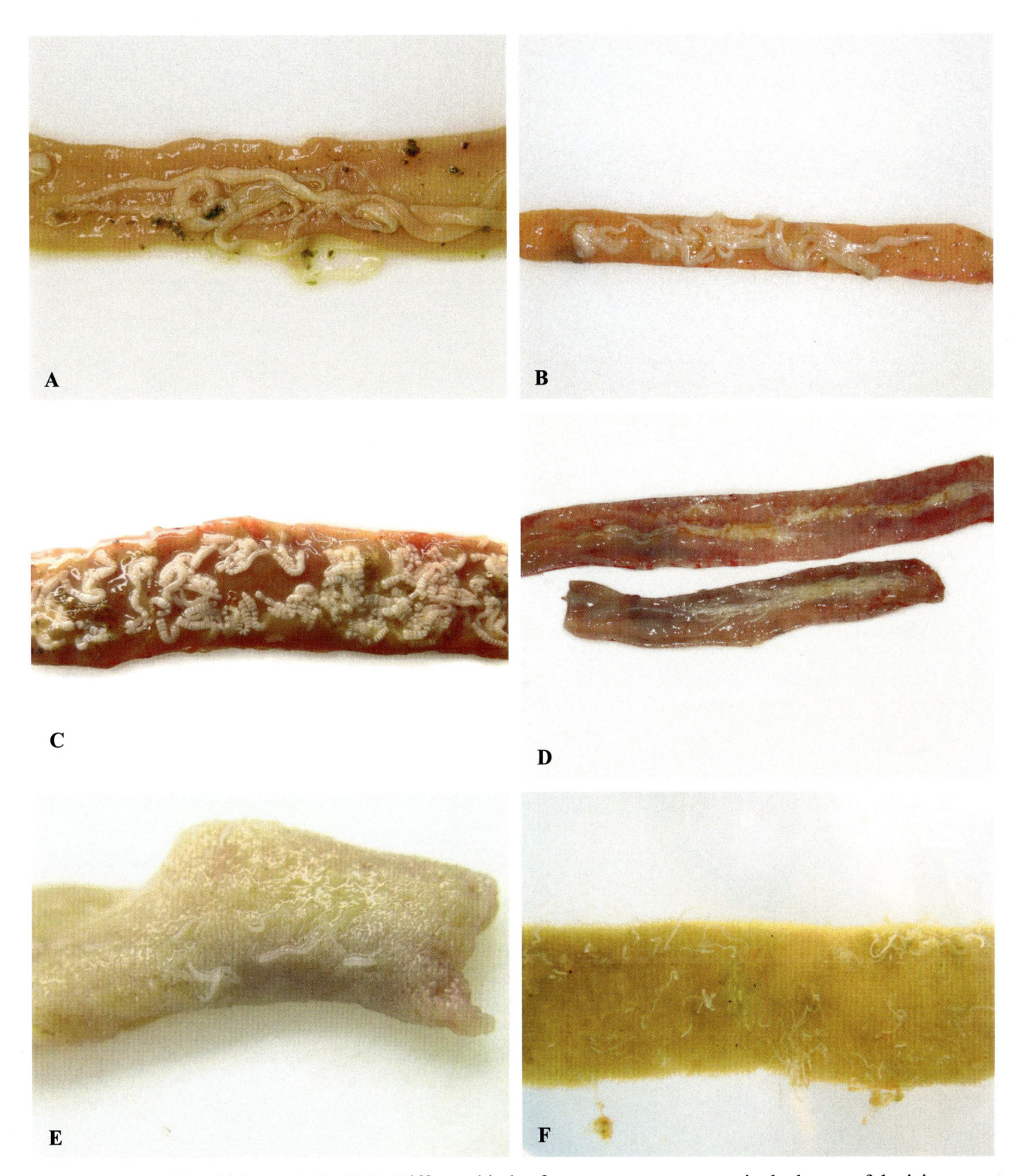

Cestodiasis. Hobby chickens. **A, B, C, D.** Different kinds of tapeworms are present in the lumen of the jejunum-ileum. Identification of the tapeworms was not attempted. **E, F.** Hobby chickens. Tapeworms protrude from the mucosal surface of duodenum.

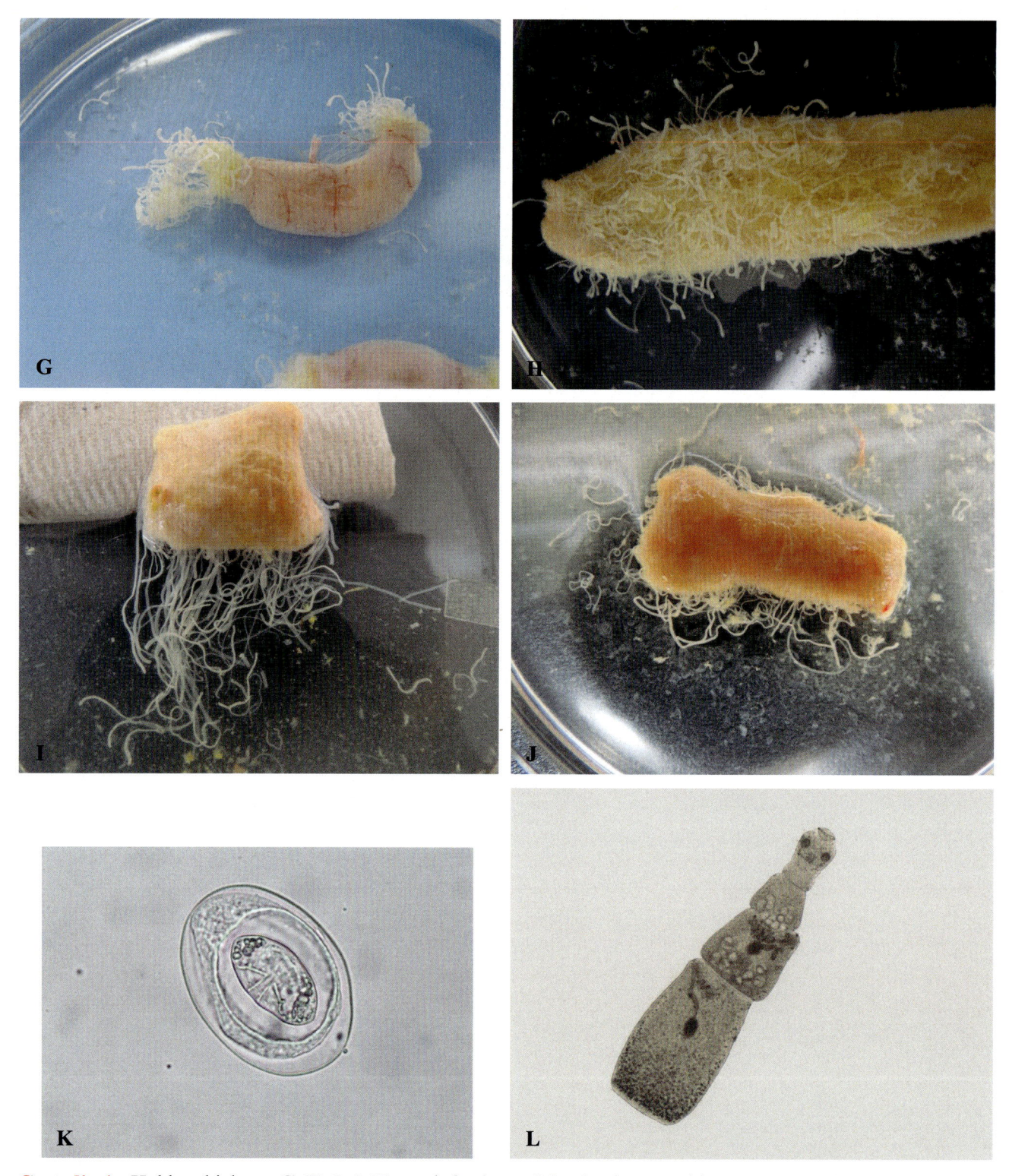

Cestodiasis. Hobby chickens. **G, H, I, J.** Heavy infections of the duodenum with tapeworms. These are likely *Hymenolepis* spp. **K.** Embryonated egg of *Hymenolepis* sp. The embryo in the middle has a prolate spheroid shape (American football shape) and 6 hooks, with characteristic granules at the poles. **L.** *Davainea proglottina*. The body consists of head, neck, and only three segments. Despite its small size, it is one of the more pathogenic tapeworms.

| M | N |

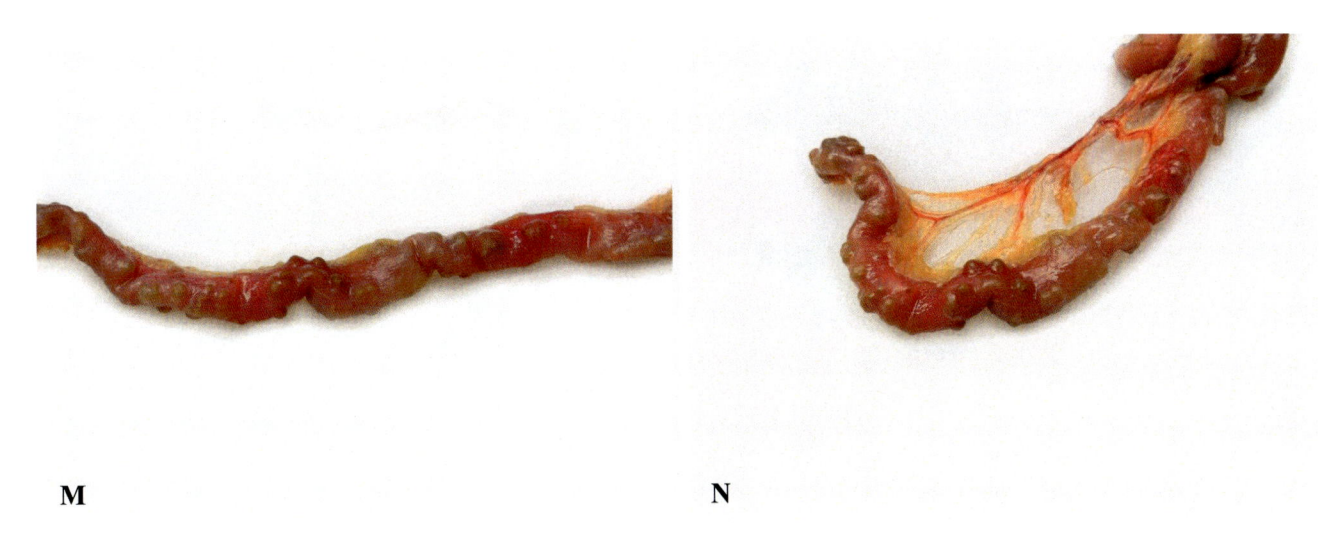

Railietina echinobothrida **infection.** Adult hobby chicken. Small nodules in the wall of the jejunum and ileum. Nodular granulomas result from penetration of the intestinal wall by tapeworm scolices.

Collyriclosis (Cutaneous Trematodiasis)

Cause. Collyriclosis is caused by the digenetic monostome fluke *Collyriclum faba*. Definitive hosts include a broad range of birds, primarily passerines. The life cycle involves two intermediate hosts. The first intermediate host is the freshwater snail *Bythinella austriaca*. Other species of *Bythinella* and the closely related genus *Amnicola* may also serve as first intermediate hosts. The second intermediate host is the mayfly (order Ephemeroptera family Heptageniidae). Other insects in the order Ephemeroptera may also serve as intermediate hosts. The fluke is almost hemispherical, dorsally convex, and ventrally flattened. It has a spiny tegument and is 4-5 mm wide. There is no ventral sucker and the oral sucker is small. Infections tend to occur in specific geographic areas where the intermediate hosts are located and during the summer following emergence of mayflies.

Gross lesions. Gross lesions of *Collyriclum faba* infection consist of single cutaneous cysts, a group of few cutaneous cysts, cutaneous mass of many small cysts, or subcutaneous mass with nodular surface. Location of lesions varies with the type of bird and includes around the vent, over the abdomen, lower limb (shank), base of the lower beak, ventral surface of the neck, and above the eye. Individual cysts are generally up to 6 mm in diameter. Each cyst has a single pore from which dark fluid may ooze. The surface of the mass is usually crusty and ulcerated. Cut surfaces of nodular masses show multiple cysts containing brownish fluid. Microscopic examination of fluid reveals many trematode eggs with brown walls. Almost hemispherical, 4-5 mm wide trematodes usually are found in pairs within each cyst, but some cysts may contain a single or no parasite.

***Collyriclum faba* infection. A.** Cutaneous mass of multiple small cysts over the abdomen of a Eurasian blackcap (*Sylvia atricapilla*) in Slovakia. **B.** Single cutaneous cyst on the back of a goldcrest (*Regulus regulus*) in Slovakia. **C.** Small cutaneous cyst at the base of the lower beak of a blue-gray tanager (*Thraupis episcopus*) in Costa Rica. **D, E.** *Collyriclum faba* cysts on the head (**D**) and leg (**E**) of a willow warbler (*Phylloscopus trochilus*). *(Photos A, B, C courtesy of Dr. Ivan Literak, Slovakia. Photos D, E. Courtesy of Turkish Journal of Zoology, © TÜBİTAK).*

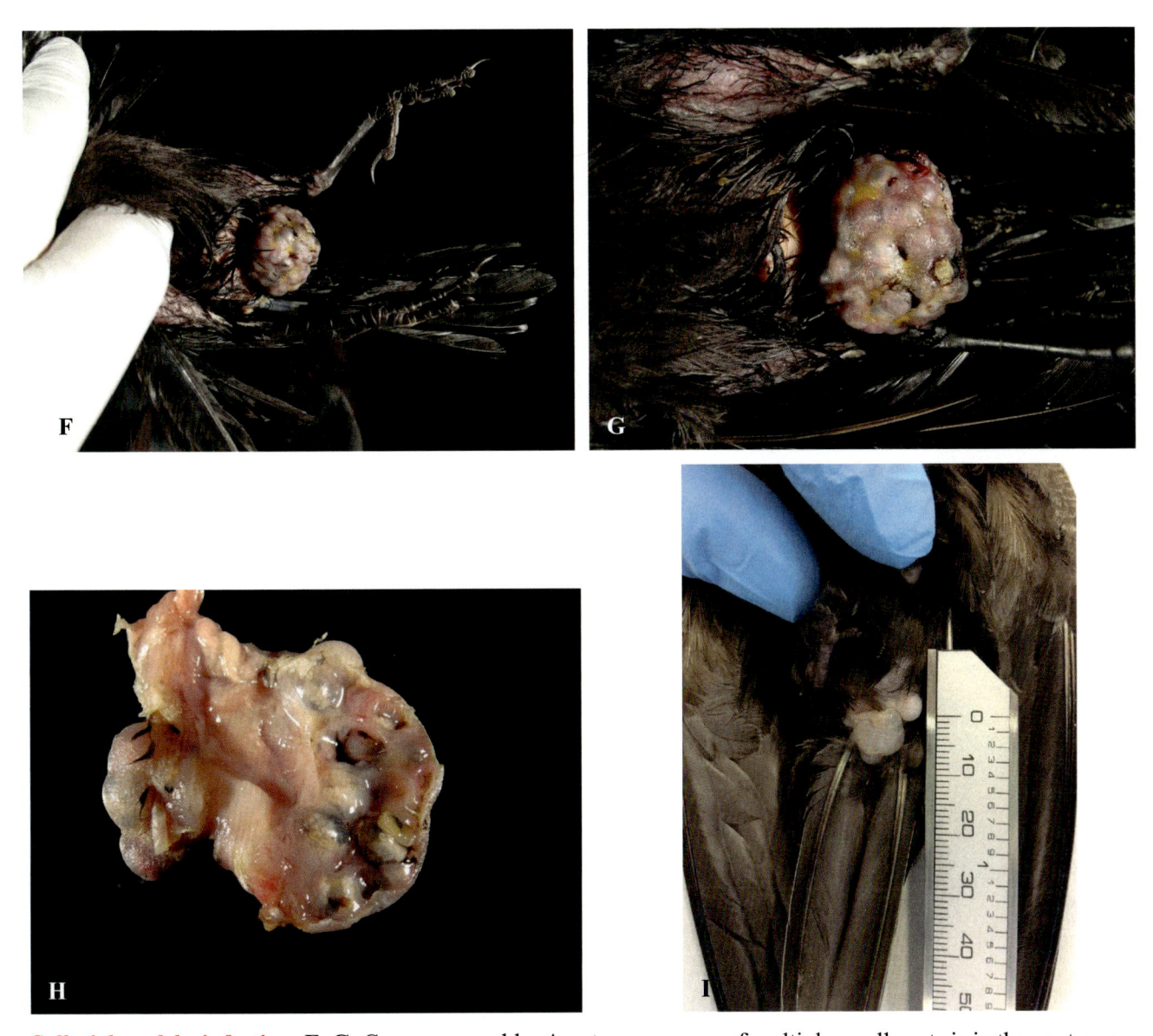

Collyriclum faba infection. **F, G.** Common grackle. A cutaneous mass of multiple small cysts is in the vent area. Surface of the mass is crusty and ulcerated. **H.** Cut surface of the mass in **G** shows cystic spaces within which *Collyriclum faba* resides, usually in a pair. **I.** Common swift (*Apus apus*). Few thin-walled cutaneous cysts are at the margin of the vent. *(Photos F, G, H. courtesy of Dr. Arno Wuenschmann, USA. Photo I. courtesy of Dr. Stamatios Alan Tahas, Switzerland).*

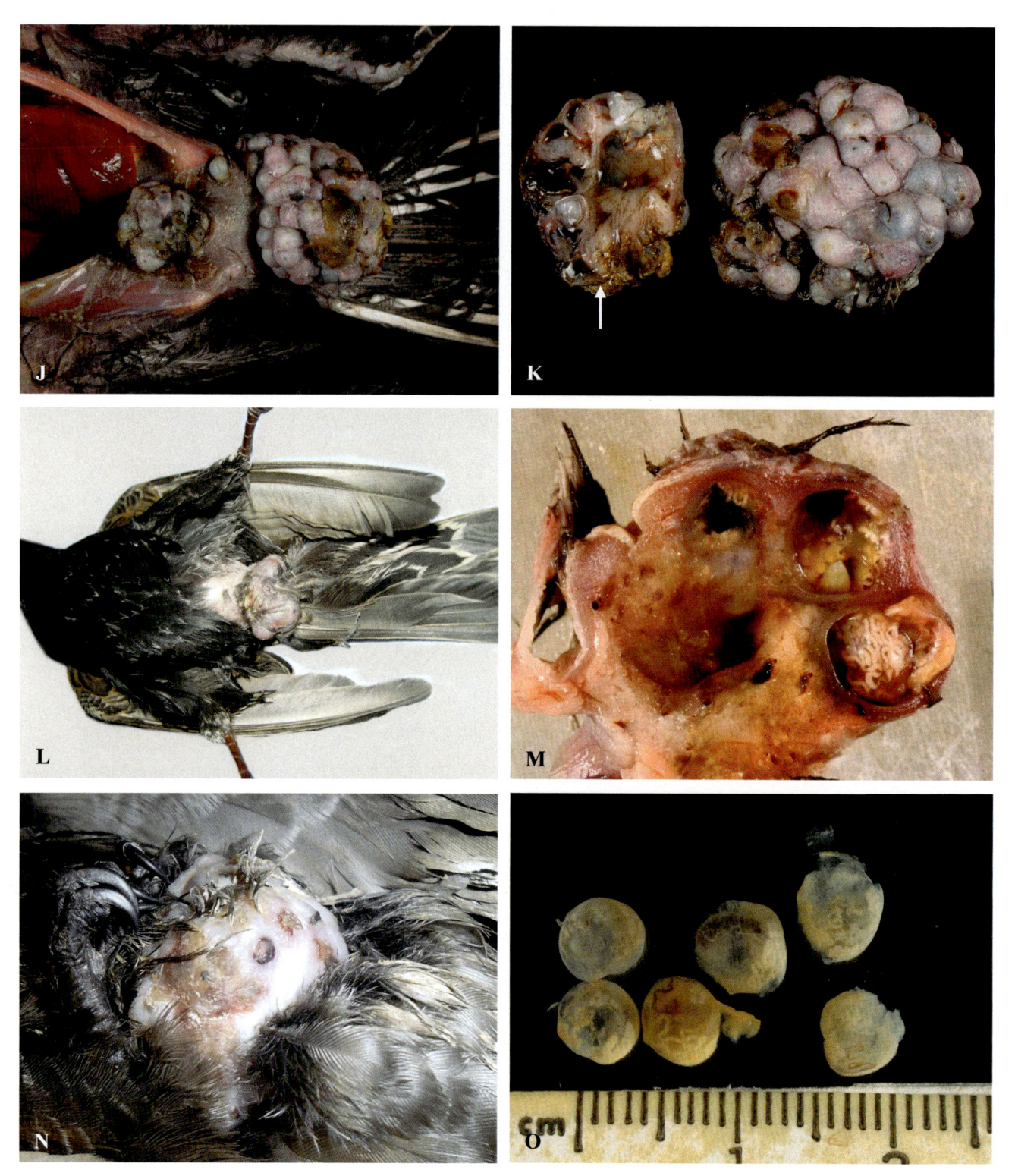

***Collyriclum faba* infection. J, K.** Crow. Two cutaneous masses of multiple small cysts. The large mass is in the vent area. The small mass is over the abdomen. The surface of the masses is multifocally crusty and ulcerated. Note the single pores in each cyst. The cut surface of the small mass (arrow) shows cystic spaces filled with dark fluid. **L.** Starling. Nodular subcutaneous cysts in the vent area. **M.** Cut surface of the mass in J shows cystic spaces containing brown fluid and small trematodes (*C. faba*). **N.** Mass with irregular, crusty, and ulcerated surface over the abdomen of a pallid swift (*Apus pallidus*). The cut surface of the mass is cystic. **O.** Cysts from *Collyriclum faba* cutaneous lesion in a cardinal. Each cyst contains a pair of trematodes. *(Photos J, K, O. Courtesy of Dr. Arno Wuenschmann, USA. Photos L, M. Courtesy of Dr. Arnaud Van Wettere, USA. Photo N. Courtesy of Dr. Carla Maia, Portugal).*

Lice, Mites, and Ticks

Lice. Poultry lice are small, straw-colored insects with a flattened body, six legs, elongated abdomen, and broad, round head. Lice infest most species of birds and several species occur on each type of poultry. They spend their entire life cycle on the bird and are primarily spread from one bird to another by close contact. Spread from one house to another is via people, fomites, or flies (phoresis). Infestations tend to be more severe in fall and winter. Free-range flocks are more likely to be infested than intensively managed commercial poultry flocks.

In contrast to lice on mammals, which pierce the skin and feed on blood, poultry lice have chewing mouthparts and do not puncture the skin; feeding on keratin debris and feathers. However, they may ingest blood if they chew into the shaft of young quill feathers. Poultry lice tend to be host-specific and usually infest specific areas of the body. They only survive for 3-6 days away from the host and cannot survive on humans or other mammals including pets. Several species of lice infest chickens, but the most common ones are the body louse (*Menacanthus stramineus*), shaft louse (*Menopon gallinae*), and head louse (*Cuclotogaster heterographa*).

During its 3-week lifespan, a female louse lays 50-300 eggs (commonly called 'nits') and glues them to host feathers. Eggs of the chicken body louse are found in clusters at the base of feathers around the vent, while eggs of the shaft louse are individual at the base of feather shafts or along the feather barbs in the breast and thigh regions. Masses of eggs at the base of feathers on the head and upper neck are produced by head lice. Eggs are elongated, white, and have a translucent wall. Eggs persist after they hatch, but a small hole can be seen in them when they are empty. Nymphs hatch from the eggs in about 4-7 days. During hatching, eggs open at one end where a small cap is lifted from the egg. Nymphs undergo several molts reaching adulthood in 2-3 weeks. Louse eggs can usually be found by carefully examining the skin and feathers of the bird around the vent, underside of the wings, head, and thighs. Lice move quickly on the skin and feathers when the feathers are parted. Clinical signs in heavily infested birds include lethargy, decreased appetite, reduced egg production, weight loss, skin redness and scabs, feather pulling, bald spots, and dull, rough, ragged-looking feathers.

Mites. Mites are just visible without magnification. They are arachnids that have a body that is not segmented and 8 legs. Mites are not as host specific as lice. The life cycle of mites is egg → larva → nymph → adult. Several different kinds of mites infest poultry.

Northern fowl mite (*Ornithonyssus sylviarum*). Northern fowl mite is a blood-sucking mite. It is the most common mite in commercial poultry, especially table-egg layer flocks. It commonly infests wild birds, especially sparrows and pigeons, and rodents, which introduce the mite into commercial poultry flocks unless sound biosecurity practices are in place. Northern fowl mites prefer cool temperatures (~65° F), which is the reason why infestations are a greater problem during cool weather. Mites primarily infest the area around the vent, but can be found on other parts of the body. They spend most of their time on the host. Females lay 2-5 eggs in the fluff of feathers after each blood meal. Larvae hatch from the eggs in 1-2 days. Larvae have only 6 legs in contrast to the 8 legs in nymphs and adults. Larvae molt to nymphs in about 9 hours. Nymphs molt twice, becoming adults in 4-7 days. The life cycle from egg to egg-laying adult is 5-7 days. A well-fed adult northern fowl mite can only live 3-4 weeks away from the host.

Heavy infestation causes dark discoloration and matting of feathers around the vent due to accumulation of mites and their eggs, excreta, and shed skins. Light infestations can be detected by seeing the mites when the feathers around the vent are parted. The skin in the area is irritated (red, thickened, scabby, cracked). Small ulcers dot the skin when there is a severe infestation and secondary bacterial infection. Severe infestations cause weight loss, anemia, and decreased egg production in layers and broiler chicken and turkey breeders. Fertility may also be affected. Mites appear as tiny, dark, slow moving specks. They often can be seen on hands and arms when affected birds are handled. Mites bite humans, causing redness, inching, and sometimes pain at the bite wound. *Ornithonyssus bursa* (tropical fowl mite), a mite similar to the northern fowl mite, is found in sub-tropical and tropical regions of the world.

Chicken mite, red mite (*Dermanyssus gallinae*). The chicken mite is primarily a warm weather pest. It has a broad host range that includes domestic and most wild birds. It is also a blood-sucking mite that feeds on birds during the night (nocturnal feeding). They leave birds during the day and hide in areas throughout the house, especially in cracks and crevices, under dirt and manure, and in nests. Females lay small groups of eggs in the environment of the poultry house. The life cycle is similar to that of northern fowl mite except this mite can survive for up to 34 weeks without feeding. Humans are also bitten by this mite, which causes small red lesions and intense itching.

Feather mites and quill mites. Feather and quill mites live in or on the feathers of birds. There are several genera that infest different avian species. Feather mites live on feather fluff and feed on feather oils, debris, and skin scales.

Quill mites live in the quill and feed on quill tissue or fluids obtained by piercing the calamus wall. Affected feathers are prone to breaking.

Ticks. While both hard and soft ticks infest a variety of birds, it is only soft ticks in the genus *Argas*, especially *A. persicus*, *A. reflexus*, and *A. walkerae* that are important poultry pathogens. They have a worldwide distribution in subtropical and tropical areas preferring warm arid regions. Ticks are not host specific and will feed on a variety of birds and other animals including humans. Adults can live for years without feeding. Similar to the northern fowl mite, nymph and adult stages of argasid ticks are intermittent, nocturnal feeders, leaving the bird during daylight to hide in cracks, crevices, or nests in the bird's environment. Feeding lasts 30 minutes to an hour. Ticks will attach to any place on the body, but legs are favored. In contrast to nymphs and adults, larval ticks are not intermittent feeders. They remain attached to the bird for 2-10 days until they are fully engorged with blood, after which, they drop off and molt to nymphs. Molting and egg laying are preceded by blood meals. Larval ticks are most numerous beneath the wing-web. Identification of a tick infestation requires finding larvae in the wing web, ticks in various stages of development in the surrounding environment, or examining the birds at night when nymphs and adults are feeding. Ticks are flat, oval, lack the scutum possessed by hard ticks, and have no visible mouthparts when viewed from above. They are 5-10 mm long, flattened, and pale brown to brown-red before feeding. After feeding, they are swollen and slate blue. Adult females can consume up to 0.3 ml blood at each feeding.

Infested birds are pale due to anemia, have small circular hemorrhagic foci where ticks have fed, especially on the legs, are weak and listless, and have depressed egg production. Severely infested birds can die from blood loss. Ticks are reservoirs and vectors of *Borrelia anserina*, the cause of spirochetosis, a serious fatal disease of poultry, and the rickettsial organism, *Aegyptianella pullorum*. When ticks are attached, birds can develop tick paralysis, characterized by flaccid paralysis of a bird that is otherwise bright, alert, and responsive.

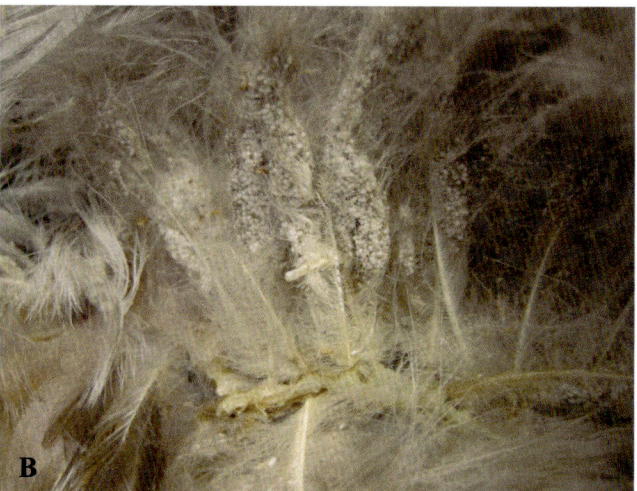

Lice infestation. Body louse. Hobby chickens. **A-C.** White clusters of eggs are located at the base of the shaft of feathers around the vent.

Lice infestation. Body louse. Hobby chickens. **D, E.** Clusters of eggs are located at the base of the shaft of feathers around the vent. In **E**, eggs with small holes are ones that have hatched and no longer contain nymphs. **F.** Eggs of body louse are elongated, white, and translucent. **G.** Body louse. The louse has six legs, broad head, and narrow segmented thorax and abdomen.

Mite infestation. Northern fowl mite. H, I. Table-egg layers. Mites appear as dark moving specks on the feathers around the vent.

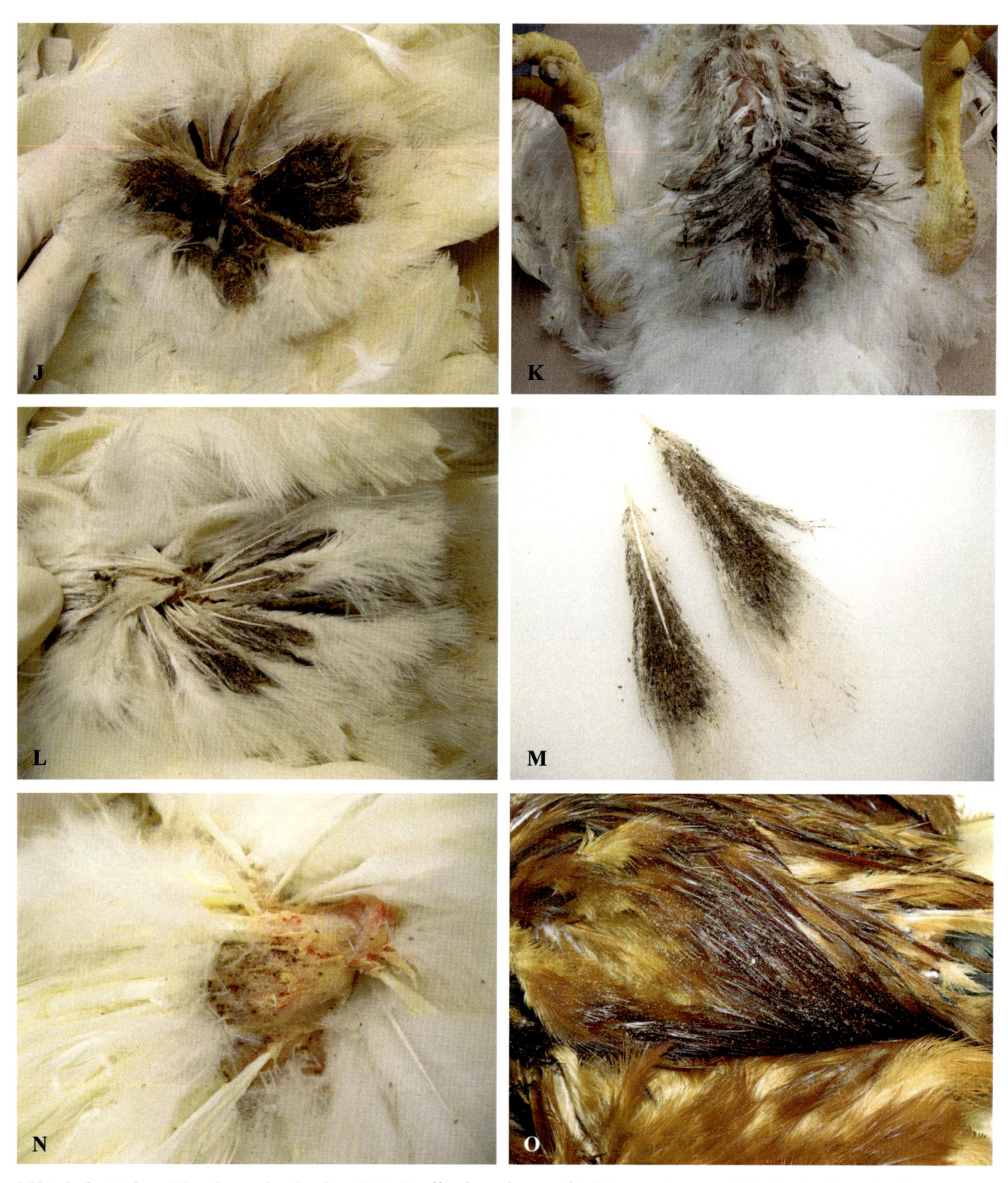

Mite infestation. Northern fowl mite. J-N. Broiler breeders and table-egg-layers. **J-L.** Dark, dirty feathers around the vent are a characteristic feature of infestation with northern fowl mites. Tiny dark mites can be seen on close examination. **M.** Two Feathers were removed from the area in **L** to show the large number of eggs, excreta, and shed skins of mites. **N.** Tiny dark mites on the surface of the skin around the vent. The skin is inflamed. **Mite infestation. Feather mite. O.** Hobby chicken. Numerous mites are on the feathers. The large population of tiny mites look like dirt material.

P

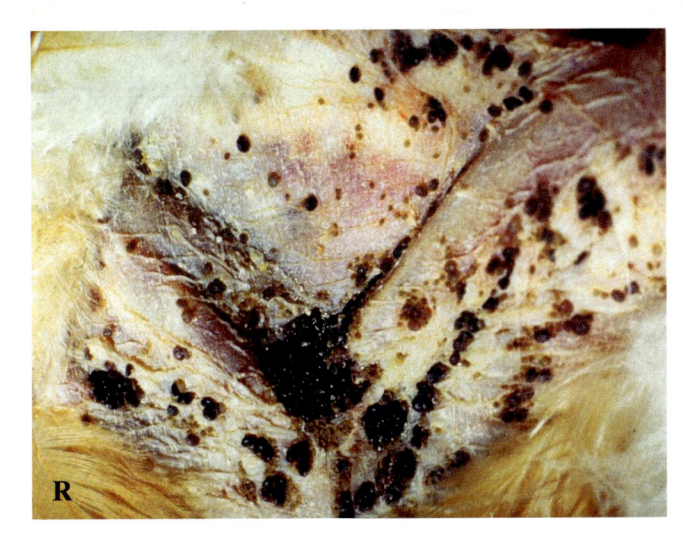

Q

Mites. P. Northern fowl mite. Note the 8 legs. The dark color is due to blood sucked from the host. **Q.** A feather mite that is different in morphology from the northern fowl mite.

Tick infestation. R. Free-range chicken, Nigeria. Numerous larval ticks, many of them engorged, are attached to the underneath side of the wing web. Punctate spots and small hemorrhages are puncture wounds where ticks were previously attached.

R

Scaly Leg Mites

Cause. Burrowing mites in the family Knemidocoptinae infest the unfeathered areas of the skin of birds producing thickened, scaly lesions. Scaly leg in poultry and raptors results from infestation with the scaly leg mite *Knemidocoptes mutans*. Other species including *K. pilae*, *K. janssensi*, *K. jamaicensis*, *K. intermedius*, *K. gallinae*, and *K. laevis* infect the legs, feet, skin, and face of a variety of commercial, captive, and free-living birds. Older chickens are affected. They lose weight, cease egg production, and, in severe cases, become lame.

Gross lesions. Feet and the unfeathered parts of the legs become excessively scaly and crusty, thickened, and discolored. Deformity of the leg and possible loss of toes occurs in severe cases. Comb and wattles are occasionally also affected.

Scaly leg caused by the mite *Knemidocoptes*. A, B. Hobby chicken. Scaly leg caused by *Knemidocoptes mutans*. Shanks and feet are markedly thickened, scaly, and discolored white. Feet are deformed. Because of the severity of the lesions, the bird was reluctant to move. **C.** Eastern towhee (*Pipilo erythrophthalmus*), male. Scaly leg caused by *K. jamaicensis*. **D.** *K. mutans* mite as seen microscopically in deep scraping of the scaly skin.

Subcutaneous Mite

Cause. The mite *Laminosioptes cysticola*.

Host. Chickens, turkeys, geese, pigeons, and pheasants are susceptible to infection with the subcutaneous mite *L. cysticola*. Free-range hobby chickens are most frequently infected. The life cycle is unknown.

Gross lesions. Small (usually 1-3 mm), oval, flattened, pale yellow to white individual hard nodules are present in the subcutaneous tissues and muscle fascia of infected birds. Rarely the mite invades other tissues including visceral organs and the central nervous system. Nodules are most frequent in the loose subcutaneous tissue of the neck, thoracic inlet, thigh, flank, breast, and vent. They are also found in the muscle fascia, especially the superficial pectoral muscles. *L. cysticola* penetrates into the subcutaneous tissue and muscle fascia where it feeds and eventually dies. When the mite dies, it is encapsulated by collagenous connective tissue, disintegrates, and undergoes mineralization. Old lesions consist of calcareous nodules composed mainly of calcium surrounded by a collagenous capsule.

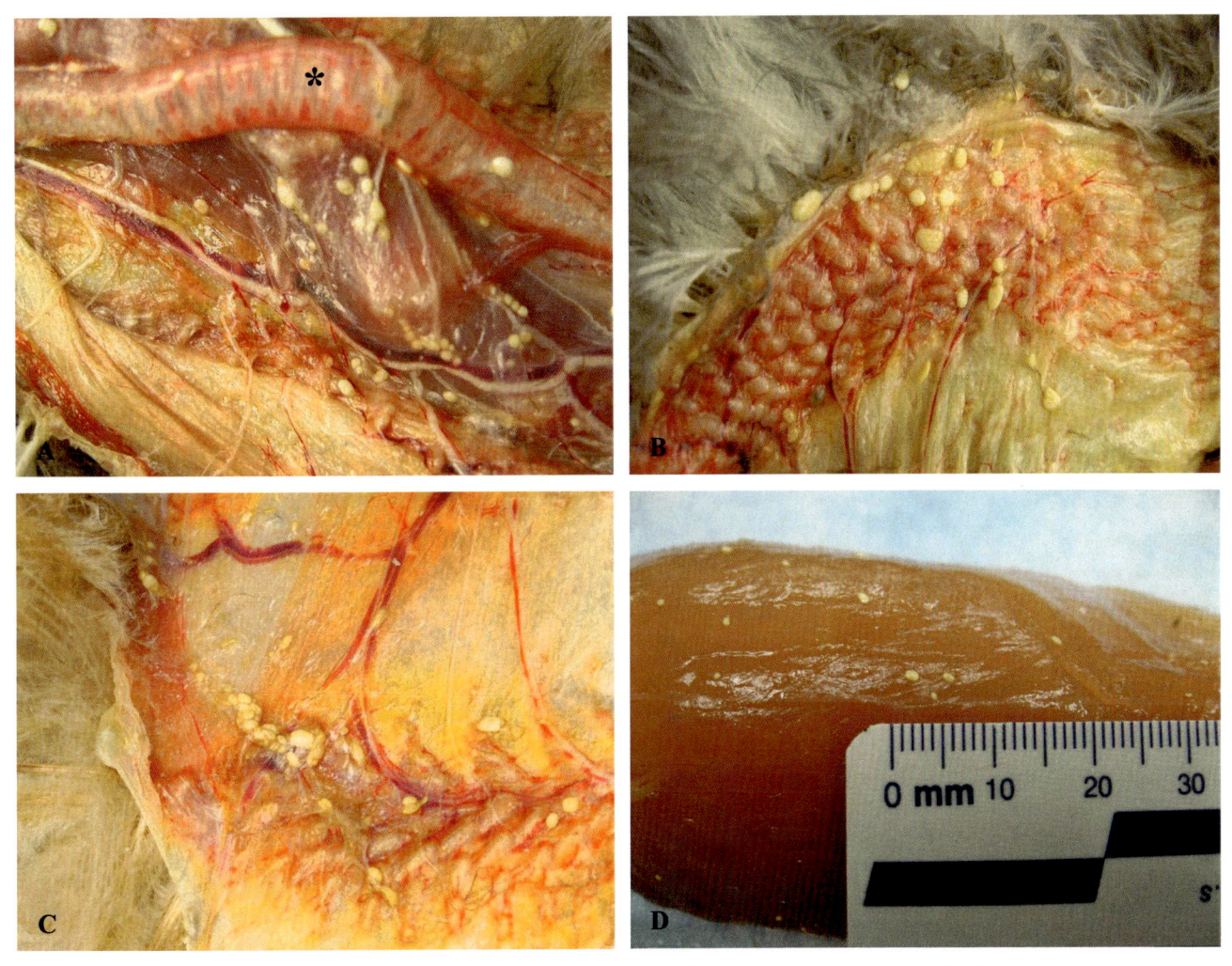

Subcutaneous mites. Hobby chickens. **A, B, C.** Small, pale yellow calcareous nodules in the subcutaneous tissue. Asterisk: trachea. **D.** Small, yellow white, calcareous nodules in the fascia of superficial pectoral muscle. *(Photo D courtesy of Dr. Richard Oliver, USA).*

Respiratory Mites

Cause. *Sternostoma tracheacolum* affects the respiratory system of small passerine birds, especially finches and canaries. *Cytodites nudus* affects the lungs and air sacs. It is uncommon in hobby chickens and other gallinaceous birds.

Gross lesions.

Sternostoma tracheacolum. Few to many mites are present in the tracheal lumen, interclavicular and thoracic air sacs, and sometimes on the outer surface of the larynx. They are usually present in the interclavicular air sacs that cover the internal surface of the sternum. Mites are visible through the tracheal wall as tiny, pinhead-sized, approximately 0.5 mm, black spots. Excess mucus surrounding mites may be found in the trachea. Mites may also be found in the abdominal cavity. Thoracic and interclavicular air sacs are thickened and contain yellow exude when mites are present. Lungs may have reddened foci.

Cytodites nudus. Small white dots moving slowly over the surface of the air sacs are seen in birds infected with air sac mites. Mites are also present in other parts of the respiratory system including pneumatic bones. Controversy exists concerning their virulence. Light infections tend to be inapparent while heavy infections are associated with clinical respiratory signs, emaciation, reduced egg production, airsacculitis, and pneumonia. Microscopically, mites cause multifocal granulomatous pneumonia and airsacculitis.

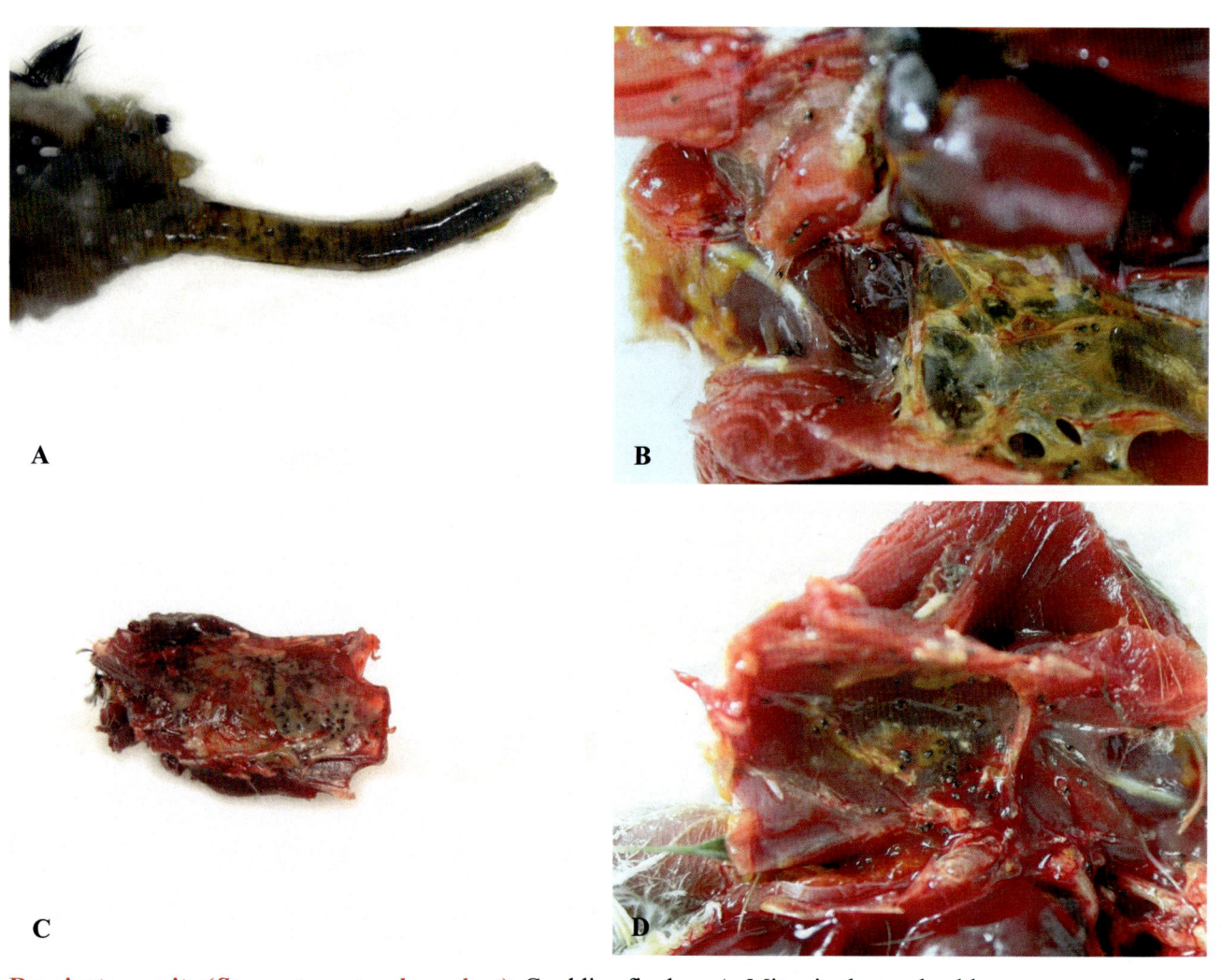

Respiratory mite (*Sternostoma tracheacolum*). Gouldian finches. **A.** Mites in the tracheal lumen are seen through the tracheal wall as black spots. **B.** Mites (black material) are in the thoracic air sac and possibly the interclavicular air sac. A thin yellow layer of exudate is present. **C, D.** Mites are in the interclavicular air sac on the inner surface of the sternum.

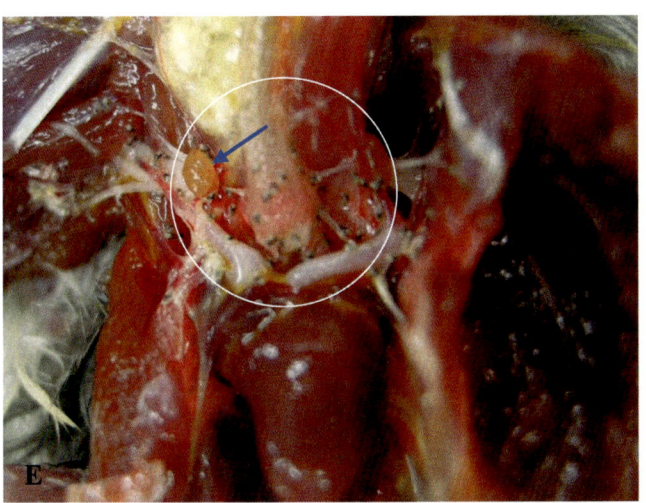

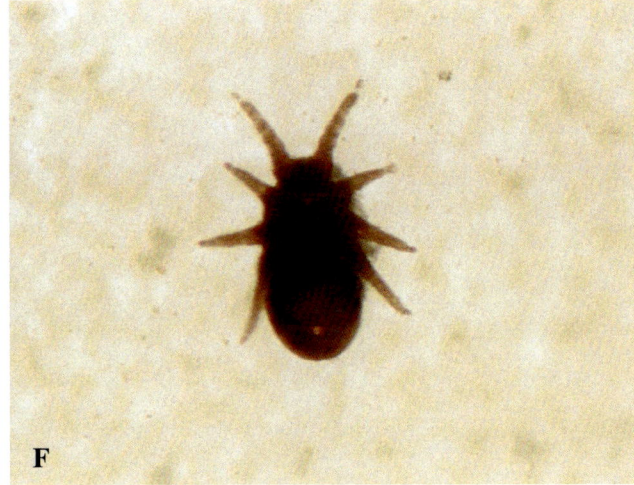

Respiratory mite (*Sternostoma tracheacolum*). Gouldian finches. **E.** Mites (dark spots in the circled area) in the interclavicular air sac. Arrow: thyroid gland. **F.** The mite *Sternostoma tracheacolum*.

Nutritional Encephalomalacia

Cause. Nutritional encephalomalacia results from low vitamin E in the diet, a high level of unsaturated fat in the diet, or enteric disease that causes malabsorption of lipids. Vitamin E is comprised of 8 lipid-soluble, naturally occurring compounds that include four tocopherols ($\alpha, \beta, \gamma, \delta$) and four tocotrienols ($\alpha, \beta, \gamma, \delta$). α-tocopherol has the highest biological activity and defines vitamin E activity. Vitamin E (α-tocopherol) is an antioxidant located mainly in the cell membrane. Its major function is to protect membrane lipids from oxidative damage (peroxidation) by endogenously produced lipid peroxyl radicals. Biologically produced reactive oxygen species, primarily superoxide anion and hydrogen peroxide, react with phospholipids in cell membranes to form peroxyl radicals (lipid peroxyl radicals), which damage membrane polyunsaturated fatty acids and initiate a chain propagation. Vitamin E is a potent scavenger of peroxyl radicals that stops the chain propagation of the radicals.

Clinical signs. Onset of clinical signs is usually abrupt. Young chickens and turkeys between 2 and 4 weeks of age are most often affected. This age correlates with depletion of maternally derived vitamin E from the liver and the need to replace it from the diet. Affected birds exhibit ataxia, backward or downward retraction of the head, somersaulting forwards or backwards, and lateral recumbency with paddling of the legs. Incoordination is more evident when birds are stimulated. Terminally, there is prostration followed by death.

Gross lesions. In mild cases, the cerebellum is swollen, soft, meningeal surface is edematous, and there is flattening of cerebellar gyri. In more advanced cases, the surface of the cerebellum often has petechial to diffuse hemorrhages, blanched areas, or brown to yellow-green, opaque areas indicative of necrosis. Cerebellar gyri may be so flattened that they are barely recognizable. Coning of the cerebellum through the foramen magnum is seen in severe cases. Lesions may be focal and barely recognizable, or extensive and involve most of the cerebellum. In cases of very severe vitamin E deficiency, the cerebellum becomes diffusely hemorrhagic and bright red. Turkey poults tend to be more affected than chicks. Turkeys also develop a form of vitamin E deficiency characterized by bilateral poliomyelomalacia of the lumbar spinal cord with minimal involvement of the brain.

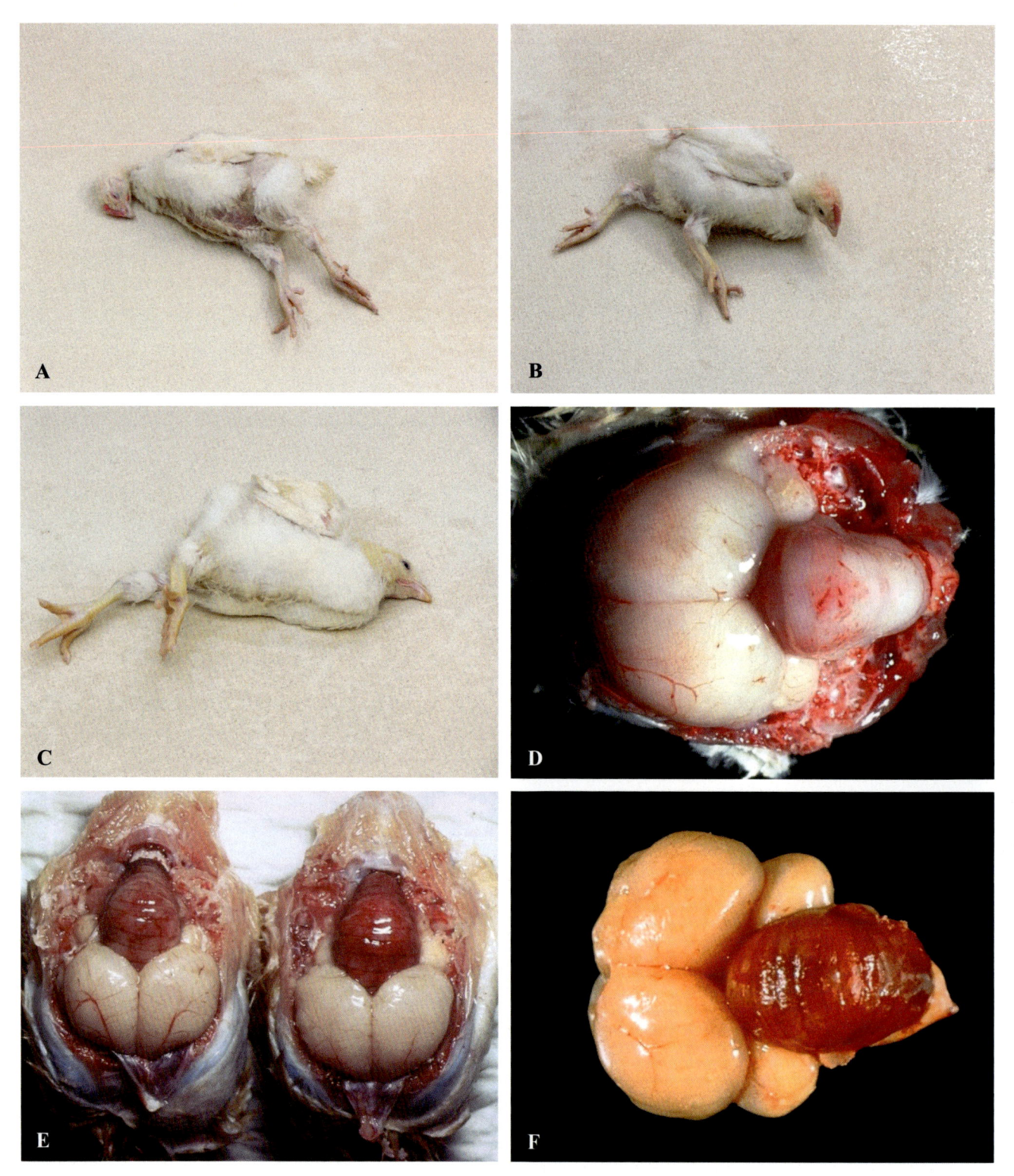

Nutritional encephalomalacia. A, B, C. 4-week broiler breeder males. Birds are on their sides and cannot stand. The bird in **A** is prostrate. **D.** 4-week layer pullet. Cerebellum is swollen, discolored with focal pallor, gyri are flattened, sulci are no longer visible, and there are multifocal hemorrhages. Note coning of cerebellum. **E, F.** 3-week turkey poults. Cerebella are similar to those in D except they are markedly hemorrhagic. This lesion is commonly referred to as "cherry brain".

Rickets

Rickets results from a nutritional deficiency. It is characterized by softening of bones due to inadequate mineralization of osteoid. Depending on severity, multiple bones become deformed as the birds grow. In chickens and turkeys, rickets usually occurs between 2 and 5 weeks of age, although it can occur in older birds. Bone deformities often persist for extended periods of time. Evidence of previous rickets can be found in adult birds.

Cause. (1) Dietary deficiency of calcium, vitamin D_3, and/or phosphorous. (2) Imbalance in calcium to phosphorous ratio in the diet (i.e., excess calcium or phosphorous). Excess calcium or phosphorus in the diet favors formation of calcium-phosphate complexes that make calcium or phosphorus unavailable for absorption from the intestine. (3) Excess dietary vitamin A interferes with vitamin D_3. (4) Small intestinal villous damage or atrophy resulting from enteric viral or protozoal (particularly coccidiosis) infections cause malabsorption of nutrients, especially lipids including fat-soluble vitamins.

Clinical signs. Affected chickens and poults stand and are reluctant to walk. They may try to walk a few steps in an unsteady stiff gate before squatting down on their hocks. Some birds will drag themselves along with their wings or use their wings to balance themselves as they attempt to walk. A spraddle-leg posture is seen in chickens with rickets caused by phosphorus deficiency. Hock joints may be swollen. Birds usually look dull and are small for their age. Lack of flock uniformity is typical of rickets following intestinal disease. This form of rickets has been called 'field' or 'infectious' rickets to differentiate it from rickets caused by incorrect nutrition.

Gross lesions with calcium or vitamin D deficiency. Tarsometatarsi are rubbery and can be bent or flexed easily without breaking. The beak is more pliable than normal. Lesions in long bones are best demonstrated in sagittal sections of the proximal medial tibiotarsi. The hallmark gross lesion is widening of the growth plate, which appears as a pale gray to white smooth band. Mushrooming of cartilage occurs in calcium/vitamin D deficiency. In advanced cases, nodular enlargements of the ribs are seen at their articulations with the vertebral column (beading, rachitic rosary). Ribs tend to bend, resulting in irregular spaces between them and the thorax becomes flattened. Curvature of the keel bone and bilateral enlargement of parathyroid glands may be seen.

Gross lesions with phosphorous deficiency. The sagittal section of proximal tibiotarsi shows widening of the zone of cartilage columns that extends downward from the lower margin of the physis. The zone of cartilage columns is dark and appears to consist of spicules. Overall shape of the bone remains normal.

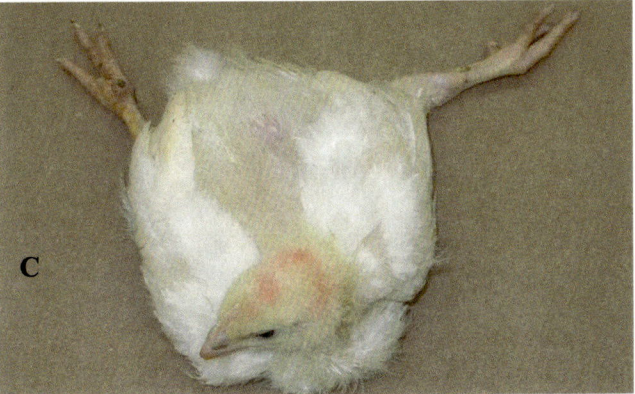

Rickets. A, B, C. 22-day broiler breeder males with rickets. Birds display spraddle-leg postures. Rickets in this case was suspected to be caused by phosphorus deficiency or excess calcium in the diet (low calcium:phosphorus ratio). Same case in figures F and G below.

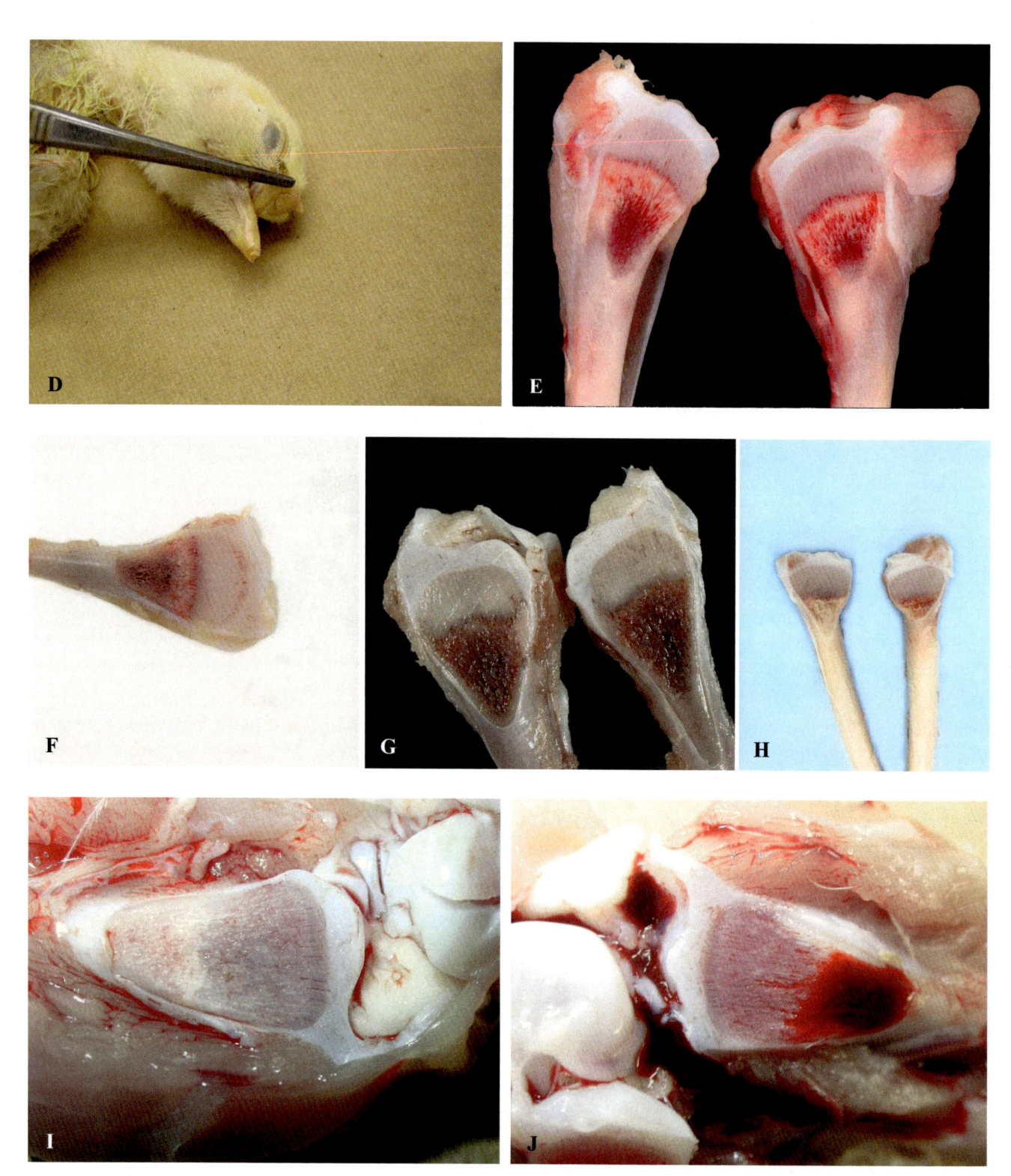

Rickets. D, F. 15-day broiler breeders. **E.** 2-week broiler chicken. **G.** 5-week broiler chicken. **H.** 8-week hobby chicken. **I, J.** 22-day broiler breeder males. **D.** Beak is pliable. **E, F, G, H.** Sagittal sections of proximal tibiotarsi showing marked widening of the growth plates. This is a characteristic lesion of rickets caused by vitamin D_3 deficiency, calcium deficiency, or excess phosphorus in the diet (low calcium to phosphorus ratio). **I, J.** Sagittal sections of proximal tibiotarsi show a wide zone of spicules of cartilaginous columns that extend from the growth plate into the diaphysis of the bone. Note that the growth plate is not widened as in **E, F, G,** and **H**. Rachitic lesions in this case are characteristic of phosphorus deficiency or excess dietary calcium.

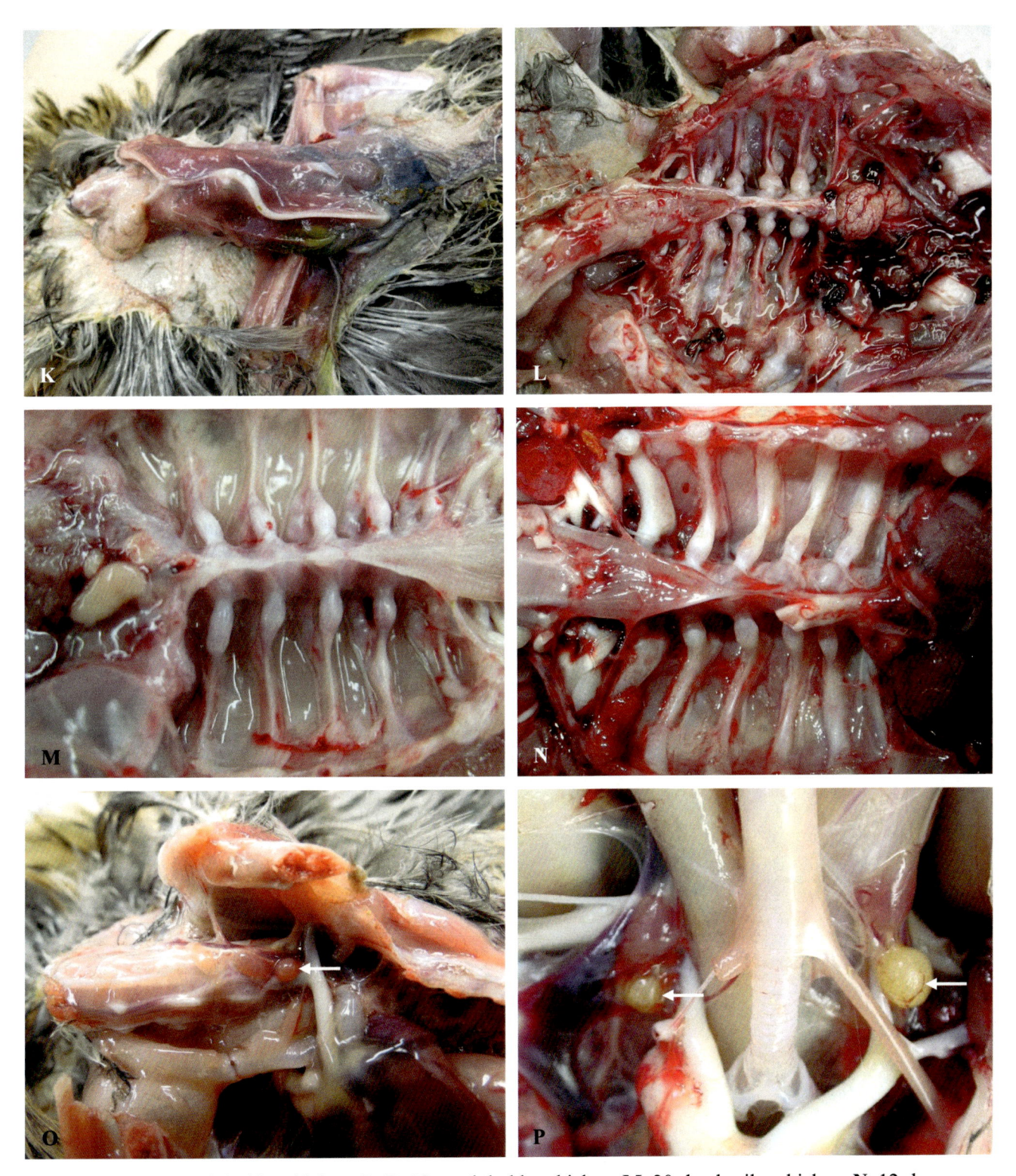

Gross Pathology of Avian Diseases: Text and Atlas   203

Rickets. K, O. 8-week hobby chicken. **L, P.** 12-week hobby chicken. **M.** 20-day broiler chicken. **N.** 12-day turkey. **K.** Chronic rickets. Lateral curvature of the keel bone. **L, M, N.** Nodular enlargements (beading) of the ribs at the articulations with the vertebrae (costovertebral articulations). This lesion is called a "rachitic rosary". Note thickening of the ribs. **O, P.** Hyperplasia of parathyroid glands (arrows). This lesion is seen in chronic rickets.

Broiler Chicken Breast Myopathy ("Wooden Breast")

Broiler breast myopathy, its most severe form commonly referred to as "Wooden or Woody Breast", has recently emerged in the broiler chicken industry as an economically significant meat quality issue. Consumer complaints of breast meat with hard, chewy areas helped recognize the condition. Grossly affected muscle is trimmed or condemned according to a new directive from the US Food Safety & Inspection Service (FSIS). Microscopically, most commercial broiler chickens have some degree of broiler breast myopathy, but only the most severely affected birds have gross lesions typical of wooden breast. Affected muscles are best appreciated by palpation. Lesions occur in the cranial part of the superficial pectoral (*pectoralis major*) muscle beneath the shoulder in the thickest part of the muscle, and extend caudally for variable distances. Affected areas are pale, hard, bulge from the surface, and may be corrugated because of accentuated swollen muscle bundles. Pale streaks are seen on cut surface. Birds with rounded rather than pointed shaped breasts are more frequently affected. Suffusive paintbrush hemorrhages occur on the surface of the breast in some birds. Less frequently, the breast is partially or completely covered with a slimy pale yellow film. In some cases this has been confused with inflammatory process but there is no caseation. White striping, another meat quality issue, is often more pronounced in broiler chickens with breast myopathy because of the increased interstitial space available for deposition of fat. Occurrence and severity of broiler breast myopathy increase with growth rate, but the cause of the condition remains unknown.

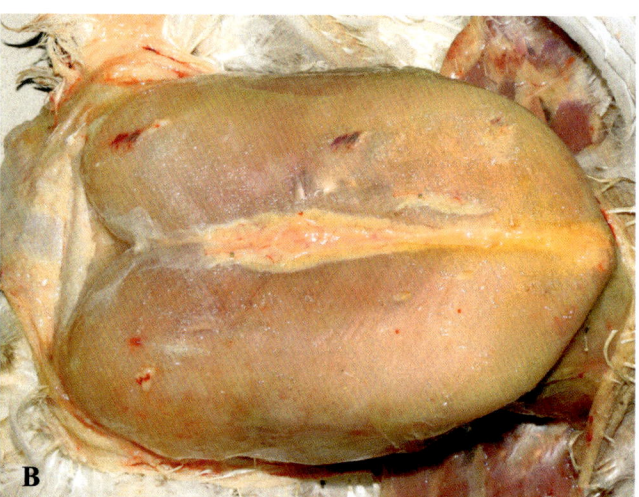

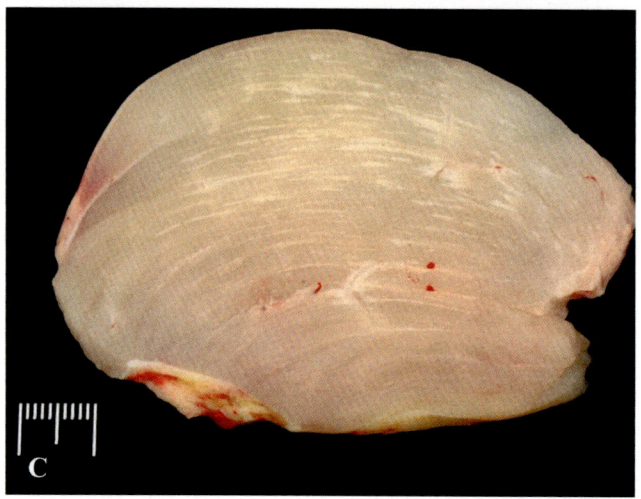

Broiler breast myopathy, *Pectoralis* muscle. **A.** 33-day broiler chicken. Breast muscles are pale, bulge beneath the shoulders, have suffusive paintbrush hemorrhages, and swollen muscle bundles that provide a corrugated appearance and feel. **B.** 54-day broiler chicken. Breast muscles are similar to those in A but are covered by a light yellow slimy film and do not have paintbrush hemorrhages. **C.** 42-day broiler chicken. Section of muscle through a severe lesion of broiler breast myopathy. Pale, linear streaks parallel to the muscle bundles are randomly distributed throughout the lesion.

Deep Pectoral Myopathy (Green Muscle Disease)

Cause. Deep pectoral myopathy results from exertional swelling of the deep pectoral muscles (supracoracoid muscles) due to prolonged violent flapping of the wings when the birds are caught and handled for routine procedures such as weighing, vaccination, and transport. Deep pectoral muscles are surrounded by a tight fascia and cannot expand when exercised. As the muscles swell within the tight fascia, their blood vessels are compressed, resulting in tissue hypoxia and ischemic necrosis.

Gross lesions. Lesions occur in the deep pectoral muscles, which function to elevate the wings. Lesions may be unilateral or bilateral. They vary considerably in appearance depending on the duration of the lesion. In the early (acute) stage, the entire muscle is pale, swollen, and edematous. Fascia over the muscle is thick, opaque, and may be covered with green, gelatinous material. When the fascia is cut, the muscle bulges through the cut. Muscle necrosis is usually limited to the middle part of the muscle, but involves the entire thickness. Necrotic muscle bundles have a boiled appearance and can be easily separated. Later, necrotic muscle turns pink or white, and green patches may be present on the surface. As the lesion progresses, the muscle becomes light green or yellow green and is dry and friable on cut surfaces. Tissue surrounding the necrotic muscle is edematous, and there may be accumulation of gelatinous fluid in the space between the superficial pectoral muscle and supracoracoid muscle. In chronic cases, the muscle is atrophied and replaced by fibro-adipose tissue.

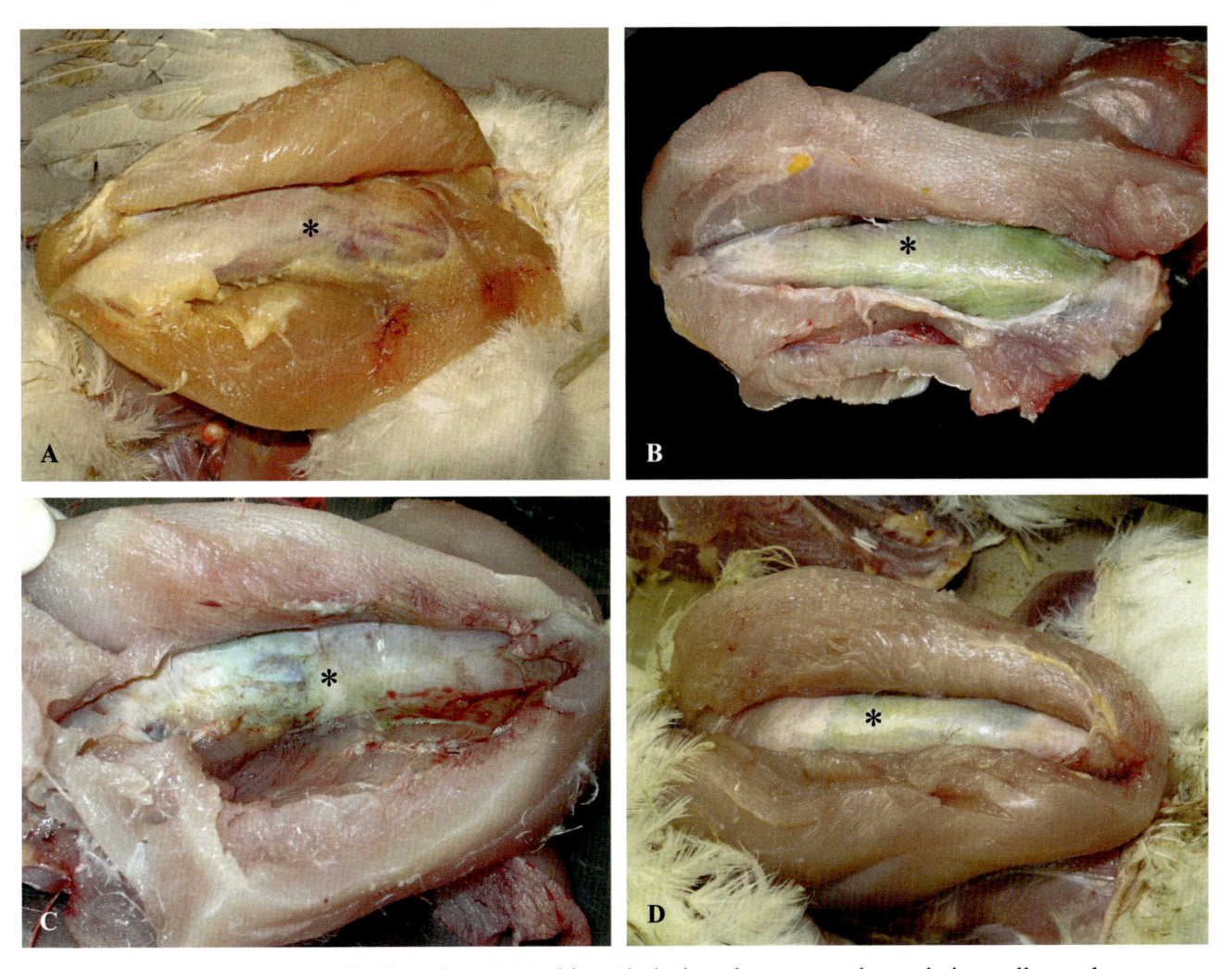

Deep pectoral myopathy. Broiler breeders. **A.** In this early lesion, deep pectoral muscle is swollen and discolored. **B, C, D.** Deep pectoral muscles (supracoracoid muscles) are discolored green. Asterisks: deep pectoral muscle.

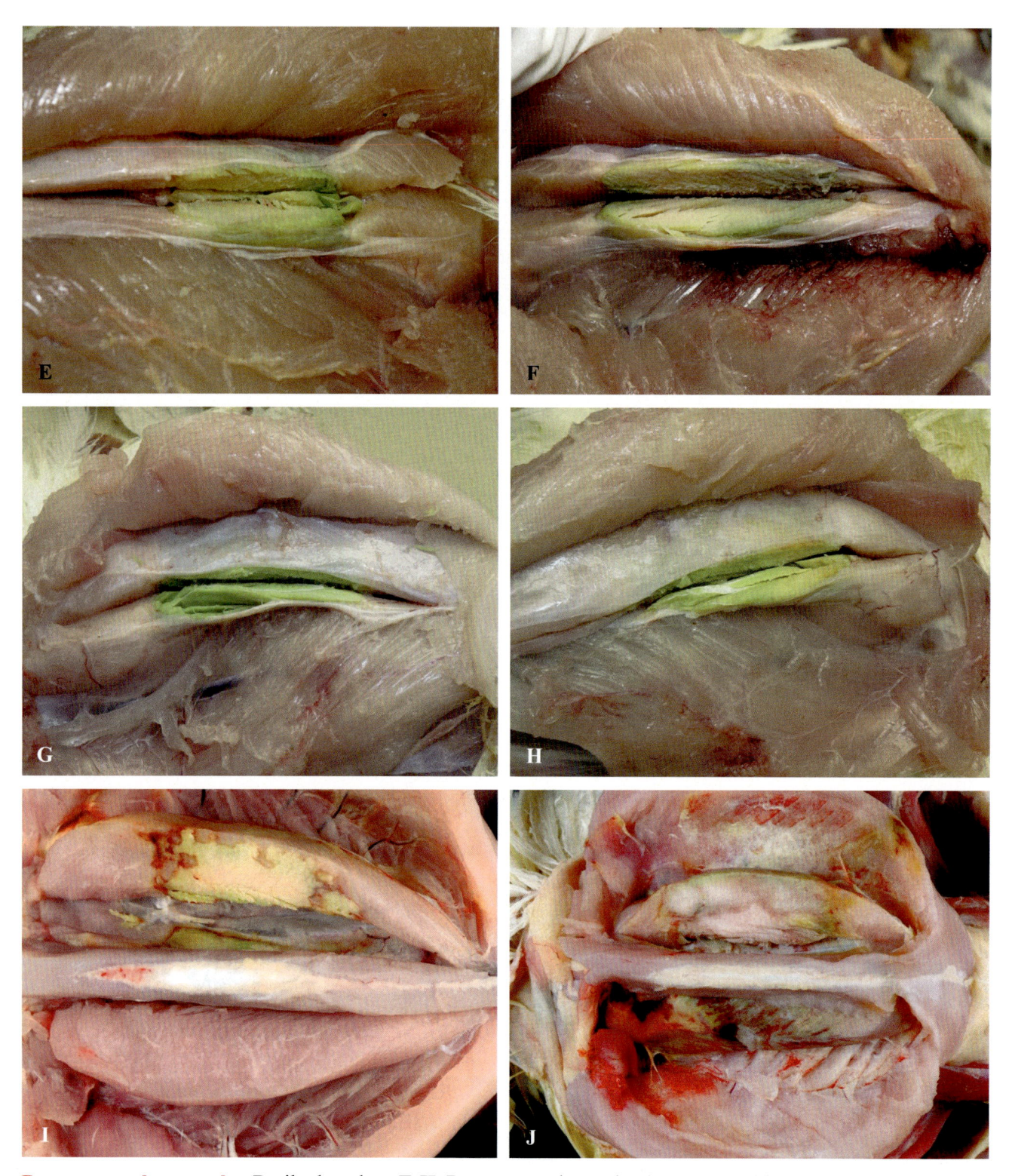

Deep pectoral myopathy. Broiler breeders. **E-H.** Deep pectoral muscles (supracoracoid muscles) are green, dry, necrotic, and friable. **I, J.** Deep pectoral muscles are necrotic and discolored green. The lesion is unilateral in **I** and bilateral in **J**.

Sternal Bursitis

The sternal bursa is a true synovial sac of variable size located in the subcutaneous tissues on the anterior aspect of the keel bone. It develops during the first few weeks of life and becomes grossly recognizable from 9-12 weeks onward in chickens and from 12 weeks onward in turkeys. The wall of the bursa is initially thin but becomes thicker and white with age due to increased connective tissue. The bursa contains trace amounts of synovial fluid. It protects the keel when the bird is resting on its breast.

Cause. Two forms of sternal bursitis occur – infectious and noninfectious. Bacteria cause infectious sternal bursitis. *Staphylococcus aureus* is the most common cause; *Escherichia coli* is isolated less frequently; and *Pasteurella multocida* may cause infectious bursitis in the later stages of fowl cholera. Noninfectious sternal bursitis, also called a breast blister, results from increased pressure on the sternal bursa. Usually this occurs when the bird is lame and rests on its breast for prolonged periods. Hard surfaces, including wire flooring, predispose to sternal bursitis. Demand for additional cushioning of the keel results in increased production of synovial fluid. Sternal bursas in these birds can become quite large and be distended with fluid.

Gross lesions. Birds with infectious sternal bursitis usually have concurrent bacterial arthritis/tenosynovitis. The early lesion is characterized by edema, slight thickening, and yellow to gray discoloration of the bursal wall. As the inflammatory process progresses, there is accumulation of thick, yellow exudate in the bursal wall and lumen, with severe damage to the bursal tissue. Inflammation may extend to the overlying subcutaneous tissues and result in cellulitis. There also may be hemorrhage. In chronic cases, caseous exudate fills the lumen of the bursa and the wall of the bursa is markedly thickened by dense connective tissue.

An enlarged, fluid-filled bursa with little to no inflammation characterizes noninfectious sternal bursitis. The wall is only mildly to moderately thickened and there is no significant fibrosis. Nodules, polyps, and villi increase the surface area of the synovium that lines the bursa. A few masses of free fibrin may be in the synovial fluid but there is no exudate or caseous material. Noninfectious sternal bursitis is seen mostly at processing where it is trimmed and the carcass is downgraded. Carcasses with infectious sternal bursitis at processing are condemned.

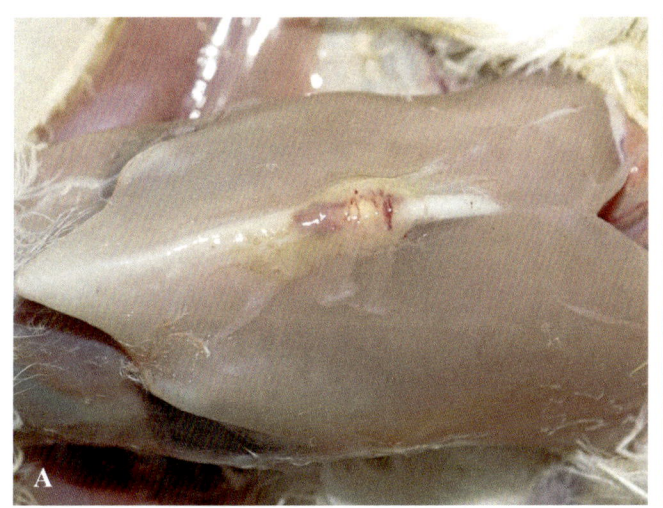

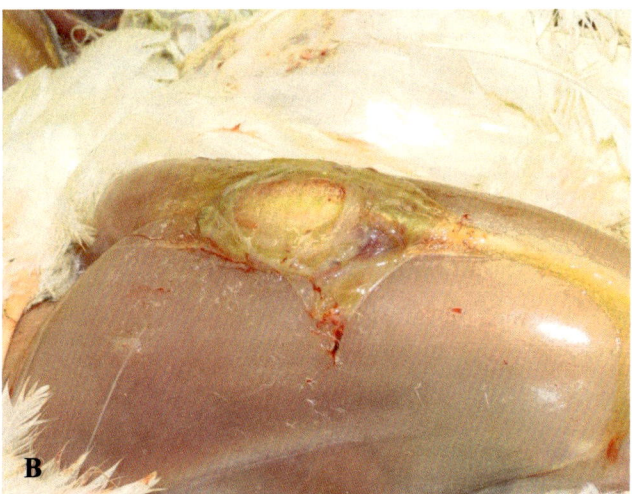

Infectious sternal bursitis. Broiler breeders (A. 6-week. B. 25-week). **A.** In this early lesion, the wall of the sternal bursa is thickened, discolored, and edematous. The bird had concurrent tenosynovitis and osteomyelitis caused by *Staphylococcus aureus*. **B.** Wall of the bursa is thickened and yellow due to inflammation.

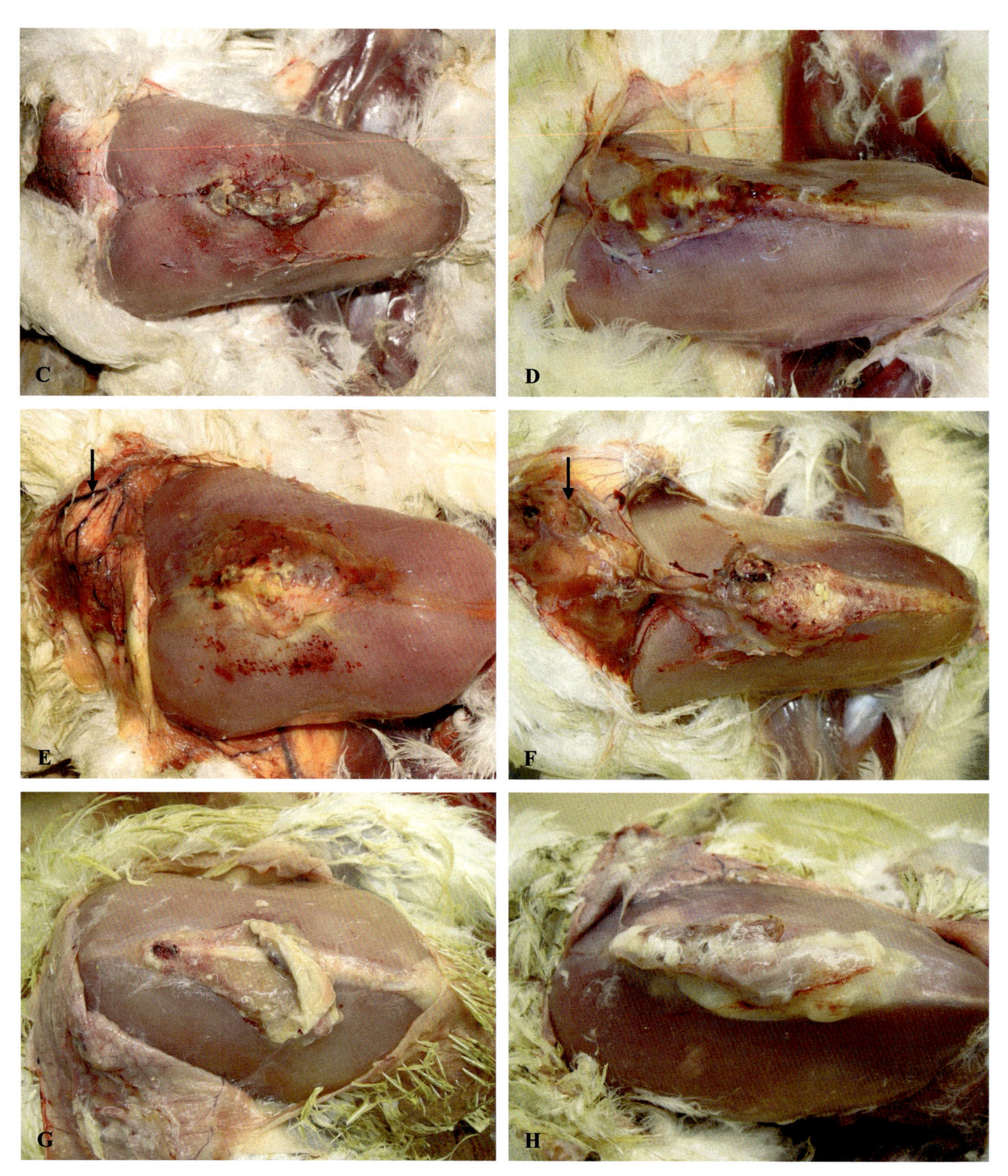

Infectious sternal bursitis. Broiler breeders (C. 31-week. D. 14-week. E. 27-week. F. 23-week. G, H. 54-week). Severe lesions of infectious sternal bursitis. **C, D** show severe inflammation of the sternal bursa and accumulation of exudate. In **D**, note hemorrhages in the severely inflamed bursa. **E, F.** Cellulitis (arrows) is present in the skin overlying the bursa. In **G** and **H**, there is yellow exudate in the affected bursas; cultures of both bursas yielded pure growth of *Pasteurella multocida*.

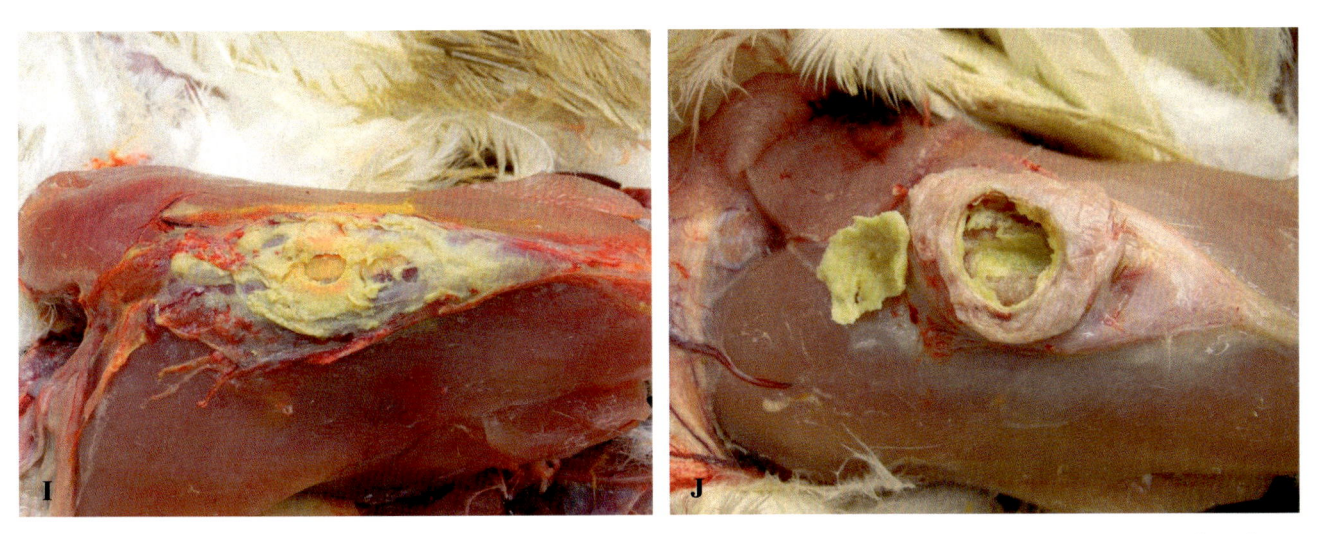

Infectious sternal bursitis. I, J. Broiler breeders (I. 27-weeks. J. 28-week). In both **I** and **J**, lesions are chronic and consist of an accumulation of caseous material in the bursa and thickening of the bursal wall due to fibrosis. Culture of the bursa in **J** yielded heavy, pure growth of *Staphylococcus aureus*.

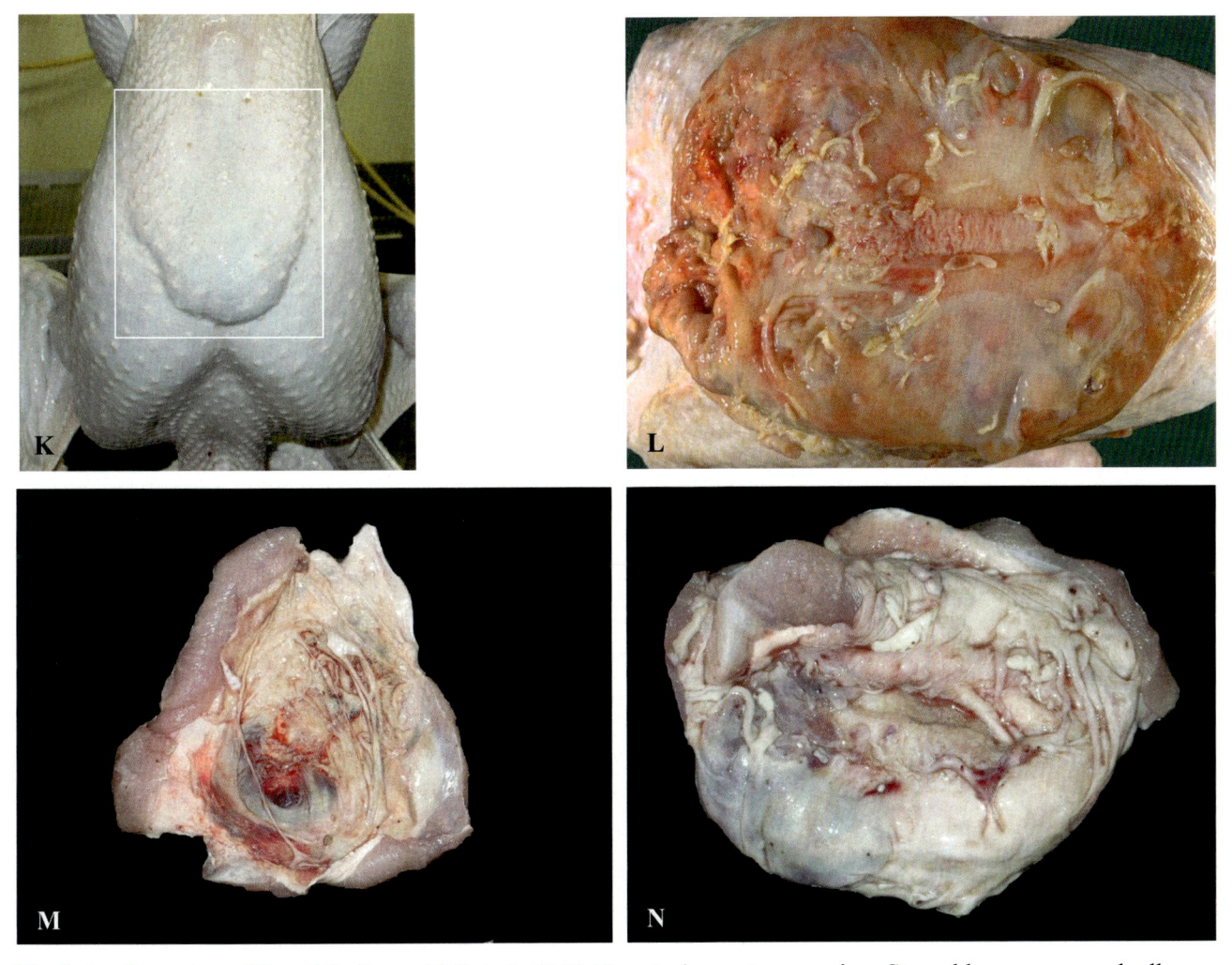

Noninfectious sternal bursitis (breast blister). K-N. Tom turkeys at processing. Sternal bursas are markedly distended and filled with excess synovial fluid. Nodules, polyps, and several villous proliferations extend into the lumen from the synovial lining. Inflammation and exudate are not present. Rectangular in K: markedly distended sternal bursa.

Ruptured Gastrocnemius Tendon

Anatomy of gastrocnemius tendon. The gastrocnemius muscle forms the entire caudal muscle mass of the lower leg and is the largest and strongest muscle of the lower leg. In most birds, it consists of 3 parts; a few passerine families have 4 parts. Two parts originate from the each of the epicondyles of the distal femur and the third originates from the medial surface of the proximal tibiotarsus. Tendons from the 3 parts unite to form a dense aponeurosis that consolidates into a single large tendon that is readily palpable above the hock (intertarsal) joint. The tendon passes over the caudal aspect of the hock joint, merges with the sheath that encloses the digital flexor tendons, and inserts on the caudal surface of the proximal tarsometatarsus. The tendon above the hock joint progressively ossifies with age at varying rates depending on the type of bird. The muscle acts to flex the stifle joint, extend the hock joint, and flex the digits.

Cause. Rupture of gastrocnemius tendons in chickens has been attributed to infectious and noninfectious factors. Tendon rupture may result from loss of tensile strength due to fibrosis occurring as a sequel to chronic infection e.g., *Staphylococcus aureus*, reovirus (reoviral tenosynovitis), or *Mycoplasma synoviae*. Spontaneous rupture of the gastrocnemius tendon may occur in chickens in the absence of any evidence of involvement of infectious agents. High slat height in broiler breeder houses has been suggested as a contributing factor to spontaneous tendon rupture. Inadequate nutrition during growth and development is considered to be another noninfectious contributing factor.

Clinical signs and gross lesions. Ruptured gastrocnemius tendons occur most frequently in older broiler breeders. Males are most frequently affected. Rupture occurs proximal to the hock joint, often at the margin of tendon ossification, and is associated with considerable hemorrhage. It may be unilateral or bilateral. If unilateral, the leg on the affected side extends laterally, or the lower leg is flexed and the bird sits on the hock joint with inward curling of the toes. If bilateral, the bird sits on both hocks with downward or inward curling of the toes. Externally, there is green or blue discoloration of the area above the hock joint, especially on the posterior aspect. An expanded firm area can be palpated. Extensive hemorrhage in the tissue is found when the discolored skin is incised. Careful dissection exposes the gastrocnemius tendon and reveals its torn ends. Partial tendon ruptures occur but are either not associated with clinical signs or cause mild lameness. Fibrosis occurring during repair of partial tendon rupture predisposes to subsequent complete tendon failure. Fibrosis of complete tendon rupture can occur in birds when only on leg is affected. There are adhesions to adjacent tissues, a large hard mass of connective tissue that is easily palpated, and impaired flexibility of the affected leg.

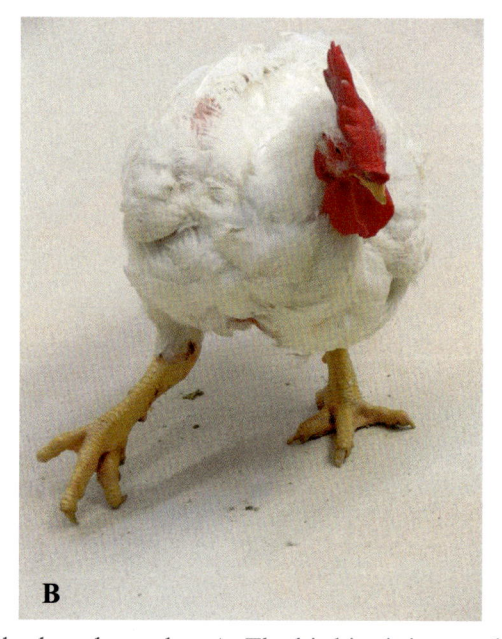

Rupture of the right gastrocnemius tendon. 37-week broiler breeder males. **A.** The bird is sitting on the right hock joint. The tibiotarsus is slightly off the ground and toes are curled downward. **B.** The right leg extends laterally, with mild downward curling of the toes.

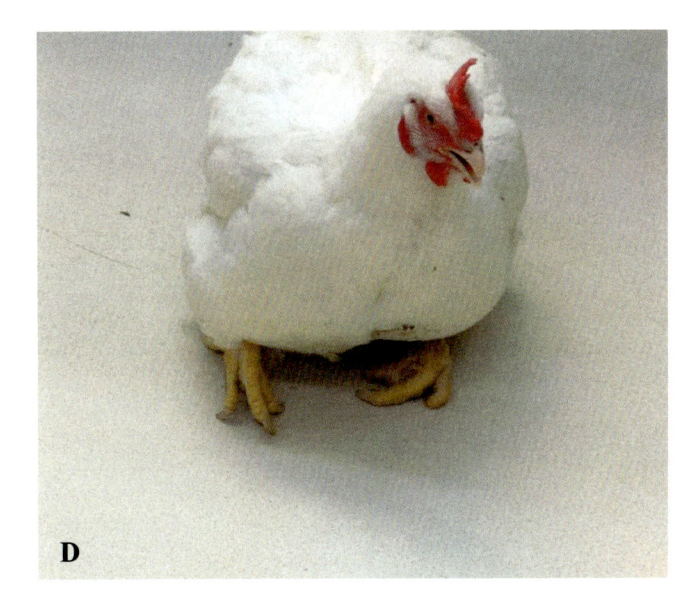

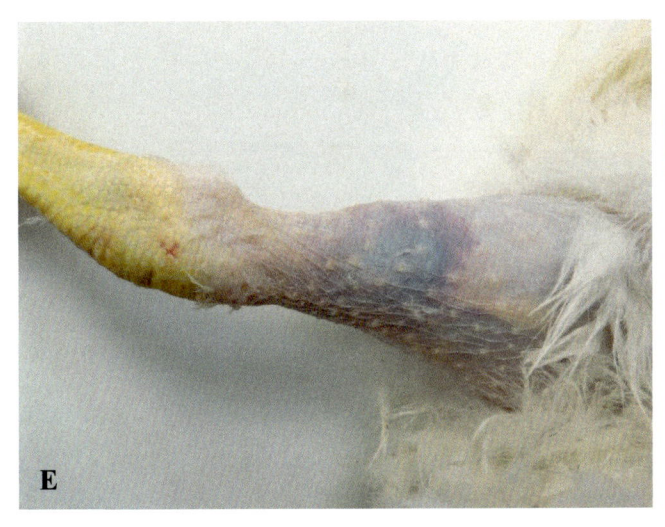

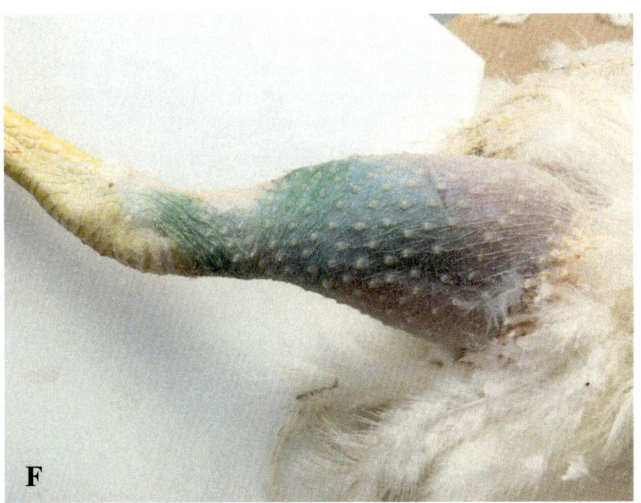

Rupture of gastrocnemius tendon. Broiler breeders (C. 37-week male, D, E, F. 30-week hens). **C, D.** Bilateral rupture of the gastrocnemius tendons in both birds. The birds are sitting on their hocks. Shanks are slightly off the ground and toes are curled downward. In **D**, note inward curling of the toes of the left leg and slight elevation of the shank and foot of the right leg. **E, F.** Blue or green discolored areas above the hock joints are characteristic lesions of ruptured gastrocnemius tendons. Discoloration is caused by hemorrhage resulting from the rupture. Advanced lesions become green due to conversion of heme from lysed erythrocytes to biliverdin.

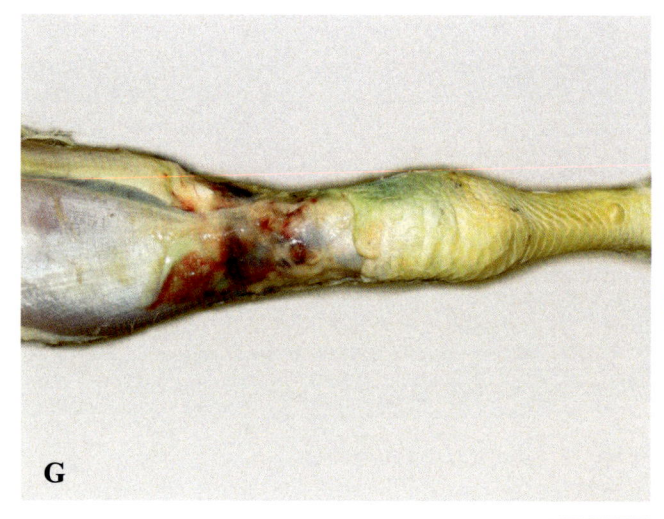

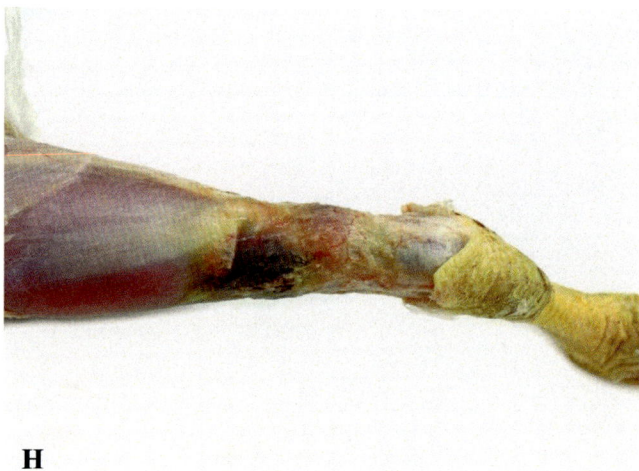

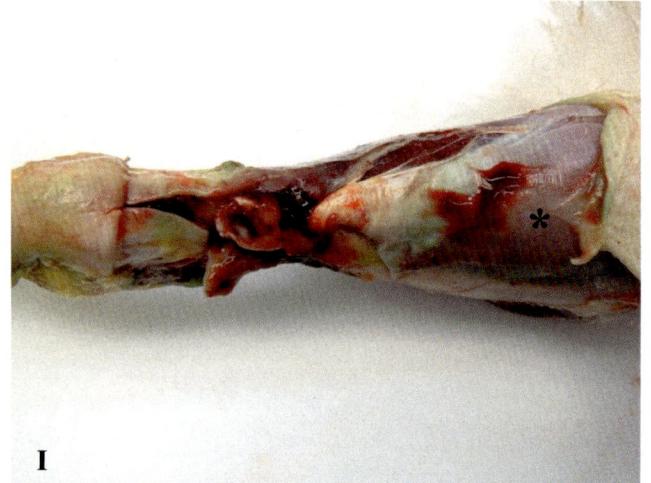

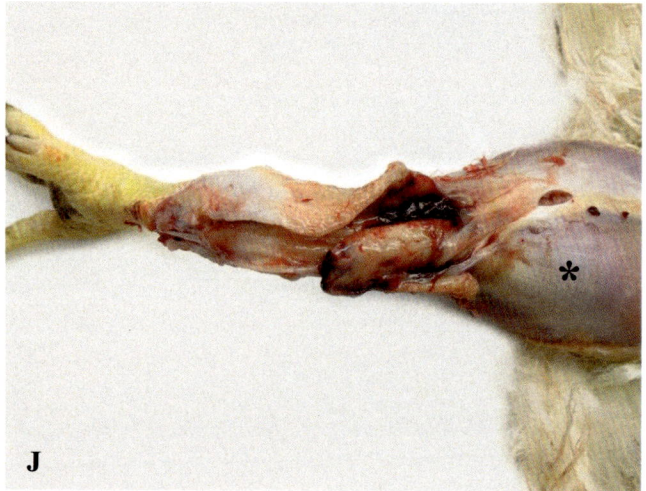

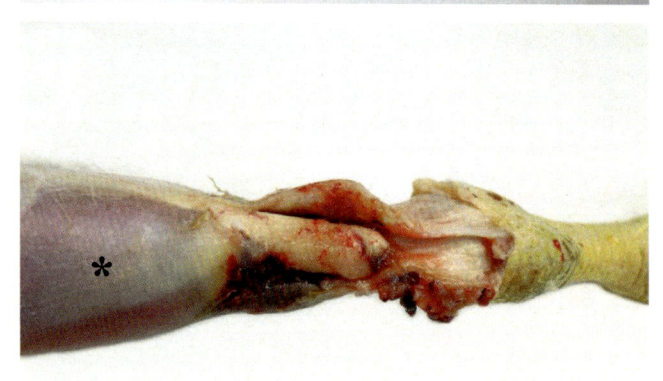

Rupture of gastrocnemius tendon. G, H. Broiler breeder hens (G. 35-week. H. 29-week). Skin is reflected to show hemorrhage just above the hock joints. Hemorrhage results from rupture of the gastrocnemius tendon. **I, J, K.** Broiler breeders (I, J. 31-week males. K. 29-week hen). Ruptured gastrocnemius tendons and marked hemorrhage above hock joints. Asterisks: gastrocnemius muscle.

Spondylolisthesis ("Kinky Back")

Spondylolisthesis in birds is a musculoskeletal disorder in which there is loss of alignment and dislocation (subluxation) of the 4th thoracic vertebra (T$_4$) [Note: Some authors identify this vertebra as T$_6$.]. T$_4$ is the only freely movable vertebra among the 5 thoracic vertebrae in several species of birds including fowls, turkeys, and quail. Cranially, T$_4$ articulates with T$_3$, which is the caudal part of the notarium, and caudally it articulates with T$_5$, which forms the cranial part of the synsacrum. In spondylolisthesis, there is ventral deviation of the cranial articulation, oblique angulation of T$_4$, and dorsal deviation of the caudal articulation. Angulation of the vertebra causes stenosis of the vertebral canal and compression of the spinal cord at the caudal articulation, which, if sufficiently severe, results in paresis (leg weakness) or paralysis. In affected flocks, examination of clinically normal broiler chickens often shows milder lesions of spondylolisthesis. Corresponding articulating vertebra deform to match the abnormal position of T$_4$. Fast-growing broiler chickens between 3 and 6 weeks of age are affected. The disease is rare in turkeys.

Clinical signs. Affected birds sit on their hock joints and tails with their feet and occasionally lower legs slightly raised off the ground. When trying to move, the birds use their wings for support, and in doing so they tend to shuffle backward, a posture characteristic of spinal cord compression. Other birds are in sterno-abdominal recumbency with legs stretched forward ("sitting dog posture"). Birds with paraplegia, lie on their sides with legs extended to the side. The back of affected birds is distinctly arched, which can be readily recognized by palpation. Dehydration and starvation may occur in severely affected birds. Mortality generally results from culling lame birds.

Gross lesions. In order to identify the lesion of spondylolisthesis, the thoraco-lumbar region of the vertebral column must be carefully cut longitudinally in the middle of the vertebral bodies along the vertebral canal. The diagnostic lesion is ventral dislocation of the anterior end of T4, with dorsal rotation of the caudal end, resulting in stenosis of the vertebral canal and compression of the spinal cord (compression myelopathy). Spondylolisthesis needs to be differentiated from spondylitis, which is characterized by necrosis and inflammation of T$_4$ and adjacent vertebrae.

Spondylolisthesis. 5-week turkey. **A.** Typical posture of a bird with spondylolisthesis. Affected birds have symmetrical paresis or paralysis. Posture is typical for birds with a spinal lesion that impinges on the spinal cord and is also seen when there is necrosis and inflammation of the spine (spondylitis) due to bacterial infection. **B.** Sagittal section of the vertebral column of this bird shows the typical spondylolisthesis deviation in the spine, compression of the spinal cord, and marked kyphosis. Birds with milder lesions may have little or no clinical signs. The disease is infrequent in turkeys compared to broiler chickens. Note the rhomboid fossa and glycogen body in the lumbar spine (arrow).

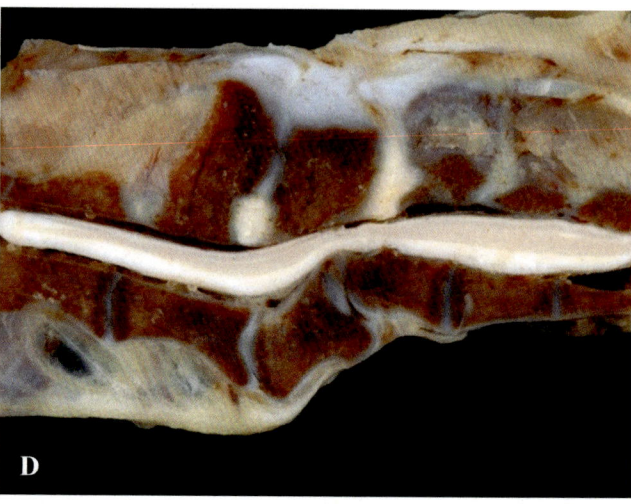

Spondylolisthesis. Broiler chickens. To diagnose spondylolisthesis, remove the thoracolumbar spine, decalcify it, and make a sagittal section. In **C** and **D**, the characteristic deviation of T4 with compression of the spinal cord is seen.

Spinal Cord Contusions in Turkeys

Vertebrae comprising the thoracolumbar spine of turkeys (and chickens) are largely fused and are included in the notarium cranially and synsacrum caudally. The next to the last thoracic vertebrae is a freely articulating vertebra (FTV) that is located between the notarium and synsacrum. Joints of the FTV are particularly labile to injury because of the considerable leverage provided by the fused vertebrae anteriorly and posteriorly and heavy musculature of the breast and legs. Excessive movement of the FTV can damage the spinal cord in the vertebral canal. Affected birds develop progressive weakness, paresis, and paralysis that begins a few days after they are handled or moved. Otherwise, they are bright, alert, and responsive. Gross lesions include possible hemorrhage, displacement, or fractures of the FTV and its joints. With time, lesions become green because of red blood cell lysis and conversion of hemoglobin to biliverdin. The spinal cord is depressed, misshapen, and has multifocal hemorrhage (hematomyelia). Birds other than turkeys may be similarly affected.

Spinal cord contusions. 30-week turkey breeder hen. **A.** Hen is unable to stand because of bilateral flaccid paralysis. **B.** Spinal cord at the free thoracic vertebra is misshapen and has multifocal hemorrhage. Note the pale green swollen area surrounding the focus of hemorrhage in the upper right.

Tibial Dyschondroplasia

Dyschondroplasia is a bone disorder characterized by persistence and accumulation of cartilage in the growth plate of bones. The lesion occurs most frequently in the proximal tibiotarsus (thus the name tibial dyschondroplasia [TD]), but it occurs in most long bones and vertebrae. Tibial dyschondroplasia occurs in different avian species, particularly meat-type chickens, turkeys, and ducks.

Cause. Despite extensive studies on TD at the morphological, biochemical, cellular, and molecular levels, it is still unclear what causes the lesion. TD is not primarily a nutrient deficiency, but the incidence and severity of TD can be influenced by nutritional and environmental factors including:

- Vitamin D3 metabolites, especially 1,25-(OH)$_2$ D3, are very effective in preventing TD. Vitamin D3 plays a major role in chondrocyte metabolism. In order for vitamin D3 to become biologically active, it must be converted (hydroxylated) in the liver to 25-(OH) D3 and then in the kidneys to 1,25-(OH)$_2$ D3. Biologically active 1,25-(OH)$_2$ D3 is required for full differentiation of chondrocytes in growth plates. Chondrocytes in TD lesions have significantly fewer receptors and a reduced affinity for 1,25-(OH)$_2$ D3 than those in normal growth plates. It is possible that chondrocytes within TD lesions have reduced ability to respond to 1,25 (OH)$_2$ D3.
- High dietary levels of sulfur amino acids (cysteine and homocysteine) increase the incidence of TD.
- Dietary copper deficiency may play a role in increasing the incidence of TD.
- High dietary levels of phosphorus (P) relative to calcium(Ca) increase the incidence and severity of TD in broiler chickens. A Ca:P ratio approaching 1:1 results in the highest incidence. Increasing the Ca:P ratio decreases the incidence and severity, but does not totally eliminate TD.
- Excess dietary chloride is an effective dietary anion for inducing TD. Excess phosphorus and chloride are believed to cause TD by causing metabolic acidosis, which interferes with conversion of vitamin D3 to 1,25-(OH)$_2$ D3.
- Dietary electrolyte imbalance may be a factor in TD development.
- Thiram, a sulfur containing dithiocarbamate used as a grain fungicide, is a potent inducer of TD.
- Fusarochromanone (from *Fusarium* spp.) is a mycotoxin that is capable of inducing TD.
- TD has a strong genetic component. The incidence of TD can be manipulated by genetic selection.
- TD may be a consequence of rapid growth in meat-type poultry. In these birds, growth and maturation of long bones may be unable to match the rate of body growth.

Due to the various, seemingly unrelated factors that influence occurrence of TD, it is possible that there are different mechanisms that impact the ability of chondrocytes to fully differentiate. Subsequent accumulation of incompletely differentiated chondrocytes results in the TD lesions.

Pathogenesis. The growth plate (physis) of bones consists of cartilage, which, through a process of proliferation, maturation, differentiation, and calcification leads to elongation (longitudinal growth) of bones. Histologically, the growth plate consists of four zones: (1) zone of proliferation of chondrocytes, (2) a thin zone of transitional or prehypertrophied chondrocytes, (3) zone of maturation and hypertrophy of chondrocytes, and (4) zone of degeneration and calcification. Chondrocytes in the growth plate proliferate, become hypertrophied (fully mature), die, and calcify before deposition of bone matrix (osteoid) on the calcified cartilage by osteoblasts occurs. Full maturation or differentiation of chondrocytes is a prerequisite for calcification and deposition of bone matrix. Failure of this sequence in the growth plate can occur at different steps and result in pathological conditions. For example, in rickets caused by vitamin D$_3$ or calcium deficiency, chondrocytes proliferate but fail to hypertrophy and become mature. In TD, there is incomplete differentiation (maturation) of chondrocytes, which results in a grossly visible mass of prehypertrophied chondrocytes in the growth plate. TD lesions develop because the collagen matrix is highly cross-linked making it impervious to vascular invasion and resistant to resorption by osteoclasts.

Gross lesions. TD lesions are recognized as a mass (plug) of white, opaque, avascular cartilage that extends from the growth plate into the proximal end of tibiotarsi. Sometimes, the lesion has areas of light green discoloration because of staining from breakdown of red blood cells. The size of the cartilage mass is variable. It can exist as a small lesion within a discrete area of the growth plate, or occupy the metaphysis along the entire width of the growth plate. Lesions occur most frequently on the medial side of the tibiotarsus. TD may be unilateral, but is more typically bilateral; lesion severity is generally similar in both legs. In young birds, TD lesions must be differentiated from those in calcium/vitamin D$_3$ rickets. Hemorrhage along the margin of TD lesions results from leg trauma. Osteomyelitis (OM) also occurs at the margin of some TD lesions. OM is a vascular lesion whereas TD is an avascular lesion. However, the abnormal blood vessels that are unable to penetrate TD lesions may provide sites for bacteria in the blood stream to lodge and initiate inflammation.

Small lesions of TD are likely asymptomatic, whereas large lesions can result in abnormal gaits and leg deformities. As birds grow, uneven and abnormal bone growth can lead to increased plateau angle and bowing of the tibiotarsus (varus deformities). Affected birds may exhibit stiff or hobbling gait and be reluctant to move.

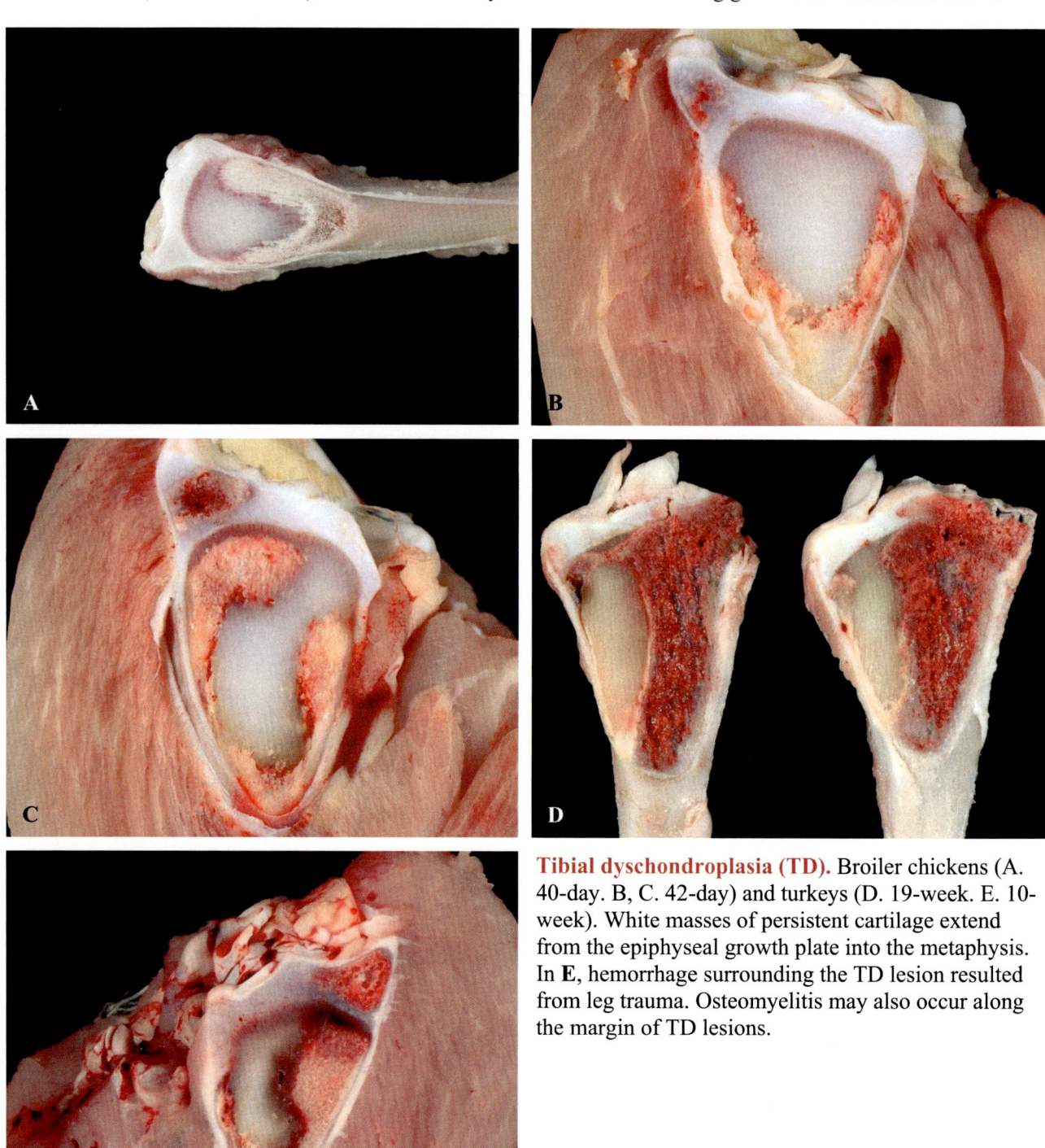

Tibial dyschondroplasia (TD). Broiler chickens (A. 40-day. B, C. 42-day) and turkeys (D. 19-week. E. 10-week). White masses of persistent cartilage extend from the epiphyseal growth plate into the metaphysis. In **E**, hemorrhage surrounding the TD lesion resulted from leg trauma. Osteomyelitis may also occur along the margin of TD lesions.

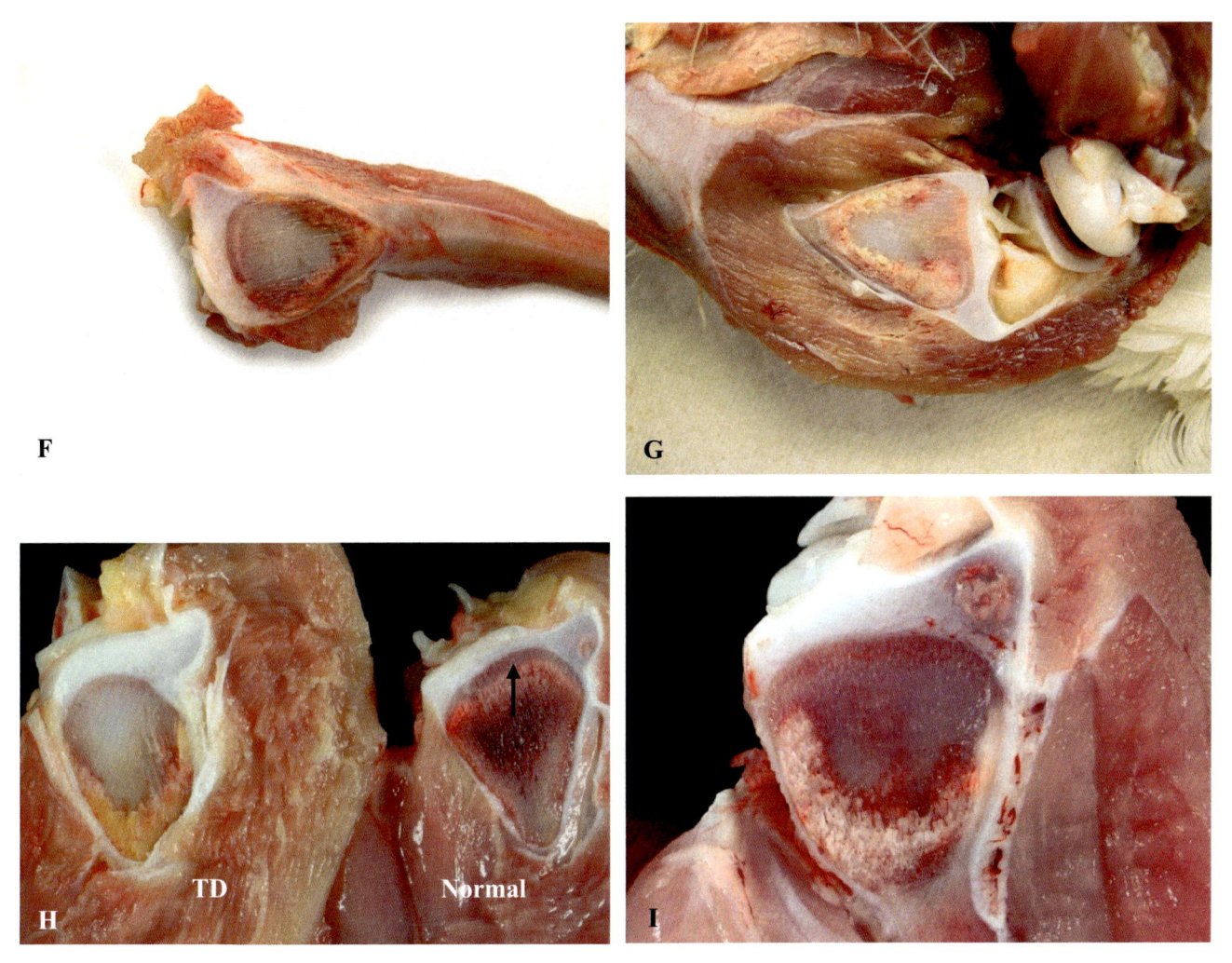

Tibial dyschondroplasia (TD). Broiler chickens (F. 46-day. G. 40-day. H. 35-day) and a turkey (I. 40-day). Proximal ends of tibiotarsi with white masses of retained cartilage extending from the epiphyseal growth plate into the metaphysis are shown. Figure **H** also shows a normal physis (growth plate) (arrow) in the proximal end of a tibiotarsus.

Osteoporosis in Caged Layers

Osteoporosis is a metabolic bone disease that mainly affects high-producing laying hens raised in cages. It is characterized by loss of structural bone mass below levels required for adequate mechanical support of the body. Osteopenia refers to thinning of bones that precedes osteoporosis. Osteoporosis is of economic significance and has animal welfare implications.

Cause and pathogenesis. Bones of laying hens are composed of cortical, trabecular, and medullary osseous tissue. Cortical bone is hard, compact external bony tissue that provides strength to bones, particularly long bones of the legs and wings. Trabecular bone provides an internal supporting framework of the bones in the vertebrae, pelvis, ribs, sternum, and limbs. Cortical and trabecular boney tissue constitute the structural elements of the skeleton and provide a mechanical supportive function. Medullary bone is a primitive type of bone peculiar to birds that provides little to no mechanical support. It consists of interconnected spicules of bone resembling trabecular bone, occurs only in sexually mature hens, has a crumbly texture, replaces trabecular bone, and is found in varying amounts in ribs, sternum, pelvis, vertebrae, femur, tibiotarsus, and fibula. Formation of medullary bone is initiated by simultaneous action of estrogen and progesterone, and coincides with maturation of ovarian follicles. At about 2 weeks prior to onset of egg production, spicules of medullary bone start to extend from the endosteal surface of cortical bone into the marrow cavity. This bone serves as a source of labile calcium that can be readily mobilized for eggshell formation.

In modern lines of high-producing layers, calcium for eggshell formation comes from a combination of dietary calcium and medullary bone reserves. Medullary bones provide approximately 40% of the calcium in the eggshell. Calcium removed from medullary bones must be replenished with dietary calcium. Throughout the laying cycle, there is continuous resorption and formation of medullary bone. As the mineral part of bones consists of both calcium and phosphorus as hydroxyapatite, when calcium is removed, phosphorus is also removed, which is excreted in urine. Calcium in medullary bones is replaced by calcium and phosphorus ($Ca_3(PO_4)_2$). If dietary calcium, phosphorus, and/ or vitamin D_3, which are required for absorption of calcium from the intestine are low or absent, medullary bone will not be re-mineralized and eventually becomes depleted of calcium.

High-producing hens have to meet the calcium demands of laying an egg every day. A hen requires about 2 grams of calcium for eggshell formation and a further 25 mg is in the yolk. Considering that the egg shell is formed in 18-20 hours before laying the egg, a hen needs to move from the blood to the egg about 100-110 mg of calcium per hour. Because the blood contains no more than 25 mg of calcium at any given time, there is a total turnover of blood calcium about every 12 minutes. A high level of calcium must be maintained in the blood to meet the continuous demands of eggshell formation and bone maintenance. The most intense eggshell formation occurs during the dark period when hens do not eat and need to mobilize calcium from medullary bones for eggshell formation. Because of the continuous demands for calcium for eggshell formation, it may be difficult to replace the minerals in medullary bone, i.e., the rate of medullary bone resorption exceeds the rate of its formation. Eventually, medullary bone become depleted of calcium. When medullary bone becomes depleted of calcium and sufficient dietary calcium, phosphorus, and vitamin D continues to be unavailable, the hen starts to break down trabecular and cortical bone to utilize the calcium in them for the formation of eggshell and re-mineralization of medullary bone. This result is a decrease in the mass of cortical and trabecular bone. The bones become light, brittle, fragile, and break easily. Other factors may also contribute to the increased incidence of osteoporosis. Hens are genetically selected for the trait of early sexual maturity. Early maturing hens are usually underweight and may not consume enough food to provide needed nutrients. Also, the structural mass of the skeleton (trabecular and cortical bone) may not be fully developed in early maturing birds, which makes the bones prone to osteoporosis.

There is no clear explanation for the occurrence of osteoporosis in caged layers but not in layers raised on the floor. It is possible that caged layers are susceptible to this condition because they do not have access to litter laden with the recycled calcium and phosphorus. Layers raised on floor litter may obtain additional calcium and phosphorus from the litter. Lack of activity/exercise in caged layers also may be an important factor contributing to the lack of bone strength in caged layers.

Clinical signs. There is leg weakness and sometimes partial or complete paralysis. Affected birds are unable to stand and usually move to the back area of the cage. They often fall onto their sides, with legs outstretched. Birds that live for several days after going down may dehydrate or emaciate, and are out of production. Although affected birds initially are alert and continue to eat, they may die from dehydration and starvation since they cannot reach water or food.

Gross lesions. Birds that die acutely from hypocalcemia are usually in active production with a partially shelled egg in the oviduct. The beak may be soft and easily bent, and bones are brittle, fragile, and easily broken. Unlike rickets, bones are not soft or rubbery. The femur is easily cut with scissors and little or no medullary bone is seen in the medullary cavity. Cranial bones are also thin and easily cut. The sternum is frequently crooked and fractures are common. Ribs are thin but swollen and roughened at the junction of their sternal and vertebral parts, with a tendency to bend at the junctions, resulting in deformation and distortion of the thorax. Collapse and infolding of the ribs due to fractures at the junction of the sternal and vertebral components are common. Fractures and collapse of thoracic vertebrae with compression of the spinal cord are usually seen in paralyzed birds. Enlargement of the parathyroid glands is evident in chronic cases.

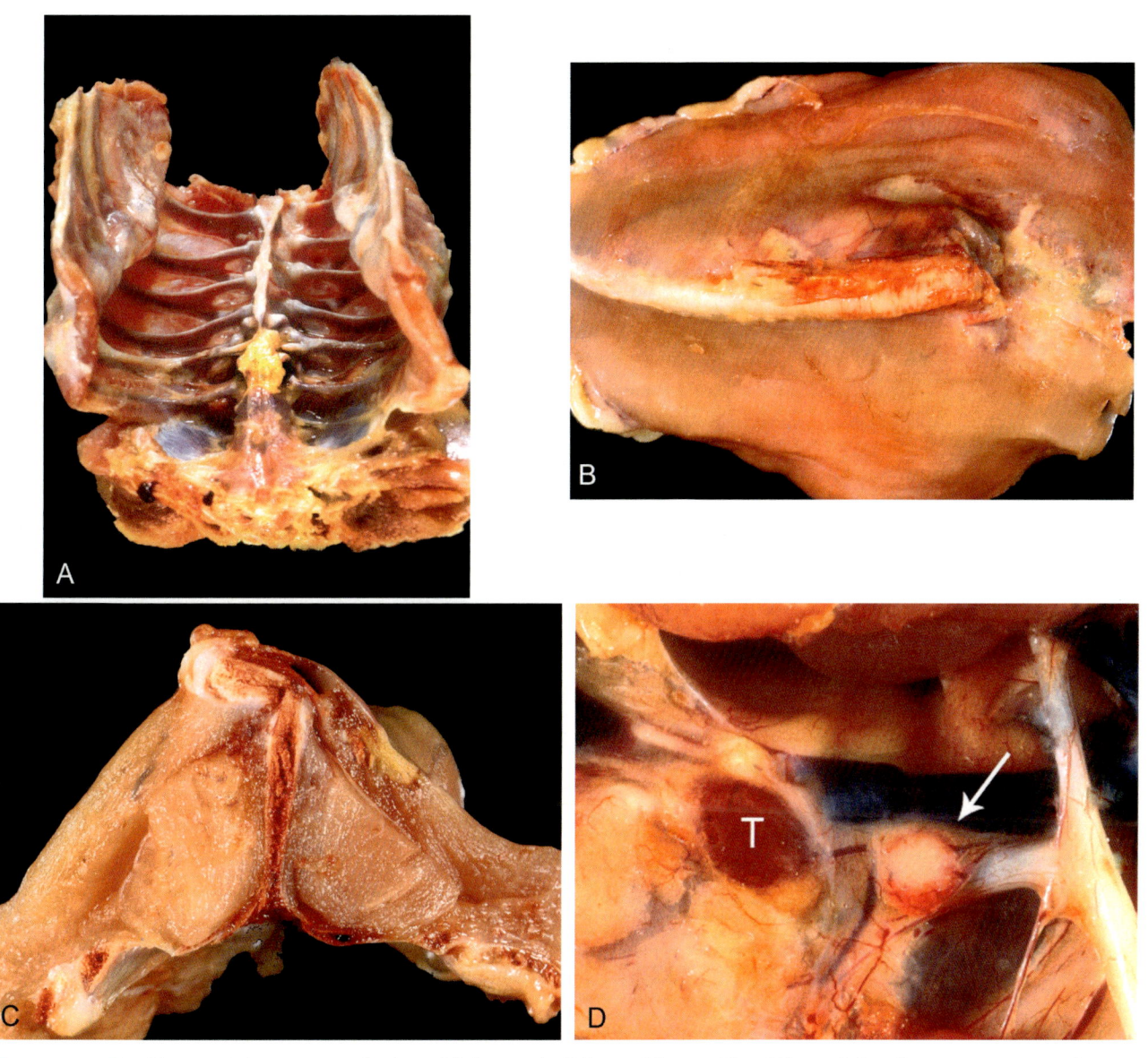

Osteoporosis. 19-month brown egg-laying chickens. **A.** Bilateral inward buckling of the ribs at costo-sternal articulations is a characteristic lesion of osteoporosis. Ribs are flattened and unable to support the weight of the bird when it rests on the breast. Palpation of ribs along the costo-sternal margin is easily done on necropsy. **B.** Keel fractures are frequently seen in laying chickens with osteoporosis. **C.** Cross-section of fractured keel in figure **B.** **D.** Parathyroid gland (arrow) is enlarged. Compare with normal thyroid gland (T).

Angular Limb Deformities (Valgus and Varus Deformities)

Valgus and varus are descriptive terms for long bone deformities characterized by angulation of the distal end of the tibiotarsus and subsequently the intertarsal joint, with displacement of the tarsometatarsus away from the midline, in the same direction as the distal tibiotarsus. Valgus-varus is the most common leg deformity in broiler chickens. The incidence is higher in males than in females. It is less common in turkeys.

Cause. The cause of valgus-varus deformity is not clear, but it is likely a combination of genetics, rapid growth rate, and nutrition.

Clinical signs and gross lesions. In valgus, there is outward (lateral) angulation of the distal end of tibiotarsus and intertarsal (hock) joint that results in displacement of the tibiotarsus away from the midline. In varus deformity, there is inward (medial) angulation of the distal end of tibiotarsus and intertarsal joint that results in displacement of the tibiotarsus toward the midline. The metatarsal bone is usually bowed in the same direction as the distal tibiotarsus. Valgus is more prevalent than varus. One or both legs are affected but not necessarily equally. Occasional broiler chickens may have a valgus deformity of one leg and a varus deformity of the other leg. Severe bilateral deformity results in hocks-in, feet-out ("knock kneed") stance in valgus and hocks-out, feet-in ("bow legged") stance in varus. Valgus-varus deformity is frequently noted between 1-4 weeks of age, but can occasionally be seen as early as one day of age. As the bird gains weight, more pressure is placed on the leg, making the deformity worse. In severe cases, the gastrocnemius tendon slips completely off the shallow distal tibiotarsal condyle groove (slipped tendon), giving a thickened appearance to the intertarsal (hock) joint. Moderately or severely affected broiler chickens walk with difficulty and tend to waddle or hobble. They prefer to sit and may have difficulty standing. As valgus deformity becomes more severe, birds walk on their hocks, particularly if both legs are involved, or go down with legs spraddled. Wing tips of these birds are abraded as they pull themselves around with their wings. If only one leg is severely affected it may be rigid in a lateral position. Severely affected birds cannot reach the feeders and slowly starve and dehydrate. Broiler chickens with only one leg affected usually survive until they go to slaughter, but they may be in poor condition.

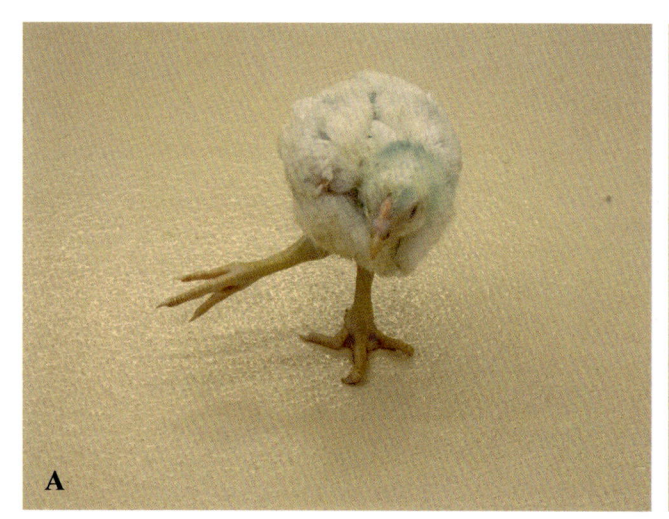

Valgus deformity. 42-day broiler chickens. **A.** Right limb is rigid and in a lateral position due to angulation of the distal tibiotarsus and intertarsal joint. **B.** Lateral deviation of the left limb (metatarsus).

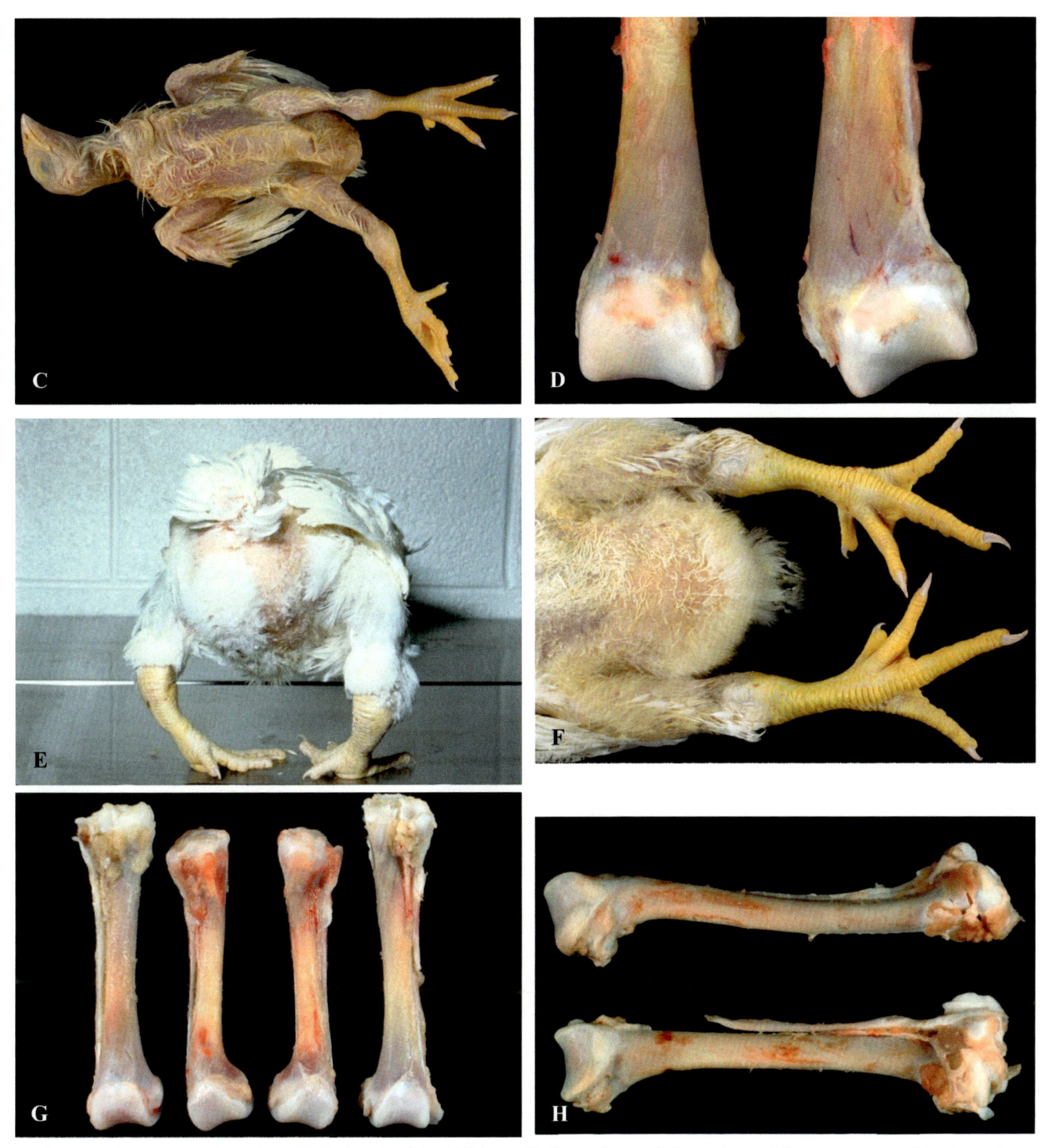

Valgus and varus deformity. C. 8-day broiler chicken. Valgus. Lateral deviation of the metatarsus. **D.** 5-week broiler chicken. Valgus. Outward (lateral) angulation of the distal end of the tibiotarsus on the right. Tibiotarsus on the left is normal. **E.** Broiler chicken. Bilateral varus deformity. Medial deviation and bowing of the tarsometatarsi results in hocks-out, feet-in ("bow-legged") stance. Hock joints are enlarged. **F.** Chicken. Bilateral varus deformity. Deviation of both limbs toward the midline (hocks-out, feet-in). **G.** Chicken. Varus deformity. Inward angulation of the distal end of the two tibiotarsi in the middle. Tibiotarsi on the right and left sides are normal. **H.** Chicken. Tibiotarsus on the top has angulation of the distal end and bowing of the bone.

Rotation of Tibiotarsus

Rotation of the shaft of tibiotarsi occurs in chickens, turkeys, and guinea fowl, but it also other birds, especially long-legged ones like cranes, storks, and ratites. The condition is particularly common in ostriches. In commercial poultry, the incidence is higher in turkeys than in chickens. In broiler chickens, the peak incidence occurs around 3 weeks of age. Varying degrees of external rotation, often 90 degrees or greater, of the shaft of tibiotarsus occurs during embryonic development. Rotation is restricted to the shaft. Unlike angular bone deformity (valgus-varus), there is no angulation of the proximal tibiotarsal head or displacement of the gastrocnemius tendon. One or both legs may be affected. Clinically, affected legs extend laterally, with rotation of the foot. If the rotation is 180 degrees, the foot of the affected leg faces in the opposite direction. The condition must be differentiated from splayed leg. The cause is uncertain but nutritional and incubation factors may be involved. Early mild rickets may also be a factor.

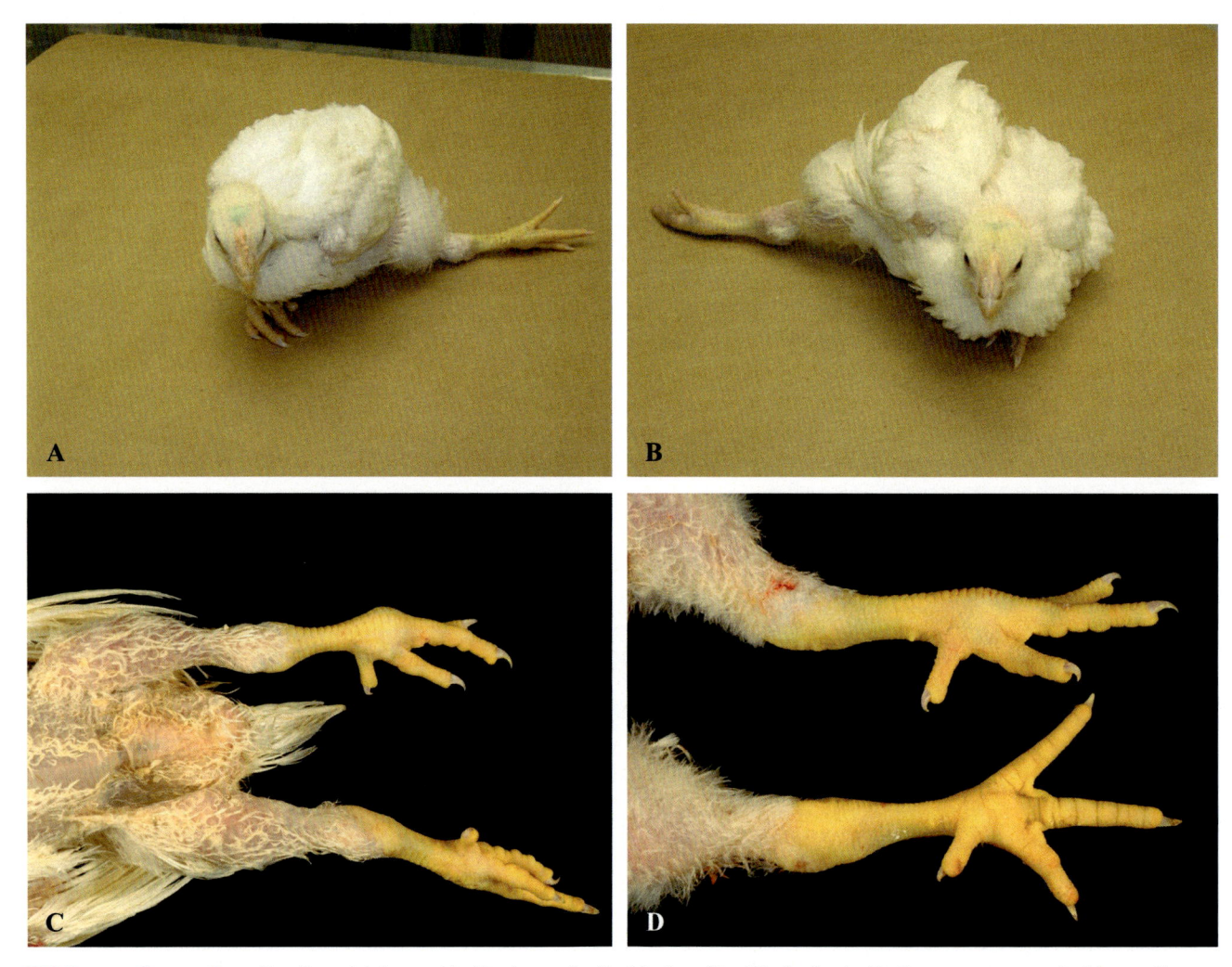

Tibiotarsal rotation. Broiler chickens (A, B. 4-week. C. 15-day. D. 18-day). **A, B.** Legs are extended laterally. Note the rotation of the feet. **C, D.** The right tibia is rotated causing the foot of the rotated leg to face in the opposite direction.

Atherosclerosis in Birds

Atherosclerosis refers to thickening of the walls of blood vessels due to the accumulation of lipid and fibrous tissue. The disease affects mainly large and medium sized arteries. Atherosclerosis is a slowly progressive disease that often starts at a young age and becomes worse over time. Early lesions are characterized by fat deposition and accumulation of lipid-laden macrophages and cellular waste products in the intima. These are atheromatous plaques or atheromas. As the diseases progresses, collagenous fibers gradually increase in atheromatous plaques, resulting in fibroatheromatous plaques or fibroatheromas. Often there are multiple cholesterol clefts. Calcium deposits and chondroid metaplasia may occur in the plaques. In advanced stages, the plaque can become entirely composed of collagenous fibrous tissue, forming a fibrous cap.

Atherosclerosis is common in parrots, particularly African gray and Amazon parrots. Incidence of the disease is reported as high as 92.1% for African grey parrots, and as high as 91.4% in Amazon parrots. The severity and incidence of atherosclerosis increases with age. Atherosclerosis is also found in other psittacines such as cockatoos, macaws, cockatiels, and Eclectus parrots, but the incidence is lower. Atherosclerotic lesions have also been seen in other birds including eagles, falcons, hawks, quail, turkeys, and pigeons. Risk factors for atherosclerosis in birds are not clear but may include genetic predisposition, high-cholesterol diet, lack of exercise, and herpesvirus infection. African gray and Amazon parrots have high plasma cholesterol levels. If plasma cholesterol is a risk factor in birds, high levels in African gray and Amazon parrots may explain their susceptibility to atherosclerosis. Marek's disease virus induces atherosclerosis in chickens. White Carneau pigeons are genetically predisposed to spontaneous atherosclerosis and are a useful animal model.

Clinical signs and gross lesions. Atherosclerosis is incidentally found in parrots that die from other diseases, but can be the only lesion identified in birds that die suddenly without premonitory clinical signs. In parrots, atherosclerotic lesions are commonly found in the ascending aorta (beginning of the aorta) and in brachiocephalic trunks and its main branches. Lesions also occur in the descending aorta and its branches, down to the femoral artery. The main pulmonary artery is less frequently affected than the aorta. Severe narrowing of the aorta or pulmonary arteries leads to left- or right-sided heart failure, respectively. Birds with heart failure may exhibit dyspnea.

On necropsy, gross lesions of atherosclerosis in parrots are usually identified as the aorta emerges from the heart or in the brachiocephalic trunk and its branches. Lesions in small arteries may be seen only on histopathologic examination. Use of a magnifying glass is often helpful to examine the arteries. Arteries affected with atherosclerosis have a thick, rigid wall that may be pale yellow. In severe cases, eccentric or circumferential narrowing of the lumen is evident in transverse sections of the vessels. Examination of the luminal surface of longitudinally dissected arteries reveals yellow or opaque plaques or diffuse and irregular thickening. Severe aortic stenosis due to atherosclerosis leads to heart failure. An early lesion in the heart is hypertrophy of the left ventricle, followed by dilation of the left ventricle and atrium. Left-sided heart failure subsequently results in dilation of the right ventricle and right-sided heart failure. Ascites with or without hydropericardium, enlargement of the heart, generalized vascular congestion, and hepatic fibrosis are common necropsy findings in birds that die of congestive heart failure. Atherosclerosis frequently affects the abdominal aorta of turkeys, which is considered to be a predisposing factor to aortic rupture.

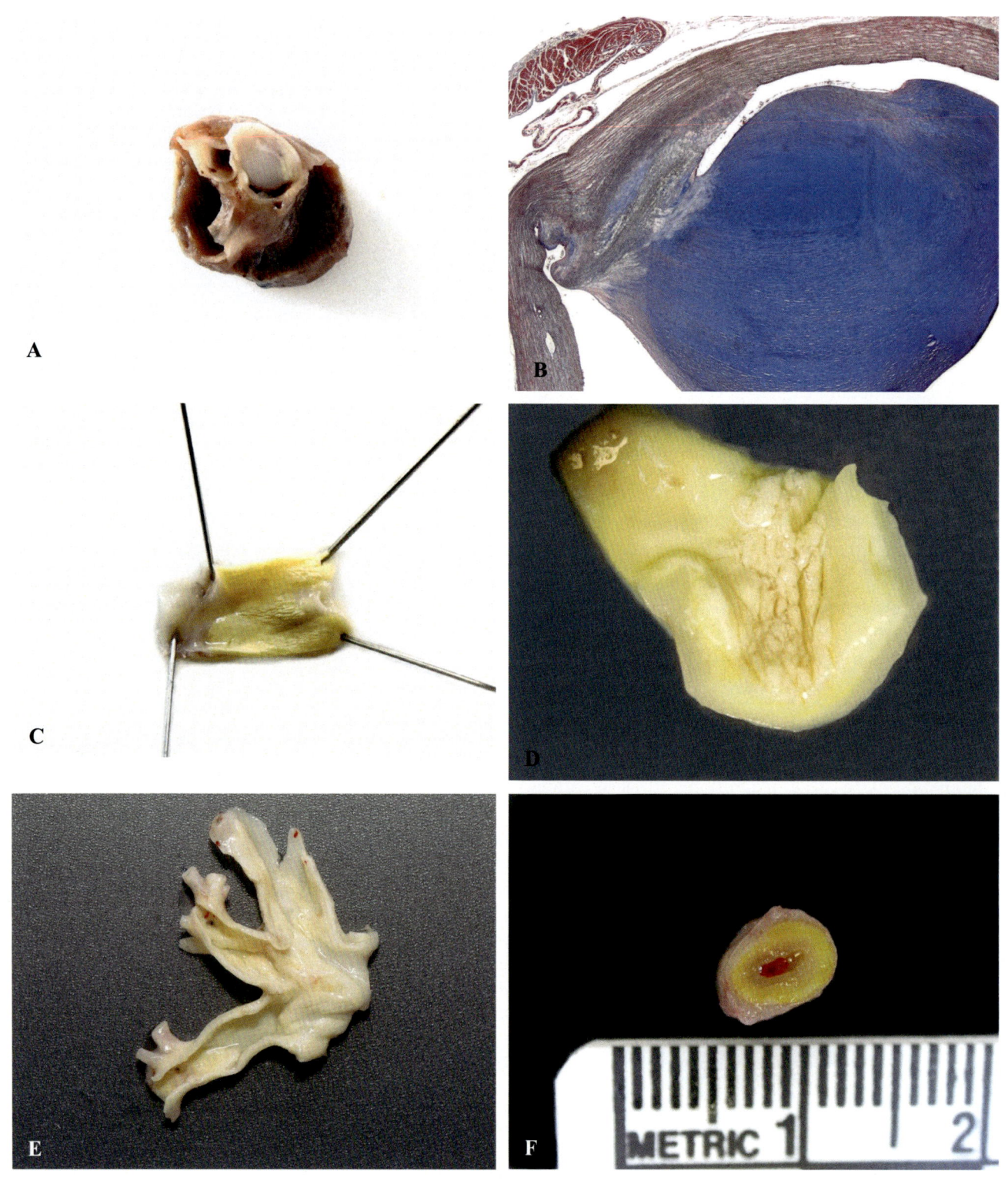

Atherosclerosis. A, B. 21-year male African gray parrot. **A.** Marked narrowing of the beginning of the aorta by a white mass represents a fibrous cap of atherosclerosis. **B.** Histologic section with Masson Trichrome stain shows the cap consists entirely of collagenous tissue. The bird also had severe atherosclerotic lesions in other parts of the ascending aorta and in the brachiocephalic trunk and its branches. **C, D.** Adult Amazon parrot. **C.** Yellow atheromatous lesion in the luminal surface of the ascending aorta. **D.** Atheromatous plaque as seen under dissection microscopy in the luminal surface of the aorta. **E.** 27-year African gray parrot. Atherosclerotic plaques in the luminal surface of the ascending aorta and brachiocephalic arteries. Plaques appear as raised areas. The diagnosis of atherosclerosis was confirmed by histopathology. **F.** Adult female hobby chicken. Severe circumferential narrowing of the lumen of the descending aorta (about the level the ovary) by a large atheromatous lesion.

Pulmonary Hypertension Syndrome (Ascites) in Broiler Chickens

Pathogenesis. Lungs of birds are molded into the thoracic cavity and are attached to the body wall. They do not expand and contract under negative pressure in a hollow cavity like mammalian lungs. To meet increased tissue demand for oxygen, the heart must increase blood flow from the right ventricle into the lungs for oxygenation. This increases the workload of the right ventricle. Expansion of pulmonary blood capillaries is limited, which restricts their ability to accommodate increased blood flow. The right ventricle has to pump against the limited capacity of the pulmonary capillary bed, which results in primary pulmonary hypertension (cor pulmonale). In response to the increased workload, cardiac myocytes increase in size (hypertrophy). If the high demand for oxygen and increased cardiac output remains uncompensated, the wall of the right ventricle becomes thickened and the right ventricle dilates to the point that the atrioventricular valve is no longer capable of covering the opening between the right ventricle and atrium. Right atrioventricular valvular insufficiency leads to progressively increasing right ventricle dilation, worsening valvular insufficiency, and eventual failure of the right heart. Hydrostatic pressure rises in the vena cava, which results in portal hypertension, increased hydrostatic pressure in splanchnic circulation, and subsequent excess production of splanchnic lymph over lymphatic return. Lymph leakage from the liver and other splanchnic organs results in ascitic fluid accumulating in the peritoneal cavities. Initially albumin leaves the vascular compartment, which increases the osmotic attraction of fluid. In advanced cases, fibrinogen also leaves the vascular compartment, which is converted into fibrin. Fibrin coagulates forming clots devoid of blood cells. Greatest accumulations are seen in the right and left dorsal hepatic peritoneal compartments, unless there is communication between them, and the intestinal peritoneal compartment. Little fluid accumulates in the ventral hepatic peritoneal compartments because of the minimal space between the liver and sternum.

Gross lesions. Usually the bird has ascites. The abdomen is distended with clear, yellow fluid and fibrin clots that accumulate in peritoneal cavities. A layer or tags of coagulated protein may be present on the ventral surface of the liver. The liver may be swollen and dark red (congested); enlarged and pale with an enhanced reticular pattern; or shrunken, firm, and somewhat lobulated. With severe ascites, the capsular surface of the liver is white and dense due to reactive thickening of the peritoneum on its surface. There may be fluid-filled blebs and cysts on the liver surface. Mild to moderate pericardial effusion (hydropericardium) with white thickening of the pericardial sac is common. The heart is enlarged and flabby and the right ventricle is swollen and bulges from the normal profile. Transverse sections of the heart show dilation of the right ventricle and occasional mild thickening of the right ventricular wall. The right atrium and vena cava are markedly dilated. Frequently, the left ventricle is also dilated with thinning of the left ventricular wall. Lungs are markedly reddened and edematous, but float in formalin fixative. When lungs are removed, pools of blood-tinged fluid often remain between the ribs. There is generalized congestion of visceral organs and other tissues. Muscles may be cyanotic. Spleen is usually small and gray, typical of a 'chronic stress' spleen. Kidneys tend to be swollen and bulge out of renal fossae in the synsacrum.

Lesions in broiler chickens that die from right-sided heart failure, but do not have ascites include swollen liver, generalized venous congestion, dilated right atrium and vena cava, thickening of the wall of the right ventricle, and pulmonary congestion and edema.

Pulmonary hypertension syndrome. 60-day broiler chickens. **A.** Ascites distends the abdomen. **B.** Yellow ascitic fluid and coagulated fibrin in the body cavity (peritoneal spaces). The surface of left lobe of the liver is covered with a thick layer of coagulated fibrin. The liver is shrunken and firm. Note the pericardial effusion. **C.** Yellow ascitic fluid in the body cavity. Pericardial sac is thickened and white. Peritoneal thickening is responsible for the white layer on the liver's surface. **D.** The affected heart is enlarged and its right ventricle is bulging (arrow). **E, F.** Two transverse sections of affected and normal hearts in D. Chambers of the right and left ventricles are dilated and the left ventricular wall is thinner than normal. RV: right ventricle. LV: left ventricle.

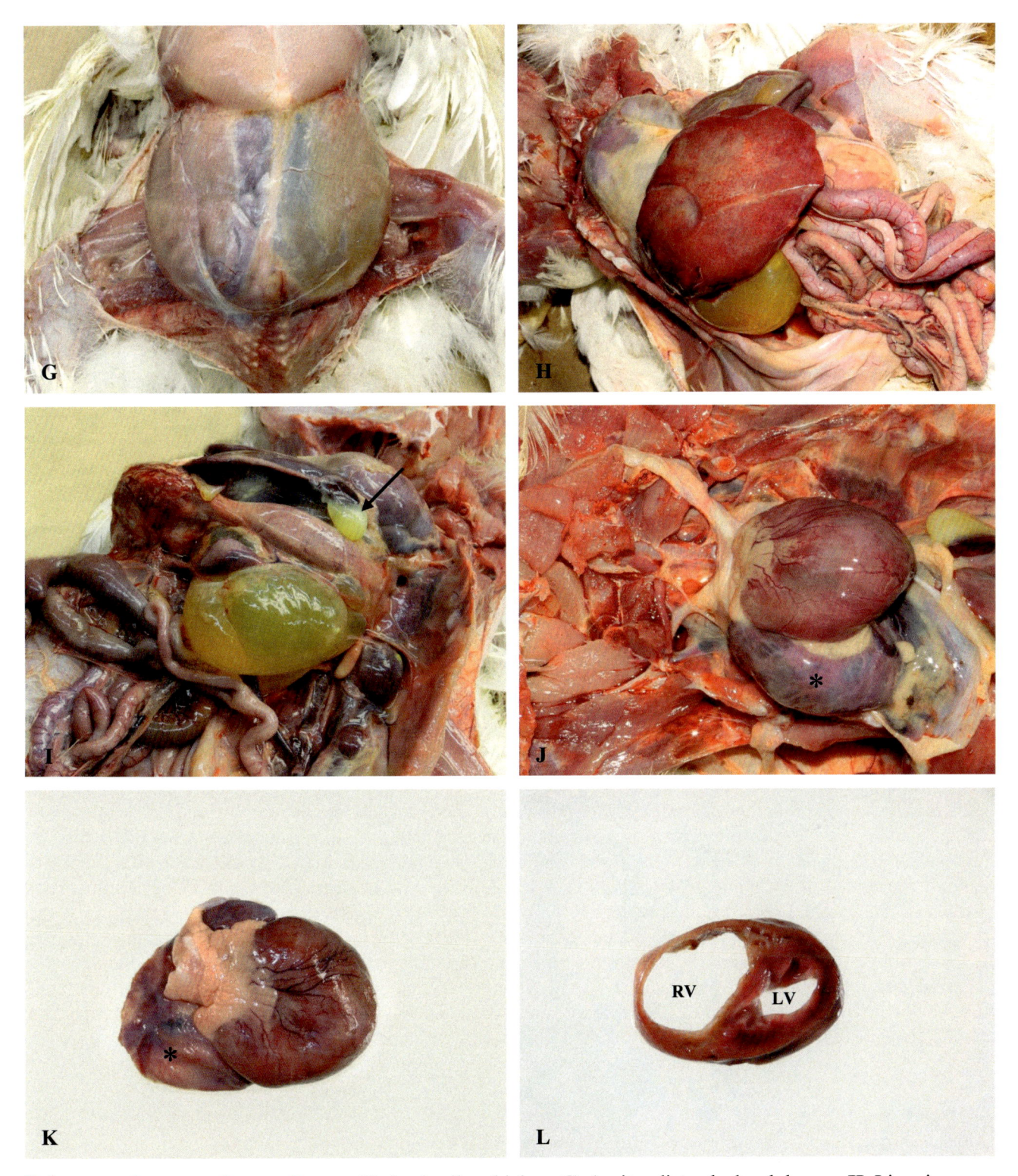

Pulmonary hypertension syndrome. 50-day broiler chicken. **G.** Ascites distends the abdomen. **H.** Liver is shrunken and pale. The right dorsal peritoneal compartment is filled with ascitic fluid and fibrin. The pericardial sac (arrow) is thickened. **I.** The fluid-filled left dorsal hepatic peritoneal cavity in **H** has resulted from an accumulation of ascitic fluid. Note also the small fluid-filled cyst (arrow) attached to the liver. **J, K.** Heart is enlarged, has a more-or-less round contour, and is flabby. Note the distended right atrium (asterisks). **L.** Transverse section of the heart in K. Chambers of both ventricles are dilated. The wall of the left ventricle is thin. RV: right ventricle. LV: left ventricle.

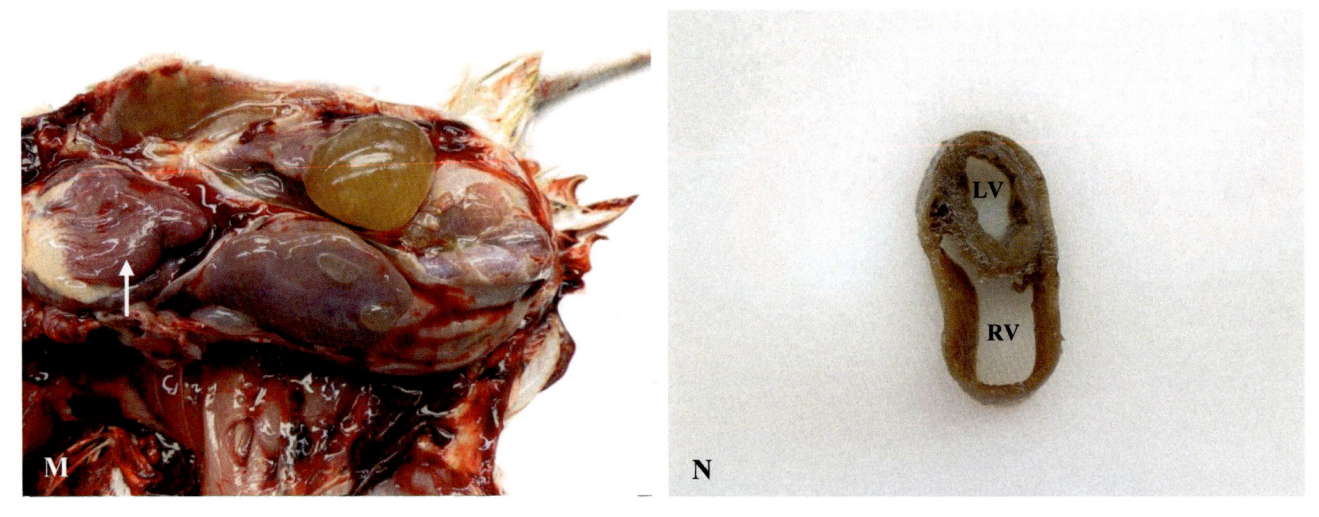

Pulmonary hypertension syndrome. 52-day broiler chicken. **M.** One large and two small cysts filled with yellow fluid are on the capsular surface of the liver. There is reactive white thickening of the peritoneum on the liver surface. Note the enlargement and flabby appearance of the heart and the bulging right ventricle (arrow). **N.** Transverse section of the heart in M. Chambers of both ventricles are markedly dilated. The wall of the left ventricle is thin. RV: right ventricle. LV: left ventricle.

Round-Heart Disease (Dilated Cardiomyopathy) in Turkeys

Cause. Uncertain. Several factors have been implicated.

Gross lesions. The primary lesion is seen in the heart, which is enlarged, has a blunted, often dimpled apex, and has lost its normal conical shape. Severity of the changes varies greatly from case to case depending on the stage of the disease. In young birds (under 3 weeks), the right ventricle is markedly dilated, flabby, and thin-walled with prominent congested vessels. In severe cases, the right ventricle becomes sac-like and makes up a major portion of the increased size of the heart. The left ventricle may be slightly to moderately dilated. At this stage, affected poults die from right-sided heart failure. Ascites with or without fibrin may present. Livers and kidneys are usually enlarged and congested. Livers become progressively fibrotic as affected birds age. In older turkeys that survive the acute stage of the disease, hearts become extremely enlarged, more or less round, and have marked thickening of the myocardium, especially papillary muscles (hypertrophic cardiomyopathy). The left ventricle is dilated and a white membrane (endocardial fibroelastosis) often covers the endocardial surface. Affected birds survive until processed or die from heart failure. Dead birds have congested, edematous lungs. Livers are shrunken, fibrotic, and pale. Affected turkeys are substantially smaller than flock mates with normal hearts.

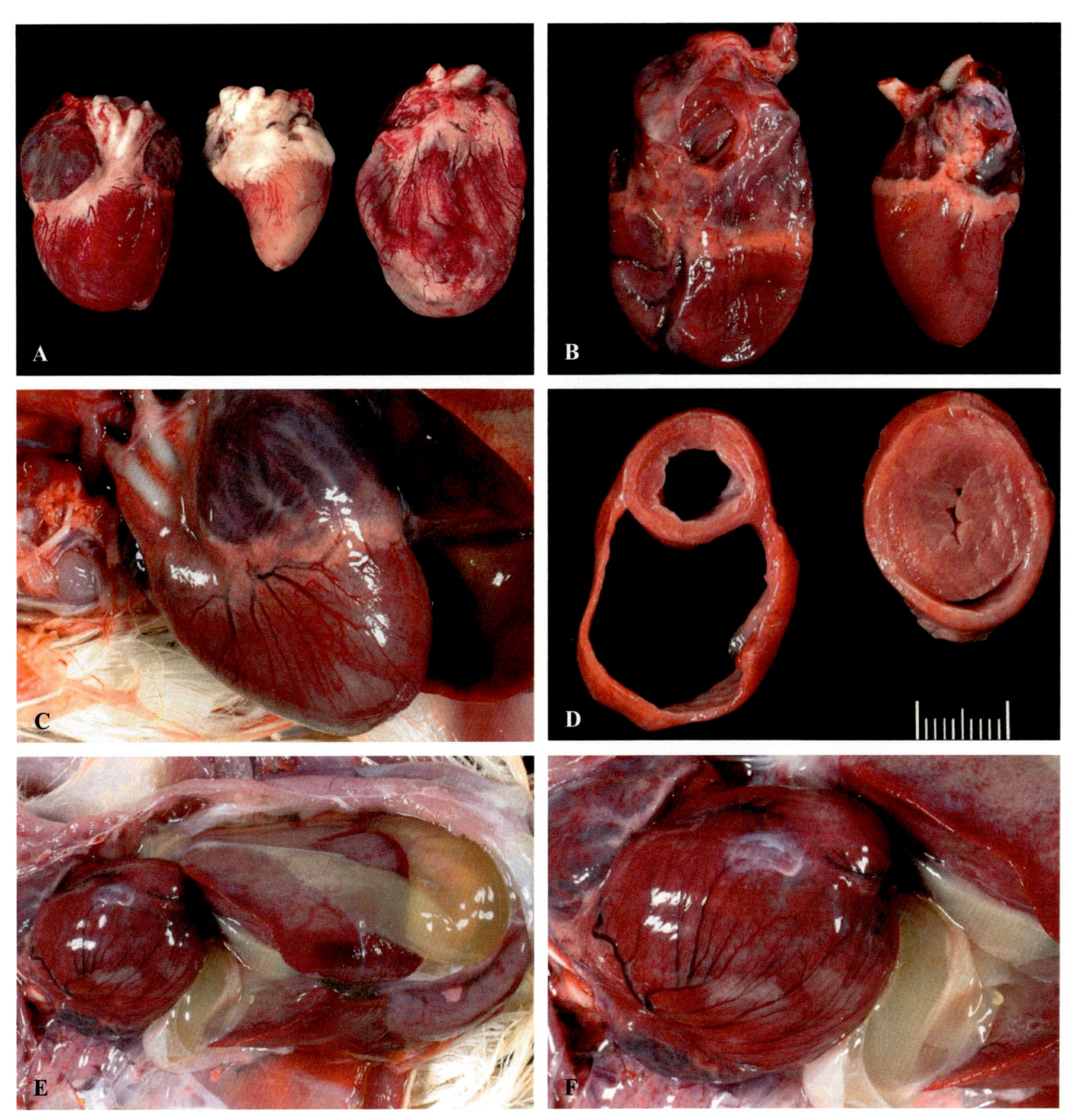

Dilated cardiomyopathy (Round-heart disease). **A.** 41-day commercial turkeys. Normal heart (middle) is flanked by two enlarged, rounded, hearts with dilated cardiomyopathy (DCM). Heart on the left is progressing to hypertrophic cardiomyopathy while the one on the right has thin-walled dilated ventricles. **B. C. D.** 43-day commercial turkeys. **B.** Normal heart (right) compared with a heart with DCM (left). Heart with DCM is enlarged, flabby, and has a rounded contour. **C.** Enlarged, rounded heart. **D.** Transverse sections. Normal heart (right) compared to heart with DCM (left). Both ventricles in the heart with DCM are dilated and have thin walls. **E, F.** 51-day commercial turkey hen. Heart is markedly enlarged and round. Right ventricle is dilated and accounts for the major portion of the increased size of the heart. Right heart vessels are prominent because of congestion. A friction rub is located at the junction of the right and left ventricles. Marked peritoneal effusion (ascites) and fibrin clot are due to congestive (right-sided) heart failure. Fibrosis of the liver has caused the mottled pale surface of the liver.

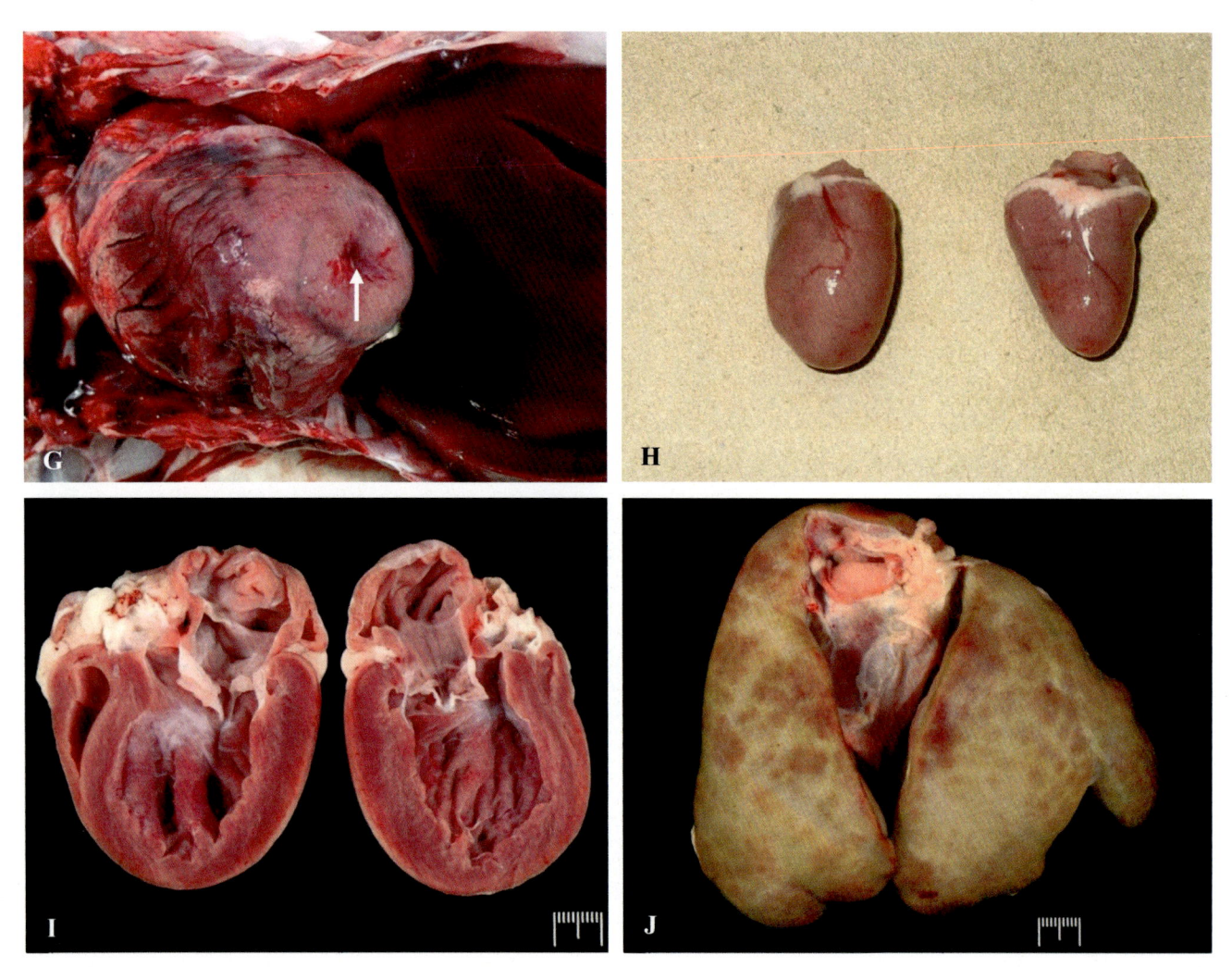

Dilated cardiomyopathy (Round-heart disease). **G.** 41-day commercial turkey hen. Apex of the heart is deeply dimpled (arrow). **H.** 3-week turkey breeder male. Normal heart (right) and heart with DCM (left). The heart with DCM is enlarged, lost its conical shape, and has a rounded apex. **I.** 19-week male turkeys at processing. Turkeys that have dilated cardiomyopathy and survive to processing often develop hypertrophic cardiomyopathy characterized by thickening of the walls of the ventricles, especially papillary muscles, which can become torturous, reduced size of ventricle lumens, and subaortic stenosis. Fibrovascular tissue develops in part or all the endocardium of the left ventricle. **J.** Liver from the same turkey as I. Liver fibrosis is often extensive because of the chronic right-sided (congestive) heart failure. Affected birds are substantially smaller than flock mates with normal hearts.

Acute Pancreatic Necrosis in Psittacines

Acute pancreatic necrosis is a distinct disease that occurs in psittacines, especially Quaker (Monk) parakeets (*Myiopsitta monachus*). Obese parakeets on high-fat diets are most likely to be affected.

Cause and pathogenesis. Diffuse severe necrosis of the pancreas most likely results from activation of trypsinogen to trypsin within the pancreas, which leads to proteolytic digestion of pancreatic tissues. Trypsinogen is the precursor or zymogen of trypsin. It is stored in acinar cells, released when needed for digestion, and activated in the duodenum by the enzyme enteropeptidase (also called enterokinase), which is secreted by crypt epithelial cells. Intrapancreatic activation of trypsinogen to trypsin leads to a chain of events that result in self-digestion of pancreatic tissue. However, the triggering event for intrapancreatic trypsinogen activation is unknown. Damaged acinar cells release other digestive enzymes that cause further damage. Lipolytic enzymes may be responsible for necrosis of mesenteric fat between the pancreatic lobes. Other pancreatic enzymes may cause disruption and destruction of blood vessels.

Gross lesions. Affected birds are in good nutritional body condition and have large amounts of subcutaneous abdominal and visceral fat. Usually an entire pancreatic lobe is involved, and more than one lobe may be affected. The affected lobe is swollen, discolored tan and/or green, firmer than normal, friable, and may contain hemorrhages. Mesenteric fat between pancreatic lobes is usually necrotic with multifocal hemorrhage. Adhesions of the pancreas and duodenum to surrounding tissues may be seen.

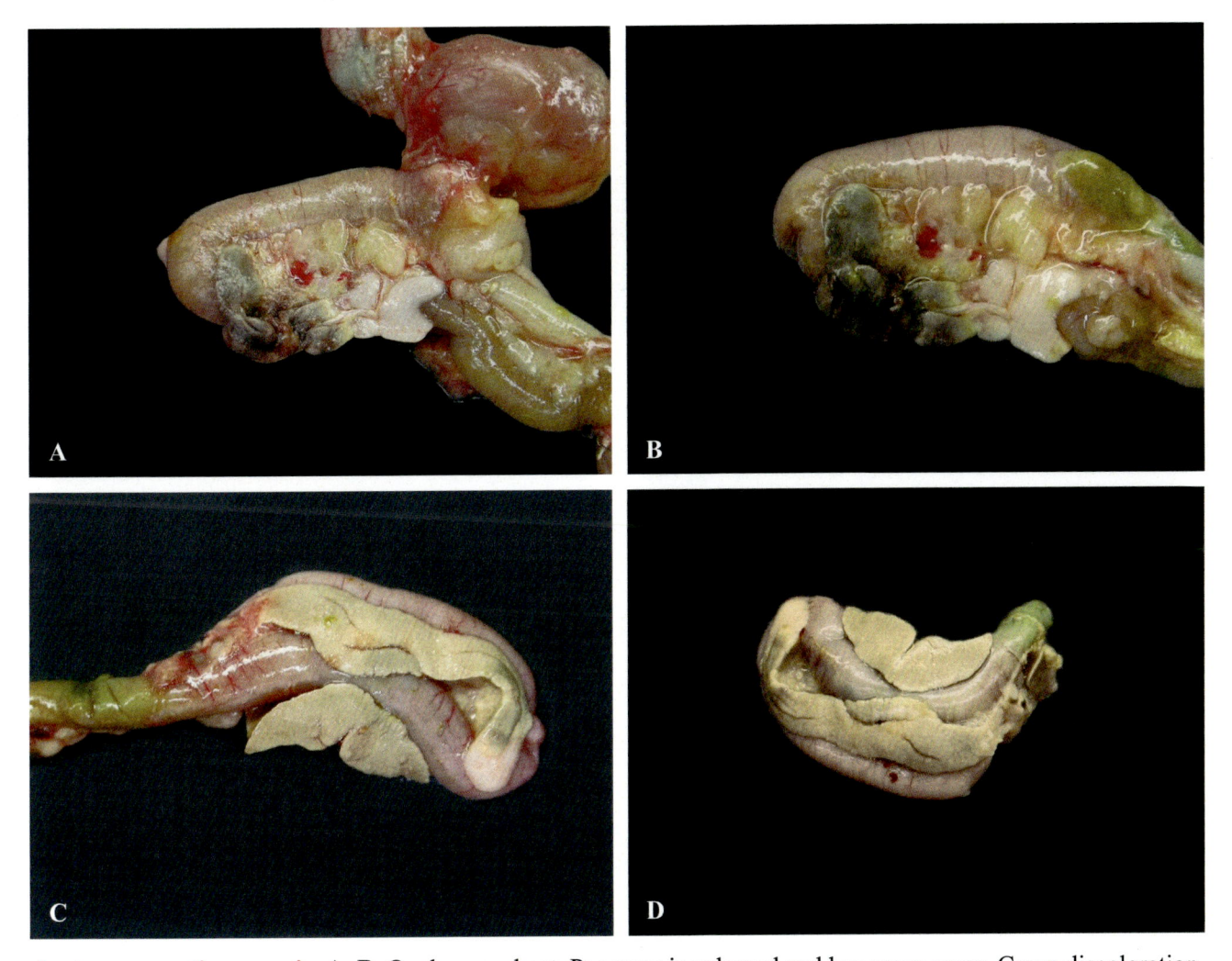

Acute pancreatic necrosis. A, B. Quaker parakeet. Pancreas is enlarged and has green areas. Green discoloration may be due to earlier hemorrhage. Mesenteric fat around the pancreas is edematous and has undergone necrosis. **C, D.** Another Quaker parakeet. Pancreatic lobes are tan, appear dry and necrotic, and are friable.

Fatty Liver Hemorrhagic Syndrome

Fatty liver hemorrhagic syndrome (FLHS) is a metabolic disorder characterized by excess accumulation of fat in the liver, with hepatic capsular tears and hemorrhage. FLHS most often affects table-egg layers, but is also a relatively common cause of sudden death in hobby hens. In hobby chickens, the incidence of FLHS is higher during hot weather.

Cause. The cause of FLHS is uncertain, but it likely results from a combination of nutritional, hormonal, genetic, and environmental factors.

Gross lesions. Birds with FLHS die suddenly without premonitory clinical signs. Usually, they are in excellent body condition, producing eggs, and obese with a thick abdominal fat pad and abundant visceral and cardiac fat. A blood clot is often found in the abdominal cavity or on the ventral surface of the liver. Affected livers are yellow, soft, friable, and may be enlarged. In some birds, hemorrhage is found within the liver. There are subcapsular hematomas (accumulation of blood between the liver capsule and liver parenchyma) and few to several parenchymal hemorrhages. Hemorrhage in recently ovulated follicles may be seen. Visceral organs are pale because of the hemorrhage. When the liver is cut, fat remains on the knife blade. Small pieces of affected livers float in formalin. Greasy debris left on the knife and floatation of liver pieces in formalin are characteristic of hepatic steatosis. Ovary is active, and there may be a developing or shelled egg in the oviduct. Liver hemorrhage with little or no hepatic lipidosis is seen in some cases of sudden death in hobby chickens. In these cases, a diagnosis of FLHS is inappropriate; *hemorrhagic liver* or *ruptured liver* is a more accurate diagnosis. Other agents that have been implicated as causing liver hemorrhage include avian hepatitis-E virus, aflatoxin, rapeseed oil, hypothyroidism, and chelated minerals.

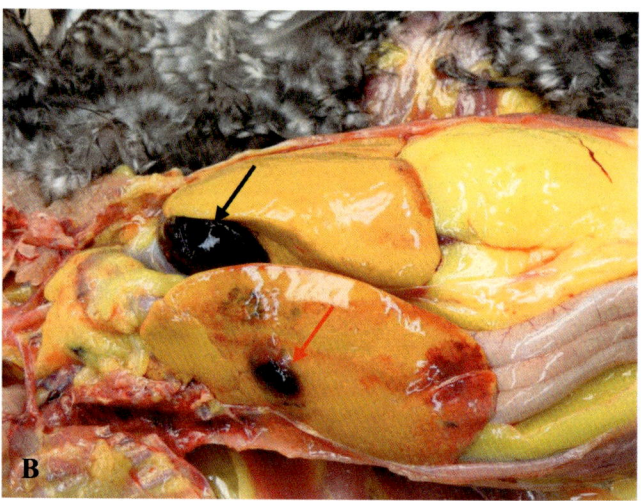

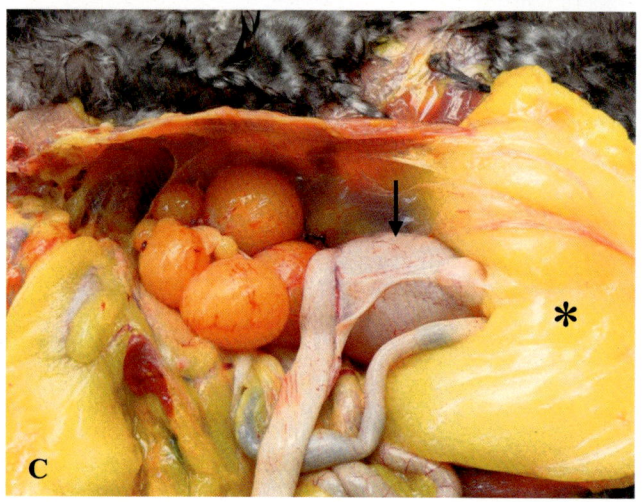

Fatty liver hemorrhagic syndrome. 2-year hobby female chicken. **A.** Liver is yellow and a large blood clot is on the surface of the left lobe. **B.** Liver is yellow and there is a small subcapsular hematoma in the right lobe (red arrow), and another larger one in the left lobe (black arrow). Note the thick layer of fat in the abdominal cavity and excessive fat around the heart. **C.** The hen has an active ovary and egg forming in the oviduct (arrow). Note the abundant fat (asterisk).

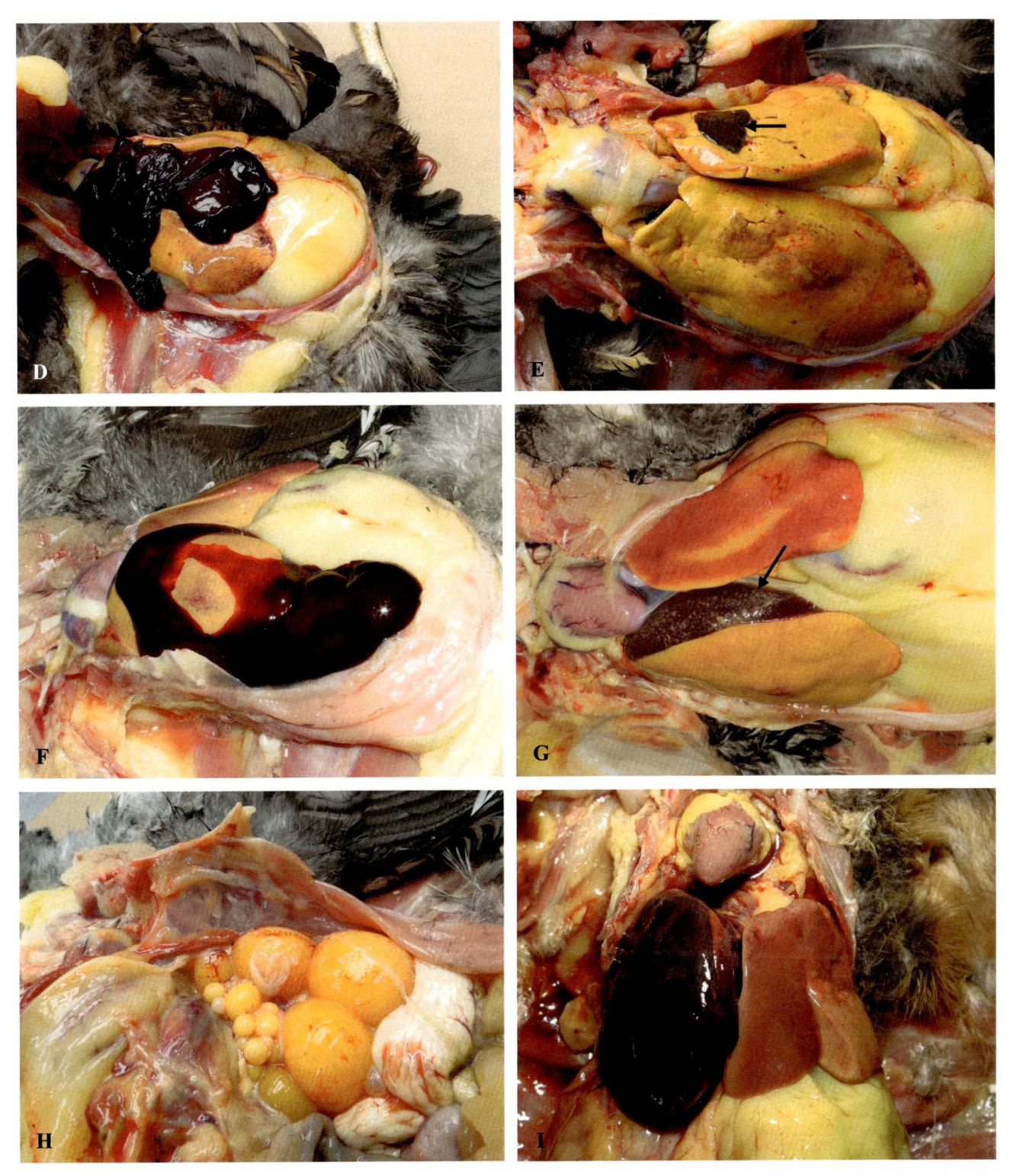

Fatty liver hemorrhagic syndrome. D, E. 3-year hobby female chicken. **D.** Liver is yellow and there is a blood clot on the surface of the right lobe of the liver. **E.** Liver is yellow, enlarged, and has a subcapsular hematoma (arrow), hemorrhages, and torn capsule. **F, G, H.** 8-month hobby female chicken. **F.** Blood clot on the surface of the right lobe of the liver. **G.** Right lobe of the liver is yellow and has a large subcapsular hematoma (arrow) on its dorsal surface. Left lobe is not as yellow as the right lobe. Note abundant visceral fat. **H.** Hen has an active ovary with yolk follicles. **I.** 10-month hobby female chicken. Subcapsular hematoma involves the entire ventral surface of the right lobe of the liver. Liver is pale but not yellow. Fatty vacuolation of hepatocytes was minimal. In this case, a diagnosis of *hemorrhagic* or *ruptured liver* is more accurate than fatty liver hemorrhagic syndrome. Avian hepatitis-E virus was suspected.

Hepatic Lipidosis Syndrome in Turkeys

Hepatic lipidosis, also called fatty liver and hepatic steatosis, is a pathological condition that occurs in humans and different animals. It is characterized by excessive accumulation of lipids, primarily triglycerides, in hepatocytes. Hepatic lipidosis syndrome (HLS) affects turkey breeder hen replacements between 12 and 25 weeks of age with most cases occurring between 20 and 24 weeks. Less frequently, HLS occurs in young commercial meat turkey hen and tom flocks. Accumulation of excessive intracellular lipid leads to rupture and death of hepatocytes. Because of extensive hepatocyte loss, the delicate meshwork of extracellular fine reticulin fibers, which support the hepatocytes and sinusoidal lining cells, collapses in some areas, resulting in extravasation of blood from sinusoids (hemorrhage).

Overview of lipid metabolism. Dietary lipids are digested in the small intestine through emulsification by bile and digestion by pancreatic enzymes. Lipid digestion produces fatty acids and monoglycerides, which enter intestinal epithelial cells where they are synthesized into triglycerides and packaged with cholesterol, phospholipids, and proteins to form chylomicrons. Triglycerides (esters of fatty acids and glycerol) are the predominant lipids in chylomicrons. Chylomicrons enter the blood stream where triglycerides are hydrolyzed by lipoprotein lipase in tissue capillaries. The released fatty acids are absorbed by adipose tissue and liver. In the liver, free fatty acids are esterified to triglycerides, converted to cholesterol or phospholipids, or oxidized to ketone bodies. Triglycerides bind with apolipoproteins to form lipoproteins, which are then transported from the liver into blood and lymph.

Energy from fat keeps the body running whenever its main energy source, glucose, is unavailable. When energy is needed, fatty acids can also be mobilized from adipose tissue by lipolysis in which triglycerides are hydrolyzed into free fatty acids and glycerol. In liver and muscle cells, fatty acids released from adipose tissue are oxidized by β-oxidation, a cyclic series of reactions that occurs mainly within mitochondria, to generate acetyl CoA. Acetyl-CoA enters the citric acid cycle to generate adenosine triphosphate (ATP), which is a primary source of energy. The series of reactions in β-oxidation involve several enzymes encoded by different genes. Carnitine is required to transport activated fatty acids from the cell cytoplasm into the mitochondrial matrix for oxidation. Carnitine is synthesized primarily in the liver and kidney from lysine and methionine, with iron, magnesium, and vitamins B_2 (riboflavin), B_3 (niacin), B_6 (pyridoxine), and C as required cofactors.

Causes of excessive accumulation of triglycerides in hepatocytes.
- Excessive energy consumption from fats or carbohydrates and reduced energy utilization. Fatty acid oxidation in the liver becomes overwhelmed and cannot keep up with excess lipid accumulation in hepatocytes.
- Excessive fatty acid influx into the liver from lipolysis of adipose tissue in obese animals.
- Decreased synthesis of lipid binding proteins with subsequent accumulation of triglycerides and other lipids in hepatocytes. Insufficient dietary protein and certain amino acids (especially lysine and methionine) or damage to hepatocytes by hepatotoxins (e.g., mycotoxins) can result in failure of hepatocytes to synthesize lipid binding proteins.
- Increased synthesis of fatty acids from glucose (lipogenesis) in the hepatocytes. Lipogenesis is regulated independently by insulin and glucose. An elevated glucose level in the blood causes increased secretion of insulin from pancreatic islets. Insulin activates lipogenesis by inducing certain molecules in the hepatocytes, which activate key genes encoding enzymes necessary for converting glucose to fatty acids. Overexpression of one or more of these molecular mediators (as seen in transgenic mice) increases lipogenesis in the liver. Furthermore, high glucose and insulin have also been shown to inhibit fatty acid oxidation. Glucose and insulin levels in turkeys with hepatic lipidosis are unknown.
- Reduced or impaired β-oxidation of fatty acids in the mitochondria of hepatocytes. In humans, there are different conditions of "fatty acid oxidation disorders" in which cells cannot oxidize fatty acids due to defects in the genes encoding synthesis of enzymes required for fatty acid oxidation. These conditions are inherited as autosomal recessives. However, it is unknown if similar conditions occur in turkeys with HLS.

Possible causes of HLS in turkeys. The cause of HLS in turkeys is still uncertain although nutritional and metabolic factors are suspected. HLS could involve the interplay of both nutritional and environmental factors. It is unknown if HLS has a genetic component in turkeys. Several factors are believed to contribute to outbreaks of HLS.
- Early feeding of low protein / high energy diets in order to control body weight.
- High and low environmental temperatures. In summer, turkeys consume large amounts of food in the cool morning hours and are inactive during the heat of the day. Lack of exercise and high temperature leads to a

positive energy balance. In contrast, during winter, low temperatures stimulate feed consumption throughout the day and the birds exercise more to keep warm.
- Short days. After 16- to 17-weeks of age, turkey breeder hen candidates are maintained in dark-out houses on 6-hours of light. Hens consume large amounts of feed in a short period of time and are inactive during the remaining 18 hours of darkness.
- Low dietary levels of the amino acids methionine, lysine, and/or cysteine.
- Overcrowding that restricts bird movements.
- Avian encephalomyelitis (AE) virus is often isolated from livers of affected birds but a possible etiologic role has not been investigated. Candidate breeders are vaccinated with a modified-live AE vaccine at around the same time that HLS usually occurs.

Clinical signs and gross lesions. Over a 2-week period, mortality without any known cause abruptly increases ranging from one to 15%. The clinical course is short. Affected hens are reluctant to stand or move and have cyanosis and labored breathing for a few hours before death. Birds that die of HLS are in good body condition and have abundant visceral fat. A yellow-tinged fluid may be found in the body cavity. The liver is typically enlarged, has rounded margins, and is yellow to yellow-beige. Usually there are well-demarcated areas of lipid accumulation or the livers are diffusely pale yellow. Some livers have numerous hemorrhagic foci. Other lesions in affected turkeys include obesity, hemorrhages on the surface of the heart and in the fat around the gizzard, and congested, edematous lungs.

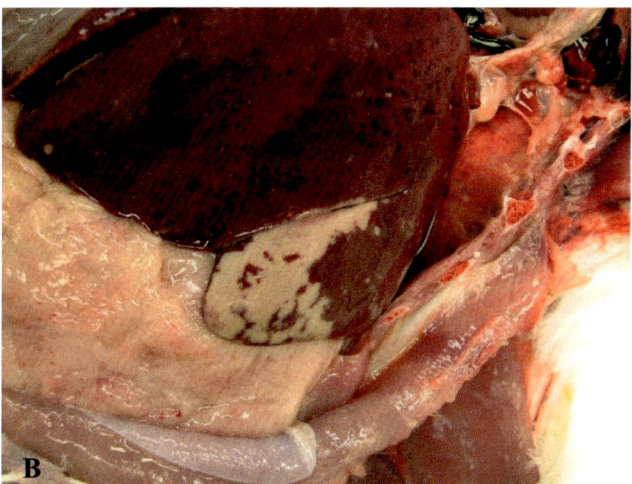

Hepatic lipidosis syndrome. Replacement turkey breeder hens. **A, B.** The yellow areas in the livers are due to marked fat accumulation in hepatocytes. In **C**, note the hemorrhagic foci on the capsule of the liver. **C.** Cut surfaces of the liver in A.

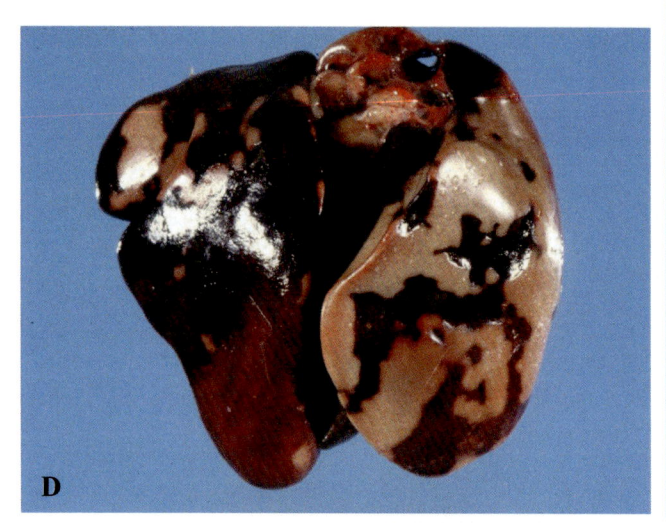

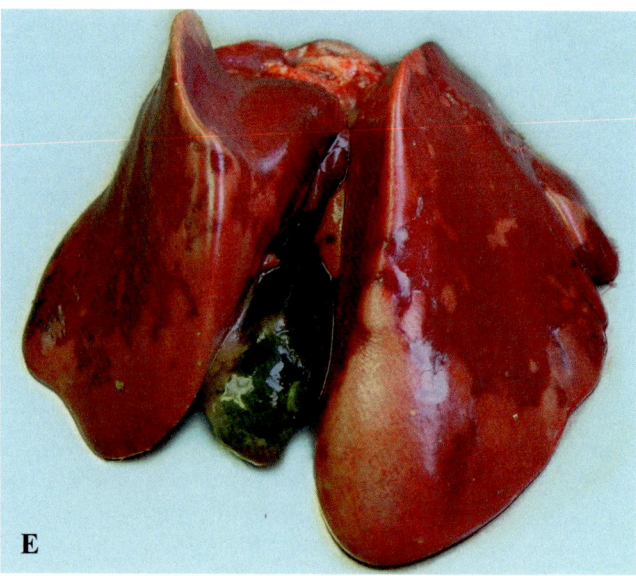

Hepatic lipidosis syndrome. Turkey breeder hen replacements. **D, E.** Pale areas of marked fat accumulation in hepatocytes. Livers are enlarged, with rounded margins. **F.** Liver is diffusely pale yellow and has many hemorrhagic foci. *(Photos courtesy of Dr. Peter Gazdzinski, Canada).*

Aflatoxicosis in Ducks

Cause. Aflatoxins are secondary metabolites produced by fungi, especially *Aspergillus* spp. At least 14 aflatoxins are known but the major ones are B1, B2, G1, and G2. *A. flavus* produces B1 and B2. *A. parasiticus* produces all four toxins but in lesser amounts. *A. flavus* and *A. parasiticus* contaminate crops (cereal grains, legumes) and processed animal feed. Under appropriate temperature and moisture conditions, they grow and produce aflatoxins. B1 is the most common and most toxic aflatoxin. Ducklings are quite sensitive to aflatoxin.

Gross lesions. In acute and subacute cases, hepatomegaly and marked yellow discoloration of the liver are the most obvious and consistent postmortem findings. The capsular surface of the liver may have an accentuated reticular pattern. Bile may be watery and pale green. Kidneys and spleen are usually pale and there is atrophy of lymphoid organs especially the bursa of Fabricius and thymus. In chronic cases, liver fibrosis and hepatic and biliary carcinomas may develop.

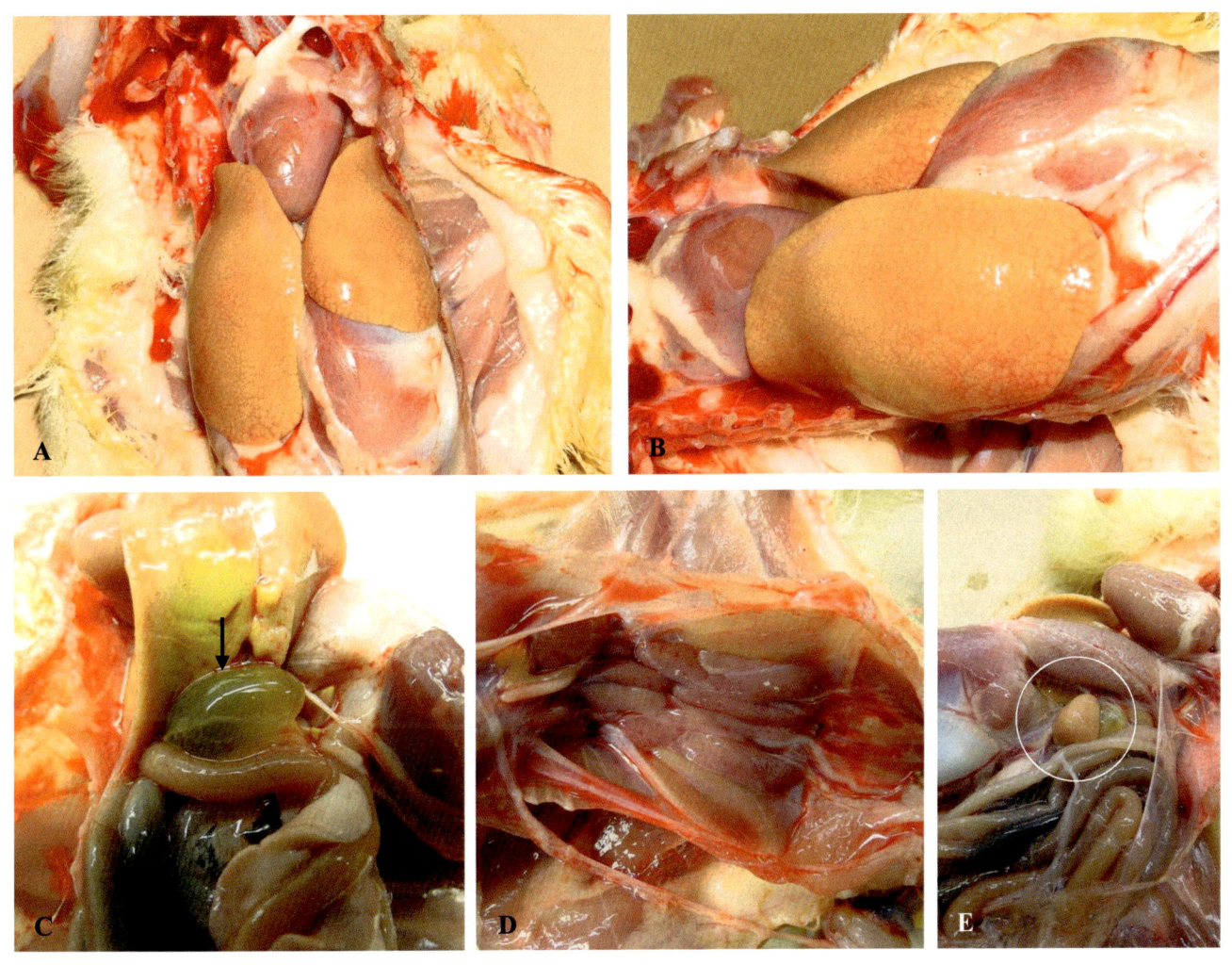

Aflatoxicosis. 2-week ducklings. **A, B.** Marked yellow discoloration of the liver due to diffuse fatty degeneration. Capsule of the liver shows an enhanced reticular pattern. **C.** Bile in the gall bladder (arrow) is thin and pale. **D.** Pale kidneys. **E.** Pale spleen (circle).

Hemosiderosis and Iron-Storage Disease

Basic metabolism of iron. To understand hemosiderosis, it is necessary to have a basic understanding of iron metabolism. Most iron required by the body (especially for erythropoiesis) is acquired by recycling it from senescent red blood cells (RBCs). Red blood cells that reach the end of their lifespan are phagocytized by reticuloendothelial macrophages in the spleen, liver, and bone marrow. Within the macrophages, RBCs are degraded by hydrolytic enzymes. Hemoglobin is released, which is further catabolized by proteolytic enzymes to separate globin and iron-containing heme. Globin is broken down into amino acids, which are used for protein synthesis. Iron liberated from the heme molecule is exported into the plasma. The mechanism by which iron is transported from macrophages to the plasma is uncertain, but is believed to be facilitated by the copper-containing protein ceruloplasmin.

Dietary iron is absorbed mainly from the duodenum and upper jejunum. Ingested inorganic ferric iron (Fe^{+++}) must be converted to ferrous iron (Fe^{++}) by the enzyme ferrireductase in the brush border of enterocytes before it can be absorbed. After ferrous iron is absorbed by enterocytes, it is transported to the plasma following conversion of Fe^{++} back to Fe^{+++} by ferroxidase hephaestin, a transmembrane copper-containing ferroxidase. Transfer of iron from enterocytes to plasma is mediated through the transmembrane protein ferroportin 1, most likely in concert with hephaestin.

In the plasma, iron binds to apotransferrin (synthesized in the hepatocytes), a copper-containing protein, to form transferrin, which transports iron to tissue. For iron uptake by cells, transferrin molecules bind to transferrin receptors on the cell surface. Transferrin receptors are highly expressed on the surface of erythrocyte precursors. Iron is taken into the cell where it is used or stored. The highest concentration of stored iron is found in hepatocytes in the liver, followed by bone marrow and spleen.

Iron is stored in the cytosol of cells as ferritin, the major intracellular iron-storing protein that stores iron and releases it in a controlled fashion when needed. Ferritin is a water-soluble, globular protein composed of multiple protein subunits that form a shell around a core of ferrous hydroxide. The protein shell sequesters iron and protects the cell from iron toxicity. Iron in ferritin does not stain and cannot be visualized with light microscopy. When iron is needed, ferritin is degraded in lysosomes to release the iron.

Hemosiderin is an iron-protein complex localized in membranous compartments within lysosomes. It has a higher content of iron than ferritin and, unlike ferritin; it is water insoluble and visible with light microscopy. In contrast to iron in ferritin, iron in hemosiderin is poorly available. Hemosiderin is formed from ferritin but the mechanism of its formation is not fully understood. It has been suggested that when there is iron overload, ferritin cannot be completely degraded by lysosomes and they cannot efficiently transport iron across lysosomal membranes to the cytosol. The protein component of hemosiderin is poorly characterized but may include apoferritin, ferritin, and their degradation products.

Hemosiderosis. Hemosiderosis refers to the accumulation of excess hemosiderin in tissues (particularly liver and spleen) that is visible microscopically. It is an indication of iron overload. Hemosiderosis in birds seems to be due mainly to high dietary iron, but can also result from excessive destruction of red blood cells as in hemorrhage and hemolytic anemia.

Iron storage disease. Iron-storage disease in birds is a pathological condition characterized by chronic, excessive accumulation of iron in cells of the liver and spleen, which damages the liver due to the direct toxic effect of iron on hepatocytes. Extensive necrosis of hepatocytes results in fibrosis (cirrhosis) with regenerative nodular hyperplasia. Not all birds are uniformly susceptible to iron storage disease. Mynahs, starlings, toucans, flamingos, and hornbills are among birds that are often affected.

Primary hemochromatosis (hereditary hemochromatosis) in humans is a genetic disease caused by inherited defective genes that encode proteins involved in regulating the absorption, transport, and storage of iron. Depending on the type of hemochromatosis, the defective gene is inherited in an autosomal recessive or dominant pattern. The overwhelming majority of primary hemochromatosis in humans is caused by mutation in the gene that encodes synthesis of hepcidin in the liver. Hepcidin plays an important role in regulating iron homeostasis. Low hepcidin levels trigger increased iron absorption from the duodenum and iron release from reticuloendothelial macrophages. Primary hemochromatosis is not known to occur in birds. There is no evidence that iron-storage disease in birds is caused by a genetically inherited defect in iron metabolism.

Gross lesions. No gross lesions are seen in the liver or spleen of birds with mild hemosiderosis. In severe hepatic hemosiderosis, the liver shows variable degrees of brown discoloration. In iron-storage disease, the liver is light to red brown, shrunken, and firmer than normal. It often has an irregular or nodular capsular surface or distorted shape due to fibrosis and formation of regenerative hepatocyte nodules. Bile stasis may cause green areas. Ascites occurs when liver damage is severe.

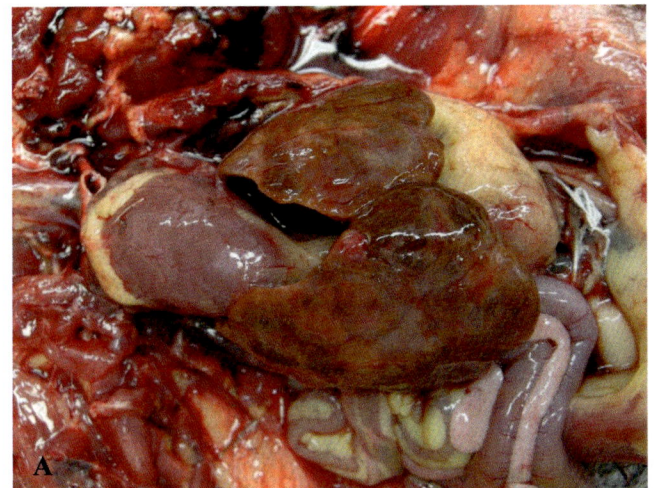

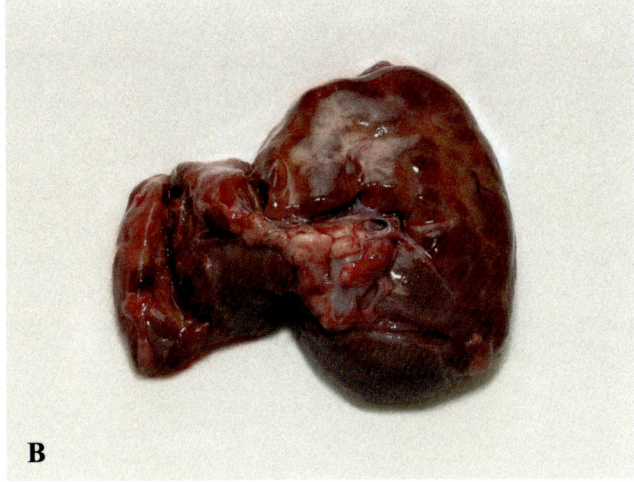

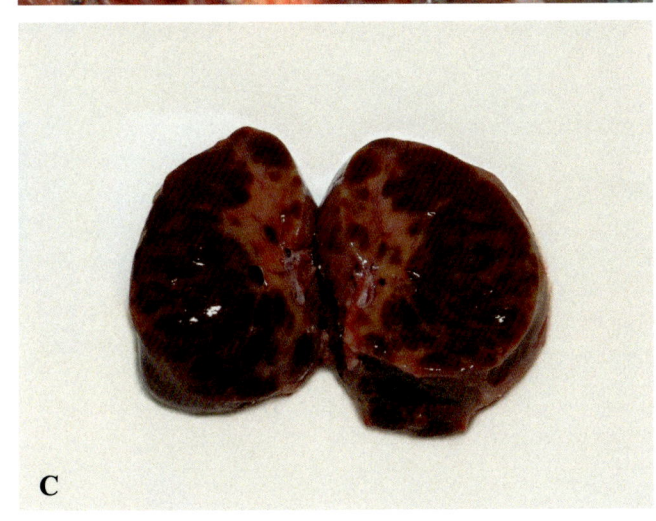

Iron-storage disease. A. 14-year parrot. Liver is mildly shrunken and discolored brown with pale and green areas due to fibrosis and bile stasis. The capsular surface is irregular. **B, C.** 24-year Macaw. **B.** Liver is red–brown and distorted and has an irregular capsular surface with slightly raised nodules. **C.** Cut surface of the liver is marbled and has pale areas of fibrous tissue.

Necrohemorrhagic Hepatopathy in Chickens Following *Salmonella* Enteritidis Bacterin Injection

Necrohemorrhagic hepatopathy occurs in broiler breeders and table-egg pullets following subcutaneous or intramuscular injections of *Salmonella* Enteritidis (SE) Bacterin.

Clinical signs. Culling and mortality are increased in pullet flocks within 2 weeks following injection of SE bacterin. Severe lethargy, weight loss, and anorexia are seen in affected pullets. Following injections in the leg, birds may show lameness and limping.

Gross lesions. Tissue damage is evident at the injection site. Frequently, the body cavity contains blood or yellow to serosanguineous fluid. The liver is often moderately enlarged, firm but friable, and has variably sized necrotic and hemorrhagic areas randomly located on the capsular surface. Enlarged livers may only have punctate red spots. Subcapsular hemorrhages are present in some birds. Spleen is usually mildly to moderately enlarged. Birds are thin and have little or no food in the crop and gizzard.

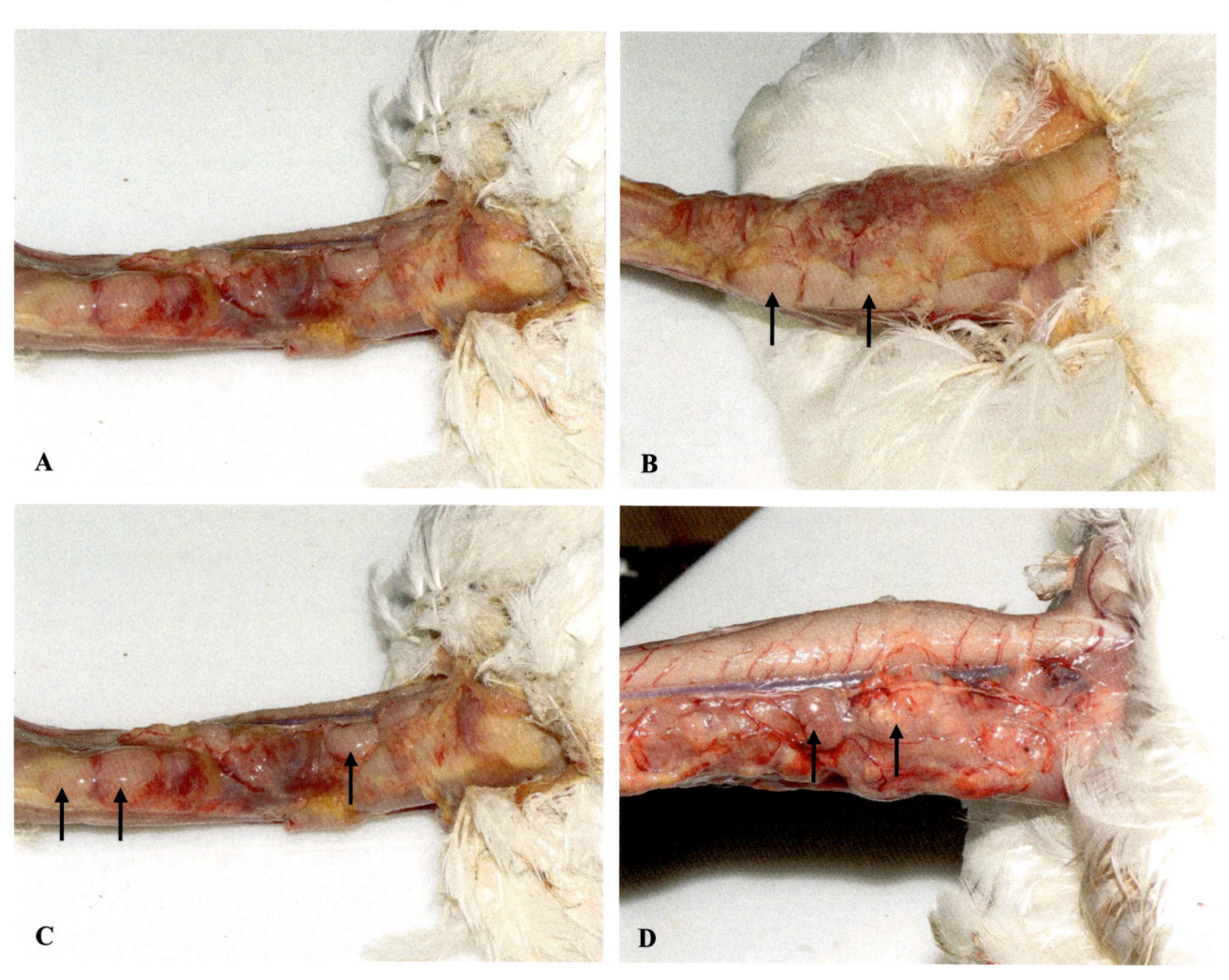

Salmonella Enteritidis bacterin injection sites (neck). 19- and 20-week broiler breeder hens. **A-D.** Severe damage to the soft tissue of the neck at the site of subcutaneous injection of the bacterin. Tissues are markedly thickened and hyperemic and contain caseous material. Thymic lobes can be identified (arrows).

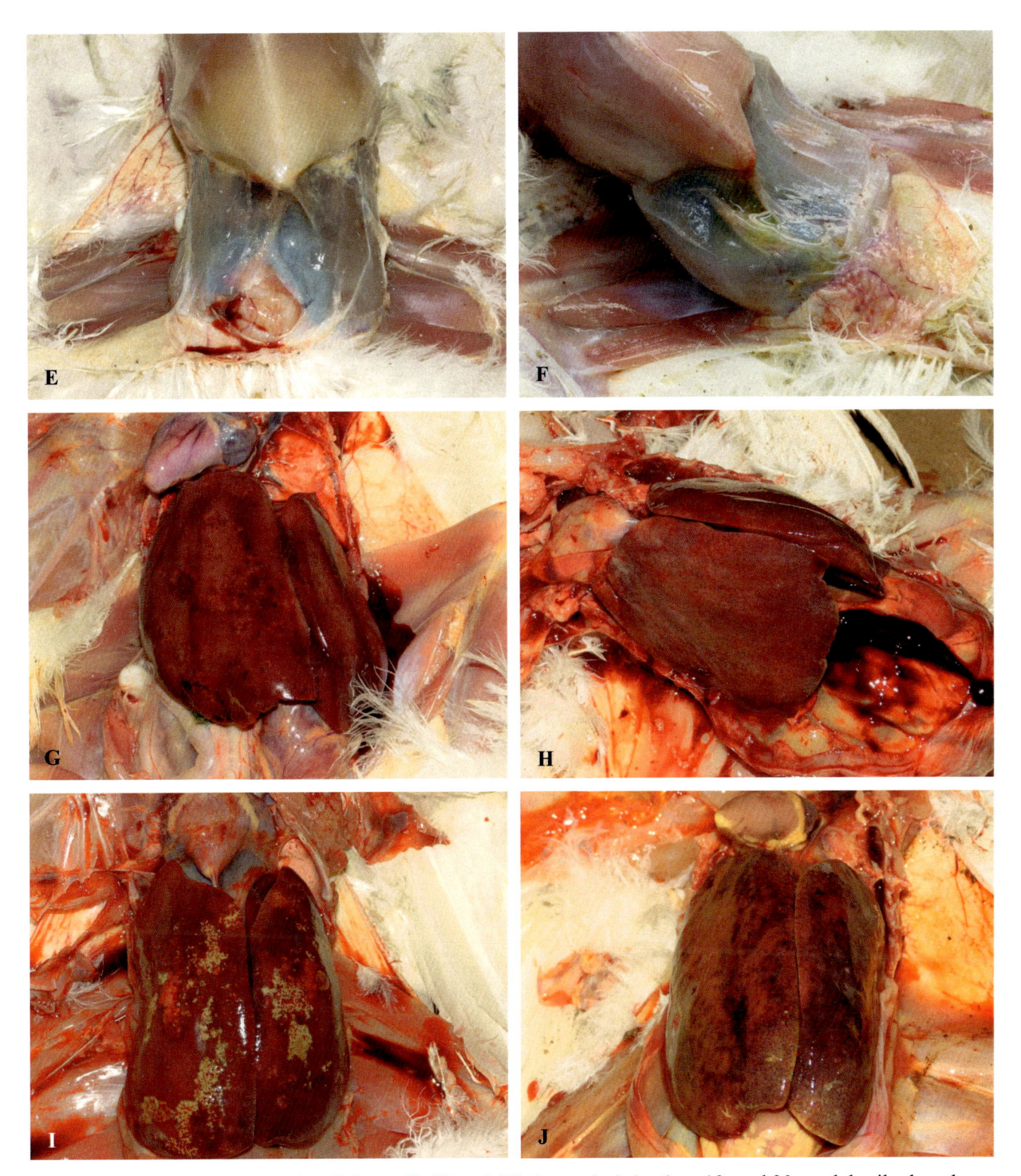

Necrohemorrhagic hepatopathy. *Salmonella* **Enteritidis bacterin injection.** 19- and 20-week broiler breeder hens. **E, F.** Body cavity contains blood. **G–J.** Liver lesions. Livers are enlarged and have hemorrhagic and necrotic areas. Livers are firm and friable. In **F**, note punctate red spots in the liver and blood in the body cavity.

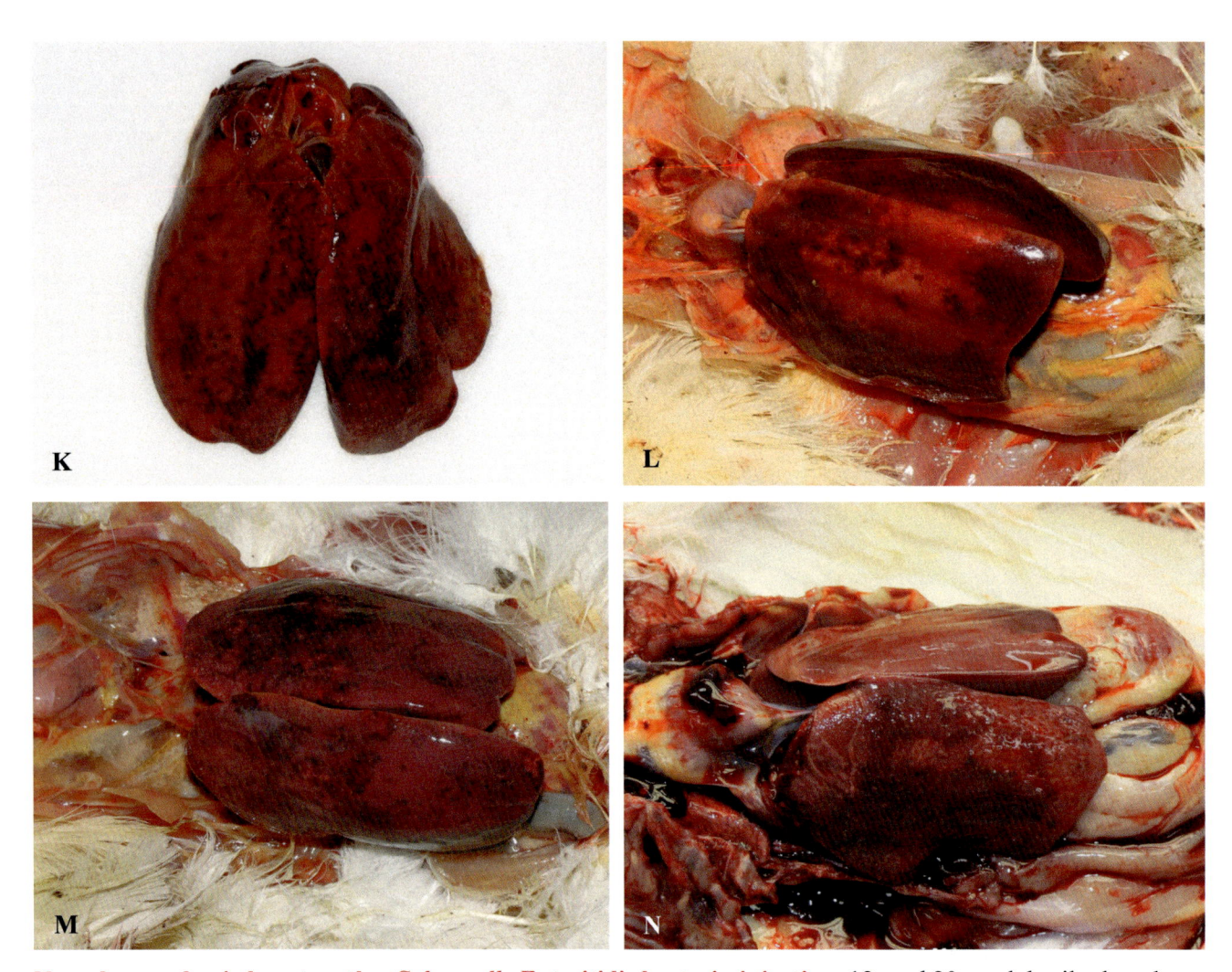

Necrohemorrhagic hepatopathy. *Salmonella* **Enteritidis bacterin injection.** 19- and 20-week broiler breeder hens. **K-M.** Livers are enlarged and have hemorrhages and necrotic areas. Livers are firm and friable. **N.** Marked subcapsular hemorrhage in the right lobe of the liver. Capsule is detached from the surface, which is roughened and pitted. Blood is in the body cavity.

Oral, Pharyngeal, Esophageal, and Laryngeal Squamous Cell Carcinoma (SCC) in Hobby Chickens

The tumor usually occurs as a caseous mass attached to and arising from the mucosal surface of the mouth (oral SCC), pharynx (pharyngeal SCC), esophageal opening (esophageal SCC), or larynx (laryngeal SCC). Careful removal of the mass reveals a roughened, ulcerated point of attachment. Laryngeal SCC fills the larynx and can occlude the glottis. Early lesions appear as thickened, raised areas in the mucosal surface.

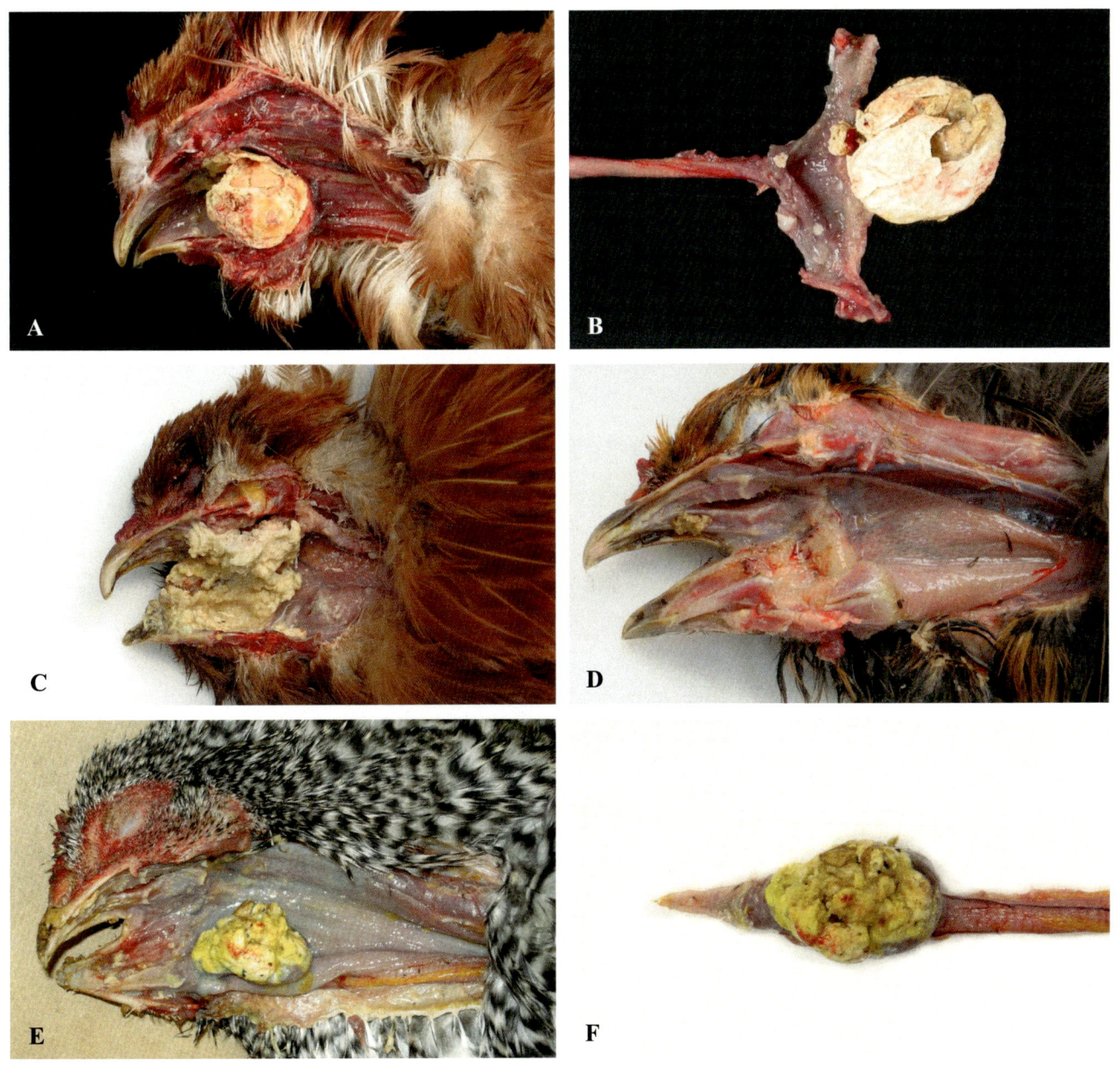

Squamous cell carcinoma (SCC). A, B. Esophageal SCC. 3.5-year hobby chicken. **A.** Tumor extends from the pharynx into the oral cavity. It has a crusty, yellow surface and contains abundant caseous exudate. **B.** Tumor is attached to the esophageal opening, indicating it is of esophageal origin. **C.** Oral/Pharyngeal SCC. Adult hobby chicken. Tumor is composed of caseo-necrotic exudate that fills the oral cavity and focally adheres to the oral mucosa. **D.** 4-year hobby chicken. Early stage pharyngeal SCC. A thickened, raised area (arrow) is in the pharyngeal mucosa. Asterisks: esophagus. **E, F.** Laryngeal SCC. 3-year hobby chicken. A caseated tumor fills the larynx and occludes the glottis. The ulcerated squamous cell carcinoma is arising from the laryngeal mucosa.

Traumatic Ventriculitis

Cause. Traumatic ventriculitis results when the ventriculus (gizzard) is perforated by a sharp foreign body. Birds ingest stones (grit) and other foreign objects to aid in grinding food in the ventriculus. If sharp objects such as pieces of wire, nails, screws, bolts, wood splinters, etc. are among the objects that are eaten; they can penetrate the wall of the ventriculus.

Gross lesions. The object may remain in the wall of the ventriculus or eventually be forced through it. An area of peritonitis develops where the object emerges from the ventriculus, which can range from small and localized to large and extensive. Sometimes the object penetrates the adjacent liver causing necrosis. The duodenum makes a sharp, 90° bend as it exits the ventriculus. Long, pointed objectives that are unable to make the bend penetrate through the wall of the duodenum. Usually the object is identified at necropsy, but sometimes, as in the case of pieces of wire and long-standing lesions, the object may dissolve and only a tract through the wall of the ventriculus remains. If the object contained iron, the tract will be black. Traumatic ventriculitis usually affects only occasional birds, but flock outbreaks occur if the birds are placed in environments where construction has occurred, sharp objects such as nails have been spilled, or litter is poor quality and contains numerous large wood splinters. An unusual case of traumatic ventriculitis occurred in a zoological collection of exotic birds that were being fed crickets. The hind legs of the insects bore several large spines and penetrated the wall of the gizzard. Removing the hind legs before feeding the insects to the birds resolved the problem.

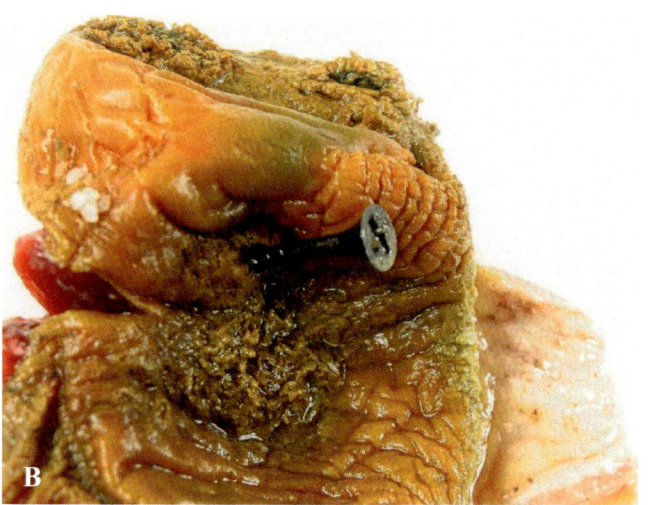

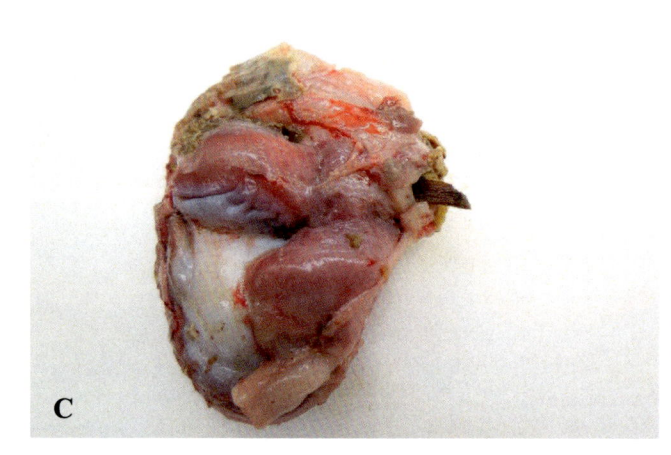

Perforation of the ventriculus by foreign bodies (traumatic ventriculitis). Hobby chickens (**A, B** [same bird]) and broiler breeder pullets (**C, D** [same bird], **E**). Foreign bodies penetrate and perforate the wall of the gizzard. In **A**, the area around where a nail has perforated the gizzard is black due to iron in the nail. In **C** and **D**, the foreign body is a piece of wood, likely from poor quality wood shavings on which the birds had been placed. In **E**, the perforating object is a screw. Note the mucosal ulcer across from the perforation that was caused by the head of the screw. In **F**, the foreign body (arrow) is a piece of metal (arrow). Leakage of gizzard contents into the body cavity leads to peritonitis.

Intussusception in Poultry

Intussusception is a condition in which a segment of digestive tract invaginates or telescopes into the lumen of an adjacent distal/posterior segment. The pattern of intussusception follows the normal direction of peristalsis. The invaginated segment is called intussusceptum and the engulfing segment is called intussuscepiens. Most commonly the lower small intestine invaginates through the large intestine, often protruding as a bloody stub from the vent. Less frequently, the proventriculus invaginates into the ventriculus. Intestinal intussusceptions often occur around 2-4 weeks of age. Proventricular intussusceptions affect young chicks a few days old that have been withheld from food and water and old commercial laying hens.

Cause. Most cases of intussusception in poultry are idiopathic, i.e., undermined cause. It has been suggested that intussusception results from intestinal hypermotility caused by coccidiosis, other intestinal parasites, *Clostridium* spp., or enteric viruses. However, there is not a consistent correlation between intussusception and enteritis, as, in many cases, no evidence of enteric infection is found in affected birds. A relatively high incidence of intussusception occurs in young broiler breeders of certain strains when they are on restricted feeding programs. In these birds, lack of feed likely causes hyperperistalsis or dysperistalsis, which results in an intussusception. A similar mechanism causing proventricular intussusception may occur in young chicks that are withheld from feed and water. How and why proventricular intussusception occurs in older laying hens is unknown.

Gross lesions. The point of intestinal intussusception is typically a short distance above the ileocecal junction. The location of intussusception is intriguing but cannot be explained. Part of the lower jejunum and ileum is invaginated into the lumen of the segment immediately posterior to it. It takes on a corrugated appearance. Initially, the intussusception is congested and edematous, but later becomes hemorrhagic and necrotic (gangrenous). Obstruction of blood vessels leads to ischemic necrosis, hemorrhage, and gangrene. The posterior end of the invaginated segment often protrudes from the vent. The protruding part is hemorrhagic and necrotic. It may be traumatized by environmental objects or pecking. Invagination of part or all of the proventriculus is seen in proventricular intussusceptions.

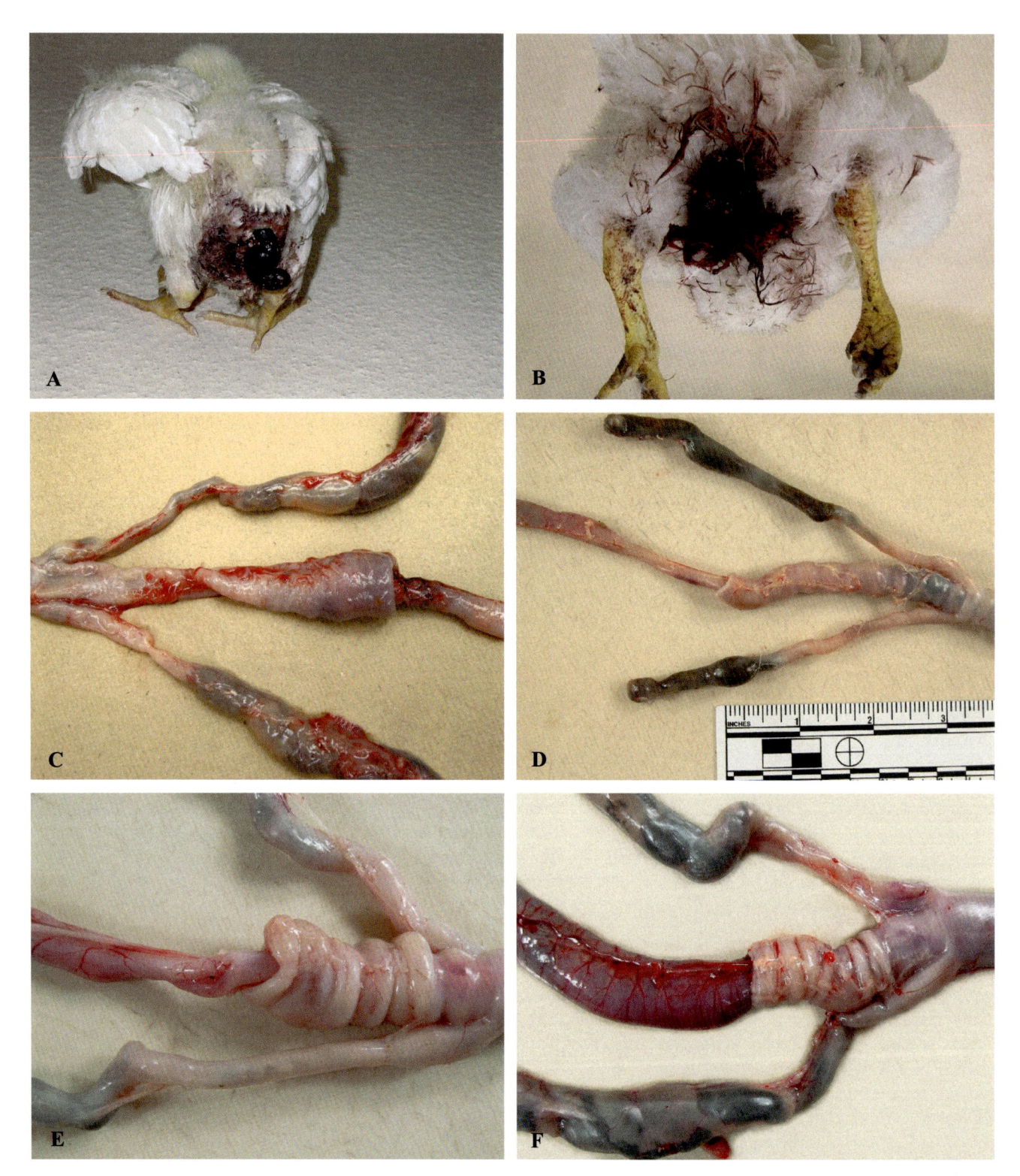

Intussusception. Broiler breeder pullets (A, B. 20-day, C. 15-weeks. D, E, F. 17-weeks). **A.** The posterior end of the invaginated segment of the intestine is protruding from the vent. The protruding piece is hemorrhagic and necrotic (gangrenous). **B.** The piece of the intestinal tract protruding from the vent is severely hemorrhagic and traumatized. **C, D, E, F.** A segment of ileum is invaginated into the lumen of another segment immediately posterior to it. In all cases, the intussusception point is a short distance above the ileocecal junction. Figure **D** shows that the point of intussusception is about 3.5 inches proximal to the ileocecal junction. In **F**, the segment of the ileum proximal to the intussusception is hemorrhagic.

Cloacitis in Broiler Breeder Hens

Anatomy of cloaca. The cloaca in birds is a pouch-like structure that communicates with the bursa of Fabricius and in which the rectum, ureters, and oviduct or ductus deferens empty. The cloaca also contains the copulatory organ in males. It is divided into three chambers: (1) the coprodeum, which is the largest and receives the contents of the rectum; (2) the urodeum, into which the ureters and genital ducts open; and (3) the proctodeum, which contains the male copulatory organs and has the bursa of Fabricius on its dorsal aspect. The lining of the cloacal lumen is a mucous membrane with epithelial cells of varying heights. There is considerable focal and diffuse lymphoid tissue in the mucosa.

Pathogenesis. As the cloaca is contaminated with feces, part of the vagina (which also has a well-developed muscular layer) and cloaca are everted to the outside (prolapsed) during ovipositioning to allow the egg to pass from the oviduct without being contaminated with fecal material. Under normal conditions, the everted cloaca retracts soon after ovipositioning, but in some birds, especially those that are obese, it remains everted for an extended period. The everted, reddened cloacal mucosa may attract and be pecked on by other birds in the flock causing traumatic injury to the cloacal wall. Additionally, the everted cloaca is subject to irritation and injury by objects and material in the environment. Although the irritated or injured cloaca will retract after transient prolapse, injury to the mucosa paves the way for secondary infection by bacteria. Occurrence of this type of cloacitis only affects in-lay hens and not pullets, out of production hens, or males, which indicates that ovipositioning and cloacal evasion are important factors in the occurrence of cloacitis. The pathogenesis of cloacitis is considered to be ovipositioning → temporary eversion of cloaca and vagina → injury to cloacal mucosa → retraction of the cloaca → bacterial infection → cloacitis. Excessive subcutaneous and visceral fat deposits, superovulation, double-yolk eggs, and hypocalcemia are among factors that predispose to cloacal prolapse because they decrease retraction of the cloaca and vagina. Other factors contributing to the pathogenesis of cloacitis include environmental factors, especially high slat height and bright light, aggressive males, newly introduced males, a high ratio of males to females, and nutrition. Vent pecking by males is associated with hormonal changes and feed restriction.

Clinical signs and gross lesions. Flocks with a high incidence of cloacitis often also have a high incidence of cloacal prolapse. Weekly mortality rates are higher than expected due to vent/cloacal pecking and evisceration of the intestinal and/or reproductive tracts. Dead birds usually have severe damage to the vent, cloaca, and tissue around the vent. Evisceration of most of the intestinal tract, with blood clots in the body cavity are common lesions in dead birds; frequently, only a piece of the duodenum remains attached to the ventriculus. A portion or the entire oviduct may also be gone, but this is less common than intestinal evisceration. Ovary is not affected.

With cloacitis, cloacae may or may not be prolapsed but show various degrees of damage, with lesions that range from mild hemorrhage and swelling to severe hemorrhage, and marked, diffuse or irregular swelling. In severe cases, areas in the cloacal mucosa are necrotic and covered by a fibrinous membrane. Often, birds with cloacal lesions have normal, uninjured vents. Feathers around the vent are often soiled with fecal and urate material and variable amounts of blood. In normal cloacae, gentle squeezing of the area around the vent is needed to expose and examine the cloacal mucosa. Eggs smeared or streaked with blood (from hemorrhagic cloacae) is another clinical finding observed in flocks with cloacitis. Postmortem examination of affected birds reveals excellent body condition, with large amounts of subcutaneous and visceral fat and; most of the affected birds are in lay (ovaries with mature yolk follicles and follicular hierarchy). In some birds, close examination of severely affected cloacae may reveal hemorrhage in the oviduct and/or rectum, near their openings into the cloaca.

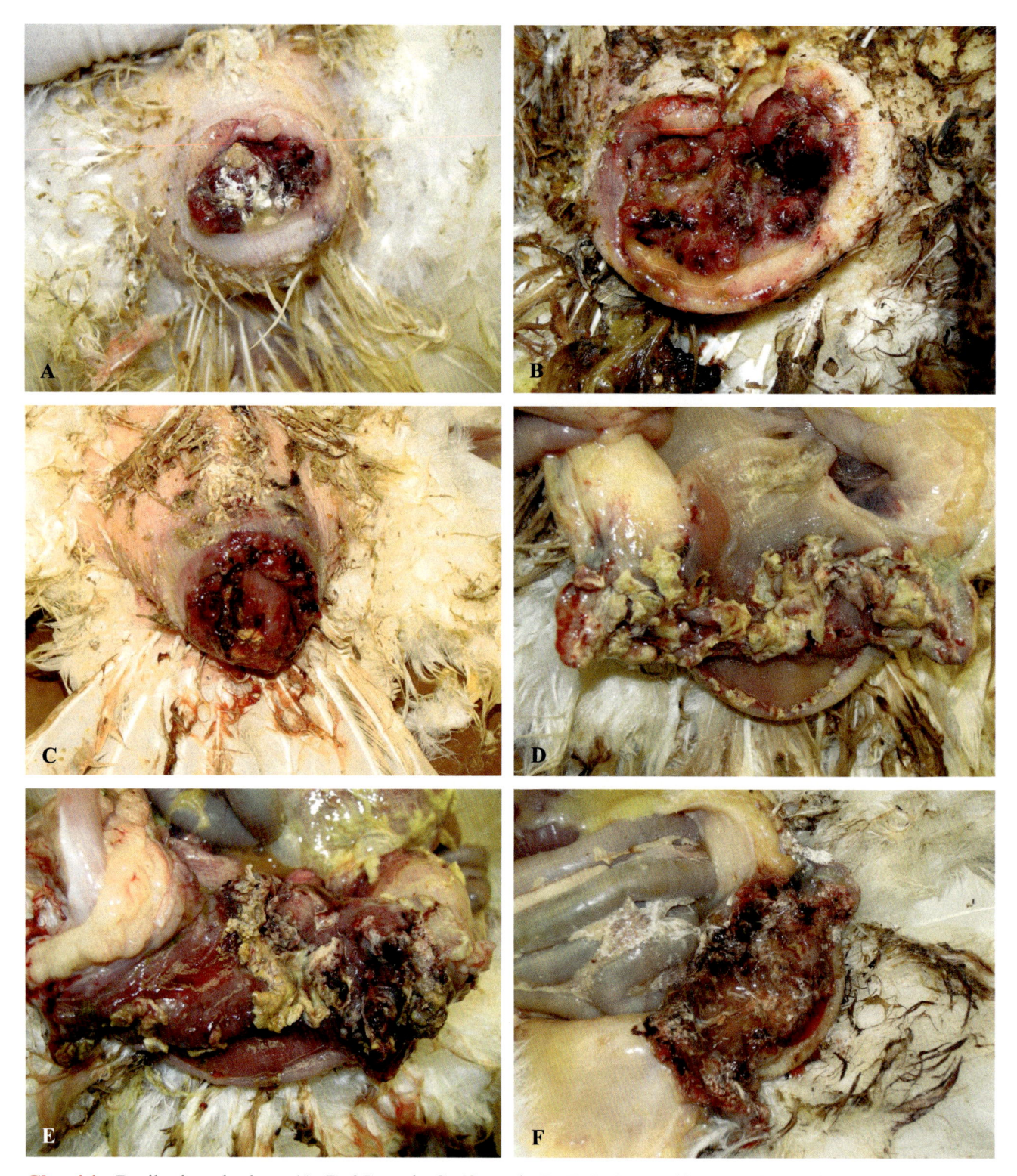

Cloacitis. Broiler breeder hens (A, B. 35-week. C. 42-week. D, E, F. 25-week). **A, B, C.** Swelling, ulceration, necrosis, congestion, and hemorrhage of the cloacal mucosa. **D, E, F.** Cloacae opened to show severe mucosal damage. **D, E.** A fibrinonecrotic membrane containing debris adheres to the underlying necrotic, ulcerated mucosa. **F.** Fibrinohemorrhagic exudate is on the surface of the underlying necrotic, ulcerated mucosa.

Dehydration in Baby Chicks (Baby Chick Nephropathy)

Gross lesions. Dehydration is an important cause of first week mortality in chicks and turkey poults. Affected birds are small for their age. Skin on the lower legs (tarsometatarsus) is dry, shriveled, and dark. A prominent fold is often located on the lateral and, to a lesser extent, medial sides of the legs. Toenails are dark and may even be black. Skin is dry and clings to the underlying tissue. The subcutis is dry and pectoral muscles are dark and dry. Kidneys in affected chicks are swollen, pale, and may show an enhanced reticular pattern or white stippling. In some birds, urates accumulate in the ureters, which become prominent. Deposition of urates on the epicardial surface of the heart, surface of the liver, and sometimes in visceral organs and tissues occurs in some cases. In chicks, the condition is called "baby chick nephropathy". Avian nephritis virus is an infectious cause of baby chick nephropathy.

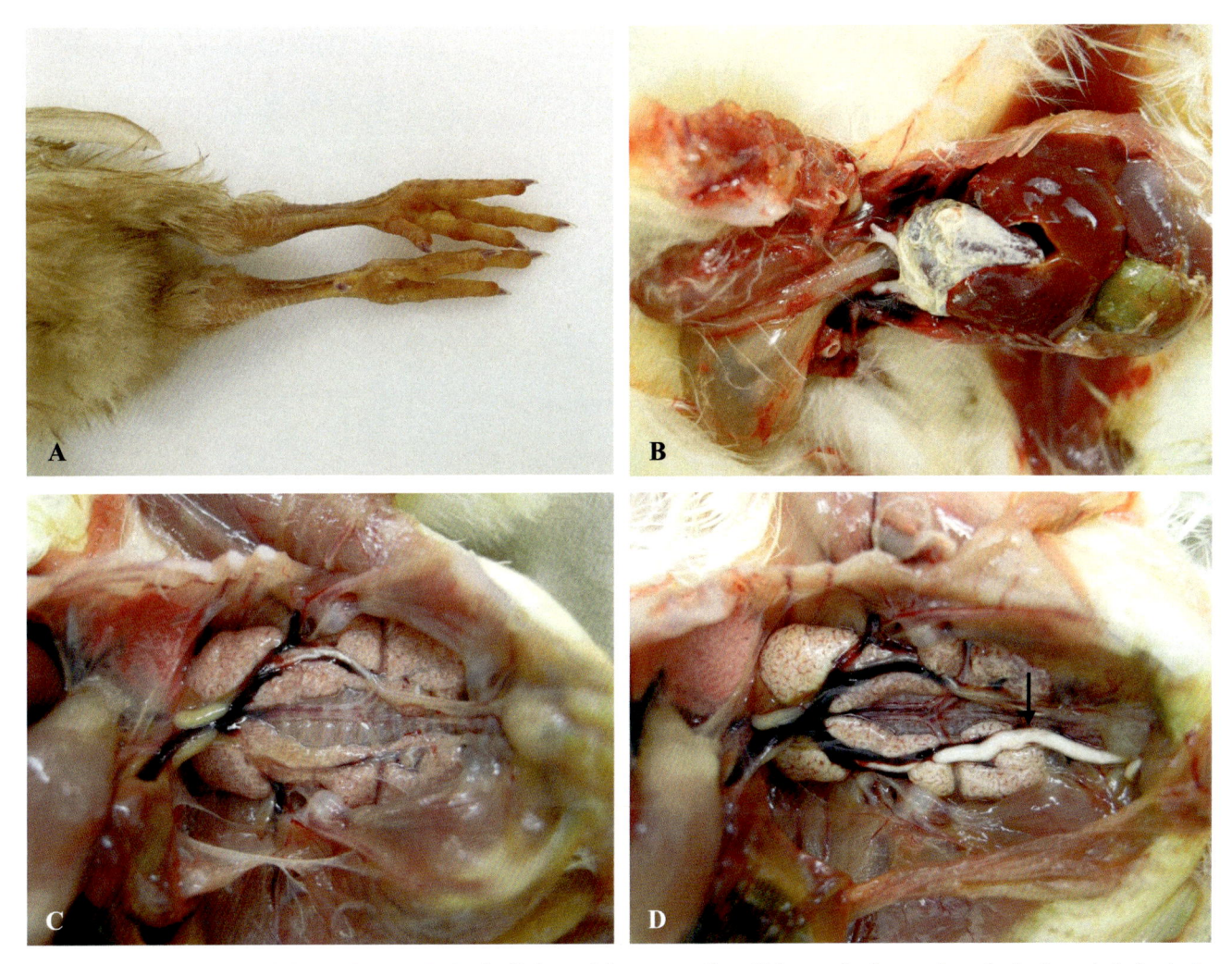

Dehydration (Baby chick nephropathy). **A.** 7-day table-egg pullet. Skin on the lower legs is dark and shriveled. Toenails are dark. **B.** 4-day broiler breeder pullet. Deposition of urates on the surface of the heart. Urates must be distinguished from exudate. **C, D.** 4-day broiler breeder males. Kidneys are swollen and pale and have an enhanced reticular pattern. In **D**, Note the accumulation of urates in the right ureter (arrow).

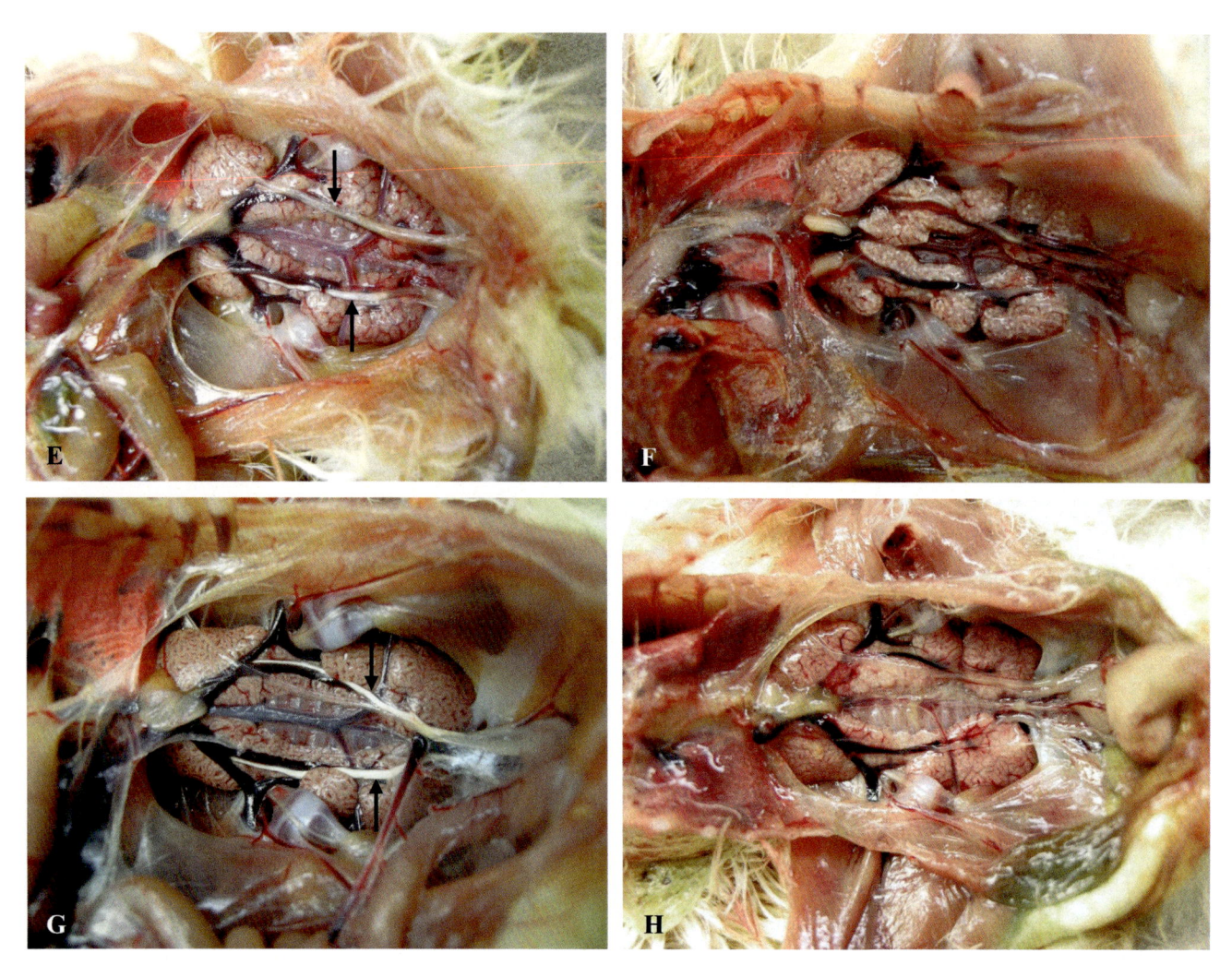

Dehydration (Baby chick nephropathy). E. 4-day broiler breeder male. Kidneys are pale, swollen, and have an accentuated reticular pattern. Ureters (arrows) contain excess urates. **F.** 4-day broiler breeder male. Kidneys are swollen, pale, and have white stippling indicative of urate deposition. **G, H.** 3-day broiler chickens. Kidneys are swollen, pale, and have a marked reticular pattern. In **G**, note the excess urates in the ureters (arrows).

Urolithiasis (Ureteral Calculi)

Urolithiasis is a metabolic disorder characterized by distension and blockage of ureters by urate concretions (uroliths), with severe damage and atrophy of one or more divisions of the kidney drained by the blocked ureter. Affected birds develop hyperuricemia because of kidney damage, with subsequent deposition of urate crystals on serosal surfaces of organs and synovial membranes of joints (visceral gout). Significant mortality can occur in table-egg layers.

Pathogenesis and cause. The pathogenesis and cause of urolithiasis are uncertain. There is progressive accumulation of uroliths in the ureter and its branches; which impedes the flow of urine from renal tubules. Urates excreted by renal tubules cannot be drained and accumulate in tubular lumens, causing tubular necrosis, tophi formation, and interstitial fibrosis. Eventually the renal division is destroyed and becomes nonfunctional. Inability to excrete urates results in hyperuricemia, which leads to visceral urate deposition. Uroliths are composed of calcium-sodium-urate crystals, with a random substitution of magnesium for calcium and potassium for sodium.

Several factors have been implicated singly or in combination in inducing or predisposing to urolithiasis including:
- Feeding relatively high calcium levels (3% or greater) for extended periods of time during the pullet period or when birds are out of egg production.
- Low available phosphorous levels (below 0.6%) may enhance development of the lesion.
- Water deprivation or reduced water intake decreases urine production and concentrates urates.
- Infection with nephrotropic strains of infectious bronchitis virus may increase the incidence of calcium-induced urolithiasis.
- Excess dietary protein (30% to 40%) increases uric acid production and may induce urolithiasis, especially if associated with water deprivation or low water intake.

Gross lesions. Affected birds are thin and in poor body condition. Often, they have urates caked around the vent. Deposition of urates in serosal membranes, especially epicardium and pericardium of the heart and capsular surface of the liver, visceral organs, and appendicular joints (visceral gout) is usually present. Dilation of one or both ureters, presence of calculi in ureters, and atrophy of kidney divisions are characteristic findings. Distended ureters are partially or totally obstructed by multiple small white calculi or large, brittle, white to pale yellow concretions (uroliths). Uroliths are surrounded by thick clear, pale yellow, gelatinous mucus that also fills the remainder of the dilated ureter. Large calculi frequently form a cast of the tubular system. One or more divisions of the kidney drained by the obstructed ureters are usually atrophied. Renal atrophy may not be evident in early stages, but in longstanding cases, renal divisions may be so atrophied as to appear absent or as only a remnant in the renal fossa. Partially atrophied divisions appear distorted due to distension of intra-renal ureteral branches by uroliths. Renal atrophy and fibrosis develop in birds instead of hydronephrosis as in mammals, because birds do not have a renal capsule; the surface of the kidney is bounded by the peritoneum. If the lesion is unilateral, the opposite functional kidney enlarges as it takes over lost function from the damaged kidney (compensatory hypertrophy). Urolithiasis must be differentiated from renal gout in which there are no ureteral calculi but both kidneys are swollen, pale, and have white pinpoint foci representing urate deposits in the renal parenchyma.

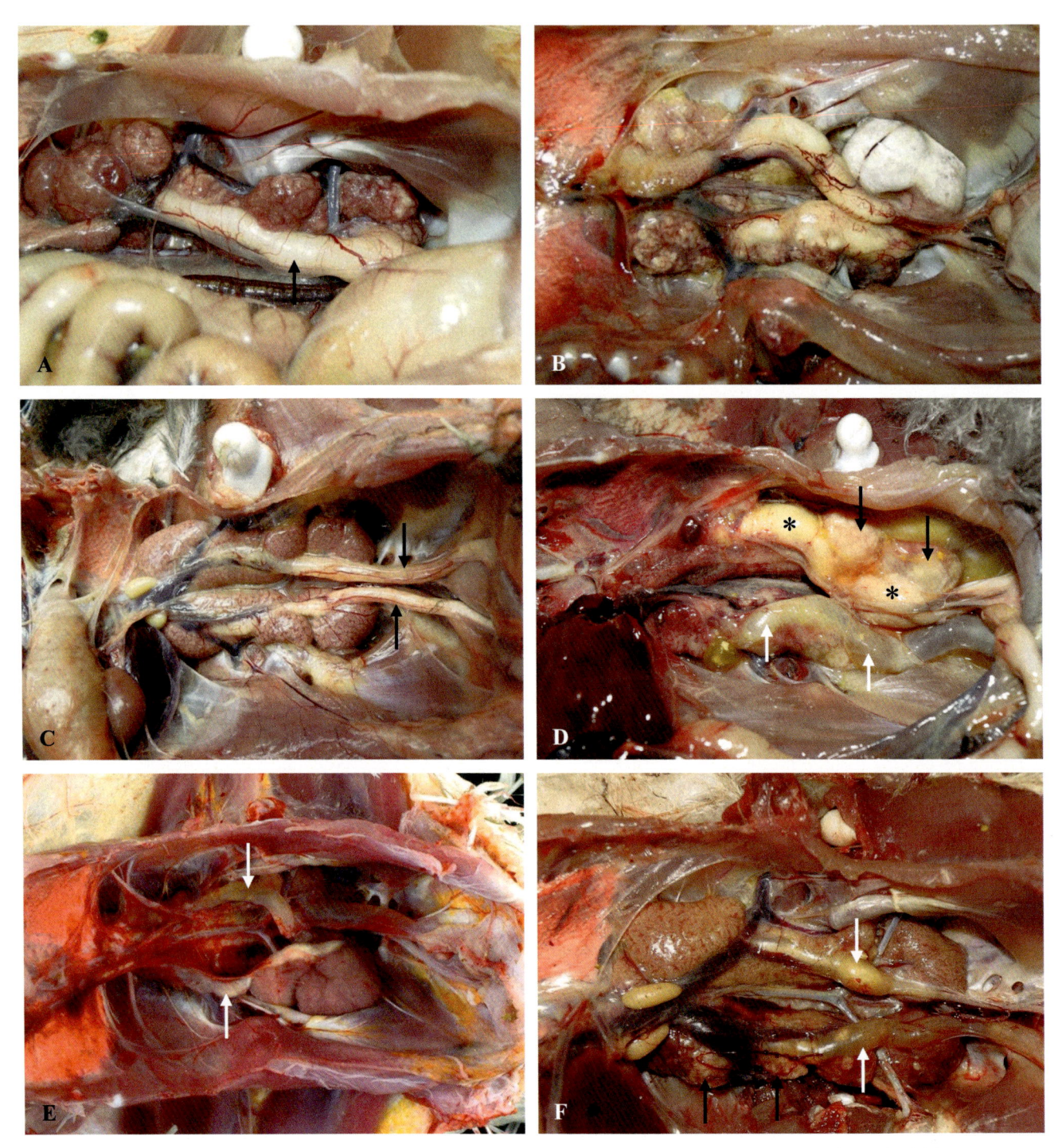

Urolithiasis. A. 11-week broiler breeder pullet. Left ureter (arrow) is distended with a urolith. The kidney is distorted by slightly raised, small white nodules representing calculi within intra-renal tubules. **B.** 11-week broiler breeder pullet. Both ureters are distended with uroliths. Both kidneys are distorted and have irregular surfaces caused by uroliths in intra-renal ureteral branches. **C.** 4-month hobby chicken. Both ureters (arrows) are distended with uroliths. Kidneys are pale. **D.** 5-month hobby chicken. Right ureter (white arrows) is distended with mucus. Left ureter (asterisks) is distended with urates and a urolith. Both kidneys are atrophied. The middle and posterior division of the left kidney (black arrows) are white due to uroliths in intra-renal ureteral branches. **E.** 57-week commercial egg layer. Ureters are distended with uroliths (arrows) and mucus. There is marked atrophy of most divisions of the kidneys. Remaining divisions show compensatory hypertrophy. **F.** 19-week broiler breeder pullet. Both ureters (white arrows) are distended with calculi and mucus. There is atrophy of the middle division of the left kidney and all three divisions of the right kidney. Raised nodules (black arrows) in the right kidney are calculi in intra-renal ureter branches.

ZZW Triploid Chicken

Triploidy is a chromosomal abnormality in which an extra set of chromosomes is present in each somatic cell. In normal birds, the male is the homogametic sex (ZZ) and the female is the heterogametic sex (ZW). During embryonic development, both testes develop in males but only the left ovary develops in females. There is little development of the right ovary, which persists as a vestigial tissue that is rarely evident grossly. If the left ovary is removed before hatching, the right ovary develops into testicular tissue capable of spermatogenesis, but there is no ductus deferens because the Wolffian duct does not develop in females. Triploid chicks are more likely to be produced by young breeder hens beginning ovulation or hens exposed to high temperatures.

Both paternal and maternal origins of triploidy are possible because of diploid spermatozoa or dispermy in the male or failure of meiosis in the female. Three genotypes of triploid embryos can occur: ZWW, ZZW, and ZZZ. Embryos with ZWW sex chromosomes do not survive to hatching; most die within the first few days of incubation. ZZW and ZZZ triploid embryos can develop, hatch, and survive to adulthood. ZZW chickens have a left ovary and right testis at hatching, but soon afterwards, the left ovary develops into an ovotestis. ZZW triploids have a normal female phenotype until they reach sexual maturity, when they undergo apparent sex reversal, developing masculine external features (comb size and shape, spur growth, and development of hackle feathers). Even though ZZW triploids appear to be males, comparison with true males shows they have a distinct phenotype that is intermediate between normal diploid males and females. Both gonads are capable of producing abnormal spermatozoa, thus ZZW triploids are sterile. The third genotype, ZZZ, have a normal male phenotype but produce abnormal spermatozoa and are sterile.

Gross appearance of the left and right gonads in ZZW triploid chickens. The left gonad (ovotestis) appears as large elongated, irregularly shaped, firm organ. Often the left gonad is yellow. The right gonad (testis) is lighter in color and may be smaller than the left gonad. It resembles a testis but is nodular and misshapen. Both oviducts are developed and often markedly enlarged. The left oviduct tends to be larger than the right oviduct.

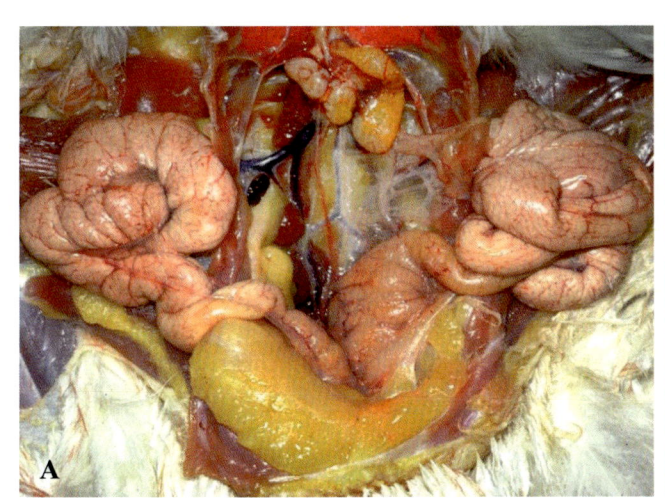

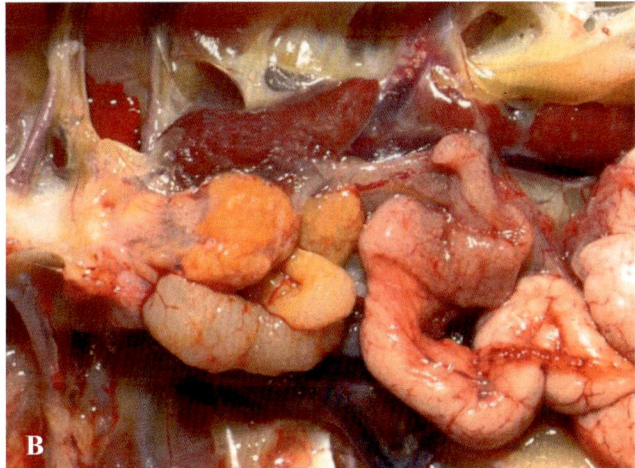

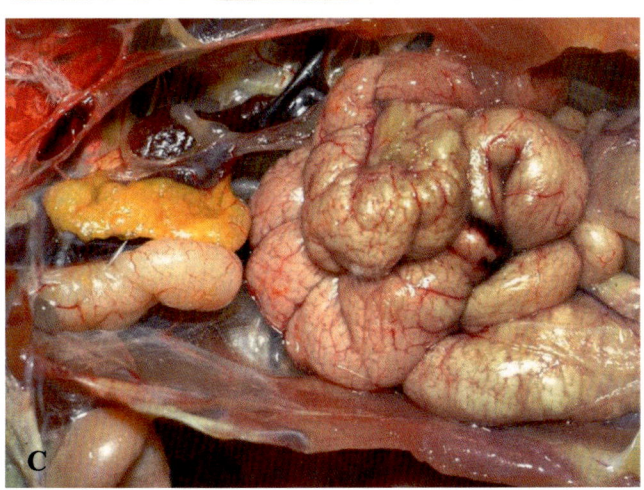

ZZW triploid chickens. 26-week white leghorn triploid egg-laying chickens. Both left and right oviducts are present and markedly hypertrophic. Left gonads are ovotestes. Yellow to tan tissue is embryonic ovary. Right gonad is testicular tissue but the shape is nodular and unlike a normal testis. Agenesis of the left kidney is also present in bird **A**.

Persistent Cystic Right Oviduct

During embryonic development of chickens and most other birds, there are left and right Müllerian (paramesonephric) ducts in both males and females. Müllerian ducts are the primordial anlage of the oviducts in females. In males, both ducts begin to regress around day 8 of incubation. In most female birds, the right duct starts to involute relatively slowly around day 12 of incubation while the left oviduct continues to develop into the functional oviduct. The regressed right oviduct persists into adulthood as a mere vestige near the cloaca at the caudal end of the body cavity. However, a segment or segments of the right oviduct may develop to varying degrees. These segments are closed at both ends (*i.e.*, have no drainage). If these primitive oviduct segments contain a significant glandular component, fluid secretions accumulate, resulting in formation of cysts that are located on the right side of the cloaca. Oviductal cysts vary in size from barely perceptible to very large ones that occupy most of the body cavity and compress visceral organs. Cysts may be multiple or separated by stalks of tissue, indicating that they developed in more than one segment of the right oviduct. Small cysts are usually somewhat elongated rather than round. Cysts have a thin, transparent wall with variable vascularization. Small cysts are usually filled with milky fluid. Larger cysts contain watery, clear or slightly white fluid. Very large cysts cause abdominal distension that can be mistaken for ascites from heart failure or reproductive tract cancers, but careful necropsy reveals that the fluid is contained within a cystic right oviduct rather than in the abdominal peritoneal cavity. Rarely, salpingitis and oviductal adenocarcinomas develop in cystic right oviducts.

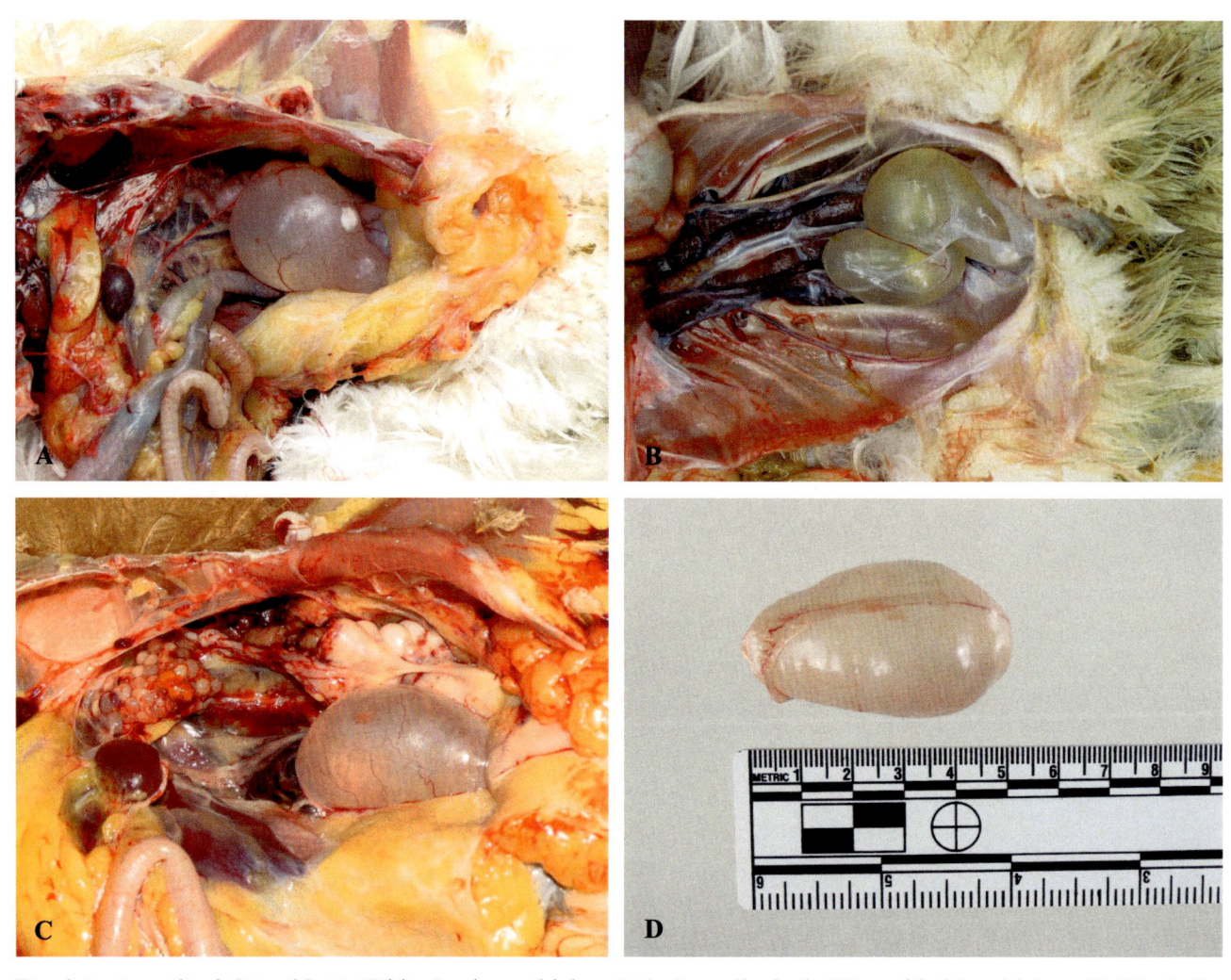

Persistent cystic right oviduct. White Leghorn chicken (A.), Juvenile duck (B), and hobby chicken (C, D). **A, B, C.** Cystic oviducts appear as a thin-walled, fluid-filled cyst located on the right side of the cloaca. The fluid, as seen through the transparent wall, looks watery. **D.** The cysts in C.

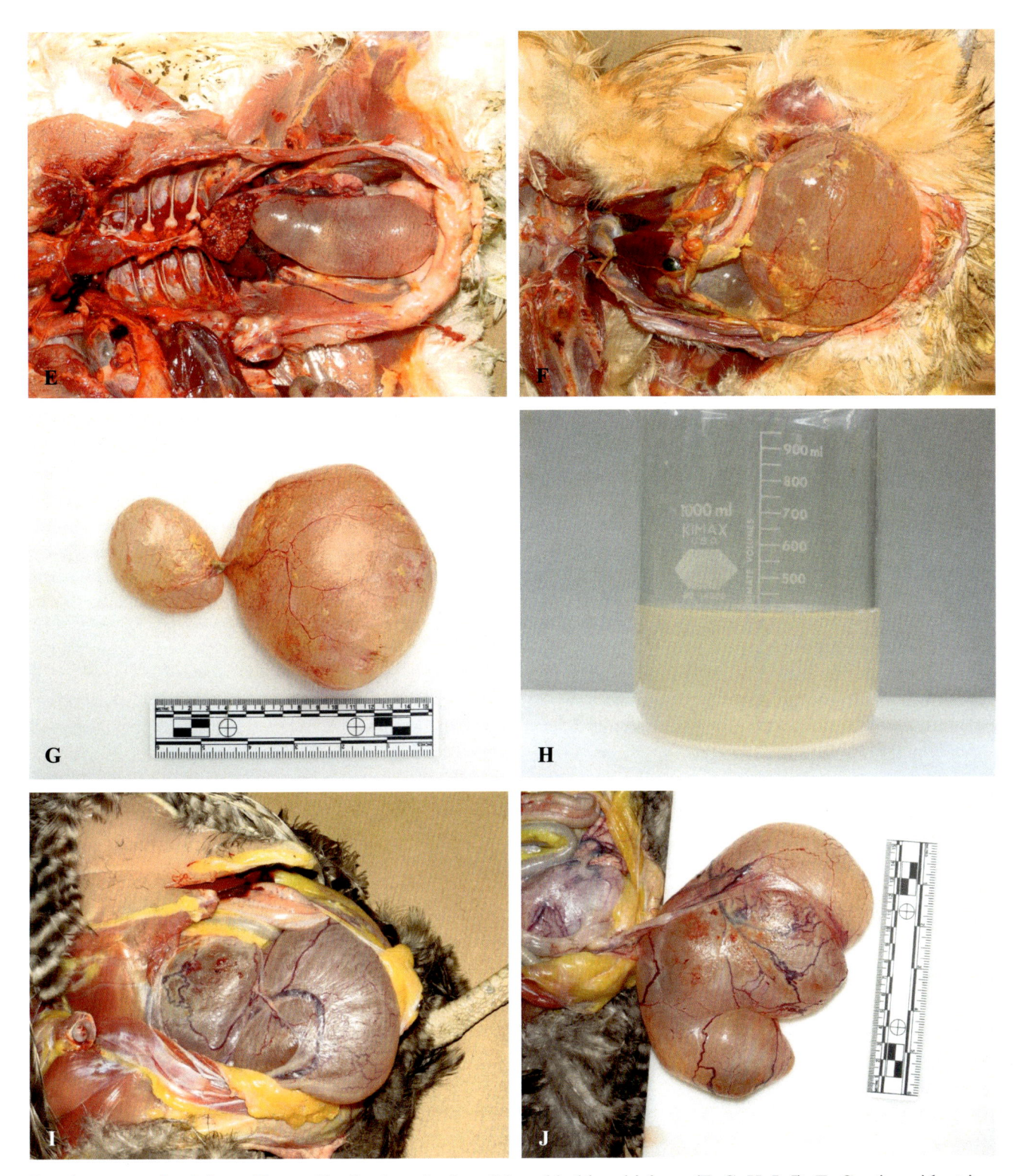

Persistent cystic right oviducts. Broiler breeder hen (E) and hobby chickens (F, G, H, I, J). **E.** Cystic oviduct is elongated in shape. **F.** Large cystic oviduct fills the body cavity. **G.** The cyst in **F** consists of two cysts separated by short stalk of tissue. **H.** Approximately 400 mL of clear, white fluid was aspirated from the cysts in **G**, **I, J**. Large fluid-filled cyst occupys most of the body cavity. Abdomen was softly distended mimicking ascites.

Regression (Involution, Atresia) of Ovarian Follicles

The ovary of a reproductively active hen contains 5-8 preovulatory yolk-filled follicles, the smallest of which is ~10-mm in diameter and the largest ~40 mm in diameter. The largest follicle is designated F1, the one next in size is designated F2, and so on. These follicles form the preovulatory follicular hierarchy. In addition to the preovulatory follicles, there are numerous microscopic quiescent primordial oocytes, many small, slow growing, cream-colored 1-5 mm follicles, and a few (generally 8-12) larger, faster growing 6-8 mm prehierarchal, cohort yolk follicles. Throughout the production cycle, primordial oocytes give rise to follicles, which increase in size overtime and eventually develop into yolk-filled preovulatory follicles. Many immature oocytes undergo obliterative atresia and do not develop into follicles, a process that is not apparent grossly. It takes about 17 days for a ~1.5 mm follicle to develop into a ~40 mm follicle. Large and small yolk-filled follicles have an avascular band termed the stigma where ovulation of the follicle occurs to release the ovum.

Normal preovulatory follicles are turgid, round, bright yellow to yellow-orange, contain viscous yolk, and are highly vascular except at the stigma. Regression (bursting atresia) of larger ovarian follicles containing yolk occurs normally at the conclusion of the hen's reproductive cycle. Acute regression also occurs when there is an adverse impact on the hen from an infectious or noninfectious disease. Responding to a disease takes precedence over maintaining reproduction when both are not possible. Ovarian regression is a non-specific lesion. Regressed follicles are wrinkled, flaccid, thin walled, and contain watery yolk that is often discolored (gray-yellow, beige, pale yellow, or green). Blood seeping into the follicle gives it a hemorrhagic appearance. Regressing follicles may rupture prematurely or the fluid yolk leak through the wall of the follicle, resulting in free yolk in the body cavity. A mild diffuse peritonitis (yolk peritonitis) develops when this happens. Normal, thick viscous yolk in the body cavity is an artifact from a follicle rupturing during handling or at necropsy. Ovarian regression generally involves the F1 follicle first, followed by the F2 follicle and so forth or may involve most of the follicles simultaneously in the case of an acute severe disease. Presence of post-ovulatory follicles indicates regression of the ovary has just begun. Regressed follicles need to be differentiated from ovarian cysts and folliculitis. Ovarian cysts occur on the surface of the ovary, have a smooth spherical shape, and are filled with clear fluid. Exudate on the surface or within a follicle indicates folliculitis. Distinguishing fully regressed and immature follicles also can be challenging. Generally, a regressed oviduct is larger and more developed than an immature oviduct. Both fully regressed and immature ovaries can look the same.

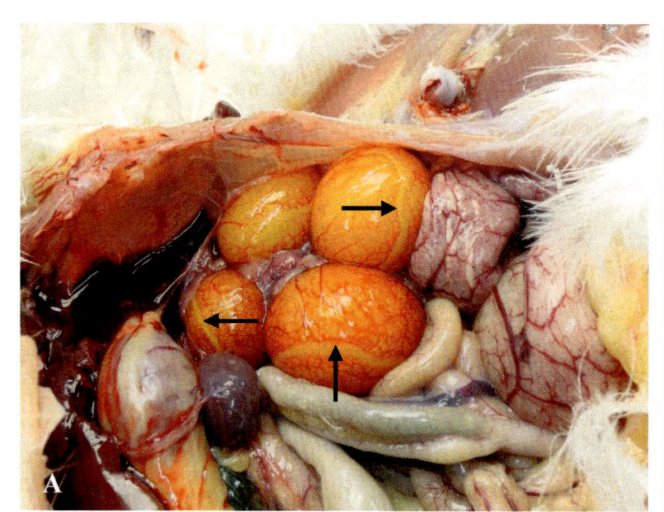

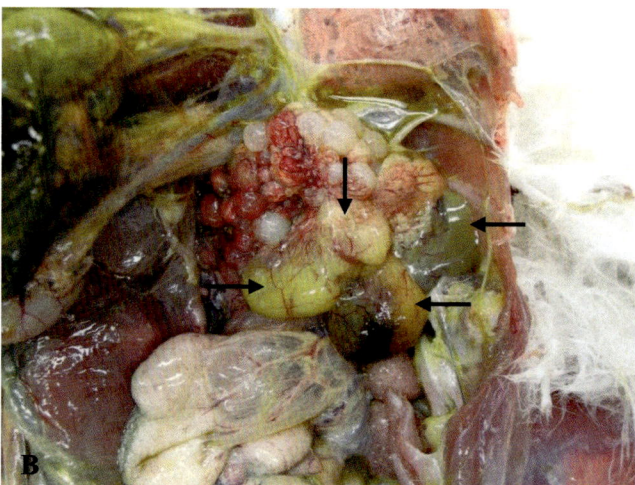

Regression of ovarian follicles. A. 31-week white leghorn chicken. Normal ovary. Preovulatory follicles are round, filled with yolk, and turgid. Arrows: stigma. **B.** Laying hen. Regressed ovarian follicles (arrows). Note the color and appearance of regressed follicles.

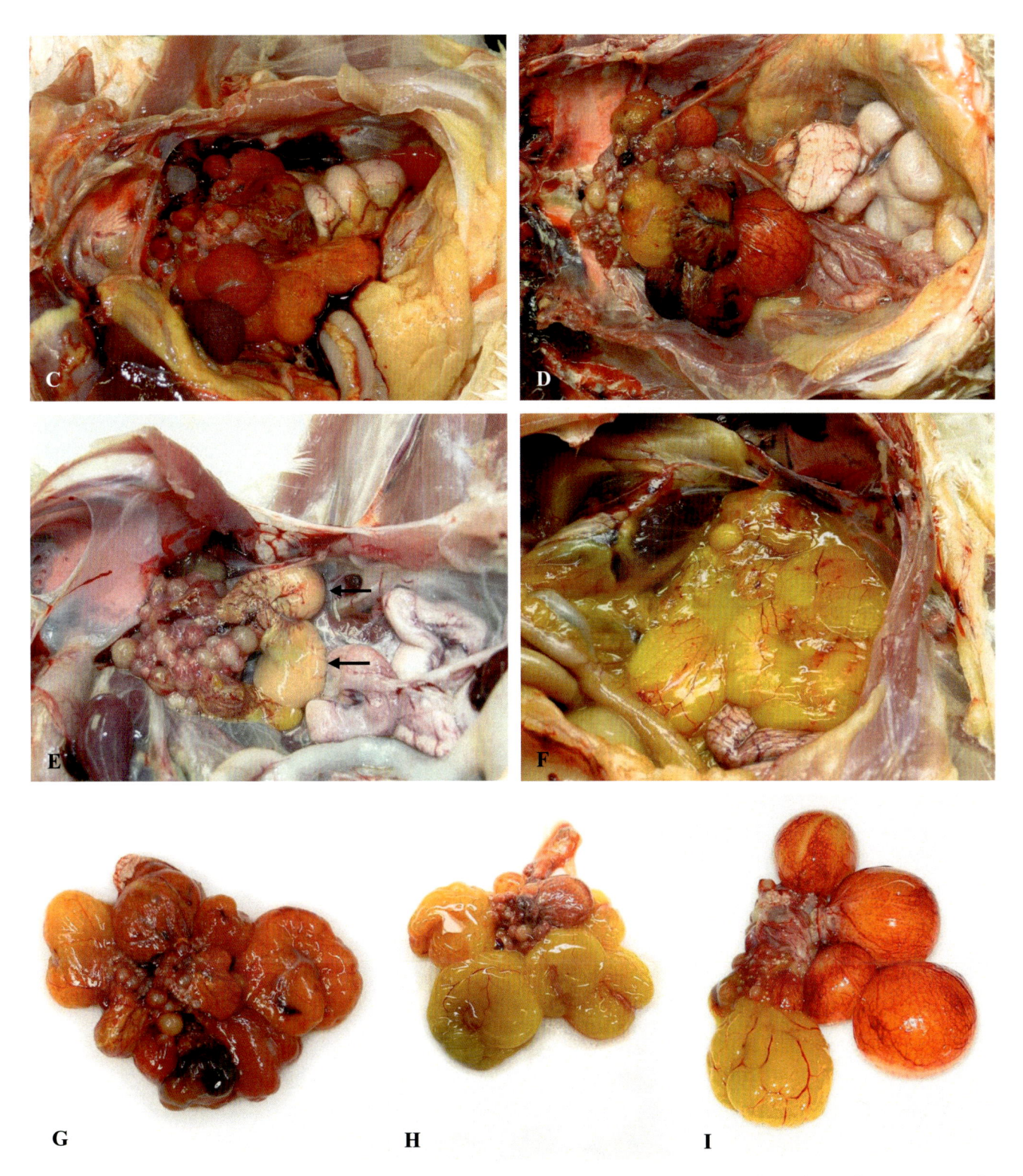

Regression of ovarian follicles. C-I. Laying hens. Regressed ovarian follicles. Note the color and appearance of the regressed follicles. In **D**, some regressed follicles are hemorrhagic. In **E**, the yolk in two regressed follicles is very thin (arrows). In **F**, ovarian regression is severe and there is some free yolk around the follicles. Free yolk results from rupture of a regressed follicle. Note in **I** that only the F1 follicle is regressing. This indicates ovarian regression has just begun.

Female Reproductive Tract Adenocarcinomas

Adenocarcinomas of the female reproductive tract are frequent in older laying hens and occasionally occur in older turkey breeder hens. Other reproductive tract tumors include Marek's disease, lymphoid and myeloid leukosis, granulosa cell tumors, ovarian Sertoli cell tumors, and mixed gonadal-stromal tumors. Hens with reproductive tumors in an early stage do not show evidence of disease and may continue to ovulate for an extended period of time as the tumors enlarge and spread. Tumors respond to the same hormonal signals as normal ovary and oviduct as long as the hen remains in production. In the late stages, hens are emaciated and have abdomens distended with ascites. The cause of reproductive adenocarcinomas is unknown, but they occur more frequently in hens with high rates of ovulation (egg production).

Adenomatous polyps. Adenomatous polyps in the oviduct are pre-neoplastic lesions. The number of polyps varies. When polyps are numerous, the term 'adenomatosis' is used. Polyps may be either sessile or pedunculated. Grossly, polyps differ from adenocarcinomas in being smaller (generally < 1 cm), have a regular smooth surface, and are uniformly colored. Pre-neoplastic lesions in the ovary have not been identified.

Adenocarcinomas. Adenocarcinomas occur in the ovary and oviduct, which are often concurrently affected. Ovarian and oviductal tumors cannot be differentiated, except by location. Almost all oviductal adenocarcinomas are in the magnum. Oviductal tumors are mural, rarely extend through the epithelium, but frequently invade muscle and serosal layers, and are often multiple. Ovarian adenocarcinomas are lobulated or nodular, firm, pale tan or white, and can become quite large replacing most or the entire ovary. Ovary with tumors may have normal or regressing follicles. Ovarian and oviductal adenocarcinomas metastasize by implantation on serosal surfaces and via lymphatics. In advanced cases, numerous tumors are located thorough out the body cavity ('carcinomatosis'). Pancreas, mesentery, intestinal peritoneal septa, visceral ligaments (e.g., mesosalpinx), and serosal surface of the spleen and proventriculus are frequently affected. The scirrhous nature of the tumors causes extensive adhesions between intestinal loops and deformity of the duodenum, which may eventually occlude the lumen. Often the body cavity is filled with a large volume of yellow, usually slightly turbid, ascitic fluid, which comes from occluded lymphatics. Metastasis to the lungs is more common than involvement of the liver and spleen. Cystadenocarcinomas are an uncommon variant of ovarian tumors. In the absence of ovarian and oviductal tumors, pancreatic adenocarcinoma is the main differential diagnosis.

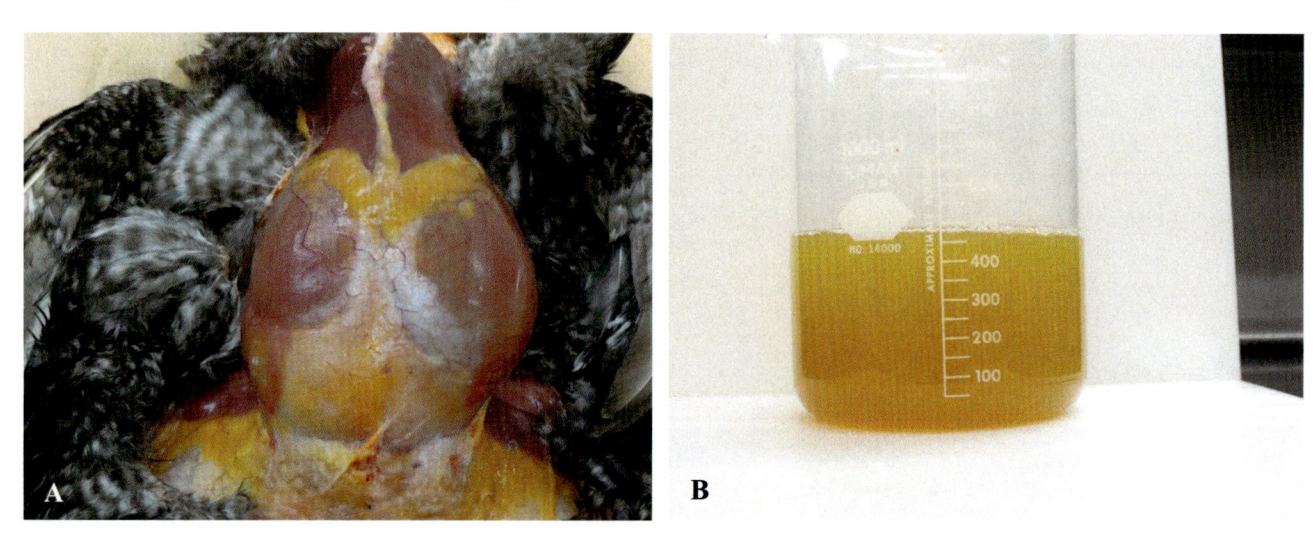

Reproductive tract adenocarcinoma. Hobby chicken. **A.** Distension of the abdomen due to ascites is a characteristic feature of reproductive tract adenocarcinoma. **B.** Large volume of yellow, usually slightly turbid fluid, is present in the peritoneal cavities (about 500 mL in this case).

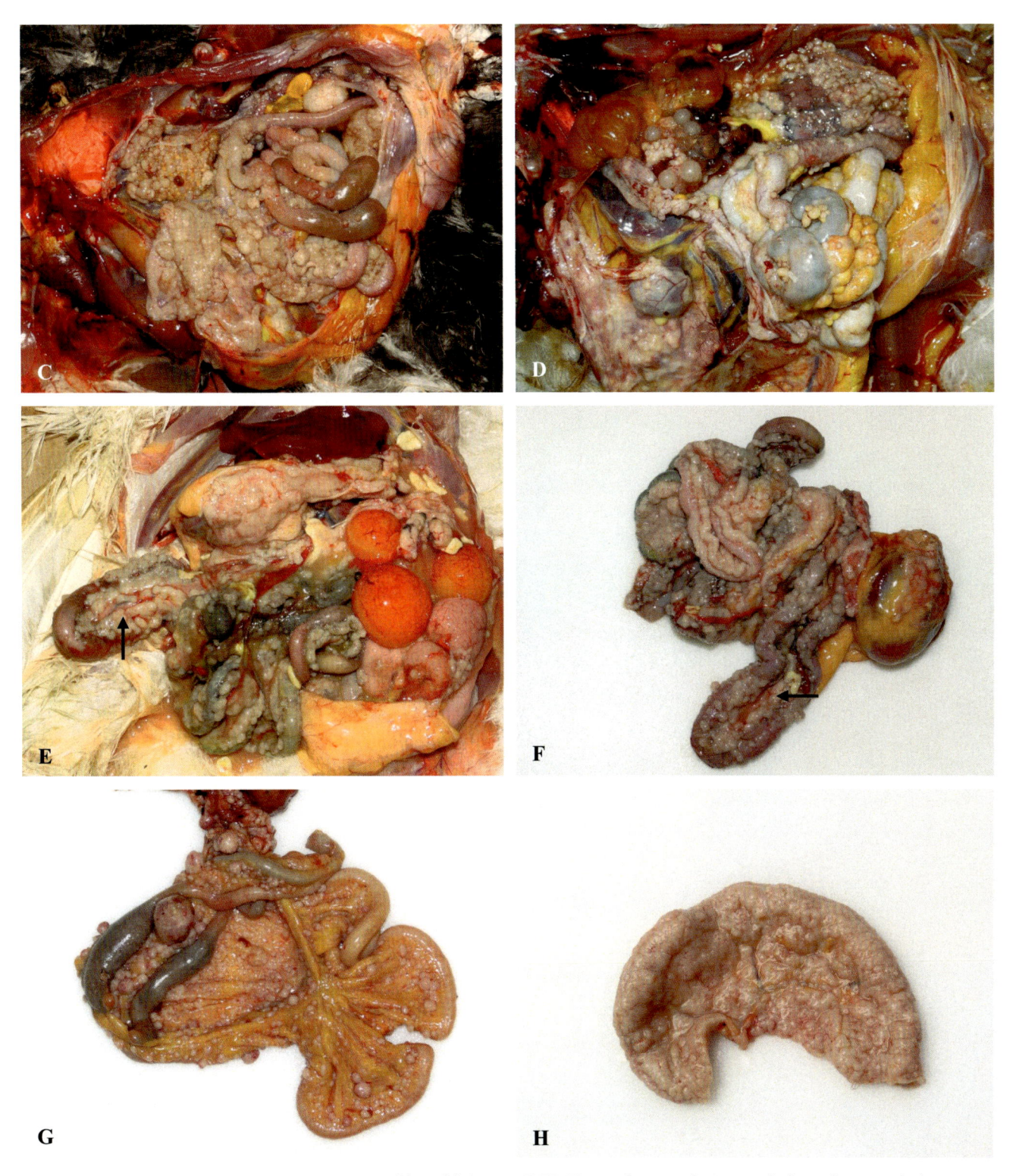

Gross Pathology of Avian Diseases: Text and Atlas 259

Reproductive tract adenocarcinomas. Hobby chickens. **C-H.** Extensive carcinomatosis is a characteristic gross lesion in hens with advanced reproductive tract adenocarcinomas. Numerous discrete or confluent firm nodules are present in the pancreas, mesentery, and serosal surfaces of intestine and proventriculus-gizzard. The pancreas is almost always involved; it becomes thickened and may have nodular tumors. **F** shows marked thickening of the intestinal wall and mesentery due to carcinomatosis. Arrows in **E** and **F** point to the pancreas, which is markedly thickened with nodular tumors.

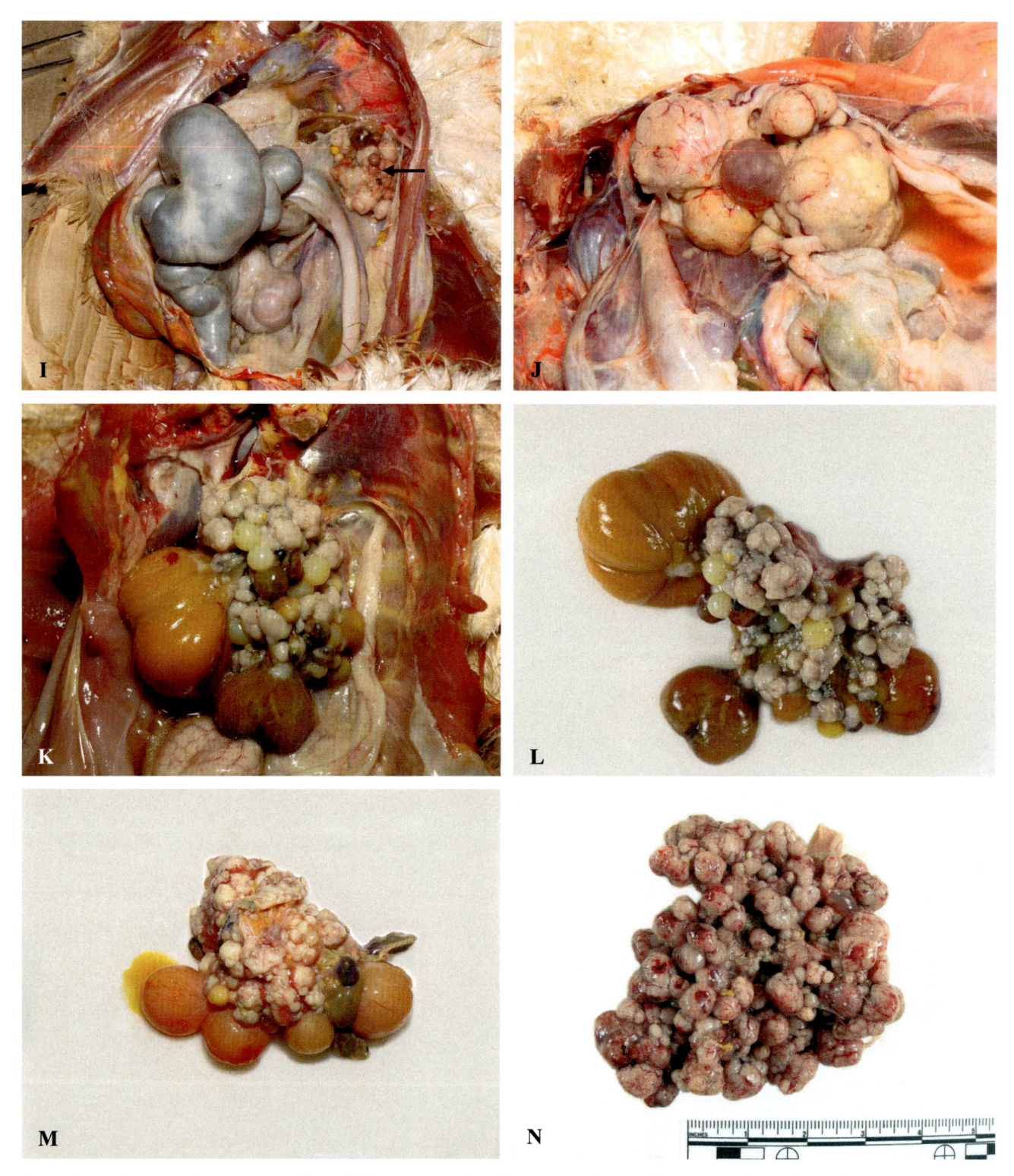

Ovarian adenocarcinomas. Hobby chickens. **I.** Deformity, occlusion, and marked distension of the duodenum. Ovary (arrow) has nodular tumors. **J.** Large, lobulated tumor in the ovary and a single large cyst. **K-N.** Many small carcinomatous nodules in the ovary. **L** is the same ovary in **K**. Note follicles that are still present but are undergoing regression.

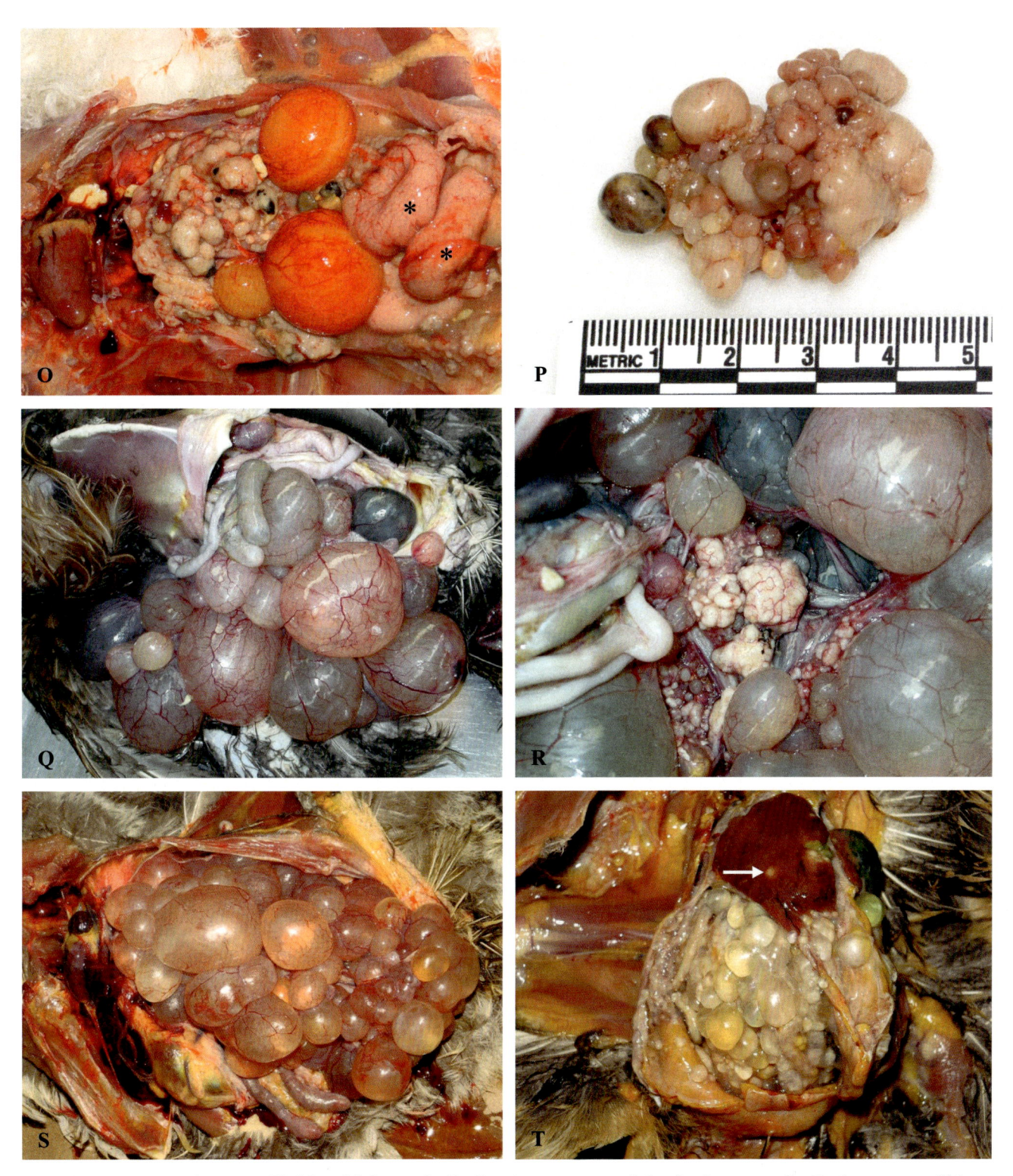

Gross Pathology of Avian Diseases: Text and Atlas 261

Ovarian adenocarcinomas. Hobby chickens. **O, P.** Carcinomatous nodules in the ovary. In **O**, the ovary still has mature follicles and the oviduct (asterisks) is well developed. **Q, R, S, T.** Cystadenocarcinomas. **Q** and **R** are the same bird. The ovary has solid tumors in the ovary, and cysts are attached to the ovary by stalks. The cystadenocarcinoma is of mixed type in **Q** and **R**, large-cyst type in **S**, and small-cyst type in **T**. Note the metastatic tumor in the liver in **T** (arrow).

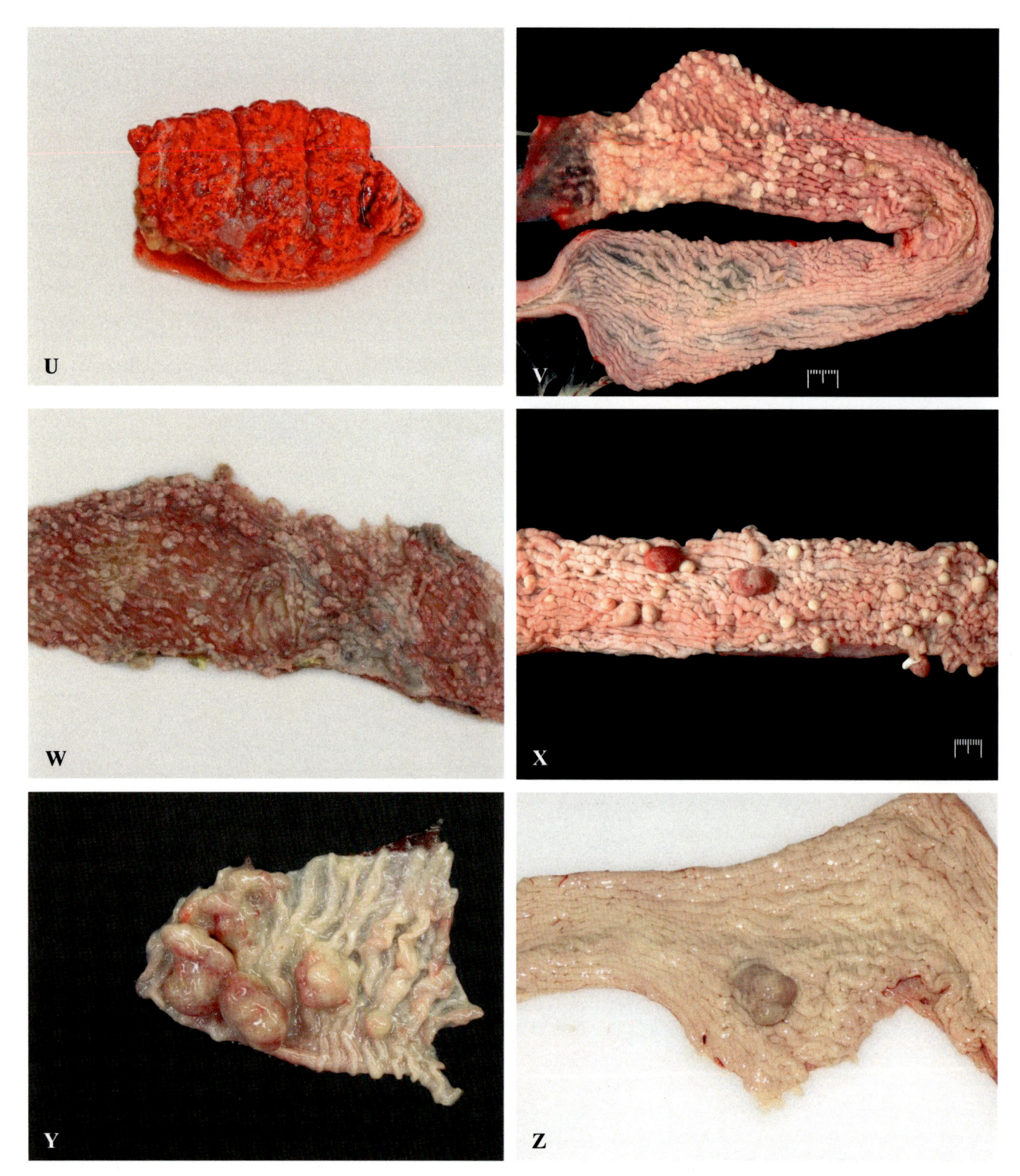

Lung metastatic of ovarian adenocarcinoma. **U.** Lung of bird with ovarian adenocarcinoma. White areas are metastatic ovarian adenocarcinomas. Metastasis probably occurs via lymphatics. Both lungs were involved.
Oviduct, adenomatous polyps. **V-Z.** Adenomatosis. Adenomatous polyps are in the mucosa. Polyps are numerous in **V, W, X.** Only a single polyp is present in **Z.** Polyps need to be differentiated microscopically from early adenocarcinomas, which develop from polyps.

Ovarian Granulosa Cell Tumor

Gross lesions. Granulosa cell tumors develop as pale yellow or yellow white, mildly or markedly lobulated or cystic mass associated with the ovary. The tumor may attain a large size, filling most of the body cavity. It is encapsulated by a smooth, vascular fibrous capsule. Extensive hemorrhages and cysts are common in the tumor. The cut surface of the tumor can be extensively hemorrhagic and usually have thin-walled cystic spaces filled with coagulated blood. Estrogenic activity of the tumor causes the oviduct to be enlarged and appear fully functional, despite the ovary being inactive. An enlarged, well-developed oviduct is an important diagnostic criterion for a granulosa cell tumor. Unlike ovarian adenocarcinoma, implantation throughout the body cavity is rare.

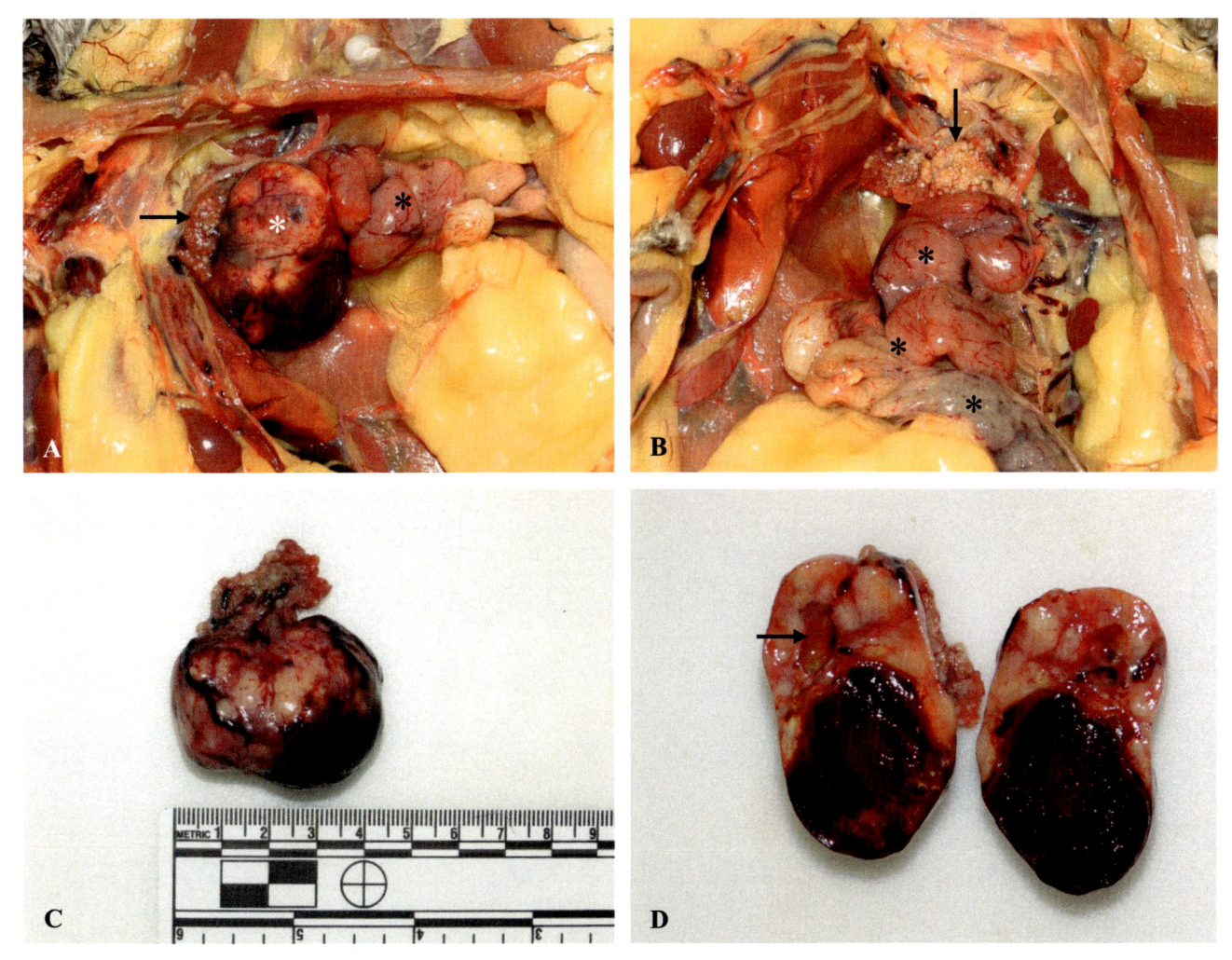

Ovarian granulosa cell tumor. 12-month hobby chicken. **A.** Large tumor (white asterisk) associated with the ovary. Tumor is more-or-less round, pale yellow, encapsulated, and mildly lobulated. Capsular surface is vascular and there is a large area of hemorrhage. Note the well-developed oviduct (black asterisk) and inactive ovary (arrow). **B.** Tumor has been removed to show the well-developed oviduct (asterisks) and inactive ovary (arrow). **C.** The tumor with part of the ovary. **D.** Cut surface is yellow-white with a cystic space (arrow) and large area of hemorrhage.

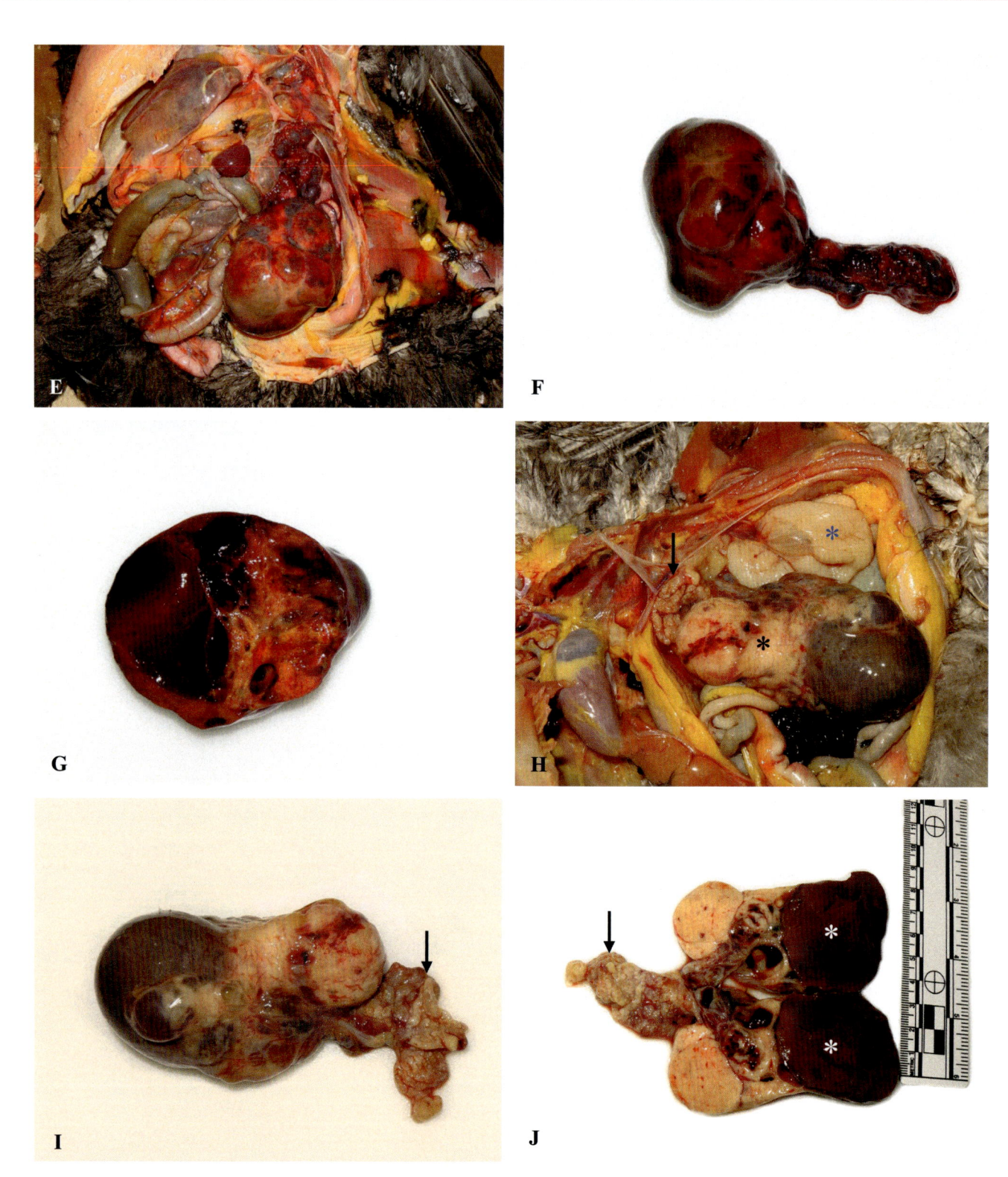

Ovarian granulosa cell tumor. E, F, G. 13-month hobby chicken. **E.** Large lobulated tumor is associated with the ovary. **F.** Tumor and ovary. Note the markedly lobulated surface of the tumor. Ovary has small blood-filled cysts. **G.** Cut surface of the tumor is yellow and has a large cystic space filled with blood. A few small cystic spaces also can be seen. **H, I, J.** 2-year hobby chicken. **H.** Large tumor (black asterisks) is associated with the ovary (arrow). The oviduct (blue asterisk) is well developed. There is a blood clot in the body cavity. **I.** Tumor and ovary (arrow). Tumor consists of solid tissue and blood-filled cysts. **J.** Cut surface of the tumor showing solid tissue, large blood-filled cyst (asterisks), small blood-filled cysts, and ovary (arrow).

Oviductal Leiomyomas

Leiomyomas are benign neoplasms of smooth muscle. Oviductal leiomyomas are a frequent incidental necropsy finding in older laying hens and broiler breeders. The most common site for the tumor is the thick free border of the ventral mesosalpinx, which has well-developed smooth muscle, especially at its caudal part. Leiomyomas also develop from the smooth muscle in the muscle layers of the magnum and isthmus and from smooth muscle in the wall of large arteries. Small leiomyomas can occasionally be identified microscopically in the ovary. Rarely, they are also found in the mesentery and along the surface of the distal digestive tract. The cause of leiomyomas is uncertain, but there is evidence that estrogen and progesterone are involved in development of the tumors.

Gross lesions. Leiomyomas usually occur as solitary or multiple discrete, firm, white, round or oval, encapsulated nodules with a smooth shiny surface. They can vary in size from a few millimeters to several centimeters in diameter. The cut surface is smooth and off white or pale yellow. Large tumors may be irregular in shape and frequently have prominent blood vessels leading into the tumor and on its surface.

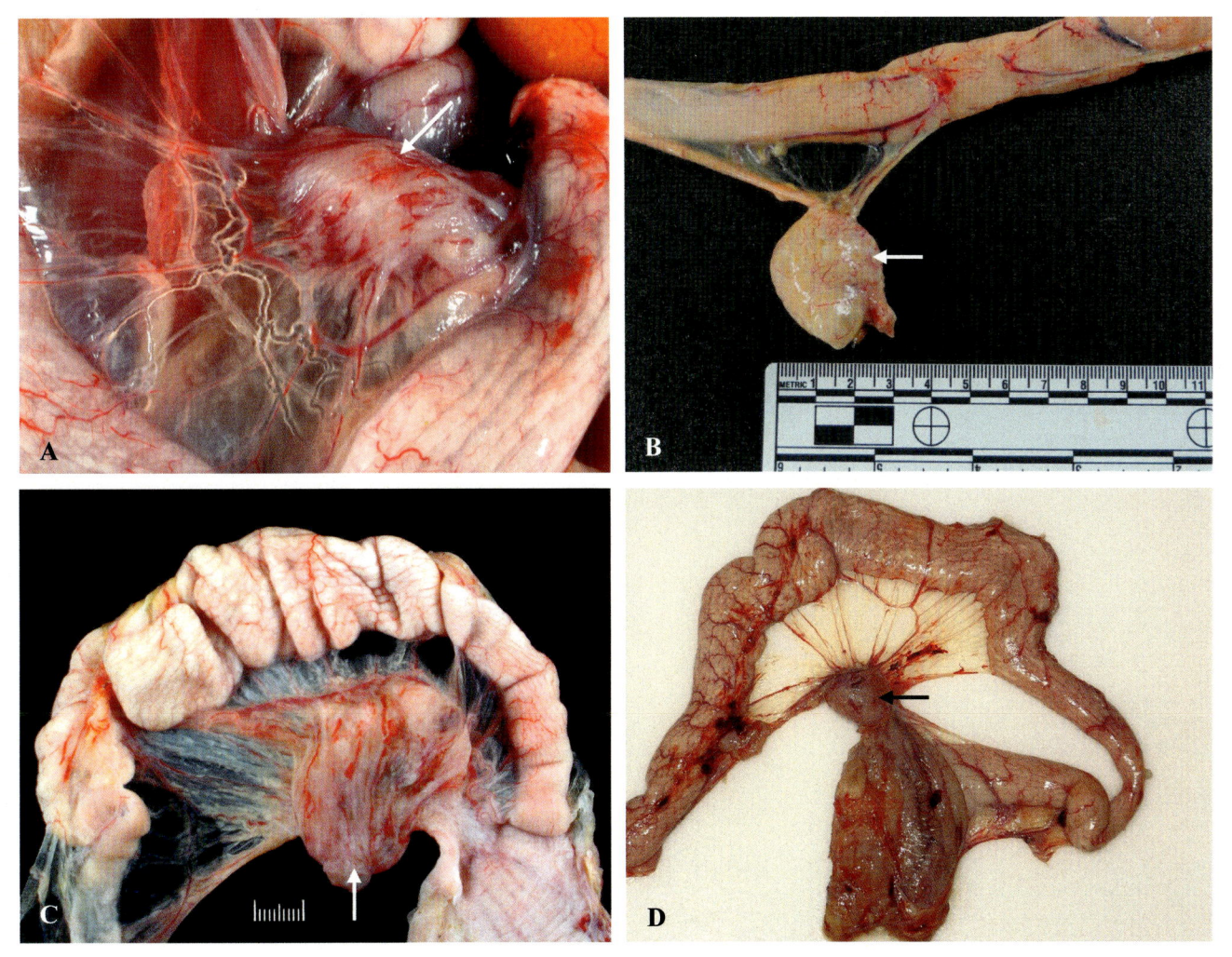

Oviductal leiomyomas. Hobby chickens (A. 65-week. B. 3-year. D. 2.5-year) and a broiler breeder hen (C. 62-week). Leiomyomas (arrows) are in the free margin of the ventral mesosalpinx of the oviduct, which is rich in smooth muscle.

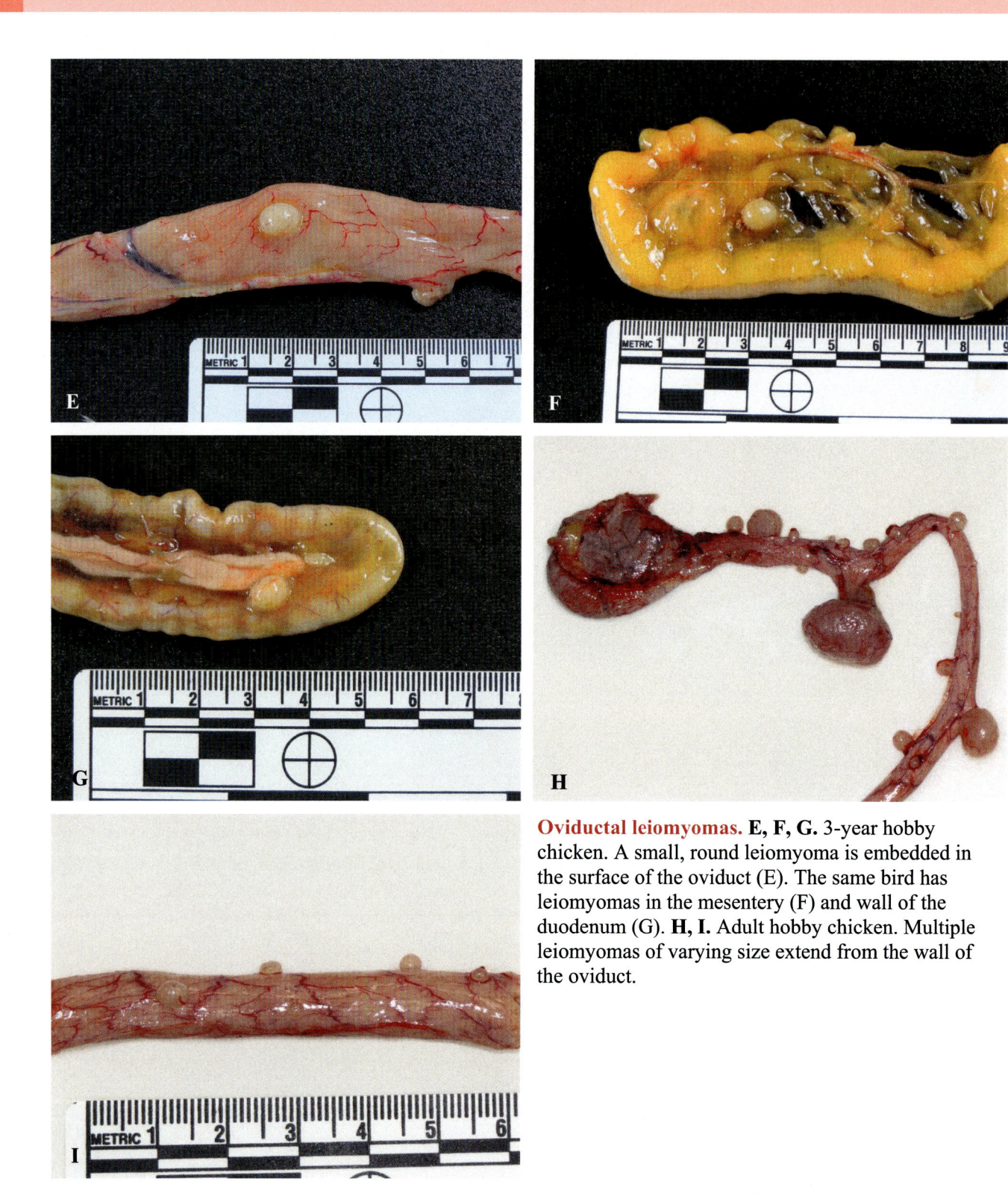

Oviductal leiomyomas. **E, F, G.** 3-year hobby chicken. A small, round leiomyoma is embedded in the surface of the oviduct (E). The same bird has leiomyomas in the mesentery (F) and wall of the duodenum (G). **H, I.** Adult hobby chicken. Multiple leiomyomas of varying size extend from the wall of the oviduct.

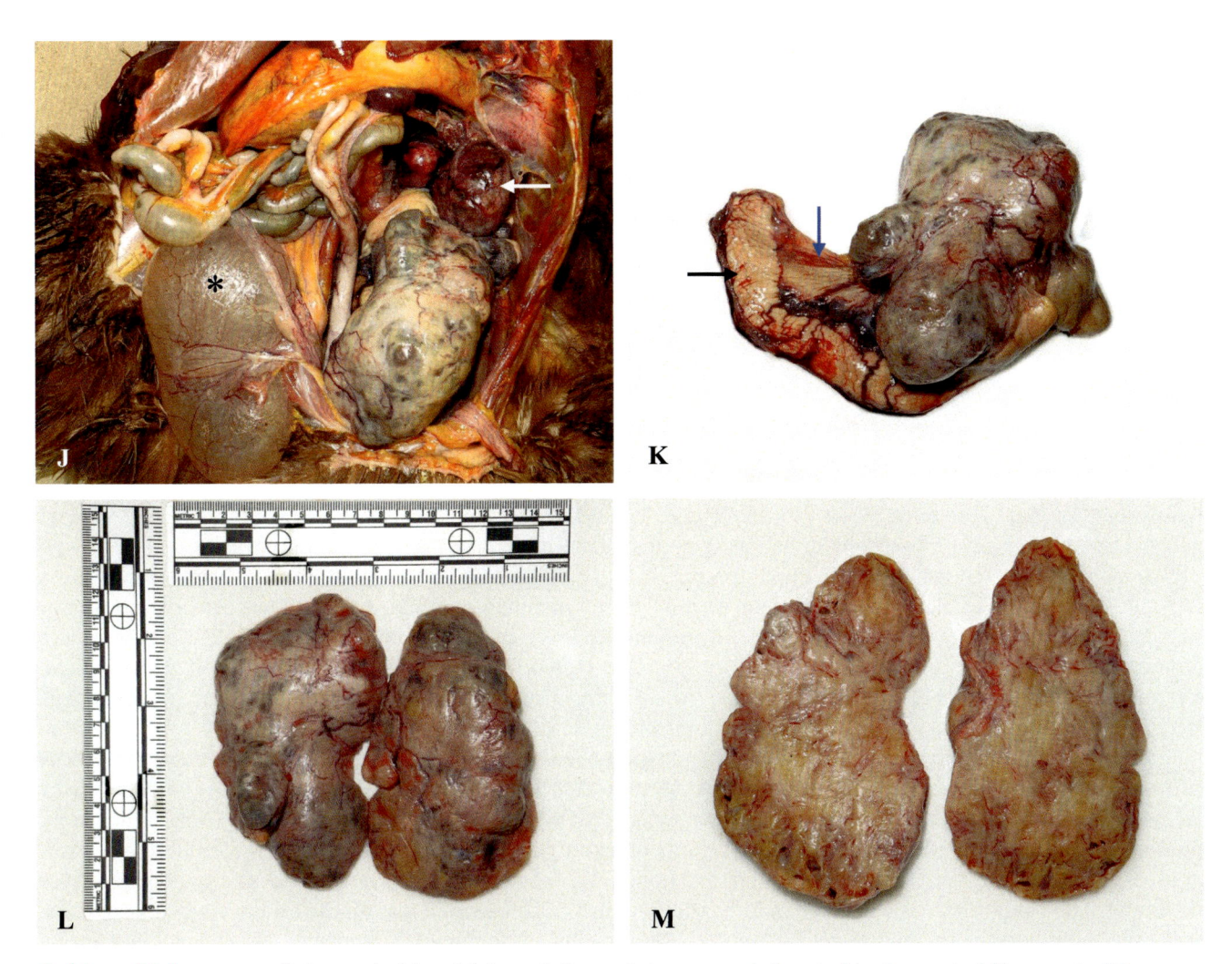

Oviductal leiomyoma. 3.5-year hobby chicken. **J.** Large leiomyoma is located in the ventral ligament of the oviduct and occupies a large portion of the abdominal cavity. Note the right cystic oviduct (asterisk). The bird also has a primary ovarian tumor (arrow). **K.** Tumor with the oviduct removed. The black arrow points to the oviduct and the blue arrow points to the ventral ligament. **L.** The outer surface of the tumor is irregular and has prominent blood vessels. **M.** The cut surface of the tumor is very firm and smooth and has off white and pale yellow areas, with a few small cystic spaces at the periphery.

Amyloidosis

Amyloidosis is a pathological condition characterized by extracellular deposition of amyloid, an abnormal, insoluble fibrillar protein derived from protein naturally produced by the body. Deposition of amyloid tends to be around vessels or sinusoids. Amyloid is a biochemically heterogeneous group that is classified into different types according to the chemical composition of the fibrillar protein. For nomenclature of different types of amyloid, the letter "A" (for amyloid) is followed by a suffix that is an abbreviated form of the precursor protein name. For example, amyloid AL refers to amyloid derived from the light chain of immunoglobulin. However, all types have similar structural properties and staining characteristics. Amyloid fibrils are non-branching and approximately 10 nm in diameter. They bind with the dye Congo red and exhibit apple-green birefringence when viewed with polarized light. When analyzed *in vivo* by X-ray diffraction, amyloid fibrils exhibit a characteristic cross diffraction pattern.

Amyloidosis in birds results from deposition of amyloid AA. Several tissues may be affected, but amyloid is most often found in the liver, spleen, adrenal glands, kidneys, and vessel walls, especially in the spleen. This type of amyloid is derived from a protein called serum amyloid-A (SAA), which is a high-density lipoprotein synthesized mainly in the liver. Normally, SAA is completely degraded by a monocyte-derived enzyme. Excess SAA is produced during chronic antigenic stimulation, *e.g.*, persistent infection or inflammation. Activated macrophages release interleukin-1 and interlekin-6, which stimulate hepatocytes to synthesize and secrete SAA. However, excess SAA secretion is not sufficient for deposition of amyloid to occur. In amyloidosis, there are certain isoforms of SAA that are incompletely degraded and partially cleaved into fragments that tend to form insoluble, fibrillar protein aggregates of amyloid. It is uncertain what causes this incomplete enzymatic degradation of SAA protein. Amyloidosis associated with chronic antigenic stimulation is also called reactive or secondary amyloidosis. Amyloidosis can be idiopathic, where no underlying antigenic (inflammatory) stimulation is found.

Among avian species, systemic amyloidosis (deposition of amyloid in different tissues) occurs in many types of birds but is particularly prevalent in waterfowl, especially ducks. It also is relatively common in other types of shorebirds (cranes, gulls, *etc.*). Amyloidosis is a progressive disease that tends to become worse with age. Severe amyloidosis can be fatal. In chickens and turkeys, hepatic amyloidosis may develop after vaccination with oil-emulsified vaccines, especially bacterins prepared from Gram-negative bacteria. Amyloid arthropathy (articular amyloidosis) is characterized by deposition of amyloid in intertarsal (hock) joints. In brown table-egg layers, it has been associated with arthritis caused by *Enterococcus faecalis*. In broiler breeders, it may be associated with arthritis caused by *Staphylococcus aureus*. Amyloidosis often results from 'bumblefoot' and mycobacterial infections.

Gross lesions. Livers with extensive, severe amyloidosis are often enlarged, have a pale or varnished appearance, and are moderately firm. In very severe cases, the liver is yellow-white with a waxy ("lardaceous") appearance. Spleens are enlarged, firm, and often have a mottled appearance. Severely affected kidneys are usually enlarged and pale tan. In amyloid arthropathy, there is deposition of orange material on the cartilaginous surfaces of intertarsal (hock) joints, joint capsule, and periarticular tissue. Amyloid stains dark brown with iodine. It can be detected by flooding the cut surface of the suspect organ with an iodine solution.

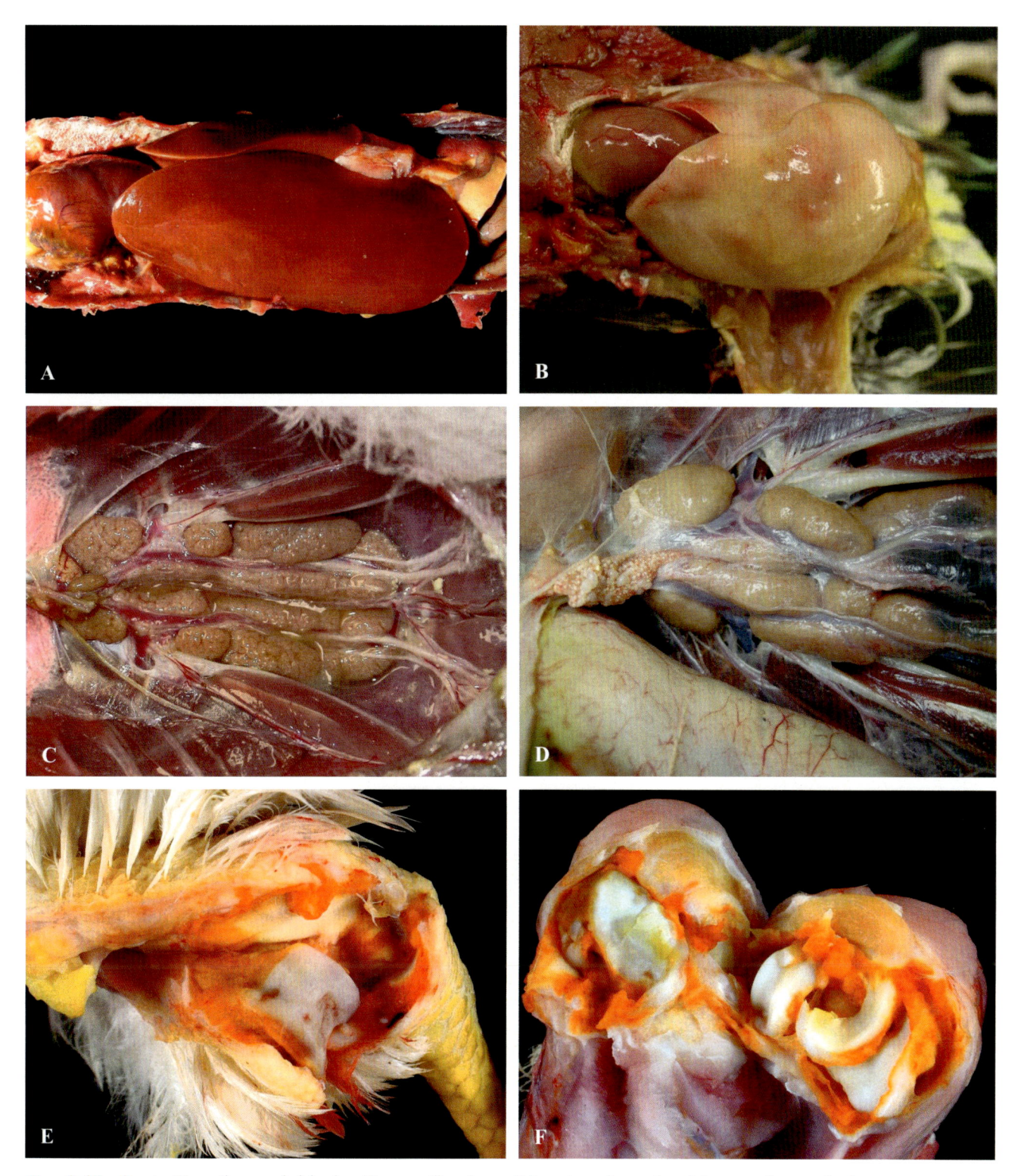

Amyloidosis. A. Hepatic amyloidosis. 42-year flamingo. Liver is enlarged and has a pale, washed-out appearance. **B.** Hepatic amyloidosis. Lovebird. Liver is enlarged, yellow-white, and has a waxy appearance. **C, D.** Renal amyloidosis. Swans. Kidneys are enlarged and pale tan. Swan in D had mycobacteriosis. **E. F.** Articular amyloidosis. 35-week broiler breeder hen. Amyloid deposits appear as orange material on the articular surfaces and in the joint capsule. *(Photograph A courtesy of Dr. Arno Wuenschmann. Photo B courtesy of Dr. Arnaud Van Wettere).*

Cerebellar Hypoplasia in Chicks

Cause. The cause is uncertain, but DNA of a parvovirus closely related to chicken parvovirus has been detected by PCR in the brains of some affected chicks. However, the role of parvovirus as the cause of cerebellar hypoplasia remains to be confirmed.

Clinical signs and gross lesions. The disease affects one to 2-day broiler chickens. They exhibit neurologic signs including lying on their sides, paddling of legs, and twisting of the neck and head (torticollis). At necropsy, the cranium must be carefully removed to avoid damaging the brain. Examining the brain *in situ* reveals cerebellums that are small and possibly misshapen, optic lobes that may be enlarged and fused dorsally, and internal hydrocephalus.

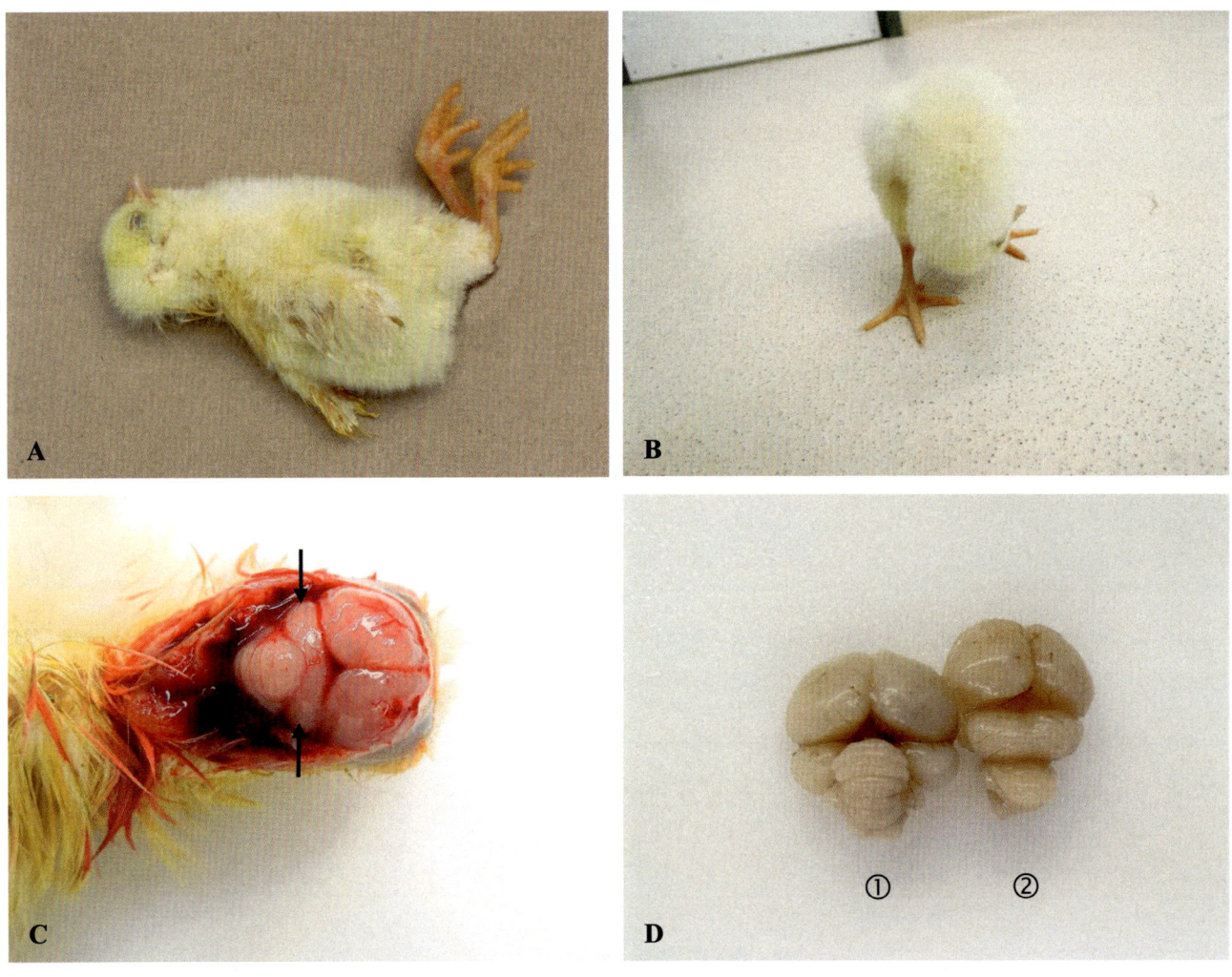

Cerebellar hypoplasia. 2-day broiler chickens. **A.** Bird is lying on its side and paddling its legs. **B.** Twisting of the head and neck (torticollis). **C.** Brain *in situ*. Optic lobes are enlarged and fused. Cerebellum is small and displaced caudally. Arrows: optic lobes. **D.** ① Normal brain. ② Enlargement and fusion of the optic lobes and hypoplasia of the cerebellum.

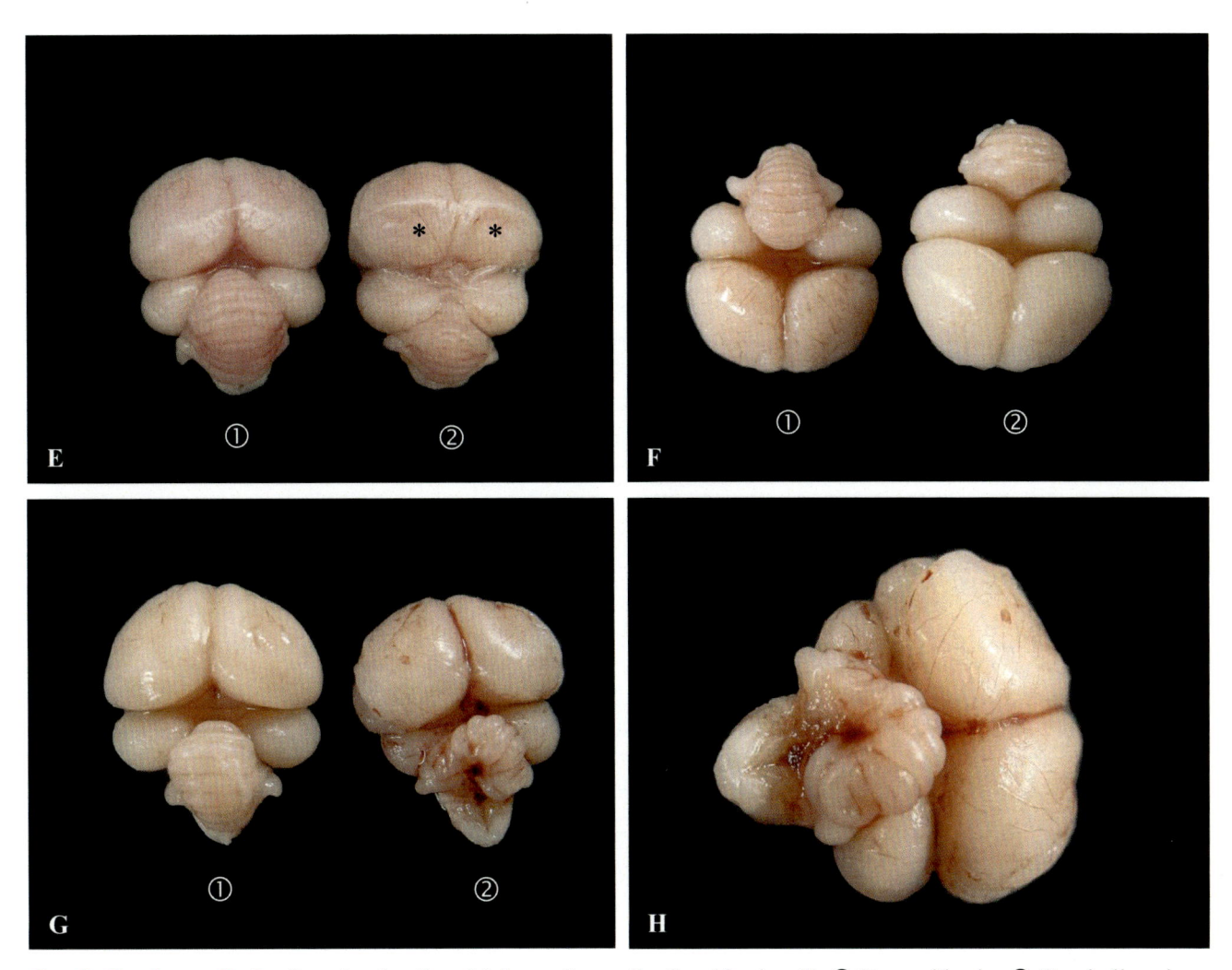

Cerebellar hypoplasia. One-day broiler chickens. Formalin-fixed brains. **E.** ① Normal brain. ② Cerebellum is notably hypoplastic. Distended right ventricles (asterisks) initially contained excess CSF (hydrocephalus) but have collapsed after fixation. **F.** ① Normal brain. ② Enlargement and fusion of the optic lobes, and hypoplasia of the cerebellum. **G.** ① Normal brain. ② Cerebellum is small and misshapen. **H.** Close-up view of the small, misshapen cerebellum in G.

Footpad Dermatitis (Pododermatitis)

Footpad dermatitis, also known as pododermatitis and footpad burn, is a type of contact dermatitis that affects the plantar region of the feet and, less frequently, the hocks and skin over the breast of poultry and other birds. The condition is characterized by necrosis and ulceration of the plantar surface of the feet. It differs from 'bumblefoot' in which there is infection and inflammation deep in the foot involving the footpad. However, footpad dermatitis can predispose to bumblefoot. Pododermatitis has become important because of the use of chicken feet in Asian diets. Additionally, the condition is a welfare concern since severe lesions likely cause pain that impairs the ability of affected birds to walk. Inability to walk results in decreased feed and water consumption, and reduced growth.

Cause and pathogenesis. Initial damage to the plantar skin of the foot results from exposure to a combination of moisture and chemical irritants in the litter. Chemical irritants include ammonia, uric acid, and volatile organic compounds. Bacteria in the litter infect the damaged skin and exacerbate the lesions. House management, nutritional, and other factors that increase moisture in the litter increase the incidence and severity of footpad dermatitis. These factors include:

- Poor airflow (ventilation) to remove moisture from the house.
- Poor quality bedding material that does not absorb and quickly release moisture.
- Poor management of drinkers (leaks, spills, etc.).
- High stocking density during brooding or growing.
- Increased condensation when relative humidity is high and temperature is low.
- Diets with high levels of protein result in increased water consumption and wet litter.
- Diets formulated with soybean meal as the primary protein source.
- High levels of minerals (sodium, magnesium, potassium) in the water.
- Increased water consumption that contributes to wet litter.
- Enteric diseases that cause loose droppings ('flushing').

Gross lesions. Lesions vary in extent and severity. Mild lesions consist of small focal areas of superficial (epidermal) necrosis and dark discoloration of the skin over the footpad. With severe lesions, multiple or a single large area in the footpad skin becomes necrotic, ulcerated, and black to brown. The lesion is best seen when the foot is washed to remove adhering material. Advanced, severe lesions consist of thick crusts covering deep ulcers. Skin over toe pads, hocks, and breast may also be affected. Focal ulcerative dermatitis ("breast button") is a similar lesion involving the breast skin over the keel in turkeys.

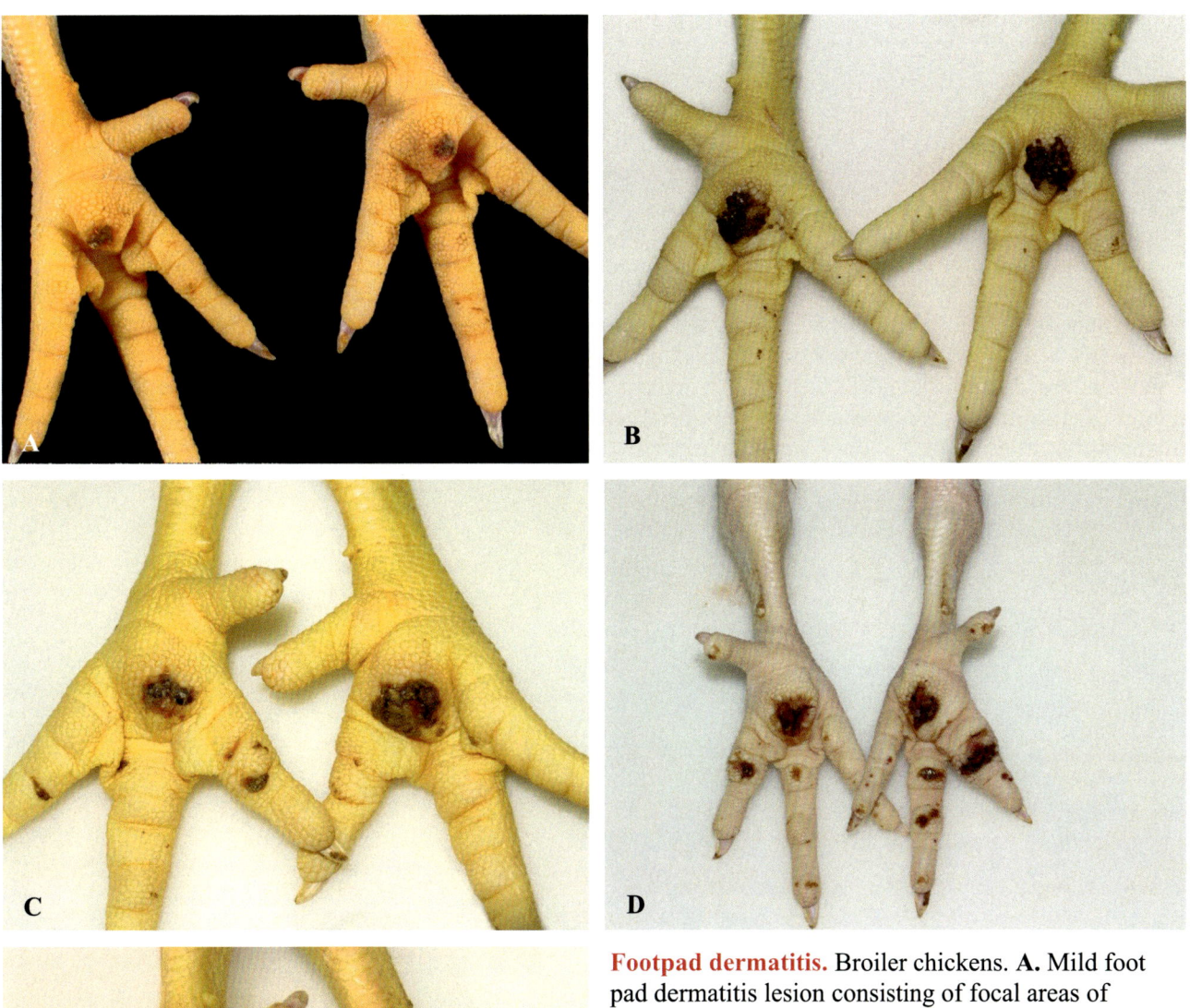

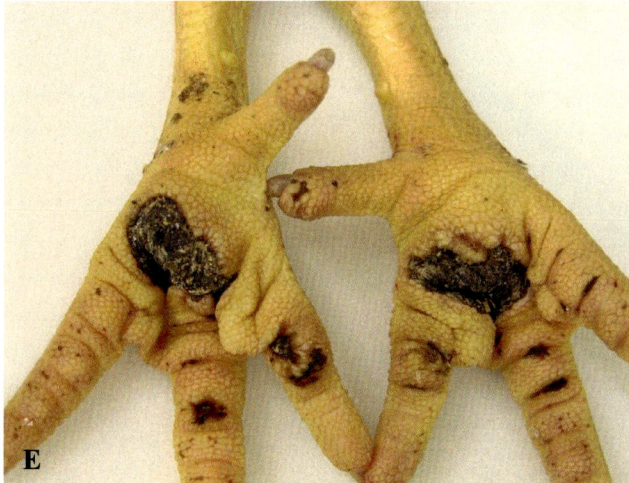

Gross Pathology of Avian Diseases: Text and Atlas 273

Footpad dermatitis. Broiler chickens. **A.** Mild foot pad dermatitis lesion consisting of focal areas of superficial necrosis (probably involving only the epidermis) and discoloration of the skin. **B, C, D.** Lesions, which are more severe than in those in A, consist of necrosis and ulceration of the skin over footpads and some of the toe pads. **E.** Lesions are severe and advanced. Black crusts fill deep ulcers.

Avian Keratoacanthoma (Dermal Squamous-Cell Carcinoma) in Broiler Chickens

Cause. Unknown.

Gross lesions. Avian keratoacanthoma differs from squamous cell carcinoma by not being malignant and spontaneously regressing with time. Lesions are restricted to the skin and are located within feather tracts; mostly those on the sides of thighs, breasts, and along the back. Few lesions occur on the wings. Lesions are usually observed at processing after feathers have been removed.

Lesions are ulcerative and nodular. Ulcerative lesions predominate and consist of individual or groups of shallow ulcers with thin, slightly raised, firm margins. Some ulcers have a crater-like appearance. Most individual ulcers are 1 cm or less in diameter. In severely affected birds, ulcers may coalesce and produce lesions that are several centimeters in diameter. Occasionally, projecting tags of keratin are associated with the ulcers.

Nodular lesions consist of raised nodules 2-3 mm in diameter adjacent to feather follicles. They progress to raised, keratin-filled cysts covered by an attenuated epidermis. Nodules ulcerate allowing the keratin core to come out as an intact plug, after which the lesion rapidly regresses. Small nodular lesions may regress before they ulcerate.

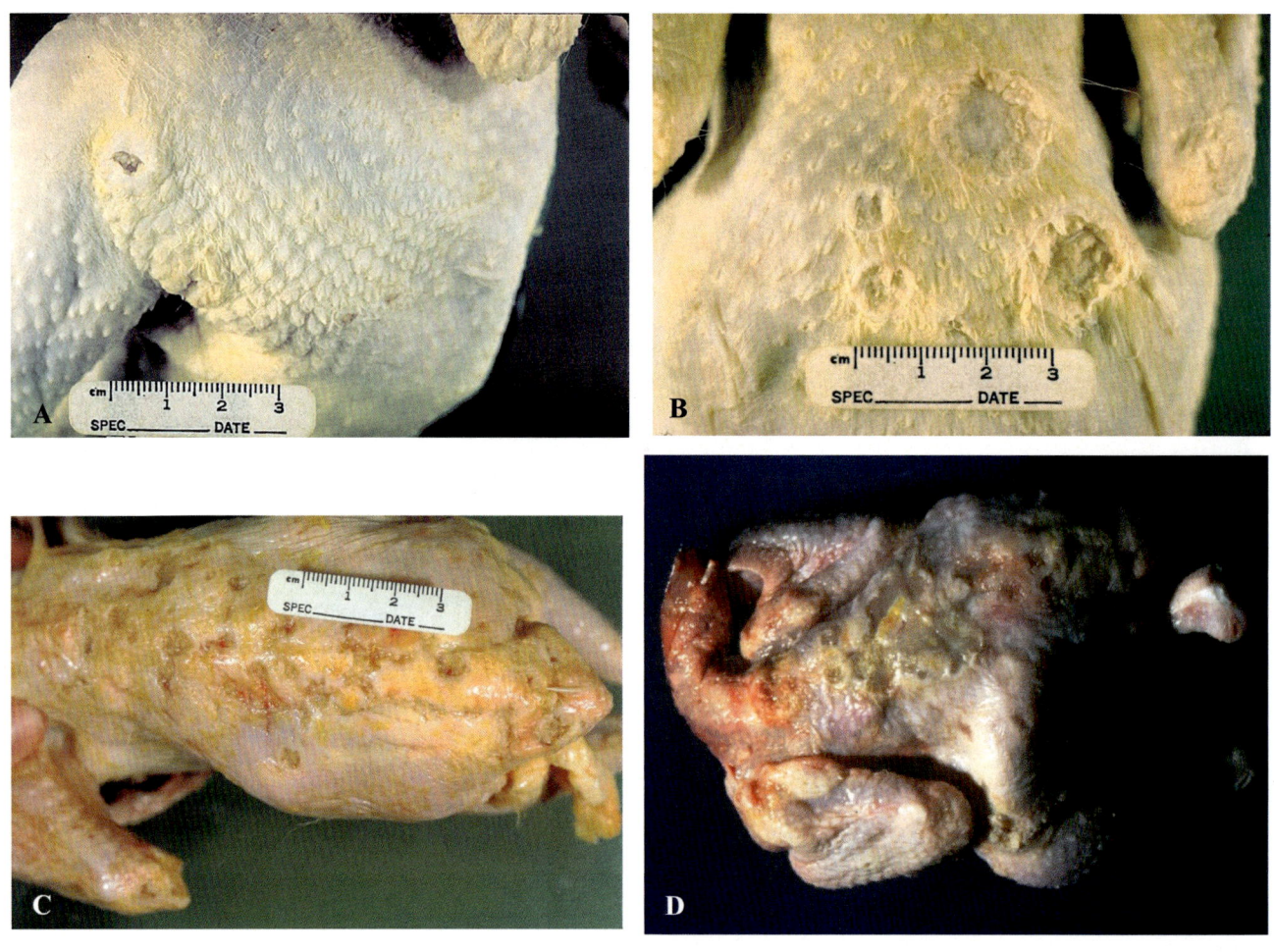

Avian keratoacanthoma. Broiler chickens. **A, B.** Individual ulcers in the skin. In **A**, note the raised border of the ulcer. **C, D.** Large lesions of coalescing ulcers. *(Photos A, B, C courtesy of Dr. Oscar Fletcher, USA).*

Cutaneous Xanthoma

Xanthoma means yellow mass (xantho = yellow, oma = mass). It is not a neoplasm but rather a localized accumulation of cholesterol-rich lipid and lipid-laden macrophages in the dermis and subcutis. The etiopathogenesis of xanthoma is not well understood. Different factors have been proposed, including high fat or cholesterol diet, genetic predisposition, obesity, hyperlipidemia (hypercholesterolemia and hypertriglyceridemia), hydrocarbon exposure, and hypothyroidism. Trauma and damage to tissue may trigger deposition of cholesterol and triglycerides. Xanthomatous lesions begin as an accumulation of cholesterol-rich lipid, followed by an influx of macrophages into the area. Macrophages phagocytize cholesterol, which causes their cytoplasm to expand and become foamy. Microscopically, the cellular inflammatory response is variable and often includes multinucleated giant cells, fibroplasia, and focal areas of distinctly shaped, empty, cholesterol clefts.

Grossly, xanthomas appear as yellow, solitary or multiple, discrete, firm, subcutaneous masses or thickenings of skin, which may be dimpled, nodular, or irregular. Overlying skin usually lacks feathers and may be traumatized, ulcerated, or hemorrhagic. Sometimes birds self-mutilate the lesions. Xanthomas are locally invasive and increase in size over time. Prognosis following complete surgical excision is favorable.

Among pet birds, xanthomas are most common in cockatiels and budgerigars. Females are more frequently affected than males. The most common sites are wing tips, breast, posterior abdomen, and around the vent.

Cutaneous xanthoma. A. Budgerigar. Yellow masses (arrows) at the shoulders of the wings. **B.** Budgerigar. Subcutaneous thickening of the posterior abdominal area just anterior to the tail. Note the yellow color of the thickened area. **C.** Ring-necked dove. Yellow discoloration, subcutaneous thickening, feather loss, trauma, and severe bruises in the wing. Xanthomatous lesion was also present in the other wing. **D.** 11-year female cockatiel. Yellow, fat-like, irregularly shaped mass in the distal left wing. *(Photos A, B courtesy of Dr. Arnaud Van Wettere, USA. Photo D courtesy of Dr. Lauren Powers, USA).*

Cataract

A cataract is any opacification or clouding of the ocular lens or lens capsule that results in loss of transparency and impaired vision. All birds are susceptible to cataract formation and they are among the more common eye disorders. The lens consists of three parts: central nucleus, peripheral cortex, and capsule that envelops the lens. In birds, an annular pad lies beneath the lens capsule at the equator, which is separated from the cortex by a fluid-filled space, the lens vesicle. Cataracts are classified into three broad types according to location: nuclear cataracts in the center of the lens, cortical cataracts that start at the periphery of the lens and extend in a spoke-like fashion to the center, and subcapsular cataracts between the fibrous capsule and lens epithelium. Most cataracts in birds are cortical. As cataracts mature there is progressive loss of lens protein, which may result in a 'dumbbell' appearance to the lens microscopically. Ultimately the lens capsule is just filled with amorphous protein (phacolysis). In young birds, lens renewal may occur around the periphery causing the abnormal tissue to be concentrated in the center of the lens.

Cause. The cause of most cataracts in birds is unknown. However, they can occur secondarily to chronic uveitis regardless of cause and retinal degeneration. Infectious causes of cataracts include viruses (avian encephalomyelitis virus, Marek's disease virus, Newcastle disease virus, West Nile virus), bacteria (*Salmonella arizonae*), fungi (*Aspergillus*, *Verruconis* [*Ochroconis*]), and protozoa (toxoplasmosis). Chicks that survive avian encephalomyelitis virus infection may develop cataracts later in life. Non-infectious cataracts include congenital, nutritional, metabolic, environmental, traumatic, toxic, radiation, and senile cataracts. Cataracts in young turkey poults are associated with vitamin E deficiency in the breeder hens. Light-induced oxidative stress causes cataracts in chickens. Cataracts can result from salt toxicosis in free-living ducks. Congenital cataracts, possibly sex-linked, affect ducklings and canaries. Senile cataracts form in companion and other captive birds as they age.

Gross lesions. Cataracts usually progress over time. They may be unilateral or bilateral. Birds with bilateral cataracts are usually affected clinically and may die. Those with a unilateral cataract tend to remain clinically normal. Cataracts resulting from infection of the eye are usually unilateral whereas cataracts from non-infectious causes are generally bilateral. In the early stages, a minute, as small as pinhead size, white clouding or opacity is visible in the center of the pupil. As the cataract advances, the opaque area in the center of the pupil increases in size and eventually the entire lens, as seen through the pupil, becomes opaque gray to white. Central clearing with a peripheral ring due to resorption of liquefied lens protein is seen in hypermature cataracts. Hypoplasia or atrophy of the optic nerve and contralateral optic lobe accompanies cataracts. Cataracts need to be differentiated from keratitis and panophthalmitis.

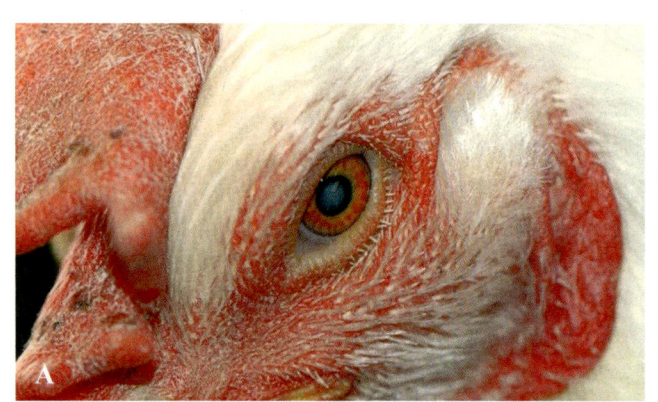

Cataract. Broiler breeders. **A, B, C.** Opacity of the pupil is the hallmark lesion of cataract. The lesion must be differentiated from keratitis. Lesions are usually unilateral.

Ammonia-Induced Corneal Erosion

Cause. Atmospheric ammonia at high concentrations causes conjunctivitis and damages the cornea of the eyes (keratoconjunctivitis). It has a pungent odor and also irritates the mucous membranes of the respiratory tract. Ammonia is generated by microbial breakdown of uric acid in the droppings of the birds. High levels result from inadequate ventilation, poor litter conditions, and temperature. Moisture and temperature promote bacterial growth and activity, which increases ammonia production. Poor ventilation, loose droppings, and faulty, over-filled, low-positioned, or leaking drinkers, are common causes of wet litter in poultry houses. Severity of eye damage depends on the ammonia concentration in the air and duration of exposure. The term "ammonia burn" is used by some to refer to ammonia-induced corneal erosion, but this term is inaccurate, as ammonia does not directly injure the corneal epithelium. Damage to the basement membrane on which the epithelium rests is responsible for detachment of the epithelial layer, which is the characteristic microscopic eye lesion resulting from excess ammonia exposure.

Clinical signs and gross lesions. Swelling and reddening of the eyelids, reddening of the conjunctiva and nictitating membrane (third eyelid), and partial or complete closure of the eyes are common clinical findings in affected birds. Eye lesions can be seen in birds of all ages, including recently placed young birds being brooded on used litter. In severe cases, eyelids are often closed shut. Eyes become almond shaped after long-term exposure to high ammonia levels because of scarring and retraction of the eyelids. The gross lesion is a roughly circular, gray-white, opaque, rough- or frosty-appearing area in the center of the cornea. Close examination of the eye using oblique light may be necessary to see early lesions that are slightly depressed with an irregular margin. The periphery of the cornea is unaffected, presumably because it is partially covered by the eyelid and receives less exposure compared to the central cornea. Both eyes are similarly affected, which helps differentiate ammonia toxicity from other eye diseases. Scarring of the central cornea occurs in chronically affected birds. Birds with corneal lesions are partially to completely blind.

Susceptibility to bacterial diseases, especially colibacillosis, is increased. High ammonia levels also have a negative impact on livability, weight gain, feed conversion, condemnation rate at processing, and the immune system of the birds. Experimentally, broiler chickens kept in an environment with ammonia concentrations of 50 and 75 ppm had reductions in body weight of 17% and 20% respectively at 7 weeks of age compared to unexposed birds.

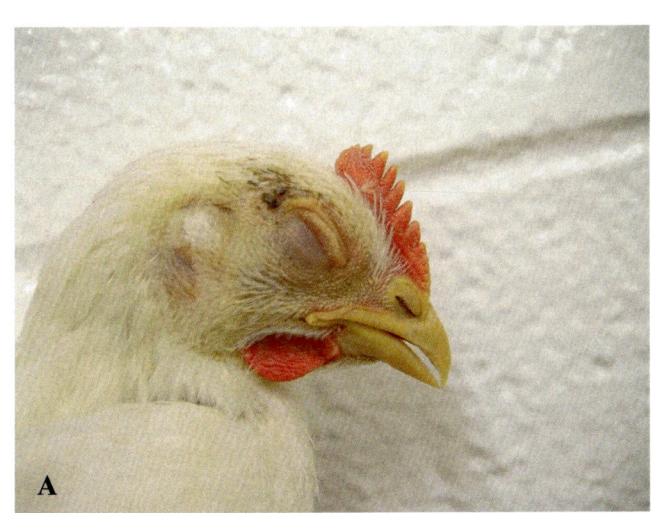

Ammonia-induced conjunctivitis. A, B. 35- and 26-day broiler chickens. Eyelids are swollen and eyes are closed. In **B**, note the crusted ocular discharge on the lower eyelid.

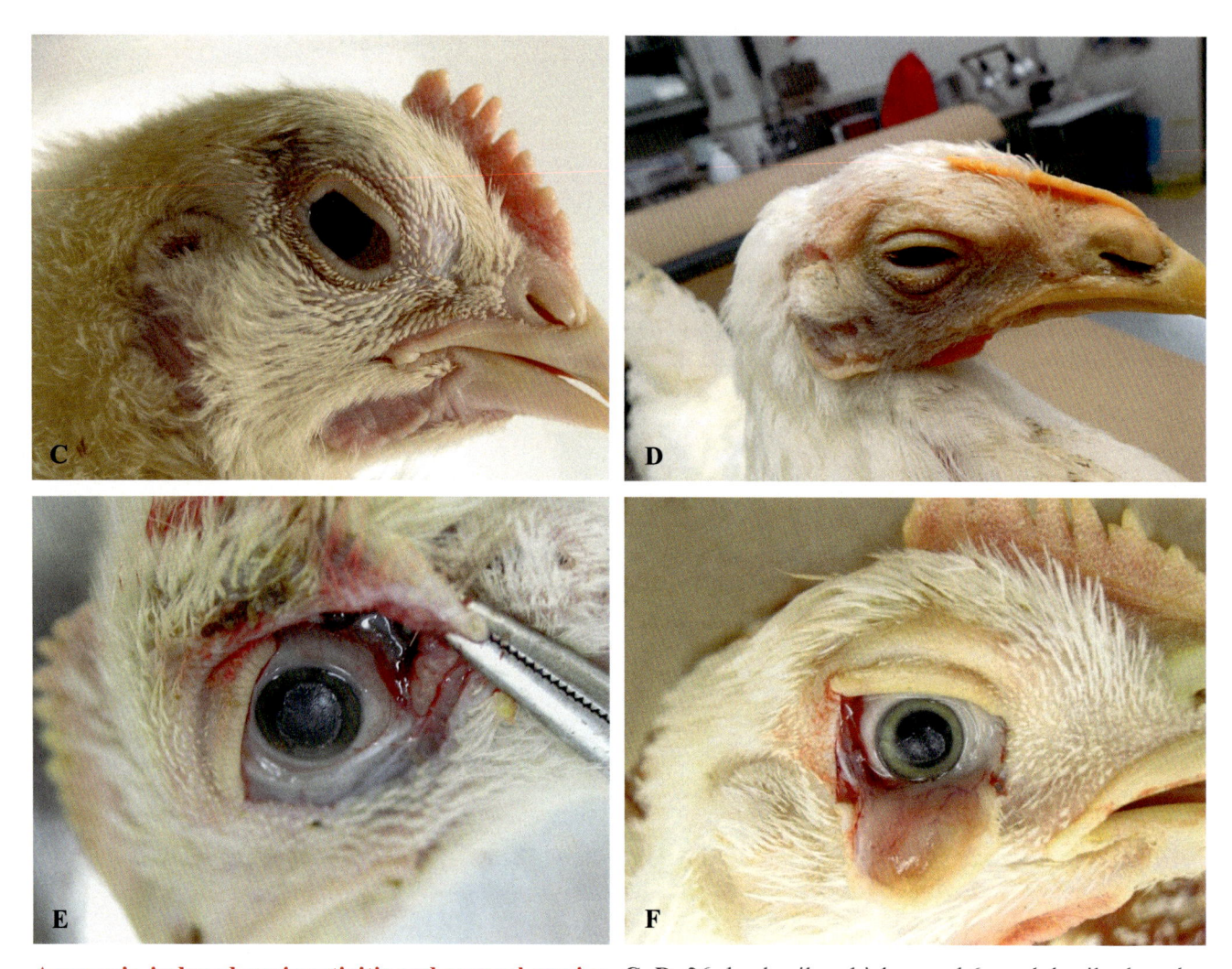

Ammonia-induced conjunctivitis and corneal erosion. **C, D.** 26-day broiler chicken and 6-week broiler breeder pullet. Thickened and misshapen eyelids due to chronic conjunctivitis. Note the almond shape of the eye in C and swollen, edematous eyelid in D. **E, F.** 26- and 35-day broiler chickens. Erosions in the center of the corneas appear as circular, gray-white, opaque, rough- or frosty-appearing areas. Note the central location of the lesions. Although not shown, the contralateral eye was similarly affected. Corneal lesion in E is more severe than the lesion in F.

Miscellaneous

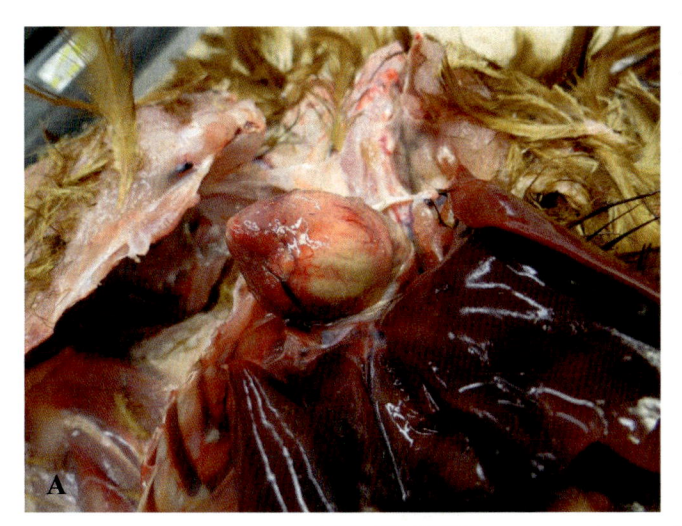

A. Listeriosis. Hobby chicken. Large necrotic area in the myocardium. Cultures of the myocardial lesion and liver yielded a pure growth of *Listeria monocytogenes*. Myocardial necrosis is a characteristic lesion of the septicemic form of listeriosis in chickens.

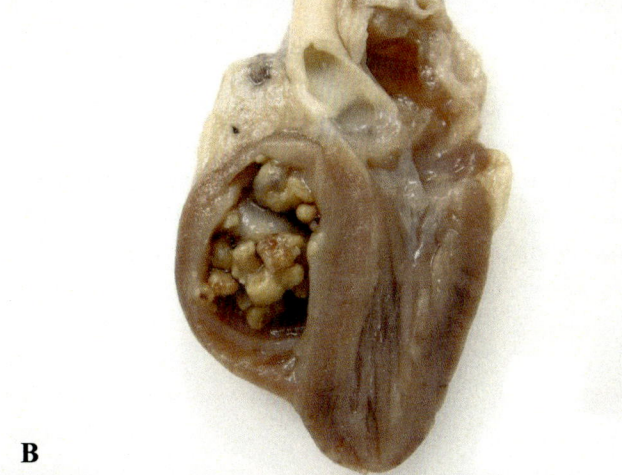

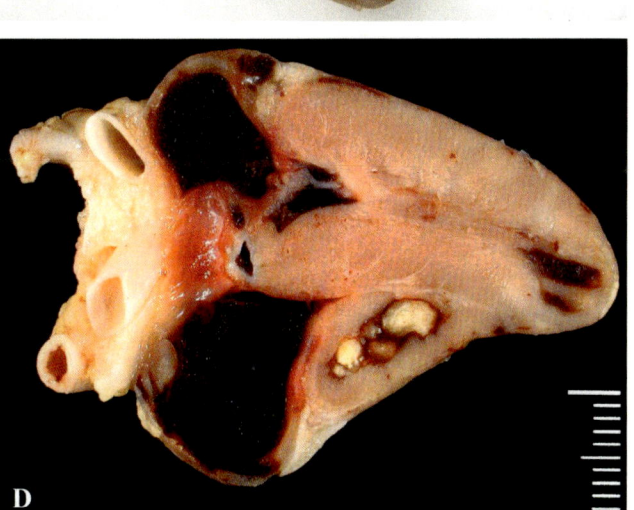

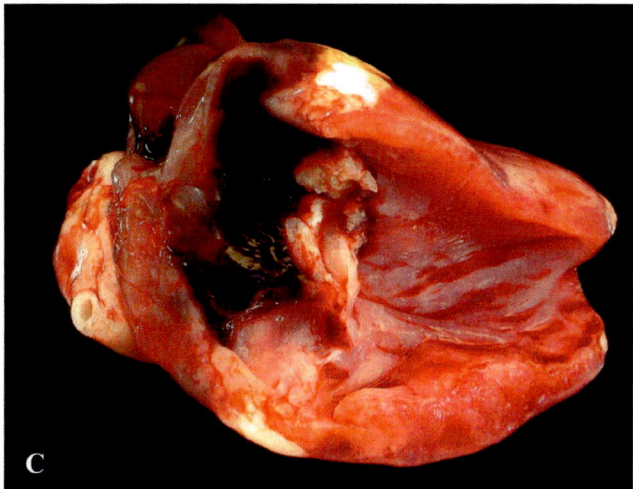

B, C, D. Vegetative valvular endocarditis. Broilers. 'Vegetative' nodular lesions are associated with the right atrioventricular valve (AV) in **B** and **D** and with the left AV valve in **C**. The lesion consists of fibrinous material admixed with myriad bacteria. *Enterococcus faecalis* is a common cause of vegetative valvular endocarditis in chickens.

Miscellaneous

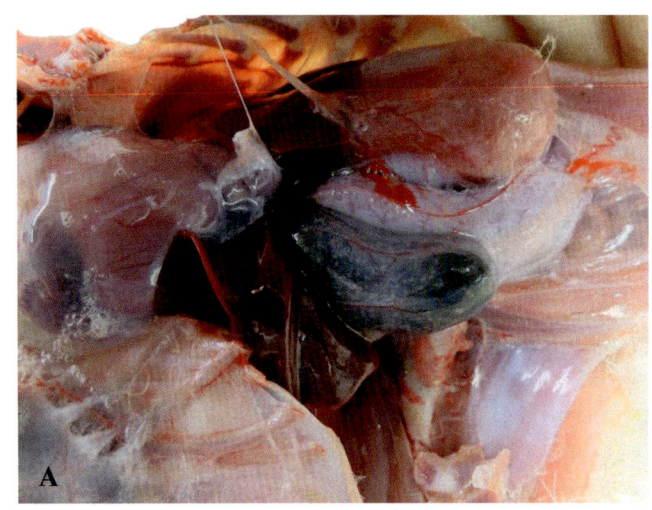

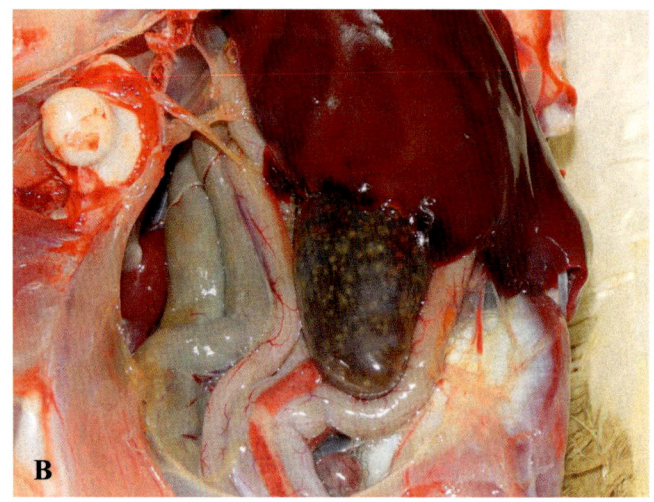

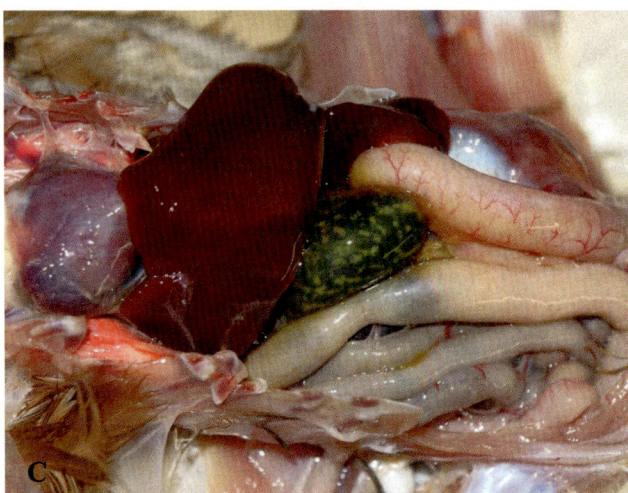

A, B, C. Cholecystitis. **A.** 14-week broiler breeder. **B.** 16-week-broiler breeder. **C.** 3-month hobby chicken. **A, B, C.** Spots are visible through the serosal surface of the gallbladder. These spots are necrotic foci in the mucosa. In **A** and **C**, culture of the bile yielded a pure growth of *Campylobacter jejuni*. In **B**, culture of the bile yielded pure growth of bacteria most closely resembling *Arcobacter*.

D, E. Keratitis caused by *Pseudomonas aeruginosa*. 18-day turkeys. A thick layer of caseous material on the corneal surface of the eyes. Approximately 1% of the flock had this lesion, which was unilateral. The exudate results from severe keratitis with perforation of the cornea. Some birds in the flock had turbidity of corneal surface, but no exudate on the corneal surface. *P. aeruginosa* is particularly capable of causing corneal ulcers through the secretion of proteoglycanase that enhances degradation of corneal tissue, which can lead to perforation.

Miscellaneous

A. *Salmonella* Typhimurium infection in a pigeon.
Commonly called a 'wing boil', swelling of the elbow joint (arrow) due to severe heterophilic arthritis is characteristic of *Salmonella* Typhimurium var. Copenhagen infection in pigeons. Other joints may be affected. *(Photo courtesy of Dr. Peter Wencel, Poland)*.

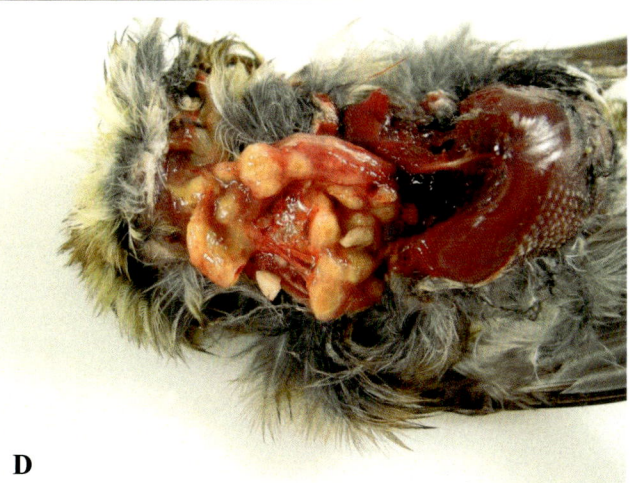

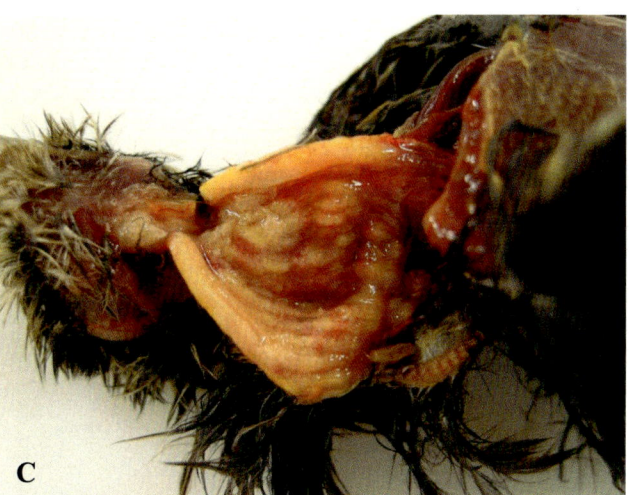

B, C, D. Necrotizing ingluvitis. *Salmonella* Typhimurium infection in American gold finches.
Necrotizing ingluvitis is a characteristic lesion of *Salmonella* Typhimurium infection in finches. **B.** The crop is yellow and has a thickened wall. **C.** The inner surface of the crop is notably thick, yellow, and irregular. **D.** Yellow, caseous nodules are visible through the serosal surface of the crop

Miscellaneous

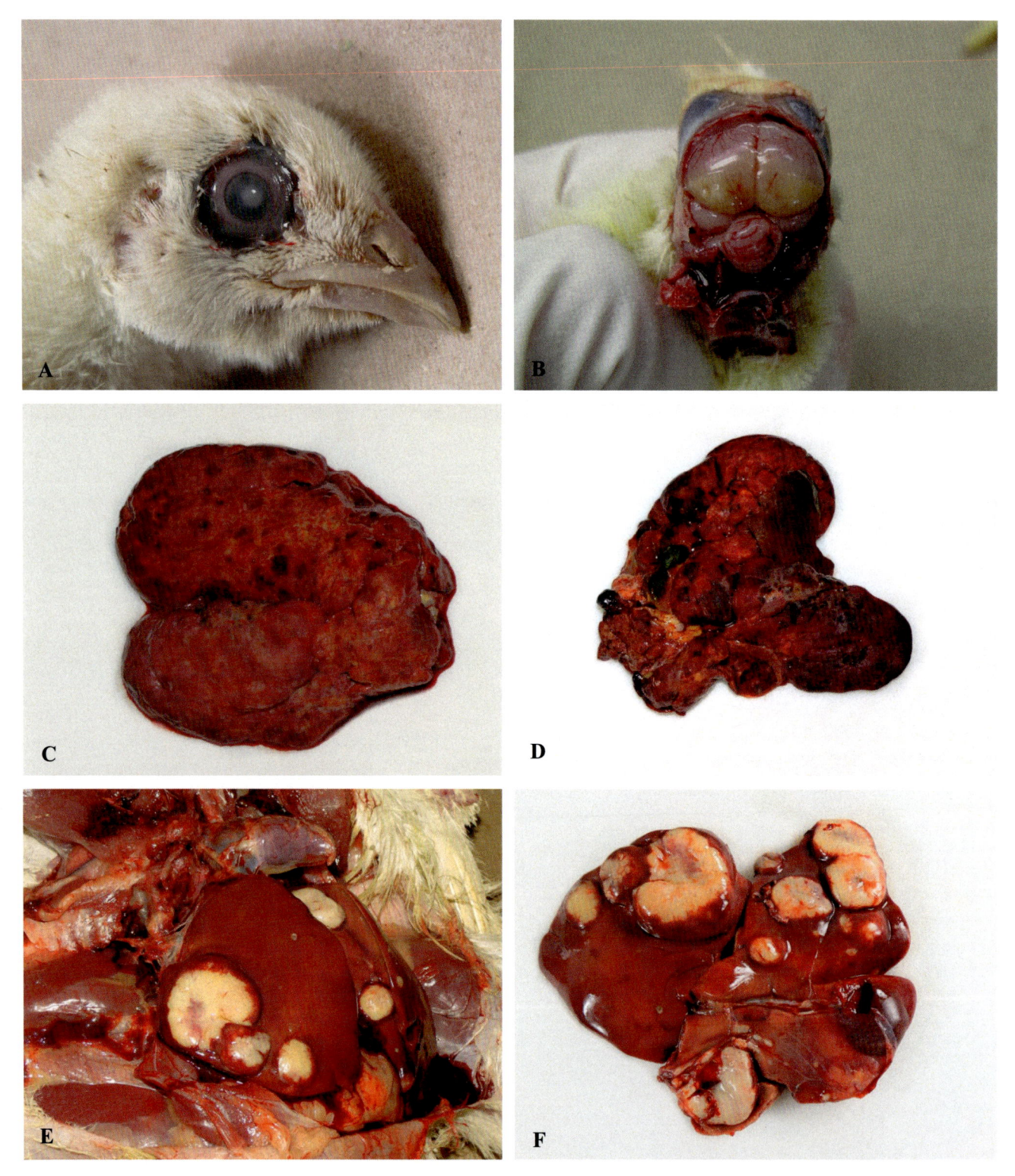

A, B. *Salmonella enterica* subsp. *arizonae* infection. 6-day broiler chickens. **A.** Gray area in the eye due to ophthalmitis. **B.** Yellow discoloration in the posterior part of the cerebral hemispheres due to encephalitis and exudate in lateral ventricles. **C, D. Hemangiosarcoma in liver.** 6-year hobby chicken. Liver is enlarged, discolored, and has an irregular surface, distorted shape, and red foci. The tumor could have been caused by lymphoid leucosis/sarcoma virus. **E, F. Fibrosarcoma in liver.** 46-week broiler breeder hen. Large protruding umbilicated nodules in the liver. The tumor could have been caused by lymphoid leucosis/sarcoma virus.

Miscellaneous

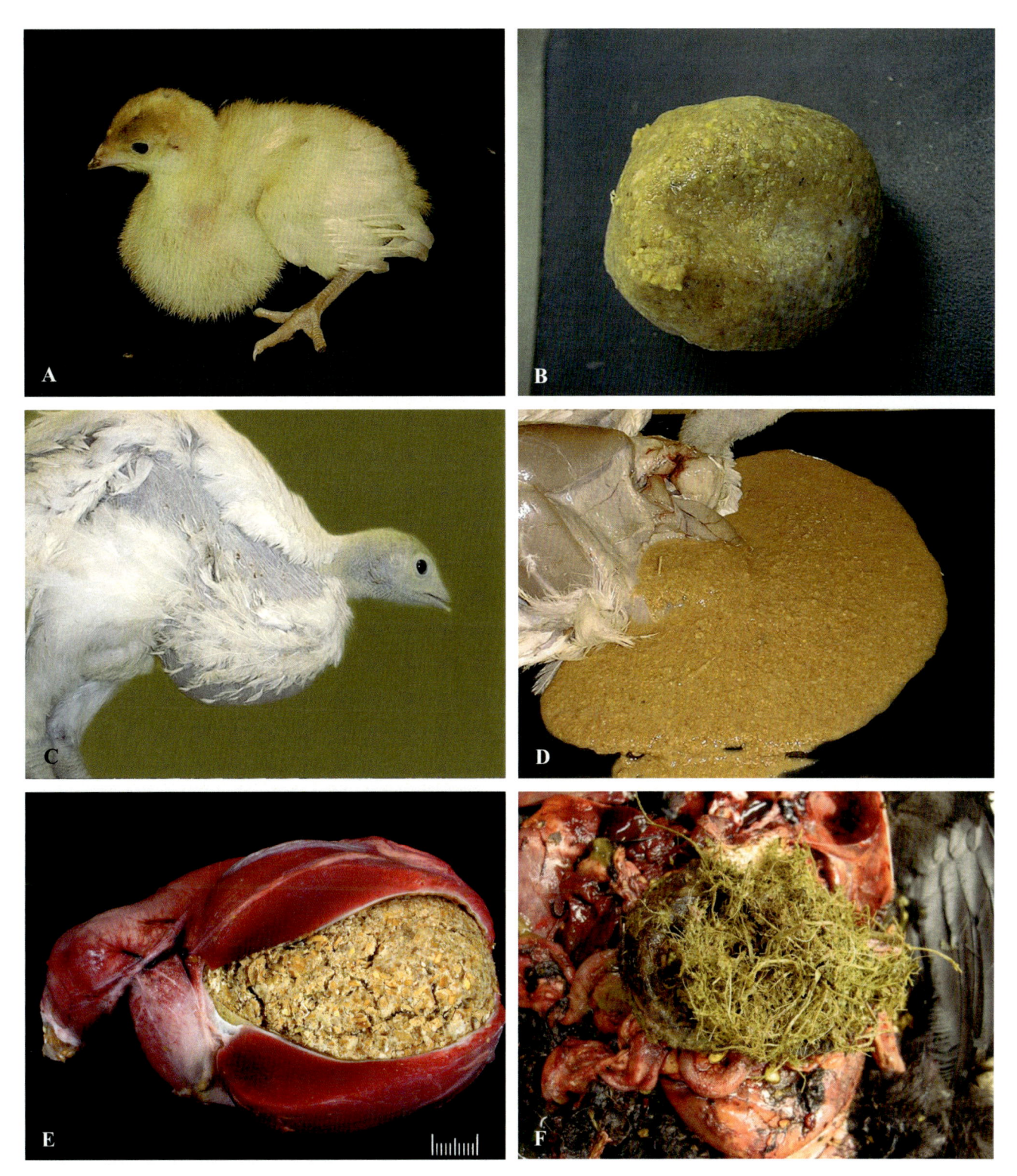

A, B. Impaction of the crop. 7-day turkey. **A.** The crop is markedly distended and firm. **B.** A compact mass of feed removed from the crop. **C, D. Pendulous crop.** Turkey. **C.** Crop is distended and soft. **D.** Thick liquid food fills the distended crop. **E, F. Gizzard impaction. E.** Broiler breeder. Gizzard is impacted with food. **F.** Hobby chicken. Gizzard is filled and impacted with fibrous material.

Miscellaneous

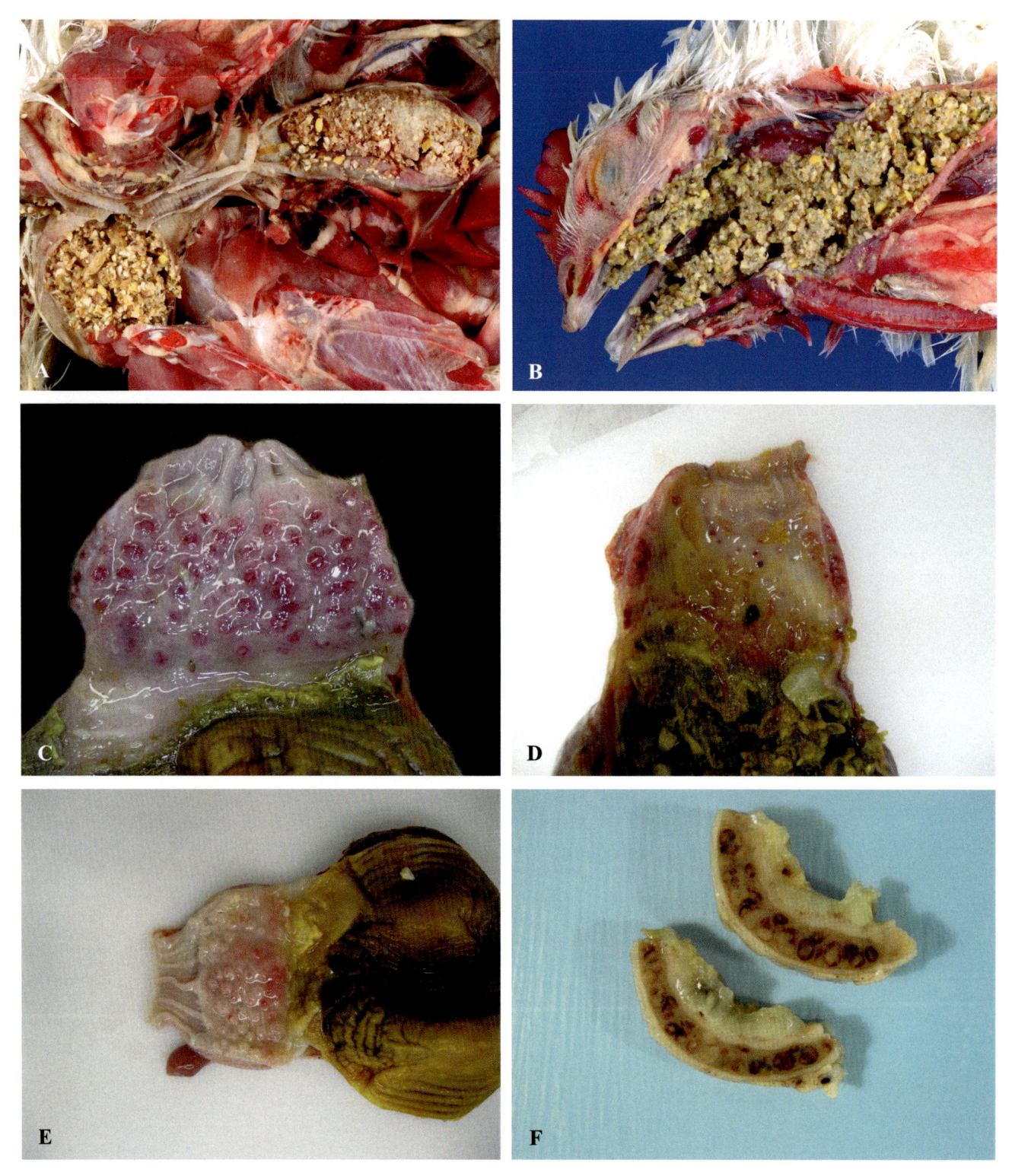

A. Impaction of the crop and proventriculus. The crop and proventriculus are impacted with food. **B. Choke.** Mouth, esophagus, and crop are filled with food. Choke is a relatively common cause of death in broiler breeder pullets on restricted feeding programs. **C, D, E, F. Necrohemorrhagic proventricular adenitis C, D, E.** Papillae of the proventricular mucosa are hemorrhagic. This lesion is seen in birds with dehydration. The pathogenesis is uncertain. The lesion is significant because it can be caused by highly pathogenic avian influenza virus, Newcastle disease virus, and copper toxicity. **F.** Formalin-fixed tissue. Cut surface of the proventriculus in **C** showing hemorrhagic proventricular glands.

Miscellaneous

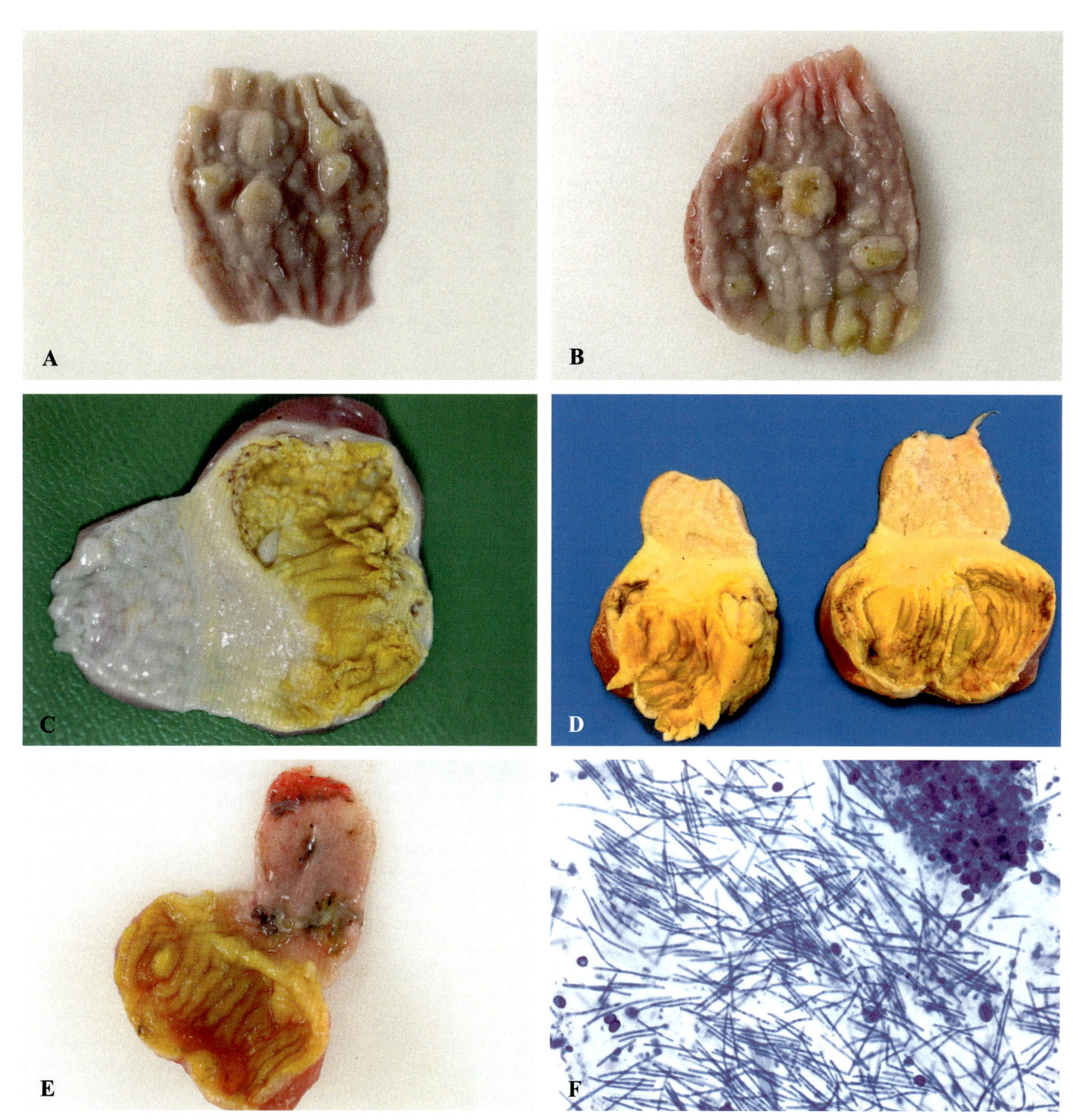

A, B. Proventricular mucosal polyp. 31-week broiler breeder hens. Mucosal polyp involving mucosal papillae. Histologically, polyps result from hyperplasia of ductal epithelium. The cause is uncertain. **C, D, E. Gizzard erosion caused by adenovirus. C.** SPF broilers were infected at day-old with fowl adenovirus and killed 10 days post-infection. Note the disruption of the koilin layer of the gizzard due to erosions *(Photo courtesy of Dr. Michael Hess, Austria)*. **D.** 19-day broilers. Field case. Clinical history indicated slow, uneven growth in the flock. There are erosions and black discoloration of the koilin layer. Adenovirus was found in the liver, cecal tonsils, and gizzard *(Photo courtesy of Dr. Ylva Lindgren, Sweden)*. Other causes of gizzard erosion include mycotoxins, biogenic amines (gizzerosine in fishmeal), and high copper level in the feed. **E, F. Macrorhabdosis (megabacteriosis) caused by *Macrorhabdus ornithogaster*.** Budgerigar. Thickening and white discoloration of the proventricular mucosa with thickening at the junction with the gizzard. Diagnosis confirmed by histopathology. Gross lesions are not always evident. **F.** *Macrorhabdus* in mucosal impression smear, Cotton blue stain.

Miscellaneous

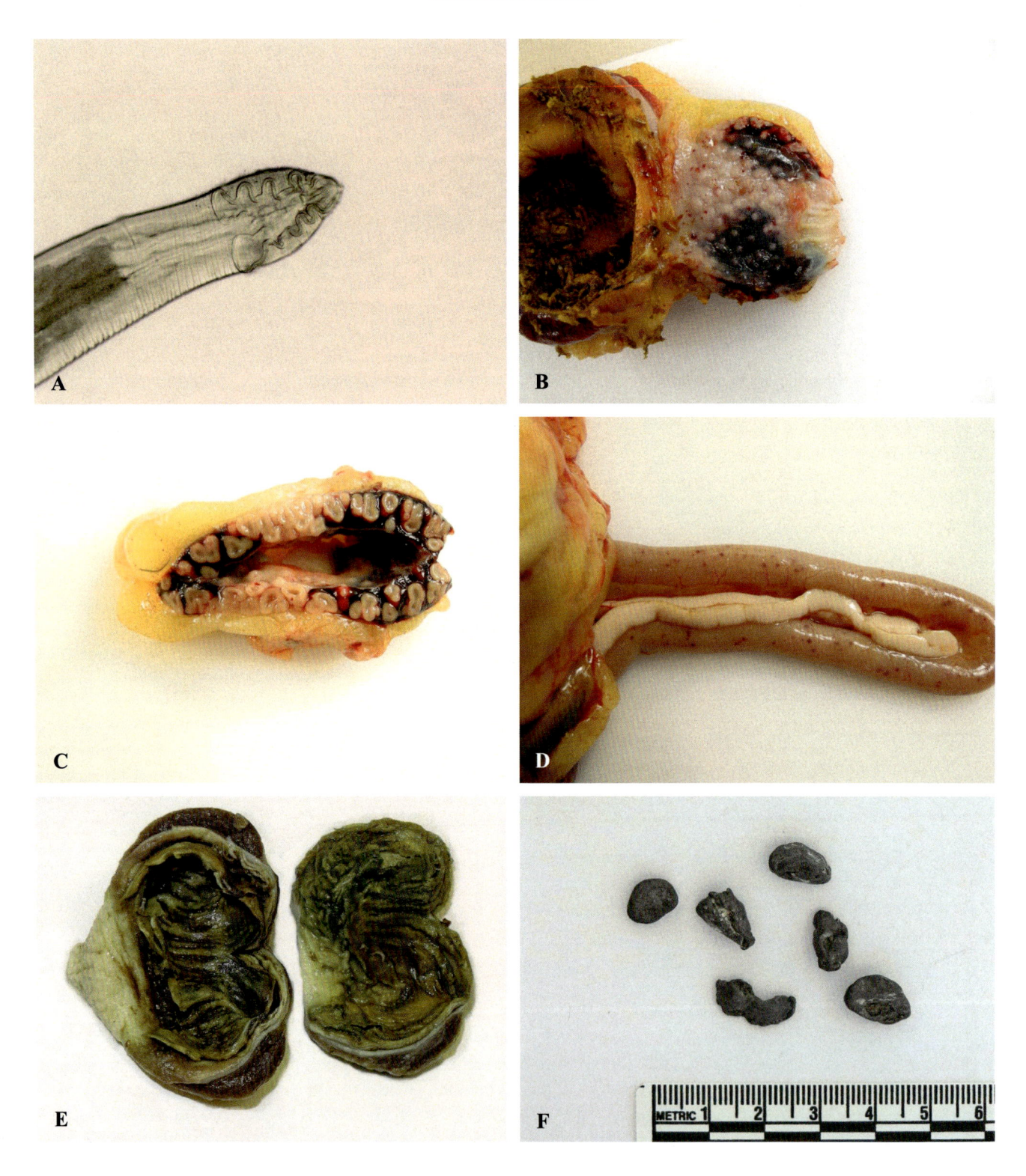

A. *Dispharynx nasuta* (proventricular nematode). This is one of several nematodes in the proventriculus of a 4-week hobby turkey. Recurrent cordons (arrows) is a characteristic feature of *Dispharynx* spp. **B, C, D. Sulfonamide toxicity.** Hobby chicken. **B.** Severe hemorrhages in the proventricular wall. **C.** Cut surface of the proventriculus in B. **D.** Petechial hemorrhages of the intestinal serosa. **D, E, F. Lead poisoning.** Hobby chicken. **E.** Laceration and sloughing of the koilin layer of the gizzard. **F.** Pieces of lead found in a gizzard. Per the owner, these are smashed 22 caliber bullets.

Miscellaneous

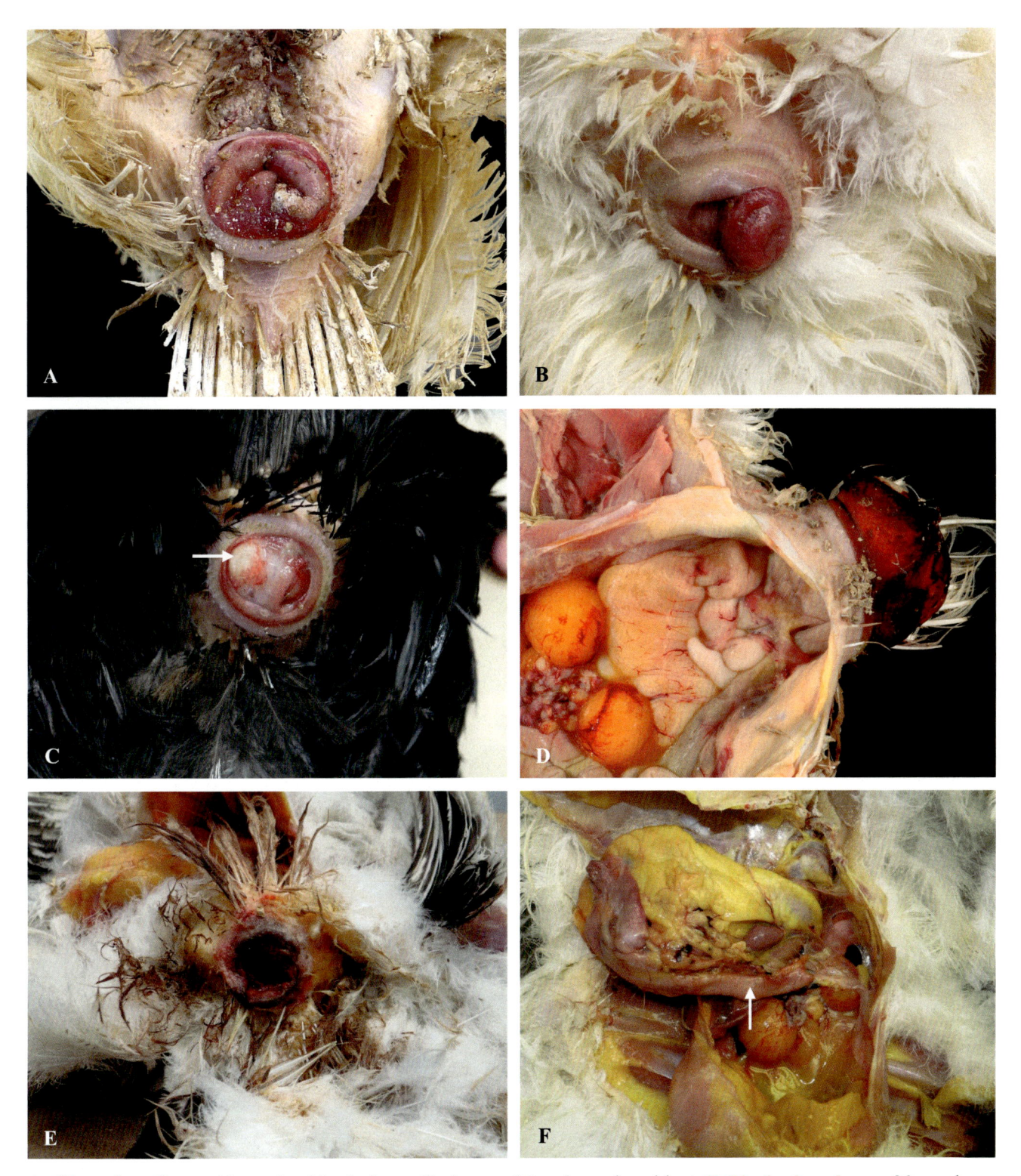

A. Cloacal prolapse. 11-week white leghorn. Prolapse of the cloaca is evident. **B. Vaginal prolapse.** 30-week broiler breeder hen. Tissue protruding from the cloaca is the vagina. **C, D. Egg bound. C.** 2.5-year hobby chicken. An egg is lodged in the cloaca. Part of the egg is seen (arrow). **D.** 62-week broiler breeder. An egg is lodged in the cloaca, which is prolapsed. **E, F. Vent persecution.** Broiler breeder. **E.** A large opening in the area of the vent due to severe vent persecution. **F.** Most of the intestine was pulled by other birds. Only the duodenum (arrow) is left.

Miscellaneous

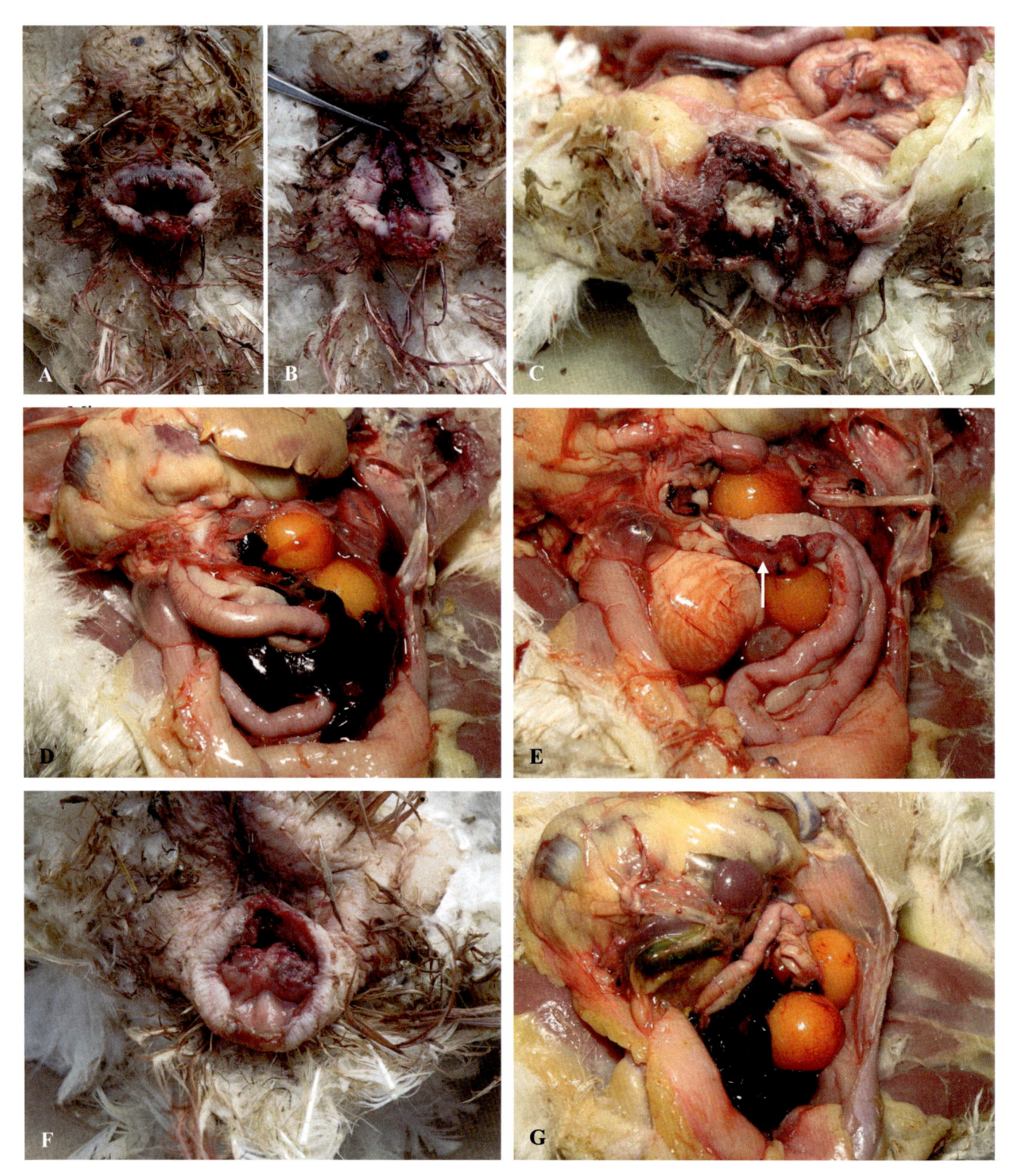

Vent/cloacal pecking and intestinal peck-out. 40-week broiler breeder hens. A-E are same bird, and E, F are same bird. **A, B, C, F.** The vent and cloaca are traumatized. In **C**, the cloaca was opened to show the traumatized cloacal tissue. **D, G.** Blood clot in the body cavity. Only the duodenum is present. The missing part of the small intestine was pulled out by other birds. Note that both birds have an active ovary. **E.** The blood clot in D was removed and the duodenum was moved to show the point of traumatic severing of the intestine (arrow).

Miscellaneous

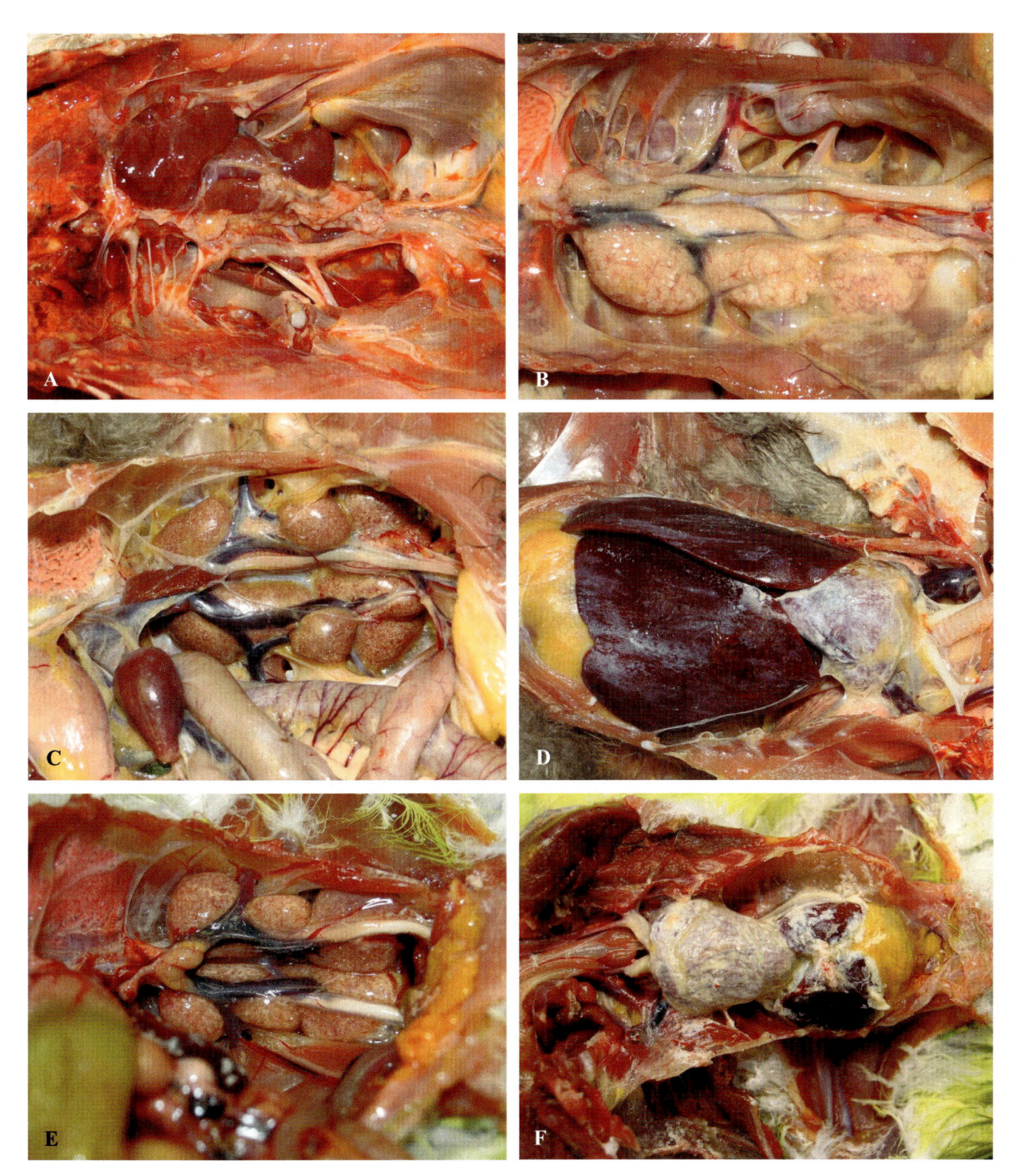

A, B. Renal agenesis (aplasia). 2-year and 10-week hobby chickens. In **A**, the right kidney is absent. In **B**, the left kidney is absent, and the right kidney is pale due to marked urate deposition (renal gout). **C, D, E, F. Renal gout and visceral urate deposition (visceral gout).** **C, D.** 9-month peafowl. **C.** Kidneys are enlarged and speckled white due to urate deposition. **D.** Urates on the surfaces of the liver and heart. **E, F.** 14-week ring-necked parrot. **E.** Kidneys are enlarged, pale, and show prominent renal tubules due to urate deposition. Marked urate deposition is on the surfaces of the heart and liver.

Miscellaneous

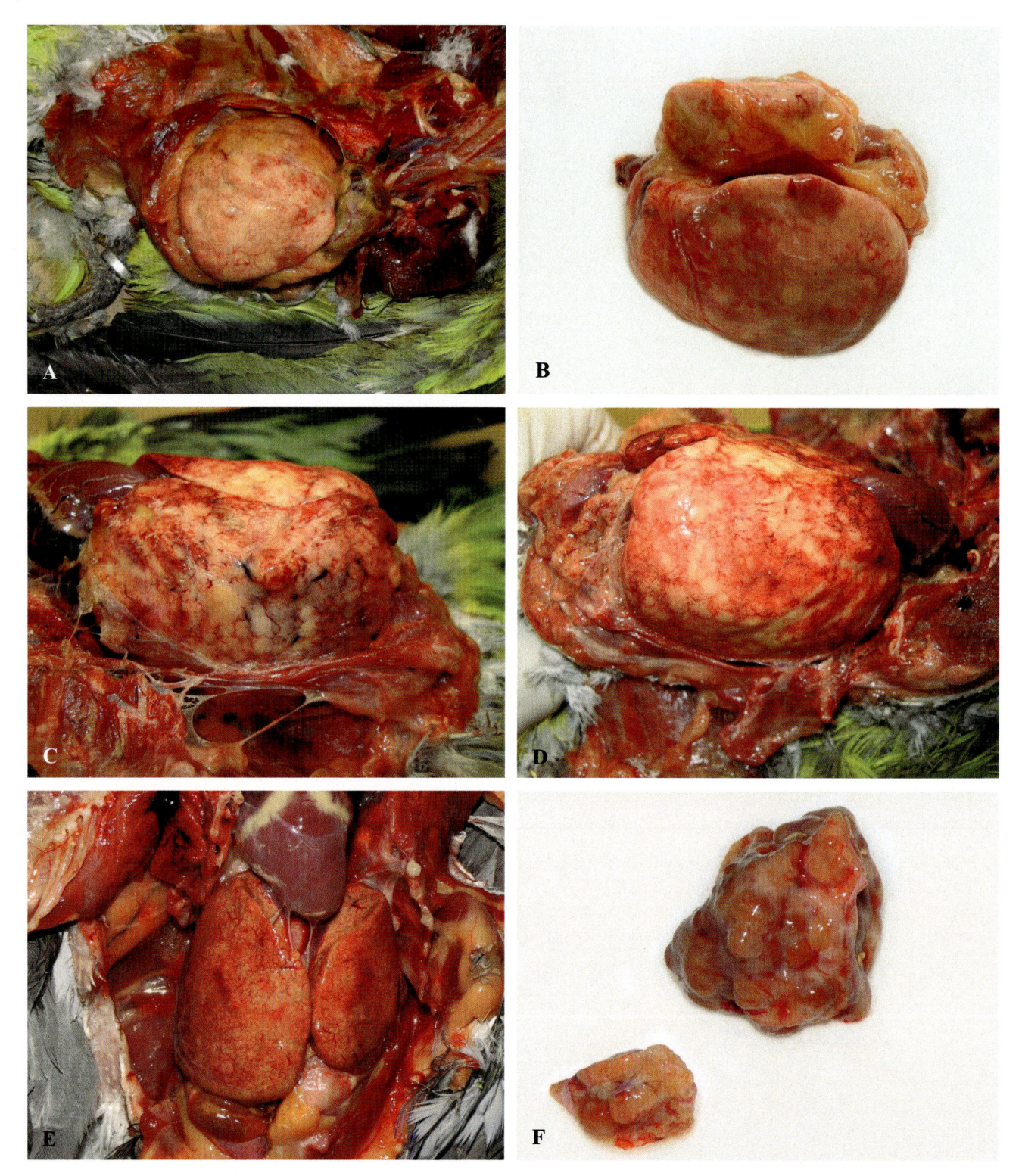

A-F. Hepatic steatosis, steatohepatitis, and cirrhosis. A, B. 10-year Amazon parrot. Steatohepatitis **C, D.** 4-year Amazon parrot. **A, B, C, D.** Livers are enlarged and discolored and have an irregular surface due to severe steatosis and extensive fibrosis (cirrhosis). In **C** and **D**, the liver has a nodular surface due to the presence of regenerative hepatocyte nodules. **E.** 20-year African gray parrot. Liver is enlarged and pale yellow due to severe hepatic steatosis. **F.** Adult Amazon parrot. Right and left Lobes of the liver are shrunken, pale, and nodular. Histologically, there was diffuse loss of hepatocytes, extensive fibrosis, multiple regenerative nodules, and marked proliferation of bile ductules.

Miscellaneous

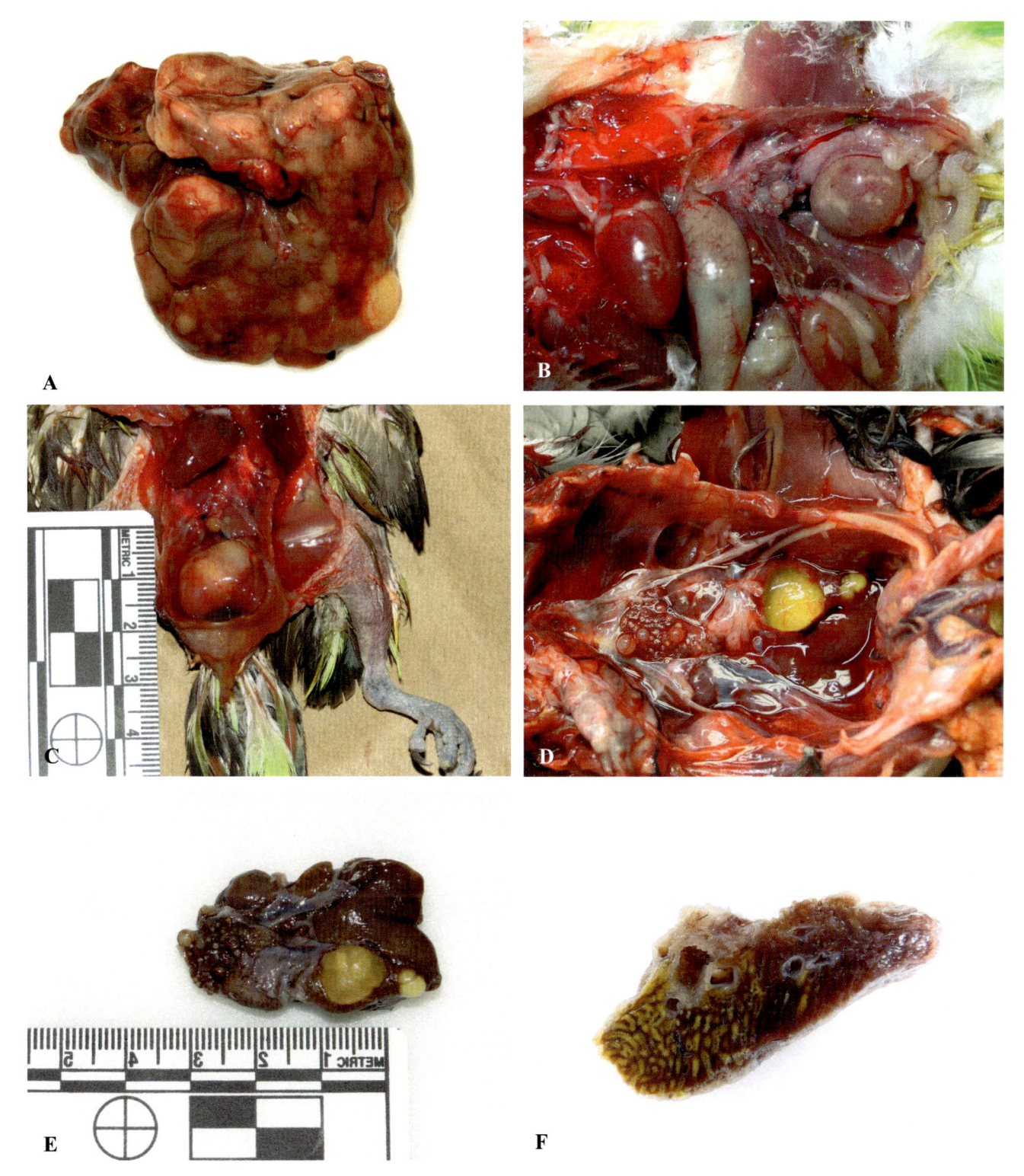

A. Cholangiocarcinoma 13-year Amazon parrot. The liver is severely distorted by protruding individual and coalescing nodules. **B, C. Renal tubular carcinoma.** Budgerigar (A. 3-year. B. 13-month). Round tumor is associated with the kidney. In B, there was metastasis to the lung and liver. **D, E. Renal cysts.** 20-year African gray parrot. Cysts filled with yellow, transparent fluid are in the left kidneys. **F. Endogenous lipid pneumonia.** 26-year African gray parrot. Airways are filled and distended with yellow material. Histologically, parabronchi were filled with lipid-laden, foamy macrophages.

Miscellaneous

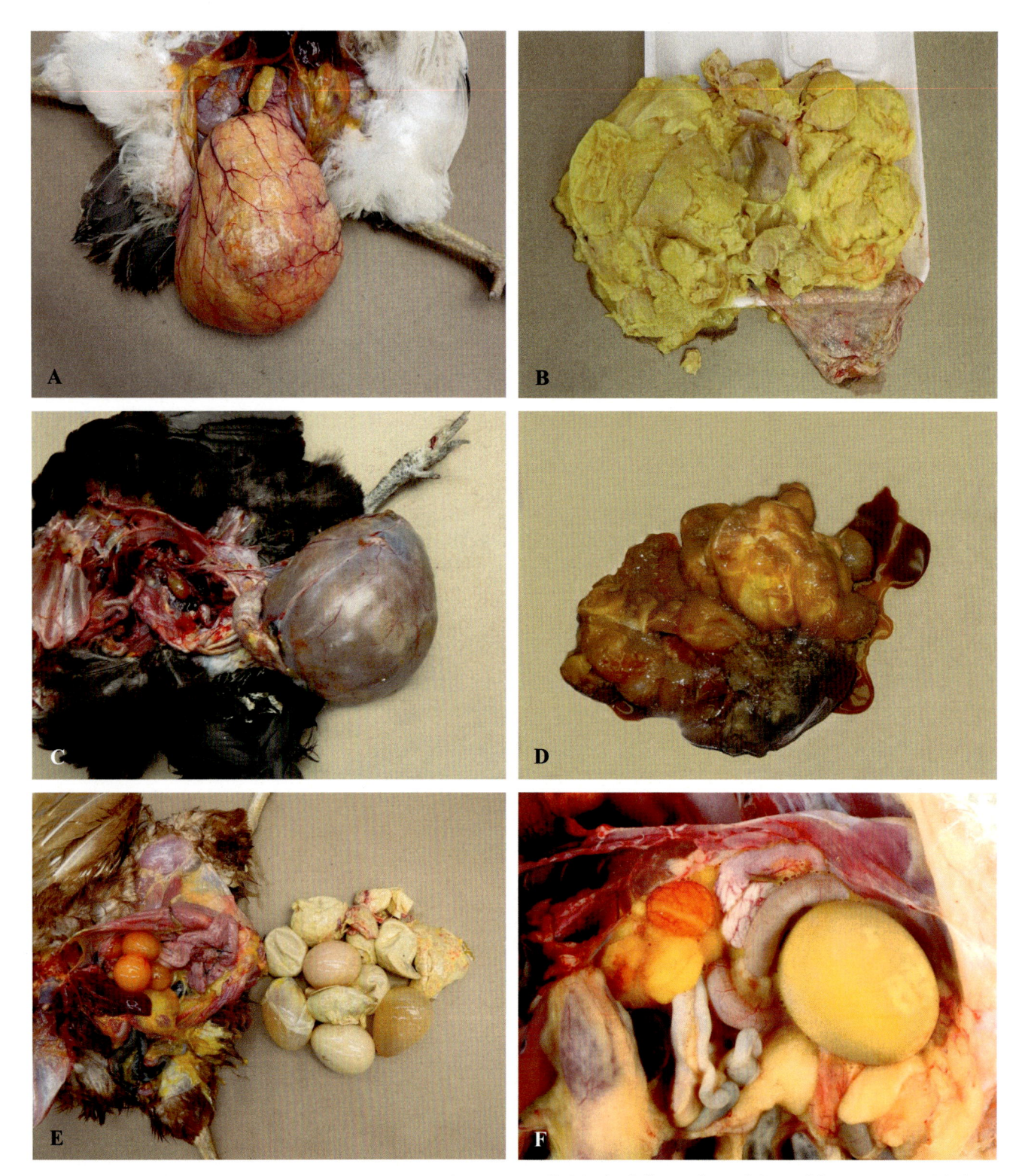

A, B, C, D. Impaction of the oviduct. Hobby chickens. A, C. Marked distension of the oviduct. **B.** same bird as A. Coagulated yolk material and membranous eggs fill the oviduct. **D.** Same bird as C. Autolyzed yolk material and probably partially formed eggs fill the oviduct. **E, F. Abdominal layers. E.** 4-year backyard chicken. Several soft-shelled eggs are in the abdominal cavity. Ovary is still active. **F.** 43-week caged layer. A thinly shelled egg is free in the abdominal cavity. Ovarian follicles are regressing. Abdominal laying follows either physical or functional obstruction of the oviduct. Propulsive waves in the oviduct reverse causing partly to fully formed eggs to be regurgitated into the body cavity where they accumulate over time.

Miscellaneous

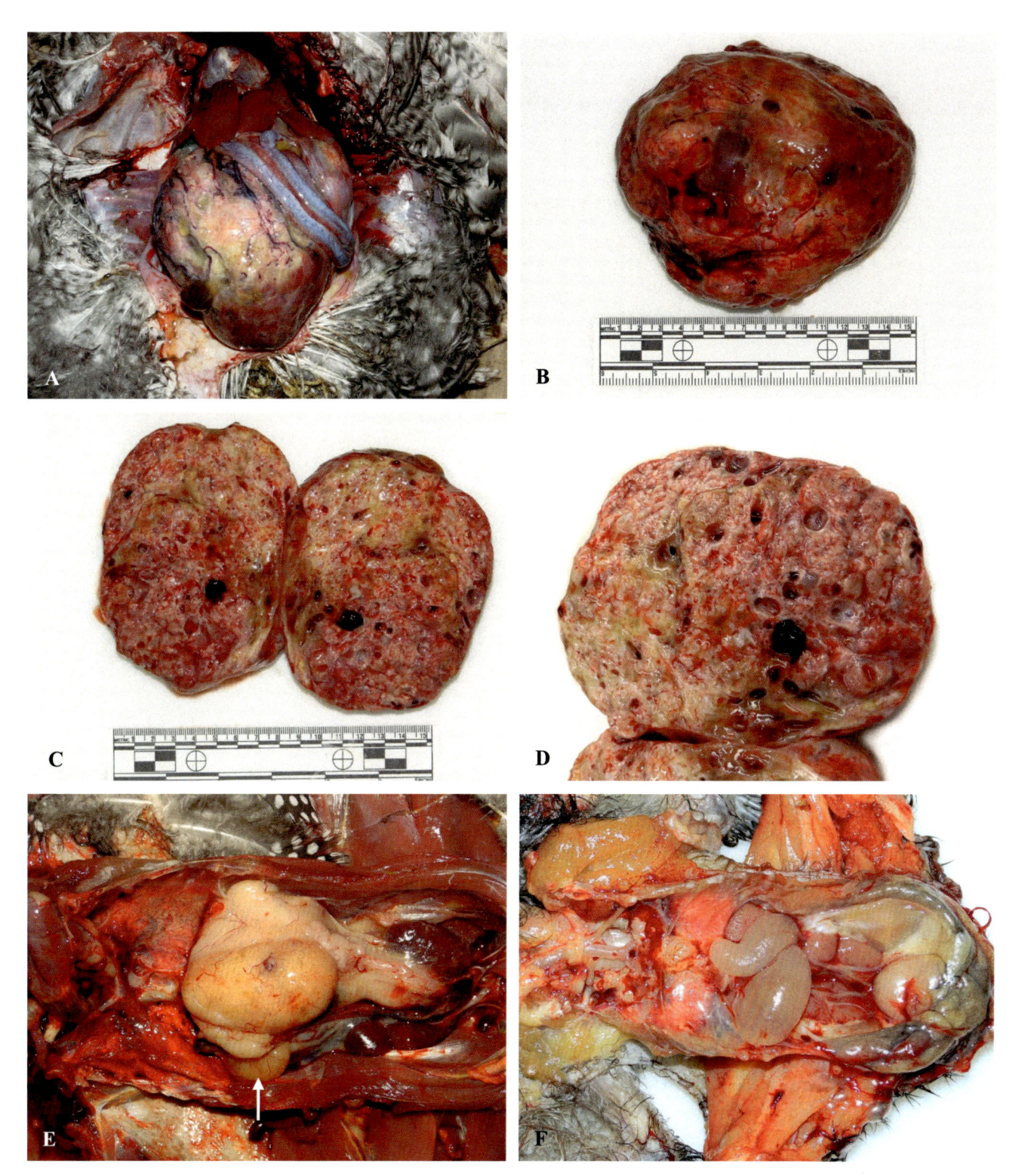

A, B, C, D. Teratoma of testis. 2-year hobby rooster. **A.** Large, firm mass occupies the body cavity and distends the abdomen. **B.** The mass is almost round and has fluid- and blood-filled cysts. **C, D.** Cut surface of the mass is irregular and shows solid tissues and cystic spaces. **E. Seminoma.** Guinea fowl. A large mass replaces the left testis. Arrow: right testis. **F. Cystic testes.** 18-day meat-type turkey. The bird had rickets, with lesions of dietary phosphorous deficiency. Cystic testes also occur in young chicks and turkeys with sodium toxicity.

Miscellaneous

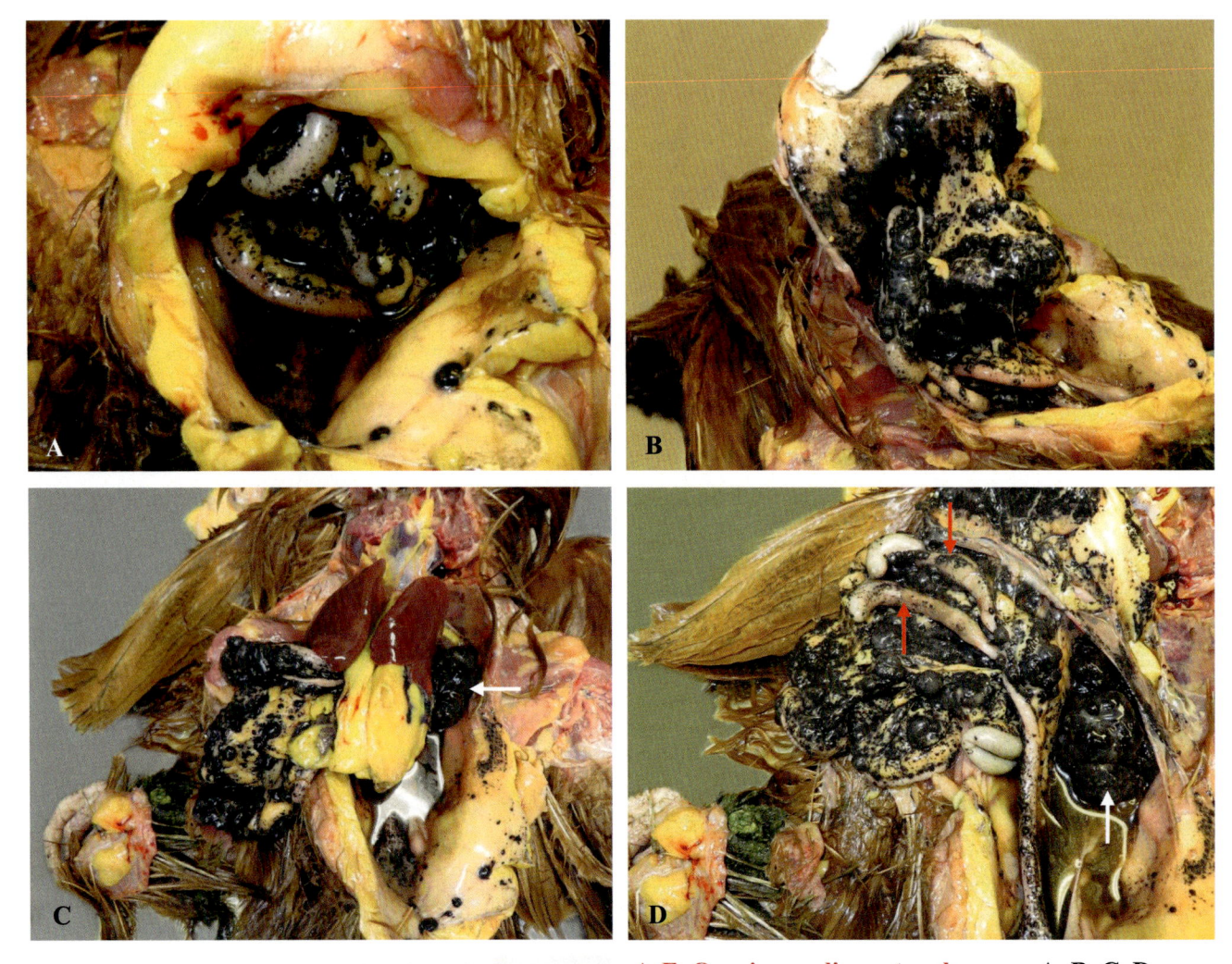

A-E. Ovarian malignant melanoma. A, B, C, D. Variably sized black coalescing nodules involve the abdominal wall, intestinal serosa, and mesentery. In **C** and **D**, white arrows point to the ovary. In **D**, red arrows point to the ceca. **E.** Malignant melanoma in the ovary. *(Photos courtesy of Dr. Jessica Kees, USA).*

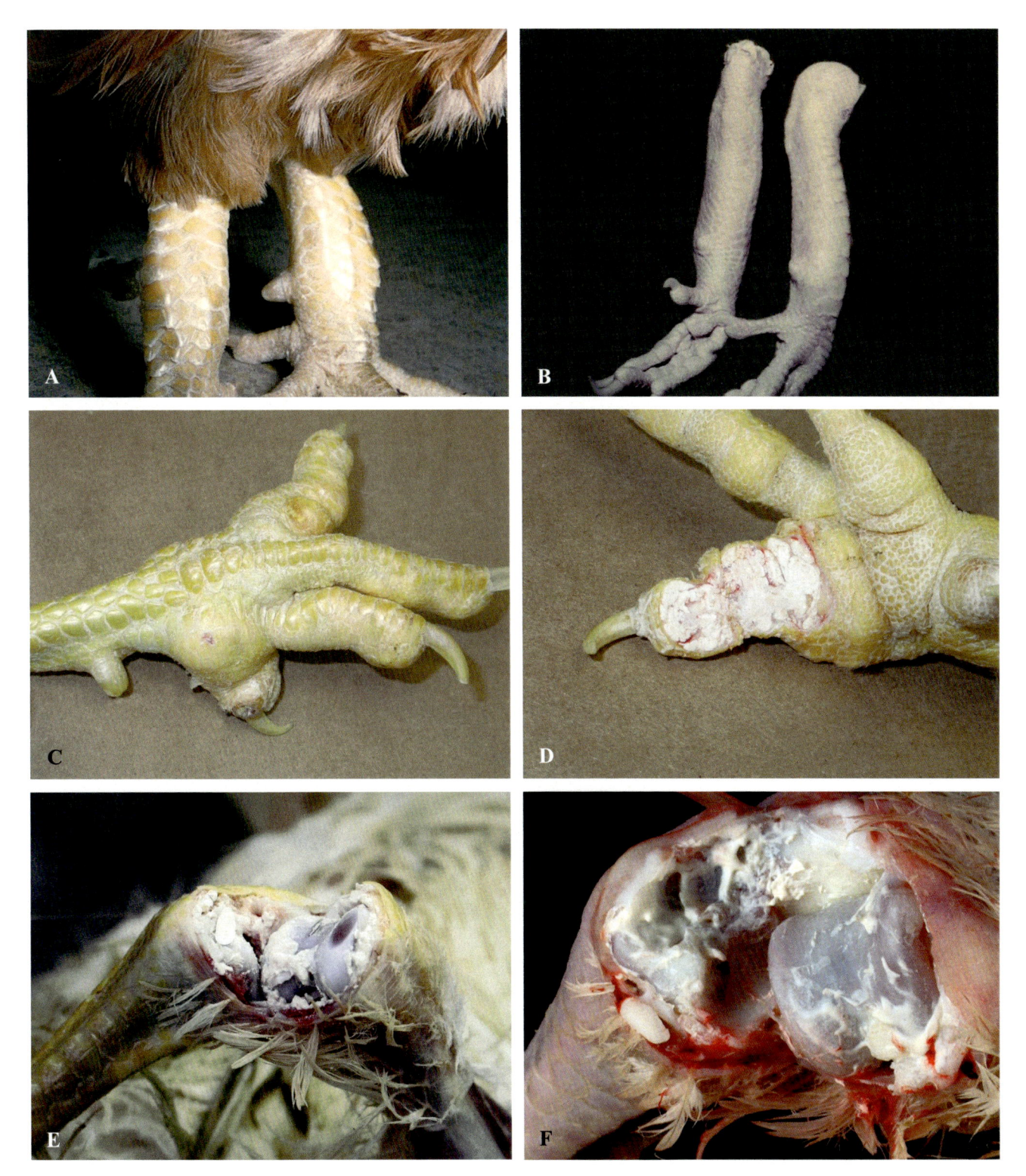

Gross Pathology of Avian Diseases: Text and Atlas 295

Miscellaneous

A, B. Osteopetrosis caused by avian leucosis/sarcoma virus. Marked thickening of the tarsometatarsus. Bone thickening is due to massive growth of porous subperiosteal bone. Only the diaphysis is affected; joints are not involved. **C, D. Articular urate deposition (articular gout).** Chickens. **C.** Swelling of the foot and toes due to accumulation of urate. **D.** Same foot in C. Toe was cut to show urates in the interphalangeal joints. Articular gout is an inherited disease, which needs to be distinguished from urate deposition in joints due to renal gout. **E, F.** Accumulation of urates in these hock joints is due to renal gout.

Miscellaneous

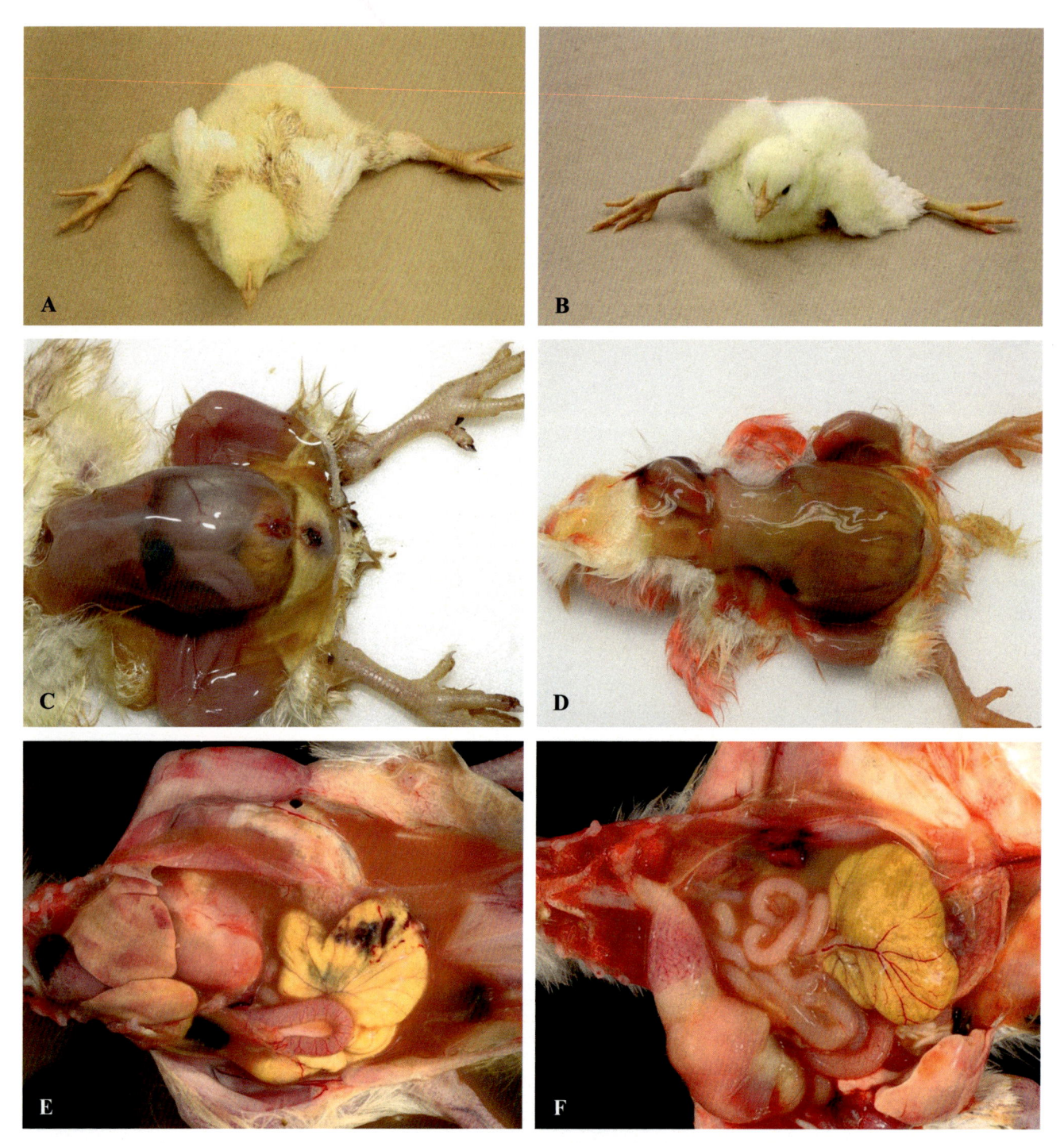

A, B. Splayed legs. Both legs are spread laterally due to dislocation of the coxofemoral joints. This condition is seen in chicks and turkey poults on slippery surfaces. One or both legs may be affected. **C, D. Subcutaneous edema.** 2-day broiler breeder pullets (2 different hatches). This is caused by suboptimal water loss from eggs due to excess humidity during incubation. Note the large yolk sac in D. **E, F. Ruptured yolk sac.** One-day turkey poults. Yolk sacs are occasionally ruptured during manual sexing. Abdomens are distended as free yolk is a mild irritant and also attracts water into the body cavity. Poults are often dehydrated and occasionally show visceral urate deposition. Hemorrhage can often be seen where the yolk sac is torn (E). Affected birds usually die within the first 2-3 days. Broiler breeder chicks also may be affected, but this is uncommon.

Miscellaneous

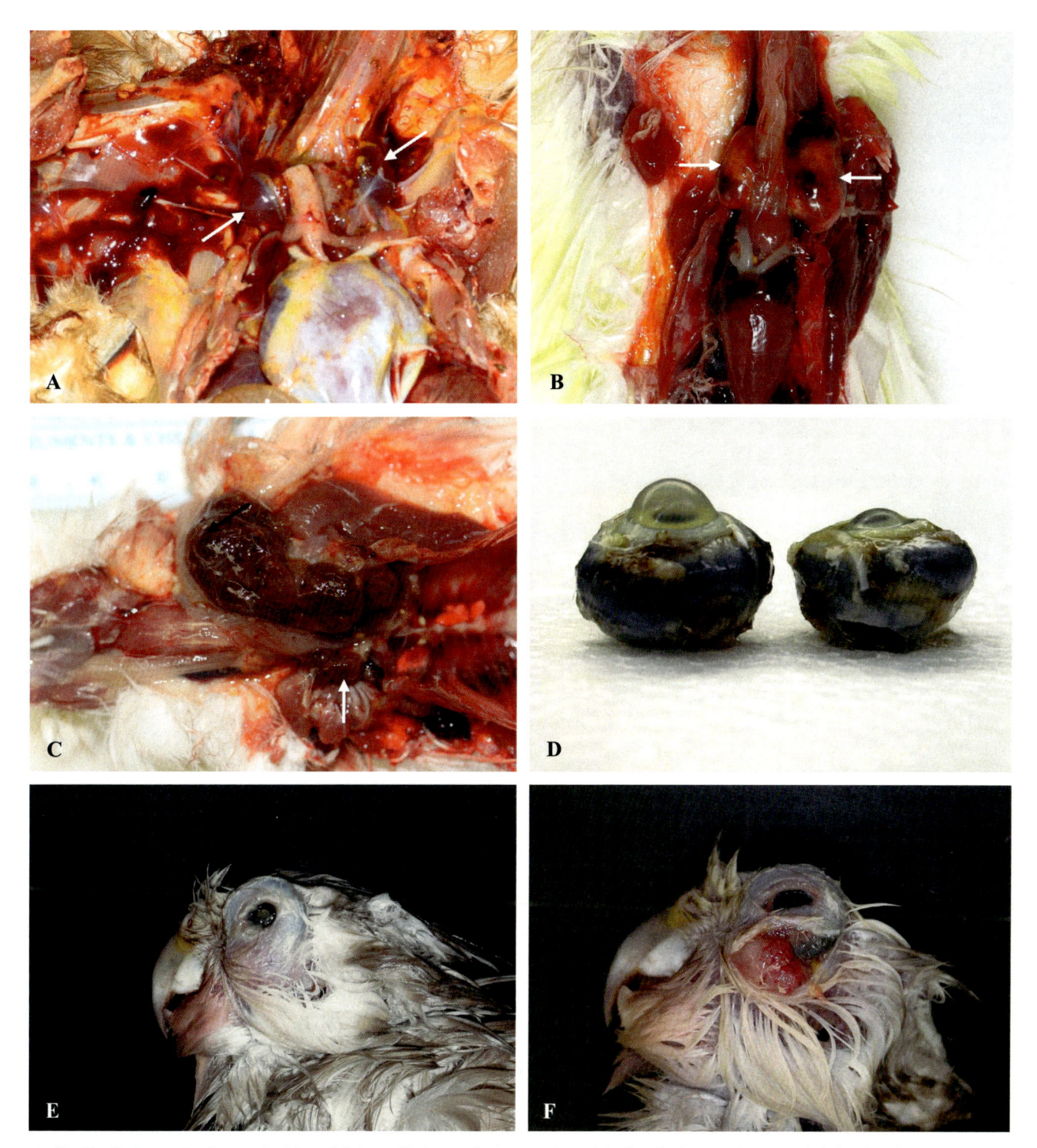

A, B, C. Goiter. A. 6-year hobby chicken. Enlarged, *in situ* thyroid glands (arrows). **B.** Adult budgerigar. Bilateral enlargement of the thyroid glands (arrows). Left gland is more affected than the right one. Enlarged glands have pale and hemorrhagic areas. **C.** Adult budgerigar. Left thyroid gland (black arrow) is markedly enlarged and has a distorted shape and irregular surface. Right thyroid gland (white arrow) is mildly to moderately enlarged. The cause was iodine-deficient diets *(Photo C courtesy of Dr. Panayiotis Loukopoulos, New South Wales, Australia)*. **D. Keratoglobus.** Hobby chicken. Globular protrusion and diffuse thinning of the cornea in the eye on the left. Eye on the right is normal. Keratoglobus is a rare non-inflammatory eye disorder. **E, F. Pituitary gland neoplasia E.** Marked exophthalmia of the left eye. **F.** The mass in the orbit causing protrusion of the eye was identified histologically as a pituitary gland carcinoma. Pituitary adenomas can also cause this lesion.

Index

A
Acute pancreatic necrosis, 231
Abdominal layers, 292
Aflatoxicosis in ducks, 237
Ammonia-induced corneal erosion, 277-278
Amyloidosis, 268-269
Arthritis/tenosynovitis in young chicks, bacterial, 10
Ascaridiasis, 178-180
Ascites in broiler chickens, 225-228
Aspergillosis
    respiratory, 146-151
    of third-eyelid, 143
Atherosclerosis, 223-224

B
Baby chick nephropathy, 249-250
Beak and feather disease, 117-119
Bordetellosis in turkeys, 31
Brain infection, bacterial, 9
Breast muscle myopathy, 204

C
Capillaria infection, crop, 170-171
Cataract, 276
Cestodiasis, intestine, 184-187
Cerebellar hypoplasia in chicks, 270-271
Cheilospirura hamulosa infection, 172
Chicken infectious anemia, 90-91
Chlamydiosis, 68-70
Choking, 284
Cholangiocarcinoma, 291
Cholecystitis, 280
Cloaca
    papillomas, 120-121
    pecking, 288
    prolapse, 287
Cloacitis, 247-248
Coccidiosis, intestinal, 154-158
Colibacillosis, 13-14
Collyriclum faba infection, 187-190
Collyriclosis, 187-190
Comb candidiasis, 153
Crop
    candidiasis (mycosis), 152
    capillariasis, 170-171
    impaction, 283
    pendulous, 283
Cutaneous papillomas, 120
Cystic right oviduct, 254-255
Cystic testes, 293

D
Deep pectoral myopathy, 205-206
Dehydration in baby chicks, 249-250
Dilated cardiomyopathy in turkeys, 228-230
Dispharynx Nasuta infection, 286
Duck viral enteritis, 103-105
Duck viral hepatitis, 105-106

E
Egg bound, 287
Eimeria acervuline, 154-155
Eimeria maxima, 154, 155-156
Eimeria necatrix, 154, 156-157
Eimeria tenella, 154, 157-158
Endogenous lipid pneumonia, 291
Erysipelas, 24-27
Esophageal squamous cell carcinoma, 243
Eustrongylidosis, 176-177

F
Fatty liver-hemorrhagic syndrome, 232-233
Femoral head necrosis, 43, 45
Fibrosarcoma in liver, 282
Focal duodenal necrosis, 55
Footpad dermatitis, 272-273
Foot tendons, tenosynovitis, bacterial, 42
Fowl cholera, 18-23

G
Gangrenous dermatitis, 48-49
Gastrocnemius tendon
    staphyloccal tenosynovitis, 40-41
    ruptured, 210-212
Gizzard
    erosion caused by adenovirus, 285
    impaction, 283
    nematodes
        Cheilospirura hamulosa, 172
        Hadjelia truncata, 175
    Traumatic ventriculitis, 244, 245
Goiter, 297
Gout
    articular, 295
    renal and visceral, 289
Granulosa cell tumor, ovary, 264-265
Green muscle disease, 205-206

H
Hadjelia truncata infection in pigeons, 175
Hemangiosarcoma in liver, 282

Hemorrhagic enteritis in turkeys, 89
Hemosiderosis, 238
Hepatic lipidosis in turkeys, 234-236
Hepatic steatosis, parrots, 290
Hepatitis E virus infection. 95-97
Hepatopathy, *Salmonella* Enteritidis bacterin-induced, 240-242
Herpesvirus infection in pigeons, 110-111
Heterakis isolonche infection in pheasants, 181
Histomoniasis, 160-164
Hydropericardium syndrome, 87-88

I
Impaction of oviduct, 292
Inclusion body hepatitis, 87-88
Infectious bursal disease, 83-86
Infectious coryza, 32-34
Infectious laryngotracheitis, 74-77
Inflammatory process, 16-17
Influenza, 78-82
Intussusception, 245-246
Iron-storage disease, 238-239

J
Joint/tendon infection in young chicks, bacterial, 10

K
Keratitis
    caused by *Pseudomonas aeruginosa*, 280
    caused by fungus, 144-145
Keratoacanthoma in broilers, 275
Keratoglobus, 297

L
Laryngeal squamous cell carcinoma, 243
Lead toxicity, 286
Lice infestation, 191-193
Listeria monocytogenes infection, 279
Liver cirrhosis, 290
Lymphoid leukosis, 134-138

M
Macrorhabdosis (megabacteriosis), 285
Marek's disease, 122-133
Melanoma of ovary, 294
Mites
    feather mite, 191, 194-195
    northern fowl mite, 191, 193-195
    chicken red mite, 191
    scaly leg mites, 196
    subcutaneous mites, 197
    quill mites, 191
    respiratory mites, 198, 199

Mucosal papillomas, 120
Mycobacteriosis, 56-58
Mycoplasma gallisepticum
    infection in hobby chickens, 60
    infection in turkeys, 59
Mycoplasma iowae infection, 64-67
Mycoplasma synoviae infection, 61-63
Mycotic keratitis, 144-145
Myelocytomatosis, 139-141

N
Navel
    omphalitis, 1, 3
    unhealed, 1-2
Necrotic enteritis, 50-52
Neonatal septicemia, 6-10
Nephroblastoma, 142-143
Newcastle disease, 71-73
Nutritional encephalomalacia, 199-200

O
Omphalitis, 1, 3
Orchitis, 38-39
Oral squamous cell carcinoma, 243
Ornithobacterium rhinotracheale infection, 30
Osteomyelitis, 43-44
Osteopetrosis, 295
Osteoporosis, 218-219
Ovary
    adenocarcinoma, 258, 260, 261
    granulosa cell tumor, 263-264
    melanoma, 294
    oophoritis, 36
    regression of yolk follicles, 256-257
Oviduct
    adenomatous polyps, 258, 262
    persistent cystic right, 254-255
    impaction, 292
    leiomyomas, 265-267
    salpingitis, 35-38
Oviductal leiomyomas, 265-267

P
Pacheco's disease, 112-113
Papillomas, cutaneous and mucosal, 120-221
Pasteurella multocida infection, 18-23
Pharyngeal squamous cell carcinoma, 243
Pendulous crop, 284
Peritonitis in layers, 35-36
Paramyxovirus infection in pigeons, 107-109
Pituitary gland carcinoma, 297
Polyomavirus infection, 115-117
Pox, 100-102
Proventricular dilatation disease, 113-114

Proventiculus
    impaction, 284
    mucosal polyp, 285
    necrohemorrhagic adenitis, 284
    nematodes
        Dispharynx Nasuta, 286
        Tetramers spp. infection, 173-174
Pulmonary hypertension syndrome, 225-228

R
Raillietina echinobothrida infection, 184, 187
Regression of ovarian follicles, 255-257
Renal agenesis, 289
Renal coccidiosis, 159
Renal cysts, 291
Renal tubular carcinoma, 291
Reovirus tenosynovitis
Respiratory mites, 198-199
Rickets, 201-203
Riemerella anatipestifer infection in ducks, 28-29
Rotation of tibiotarsus, 222
Round-heart disease in turkeys, 228-230
Rupture of gastrocnemius tendon, 210-212

S
Salmonella Enterica subsp. *arizonae* infection, 282
Salmonella Enteritidis infection, 11-12
Salmonella Enteritidis-induced hepatopathy, 240-242
Salmonella Typhimurium infection, finches, 281
Salmonella Typhimurium infection, pigeon, 281
Salpingitis, 35-38
Sarcocystis falcatula infection, 169
Sarcocystis rileyi infection, 169
Scaly leg mites, 196
Seminoma, 294
Septicemia, neonatal, 6-10
Spinal cord contusion in turkeys, 214
Spironucleosis (hexamitiasis), 167-168
Splayed legs, 296
Spondylitis, 46-47
Spondylolisthesis, 213-214
Staphylococcal tenosynovitis, 40-41
Steatohepatitis, 290
Sternal bursitis, 207-209
Subcutaneous edema in chicks, 297
Subcutaneous mite, 197

Sulfonamide toxicity, 286
Swollen head syndrome, 15
Syngamus trachea infection, 182-183

T
Tapeworms, intestine, 184-187
Tenosynovitis of foot tendons, bacterial, 42
Tenosynovitis caused by reovirus, 98-99
Teratoma of testes, 294
Testes
    cystic, 293
    seminoma, 293
    teratoma, 293
Tetrameres spp. infection, 173-174
Third-eyelid aspergillosis, 143
Tibiotarsus, rotation, 222
Tick infestation, 192, 195
Traumatic ventriculitis, 244-245
Trichomoniasis, 165-166
Triploid chickens, 253
Turkey viral hepatitis, 102-103

U
Ulcerative enteritis, 53-54
Urolithiasis, 251-252

V
Vaginal prolapse, 287
Valgus leg deformity, 220-221
Varus leg deformity, 220-221
Vegetative valvular endocarditis, 279
Vent pecking, 288
Vent persecution, 287
Vertebral osteoarthritis, 46-47

W
White chick syndrome, 92-94
Wooden breast in broilers, 204

X
Xanthoma, cutaneous, 275

Y
Yolk peritonitis, 35-36
Yolk sac, normal, 5
Yolk sac infection, 1, 3-5
Yolk sac rupture, 296